THE OXFORD HANDBOOK OF

SKILLS AND TRAINING

THE OXFORD HANDBOOK OF

SKILLS AND TRAINING

Edited by

CHRIS WARHURST, KEN MAYHEW,
DAVID FINEGOLD,
and
JOHN BUCHANAN

OXFORD
UNIVERSITY PRESS

OXFORD
UNIVERSITY PRESS

Great Clarendon Street, Oxford, OX2 6DP,
United Kingdom

Oxford University Press is a department of the University of Oxford. It furthers the University's objective of excellence in research, scholarship, and education by publishing worldwide. Oxford is a registered trade mark of Oxford University Press in the UK and in certain other countries

Impression: 1

Published in the United States of America by Oxford University Press
198 Madison Avenue, New York, NY 10016, United States of America

British Library Cataloguing in Publication Data
Data available

Library of Congress Control Number: 2016944776

ISBN 978–0–19–965536–6

Printed in Great Britain by
Clays Ltd, St Ives plc

Acknowledgements

The editors would like to thank David Musson of the Oxford University Press for his unwavering encouragement with this handbook, and Clare Kennedy and Emma Booth, also of the OUP, for their editorial support. We are grateful to Amanda Kerry of the University of Warwick for providing secretarial support. Finally, we would like to acknowledge the efforts of all of our contributors. Contributors need to have acquired extensive specialist expertise in their subject over many years. Handbooks then require them to synthesize, distil, and demonstrate this expertise in limited space. It can be a tough task and we thank them for their generosity in agreeing to take part in this venture and for being patient with us while we edited the handbook.

Contents

SECTION II EDUCATION, TRAINING, AND THE DEVELOPMENT OF WORKFORCE SKILLS

SECTION III SKILLS DEMAND AND DEPLOYMENT

SECTION IV SKILL OUTCOMES

SECTION V DIFFERING SKILL SYSTEMS: THE LEVELS OF DETERMINATION

SECTION VI DIFFERING SKILL SYSTEMS: THE DYNAMICS OF DEVELOPMENT IN A GLOBAL ECONOMY

SECTION VII CURRENT CHALLENGES

List of Contributors

Pauline Anderson PhD is Chancellor's Fellow at the Department of Human Resource Management at the University of Strathclyde in the United Kingdom. Her research focuses on the articulation of the relationship between education/training and work. She has a particular interest in 'middle-skill' or intermediate-level jobs and green jobs' growth. Contact: pauline.anderson@strath.ac.uk.

David Ashton is Emeritus Professor at Leicester University and Honorary Professor at Cardiff University. He has published extensively on skill formation, HRM, and workforce development. His latest book with Johnny Sung is *Skills in Business: The Role of Business Strategy, Sectoral Skills Development and Skills Policy*, Sage, 2014. He has provided consultancy services to government departments within the United Kingdom, South Africa, Singapore, the European Union, and international agencies such as the International Labour Organisation (ILO) and World Bank. Contact: davidashton8@gmail.com.

Gerhard Bosch is Director of the Institute for Work, Skills and Training (Institut Arbeit und Qualifikation) and full Professor of Sociology at the University of Duisburg-Essen. He has published a number of books and articles on wages, employment systems, working time, industrial relations, wages, and skills including, with Jean Charest, *Vocational Training: International Perspectives* (Routledge 2010). He has been expert advisor on employment and skills policy to the German government, the European Union, the ILO and the Organisation for Economic Cooperation and Development (OECD). Contact: gerhard.bosch@uni-due.de.

Phillip Brown is Distinguished Research Professor in the School of Social Sciences, Cardiff University. He worked in the auto industry in Oxford before training as a teacher. His academic career took him to Cambridge University and the University of Kent at Canterbury before joining Cardiff University in 1997. He has written, co-authored, and co-edited 16 books including *The Global Auction: The Broken Promises of Education, Jobs and Incomes* with Hugh Lauder and David Ashton (Oxford University Press, 2011). Contact: BrownP1@cardiff.ac.uk.

Jane Bryson is Associate Professoxr in Human Resource Management and Industrial Relations at Victoria Business School, Victoria University of Wellington, New Zealand. She researches the range of factors (institutional, organizational, and individual) which influence human capability at work. Most recently she has examined the impact of employment law on workplace management practices.

John Buchanan is Professor in Working Life and currently Chair of Business Analytics and Principal Advisor (Research Impact) at the University of Sydney Business School. Up to 2014 he was Director of the Workplace Research Centre. His key domains of expertise are in the areas of wage determination, workforce development, health workforce, and the work-health nexus. His current role is principally concerned with deepening the capacity for high impact research and education in the field of data science. He is also helping build capacity for research and education activity of the Business School to assist in the transformation of health and wellbeing in Western Sydney. His most recent co-edited book is *Inclusive Growth in Australia: Social Policy as Economic Investment* (2013). Contact: John.Buchanan@sydney.edu.au

Paul Dalziel PhD is Professor of Economics and Deputy Director of the Agribusiness and Economics Research Unit at Lincoln University, New Zealand. He has more than 100 refereed publications on economic policy, including *Wellbeing Economics* (Wellington: Bridget Williams Books, 2014). He has been involved in four OECD projects and was Science Leader for a national trans-disciplinary research programme on education and employment linkages (2007–2012). Contact: paul.dalziel@lincoln.ac.nz.

Stuart W. Elliott PhD is an analyst in the Directorate of Education and Skills at theOECD. For ten years he directed the Board on Testing and Assessment of the National Research Council in the United States, leading numerous studies on educational tests and indicators, assessment of science and twenty-first-century skills, applications of information technology, and occupational preparation and certification. Contact: stuart.elliott@oecd.org.

Alan Felstead is Research Professor at Cardiff School of Social Sciences, Cardiff University in the United Kingdom. He has published numerous books and articles on skills, training, and employment. Recent books include *Improving Working as Learning*, co-authored with Alison Fuller, Nick Jewson, and Lorna Unwin (Routledge, 2009), and *Unequal Work in Britain* (Oxford University Press, 2015), co-edited with Duncan Gallie and Francis Green. Contact: alanfelstead@cf.ac.uk.

David Finegold is Distinguished Professor at Rutgers University and is the founding Chief Academic Officer for American Honors. He is a leading international expert on skill development systems and their relationship to the changing world of work and economic performance. Contact: david.finegold@americanhonors.org.

Duncan Gallie is Professor of Sociology, University of Oxford, and Emeritus Fellow of Nuffield College, Oxford. His research has examined the changing nature of job quality both in Britain and Europe, the social consequences of unemployment, and attitudes to inequality. He recently published a comparative study of the effects of economic crisis on work and employment relations in Europe, titled *Economic Crisis, Quality of Work and Social Integration* (Oxford University Press, 2013). He has been Vice-President and Foreign Secretary of the British Academy. Contact: duncan.gallie@nuffield.ox.ac.uk.

Lynn Gambin PhD is an economist based at the University of Warwick Institute for Employment Research where she is leads a programme of research on methodological approaches to assessing the rates of return that accrue to individuals obtaining various qualifications, especially those related to vocational education and training (VET). She is also an expert in the evaluation of programmes designed to increase participation in VET and was an adviser to the House of Commons on apprenticeships. Contact: Lynn.Gambin@warwick.ac.uk.

Mary Gatta PhD is Senior Scholar at Wider Opportunities for Women in Washington DC. She leads research on job quality for low-wage workers; workforce development training programmes; and non-traditional jobs for women. Mary's expertise includes integrating a gender lens into policy analysis. She has published numerous books and articles including: *All I Want Is A Job! Unemployed Women Navigating the Public Workforce System* (Stanford University Press, 2014). Contact: mgatta@wowonline.org.

Francis Green is Professor of Work and Education Economics at the LLAKES Centre, UCL Institute of Education, London. His research focuses on skills, training, work quality, and industrial relations issues. His most recent book is *Skills and Skilled Work: An Economic and Social Analysis* (Oxford University Press, 2013). In recent years he has been an expert advisor on skills-related issues to the OECD and the European Union, and to the UK and Singapore governments. Contact: f.green@ioe.ac.uk

Irena Grugulis is Professor of Work and Skills at Leeds University Business School in the United Kingdom. Her specialist area of research is skills, and she has been funded by the ESRC, the EPSRC and the EU. She is Associate Fellow of SKOPE, held a UK AIM/ESRC Research Fellowship and has worked as both editor and editor-in-chief of *Work, Employment and Society*. She sat on the academic advisory board of the UK Commission on Employment and Skills (UKCES) and worked with many government skills enquiries including the Leitch Review.

Michael J. Handel is Associate Professor in the Department of Sociology and Anthropology at Northeastern University in the United States. He studies trends in earnings inequality and job skill requirements, and their relationships to computer technology and the organization of work, including employee involvement practices. His STAMP survey is the basis for sections and items on job skill requirements used in the World Bank's multi-country STEP survey and the OECD's multi-country PIAAC survey.

Terence Hogarth is based at the University of Warwick Institute for Employment Research in the United Kingdom where he leads a programme of research on the costs and benefits related to employers' and individuals' investments in skills. Since the mid-1990s he has directed the Net Costs of Training to Employers series of studies that have been periodically undertaken in England. Contact: T. Hogarth@warwick.ac.uk.

Craig Holmes is a labour economist at Pembroke College, Oxford University; Research Fellow on the Employment, Equity, and Growth programme with INET Oxford; and Research Associate of the Centre on Skills, Knowledge and Organizational Performance

(SKOPE) also at Oxford University. His research interests include earnings inequality, social mobility, behavioural economics, and the economics of education, skills, and skills policy.

Martin Humburg is a former researcher and PhD candidate at the Research Centre for Education and the Labour Market (ROA) at Maastricht University, and is now a senior consultant at ICF International in Brussels. In his dissertation, he examined the relationship between university graduates' skills and their employability. Contact: martin.humburg@icf.com.

Tony Huzzard is Professor of Organization Studies at the Department of Business Administration, Lund University. He has researched and published widely on organizational development, work organization and industrial relations including recent books, with others, *Critical Management Research—Reflections from the Field* (Sage) and *Corporate Governance, Employee Voice and Work Organization: Sustaining High Road Jobs in the Automotive Supply Industry* (Oxford University Press). Contact: tony.huzzard@fek.lu.se.

Ewart Keep PhD is Professor of Education, Training and Skills at the Department of Education, Oxford University. He has published extensively on apprenticeship, lifelong learning, employers' investment in skills, and skill policy formation. He has advised governments and parliamentary committees across the UK, is a member of committees for all three British higher education funding bodies, and has also advised the Australian and New Zealand governments. Contact: ewart.keep@education.ox.ac.uk.

Alice Lam is Professor of Organization Studies at Royal Holloway, University of London. She has researched extensively on how societal institutions influence work organization, learning and knowledge creation within firms. More recently she has examined the role of knowledge in collaborative ventures between organizations, and the role of careers as a vehicle for knowledge transfer between organizations. Contact: Alice.Lam@rhul.ac.uk.

Hugh Lauder is Professor of Education and Political Economy and Director of the Institute for Policy Research at the University of Bath. He worked as a teacher in inner London before taking his doctorate at the University of Canterbury in New Zealand. He has written and co-authored many books, including *The Global Auction: The Broken Promises of Education, Jobs and Incomes* (Oxford University Press, 2011) and has, for over a decade, worked with Phillip Brown on skill formation and the global economy. Contact: h.lauder@bath.ac.uk.

Robert I. Lerman PhD is Institute Fellow at Urban Institute, Professor of Economics at American University, and a Research Fellow at IZA in Bonn, Germany. An expert on apprenticeships, he established the American Institute for Innovative Apprenticeship (www.innovativeapprenticeship.org). His published research covers employment issues, inequality, family structure, income support, and youth development. He earned his BA at Brandeis University and his PhD in economics at MIT in the United States.

Mingwei Liu PhD is Assistant Professor of Labor Studies and Employment Relations at Rutgers University. His research interests include labour relations, trade unions, and skill development in China; high performance work practices; and labour standards and corporate social responsibility in global value chains. He has published articles in leading journals such as the *Industrial and Labor Relations Review* and *British Journal of Industrial Relations* as well as chapters in many books.

D. W. Livingstone is Canada Research Chair in Lifelong Learning and Work, and Professor Emeritus at OISE/University of Toronto. His books include: *Education and Jobs* (University of Toronto Press, 2009), *Lifelong Learning in Paid and Unpaid Work* (Routledge, 2010), *Manufacturing Meltdown* (Fernwood, 2011), *The Knowledge Economy and Lifelong Learning* (Sense Publishers, 2012), *Teacher Learning and Power in the Knowledge Society* (Sense Publishers, 2012), and *Restacking the Deck* (CCPA, 2014). Contact: dwlivingstone@gmail.com.

Caroline Lloyd PhD is Professor in the School of Social Sciences, Cardiff University in the United Kingdom. Her research focuses on the relationships between product markets, labour markets, work organization, and skills. She has published widely on the issue of low-wage work, including co-editing *Low-Wage Work in the UK* (Russell Sage Foundation, 2008) and is currently working on a comparative study of work organization in the service sector. Contact: lloydc4@cardiff.ac.uk.

Wendy Loretto PhD is Professor of Organizational Behaviour at the University of Edinburgh Business School. She has published widely in the field of age and employment, with a particular focus on the ways in which gender and age interact to affect work and retirement experiences (*Human Relations, Work, Employment, and Society*). Her research has been funded by research councils, Scottish and UK governments, charities, trade unions, and employers. Contact: W.Loretto@ed.ac.uk.

David Marsden is Professor of Industrial Relations at the London School of Economics, and a member of the Centre for Economic Performance. He is the author of *The End of Economic Man?* and *A Theory of Employment Systems*, and has researched extensively on how societal institutions shape labour markets, as well as on pay systems and incentives. Contact: D.Marsden@lse.ac.uk.

Cathie Jo Martin is Professor of Political Science at Boston University in the United States and former chair of the Council for European Studies. Her book with Duane Swank, *The Political Construction of Business Interests* (Cambridge, 2012), received the APSA Politics and History Book Award. She also wrote *Stuck in Neutral: Business and the Politics of Human Capital Investment Policy* (Princeton 2000) and *Shifting the Burden: The Struggle over Growth and Corporate Taxation* (Chicago 1991). She held fellowships at the Radcliffe Institute and the Russell Sage Foundation, and co-edited with Jane Mansbridge an APSA presidential task force report, *Negotiating Agreement in Politics* (Brookings 2015).

Ken Mayhew is Emeritus Professor of Education and Economic Performance, at Oxford University, Emeritus Fellow in Economics at Pembroke College Oxford, Extraordinary Professor at Maastricht University, and a member of the Armed Forces Pay Review Body. He was founding director of SKOPE, an ESRC research centre on skills, knowledge, and organizational performance. He has published widely in labour economics and policy analysis, and advised many private and public sector organizations at home and abroad.

Jonathan Payne is Reader in Employment Studies in Leicester Business School at De Montfort University in the United Kingdom. His research interests and publications span the political economy of skill formation and use, vocational education and training policy in the United Kingdom, the changing meaning of "skill", workplace innovation, and job quality.

Chris Phillipson is Professor and Co-Director of the Manchester Interdisciplinary Collaboration for Research on Ageing (MICRA). He is co-editor of the *Sage Handbook of Social Gerontology* (Sage Books, 2010), and author of *Ageing* (Polity Press, 2013). His present research focuses on developing 'age-friendly cities' and changing retirement transitions. He is Fellow of the Gerontological Society of America and a past president of the British Society of Gerontology. Contact: christopher.phillipson@manchester.ac.uk.

John Polesel is Professor and Associate Dean International in the Melbourne Graduate School of Education in the University of Melbourne. He has written over 100 journal articles, book chapters, and commissioned reports, including articles in *Oxford Review of Education*, *Comparative Education*, and *Journal of Education Policy*. His research focuses on youth transitions. He is currently leading a national study for the UK Schools Partnership Forum to deliver vocational learning. Contact: jpolesel@unimelb.edu.au.

Gail Power is currently manager (advisory, people and organizations) in Ernst and Young's Sydney Office in Australia. Prior to this appointment she was a senior research analyst at the Workplace Research Centre in the University of Sydney Business School. She has had extensive experience in evaluating and reforming sectoral systems of workforce development. In recent years she has examined the changing skill requirements and evolving communities of trust concerning workforce development in the Australian agricultural sector, especially cotton growing.

Arwen Raddon PhD is Project Manager at Singapore's Institute of Technical Education. Formerly an academic at the Universities of Warwick and Leicester, she has been a consultant/researcher since 2011. She recently completed a comprehensive World Bank study on Singapore's workforce development system, and researched 'back to work women' for the Institute of Adult Learning and Singapore Workforce Development Agency. Contact: arwen_raddon@ite.edu.sg.

Mari Sako is Professor of Management Studies at Saïd Business School, University of Oxford. Her research on the comparative analysis of supplier relations, employment systems, and education and training resulted in numerous publications, including *Are*

Skills the Answer? (OUP, with Crouch and Finegold), *Prices, Quality and Trust* (CUP), and *Shifting Boundaries of the Firm* (OUP). In 2011–12 she was President of the Society for the Advancement of Socio-Economics (SASE). Contact: mari.sako@sbs.ox.ac.uk.

Günther Schmid is Emeritus Director at the Berlin Social Science Centre (WZB) and has been a professor at the Freie Universitaät Berlin. He has written a number of books, including the *International Handbook for Labour Market Policy and Evaluation* (Edward Elgar, 1996) and *Full Employment in Europe: Managing Labour Market Transitions and Risks* (Edward Elgar, 2008). He has been a member of various advisory bodies, in particular the committee preparing the German labour market reforms under chancellor Schröder, and he is Honorary Doctor at the Universities of Aalborg and Linnaeus. Contact: www.guentherschmid.eu.

Caroline Smith PhD is Deputy Chief Executive Officer, National Employment Services Association (Australia). Her career spans 18 years in employment, skills, and labour market research, and policy roles across government, academia, industry, and the not-for profit sector in Australia and the United Kingdom. Caroline has published a number of related articles and book chapters and was the 2012 Australian-American Fulbright Commission Professional Scholar in VET. Contact: drcarolinefsmith@gmail.com.

Gordon Stanley is Honorary Professor of Education at the University of Sydney. He was the inaugural Pearson Professor of Educational Assessment and Director, Oxford University Centre for Educational Assessment. He has had considerable experience of quality assurance, assessment, and accreditation issues in vocational education as a member of vocational education and training boards in Australia and Hong Kong. Research interests include quality metrics, and competency-based and standards-based assessment systems.

Mark Stuart is Montague Burton Professor of Employment Relations and Director of the Centre for Employment Relations Innovation and Change, University of Leeds. He has published extensively on union change, skills, restructuring, and employment relations, including, with others, *Partnership and the Modernisation of Employment Relations* (Routledge, 2005) and *Trade Unions and Workplace Training: Issues and International Perspectives* (Routledge, 2012). He has led numerous evaluations of the UK Union Learning Fund. Contact: ms@lubs.leeds.ac.uk.

Johnny Sung PhD is Professor and Head of Centre for Skills, Performance, and Productivity at the Institute for Adult Learning (IAL) in Singapore. He has published books, book chapters, reports, and journal articles on high performance working, national skills formation systems, and skills policy. He has provided research input to the UK and Singapore governments as well as international agencies, such as the World Bank and ILO. Contact: johnny_sung@ial.edu.sg.

Chris Tilly is Professor of Urban Planning and Director of the Institute for Research on Labor and Employment at the University of California Los Angeles. He is a labour economist specializing in job quality. His books include *Half a Job: Bad and Good*

Part-Time Jobs in a Changing Labor Market (Temple University Press, 1996), *Stories Employers Tell: Race, Skill, and Hiring in America* (Russell Sage Foundation, 2003), and Are Bad Jobs Inevitable? (Palgrave, 2012). Contact: ctilly@irle.ucla.edu.

Lorna Unwin PhD is Professor Emerita (Vocational Education) and Honorary Professor in the LLAKES Research Centre, UCL Institute of Education, University College London in the United Kingdom. She has published many articles and books on skill formation, including, with colleagues, *Contemporary Apprenticeship: International Perspectives on an Evolving Model of Learning* (Routledge 2013). She advises the UK government and regional bodies and the OECD. Contact: l.unwin@ud.ac.uk.

Rolf Van der Velden is a professor at Maastricht University and Director of the Research Centre for Education and the Labour Market (ROA). He supervised several (inter-) national studies on the transition from school to work (e.g. the REFLEX project: www.reflexproject.org) and was involved in the PIAAC project (http://www.oecd.org/site/piaac). He has published on many studies in the field of education, training, and the labour market. Contact: R.vanderVelden@Maastrichtuniversity.nl.

Sarah Vickerstaff PhD is Professor of Work and Employment, and Head of the School of Social Policy, Sociology, and Social Research at the University of Kent. Her research focuses upon paid work and the life course especially at the beginning and end of working life. She is currently PI for an ESRC/MRC-funded research consortium undertaking a study of: *Uncertain Futures: Managing Late Career Transitions and Extended Working Life*. Contact: S.A.Vickerstaff@kent.ac.uk.

Chris Warhurst PhD is Professor and Director of the Institute for Employment Research at the University of Warwick in the United Kingdom, a Trustee of the Tavistock Institute in London, and a Research Associate of SKOPE at Oxford University. He has published a number of books and articles on skills, including, with colleagues, *The Skills that Matter* (Palgrave, 2004) and *Are Bad Jobs Inevitable?* (Palgrave, 2012). He has been expert advisor on skills policy to the UK, Scottish, and Australian governments, and an international expert advisor to the OECD's LEED programme. Contact: c.warhurst@warwick.ac.uk.

Leesa Wheelahan is an associate professor and the William G. Davis Chair of Community College Leadership at the Ontario Institute for Studies in Education at the University of Toronto. She has published widely on vocational education and training, competency-based training, the links between education and work, and post-secondary education policies. Her publications include *Why Knowledge Matters: A Social Realist Argument* (Routledge, 2012). Contact: leesa.wheelahan@utoronto.ca.

James Wickham PhD is Fellow Emeritus of Trinity College Dublin in Ireland where he was Jean Monnet Professor of European Labour Market Studies, Professor in Sociology, and Director of the Employment Research Centre. He has researched and published on employment, migration, and mobility in Ireland and the European Union including most recently with colleagues, *New Mobilities in Europe: Polish Migration to Ireland Post-2004* (Manchester UP, 2013). Contact: jwickham@tcd.ie.

INTRODUCTION

Skills and Training: Multiple Targets, Shifting Terrain

JOHN BUCHANAN, DAVID FINEGOLD,
KEN MAYHEW, AND CHRIS WARHURST

Skill Matters

Academic concern with skill is longstanding. Indeed, over the last half century, skill has been at the heart of much research on work, employment, and management across sociology, economics, labour/industrial relations, human resource management, education, and, more recently, geography. In the 1950s and 1960s there was a strong optimistic argument made by sociologists and economists, for example, about economic developmental trajectories that centred on upskilling in the advanced economies (Kerr et al. 1960; Bell 1973) and which was qualified in the 1970s and 1980s by more pessimistic claims of deskilling (Braverman 1974; Wood 1982), with a return to greater optimism in accounts of knowledge and creative economies in the 1990s driven largely by academics based in business schools (Reich 1992; Darr and Warhurst 2008). In the 2000s the rhetoric of the knowledge economy remained but the discourse partially shifted terrain again with assertions of a skill polarization led by economists such as Goos and Manning (2007) and largely accepted by other disciplines and which in turn is now also being challenged by other economists (e.g. Holmes and Mayhew 2012).

If skills are often at the heart of academic debate about work, employment, and management, throughout the advanced and developing economies, governments too cling to skill, believing that skills are the answer to a range of policy challenges. Huge expectations now rest on the shoulders of skill (Keep and Mayhew 2010). Skills are commonly regarded as a driver of economic development, as a panacea for social ills (e.g. Leitch 2006; UKCES 2009), and an essential tool of economic recovery and a route out of recession (e.g. EC 2009). Skill has become not just a silver bullet but also a sponge, absorbing many other work and employment issues such as job quality (Gautié and Schmitt 2010) and social equity (Goldin and Katz 2010). Moreover, skills have also become a springboard into other work, employment, and management roles. For example, Skills Australia (2012), in trying to discern the best environment within workplaces to lever skill utilization, stumbled across an underpinning need for good leadership and good human resource management practices.

Thus skills matter not just in and of themselves because they offer a window into a range of academic and policy matters. However, debates and developments are dynamic. What skills are expected to deliver changes, as does the general understanding of 'skill'.

The Multiple Targets Skills are Expected to Hit

It is recognized that 'skill' is both a narrow and blunt concept—used to address productivity and efficiency issues, and more recently workforce and organizational development—and a wider, amorphous concept that masks a myriad of disciplinary, social and historical understandings as well as operational and analytical definitions (e.g. Attewell 1990; Vallas 1990; Appelbaum and Gatta 2005; Bryson 2010; Grugulis and Lloyd 2010). Furthermore, as compared to the 1970s and 1980s, there is increasing recognition of the need to appreciate that skill trajectories in the advanced economies cannot be disentangled from skill developments in the developing economies, as Sung and Raddon, and Liu and Finegold, Chapters 24 and 25, respectively, this volume, illustrate.

At the same time, other debates have become important. In part these new debates relate to the shift from manufacturing to services in the advanced economies as well as to changes in the relative power of the key economic players—the state, employers, and organized labour. In this respect, a key new debate centres on the morphing of understandings and control of skill, and on exactly what these entail as the contributions to this volume, by Payne and Warhurst et al. (Chapters 3 and 4, respectively) highlight. Moreover, as the literature expands to include developing economies, there is a greater emphasis on skills in the informal economy, where a high percentage of the population continues to be employed but which often evades the gaze of official classification and count.

What has been particularly striking most recently has been growing recognition of the need to nest skills initiatives in wider strategies of economic renewal, which involves both the redistribution and not just the growth of income. The importance of dealing directly with the inequality and not expecting too much from skills policies alone has been cogently argued for by Piketty (2014, 304–335). International agencies, such as the OECD, which previously strongly advocated supply-side initiatives, based on the assumption that increased skills boost economic development, have argued in recent pronouncements for the need to engage with a wider range of factors. Along with the International Labour Organization (ILO) and the World Bank, the OECD now explicitly acknowledges that skills alone cannot solve the major economic challenges of our time and that unless the broader forces shaping inequality are tackled, initiatives in particular domains, such as skills, will be of limited impact (OECD 2012; ILO, OECD, and World Bank 2014).

The Shifting Terrain of Debates about Skill

Within these academic debates and policy initiatives, different aspects of skill are given priority over time. What matters about skills frequently shifts. In the context of who pays for post-compulsory education, training, and skill development (see Gambin and Hogarth, Chapter 31), accompanying attempts to make individuals pay (more) for their own education and training, the returns on skills acquisition for individuals have become a concern. Mainstream economic thinking, in the form of human capital theory, suggests that higher skills acquisition provides higher income for individuals. It also posits that firms benefit from higher-skilled individuals through productivity gains. As a consequence, over the past few decades, governments across the world have invested massively in supply-side polices to create more and better skilled workforces. The various beneficiaries of skill are considered in two chapters in this volume: by Holmes (Chapter 17) and Grugulis et al. (Chapter 18). These new debates are, in part, recognition of the failure of skill alone to deliver the anticipated economic, as well as social, improvements. The potential for wage premiums can, for example, decline as the labour markets of the advanced economies become flooded with more individuals with more skills. Relatedly, there is a now a growing concern amongst academics and policymakers about workforces being over-qualified for the jobs available (Smith, Chapter 23).

This failure to deliver has triggered appreciation of the need to move beyond supply-side policies to ones sensitive to demand, deployment, or what government and academics call 'skill utilization'. The Scottish Government is an exemplar in this respect (Warhurst and Findlay 2012). Although not yet underpinned by a robust body of research (Buchanan et al. 2010), skill utilization has become a concern because of its links to issues of business strategy, leadership and management, job design and work organization, and human resource practices (Lloyd 2005; Buchanan 2006; Hall and Lansbury 2006; Skills Australia 2012). The various strands of these debates are covered in this volume by Livingstone (Chapter 14), Ashton et al. (Chapter 15), and Felstead et al. (Chapter 16). The focus on skills utilization has intensified after the global financial crisis of 2008 since both advanced and developing economies have struggled during the slow recovery to create enough good jobs to employ the increasingly well-qualified students graduating from schools and universities. However, such issues are not new; skill has long been a springboard for examining wider issues about, for example, job quality, gender and control in the workplace, social and occupational mobility, and national and regional competitive advantage (e.g. Cockburn 1983; Finegold and Soskice 1988; Reich 1993; Crouch et al. 1999; Gautié and Schmitt 2010).

Once, charting how workers become skilled seemed easy. Becoming a 'skilled worker' involved a time-served apprentice involving on- and off-the-job accredited training and was framed around the so-called 3Ms workforce—male, manual and manufacturing. Now, with a focus on the growth of the services economy, not only is what constitutes a skilled worker contested (see, for example, Payne 2009 and Bolton 2004), as the definition of skill widens, there is new interest in how and where skills are developed. The answer seems to be not just in firms and formal institutions of technical education but also in schools, colleges, and universities as well as through family, friends and peers (Warhurst et al. 2004; Gatta 2005; Warhurst and Nickson 2007; James et al. 2013; also Polesel, Chapter 8 in this volume). However it should be recognized that at least some of the so-called 'soft skills' needed to get and do jobs in services are not new—they are important too *amongst employees* in all workplaces past and present, and are not just about relationships *between employees and clients/customers* in today's service organizations (Moss and Tilly 2001).

This shifting focus from supply to demand, deployment and development, and all that it entails, has raised calls for a more holistic and more nuanced appreciation of the 'skills cycle' (James et al. 2013) encompassing all four of these dimensions and the connections between them. Of course complexity now becomes an issue as treating each point on the skill cycle becomes more difficult. For example, some firms with skill utilization problems that are due to a skills mismatch can be tempted to muddle through, hire new staff, or train existing staff (Gambin et al. 2015). This complexity is compounded by comparative international analyses that show that even 'training' and 'apprenticeship' definitions and delivery systems vary by country, and that these variations have their roots in historical and equally varied settlements between capital, labour, and the state. These settlements are, moreover, subject to change, as the contributions to this volume by Martin (Chapter 2), Buchanan et al. (Chapter 21), and Bosch (Chapter 20) show. Unfortunately this complexity runs counter to many policymakers' (and academics') desire for simplicity. Indeed, the advent of so-called Big Data fuels this desire with the promise that a few algorithms applied to newly available machine-readable data will reveal all that needs to be known. This volume offers a middle way: coherence, but generated in ways that respect the complexity that surrounds skills today.

Capturing the Debates and Developments: A Framework

To capture the richness and diversity of current debates this book has been structured around three basic questions:

1. How are skills and training currently conceptualized and defined in scholarly and policy discourse (Section I)?
2. What are the core factors currently shaping skills in practice (Sections II–VI)?
3. What are the key challenges shaping them for the foreseeable future (Section VII)?

Section I deals with the key frames of reference (and how they are combined) for understanding skills covering conceptualization, and definitional and measurement issues. Perspectives covered include comparative political economy, sociology, education, philosophy, human resource management, and labour relations. The bulk of the book covers the vast, and often growing, literatures on skill formation with its attendant education and training (Section II), the demand for and deployment of skills, including skills utilization (Section III), and the outcomes of these processes for individuals, organizations and society (Section IV). Within any particular 'skill system', approaches to skill formation, use, and associated outcomes are intimately connected. The systems that prevail arise from four levels of determination: the global, the national, the meso (i.e. regional and sectoral), and the enterprise or organizational. The nature of these different levels of determination is examined in Section V. How these levels connect to form identifiable and different skill systems is profoundly shaped by the level of social and economic development within a nation state (Section VI). Skill systems involve more than state-driven projects or individuals making supposedly rational calculations about the rates of return to years of education. Rather, they reflect the balance of forces arrayed around different notions of the role of labour in social life in general and in production in particular—what can be called 'skill settlements'. However, these settlements are rarely static. The forces disrupting them and the factors currently shaping emerging skill settlements are considered in the final section (VII) on current challenges.

Concepts, Definitions, and Measurements of Skill

Section I is concerned with the frames of reference researchers draw upon to make sense of skills and training. While a wide range of disciplines analyse skill in their own distinct ways, scholars are increasingly combining insights from multiple disciplines to make sense of the issues and problems noted above. Bryson (Chapter 1) examines the strengths and weaknesses of the contrasting ways in which different disciplines such as economics, political science, organizational studies, and psychology contribute to understanding the various dimensions of skill from acquisition through recognition to utilization. In Chapter 2, Martin—drawing on comparative historical-political economy, industrial relations, and educational sociology—describes the historical evolution of different national training systems, contrasting them along two axes. The first is whether skills are taught in the regular secondary education system or through vocational schools and apprenticeships. The second is what is taught, some systems emphasizing the acquisition of general skills, others the acquisition of field-specific skills. As Martin shows, skill had a clear meaning in the context of manufacturing industry. However, as the composition of production has altered in developed countries, so the meaning of skill has widened massively. The sort of qualities needed by relatively low-level service sector workers—pleasant demeanour and pleasing appearance, for instance—were once thought of as personal characteristics. Increasingly they are now described as 'skills'. Payne (Chapter 3) in this volume analyses why and how this change has happened and considers its possible consequences. Even when there is agreement on exactly what is meant by 'skill', there are still massive measurement problems. The early days of human capital theory saw years of schooling as the most common measure of human capital acquired in the education system, and the number and duration of training episodes as the measure of skills acquired through workplace training. As better and better data became available on these matters, qualifications obtained became a common metric. However, it is an imperfect measure privileging, as it does, formal education as the key variable of interest and tending to neglect other dimensions of skill. That there are at least three accounts of skill has long been recognized: that which resides with the person, that which resides with the jobs, and that which is socially constructed (Grugulis et al. 2004). Warhurst et al. (Chapter 4) examine how the social construction of skills has changed in recent years with shifts in the balance of power between capital and labour and how the new social construction of skills affects different types of workers by sex, class, and race, variously helping and hindering the employment prospects of these workers. Handel (Chapter 5) grapples with similar issues but with a view to devising a measurement system that draws on the best techniques and insights associated with sociology, labour economics, industrial relations, education, occupational psychology, and human resource management. His survey of skills, technology, and management practices (STAMP) provides a robust way of measuring the content of work based on these variables. Drawing on more tightly defined educational debates, Stanley (Chapter 6) discusses accreditation and assessment methods, contrasting competency-based assessment with standards referenced approaches to defining and measuring skill. All these chapters serve to reinforce caution when interpreting currently available summary statistics about a country's or organization's skill performance.

Skill Formation, Use, and Outcomes

How and why skills are formed, principally through education and training, has been a matter of longstanding interest to researchers and policymakers alike (Section II). Over the last 50 years one of the most influential intellectual traditions shaping analysis of these matters has been human capital theory—a narrative originally developed by Mincer (1958), Schultz (1961) and Becker (1962, 1964). While initially novel in the insights it generated, especially concerning the education–earnings nexus, it is a research tradition more noted now for its narrowing of analytical concerns than for any new knowledge created (Dalziel, Chapter 7). In recent decades most original insights into the dynamics of workforce development have emerged beyond—and often in explicit opposition to—this approach. The other chapters in Section II provide an overview of these rich analytical streams. Schools have long been recognized as important sites for preparing citizens for work—but their contribution involves more than 'years of education'. An overview of the different ways they deliver pre-employment skills formation is provided through a comparison of the German (tracked) and Australian (generalist) approaches to vocational education at secondary school level (Polesel, Chapter 8). Understanding how universities develop higher-level technical and cognitive capacities requires far more than understanding the years of education–earning nexus. In Chapter 10, Humburg and van der Velden assess the wide array of forces at work in the sector dealing with preparation of professional and senior managerial employees. At a formal level human capital theory acknowledges learning occurs both on and off the job. Its stylized approach to this matter, however, fails to grapple with the complexities within both domains and how they interact. The rich dynamics associated with how the apprenticeship model of learning combines both is documented by Lerman (Chapter 9). The human capital tradition is equally weak in engaging with how employers differ in the way in which they either contribute to or hinder the development of human capability on the job. The growing literature on this issue is considered by Unwin (Chapter 11). How workplaces shape learning is not solely determined by employers. Unions have also had a longstanding interest in this matter—a role that has changed dramatically in both content and scale in countries such as Sweden and the United Kingdom in recent times (Stuart and Huzzard, Chapter 12). Finally, skill formation evolves over individuals' working lives. The manner in which this evolution occurs depends greatly on how societies either help or hinder citizens' capacities to navigate transitions between work and non-working spheres of life. Schmid (Chapter 13) summarizes the latest developments concerning this dimension of workforce development.

While interest in skill formation has been of longstanding analytical and policy concern, interest in skill utilization is of more recent origin. The key aspects of this emerging literature are dealt with in Section III. As levels of educational attainment have increased it has become increasingly clear that while we may live in knowledge society we are yet to live in a knowledge economy (Livingstone 1999). This reality has made skill under-utilization a matter of growing policy attention. The limited evidence that is available shows how extensive the problem can be: in the United Kingdom, for example, almost half (48%) of employers report skills under-use amongst their workforce (UKCES 2014). Under-utilization is thought to be bad for individuals, firms and nations. However, as Livingstone (Chapter 14) points out and explores, there are two key challenges in assessing the extent of skill under-utilization: first, resolving how to define skill utilization; second, understanding who uses the skill available and for what purpose. Ashton et al. (Chapter 15) explore some of the implications of this challenge by examining how differing business strategies in manufacturing and services influence skill use. Their analysis challenges the widely held belief that the 'right' workforce skills are an essential element of organizational competiveness. They note that the framing of this belief tends to be underpinned by prescriptive rather than descriptive supporting evidence. In reality the hard evidence is mixed. What is clear, however, is that there is some relative autonomy for employers to make choices about their business strategies and the skills of their workforces. It would seem therefore that skill under-utilization is a product of employers' business models and the policy environments in which they operate. Felstead et al. (Chapter 16) review the different types of international and national skills data currently available on skill stocks, job skills, and skill mismatches, critically appraising the underlying concepts of skill and the collection techniques used to generate these data. As they point out, this is not merely a technocrat exercise of purely academic interest but one that impacts how governments around the world make decisions about investment in education and training for their citizens and which affects international comparisons of national competitiveness.

The two chapters in Section IV consider the outcomes associated with skill acquisition. Research in this area has been at the heart of economists' approach to the subject and has been highly influential with policymakers, not least in deciding what areas of training activity to subsidize. Holmes (Chapter 17) reviews research on the economic returns to individuals, demonstrating that there are still a number of unresolved methodological difficulties with conventional econometric approaches. Prominent amongst these difficulties is the use of misleading or inappropriate control groups. This theme is pursued by Grugulis et al. (Chapter 18). They discuss the possible returns of skill acquisition to the employer and to the national economy in terms of higher productivity and faster economic growth. The authors of both chapters argue that the contingent nature of many of the econometric results has not always been fully appreciated by policymakers and that this problem has led to some faulty policy interventions, and to a tendency to over-estimate both the private and social economic returns. Grugulis et al. note, however, the broader non-economic benefits to skill acquisition in terms of individuals' lifestyles and their behaviour in civil society. Treating knowledge and skills as primarily leading to narrowly defined economic benefits can result in the neglect of the benefit of skills for the quality of life more broadly.

Skill Systems: Levels of Determination and Dynamics of Development

Given that skills involve more than benefits to individuals and are shaped by significantly more than individuals making self-interested, rational calculations about their own rates of return, it is necessary to consider what actually does shape the formation, uses, and outcomes of skills. The four chapters in Section V deal with such questions at the global, national, meso, and organizational levels. Whilst each chapter deals with a different level of analysis, they share a common understanding of how the different levels are connected. Whilst each has a distinct impact, none operate independently of the others. Indeed, each level shapes the operation of the others.

Lauder et al. (Chapter 19) consider the global level. They begin with an evaluation of the main theories of skill formation, which they term 'universal' and 'particularistic'. They assess the utility of these theories against developments in the globalization of the world economy. They argue that, in this context, a new agenda for skill formation is needed that uses insights from the particularistic theories but within an emergent model of global skill formation driven by transnational companies. Doing so, they further argue, highlights an additional need—for national governments to develop industrial policies that match the supply of skills to demand in this new context.

Bosch (Chapter 20) considers the nature of different national skill systems. He notes that skill systems are not pre-determined by technology or other practical constraints but are social (and often quintessentially national) institutions within which there is scope for independent action. Drawing on different disciplinary approaches to understanding these social institutions, he outlines various typologies of national skill systems, focusing particularly on vocational training, and noting that some systems are perceived to function better than others. The bad news for governments is that it is difficult to transpose these better systems—which, of course, does not stop governments wanting (and trying) to do so. The consequence is that differences in national skill systems and their functionality are likely to remain.

Even within national systems there is often considerable variation in practice at the regional and sectoral levels. Buchanan et al. (Chapter 21) shift the focus to understanding skills in this context. Recent efforts to reshape skill systems at this level have centred on what are referred to as 'skill ecosystems'. Although this notion emerged out of reflections on novel experiences in the United States, they note that most practical initiatives to reform ecosystems have occurred in Australia, though strongest political support has occurred in Scotland. Whilst welcome, these efforts have not been sufficiently ingrained or sustained to achieve lasting change. Unless there is an alignment of activity at national, regional, and enterprise level—as well as at sector/regional level—significant, lasting reform to skill ecosystems is all but impossible to achieve.

The firm level is examined by Lam and Marsden (Chapter 22). They analyse skill development within different types of employment systems in the context of organizational change. No firm is an island—and Lam and Marsden highlight how enterprise level choice and practice is profoundly shaped by 'societal effects' such as wider 'educational' and 'employment relations'. Their focus is on learning-by-doing and the accumulation of practical experience and skill in this context, mindful that there are different and dynamic interests at play amongst workers, managers, and investors. They argue that societal influences affect the current operation of employment systems. These influences come from two directions: the nature of skills and knowledge that employees bring to the labour market from educational systems; and the way societal institutions affect the operation and choice of firm governance arrangements for skills and knowledge. Whilst there is room for some autonomy at the enterprise level, these broader 'societal effects' profoundly limit the realm for discretionary action.

Most of the analysis of skill systems has been concerned with developments in the advanced capitalist economies. The nature of skill systems varies with—and often plays a critical role in shaping—the levels and character of development within countries. What is striking, however, is the commonality of the skill mismatching problem across countries at very different stages of development. This is a common theme of the chapters in Section VI. For the advanced industrial economies, where the vast majority of individuals complete secondary education and a high percentage continue into some form of tertiary education, having a sufficient supply of skills is rarely a serious concern. Instead, as Smith (Chapter 23) notes, the focus of policy debates is shifting toward skills demand and whether there will be a sufficient quantity of good jobs for individuals to use the skills that they and society have invested in, and if the skills that are being developed are the right ones for today's global economy. Singapore and South Korea are starting to confront similar issues, as their developmental states have been extremely successful in moving their economies rapidly up the skill ladder (Sung and Raddon, Chapter 24). In both countries, strong governments have simultaneously used industrial policy to help foster more higher-value-added sectors and corporate strategies and continuously upgraded the education and training system to ensure companies have a well- and appropriately-prepared workforce to meet their needs. As their development has matured, these economies have struggled to make full use of their increasingly educated populations. China and India, by contrast, are still at the early stages of this transition from low- to high-skill equilibria (Liu and Finegold, Chapter 25). The world's two largest workforces, which together will account for over one-third of human capital in the first part of the twenty-first century, have very rapidly increased their investments in education and training over the last two decades, but continue to struggle with uneven quality of much provision and the failure of skills demand to keep pace with the increase in supply.

What Are the Current Challenges?

The final Section (VII) explores the forces making for change and the key challenges that will shape the character of these changes. Whilst this volume highlights the diversity of institutional systems and approaches to skill development, the concluding chapters highlight the common set of challenges that most nations are facing today. Arguably, the greatest change emerging is that affecting demand, especially the character (and not just the level) of labour required for productive activity. Perhaps top of this list is the likely disruption posed by technological change, as the integration of advances in artificial intelligence, sensors, robotics, and other fields have the potential to fully automate 60% or more of all jobs by 2030 (Elliott, Chapter 26). At the same time that technology is eliminating many good jobs, it is also intensifying competition for those jobs that remain by facilitating the process of globalization. The most visible manifestation of this process in skills systems is the rise of international skill flows and migration. Wickham (Chapter 27) describes the increasing flow of labour (low- and high-skill, temporary and permanent) across borders, as individuals from populous emerging nations seek opportunities in richer, lower birth rate OECD countries. Initially the most acute manifestations of increased global competition in labour markets were felt amongst lower-skilled, blue and white collar workers undertaking routine tasks. But Sako (Chapter 28) shows that even very advanced education provides no guarantee of job security as high-end work in many professions that until recently was almost exclusively performed in-country has been routinized and standardized, enabling firms to move it around the world to where they can find the most available talent at the best price. Compounding problems of increasing competition on the supply-side of the labour market originating from rising global integration are increases in labour supply from domestic sources. As

Loretto et al. (Chapter 29) show, advances in medicine and public health have generated major gains in life expectancy around the world, with an accompanying increase in the age of the of the workforce and need to help individuals prepare for multiple and more varied career changes.

Whilst changes in the conditions of labour demand and supply will make change inevitable, the actual nature of the change that will prevail will be shaped by how skills are defined and how the financial burden associated with skill development and the benefits of their use are distributed and organized. Wheelahan (Chapter 30) identifies the need to question the increasingly narrow vision of work-related skills training currently prevailing in the United Kingdom and many Commonwealth countries. Moving beyond the age-old 'education' versus 'training' dualism, she highlights the importance of redefining skills on the basis of Sen's (1999) and Nussbaum's (2000) notions of capability and argues for nurturing what she calls a modern notion of vocation and vocational streams. Recasting skill regimes along these lines has the potential for providing both rewarding careers for individuals and adaptive capacity for organizations and sectors facing increasingly uncertain futures. The last two chapters engage with the thorny question of financing and organizing skill development. As education and training vie with a range of competing policy priorities for tightly constrained public funding, a core issue that governments will face is who should pay (Gambin and Hogarth, Chapter 31). In the context of the financial squeeze on education and training, Keep (Chapter 32) seeks to synthesize key lessons from the research across the volume to help guide policymakers as they confront these difficult challenges. He concludes that the issue is not just the level and distribution and funding—but how skill systems are organized and what funding models are used to nurture effective responses to the change and turbulence faced by all economies.

Conclusion: 'The Old Is Dying and the New Is Waiting to Be Born'

Gramsci's observation concerning the situation prevailing at the end of the Great War[1] neatly captures the nature of our times. The skills of a population—how and what human capability is developed and used—are matters of perennial policy and analytical concern. The contributions to this handbook highlight that, whilst there are in fact diverse perspectives on this matter, the divergence in disciplinary outlooks is not as great as it once may have been. Nearly all the contributions question explicitly or implicitly the simple-minded human capital framing that until recently has had

[1] This quote is a variant on Gramsci's observation on the upheavals in Europe following the end of the First World War. In the original it reads: 'The crisis consists precisely in the fact that the old is dying and the new cannot be born; in this interregnum a great variety of morbid symptoms appear' (1971, 276).

such pervasive influence, not just in mainstream economics but also, more importantly, amongst many public policymakers. Whilst interest in moving beyond a preoccupation with supply-side concerns is growing, much work remains to be done. This handbook provides a benchmark of the current understanding of the dynamics and dilemmas of skill demand and deployment. With this understanding has also come a greater appreciation of the difficulty of changing both utilization and of achieving a fairer and more sustainable distribution of the costs and benefits of skill development. Whilst scholarly understanding of these matters is on the rise, the reality of who pays is becoming more narrowly defined. Individuals are finding themselves bearing more of the burden as employers and the state shift the costs and risks of skill development onto workers. This outcome is a legacy not of human capital theory's superior understanding of skills issues; rather, it is occurring because more workers are finding themselves in labour markets with increasing numbers of highly skilled competitors both domestically and internationally. In a situation of excess supply of skilled labour and weakened organized labour, employers and the state are in a position to shift costs relatively easily.

As the chapters on skills systems show, the determinants of the current situation reflect forces at work at the global, national, meso, and enterprise level. Affecting policy-induced change is, therefore, very difficult. But equally, as the final section demonstrates, profound changes in skill demand and use are already well underway. Shifts in the level as well as the content of skill demand consequent upon the most recent round of technological change is (and will continue to be) significant. The shifts in labour supply will be just as important—globally as well as domestically. How these forces play out will be shaped directly by how the nature of skill requirements is defined (for example, narrow conception of immediately relevant 'competence' on the British Commonwealth model versus a more expansive notion of capability, elements of which already prevail in some European systems). They will also be shaped by policies concerning the distribution of the costs and benefits of productivity gains that come from skills and allied innovations at enterprise, sectoral, and national levels.

Arguably the key issue requiring closer attention is how new institutional capacity to respond to these new understandings and challenges can be established. The dynamics shaping current and emerging systems are documented in this book. Just how they will evolve is an open question. Whilst the policy legacy of human capital theory, with its preoccupation with supply issues is still strong (especially in a situation of expanding skilled labour supply), the analytical and policy resources to transcend it are stronger than ever. The outcome in terms of the types of skills systems that prevail will ultimately be settled at national and sectoral/regional level. As such, whilst the forces for change are common and appear to be converging around the globe, the diversity in skill systems and regimes is set to continue—but in different forms. This handbook includes the key thinkers and offers state of the art understanding of these skill debates and developments. As the targets and terrain continue to expand and shift, what is known and understood now about skill will inevitably change and will be informed by the contributions to this handbook.

References

Appelbaum, E. and Gatta, M. (2005) *Managing for the Future: 21st Century Skills and High School Educated Workers*, New Brunswick, NJ: Center for Women and Work, Rutgers University.

Attewell, P. (1990) 'What is Skill?', *Work and Occupations*, 17(4): 422–448.

Becker, G. (1962) 'Investment in Human Capital: A Theoretical Analysis', *Journal of Political Economy*, 70(5) (Part 2): 9–49.

Becker, G. (1964) *Human Capital: A Theoretical and Empirical Analysis with Special Reference to Education*, New York: Columbia University Press.

Bell, D. (1973) *The Coming of Post Industrial Society*, New York: Basic Books.

Bolton, S. (2004) 'Conceptual Confusions: Emotion Work as Skilled Work', in C. Warhurst, E. Keep, and I. Grugulis (eds), *The Skills That Matter*, London: Palgrave: 19–37.

Braverman, H. (1974) *Labor and Monopoly Capital*, New York: Monthly Press.

Bryson, J. (2010) *Beyond Skill*, Houndmills: Palgrave Macmillan.

Buchanan, J. (2006) *From 'Skill Shortages' to Decent Work: The Role of Better Skill Ecosystems*, Sydney, NSW Board of Vocational Education and Training.

Buchanan, J., Scott, L., Yu, S., Shutz, H., and Jakubauskas, M. (2010) *Skill Utilisation: An Overview of Current Approaches to Measurement and Improvement*, Sydney: Workplace Research Centre, University of Sydney.

Cockburn, C. (1983) *Machinery of Dominance*, London: Pluto.

Crouch, C., Finegold, D., and Sako, M. (1999) *Are Skills the Answer?* Oxford: Oxford University Press.

Darr, A. and Warhurst, C. (2008) 'Assumptions, Assertions and the Need for Evidence: Debugging Debates about Knowledge Workers', *Current Sociology*, 56(1): 25–45.

European Commission (EC) (2009) *Economic Crisis in Europe: Causes, Consequences and Responses*, Luxembourg: Office for Official Publications of the European Communities.

Finegold, D. and Soskice, D. (1988) 'The Failure of Training in Britain: Analysis and Prescription', *Oxford Review of Economic Policy*, 4(3): 21–53.

Gambin, L., Hogarth, T., Murphy, L., Spreadbury, K., Warhurst, C., and Winterbotham, M. (2015) *Research to Understand the Extent, Nature and Impact of Skills Mismatches in the Eeconomy*, London: BIS.

Gautié, J. and Schmitt, J. (eds) (2010) *Low Wage Work in the Wealthy World*, New York: Russell Sage.

Goldin, C. D. and Katz, L. F. (2010) *The Race between Education and Technology: The Evolution of US Educational Wage Differentials, 1890–2005*, Cambridge, MA: Belknap Press.

Goos, M. and Manning, A. (2007) 'Lousy and Lovely Jobs: The Rising Polarization of Work in Britain', *Review of Economics and Statistics*, 89(1): 118–133.

Gramsci, A. (1971) *Selections from the Prison Notebooks* (translated and edited by Q. Hoare and G. Nowell-Smith), London: Lawrence and Wishart.

Grugulis, I., Warhurst, C., and Keep, E. (2004) 'What's happening to "skill"?', in C. Warhurst, I. Grugulis, and E. Keep (eds), *The Skills that Matter*, Basingstoke: Palgrave: 1–18.

Grugulis, I. and Lloyd, C. (2010) 'Skill and the Labour process: The Conditions and Consequences of Change', in P. Thompson and C. Smith (eds), *Working Life*, Houndmills: Palgrave Macmillan: 91–112.

Hall, R. and Lansbury, R. (2006) 'Skills in Australia: Towards Workforce Development and Sustainable Skill Ecosystem', *Journal of Industrial Relations*, 48(5): 575–592.

Holmes, C. and Mayhew, K. (2012) *Is the UK Labour Market Polarising?* London: Resolution Foundation.

ILO, OECD, and World Bank (2014) *G20 Labour Markets: Outlook, Key Challenges and Policy Responses*, Report prepared for the G20 Labour and Employment Ministerial Meeting, Melbourne, 10–11 September.

James, S., Warhurst, C., Tholen, G., and Commander, J. (2013) 'What We Know and What We Need to Know about Graduate Skills', *Work, Employment and Society*, 27(6): 952–963.

Keep, E. and Mayhew, K. (2010) 'Moving beyond Skills as a Social and Economic Panacea', *Work, Employment and Society*, 24(3): 565–577.

Kerr, C., Dunlop, J. T., Harbison, F., and Myers, C. A. (1960) *Industrialism and Industrial Man*, Boston, MA: Harvard University Press.

Leitch Review of Skills (2006) *Prosperity for All in the Global Economy: World Class Skills*, Final Report, London: Stationery Office.

Lloyd, C. (2005) 'Competitive Strategy and Skill in the Fitness Industry', *Human Resource Management Journal*, 15(2): 15–34.

Livingstone, D. W. (1999) 'Lifelong Learning and Underemployment in the Knowledge Society: A North American Perspective', *Comparative Education*, 35(2): 163–186.

Mincer, J. (1958) 'Investment in Human Capital and Personal Income Distribution', *Journal of Political Economy*, 66(4): 281–302.

Moss, P. and Tilly, C. (2001) *Stories Employers Tell*, New York: Russell Sage Foundation.

Nussbaum, M. (2000) *Women and Human Development: The Capabilities Approach*, Cambridge: Cambridge University Press.

OECD (2012) *Better Skills, Better Jobs, Better Lives: A Strategic Approach to Skills Policies*, Paris: OECD Publishing. http://skills.oecd.org/documents/OECDSkillsStrategyFINALENG.pdf.

Payne, J. (2009) 'Emotional Labour and Skill: A Reappraisal', *Gender, Work & Organization*, 16(3): 348–367.

Piketty, T. (2014) *Capital in the Twenty-First Century*, Cambridge, MA: Belknap Press.

Reich, R. (1992) *The Work of Nations*, New York, Vintage Books.

Schultz, T. W. (1961) 'Investment in Human Capital', *American Economic Review*, 51(1): 1–17.

Sen, A. (1999) *Development as Freedom*, New York: Knopf.

Skills Australia (2012) *Better Use of Skills, Better Outcomes: A Report on Skills Utilisation in Australia* (April), Canberra: Department of Education, Employment and Workplace Relations. http://www.industry.gov.au/skills/Publications/Documents/Skills-utilisation-research-report-15-May-2012.pdf.

UK Commission for Employment and Skills (UKCES) (2009) *Ambition 2020: World Class Skills and Jobs for the UK*, Wath-upon-Dearne: UKCES.

UK Commission for Employment and Skills (UKCES) (2014) *Employer Skills Survey 2013: UK Results*, Wath-upon-Dearne: UKCES.

Vallas, S. (1990) 'The Concept of Skill: A Critical Review', *Work and Occupations*, 17(4): 379–398.

Warhurst, C., Grugulis, I., and Keep, E. (eds) (2004) *The Skills that Matter*, Basingstoke: Palgrave.

Warhurst, C. and Nickson, D. (2007) 'Employee Experience of Aesthetic Labour in Retail and Hospitality', *Work, Employment and Society*, 21(1): 103–120.

Warhurst, C. and Findlay, (2012) 'More Effective Skills Utilisation: Shifting the Terrain of Skills Policy in Scotland', SKOPE Research Paper no.107, SKOPE, Universities of Oxford and Cardiff.

Wood, S. (ed) (1982) *The Degradation of Work* London: Hutchinson.

SECTION I

CONCEPTS, DEFINITIONS, AND MEASUREMENTS OF SKILL

CHAPTER 1

DISCIPLINARY PERSPECTIVES ON SKILL

JANE BRYSON

'SKILL' is a term that everyone thinks they understand. From infancy through adulthood to old age we all lay claim to a range of skills, or have them attributed to us or to the activities we engage in. They are developed, recognized and utilized in different ways for different purposes. Commonly we assume skill refers to one's ability to do things, but when one approaches skill from different perspectives it shows us that skill is also located in the job or activity, and that skill is socially constructed.

Skill is deceptively simple and complex at the same time. From a child development perspective, the marvel of growing skills is complicated by factors which enhance or inhibit physiological and psychological processes. For example, environmental conditions influencing nutrition and nurturing such as access to food and education, quality of parenting, and circumstances in the home can all impact whether skills are developed, which ones, and to what level of expertise. Also as adolescents and adults, in our work and non-work lives, skills are complicated by how they are developed, recognized, and valued. For example, skills developed in one employment setting may not be recognized and valued in another, a phenomenon most starkly illustrated by migrants unable to utilize their foreign-developed skills and qualifications, or by locals with years of practical experience but no recognized qualification, or by young people with base qualifications but no work experience.

Skill is instrumental. It serves us in individual, social and economic life, aiding our survival and wellbeing. It also serves others. In the broadest sense skill is mutually relied upon in everyday interactions in various communities and contexts (for example, through skills of communication and organization). Skill is used by both paying employers and voluntary organizations to contribute to business goals. Skill may be developed and shaped in the context of its use. It is in the access to skill development opportunity, and in the recognition, utilization and valuing of skills, that complexity emerges and skill becomes intensely politicized. These complicating factors bring skill within the realm of political decision-making over allocation and distribution of education resources, state involvement, and social valuing of skill.

Academic interest in skill examines, theorizes, or directs the shaping of that instrumentality. Disciplines such as psychology and education explore how an individual develops skills: how skill can be taught, or learnt, or reshaped. The interests of other disciplines, such as economics, sociology, industrial relations, and human resource management, canvass skill formation and value but more often through a view based on economic instrumentality, that is, how skill is shaped to serve economic ends. Thus, although there are strands of literature that take a broader view of skill for living in society, recent interest and public policy have been dominated by skills for vocational purposes in order to drive economic growth.

This chapter's objective is to assist the reader's critical comprehension of different perspectives on skill. In order to analyse skill discussions, one needs to appreciate the variety of ways in which skill is framed and theorized depending on the disciplinary paradigm underpinning the view. This chapter introduces some of these different disciplinary perspectives on skill. It would simplify analyses such as this if we all adhered to a single discipline and each discipline had a single world view. But, of course, neither of these things happens. The topical context and issues associated with studying work, workers, economies, societies, and skill requires a cross-disciplinary lens, examining both institutional- and individual-level influences thus combining the political, economic, sociological, organizational, and psychological. However, unpicking cross-disciplinary approaches, or indeed trying to knit them together, can be confusing. Skill is discussed as both a quality (what it is, how one develops it or uses it) and a quantity (high-skilled versus low-skilled, or calculating the cost and the financial benefit of skill). There are differences in the interests of researchers within each discipline about skill; consequently, they ask different questions and use different methods to explore them.

For example, a psychologist is usually more concerned with how we acquire skill; an educationalist focuses on teaching of skill for optimal learning and education outcomes such as successful course completion. An economist is more interested in the economic value of specific skills, the incentives to invest in their development, and their contribution to the economy; a sociologist may be more concerned with which skills are recognized by society, how they are valued and why; and a political scientist with how different national institutions and policies impact skill formation and distribution.

In a related vein, Fenwick reviews a variety of disciplinary accounts of workplace learning and argues that the differences are 'not perspectival, but ontological' (2010, 79). She demonstrates that, under the label of 'learning', disciplines such as adult education, human resource management (HRM) and organization studies, 'actually delineate different objects of study' (2010, 80). The same may be true of skill. Hence this chapter identifies three cross-disciplinary lenses on skill, and within these discusses the features and focus brought by the different disciplines commonly utilizing each lens. The first discussed is political economy of skill approaches, which tend to be the preserve of economics, political science, sociology, and industrial relations; the second I have labelled skill as organizational resource, which is a view of skill typified by organization studies and HRM; the third is learning theory approaches to skill dominated by psychology and education. There is of course blurring of the artificial boundaries I have delineated here; in fact, they are not boundaries at all, merely broad categories to aid analysis. In practice, different disciplines, to varying degrees, do take account of other disciplinary approaches, for example, sociology takes account of the economic consequences of having skill. Hopefully awareness of different perspectives allows one to span or integrate them in ways that could lead to advances in theorizing and policymaking in the future.

Table 1.1 poses a series of questions in order to interrogate different disciplinary perspectives on skill. Disciplines differ in that they may:

- have different views on each of these questions
- be more concerned or place greater weight on some questions rather than others (and/or have different goals in mind)
- have different ways of investigating these questions.

Table 1.1 Different perspectives on skill

Typical broad theoretical approach	Political economy of skill		Skill as organizational resource	Learning theory
Underpinning disciplines	Economics	Political science, sociology, industrial relations	Organization studies, HRM	Psychology and education
What is skill?	Economic resource Skill as the input Skill as an independent variable Skill is technical, firm-specific, or general	Individual and social or collective resource (interdependency of skills) Skill as a dependent variable Skill is in the job	Organizational resource (RBV) Skill in person and job	Individual attribute, competency Skill as the product or output Skill as an independent variable Skill is in the person
How do we acquire skill?	Institutional arrangements for systems of skill formation	Socially constructed; social networks, institutions	Buy it in, develop on the job—dependent on organization strategy	Learning processes, pedagogical processes, skill transfer

(continued)

Table 1.1 Continued

Typical broad theoretical approach	Political economy of skill		Skill as organizational resource	Learning theory
Underpinning disciplines	Economics	Political science, sociology, industrial relations	Organization studies, HRM	Psychology and education
Why have skill? How is it used?	Individual investment for personal gain or public good?	Human/social right/ entitlement to a level of skill	Organizations as learning environments; communities of practice	Individual performance and/or communities of practice
How is skill recognized?	Qualifications signal skill. Differing pay levels as labour market supply and demand dictates	Occupational/ skill hierarchies/ ecosystems	Qualifications and matching at recruitment; performance on the job; completion of company-endorsed training	Formal assessment processes for task mastery and competence
What impacts does skill have?	Source of competitive advantage and economic growth	Personal and societal	Contribution to organization performance	Personal and interpersonal wellbeing

Political Economy of Skill

Political economy approaches study the interrelationship of political action, policy, and economic process. It has been regarded as a hybrid of political science and of economics, but is a cross-disciplinary perspective utilized also by sociology, industrial relations, and other social sciences. Broadly speaking, the political economy of skill examines the range of institutions and actors of modern economies (particularly varieties of capitalism) in relation to skill formation, utilization, and value. This may involve analysing the social and economic consequences or impact of different skill-formation regimes, such as investigating the behaviour of governments and employers in relation to investment and provision of vocational education and training, and issues of skill supply and demand in the labour market, or analysing how skill demands can drive income inequality and other consequences. In some instances the wider purview of political economy has given rise to overarching analytical models. For example, the notion of skills equilibria and skill ecosystems has assisted examination of the range of institutions, policies, practices, and conditions at region, industry and firm level which impact the skill demand and supply in a particular industry or location (Finegold 1999; Buchanan 2006).

Political economists are interested in outcomes associated with skill and in how institutions such as vocational training systems, industrial relations systems, and welfare policies shape how skill is regarded and distributed in society (locally and globally). Economists tend to approach political economy with an emphasis on the operation of the market for skills—the labour market—as a central feature of their considerations. This reflects their disciplinary roots. Similarly, sociologists, political scientists, and industrial relations experts all engage in the political economy of skill debates with more of a sociocultural perspective than an economic one. In particular, political scientists appreciate that politics significantly influence 'what kind of skilled labour market employers (and trainees) faced, as well as the kinds of solutions available for redressing the particular market failures that emerged in different contexts' (Thelen 2004, 16). Hence, political economy in the hands of a neoclassical economist is quite different to political economy in the hands of a political scientist or sociologist. So at the risk of over simplification the following summarizes perspectival differences in what is attended to or prioritized.

Economics

Economics as a discipline has been described as 'the study of how people choose to use resources' (American Economic Association), and as the analysis of the production of wealth and its distribution. Microeconomics examines individual decisions and economic behaviour (of people, firms, and markets), whilst macroeconomics is the study of the whole economy, usually national economies but also the global and regional economies. Macroeconomics defines and analyses relationships between broad economic aggregates representing the sum of behaviours, transactions, and financial flows in the economy: for instance, national income, saving and consumer expenditure, investment, aggregate employment, quantity of money (money supply), and balance of payments. Macroeconomic outcomes are a function of many micro-outcomes (individual behaviours), and micro-outcomes are influenced by events at the macro-level. Thus macroeconomics examines economy-wide phenomena, finding the conditions under which the economic system is in equilibrium and noting the characteristics of this in order to make predictions. A common difference amongst economists is their views on what influences macroeconomic conditions, in particular the role of government policy in guiding the macroeconomy.

The interests and priorities of economics are reflected in its research tools and methods. Uppermost for many economists has been a desire to explain, forecast, or predict economic behaviour (of individuals, businesses, nations) and thereby to shape future actions. The explanation and forecasting of economic behaviour is done by creating models of markets or economies often based on statistical analysis of large datasets. For instance, labour economists (those specializing in the economics of labour or work) analyse the operation of labour markets for various types of labour or skill. They form models of the demand for and supply of labour, and the influencing factors that bring these two features into equilibrium, such as wages offered, training available, jobs available, etc. Generally, however, economics is not good at labour market forecasting because of an inability to project changes in demand—that is, employer behaviour.

Therein lies the challenge for economics: the inability to accurately predict some aspects of economic behaviour undermines its models.

Thus economics, like many disciplines, does not have a consensus view on how best to shape or understand an economy. Various schools of thought have competed for intellectual dominance such as classical, neoclassical, Keynesian, Chicago, and monetarist beliefs, to name a few. These differ either in the assumptions they make about economic behaviour or the priority they accord to specific features of the economy. For example, a central assumption of neoclassical approaches is to separate economic theory from social context: a rather mechanical view of the economy and its operation is the result. This view had a significant impact on the economic policies and institutions of many English-speaking countries in the 1980s 1990s. However, there are certain pervasive assumptions that cut across various economic orientations such as a presumption of rational behaviour by economic actors, and markets as a key unit of analysis and as economic drivers. Turning attention to economic perspectives of skill we also find common ground.

From an economist's perspective, skill is an economic resource. Economics tends to look at skill in terms of cost, value, and returns on investment in skills to the economy, the firm, and the individual. Thus there is a focus on the rational investment in skill and associated market behaviour, and an absence of consideration of other factors, such as emotional investment in skill (e.g. driven by individual interest, skill heritage, or cultural valuing). Although it is interested in the pay-off of skill to individuals, by and large economics assesses skill disembodied from the person.

Skill is seen as an input to the production process or economic activity which increases the value of raw materials or interactions, and is thus an essential element of the economy. Economists are particularly interested in using skill differences to explain different economic outcomes, both at a macro- and a micro-level: for instance, examining gross domestic product (GDP), prosperity, and wellbeing in relation to national skill levels, or calculating the return on investment in education and training to the firm, or the return to the individual in the form of increased wage-earning capacity over time. Indeed, skill is often used as the independent variable in economic research, which is used to predict or explain variations in some other variable.

Economic interest in skill has thus had an instrumental focus: how skill contributes to the economy. Economists have historically emphasized the difficulties of the labour market in meeting the skill needs of industry. In particular, attention has been paid to the failure of markets to provide skill formation for workplaces, the argument being that firms lacked the incentive to invest in training their workers for fear that they might quit and join a competitor. This thinking was extended by human capital theory (HCT), which has been one of the most influential conceptual developments in modern labour economics. Becker's (1964) theorizing in this area reinvigorated economic interest in issues of labour supply, education, and skill development. The core of HCT brought economic attention back to individual behaviour. HCT framed individual choices about skill development (through schooling to tertiary education and on-the-job training) as *investment* decisions which yield individual rewards in the short- and long-term such as access to better jobs, improved wages, and opportunities. Thus, true to its economic roots, HCT theorizes skill as a quantifiable cost, return on investment and value to both the individual and to employers and the economy. It is this framing that underpins the view that organizations are better to invest in firm-specific skills rather than generalizable or portable skills which employees can take to other employers. It also underpins the view that individuals should bear the cost of their higher education, theoretically because they will derive the financial benefit from it.

HCT has been challenged and developed further on the grounds that most skills, rather than being firm-specific, are more likely industry-specific and thus transferable (Stevens 1994; Acemoglou and Pischke 1998). Acemoglou and Pischke (1998) observe the impact of different regulation regimes, challenging HCT at both macro- and micro-levels. Stevens (1999) extends an HCT analysis to demonstrate that the main causes of under-investment in vocational training are: capital-market imperfections, labour-market imperfections, and informational problems (about types and quality of training). Thus, although subject to challenge and development, HCT remains a very influential driving set of assumptions within skill debates.

Not only is economics concerned with institutional arrangements for skill formation—who pays, who benefits—but also, as already alluded to, with the operation of the labour market for skill. Because economic research methods involve modelling and forecasting they require measures of the various factors being modelled, such as skill, return on investment, etc. Most commonly qualifications (or years of education) are used as a proxy for skill or productive potential (Spence 1973; Bills 2003), and the return on those is measured by pay levels or earning capacity in the labour market. Thus economics provides a predominantly quantitative view of skill as a resource with costs and payoffs that is traded in the labour market. This perspective has also been highly influential in industrial relations, HRM, and organization studies.

Political Science, Sociology, and Industrial Relations

Social sciences, such as political science, sociology, anthropology, economics, and human geography, all share a certain range of common interests, concepts, and methods (Giddens 2009). However, despite these commonalities each discipline has a distinctive orientation to issues.

Political science is concerned with how society governs itself, political systems, and political behaviour. Through this it is also interested in how power and resources are allocated in society, that is, how political processes and governance confer power on some and not others in society. Hence political scientists' interest in skill tends to relate to examining the influence of government policies on the formation and distribution of skills and skill outcomes in society.

The 'varieties of capitalism' debates in political science (Hall and Soskice 2001) have given rise to increased interest in skills at the level of national political economy, that is, the impact of different national institutions or regimes on skill formation, utilization, and societal outcomes. This approach underpins a range of studies comparing skill formation in different countries and how it is influenced by the distinctive institutional structures of each nation (Thelen 2004; Lauder et al. 2008). In particular, varieties of capitalism originally contrasted liberal market economies (such as Britain, the United States, and Australia) with coordinated market economies (such as Germany, Japan, and Denmark), and explored how the strategies and business practices of a firm are shaped by and interact with the institutional structures, such as industry or sector training bodies, apprenticeship systems or other educational systems, and incentives. This approach permits a more nuanced appreciation of the production and reproduction of skill in jobs and in people, and the powerful impact of government policies. Thus the political scientist deploys a wide range of methods: qualitative, quantitative, historical, comparative, interpretive, and critical. Historical approaches document and analyse past institutional arrangements. Comparative methodology may analyse contemporary arrangements compared with those of the past, or, as in varieities of capitalism, it may compare across different countries. The comparative approach may use both qualitative and quantitative data in its analyses. Interpretative methodologies see human action as meaningful and historically contingent, thus they explore the lived experience of people. Interpretative approaches do not start with predetermined concepts, nor search for generalizable laws; rather, they search for meaning in a specific context (see Bevir and Kedar 2008). Critical approaches assess and question dominant understandings and modes of operation in society and culture. They have their roots in the thinking of Hegel and Marx, critically analysing society to expose political structures of constraint, and arbitrary exercise of power (Bonner 2010).

Sociology studies society, social processes and human social behaviour. It seeks to understand how and why a society is structured in the way it is, and how societies change. Hence, it has been argued that a sociological perspective can be regarded as an overarching view of 'all studies of human kind, including history, psychology and economics' (American Sociological Association). As a result it tends to take a broader view of skill than economics.

Sociologists tend to focus on 'skill in the job' as opposed to in the person (Vallas 1990; Grugulis and Stoyanova 2011). Thus the sociologist questions why some jobs are regarded as unskilled and others as highly skilled. They explore, for instance, whether this is because some jobs are structured to be tightly controlled with no room for discretion or have only a small range of simple tasks to perform, whilst other jobs require more decision-making and rely on the judgement of the incumbent. Alternatively, sociologists also consider whether society has defined some work as skilled or unskilled, professional or menial, and thus creates skill or occupation hierarchies that become entrenched if they are not challenged. As Vallas (1990) discusses, 'sociologists typically view skill as a dependent variable, as when we attempt to explain variations in the level of skill within occupations, firms, or economies over time' (1990, 380). Thus sociologists are interested in explaining or accounting for skill largely by looking at the nature and structure of work, whereas other disciplines (such as economics) tend to prefer to use skill to explain or account for other phenomena like wage inequality, economic growth, or organizational performance. Sociologists are also interested in social inequalities and their antecedents and consequences, for instance, how they are affected by and affect access to skill development or access to skilled jobs—again skill is the factor being accounted for. Because of this desire to explain skill, and to regard it as in the job or occupation, the research methods of sociologists have tended to be case studies of occupations or industries or regional conditions, and more recently also large-scale quantitative research such as surveys of skill requirements in jobs (see Felstead et al. 2007).

Attewell (1990) discusses the concept of skill in sociological research, identifying four schools of thought: positivism, ethnomethodology, neo-Weberian or social constructionist, and Marxist. The positivist regards skill as something that can be measured quantitatively; thus the challenges for positivists centre on what is being measured (e.g. skill in the person or in the job?) and how it is measured (e.g. can all skills be measured the same way? If not, how does one compare across measures?). Positivist approaches to skill are dominant in economics and psychology; they are also used in sociology but tend to focus on skill in the job. In contrast, ethnomethodology argues that all human activity (and thus skill) is complex and much of it is unconscious, leading to many skills being taken for granted. In this way, many skills become invisible, and measuring skill becomes highly problematic. The ethnomethodologist is sceptical of positivist approaches; instead they prefer to either understand why occupational members regard some work as 'skilled' or to research, through observation, of the detail of everyday work for a sense of both the acknowledged and the invisible skills. Similar to this, in many respects, is the social constructionist view, which attempts to understand why some jobs and occupations are considered skilled or more skilled than others. It also examines how occupations construct themselves to perpetuate a certain status, for example, through restricted entry to the occupation, or a distinctive vocabulary—both strategies that exclude others. As a result, social constructionists tend towards research methods such as case studies or historical studies of occupations. On the final point, Attewell (1990) notes that there are varying interpretations of the Marxist school of thought owing to Marx's own lack of theoretical development of the notion of skill. This has been compounded by the different development paths of contemporary Marxist and neo-Marxist approaches. On the one hand, the social constructionist perspective is reflected in Marxist analyses, which account for the social status and perceived skill of an occupation as deriving from the power of the workers rather than from the complexity of their work. On the other hand, more positivist conceptualizations of skill are evident in some neo-Marxist views on deskilling, which equate deskilling with rule-governed work and 'give pride of place to intellect over manual dexterity and decry the loss of conceptual content in work' (Attewell 1990, 442).

Labour market categorization of skill in 'standard classifications of occupations' and, in the United States, the *Dictionary of Occupational Titles* have been the subject of sociological scrutiny. A positivist view would critique the bases of these definitions and how they are measured, and an ethnomethodologist or social constructionist view would interrogate the hierarchies such definitions create or embed. And yet such classifications are the pervasive public policy measure of skill underpinning many national statistics and quantitative research.

Both sociology and political science are interested in institutional frameworks, social or political processes, and behaviour as they account for skill. Similarly, the field of industrial relations draws on all the social sciences as well as law and psychology in its study of the regulation, control, and governance of work and employment relationships (BUIRA 2008). Thus industrial relations research often takes a broader political economy perspective and links this to workplace behaviour (Hamann and Kelly 2008). Industrial relations research encompasses many different levels, from the workplace to the global (Heery et al. 2008) as it is essentially an applied and policy-oriented field. In particular, industrial relations is concerned with the competing interests of different parties in employment, the balance of power between employer and worker, and the institutional and regulatory balancing of those relationships particularly through labour market mechanisms such as collective bargaining and trade union representation. Skill concerns are a large part of that, for example, how skill (in the job) is recognized and valued by employers in the form of wages and other rewards; how skill is designed into or out of jobs, and the division of labour; and how individuals access the skill development they need (Grugulis 2008).

The multidisciplinary base of industrial relations means that a range of qualitative and quantitative research methods are used, from ethnographic interviewing, comparative historical analysis, and case studies, through to surveys of individual workplaces or of whole industries (Strauss and Whitfield 2008). In recent years quantitative research in industrial relations has been boosted by regular national surveys of workplace employment relations practices, such as the Workplace Employment Relations Study in the United Kingdom, the Austrialian Workplace and Industrial Relations Survey, and its successor, Australia at Work. These repeated surveys have the benefit of allowing researchers to track change in practices, including those related to skills and training, and outcomes over time. This type of research, combined with analyses of the outcomes of collective bargaining or changing wages and work conditions, often underpins industrial relations advocacy for policy change.

From a theoretical perspective labour process theory has been a key driver of skill discussions in industrial relations (see Braverman 1974; Thompson 1983; Adler 2004). Building on Marx's theory of surplus value it focuses on managers' desire to control how work is organized, its pace and duration (i.e. the labour process), thus potentially removing autonomy, enjoyment, and skill from the work and worker. Many interpret it as arguing that the advance of capitalism has led to increasing deskilling in the workplace. However, the pervasiveness of this alleged phenomenon has been challenged by views that the general trajectory of capitalism has been an upgrading of skill in the workforce and in jobs (see Adler 2004). A central debate in industrial relations and sociology concerns whether deskilling, upskilling, or reskilling has been the main result of economic change. Regardless, industrial relations is concerned with mechanisms to ensure fair access to, use of, and reward of skill at work.

Summary

Economic, political, and social phenomena are all analysed by political economy approaches. In the last few decades, this has been one of the fastest-growing approaches in the social sciences (Plumper 2009). Undoubtedly the appeal of political economic reasoning is its consideration of a broader range of factors. In recent years, political economy of skill approaches have acknowledged the desirability of taking an even more holistic view by also embracing organizational and individual influences on skill, thus integrating workplace dynamics with institutional change (Lloyd and Payne 2004). Priorities in political economy (of skill) have therefore changed—and are changing—to reflect an expanding cross-disciplinary perspective.

Each discipline brings a distinctive starting point (and set of assumptions) which a political economy approach facilitates, blending into a wider consideration of skill. It is not surprising that economics starts from considerations of the economy (either macro or micro or both), political science starts from a consideration of institutions and policies, sociology starts from concerns with social processes and norm construction, and industrial relations starts from a concern for social justice in the workplace (i.e. decent work, fair reward, good work conditions).

Skill as an Organizational Resource

The fields of HRM and organization studies both have their roots in elements of all the disciplines presented in this chapter. As an applied field, HRM concerns itself with understanding the management of people and work in order to achieve the goals of the organization. HRM is heavily influenced by industrial and organizational (I/O) psychology, and as a result places an individual focus on skill (in the person) and job characteristics (skill in the job). Organization studies, on the other hand, whilst taking the psychological view, is also influenced by sociology, and is concerned with issues such as the social construction of skill or the impact of different institutional arrangements. This reflects the organizational studies remit as 'the examination of how individuals construct organizational structures, processes, and practices and how these, in turn, shape social relations and create institutions that ultimately influence people' (Clegg and Bailey 2008). Arguably this lends organization studies a critical perspective in contrast to HRM's applied and functional approach.

However, one could argue that for both HRM and organization studies a microeconomic perspective tends to dominate in which skill is treated essentially as a resource for the firm. This is clearly evidenced in the prominence of the resource-based view of the firm (RBV), which originated in economics (Penrose 1959) and, in modern form, emerged as a strategic management theory (Barney 1991). The RBV suggests that organizations derive their competitive advantage from their tangible and intangible resources, particularly from resources that are valuable (i.e. successful), inimitable (i.e. hard to copy), and appropriable (i.e. that benefit shareholders). It has become a dominant force in strategic HRM (Barney and Wright 1998), particularly the view that the blend of skills, knowledge, experience, and personalities of individual workers and collectively of work groups can be rare and hard to copy. Thus skill is of central importance to HRM.

In addition HRM is also driven by the economically inspired HCT. As already traversed in the discussion of economic perspectives, HCT provides a logic encouraging employers to invest in developing firm-specific skills, and justifying the individual bearing the cost and benefit (and, one might add, the risk) of all other skill development. This has appeal in HRM thinking, at least in the short-term, to develop and retain the skills the firm requires. From an HRM perspective, the skill of the workforce is regarded as a key ingredient in an organization's performance. Thus, HRM interests spread across how jobs are designed (the skills they require and develop), how to access the skills required (training for them, recruiting for them, contracting out), how to reward and motivate people to use their skills (pay systems, management practices), and how to ensure skills are contributing to organizational goals (HR planning, performance management). Consequently, HRM strives to find ways to measure skill, both in the person and in the job. In this regard, apart from the influence of economics, most of the theories that underpin HRM thinking draw on social or I/O psychology. For example, employee recruitment and selection practices are driven by a desire to match the job and the person. Based on the psychological theory of person–environment fit, the search for person–job fit accompanies a greater emphasis on technical skills; however, in recent years, as employers have pursued flexible firm strategies, the emphasis has shifted to person–organization fit. This reflects an HRM trend away from technical skills to softer skills such as teamwork, problem-solving, customer focus, resilience to change, and positive attitude. These softer skills are often referred to as competencies, which Heery and Noon (2009) define as behaviour-based personal characteristics or attributes; they also identify specific skills and abilities for job performance that are labelled work-based competencies such as use of software, budget management, etc. This changing notion of skill has accompanied national policies of increasing labour market flexibility, the hope being that a generally competent person can turn their hand to a range of different projects and tasks as required by the employer and thus be more flexible to changing circumstances than a specialist in a strictly demarcated job. This blurring of the division of labour and drive to skill flexibility, whilst promoted as desirable strategy, most recently in the notion of the high-performance workplace that dominates much HRM discussion and policy agendas, has been widely criticized and debated in the political economy, sociology, and industrial relations literature (see Ramsay et al. 2000; Brown and Hesketh 2004; Lloyd and Payne 2004). Indeed, some of the more interesting analyses of HRM practice in relation to skill come from researchers bringing a broader political economy perspective (see Ashton et al. 2010; Grugulis and Stoyanova 2011; Thompson 2011). For instance, at a strategic HRM level, Ashton et al. (2010), investigating the handling of skills issues in transnational companies, show that these organizations are starting to take advantage of different national systems of skill formation.

Human resource development, a subfield of HRM, concerns itself with skill development for the workplace. The literature is split in its focus, one side emphasizing learning and the other organizational performance (Bryson 2007). The emphasis on learning connects with the psychology and adult education literature on issues such as workplace learning, training theory, and transfer of training, and also with the organization studies literature on issues of organization development, career development, learning organization, and communities of practice (Senge 1990; Lave and Wenger 1991; Schein 1996). Despite the range of disciplines contributing to HRM knowledge, it has struggled to prove the link between HRM practices and organizational performance (Guest 2011). Grugulis and Stoyanova (2011) discuss the difficulty HRM has had in measuring the link between skills and performance. They argue that this is, in part, because of the tendency for research to focus on HRM practices as a whole rather than skill per se. In addition, due to the influence of psychology and economics, research methods in HRM are often positivist, using quantitative surveys of employers, human resources staff, and workers, thus reliant on either self-report (perceptions rather than actual practice) or on crude proxies for skill and performance. Seldom does HRM research actually observe the utilization of skill in the workplace. Perhaps more worryingly, Grugulis and Stoyanova (2011) point out that very influential HRM research does not allow for the time lag between skill improvement initiatives and better performance because it tends to measure input, output, and outcome at the same time in a single survey. HRM also engages in qualitative research, interviewing workers, employers, and other stakeholders. Such research yields richer accounts of skill development and utilization but often they are not generalizable to other organizations or they are again a single snapshot in time.

In summary, HRM's main interest in skill is how to acquire it for the organization and then how to use it, recognize or value it—all based on a relatively unexplored assumption that skill impacts organizational performance. Organization studies, whilst holding the same assumptions, is more concerned with why organizations have skill and how it is used, for instance, investigating notions of organizations as learning environments and the skill benefits of communities of practice. Organization studies also brings a critical perspective to analysing the social and political dimensions of skill in organizations, thus incorporating concerns also rehearsed in sociology, political science, and industrial relations.

As already mentioned, contributing to both HRM and organization studies is a substantial body of work from the education discipline, which is specifically focused on understanding workplaces as learning environments (see Billett 2002; Fuller and Unwin 2004). This reflects an interest in how skill is developed and takes us to the final broad category of disciplinary perspectives on skill—those underpinning learning theory.

Learning Theory

At the other end of the spectrum from the broad view of political economy is a focus on learning theory and how skill is developed in the individual, which is mainly the concern of the disciplines of education and psychology. Education explores how knowledge is transmitted in human society and is dominated by a pragmatic focus on teaching practice or the learning environment. Psychology is generally regarded as the science of mind and behaviour and its branches are applied to particular fields of knowledge or activity, for example, I/O psychology focuses on organizations, work, and people at work. As we have discussed, HRM relies on I/O psychology for many theories of behaviour in the workplace. With regard to skill, I/O psychology assists in understanding both skill in the job (for instance, theories of job characteristics, job design, and job evaluation—see Hackman and Oldham 1976) and skill in the person (for instance, theories of training needs assessment, training design, delivery, training transfer to the workplace, and evaluation—see Tharenou 2009; or, on managing performance, see Cooper and Locke 2000).

Educational psychology marries both disciplines and studies how people learn throughout their entire lifespan. Its emphasis is predominantly on skill in the person and how it is developed, thus it treats skill as a product or output of specific formal or informal educational interventions or learning opportunities. Much of that literature is devoted to the development of children and adolescents, but there is also an established body of research on adult learning and vocational education.

Learning theory is central to this segment of the skill literature, which seeks to understand and improve learning in order that people can become skilled. There are at least four competing schools of thought in learning theory (Merriam et al. 2007) that differ in their views on learning processes, the purpose of education, and the educator's role. All relate in some way to developing skill, whether it be learning how to learn (cognitivist views, e.g. Lewin 1951), becoming socialized (social/situational views, e.g. Lave and Wenger 1991), engaging in self-directed learning (humanist views, e.g. Rogers 1969), or achieving a specific competency (behaviourist views, e.g. Skinner 1953). As a result, evaluating the success of the learning process depends on the orientation to learning and may range from self-assessment to course completion or passing a competency test.

It is from this focus on learning as a key ingredient of skill that a growing literature on workplace learning has emerged (see Fenwick 2006, 2010; Eraut 2007; Eraut and Hirsch 2007; Unwin et al. 2007). This literature explores issues such as how people learn in the workplace, influences on that learning, what is learnt, how to embed learning in work processes, and how to improve learning in the workplace. Although this topic area is increasingly multidisciplinary, the core focus is learning, either as process or outcome, and thus the contribution of the education discipline is central to its discussions. Within this literature, skill contributes to, and is, a product of learning.

The research methods draw on psychology and the social sciences, ranging across full experimental design testing of hypotheses to case studies and interviews in workplaces. Generally, skill is an independent variable in education research (Vallas 1990), a feature that helps explain or predict other variables such as variations in learning.

Finally, it should be noted that many education researchers are also interested in how education policy can facilitate moving from school to work. In such instances, a political economy as well as a learning perspective may prevail.

Conclusion: An Example of Applying Disciplinary Perspectives

What do the perspectival variations tell us? Is it, as Fenwick (2010) suggested for workplace learning, a situation in which different disciplines are not all talking about the same thing under the label of skill? Or do they reveal different facets of skill? When we look at the range of disciplinary perspectives and their overlaps, four key areas of difference emerge: (1) level of focus—national, organizational, individual, and policy or personal; (2) location of skill—in the person, the job, or a social construction; (3) skill definitions—technical, behavioural, cognitive; and (4) type of variable—dependent or independent, mediator, or outcome. As a result, each disciplinary perspective reveals and explores only part of the full picture of skill.

Here is an example to illustrate, rather crudely, the impact of different disciplinary perspectives on skill. The scenario examined is unpaid graduate internships. One of the challenges facing government skills policy is the transition from education to employment. In the case of tertiary education in the United Kingdom, whilst employers have cut graduate positions, one consequence has been an increase in university graduates taking on unpaid internships in order to develop relevant work experience. In the worst cases, graduates occupy a series of unpaid internships in the hope of ultimately securing a paid job (see BBC News, 7 March 2010; *Guardian*, 5 September 2011).

A political economy of skill perspective on unpaid internships might embrace all or some of the following disciplinary perspectives. In particular, it would seek to explore the short- and long-term impact of these employer initiatives on firms, on the labour market generally, and on graduates; and the relationship or compatibility of these actions with a range of government policy.

From an economic perspective, analysis might address whether internships facilitate entry to the labour market. Do internships serve as a viable signal to prospective employers of a graduate's employability? Are the costs and benefits of internship borne appropriately? What are the knock-on effects to other positions and to the graduate labour market? Research methods will be primarily quantitative and may include, for example, tracking the prevalence of internships over time, tracking the rate of conversion from unpaid intern to paid employee, and calculating costs and benefits to the employer and the intern over both the short- and long-term.

From a political science perspective, analysis may question how unpaid internships relate to existing skill formation policies and other government policies, relating, for example, to welfare. Research approaches might include examining unpaid internship policies relative to other government policies both current and historical, and comparing them to policies in other countries and their outcomes.

From a sociological perspective, analysis may examine how internships construct skill. Are the roles perceived as unskilled or as novice? If they are unpaid, how are they valued by the organization? Do they perpetuate certain social structures that disadvantage some groups whilst privileging others? What is the immediate and long-term impact on skill utilization and social mobility? Research approaches may involve longitudinal case studies, or surveys, of specific occupational groups or industries using interns. Thus the research may chronicle the changing impacts of unpaid internships on individuals, occupations, organizations, and communities.

From an industrial relations perspective, analysis would focus on issues of fair treatment of the intern and institutional or regulatory mechanisms to ensure fairness. Is this skill development or skill exploitation? What is the legal employment status of the intern and how are they protected in the workplace and in the work relationship? How does the graduate have a voice in their internship and skill development? Are unpaid internships a socially just arrangement? Research methods might include interviewing or surveying interns and host organizations to discover internship conditions, experience, and outcomes; examining any internship agreements or documentation of conditions of the internship; and tracking the prevalence of unpaid internships and in which sectors.

From an HRM perspective, analysis would focus on the costs and benefits to the organization of internships. How does the intern contribute to organizational goals? How does one structure intern tasks and learning to optimize productivity? What does this do to the employer brand? What does this do to the retention, development, and contribution of other employees? How does this fit the talent-management strategy of the organization? How does the organization minimize legal and other risks associated with unpaid internships? Research methods might include interviews with managers and with interns, focusing on assisting organization productivity and individual development. Similarly, organization studies may consider these factors but may also examine the dynamics between paid and unpaid workers, the impact on organizational learning, and overall strategy.

From an education and psychology perspective, analysis might centre on what skill is developed in the internship. How is the learning structured and supported in the internship? How are graduates' existing skills transferred to the intern situation? Methods might include surveys or interviews with the intern and with others in the host organization and observation of the intern work, work processes, and documentation. There may also be interest in examining whether the internship eases transition from education to paid employment.

So, what can one conclude about the implications of taking different disciplinary perspectives on skill? It is obvious from this example that to analyse from only *one* of these perspectives results in a limited view of the issue. The consequence of this for policy formulations is worrying as a narrow perspective on skill will result in policy that is, at best, ineffective or, at worst, harmful. In the case of unpaid internships the temptation may be, under pressure from employers, to take only the HRM perspective. This then takes no account of compatibility with other skills-related government policies, or of the immediate and longer-term impacts on students or other workers, nor any concern for the labour market as a whole. Alternatively, even when taking a broader political economy perspective the resulting policy may lack an appreciation of how internships are implemented in organizations, and how skill development can be enhanced or inhibited by internship arrangements. The full picture requires an appreciation of multiple disciplinary perspectives.

Examining skill from multiple perspectives is a challenging but important task in order to increase our understanding, develop effective policy, and positively influence individual and societal wellbeing. The examples in this chapter illustrate the need to ensure that there are cross-disciplinary teams working collaboratively on skills policy issues, or at miminum facilitating debate from different disciplinary perspectives in order to generate policy solutions of sufficient breadth and depth to be effective.

References

Acemoglou, D. and Pischke, J-S. (1998) 'Beyond Becker: Training in Imperfect Labour Markets'. NBER Working Paper Series, 6740.

Adler, P. (2004) 'Skill Trends under Capitalism and the Socialisation of Production', in C. Warhurst, I. Grugulis and E. Keep (eds), *The Skills that Matter*, Basingstoke: Palgrave Macmillan: 242–260.

Ashton, D., Brown, P., and Lauder, H. (2010) 'Skill Webs and International Human Resource Management: Lessons from a Study of the Global Skill Strategies of Transnational Companies'. *The International Journal of Human Resource Management*, 21(6): 836–850.

Attewell, P. (1990) 'What is Skill?' *Work and Occupations*, 17(4): 422–448.

Barney, J. (1991) 'Firm Resources and Sustained Competitive Advantage', *Journal of Management*, 17(1): 99–120.

Barney, J. and Wright, P. (1998) 'On Becoming a Strategic Partner', *Human Resource Management*, 37: 31–46.

Becker, G. (1964) *Human Capital*. New York: National Bureau of Economic Research.

Bevir, M. and Kedar, A. (2008) 'Concept Formation in Political Science: An Anti-naturalist Critique of Qualitative Methodology'. *Perspectives on Politics*, 6(3): 503–517.

Billett, S. (2002) 'Workplace Pedagogic Practices: Co-participation and Learning', *British Journal of Educational Studies*, 50(4): 457–481.

Bills, D. B. (2003) 'Credentials, Signals, and Screens: Explaining the Relationship Between Schooling and Job Assignment'. *Review of Educational Research*, 73(4): 441–469.

Bonner, S. (2010) 'Sketching the Lineage: The Critical Method and the Idealist Tradition'. *New Political Science*, 24(2): 265–292.

Braverman, H. (1974) *Labor and Monopoly Capital: The Degradation of Work in the Twentieth Century*. New York: Monthly Review Press.

British Universities Industrial Relations Association (October 2008) 'What's the Point of Industrial Relations?'

Brown, P. and Hesketh, A. (2004) *The Mismanagement of Talent: Employability and Jobs in the Knowledge Economy*. Oxford: Oxford University Press.

Bryson, J. (2007) 'Human Resource Development or Developing Human Capability?', in S. Bolton and M. Houlihan (eds), *Searching for the Human in Human Resource Management*, Basingstoke: Palgrave Macmillan: 171–192.

Buchanan, J. (2006) *From Skill Shortages to Decent Work: The Role of Better Skill Ecosystems*, Sydney: NSW Department of Education and Training.

Clegg, S. and Bailey, J. (2008) 'Introduction', *International Encyclopedia of Organization Studies*, Online library resource.

Cooper, C. and Locke, E. (eds) (2000) *Industrial and Organizational Psychology: Linking Theory with Practice*, Oxford: Blackwell.

Eraut, M. (2007) 'Learning From Other People in the Workplace', *Oxford Review of Education*, 33(4): 403–422.

Eraut, M. and Hirsh, W. (2007) *The Significance of Workplace Learning for Individuals, Groups and Organizations*. SKOPE Monograph 9, Oxford: SKOPE.

Felstead, A., Gallie, D., Green, F., and Zhou, Y. (2007) *Skills at Work, 1986–2006*, Oxford: SKOPE.

Fenwick, T. (2006) 'Tidying the Territory: Questioning Terms and Purposes in Work-learning Research'. *Journal of Workplace Learning*, 18(5): 265–278.

Fenwick, T. (2010) 'Workplace "Learning" and Adult Education: Messy Objects, Blurry Maps and Making Difference', *European Journal for Research on the Education and Learning of Adults*, 1(1–2): 79–95.

Finegold, D. (1999) 'Creating Self-sustaining High-skill Ecosystems', *Oxford Review of Economic Policy*, 15(1): 60–81.

Fuller, A. and Unwin, L. (2004) 'Expansive Learning Environments: Integrating Organizational and Personal Development', in H. Rainbird, A. Fuller, and A. Munro (eds), *Workplace Learning in Context*, London: Routledge: 126–144.

Giddens, A. (2009) *Sociology*, Cambridge: Polity Press.

Grugulis, I. (2008) 'Skill Formation', in P. Blyton, N. Bacon, J. Fiorito, and E. Heery (eds), *The Sage Handbook of Industrial Relations*, London: Sage: 606–622.

Grugulis, I. and Stoyanova, D. (2011) 'Skill and Performance', *British Journal of Industrial Relations*, 49(3): 515–536.

Guest, D. (2011) 'Human Resource Management and Performance: Still Searching for Some Answers', *Human Resource Management Journal*, 21(1): 3–13.

Hackman, J. and Oldham, G. (1976) 'Motivation through the Design of Work: Test of a Theory', *Organizational Behaviour and Human Performance*, 16: 250–279.

Hall, P. and Soskice, D. (eds) (2001) *Varieties of Capitalism: The Institutional Foundations of Comparative Advantage*, Oxford: Oxford University Press.

Hamann, K. and Kelly, J. (2008) 'Varieties of Capitalism and Industrial Relations', in P. Blyton, N. Bacon, J. Fiorito, and E. Heery (eds), *The Sage Handbook of Industrial Relations*, London: Sage: 129–148.

Heery, E. and Noon, M. (2009) *A Dictionary of Human Resource Management*, 2nd ed., Oxford: Oxford University Press.

Lauder, H., Brown, P., and Ashton, D. (2008) 'Globalisation, Skill Formation and the Varieties of Capitalism Approach', *New Political Economy*, 13(1): 19–35.

Lave, J. and Wenger, E. (1991) *Situated Learning: Legitimate Peripheral Participation*, Cambridge: Cambridge University Press.

Lewin, K. (1951) *Field Theory in Social Science: Selected Theoretical Papers*, New York: Harper and Row.

Lloyd, C. and Payne, J. (2004) 'The Political Economy of Skill: A Theoretical Approach to Developing a High Skills Strategy in the UK', in C. Warhurst, I. Grugulis, and E. Keep (eds), *The Skills that Matter*, Basingstoke: Palgrave Macmillan: 207–224.

Merriam, S., Caffarella, R., and Baumgartner, L. (2007) *Learning in Adulthood*, 3rd ed., San Francisco: Jossey Bass.

Penrose, E. (1959) *The Theory of the Growth of the Firm*. New York: John Wiley and Sons.

Plumper, T. (2009) 'Comparative Political Economy', in T. Landman and N. Robinson (eds), *The Sage Handbook of Comparative Politics*, Thousand Oaks, CA: Sage: 144–159.

Ramsay, H., Scholarios, D., and Harley, B. (2000) 'Employees and High-Performance Work Systems: Testing Inside the Black Box', *British Journal of Industrial Relations*, 38(4): 501–531.

Rogers, C. (1969) *Freedom to Learn: A View of What Education Might Become*, Columbus, OH: C. E. Merrill.

Schein, E. (1996) 'Career Anchors Revisited: Implications for Career Development in the 21st Century', *The Academy of Management Executive 1993–2005*, 10(4): 80–88.

Senge, P. (1990) *The Fifth Discipline: The Art and Practice of the Learning Organization*, New York: Doubleday.

Skinner, B. (1953) *Science and Human Behavior*, New York: Macmillan.

Spence, M. (1973) 'Job Market Signalling', *The Quarterly Journal of Economics*, 87(3): 355–374.

Stevens, M. (1994) 'A Theoretical Model of On-the-job Training with Imperfect Competition', *Oxford Economic Papers*, 46: 537–562.

Stevens, M. (1999) 'Human Capital Theory and UK Vocational Training Policy', *Oxford Review of Economic Policy*, 15(1): 16–32.

Strauss, G. and Whitfield, K. (2008) 'Changing Traditions in Industrial Relations Research, in P. Blyton, N. Bacon, J. Fiorito, and E. Heery (eds), *The Sage Handbook of Industrial Relations*, London: Sage: 170–186.

Tharenou, P. (2009) 'Training and Development in Organizations', in A. Wilkinson, T. Redman, S. Snell, and N. Bacon (eds), *The Sage Handbook of Human Resource Management*, Thousand Oaks, CA: 155–173.

Thelen, K. (2004) *How Institutions Evolve: The Political Economy of Skills in Germany, Britain, the United States, and Japan*, Cambridge: Cambridge University Press.

Thompson, P. (1983) *The Nature of Work: An Introduction to Debates on the Labour Process*, London: Macmillan.

Thompson, P. (2011) 'The Trouble with HRM', *Human Resource Management Journal*, 21(4): 355–367.

Unwin, L., Felstead, A., Fuller, A., Bishop, D., Jewson, N., Kakavelakis, K. (2007). 'Looking Inside the Russian Doll: The Interconnections Between Context, Learning and Pedagogy in the Workplace', *Pedagogy, Culture and Society*, 15(3): 333–348.

Vallas, S. P. (1990) 'The Concept of Skill: A Critical Review', *Work and Occupations*, 17(4): 379–398.

CHAPTER 2

SKILL BUILDERS AND THE EVOLUTION OF NATIONAL VOCATIONAL TRAINING SYSTEMS

CATHIE JO MARTIN

Introduction

This chapter investigates the origins of diverse forms of skills training for industrial workers. In particular, one must understand why some countries largely rely on regular secondary education systems to provide workers with general skills, whilst others develop industrial schools and apprenticeship programmes to offer credentialed, industry, or firm-specific occupational skills.

We consider four broad factors contributing to the evolution of varied systems to cultivate vocational skills. Firstly, patterns of industrial development and economic cleavages have bearing on skills training: for example, stark regional heterogeneity works against the emergence of national training systems. Secondly, the legacies from pre-industrial patterns of cooperation—most prominently, from the guild system—make both employers and workers in some countries more inclined to negotiate collective vocational training institutions. Thirdly, the political features of the state (most importantly, the structure of party competition and degree of federal power sharing) reinforce or work against collectivist solutions to skills needs, cooperative industrial relations systems, and entrenched regional cleavages.

Finally, the characteristics of industrial relations systems and, in particular, employers associations' and unions' capacities for collective action, give rise to the medley of forms of skills training. The structure of business and labour associations mattered to the venue of skills training (and balance between general education, apprenticeship, and school-based learning) and to the portability of *specific assets*. Both venue and type of specific assets reflect the degree of oversight by the social partners; moreover, the associational structure and consequent involvement of the social partners have an enormous impact on levels of spending on vocational training. Both employers and workers become more committed to skills training when well-organized social partners are given a significant role in the creation and oversight of training programmes.

Varieties of Vocational Training Regimes

Skills in modern industrial economies are typically grouped into two to three ideal types: general skills and specific skills (either at the firm or industry level). Industrial workers with general skills have basic knowledge but may not claim certification in skills for a specific industry nor portable skills that translate from one job to another. Alternatively, specific skills constitute portable, certified occupational skills and usually involve employers' associations and labour unions in the oversight or administration of skills training (Busemeyer and Trampusch 2010). Social scientists believe that countries develop characteristic skills profiles that enable distinctive forms of capitalist development; for example, whereas coordinated market economies utilized highly trained workers with specific skills to produce for high-value-added markets, liberal market economies tend to compete on the basis of price with less skilled labour. Therefore, employers who utilize specific skills are more motivated to develop collective institutions than employers dependent on general skills (Hall and Soskice 2001; Estevez-Abe et al. 2001; Bosch, Chapter 20 in this volume).

Venues vary for the development of these diverse types of skills. *General skills* are nurtured within the regular K-12 education system; however, the creation of specific, occupational skills seems to require a separate educational track with significant involvement of employers and unions. Countries such as France and Sweden have chosen to create specific skills within special industrial schools; this classroom instruction—with input from the social partners—produces *industry-specific skills*, which are easily transferable within companies at the industry level). Other countries such as Germany and Switzerland rely on a dual model to produce *firm-specific skills*, in which firm-based apprenticeships are combined with school-based instruction, with the apprenticeships being most important. Denmark (producing industry-specific skills) and Austria have a dual system but the school-based component is much more important than in Germany and these countries hug the line between the industrial school and dual system models.[1]

[1] Greinert (2005) roots the distinctive venues for developing and controlling skills in the hegemonic culture of work found within nations, thus: the British liberal market economy located the institutions to cultivate vocational skills within markets; the French statist tradition cultivated state bureaucratic institutions to nurture an industrial workforce; and Germany, with its corporatist values, accorded control of skills training to societal actors.

Table 2.1 Variations in vocational training systems

Vocational training provider	Certified, portable skills	Non-certified, non-portable skills
Apprenticeships are dominant institutions for training skilled workers and schools play a supplementary role	Germany Denmark is on the border	Japan
Schools are the dominant institutions for initial training skilled workers and apprenticeships play a supplementary role	France: schools are dominant, with some apprenticeships but largely for more highly skilled workers	UK/US initial general skills In-firm practical training Very few apprenticeships except for management

For example, the firm-based specific assets of Germany have many more categories of occupations than the industry-based specific assets of Denmark (Busemeyer 2015). But all types of collectivist skills systems offered skills that are certified, closely matched to real job needs, and developed with strong oversight by employers and workers (Greinert 2005; Busemeyer 2009.) Table 2.1 suggests variations in vocational training systems along the broad cleavages of apprenticeship-based versus school-based venues and certified, portable skills versus non-certified portable skills.

Our mandate is to reflect on the factors causing these divergent skills formation systems: why did some countries rely on school-based training to produce general skills, some on school-based training to create portable, occupational, industry-specific skills, and some on apprenticeships with supplemental schooling to deliver portable, occupational, firm-specific skills? These models largely solidified during the interwar period and by the 1920s virtually advanced, industrialized countries had national legislation for publicly funded vocational training, either in separate vocational schools or in dual-stream secondary schools (Benavot 1983, 61–65).

The Determinants Of Skills Regimes

Industrialization and Vocational Training Systems

Modern vocational training systems, at the most basic level, are driven by the process of industrialization, in that the industrial revolution put an end to the old system of class and craft-based education administered by guilds. The guilds model extended across Europe in fairly standardized form from the Middle Ages on, but this model, rooted in the close mentoring relationships between masters and journeymen, was unable to meet the skills requirements of industrial workers. Guilds had declined enormously by the middle of the eighteenth century and more sharply differentiated national training models emerged to fill this void (Wilensky 2002; Greinert 2005, 8–25).

Differences amongst the new models of vocational training undoubtedly reflected, to some extent, cross-national differences in patterns of industrialization. Political actors within late developing countries were motivated to catch up with the early leaders in the industrial race and adopted social protections to narrow the gap (Gershenkron 1962). Thus anxious about the path of late industrialzation in the Netherlands, Dutch political leaders developed industrial schools to close the gap with foreign powers (Andersen and Nijhuis 2012). The yearning to export drove the early expansion of primary education and spending on skills formation might also be linked to competitiveness in world markets (Ansell 2008). Greater 'firm specificity' in training happens more readily in countries with large-sized firms and with oligarchical industry sectors, in which a few large firms dominate each industrial sector. Germany, for example, might specialize in firm-based training because it has larger firms, whereas Danish employers might develop collective, school-based training systems because these small and medium-sized enterprises are less able to provide in-house training and because the firms recruit from the same occupational labour markets (Kristensen and Sabel 1997; Busemeyer 2015).

Yet industrialization is but a blunt tool for capturing the full portraiture of vocational training differentiation. For example, British firms (with an average of 64 workers) were much larger than German ones (with an average of 14) at the beginning of the twentieth century; yet, these firms did not develop higher levels of in-house training (Kinghorn and Nye 1996, 97). Sweden had larger firms than Denmark but relied even more on school-based vocational training. Thus, it makes sense to look more deeply at other types of factors and at the historical record for an understanding of the evolution of vocational training.

Legacy of Guilds and Vocational Training Systems

The legacy of pre-industrial guilds constitutes another salient factor in the emergence of diverse forms of vocational training institutions and industrial skills as countries with strong vocational training programmes also tend to have robust guilds well into the early industrial era. Guilds encourage a culture of economic cooperation, so important to ventures in skills training, because they enhance solidarity amongst economic actors at various levels in the production hierarchy. Masters and journeymen are brought together within the guild organization and the fraternal ties between more and less skilled workers extend to small employers in the handicraft sector during the industrial period, dividing the small handicraft firms from the large industrial ones. Thus, the structure fosters considerable cooperation over skills development amongst small firms, skilled workers (masters) and unskilled workers (journeymen); and these alliances encouraged the emergence of a highly skilled labour pool and competitive practices based on high quality rather than on low wages (Unwin 1966; Hanson 1997; Thelen 2004).

The guilds are also crucial to the evolution of vocational training systems in their important impact on the emergence of varied types of worker organizations (i.e. craft versus industrial unions). Countries with historically vibrant guilds tend to develop industrial unions, and countries such as Britain, which abandoned guilds at an early stage in history, produce craft unions. Craft and industrial unions have divergent capacities for cooperation in general and for collective skills development in particular, because craft unions bring together workers within an occupation (i.e. metal workers) but from different companies and industries, whereas industrial unions represent all workers within the same firm or industry. Craft unions divide workers within the same industry; accordingly, this produces reduced solidarity amongst high- and low-skilled workers within an industry and lower labour power. Politically weak craft unions have incentives to restrict the pool of skilled workers to bolster their strength and to drive up wages; and these strategies tend to harm unskilled workers and other vulnerable workers. In comparison, stronger industrial unions—in countries where robust guilds created norms of non-wage competition—do not need to assert their power by restricting the pool of skilled workers. In Britain, for example, worker skills became a battleground and the mutual interests of labour and management in cultivating human capital got lost in the tussle. Ultimately the strong British craft unions, with their efforts to control skills production, motivated employers to adopt labour-saving strategies that relied on less skilled workers (Unwin 1966; Thelen 2004).

The persistence of robust guilds explains much about cross-national differences in the capacities for collective investments in vocational training; and in particular, offers important insights into the different paths taken by coordinated and liberal market economies. Yet this explanation tells us less about why training institutions within coordinated market economies vary. In addition, guilds' practices varied across countries; for example, Danish guilds created sharper divisions between skilled and unskilled workers than German ones and employers in the handicraft sectors formed a tight alliance with large industrial firms. Moreover, cross-national differences in capitalism and skills were less starkly different amongst coordinated and liberal nations in the nineteenth century, and employers and unions sought to improve skill formation systems before the 1920s across the industrial world. Coordinated market economies with high levels of workers skills could be found at the regional level throughout Europe and North America in the nineteenth century before the first 'industrial divide'. Many American communities had extensive apprenticeship and training systems during the nineteenth century and American manufacturing processes in many sectors resembled those in continental Europe; thus, a diversity of models or economic dualism may best characterize American manufacturing during this period (Bureau of Labor 1911; Galenson 1952; Piore and Sabel 1984; Hanson 1997; Martin 2011). Skills in the British metalworking and engineering sectors remained quite high at the end of the nineteenth century and the British apprenticeship system was far from dead. At a series of critical junctures (1910s, 1940s, and 1960s), employers and unions sought to create broad frameworks for vocational training that looked much more like European models than the patchwork system that ultimately evolved (Zeitlin 1996).

Recently scholars have acknowledged indeterminacy in the relationship between the guilds' traditions and newer structures for training industrial workers. In particular, attention has been given to the impact of political institutions on the development of vocational training systems, and it is to this issue that the chapter now turns.

Features of the State and Vocational Training Systems

Two structural features of governing institutions seem particularly crucial to the evolution of diverse forms of vocational training institutions: the structure of party competition and degree of power sharing amongst levels of government. The degree of proportionality in electoral rules matters because proportional systems offer a more complete coverage of interests than majoritarian systems and provides citizens with the assurance to make risky, collective human capital investments. When social groups are represented in parties dedicated to their interests, constituents are more willing to believe politicians' and party leaders' promises to protect their interests in the future. Party platforms do not fluctuate to appeal to the median voter as these do in two-party systems. Party leaders are viewed as making *credible* commitments and this makes constituents more willing to coordinate in making contributions to collective ambitions such as a well-trained workforce. Coalition governments—the norm in multiparty systems—further encourage cooperation amongst competing interests (who must form governments) and stable policy outcomes. In a two-party system, parties compete for the medium voter, competition takes on a two-dimensional space, and commitments by politicians seem unlikely to endure over time (Kitschelt 1933; Cusack et al. 2007).

The ideological content of party control also matters. In this vein, Iversen and Stephens (2008) draw our attention to three separate worlds of human capital formation, that are analogous to the dominant welfare state regimes because they reflect mutually reinforcing relationships between protections against social risk and skill formation. In social democratic countries, a commitment to redistribution goes hand in hand with a commitment to nurturing a high level of skills amongst the industrial workforce. In continental countries, extensive social insurance coverage is philosophically and programmatically congruent with high specific skills provided by extensive firm-based vocational training; however, Christian democratic parties accept a higher degree of class stratification and dualism in skills. Finally, liberal welfare states (with extensive privately provided benefits but few public ones) nurture heavy private investment in general skills but modest spending on vocational training.

Busemeyer (2015) traces the origins of diverse skills training systems to the differences in party, suggesting that the policy proposals of diverse political parties may have quite different impacts on cross-class coalitions. Social democratic parties generally prefer statist systems, which commit extensive resources to nurturing the economic interests of workers; whereas, Christian democratic parties favour a politics of mediation and a reliance on the social partners. Liberal parties tend to favour market systems that accord maximum freedom to their business supporters. On a similar note, Trampusch (2010) suggests that training regimes evolve in tandem with unemployment insurance regimes, which differ significantly across social democratic and Christian democratic countries.

The degree of power sharing within government also has bearing on the evolution of vocational training regimes. Federalism worked against centralization of primary education and one might assume that a centralized network of industrial schools would also flourish more easily in countries with unitary governments (Ansell and Lindvall 2013).

The structural features of government also have an indirect impact in evolution of vocational training systems in their role in shaping diverse industrial relations institutions. Majoritarian versus proportional electoral institutions and unitary versus federal distributions of governing authority instil in politicians quite varied incentives for nurturing strong encompassing employers' associations and unions.[2] Institutions for business and labour representation, in turn, influence preferences for investments in skills (Martin and Swank 2008, 2012). We turn now to the impacts of these institutions on the evolution of vocational training systems.

Industrial Relations Institutions and Vocational Training Systems

The organization of business and labour is important to skills-building institutions because industrial relations institutions influence the willingness of the social partners to make collective investments. In macro-corporatist countries, peak employers' associations and unions are centrally organized, exert considerable influence over industrial groups, and are privileged to speak for broad class interests in policymaking. In countries with sectoral coordination, industry-level groups are more powerful than centralized, peak associations and the latter play a less influential role in policymaking. In pluralist countries, diverse groups compete for political power.

On the business side, the nature of employer representation has an impact on collective training institutions because the provision of skills through institutions outside of the firm requires greater collective effort, which is facilitated by strong associations.

[2] Leaders of business parties in proportional, multi-party systems have incentives to delegate policymaking authority to private channels, because they are unlikely to win electoral majorities when pitted against possible coalitions of workers and agricultural interests and calculate that their constituents are more likely to secure favourable policy outcomes in direct negotiations with workers than in parliamentary processes. Party leaders in two-party systems are less willing to delegate policymaking authority to private actors, because they have greater hopes of winning outright electoral victories. Unitary as opposed to federal governments engender macro-corporatist associations because the political action largely takes place at the national level (Martin and Swank 2008, 2012).

Firstly, the profiles of employers' associations have implications for the *venue and scope* of training. Because apprenticeships are more geared to the most highly skilled workers, more encompassing employers' associations are both more likely to deliver higher levels of training for less skilled industrial workers and to create systems with a broader reliance on schools. Industrial schools were initially developed to meet the needs of less skilled industrial workers, who could not obtain training through the old guild-controlled apprenticeship systems (largely oriented towards journeymen.) Thus, countries with more encompassing employers' associations are more likely to produce more inclusive and encompassing skills systems that transcend sectoral and regional variation and provide skills training for a broader cross-section of workers. For example, the evolution of the Austrian vocational education system was enabled by a system of small state corporatism, in which the social partners mediated the country's responses to changes in socioeconomic conditions (Graf et al. 2012).

Secondly, the profile of employers' associations matters because of the *types and portability of assets*: the programmatic oversight of the content of training institutions influences the development of specific versus general skills and firm-level versus industry-level skills. In particular, more encompassing employers' associations are more likely to have the capacity to link skills obtained through training to the real needs of firms. This is especially important to school-based skills development, where there is a greater possibility that course-work will not deliver the appropriate skills and it is not by accident that liberal countries lacking strong employers' associations have great difficulty delivering portable, certified occupational skills. Moreover, when school-based training institutions are developed through collective bargaining and tripartite policy-making channels, the needs of the social partners are likely to be given greater attention vis-à-vis the interests of professional educators.

Thirdly, the nature of employers' associations has implications for the *levels of training* and *public subsidies* in solving collective action problems and in exposing employers to positive information about human capital investment. The interests of employers in securing a skilled workforce can be a major *political* boon in the creation of collectivist systems, either through legislative channels or through private policymaking channels. Legislation is more likely to be passed when the right joins with the left and encompassing employers' associations have been shown to offer greater support for welfare state spending and labour market initiatives (Martin and Swank 2004). More encompassing employers' associations also are more likely to develop collectivist systems in collaborations with the state and/or employers through private policymaking channels such as tripartite commissions and collective bargaining rounds. Thus more encompassing associations are more likely to overcome the collective action problems associated with maintaining a sufficient level of investment in skills. We might also hypothesize that more encompassing employers' associations are more likely to tolerate a higher tax burden in order to create higher subsidies for skills training, which, in turn, result in more highly skilled workers. Rothstein has observed that employers on corporatist oversight committees have been co-opted into supporting expansion of the budgets for the governmental departments under their jurisdiction and this constitutes a reason for the growth of welfare states.

Moreover, once a system of coordinated labour relations has been set into place, employers have reduced incentives to use their apprentices either as a source of low wage labour and or as a reserve army of the semi-employed to break strikes. Employers' associations and unions seek to preserve peaceful labour relations, in part to sustain their jurisdictional authority over policymaking; consequently, they have incentives to sustain apprenticeships that fit easily into the broader parameters of the labour market relationship for reasons of associational control.

Finally, the profile of the employers' associations will have an impact on training systems' *flexibility and capacity for adjustment* and in particular on the extent to which skills production can be adjusted to economic transformations and tailored to diverse regional needs. More encompassing employers' associations are more likely to unite manufacturing and services sectors, to reconcile the diverse needs of sectors in achieving an overarching framework for vocational training, to aid in the movement of workers from declining into emerging sectors, and to help to renegotiate collective business identities during moments of economic and generational transformation.

On the labour side, encompassing unions and highly centralized coordinated bargaining bring skilled workers to support vocational training for their less skilled colleagues. Within industrial sectors, semi-skilled workers are a complement to skilled workers in the production process; therefore, the consent of the former must be reached before deals with employers can be made and this increases the bargaining power of the unskilled workers (Iversen 2005). Clark and Winch (2007) agree that the development of vocational education and training is intertwined with the formation of national labour markets.

A brief recounting of the evolution of vocational training in Germany, Denmark, and the United States gives one a sense of how these various factors interact in producing cross-national variations in training institutions.

The German Vocational Training System

Firm-based apprenticeships are the core of the German system of vocational training, with school-based instruction playing a secondary role. Workers are trained within small companies, which use apprentices as a source of cheap labour and then pass them on to the larger firms. A marked regional diversity creates much unevenness in the German system and the social partners play a more limited role, with comprehensive, national framework for oversight by business and labour only emerging in a 1969 law (Smart 1975, 153).

In Germany, a strong guilds tradition created norms of non-market competition and expectations of a highly skilled workforce. The government vested power in the handicrafts sector to educate these workers with the Crafts Trades Protection Act of 1897, which established compulsory chambers of trades as bodies for determining skills. The suring up of guilds and handicraft control reflected party competition for bourgeois electoral support and an effort by the authoritarian state to prevent labour from gaining control over skills (Thelen 2004, 53–54; Greinert 2005, 40).

The handicraft system could not, however, adequately address the skills needs of factory workers in large firms; and the first world war made training gaps even more salient, as youths seeking apprenticeships dropped from two-thirds of males between 14 and 18 in 1907 to well below 40% by 1917 (Hanson 1997, 572–574). Industrialization fuelled an interest in technical schools for less skilled factory workers, such as the Kerschensteiner continuation schools, production schools, and course-based training. The Association of German Engineers lobbied the Prussian Ministry of Trade and Industry to provide technical middle schools, and by 1911 Prussia had an elaborate network of schools (Greinert 2005, 42–43, 56, 63–65). Many large industrial firms developed in-house training programmes but these could not grant certificates. The German Committee for Technical Education developed certifications, mechanisms for the standardization of skills, and training course material appropriate to diverse trades (Hanson 1997, 595–599; Thelen 2004, 55–61).

But regional economic and political diversity, coupled with weak national associations for the social partners and opposition from the handicraft sectors, restrained collectivist training options and large German firms experimented with segmentalist firm-based training strategies (Sweeney 2001, 712–718; Dunlavy and Welskopp 2007). Cooperation did not come easily to the regionally diverse German firms and political fragmentation—federalism and regionally dominated political parties—reinforced the fault lines. In Germany, the absence of a single dedicated business party constrained the emergence of full-blown macro-corporatism. For example, after the war, employers were distributed across parties and this heightened employers' distrust of the political system (Pollock 1929).

The absence of a unifying centralized employers' association or union added to the difficulty of national cooperation. The newly formed peak association, the Reich Association of German Industry, never gained any real authority, decision-making power largely transpired at the industry level and business–labour negotiations over training and other social issues were stalled (Rogers and Dittmar 1935, 483–484; Wolff-Rohe 2001). Business and labour sought a national certificate system and social partner oversight of firm-level training to improve the human capital of industrial workers, the government considered an extensive vocational training reform, and the Prussian Ministry of Trade lobbied for comprehensive national legislation; but these initiatives failed to gain traction. Attempts to create oversight committees of business and labour were thwarted by the special position of the handicraft sectors in controlling apprenticeships and the way in which the handicraft sectors' interests connect to employers' history of fighting amongst themselves (Hanson 1997, 585–593; Thelen 2004, 73–87; Greinert 2005, 81).

United States

Unlike Germany, the United States had a very weak tradition and this, undoubtedly, contributed to its failure to establish strong, collectivist skills training institutions for workers with specific assets. Yet the United States had a rather extensive system of industrial schools in the nineteenth century and American employers were very eager to obtain portable, certified skills for their workers. Many employers believed that in order to be an industrial power, US industry required skills and workers with 'industrial intelligence', and employers expressed considerable support for differentiating the educational experience into two tracks, beginning with the sixth grade (Cohen 1968, 100). Many managers became active in the 'manual training movement', to incorporate practical skills in the educational content of public schools. The National Association of Manufacturers (NAM) provided an epicentre of the business support for vocational training and, in particular, the NAM Committee on Industrial Education sought the creation of industrial schools for blue-collar workers that followed the German model (Miles 1911). The National Society for the Promotion of Industrial Education, a group composed of diverse interests, sponsored a multi-city tour for Georg Kerschenstelner to educate America about the German continuation schools ('To Lecture on Education') and lobbied for federal financing of vocational training within new continuation schools ('Plan to Train the Workers').

The wave of support for vocational education crested with the legislation of the Smith-Hughes Act in 1917, which created a national mandate for vocational education, federal funds to the states to support part-time and full-time vocational education, and a Federal Board of Vocational Education to oversee ventures in pushing this model. However, individual states were accorded the right to determine the form of vocational education—in particular, whether schools would remain separate or be incorporated into the mainstream —and a small minority of states moved to the dual track (Kantor and Tyack 1982; Benavot 1983; Kliebard 1999).

Yet the emergence of an effective vocational training system with high levels of coordination and certified, occupational skills was severely constrained by strong economic sectional divisions, the political features of government, and the low level of organized labour market coordination. Southern elite agricultural interests were dead set against any national initiative to develop portable, certifiable skills for southern African-American plantation workers and northern industrial interests ran up against the stonewalling techniques of southern agrarian elites. These southern agricultural elites won because they were represented by southern democrats, who held key Congressional chairs responsible for reporting out legislation and the concept of state's rights was used to strike down amendments permitting the evolution of a more viable skills training policy (Margo 1990; Werum 1997, 400–404, 414).

Weak employers' associations and unions also contributed to the failure to develop a comprehensive training system for vocational workers. School boards rather than social partners were responsible for proscribing the content of vocational education in the United States and the absence of systematic input by the social partners worked against the development of real qualifications. Organized labour had legitimate reasons to distrust employers' (and especially NAM's) interests in vocational training, as organized business seemed so determined to stifle the power of the working class and the American Federation of Labor favoured encompassing public schools with both academic and vocational tracks to avoid a second-tier system.

After the passage of the Smith-Hughes Act, only eight states moved to form vocational schools; moreover, the absence of highly organized institutions for coordination with business worked to dampen the social partners' input into the content of school-based instruction. Consequently, a system of school-based courses tailored to certified skills failed to emerge. Finally, the High School Act of 1926 incorporated vocational training back into the mainstream education system and the era of experimentation with a separate track for vocational training came to an end.

The Danish Vocational Training System

A puzzle is why Denmark developed a strong network of industrial schools with extensive oversight by the social partners and chose not to leave control in the handicraft sectors, as happened in Germany. Danish vocational training relies on a dual system, with apprenticeship positions playing a secondary role to school-based instruction (although the state began a campaign to expand the number of apprenticeship positions in the late 1980s). The social partners have played a strong role in determining the content and in providing oversight of vocational training since the beginning of the twentieth century (Nielsen and Cort 1999, 4; Nelson 2012).

Denmark had strong guilds until the beginning of the nineteenth century and this laid the foundation for strong norms of non-market competition and collectivist skills training within the handicraft sectors. The handicraft system of apprenticeship training, however, was threatened by the introduction of free trade in 1857, after apprentice examinations declined sharply, industrial production expanded, and industrial schools grew in response to a growing need for semi-skilled workers. Technical schools were better suited than apprenticeship programmes to the training needs of larger industrial firms (Boje and Fink 1990, 126–135). Yet a mystery remains: why Denmark created such strong schools to meet the competency needs of both high- and low-skill workers and why these skills are developed at the industry- rather than firm-level.

The very high levels of coordination amongst business and labour groups also contributed to the expansive provision of certified skills by vocational training schools (Juul 2009). The initial experiment in the expansion of vocational training arrangements by the social partners occurred in 1909, when a tripartite negotiation in the molder industry established an apprenticeship committee, composed of representatives from the employers' association and the union. The committee developed an educational plan for a trade school and this marked a vast improvement in the education of molders. This innovation—to have the social partners specify the content of industrial education rather than leaving it to the traditional educational process—came to constitute the model for all industrial and handicraft education (Boje and Fink 1990, 137–138).

After the war, industrial violence prompted employers to nurture workforce skills as a means of diminishing labour radicalism (Dansk Arbejdsgiverforening 1946, 9–14). The Apprenticeship Law of 1921, passed with support from a centre-right coalition, gave the social partners some shared, formal responsibility over apprenticeships and incorporated semi-skilled workers into policies covering apprenticeships and training (Arbejdsgiveren 1921, 124–125, 155; Boje and Fink 1990, 137–138). Whilst the 1921 Apprenticeship Act extended social partners' jurisdiction over apprenticeships, the technical education part of the formula remained beyond their jurisdiction and the plethora of trade schools and technical institutes continued to grow in spontaneous, pluralist fashion without any oversight from the state or society. Schools became increasingly differentiated with technological change; for example, Fordism created a need for both entry-level technical education for semi-skilled workers and technical schools for those playing a supervisory role in the production process. What was lacking, however, were steering, coordination, and a formal integration of practical training and technical education. Growing specialization and the emerging army of low-skilled workers—particularly in the iron and metal industries—posed a significant problem for quality control of work output, in the absence of much direction in formal education and employers in the metal industry were inspired by the earlier experiments by the molders in 1909 to oversee the development of an educational course that sufficiently met the skills needs of the industry (Boje and Fink 1990, 140–144). The Apprenticeship Act of 1937 extended social partners' control to technical schools, in giving occupational committees the authority to monitor vocational education in the classroom as well as on the shop floor. The peak employers' association, the Federation of Danish Employers, viewed the occupational committees as 'an overwhelmingly valuable organ for carrying out training and education and that can give apprenticeships a higher quality … This is a social act in which employers and workers operate completely together' (Dansk Arbejdsgiverforening 1946, 67).

Concluding Thoughts: Twentieth-Century Legacies for Twenty-First Century Choices

By way of conclusion, the chapter contemplates what the past bodes for the future and how trajectories of skills training determine national struggles to prepare workers for the post-industrial age. The rise of a services economy poses fundamental challenges to national models of training. Manufacturing workers with mid-range skills are being replaced with higher- and lower-skilled service sector workers (in a 'hollowing out' of skills) (Lash and Urry 1987). Service sector employment may also entail a larger predominance of low-skilled workers, although others suggest that the services economy has a higher proportion of professional and managerial workers (Fagan et al. 2004; Bosch 2005). Service sectors have lower levels of productivity growth, making it difficult for countries to sustain solidaristic wage policies. Whereas solidaristic wage policies tended to squeeze out the least productive workers in manufacturing sectors and shift resources to high-growing sectors, solidarist wage bargaining in the service economy keeps wages high in the least dynamic sectors. Because vocational training for low-skilled workers has historically focused on manufacturing skills development, policymakers face a skills barrier (at both the individual or institutional levels) in training and retooling service sector workers (Iversen 2006, 16–17).

Countries have responded quite differently to the threats of deindustrialization, and early innovations in workforce training set policy legacies for these later struggles and for flexibility in adjusting to the new economic climate. General and specific skills training systems both exhibit pros and cons in the transition to services.

First, general skills training systems may do somewhat better in preparing service workers than in training skilled manufacturing workers,as vocational training has been the weak link in liberal market economy (LME) educational systems (King 1995; Hall and Soskice 2001; Wood 2001). Moreover, the distribution of jobs into high-skilled and low-skilled groups found in the services economy more closely matches the LME profile; therefore, as manual skilled-labour jobs disappear, these countries will more comfortably deliver appropriate skills. Some evidence suggests that the United Kingdom narrowed the skills gap with Germany (Steedman et al. 1998, 6).

Yet the limited historic commitment to skills development in liberal market economies may bode ill for the transition to services. Labour market policies for low-end workers have been conceived of as a residual service for the unemployed (King 1995; Wood 2001). Firm-based training is voluntary and training levies have been largely absent; consequently, training in most sectors is under-supplied. Low-skilled individuals in Britain are less likely than their Danish counterparts to have permanent, full-time employment, and these bouts of unemployment create lasting scars on the career paths of the unemployed (Gangl 2006). Spending on vocational training in the United States continues to be exceedingly low from a cross-national perspective and green-card immigration has become a functional equivalent for skills training programmes. This sheds light on why immigration reform has become such a cause célèbre amongst the American business community. Second, the expansive commitments to specific skills production in coordinated market economies in collectivist skills training systems also provide advantages in the training of post-industrial workers. Coordinated market economies have stronger training traditions for blue-collar workers and this excellence might translate into better skills development of low-skilled service sector workers. For example, Danish training programmes for retail workers have simply slipped into the well-worn grooves of the training system for manual workers (Martin and Knudsen 2010). Job retention within the firm might continue to be higher in these countries than in LMEs and it may bring companies to make more costly investments in skills development (Hall and Soskice 2001; Estevez-Abe et al. 2001).

Yet collectivist training institutions have also demonstrated problems making the adjustment to services. Lower-skilled workers may well have difficulty making a commitment to a lengthy vocational training programme and whilst extensive training may seem appropriate for highly skilled manufacturing workers, a comparable commitment may not make sense for service workers. In countries with highly regulated training options, low-skilled workers may be forced to choose between all and nothing. In addition, general education programmes may meet the skills needs of low-end service workers better than vocational training (Martin and Knudsen 2010). Even at the low end of the skills continuum, service sector workers have a greater need for soft skills than manufacturing workers (see Warhurst et al., Chapter 4 in this volume), and store and office clerks may benefit the most from learning basic maths and literacy skills through schools that aid in emotional work (Hochschild 1983).

Moreover, the politics of training for low-skilled workers may be in transition, because social democratic parties are more anxious to represent the interests of their core constituents than those of low-skilled service workers (Rueda 2007). Core working class strength also works to diminish attention to marginally skilled workers through extra-political channels, when core business and labour associations negotiate vocational training arrangements that largely ignore the needs of low-skilled workers (Marsden 2002). German social democrats have been increasingly committed to spending on higher education, even whilst cutting back spending on certain social programmes and the decline of union membership might further cut support for training (Busemeyer 2015).

Third, the venue of training within coordinated market economies—industrial schools versus apprenticeships—also contributes to countries' capacities to adapt to the post-industrial economy. Countries with a heavier reliance on apprenticeships than industrial schools in the dual system have shown the greatest difficulty adapting to the post-industrial economy. Past practices of crafts sector firms supplying semi-skilled labour to big industrial firms have declined with increased educational requirements and rising costs of training, and these small companies are less willing to supply many apprenticeship slots (Thelen 2004; Busemeyer 2015). German apprenticeships have been declining steadily over the years, and service firms have been less proactive in developing apprenticeship programmes for their workers than manufacturing companies (Busemeyer 2015; see also Ashton et al., Chapter 15 in this volume). Indeed, Germany is moving to rely more on industrial schools for training in semi-professional occupations and these skills are becoming less standardized than they were in apprenticeship programmes (Shire and Gottschall 2006, 12). These factors may well contribute to the growing dualism separating labour market insiders and outsiders in Germany and other continental countries (Palier and Thelen 2010; Busemeyer 2015).

Countries making greater use of schools (especially in Scandinavia) have demonstrated weaker dualist tendencies than those relying primarily on apprenticeships. Their greater reliance on schools to train workers at all skills levels has enabled skills development for all manual workers and this may well contribute to lower rates of dualism found in the continental countries. The Scandinavian countries with the strongest, collective deliberative institutions are better positioned to make post-industrial reforms than those that leave workers to fend for themselves in adjusting to shifting skills needs. Denmark's early development of corporatist committees involving the social partners in oversight of training programmes at the beginning of the twentieth century left a legacy of strong business–labour commitment to training. Both sides of the industrial divide continue to be crucial actors in training developments today.

REFERENCES

Ansell, B. (2008) 'Teachers, Traders, and Tyrants: Democracy, Globalization and Education Spending', *International Organization* (Spring).

Ansell, B. and Lindvahl J. (2013) 'The Political Origins of Primary Education Systems: Ideology, Institutions, and Interdenominational Conflict in an Era of Nation-Building', *American Political Science Review*, 107(3) (August): 505–522.

Arbejdsgiveren (1921) 'Lærlingeloven', 22 (16) (22 Avril): 124–125.

Benavot, A. (1983) 'The Rise and Decline of Vocational Education', *Sociology of Education*, 56 (2 April): 63–76.

Boje, P. and Fink, J. (1990) 'Mesterlære og teknisk udannelse I Danmark 1850–1950', *Erhvervshistorisk Årbog*, Aarhus: Erhvervsarkivet.

Bosch, G. and Lehndorff, S. (eds) (2005) *Working in the Service Sector*, New York: Routledge.

Busemeyer, M. (2009) 'Asset Specificity, Institutional Complementarities and the Variety of Skill Regimes in Coordinated Market Economies', *Socio-Economic Review*, 7: 375–406.

Busemeyer, M. (2015) 'Skills and Inequality: Political Parties and the Political Economy of Education Reforms in Western European Countries', Cambridge: Cambridge University Press.

Busemeyer, M. and Trampusch, C. (2011) 'Review Article: Comparative Political Science and the Study of Education', *British Journal of Political Science*, 41: 413–443.

Clark, L. and Winch, C. (2007) 'Introduction', in L. Clark and C. Winch (eds), *Vocational Education, International Approaches, Developments and Systems*, London: Routledge: 1–17.

Cohen, S. (1968) 'The Industrial Education Movement, 1906–1917', American *Quarterly*, 20(1): 95–110.

Cort, P. and Hansen, S. (2002) *Vocational Education and Training in Denmark*, Luxembourg: Cedefop.

Cusack, T. Iversen, T., and Soskice, D. (2007) 'Economic Interests and the Origins of Electoral Systems', *American Political Science Review*, 101(3): 373–91.

Dansk Arbejdsgiverforening (1946) *Arbejdsgiver Foreningen Gennem 50 Aar*, Copenhagen: Langkjærs Bogtrykkeri.

Dunlavy, C. and Weiskopf, T. (2007) 'Peculiarities and Myths: Comparing U.S. and German Capitalism', *German Historical Institute Bulletin*, 41 (Fall 2007): 33–64.

Estevez-Abe, M., Iversen, T., and Soskice, D. (2001) 'Social Protection and the Formation of Skills', in P. Hall and D. Soskice (eds), *Varieties of Capitalism*, Oxford: Oxford University Press: 145–183.

Fagan, C., Halpin, B., and O'Reilly, J. (2005) 'Service Sector Employment in Germany and the UK', *Arbeitsmarktpolitik und Strukturwandel. Empirische Analysen, Journal of Applied Social Science Studies/Zeitschrift für Wirtschafts- und Sozial wissenschaften*, Schmollers Jahrbuch, 125(1): 97–108.

Galenson, W. (1952) *The Danish System of Labor Relations: A Study in Industrial Peace*, Cambridge: Harvard University Press.

Gershenkron, A. (1962) *Economic Backwardness in Historical Perspective*, Cambridge, MA: Harvard University Press.

Graf, L., Lassnigg, L., and Powell, J. (2012) 'Austrian Corporatism and Institutional Change in the Relationship between Apprenticeship Training and School-Based VET', in M. Busemeyer and C. Trampusch (eds), *The Political Economy of Collective Skill Formation*, Oxford: Oxford University Press.

Greinert, W-D. (2005) *Mass Vocational Education and Training in Europe*, Luxembourg: Cedefop.

Hall, P. and Soskice, D. (eds) (2001) *Varieties of Capitalism: The Institutional Foundations of Comparative Advantage*, New York: Oxford University Press.

Hanson, H. (1997) 'Caps and Gowns: Historical Reflections on the Institutions That Shaped Learning for and at Work in Germany and the United States'. PhD thesis, University of Wisconsin, Madison, WI.

Hochschild, A. (1983) *The Managed Heart: The Commercialization of Human Feeling*, Berkeley: University of California Press.

Iversen, T. (2005) *Capitalism, Democracy and Welfare*, New York: Cambridge University Press.

Iversen, T. and Stephens, J. D. (2008) 'Partisan Politics, the Welfare State, and Three Worlds of Human Capital Formation', *Comparative Political Studies*, 41 (4–5): 600–637.

Juul, I. (2009) 'Fra lavsvæsen til fagligt selvstyre. Arbejdsgivelserne indflydelse på erhvervsuddannelserne i perioden 1857–1937', *Økonomi & Politik*, 82(3): 3–14.

Juul, I. (2005) *På sporet af erhvervspædagogikken*, Copenhagen: The Danish University of Education.

Kantor, H. and Tyack, D. (eds) (1982) *Work, Youth and Schooling*, Stanford, CA: Stanford University Press.

King, D. (1995) *Actively Seeking Work*, Chicago: University of Chicago Press.

Kinghorn, J. R. and Nye, J. V. (1996) 'The Scale of Production in Western Europe: A Comparison of the Official Industry Statistics in the United States, Britain, France and Germany, 1905–1913', *The Journal of Economic History*, 56(1): 90–112.

Kitschelt, H. (1993) 'Class Structure and Social Democratic Party Strategy', *British Journal of Political Science*, 23(3): 299–337.

Kristensen, P. H. and Sabel, C. (1997) 'The Small-Holder Economy in Denmark', in C. Sabel and J. Zeitlin (eds), *World of Possibilities: Flexibility and Mass Production in Western Industrialization*, New York: Cambridge University Press: 344–378.

Lash, S. and Urry, J. (1987) *The End of Organized Capitalism*, Oxford: Polity Press.

Marsden, D. (2002) 'National Vocational Qualifications, Modern Apprenticeship and the Revival of Intermediate Skills in Britain', Japan Institute of Labour, report no. 127, Tokyo.

Margo, R. (1990). *Race and Schooling in the South*, Chicago: University of Chicago Press.

Martin, C. J. (2012) 'Vocational Training and the Origins of Coordination: Specific Skills and the Politics of Collective Action', in M. Busemeyer and C. Trampusch (eds), *The Comparative Political Economy of Collective Skill Systems*, Oxford: Oxford University Press.

Martin, C. J. and Swank, D. (2008) 'The Political Origins of Coordinated Capitalism', *American Political Science Review*, 102(2) (2 May): 181–198.

Martin, C. J. and Swank, D. (2012) *The Political Construction of Business Interests: Coordination, Growth and Equality*, Cambridge: Cambridge University Press.

Martin, C. J. and Knudsen, J. S. (2010) 'Scenes from a Mall: Retail Training and the Social Exclusion of Low-Skilled Workers', *Regulation & Governance*, 4(3): 345–364.

Martin, C. J. and Thelen, K. (2007) 'The State and Coordinated Capitalism', *World Politics*, 57(1) (1 October): 1–36.

Miles, H. E. (1911) *Industrial Education: Report of the Committee on Industrial Education*, Washington, DC: National Association of Manufacturers Committee on Industrial Education.

Nelson, M. (2012) 'Comparative Political Economy of Collective Skill Systems: Denmark', in M. Busemeyer and C. Trampusch (eds), *The Political Economy of Collective Skill Systems*, Oxford: Oxford University Press.

New York Times (1910) 'To Lecture on Education', 29 October: 18.

New York Times (1914) 'Plan to Train the Workers', 19 April: 12.

Nielsen, S. and Cort, P. (1999) *Vocational Education and Training in Denmark*, Thessaloniki: Cedefop, European Centre for the Development of Vocational Training.

Palier, B. and Thelen, K. (2010) 'Institutionalizing Dualism: Complementarities and Change in France and Germany', *Politics & Society*, 38 (1): 119–148.

Pollock, J. (1929) 'The German Party System', *American Political Science Review*, 23 (4 November): 859–91.

Rogers, L. and Dittmar, W. R. (1935) 'The Reichswirtschaftsrat', *Political Science Quarterly*, 50 (4 December): 481–501.

Rothstein, B. (1988) 'State and Capital in Sweden', *Scandinavian Political Studies*, 11 (3): 235–260.

Rueda, D. (2006) 'Social Democracy and Active Labour-Market Policies', *British Journal of Political Science* 36: 385–406.

Shire, K. and Gottschall, K. (2006) 'Understanding Employment Systems from a Gender Perspective'. ZeS-Arbeitspapier Nr. 5/2007 (Zentrum für Sozialpolitik, Bremen University).

Smart, K. (1975) 'Vocational Education in the Federal Republic of Germany', *Comparative Education*, 11(2 June): 153–163.

Steedman, H. and Wagner, K. (2006) 'Changing Skill Needs in Europe and Responsiveness of Apprenticeship/Work-based Learning'. Unpublished paper.

Steedman, H., Gospel, H. and Ryan, P. (1998) *Apprenticeship: A Strategy for Growth*, London: Centre for Economic Performance, London School of Economics.

Sweeney, D. (2001) 'Corporatist Discourse and Heavy Industry in Wilhelmine Germany', *Comparative Studies in Society and History*, 43 (4 October): 701–734.

Thelen, K. (2004) *How Institutions Evolve*, New York: Cambridge University Press.

Trampusch, C. (2010) 'Co-evolution of Skills and Welfare in Coordinated Market Economies?', *European Journal of Industrial Relations*, 16(3); 197–220.

Unwin, G. (1966). *The Guilds and Companies of London*, 4th ed., London: Frank Cass & Co.

Werum, R. (1997) 'Sectionalism and Racial Politics: Federal Vocational Policies and Programs in the Predesegregation South', *Social Science History*, 21(3): 399–453.

Wilensky, H. (2002) *Rich Democracies*, Berkeley, CA: University of California Press.

Wolff-Rohe, S. (2001) *Der Reichsverband der Deutschen Industrie 1919–1924/25*, Frankfurt am Main: Peter Lang.

Wood, S. (2001) 'Labour Market Regimes Under Threat?', in P. Pierson (ed.), *New Politics of the Welfare State*, New York: Oxford University Press: 394–398.

Zeitlin, J. (1990). 'The Triumph of Adversarial Bargaining: Industrial Relations in British Engineering, 1880–1939', *Politics and Society*, 18(3): 381–404.

CHAPTER 3

THE CHANGING MEANING OF SKILL

Still Contested, Still Important

JONATHAN PAYNE

INTRODUCTION

'SKILL' has acquired almost totemic status in recent policy debates as a, or even *the*, critical factor in economic competitiveness, productivity growth, and social cohesion (Green 2011). Much of this has been driven by the seductive rhetoric of the knowledge economy, with its promise of a new workplace populated by teams of knowledge workers enjoying high levels of autonomy, creativity, and authorship at work (Reich 1991; Leadbetter 2000). For many policymakers across the advanced industrialized world, this *is* the present and the future—one where demand for skill rises inexorably as organizations adjust to the new rules of global competition (Grugulis and Lloyd 2010).

Such optimistic scenarios, however, downplay the rapid growth, particularly in the United States, United Kingdom, and Australia, of routine service jobs in areas such as hospitality, retailing, and personal services, and labour markets that are becoming increasingly polarized in terms of incomes and job quality (Grugulis et al. 2004). Low-skill, low-wage work is not disappearing; neither is it confined to liberal market economies (Gautié and Schmitt 2010). Such critical perspectives assume, of course, that we know what a 'skilled job' is, or at the very least that there is some way of distinguishing different jobs in terms of their relative skill level. However, skill is a notoriously complex as well as contested concept (Attewell 1990; Green 2011), and notions of skill, competence, and skilled work(er) often mean different things in different countries (Brockmann et al. 2011).

Matters have become even more complicated as the meaning of skill has widened within official policy discourse (Payne 2000). Forty years ago, 'skill', when talked about in UK policy documents, mainly referred to the educational qualifications, manual dexterity, spatial awareness, and technical know-how of the skilled craft worker or technician. To be skilled was to be unionized and male, to have undergone a lengthy apprenticeship, to exert a degree of control over one's work, and to be well rewarded.[1] With the shift towards a service-based economy, such traditional notions of skill are widely seen as 'neither descriptively robust nor versatile enough to handle contemporary questions of skill' (Gatta et al. 2009; Green 2011; Hurrell et al. 2013, 164). New categories of 'generic', 'transferable', 'basic', 'employability', 'soft', and 'social' skills have emerged. Today, the 'skills' label is applied to everything from thinking, communication, reading, writing and numeracy, team working, problem solving, customer handling, leadership, motivation, initiative, a positive attitude, punctuality, personal appearance, stress management, and even plain obedience (Grugulis 2007, ch. 5).

Some worry that the concept of skill is being stretched so far that it risks losing any analytical or operational meaning, and that it may end up fuelling policy myths around universal upskilling (Lafer 2004; Payne 2009; Lloyd and Payne 2009). Others argue that this should not detract from attempts to render visible the real skills required in interactive service work, and have put forward new skill concepts of 'emotion work' (Bolton 2004), 'aesthetic labour', and 'articulation work' (Hampson and Junor 2010; for a more general discussion, see Gatta et al. 2009). They argue that many routine service jobs have been too readily dismissed as low-skilled because of a preoccupation with conventional measures, or proxies, such as qualification requirements and length of education or training times, which fail to capture the actual skills in use. Furthermore, because these jobs are performed mainly by women, skills such as emotion work tend to be dismissed as 'natural' feminine abilities so that their real skill content goes unrecognized and unrewarded (Korczynski 2005). By holding out the prospect of a revaluation of such skills, these discourses provide a modicum of relief from the pessimism that might otherwise be associated with labour markets that are becoming increasingly polarized. However, many of these new skills remain problematic and have prompted considerable debate (Grugulis et al. 2004, 6).

The purpose of this chapter is to guide the reader through the thickets of controversy, and to try and chart a way forward. The argument is that there is a need for a robust and meaningful concept of skill that can be applied to both manufacturing and service-based settings, one which sets skill in its societal and workplace context, is rooted in political economy, and takes seriously issues of power, job complexity, and worker autonomy (Grugulis and Lloyd 2010). With the label 'skill' having acquired a much broader application, it is more important than ever to have clarity about the actual level of skill required to perform the job. Often it is confusion over this issue that has tended to cloud meaningful debate. It would be naïve, however, to believe that a consensus is possible or achievable. Rather, the aim is to highlight some of the problems and pitfalls that surround current understandings of skill, the consequences of which are far from benign, and, in doing so, stimulate further debate.

[1] The concept of skill was not exclusively reserved for skilled manual workers but was also applied more broadly to professional groups, such as doctors, accountants, and teachers, whose expert knowledge and certified competence helped to underpin claims to professional autonomy.

Skill: A Contested Concept

Skill has always been a slippery concept within the social sciences. Reviewing what he labelled positivist, ethnomethodological, Weberian, and Marxist understandings of skill, Attewell (1990, 422) found that these not only varied markedly but were often 'blind to their preconceptions'. More recently, Green (2011) has argued that the disciplines of economics, sociology, and psychology have tended to talk past each other, and that this lack of dialogue is impeding attempts to grapple with contemporary analytical and policy issues.

In economics, the dominant analytical framework has been supplied by human capital theory (HCT) (Becker 1964). Put simply, human capital is *any* capacity that makes a worker more productive and adds to their present and future earnings. In theory, rationally calculating individuals make decisions to invest in education and training in anticipation of expected returns on their investment. Combined with the rhetoric of the knowledge economy, this has helped to seal in many policymakers' minds a simplistic link between skills supply (as proxied by qualifications) and productivity, upon which large rafts of public policy have come to depend (see Keep and Mayhew 2010). As Green (2011, 7) notes, it is a perspective with well-known shortcomings. Based on a highly individualized conception of skill as a 'thing to be acquired', HCT is prone to ignore societal factors, such as class, which structure individuals' educational choices and opportunities. By treating skill, like physical capital, as simply another factor input within the 'black box' of the firm, it posits a 'world with exogenously determined technologies and optimum management policies' in which issues of skill recognition, reward, and utilization are assumed to be unproblematic (Green 2011, 7; see also Grugulis 2007, 18).

Green (2011, 7, 22) reminds us that the *valuation* of skill is far more complex than HCT allows, and remains deeply political (with a small *p*). As he points out, 'social processes, including power, affect who can sport the label of "skilled labour", and who can claim the rewards' with '[M]ultiple actors vying for advantage' and apt to privilege their own particular definitions and interests. Take the case of those within the top one per cent of the earnings distribution, who are often said to possess that rare commodity called 'talent'. Their incomes have experienced a meteoric rise in countries such as the United Kingdom and the United States in recent decades, far outstripping even the rest of those within the top decile. HCT would say that the wage paid to such talented individuals reflects the market valuation of their productivity which, in turn, reflects their human capital. In reality, however, we know very little about what this talent consists of, and, crucially, whether their abilities impact on productivity and performance in a way that can make any sense of the scale of rewards provided (see High Pay Commission 2011).

Sociological accounts have focused on the skills required *within* the job and skill as a social construct. Jobs can be designed to restrict the scope available to the worker to exercise discretion and skill, but they can also be designed in ways that expand such opportunities. Since Braverman's (1974) influential account of the deskilling of craft-work through the Taylorist division of labour, the idea that skilled work is intrinsically bound up with workers' autonomy and job control has been a defining principle for many commentators. Littler (1982, 9) argued that it was 'not possible to define "skill" independently of organizational control and control processes', while Thompson (1989, 92) defined skill as 'knowledgeable practice within elements of control'. In contrast, Green (2011, 9) argues that fusing autonomy into the definition of skill misses the point that 'even closely rule-bound operations can be complex'. However, he acknowledges that 'Complex tasks are likely to be less easily specified, more infused with contingencies and subject to uncertainty; so greater worker autonomy is likely to be found in the organisation of complex work.'

The other major contribution of sociology has been to highlight the *social construction* of skill (Littler 1982; Cockburn 1983). The concept of *social closure* focuses upon the ability of a particular group to insulate its members from market competition by erecting barriers to entry through qualification requirements (Noon and Blyton 2002).[2] Thus, the ability of British craft unions to restrict entry to certain jobs by exercising control over apprenticeship training once played a crucial role in securing skilled status and higher rewards for their male membership (Turner 1962).[3] Feminist commentators have long recognized this (Cockburn 1983), as skilled work frequently becomes simply 'work women don't do' (Phillips and Taylor 1980, 79). The upshot is that women's skills can go unrecognized, resulting in lower pay compared with skilled male jobs that, in objective terms, may be less or no more complex. Social structures and power-based inequalities, including gender, race (Moss and Tilly 1996), and class (Brown and Hesketh 2004), can also affect judgements of what counts as skill as well as lead to forms of social stereotyping that may disadvantage particular groups, both in the workplace and the wider labour market.

Green (2011, 11) argues that sociological accounts have been less inclined to engage with 'theories of value', tending to 'fall back on complexity of production as skill's true measure'. This, he argues, is problematic given the difficulties that surround defining what is and is not 'complex' (see Attewell 1990). Detailed ethnographic studies of work, along with theories of work-based learning (Lave and Wenger 1991), have highlighted the often complex tacit or unarticulated skills that underpin many work processes, and which can remain invisible both to outside observers and even those who perform them. Green (2011, 9) includes 'emotional and aesthetic skills' among them, describing these as 'complex tasks', a point that has not escaped controversy and which we return to below.

In occupational and educational psychology, the focus is on exploring the skill content of particular jobs, and how skills are learnt and used within their particular context. As Green (2011) notes, recent debates have been dominated by the notion of 'competence',

[2] Economists use similar terms such as 'non-competing groups' and 'labour market segmentation'.

[3] The concept is now reserved mainly for professional groups, for example, lawyers, doctors, and accountants.

an approach that has not been without its problems, not least in the United Kingdom where the introduction of national vocational qualifications in the mid-1980s served to entrench a narrow view of skill as the ability to perform particular tasks with prescriptive accuracy (Jessup 1991). This gave rise to qualifications that heavily discounted the importance of underpinning knowledge and theory and, in some cases, any connection with a learning programme (Green 1998). English vocational programmes are also characterized by a lack of substantive general education content, with a restricted diet of 'core', 'key', and now 'functional' skills acting as a poor surrogate for the much broader and more substantive general education offered to vocational students in many European countries as a basis for future progression, learning, and citizenship (Green 1998).

Other European countries have managed to develop and sustain much broader notions of competence and what it means to be skilled (Clarke and Winch 2006; Brockmann et al. 2011). In Germany, a 'skilled worker' is someone who has undergone an apprenticeship and who has acquired, through an extensive learning programme, a high but broad base of knowledge and skills required to operate and progress within an occupational field.[4] This model is embedded within an institutional context, where apprenticeship training is regulated through tripartite arrangements, and the value of skilled, qualified labour is negotiated and recognized through collective agreements.

This marks a significant contrast with the United Kingdom, where 'skilled' and 'qualified' remain distinct, and vocational qualifications bear little relation to wage structures and collective agreements. As Clarke and Winch (2006, 262) note, 'In Britain ... a "skilled worker" is someone whose operational ability to carry out particular tasks is recognised by the immediate employer but who is not necessarily formally trained or "qualified" with the potential to carry out a wider range of tasks than those immediately confronted.' In the United Kingdom, skill is understood in very narrow terms, while the focus of vocational education and training is almost solely on *training* for work. Elsewhere in Europe, there is an assumption that those pursuing vocational programmes require much broader training and an education for life and citizenship.

Towards an Integrated Concept of Skill

Notwithstanding the profound differences in the way that skill is understood both across disciplines and countries, there have been attempts to develop an integrated conceptual approach. Following Cockburn (1983), Grugulis et al. (2004, 5) distinguish between 'the skill that resides in the worker', 'the skill that is required of the job', and 'socially constructed skill arising from negotiation between economic actors, collectively or as

[4] In Germany, these notions are captured by the term *beruf*, which implies professional status.

individuals'. In an attempt to encourage greater interdisciplinary dialogue, Green (2011, 5) proposes a 'simple' definition as any 'personal quality' that is *productive* of value, *expandable* (capable of being enhanced), and *social* (that is, socially determined).[5] This is a broad definition, which includes attitudes, behaviours, dispositions, and personal attributes. Apart from qualities outside the world of work (for example, sporting abilities) or those that cannot be improved upon (for example, human height), very little is excluded. Indeed, he argues that 'virtually no work should be called "unskilled"', adding that it is 'practical only to make distinctions along the spectrum between low-skilled and high-skilled work' (Green 2011, 22).

Such a definition certainly accords with the broader usage of the term 'skill' within current policy and popular discourse. However, a loose definition of skill, particularly one which embraces appropriate work behaviours and attitudes, raises important analytical, conceptual, and normative issues. Some of these may be usefully illustrated through the current debates surrounding 'soft skills', particularly in relation to interactive service work.

Skilling Me Softly

'Soft skills' is a broad umbrella term for what Grugulis (2007, 73) describes as a 'confused morass' of attitudes, behaviours, dispositions, and personal characteristics. They can include anything from team working, problem solving, communication, motivation, customer handling, a positive attitude to change, punctuality, and the willingness to accept authority and follow orders (see Keep and Payne 2004). The new skill currencies have courted considerable controversy, in particular the association of skill with a positive work ethic. Lafer (2004, 116) insists that compliance and motivation are not skills and are better viewed as 'acquired habits' or 'commitments which one chooses to offer or withhold on the basis of the wages and conditions provided'. The skills-as-discipline curricula that he identifies in US welfare-to-work programmes are simply about getting people to work hard for poverty wages and to submissively accept their lot.

Green (2011, 16–17) also raises the question of whether 'subservience' should be treated as a skill, and asks whether employees ought to be taught 'boredom coping skills' or 'resistance' when it comes to jobs that are dull, repetitive, and monotonous. Such questions raise serious moral, political, and policy issues. Responsibility for developing a motivated workforce can be shifted onto the education and training system or turned into a self-development or training issue for individuals, thereby allowing employers and policymakers to avoid addressing the problem of 'bad jobs' (Gugulis et al. 2004; Keep and Payne 2004; Lafer 2004).

[5] Green (2011) also distinguishes between job skill and the skill of the job holder.

New Skill Concepts in Service Work

Critical commentators draw a firm line when it comes to treating 'submissiveness' as a skill, and acknowledge that the policy discourse around skill is deeply politicized (Lloyd and Payne 2009; Hampson and Junor 2010; Hurrell et al. 2013). However, there remains the need for robust conceptual tools that are capable of handling contemporary questions of skill in today's economy. To this end, commentators have sought to develop new conceptual vocabularies—'emotion work', 'articulation work', and 'aesthetic labour'—that can help render visible the 'real skills' required in interactive service work.

Skilled Emotion Work

The starting point for much of the discussion is Hochschild's (1983) *The Managed Heart*, which developed the concept of 'emotional labour'. Emotional labour occurs when service workers transform their emotions in order to produce an emotional state in the customer that is of commercial benefit to the organization. Organizations not only expect employees to be friendly, cheerful, and polite when dealing with customers but will often go to considerable lengths to mould, shape, and control their 'emotional displays' through induction and training programmes and the imposition of prescribed 'feeling rules' (Callaghan and Thompson 2002).

Some have argued that the management of emotions during customer interactions is a real but unrecognized element of skilled work performance (Bolton 2004; Korczynski 2005; Gatta et al. 2009). Using Littler's (1982) criteria for defining skilled jobs, Bolton (2004, 32) contends that 'emotion work is indeed skilled work which contains recognisable elements of discretionary content, task variety and employee control'. Given the unpredictability and variability of service encounters, managerial control can never be absolute, meaning that even 'the lowest order of emotion workers' (Bolton 2004, 28) must learn to adapt their emotional displays to the demands of different customers and situations. Service workers do not simply perform emotional labour in line with organizational feeling rules; they may also engage in what Bolton terms 'emotion work', electing to provide emotional 'gifts' to customers and colleagues. One example cited is the call centre worker who, when faced with the pressure of management-imposed call targets, sympathizes with a lonely pensioner and takes time to chat with them. For Bolton (2004, 33), a successful service episode is nothing less than 'a fragile accomplishment requiring high levels of skilled emotion work'. The implication would seem to be that *all* interactive service jobs, even the most routine, can be seen as a form of skilled work (see Payne 2009, 353; Hurrell et al. 2013).

Aesthetic Labour

The concept of 'aesthetic labour' was originally coined by researchers investigating the recruitment and selection practices of 'upmarket' service employers in Glasgow (Witz et al. 2003). Aesthetic labour arises when organizations hire workers for the way they look and sound and then seek to shape these elements through training and regulation so that they come to embody a particular 'style' that is appealing to customers (Warhurst and Nickson 2009). While it can be difficult to draw a clear distinction between emotional labour and aesthetic labour, the latter refers specifically to embodied aspects of employee corporeality such as physical appearance, weight, body size/shape, grooming, deportment, accent, dress sense, and the ability to respond to fashions or trends. Subsequent research reveals that demands for workers to look good and sound right are not confined to upmarket niches but also figure prominently among more prosaic retailers and hospitality outlets.

As Warhurst and Nickson (2009, 388, emphasis added) note, 'It is this other "skill", *as it is deemed by management*, that underpins the analytical concern with aesthetic labour.' Although the original architects of the concept recognize that many employers regard appearance as a skill, they themselves have been quite careful to avoid such labelling. Other commentators have been less circumspect, and aesthetic labour has duly entered the lexicon of skill in service work (Korczynski 2005; Gatta et al. 2009).[6]

Articulation Work Skills

Hampson and Junor (2005; 2010) have argued that many routine interactive service jobs may also require 'articulation work' or 'work process skills' that go beyond emotion work. These involve employees learning how to juggle, under pressure of time, the demands of technology, information, and emotion management. The authors provide a number of examples. Call centre workers, even those operating in low discretionary work contexts, are said to manage 'complex articulations' between computer work, customer needs, supplementary work processes (for example, data inputting and 'after call' work), and emotion work. The ability to work under 'stressful conditions to maintain information flows and to keep work routines functioning smoothly' is presented as an unrecognized aspect of skill in call centre environments (Hampson and Junor 2005, 177–178). In a similar vein, Bolton and Houlihan (2007, 258) argue that call centre work involves 'extensive but under recognised discretionary skills in terms of constructively managing the call process and coping with the work', including the

[6] Unlike with emotion work, an explicit argument that aesthetic labour is skilled labour has yet to be expressly formulated. The claim tends to proceed from the observation that employers have defined it in this way.

ability to 'multi-task', 'cope with complex and competing demands', and 'absorb and yet decompress stress'.

Among other examples cited by Hampson and Junor (2010, 537–538) is a special education support worker responsible for children in a special-needs centre who found it difficult to articulate the 'non-verbal communication skills she used in "quietly encouraging" school-refusers into the classroom, blocking out the screaming and maintaining a reassuring firmness'. Gatta et al. (2009, 978) apply the concept of 'articulation work skills' to restaurant servers who must 'greet customers, take orders, get drinks, process orders in computers, bring food, balance as many plates as possible ..., make change for customers, and be friendly'. They also cite Newman's (1999) study of fast-food workers who must be able to 'listen to orders, communicate with customers, send out a stream of instructions to co-workers who prepare food, pick up the food, check orders, and process customers' payments'. The ability to coordinate such tasks under time pressure is said to require 'higher-order skills' (Gatta et al. 2009, 978). Clearly the concept has been applied across an extensive range of service jobs with very different demands.

Problems with the New Skill Concepts

The new skill concepts are not unproblematic, with some commentators arguing that there is a risk of conceptual confusion (Payne 2009; Lloyd and Payne 2009; Hurrell et al. 2013). Three key issues have come to the fore. First, if these are indeed skills, at what *level* of skill are they displayed within particular work settings (on emotion work, see Payne 2009, 358–359)? Second, when is it 'appropriate to describe work reliant on soft skills as skilled work' (Hurrell et al. 2013, 162)? Third, to what extent might better recognition help to improve the pay and conditions of low-paid service workers?

Are Soft Skills Really Skills?

Many commentators have pointed to the tendency to re-label as skills what in the past would have been considered dispositions, behaviours, or personal characteristics (Keep and Mayhew 1999; Payne 2000). It is hard to deny, however, that there is an element of *acquired* human capability in our social dealings with other people, which involves managing emotions (Bolton 2004; Hurrell et al. 2013). Such capacities are not equally distributed across individuals, with their development linked to social class, parental upbringing, and education. Referring to emotion work, Bolton (2004, 31) cites Hochschild's (1983, 158) observation that it is the middle-class child who 'grows sensitive to feeling and learns to read it well'. Commenting on aesthetic labour requirements in fashion retailing, Nickson et al. (2010, 84) also suggest that 'middle classness is being recast as a skill'. This clearly has important implications in terms of reinforcing middle-class advantage in the labour market, threatening to crowd out employment opportunities for those from less privileged backgrounds. Other commentators have highlighted the problem of discrimination according to race, with some US retail employers tending to see soft skills as 'white' (Moss and Tilly 1996).

There is no doubt that service organizations want employees who deal appropriately with customers, and that many recruit on the basis of 'attitude' and 'appearance'. Employers clearly believe that these are important in terms of customer satisfaction and retention and that they contribute to the bottom line, even if they attract no wage premium (Bolton 2004; Felstead et al. 2007). The link with productive value, however, is not straightforward. Vincent (2011, 1372) notes that 'voluntary kindness over and above that prescribed by an employer can result in "happy customers" returning for further products and services'. But it may also conflict with efficiency targets and may even annoy some customers who simply want to be served quickly, suggesting that an ability to read customer preferences may be required. An elderly person living alone may genuinely value a care worker who takes the time to sit and chat with them, even if this breaches the time slots allotted by the organization and adds to its costs. Kindness is not always good for the bottom line. Furthermore, there are many aspects of labour that create value for an employer, including simply working harder, although this is far removed from what many would regard as skill.

Even where emotion work can be said to satisfy Green's (2011) criteria of skill as being 'productive of value', it would still leave open the question of whether kindness or compassion might be trained or expanded. It might be argued that when a care worker displays compassion for an elderly person this says more about the type of person they are, their ethical and moral self, than it does about their skill set (Payne 2009, 357). Vincent (2011, 1379–1380) worries that posing such questions 'risks reproducing existing taken-for-granted prejudice: "hard" male skills are technically measured and valued; "soft" female skills are unmeasured and undervalued'. Nevertheless, value creation remains a rather blunt criterion for identifying skill, and certainly does not provide any indication, let alone measure, of the level of complexity of the skills in use or the degree of autonomy afforded to employees within specific job contexts.

Do They Constitute Skilled Work?

If social skills are real at an individual level, what are we to make of Bolton's (2004, 32) argument that 'emotion work is indeed skilled work'? The question takes us back to the critical distinction between 'skill in the person' and 'skill in the job' (Cockburn 1983). One can certainly question how complex or skilled many service interactions are across large tracts of the mass service economy. For many who make up the ranks of the 'emotional proletariat', such interactions are often highly routinized and limited affairs, lasting only a few minutes or sometimes even seconds, as those familiar with many a supermarket checkout, hamburger joint, or retail outlet will no doubt be aware. Product knowledge is, in many cases, extremely limited, with employees afforded little discretion over their emotional displays, and interactions with customers reduced to a 'perfunctory politeness' that hardly warrants the label 'skilled' (Payne 2009, 359).

The majority of studies of high-volume call centres, while acknowledging demands on agents in terms of their emotional labour, point towards a labour process characterized by what Taylor et al. (2002, 136) refer to as 'routinization, repetitiveness and a general absence of employee control'. Even allowing for the requirement to perform emotion work (Bolton 2004) or to multitask under time pressure (Hampson and Junor 2005), defining *work* as skilled where employers have sought to design skill and autonomy out of the job is clearly problematic. As Hurrell et al. (2013, 164) note in reply to Bolton (2004), 'The fact that employers cannot design jobs that completely eliminate uncertainty and variety, or that workers choose to fill gaps in service delivery via their soft skills, does not make a job de facto skilled.' Just because workers sometimes choose to show kindness or compassion to customers, in acts of philanthropic emotion management, does not mean that they are doing a skilled job any more than it makes sense to 'redefine a fast food context as skilled, just because some employees are prepared to depart from a script' (Hurrell et al. 2013, 167). This may be discretion of a sort but it takes place in a job where overall employee autonomy is very tightly bounded. As noted above, discussions of skilled emotion and articulation work also have a worrying tendency to equate skill with the ability to cope with monotonous and stressful working conditions, an application that many would dispute (Lloyd and Payne 2009).

Of course, one can argue that no job, even those that are highly routinized, are completely devoid of skill (Green 2011); they are simply *low-skilled* in terms of their overall design and what they allow workers to do. Again, however, the problem is that some commentators appear to suggest that the 'low-skill' label should be avoided in the case of *any* service job, even the most routine, that involves emotion and articulation work. Take Bolton's (2004, 25) comment that 'emotion workers have never before required such a high level of skill'. Similarly, Gatta et al. (2009, 976) claim that many ostensibly routine service jobs that have 'traditionally been treated as "low skilled" … may indeed represent higher-skilled work that cannot be recognized with conventional measures' (see also Korczynski 2005). By emphasizing the high(er) skill content of such jobs, such discourses may, inadvertently, end up fuelling policymakers' claims around universal upskilling (Payne 2009). For these reasons, some critics have urged caution, arguing that that there is a need for a more demanding definition of skilled service *work*, which takes seriously 'the critical issues of knowledge, control and autonomy which have always lain at the heart of skill' (Lloyd and Payne 2009, 630).

Drawing upon Thompson's (1989, 92) view of skill as 'knowledgeable practice within elements of control', Hurrell et al. (2013, 162) seek to 'extend our understanding of when it may and may not be appropriate to describe work reliant on soft skills as skilled work'. Taking the example of mass service call centres, they argue that were management to train 'employees to have substantive knowledge of products and allowed discretion in word and deed, that could then be described as skilled work' (Hurrell et al. 2013, 166). They point to Jenkins et al.'s (2010) study of a high-commitment, mass customized call centre as one illustration. Drawing on their own research conducted in two premium Glasgow hotels (dubbed 'Fontainebleau' and 'Oxygen'), they seek to illustrate how differences in work organization and employer practice were crucial in shaping low- or high-skill environments for customer-facing staff. In Fontainebleau, employees were permitted limited discretion in terms of how they interpreted prescribed service standards, whereas at Oxygen employees were allowed 'to conduct the service experience, as they felt best, within broad guidelines', with training and other socialization processes used to embed knowledge of the brand (Hurrell et al. 2013, 174). With induction training limited to three days, it is perhaps open to debate whether the latter constitutes a high-skill environment, but it certainly provided, in relative terms, greater scope for employee autonomy and decision-making. The key point, however, is that context matters and it is not possible to define soft skills as 'skilled work' in the absence of substantive levels of employee knowledge and autonomy.

What seems important is that there is a way of dealing with the heterogeneity of interactive service work that is sensitive to context, which addresses the scope for discretion, complexity, and knowledge within the job, and avoids 'the tendency to lump all emotion workers and all jobs involving emotion work together' as examples of skilled work (Payne 2009, 359). While it may be true that no job is 'unskilled' (in a fairly weak sense of the term), it is equally important to recognize that many jobs with an interactive service component remain highly routinized and low skilled by virtue of their actual design. The more broadly the term 'skill' comes to be used within contemporary academic and policy discourses, the more vital it is then to try and hang on to some notion of *relative* skill levels.

Though they are themselves critical of the way the new skill concepts have been applied, Hurrell et al. (2013) also take issue with other critics, notably Payne (2009), and Lloyd and Payne (2009). The latter are taken as suggesting that 'soft skills' are merely a chimera and that work which relies on such skills is, *ipso facto*, unskilled. This makes for neatness in that it allows the presentation of a polarized set of positions between commentators who treat soft skills as 'either ubiquitously skilled ... or unskilled' (Hurrell et al. 2013, 162). A close reading of the critics' work, however, indicates that they are careful to avoid such sweeping generalizations. It is certainly the case that Payne (2009, 357) questions whether empathy and kindness can be adequately viewed through the lens of skill and, like Hurrell et al., asks whether displaying such *humanity* in routinized service environments necessarily makes a job skilled. It is also true that Lloyd and Payne (2009, 631) argue for a concept of skill that has a 'clear link to technical competence and knowledge', the latter often adding depth and sophistication to skills such as problem solving, for example (see also Grugulis and Lloyd 2010). However, they also recognize that 'If service workers had substantive knowledge of a sophisticated product, process or technique and considerable autonomy in terms of how they did their job and interacted with customers and clients, one may be much closer to a workable definition of skilled service work' (Lloyd and Payne 2009, 630). Indeed, there seems to be more common ground here than might appear at first sight.

Can Recognition Act as a Lever for Better Pay?

Finally, what might be said of the opportunities available to win higher rewards for low-paid service workers? This has been an important motivation behind the development of the new skill concepts, the argument being that these 'skills' are misrecognized and under-rewarded, in part owing to their gendered construction as 'natural', feminine abilities (Bolton 2004; Korczynski 2005; Gatta et al. 2009). However, with increasing numbers of men working in areas such as call centres and retailing, there may be other plausible explanations as to why many of those who make up the emotional proletariat are likely to find it difficult to use the new skill concepts to secure higher rewards.

Given the way some service jobs have been designed (one might think of fast-food workers, supermarket checkout operatives, or agents in high-volume call centres), the customer handling skills required of the worker may not extend far beyond the basic requirement to remain polite and courteous to customers, abilities that are likely to be in relatively plentiful supply among the overall population as a result of primary socialization (Payne 2009). While employers are apt to complain of shortages of 'customer handling skills' (Bolton 2004), they generally have little difficulty in filling such positions. Given the available labour supply, it is extremely difficult to imagine what would persuade employers to offer higher levels of remuneration. In these cases, rendering visible the emotional, aesthetic, and articulation skills required in the job may turn out to be little more than a 'rhetorical device that carries with it no material benefits' (Grugulis et al. 2004, 12).

This is not to say that there are no prospects for emotion workers, but certainly much will depend on the specific context. As Vincent (2011, 1381) notes, in some areas such as health and social care, measures of 'emotional intelligence' (Goleman 1998; Mayer et al. 2008) might offer hope for those who can demonstrate substantive emotional demands in their role and get them recognized within job-regrading schemes (also Payne 2009, 360). However, as Vincent acknowledges, such schemes tend to be expensive to implement and manage, with employers likely to resist any mechanism that raises labour costs. Progress, he argues, may be aided by national legal frameworks that support 'equal pay for equal value', although this assumes the existence of a suitable job comparator and 'assertive action' (presumably on the part of trade unions), both of which can be problematic for many low-paid service workers. Again there are potential dangers. Management may find themselves with a new 'tool for disciplining employees' (Vincent 2011, 1381), and yet more grist for the mill of performance management (Lloyd and Payne 2009; Grugulis and Lloyd 2010). Hampson and Junor (2010, 541, 527) concede that rendering work process skills visible is a two-edged sword that may facilitate employer control. For them, this is a risk worth taking in order to achieve 'justice in remuneration', even if the latter requires more than visibility and can be 'advanced only through political contestation'.

Grugulis and Lloyd (2010) make the important point that soft skills and technical skills/knowledge are interdependent, with the latter adding depth and complexity to problem solving, communication, and relationship building with customers/clients (see also Keep and Payne 2004).[7] Recognizing that there is no wage premium accruing to social skills except when linked with technical skills (Bolton 2004; Felstead et al. 2007), Vincent (2011, 1382–1384) calls for an analysis that is sensitive to the synergies between 'emotion at work, technical know-how and organizational performance' that might aid understanding of the 'situations and contexts within which additional value creation and redistribution are more likely'.

In search of answers, he turns to the literature around 'high performance working' (Appelbaum et al. 2000). The latter invokes a new psychological contract, or 'mutual gains' bargain, in which workers trade increased commitment, effort, and responsibilities in the sphere of production, through team working for example, in return for performance-based pay, employment security, and investment in training and career paths. Such claims have been challenged by many studies that suggest that they can, in some cases, be associated with work intensification and a loss of employee control (Lloyd and Payne 2006). Vincent (2010, 1383) notes that 'positive outcomes are contingent', being more likely to accrue where firms pursue 'quality strategies', and are affected by national institutional environments. Neoliberal economies are seen to suffer from the dominance of shareholder value, weak employment protections, and a lack of institutional supports for collective bargaining, which corrodes trust by leaving employees exposed to the threat of downsizing and redundancy and without adequate social protections (Godard 2004). Indeed, he concludes that for '*routine* customer services workers ... the *ubiquity* of the skills in use and the ability of managers to prescribe and regulate emotional displays' makes it unlikely that organizations, wedded to cost-based strategies, will be interested in introducing systems that 'may actually improve worker experiences' (Vincent 2011, 1384, emphasis added).

Similarly, Gatta et al. (2009, 983–984) note that rewarding service-work skills may have more chance of success if linked with efforts to 'improve the quality of service jobs and the quality of services provided'. They also refer to the importance of 'high-road management practices', to 'direct[ing] firms to move from low-cost, low-skills strategies to higher value product markets where higher skills are needed', and to the role of 'national labor-market institutions' in restricting the ability of employers 'to pay lower wages and to reduce employment security'. Concerned about the 'focus on skill to the detriment of other areas of job quality' and the 'danger of being side tracked into an ever-narrowing agenda', Grugulis and Lloyd (2010, 107) argue that researchers might do better to concentrate their attention not on seeking out new skills, but on 'the conditions and actions required to make work better.' They cite examples of countries, such as Denmark, where strong trade unions, limited income differentials, and a high reservation wage have helped to provide incentives to employers to improve job quality and make better use of skills.

[7] Problem-solving skills, for example, depend on the nature of the problem to be solved, whether it be invasive heart surgery, a broken gas boiler, giving a refund, or finding where curry sauce is located in a supermarket.

Conclusion

'Skill' is one of the most slippery of concepts within social science. It has both objective and subjective properties, owing to the way in which skill is socially constructed and embedded within social and power relations. Controversy has intensified as the meaning of skill has broadened both in policy and academic usage. Today, skill can be about turning up for work on time, suitably washed and dressed, with a positive 'can-do' attitude, and ready to smile for the customer. In this rather impoverished sense, we are all 'skilled' now, regardless of the type and quality of the work we do, the level of personal control or autonomy we enjoy, or the pay we receive.

The polarization of labour markets in liberal market economies, together with the rapid expansion of low-paid, routine service jobs in areas such as hospitality, retail, and personal services, may have dented the fantasy of an all-inclusive knowledge economy that demands universal upskilling. However, the broadening meaning of skill affords policymakers a convenient ideological smokescreen for obscuring the reality of work for many and another excuse for avoiding tackling the problem of 'bad jobs'. The need for a robust and meaningful understanding of skill that can address contemporary realities of work, of course, is not in doubt. Some commentators have therefore put forward new skills concepts in an attempt to render visible the real skills required in routine customer-service jobs as well as help support claims to improved status and pay.

The concern among critics is that such blanket discourses exaggerate the skill content of many highly routinized service jobs and threaten to remove the category of 'low-skilled' from across large swathes of the service sector. In doing so, these discourses risk trivializing the notion of skilled work in ways which may, unwittingly, let policymakers off the hook when it comes to addressing very real deficiencies in work design and job quality. The challenge of revalorizing service work skills has been led by critical workplace scholars within liberal market economies, where issues of low pay and income inequality loom large and where there is a concern to find ways of advancing remunerative justice in an extremely challenging political and policy context. While attempting to secure better pay for low-paid service workers is certainly a laudable goal, it is open to serious doubt as to how effective a vehicle the new skill concepts will prove in this respect. Where jobs have been designed to require skills that are in relatively plentiful supply, the law of supply and demand tends to dictate that their holders will struggle to exact a wage premium. Even those who support such attempts appear to accept the danger that employers may acquire insight into what workers do, along with new tools for monitoring and control.

It might be easier to simply accept that there are many jobs that are low-skilled and have many unattractive features built into them. This does not mean, however, that they necessarily have to be so poorly paid, as is currently the case in countries such as the UK and US. One need only look to Scandinavia, with its extensive collective bargaining arrangements, or France, with its higher national minimum wage, to realize that, even under conditions of globalization, there is still space for political choice when it comes to mitigating income inequality and reducing the incidence of low pay among the working population (Gautié and Schmitt 2010). These countries have also managed to sustain more robust notions of what it means to be a 'skilled worker' and accept that all learners, including those on vocational programmes, need a broad general education for life and citizenship, irrespective of the jobs they end up doing.

While the new skill concepts have divided commentators, there does seem to be agreement around the need to address broader aspects of political economy and the role that national institutions and regulations play in shaping skill and its rewards, along with job quality more generally. Inevitably, however, this trails difficult questions in its wake, such as where progressive change might come from within liberal market economies that currently lack such arrangements (Lloyd and Payne 2005). Perhaps the final word should go to Lafer (2004, 126), who reminds us that progress 'lies not in winning the hearts and minds of those in power, but in changing the political constraints under which they operate. In this case, the most important skill for working people to acquire is ... the solidarity required for collective mobilisation'.

References

Appelbaum, E., Bailey, T., Berg, P., and Kalleberg, A. L. (2000) *Manufacturing Advantage*, Ithaca, NY: Cornell University Press.

Attewell, P. (1990) 'What is Skill?' *Work and Occupations*, 17(4): 422–48.

Becker, G. (1964) *Human Capital: A Theoretical Analysis with Special Reference to Education*, New York: Columbia University Press.

Bolton, S. C. (2004) 'Conceptual Confusions: Emotion Work as Skilled Work', in C. Warhurst, I. Grugulis, and E. Keep (eds), *The Skills That Matter*, Basingstoke: Palgrave MacMillan: 19–37.

Bolton, S. C. and Houlihan, M. (2007) 'Risky Business: Re-thinking the Human in Interactive Service Work', in S. Bolton and M. Houlihan (eds), *Searching for the Human in Human Resource Management: Theory, Practice and Workplace Contexts*, Basingstoke: Palgrave MacMillan: 245–262.

Braverman, H. (1974) *Labor and Monopoly Capital*, New York: Monthly Review Press.

Brockmann, M., Clarke, L., and Winch, C. (2011) *Knowledge, Skills and Competence in the European Labour Market: What's in a Vocational Qualification?* Abingdon: Routledge.

Brown, P. and Hesketh, A. (2004) *The Mismanagement of Talent: Employability and Jobs in the Knowledge Economy*, Oxford: Oxford University Press.

Callaghan, G. and Thompson, P. (2002) '"We Recruit Attitude": The Selection and Shaping of Routine Call Centre Labour', *Journal of Management Studies*, 39(2): 233–254.

Clarke, L. and Winch, C. (2006) 'A European Skills Framework?—But What Are Skills? Anglo-Saxon Versus German Concepts', *Journal of Education and Work*, 19(3): 255–269.

Cockburn, C. (1983) *Brothers: Male Dominance and Technological Change*, London: The Pluto Press.

Felstead, A., Gallie, D., Green, F., and Zhou, Y. (2007) *Skills at Work, 1986–2006*, Oxford: University of Oxford, SKOPE.

Gatta, M., Boushey, H., and Appelbaum, E. (2009) 'High-Touch and Here-to-Stay: Future Skills Demands in US Low Wage Service Occupations', *Sociology*, 43(5): 968–989.

Gautié, J. and Schmitt, J. (eds). (2010) *Low-Wage Work in the Wealthy World*, New York: Russell Sage Foundation.

Godard, J. (2004) 'A Critical Assessment of the High-Performance Paradigm', *British Journal of Industrial Relations*, 42(2): 349–378.

Goleman, D. (1998) *Working with Emotional Intelligence*, New York: Bantam Books.

Green, A. (1998) 'Core Skills, Key Skills and General Culture: In Search of the Common Foundation in Vocational Education', *Evaluation and Research in Education*, 12(1): 23–43.

Green, F. (2011) 'What is Skill? An Inter-Disciplinary Synthesis'. LLAKES research paper 20. London: Institute of Education. Available at: http://www.llakes.org.

Grugulis, I. (2007) *Skills, Training and Human Resource Development: A Critical Text*, Basingstoke: Palgrave MacMillan.

Grugulis, I. and Lloyd, C. (2010) 'Skill and the Labour Process: The Conditions and Consequences of Change', in P. Thompson and C. Smith (eds), *Working Life: Renewing Labour Process Analysis*, Basingstoke: Palgrave MacMillan: 91–112.

Grugulis, I., Warhurst, C., and Keep, E. (2004) 'What's Happening to "Skill"?', in C. Warhurst, I. Grugulis and E. Keep (eds), *The Skills That Matter*, Basingstoke: Palgrave MacMillan.

Hampson, I. and Junor, A. (2005) 'Invisible Work, Invisible Skills: Interactive Customer Service as Articulation Work', *New Technology, Work and Employment*, 20(2): 166–181.

Hampson, I. and Junor, A. (2010) 'Putting the Process Back In: Rethinking Service Sector Skill', *Work, Employment and Society*, 24(3): 526–545.

High Pay Commission (2011) 'Cheques with Balances: Why Tackling High Pay is in the National Interest', Final Report of the High Pay Commission. Available at: http://highpaycommission.co.uk/wp-content/uploads/2011/11/HPC_final_report_WEB.pdf.

Hochschild, A. (1983) *The Managed Heart: Commercialization of Human Feeling*, Berkeley: University of California Press.

Hurrell, S., Scholarios, D., and Thompson, P. (2013) 'More Than a "Humpty Dumpty" Term: Strengthening the Conceptualization of Soft Skills', *Economic and Industrial Democracy*, 34(1): 161–182.

Jenkins, S., Delbridge, R., and Roberts, A. (2010) 'Emotional Management in a Mass Customised Call Centre: Examining Skill and Knowledgeability in Interactive Service Work', *Work, Employment and Society*, 24(3): 546–564.

Jessup, G. (1991) *Outcomes: NVQs and the Emerging Model of Education and Training*, Brighton: Falmer.

Keep, E. and Payne, J. (2004) '"I Can't Believe It's Not Skill": The Changing Meaning of Skill in the UK Context and Some Implications', in G. Hayward and S. James (eds), *Balancing the Skills Equation—Key Issues and Challenges for Policy and Practice*, Bristol: Policy Press: 53–76.

Keep, E. and Mayhew, K. (2010) 'Moving Beyond Skills as a Social and Economic Panacea', *Work, Employment and Society*, 24(3): 565–577.

Korczynski, M. (2005) 'Skills in Service Work: An Overview', *Human Resource Management Journal*, 15(2): 3–14.

Lafer, G. (2004) 'What Is "Skill"? Training for Discipline in the Low-Wage Labour Market', in C. Warhurst, I. Grugulis, and E. Keep (eds), *The Skills That Matter*, Basingstoke: Palgrave MacMillan: 109–127.

Lave, J. and Wenger, E. (1991) *Situated Learning: Legitimate Peripheral Participation*, Cambridge: Cambridge University Press.

Leadbetter, C. (2000) *Living on Thin Air: The New Economy*, London: Penguin.
Littler, C. (1982) *The Development of the Labour Process in Capitalist Societies*, London: Heinemann.
Lloyd, C. and Payne, J. (2005) 'The Political Economy of Skill: A Theoretical Approach to Developing a High Skills Strategy in the UK', in C. Warhurst, I. Grugulis and E. Keep (eds), *The Skills That Matter*, Basingstoke: Palgrave MacMillan: 207–224.
Lloyd, C. and Payne, J. (2006) 'Goodbye to All That? A Critical Re-evaluation of the Role of the High Performance Work Organization within the UK Skills Debate', *Work, Employment and Society*, 20(1): 151–165.
Mayer, J., Salovey, P., and Caruso, D. (2008) 'Emotional Intelligence: New Ability or Eclectic Traits', *American Psychologist*, 63(6): 503–517.
Moss, P. and Tilly, C. (1996) '"Soft" Skills and Race: An Investigation of Black Men's Employment Problems', *Work and Occupations*, 23(3): 252–276.
Newman, K. (1999) *No Shame in My Game: The Working Poor in the Inner City*, New York: Russell Sage Foundation.
Nickson, D., Hurrell, S., Warhurst, C., and Commander, J. (2011) 'Labour Supply and Skills Demand in Fashion Retailing', in I. Grugulis and O. Bozkurt (eds), *Retail Work*, Basingstoke: Palgrave MacMillan: 68–87.
Payne, J. (2000) 'The Unbearable Lightness of Skill: The Changing Meaning of Skill in UK Policy Discourses and Some Implications for Education and Training', *Journal of Education Policy*, 15(3): 353–369.
Payne, J. (2009) 'Emotional Labour and Skill: A Reappraisal', *Gender, Work and Organization*, 16(3): 348–367.
Phillips, A. and Taylor, B. (1980) 'Sex and Skill: Notes Towards a Feminist Economics', *Feminist Review*, 6: 78–88.
Reich, R. (1991) *The Work of Nations*, London: Simon and Schuster.
Taylor, P., Mulvey, G., Hyman, J., and Bain, P. (2002) 'Work Organization, Control and the Experience of Work in Call Centres', *Work, Employment and Society*, 16(1): 133–150.
Turner, H. A. (1962) *Trade Union Growth, Structure and Policy*, London: Allen and Unwin.
Thompson, P. (1989) *The Nature of Work: An Introduction to Debates on the Labour Process*, London: MacMillan.
Vincent, S. (2011) 'The Emotional Labour Process: An Essay on the Economy of Feelings', *Human Relations*, 64(10): 1369–1392.
Warhurst, C. and Nickson, D. (2009) '"Who's Got the Look?" Emotional, Aesthetic and Sexualized Labour in Interactive Services', *Gender, Work and Organization*, 16(3): 385–404.
Witz, A., Warhurst, C., and Nickson, D. (2003) 'The Labour of Aesthetics and the Aesthetics of Organization', *Organization*, 10(1): 33–54.

CHAPTER 4

A NEW SOCIAL CONSTRUCTION OF SKILL

CHRIS WARHURST, CHRIS TILLY, AND MARY GATTA

Introduction

Analyses of skill tend to coalesce around three positions. The first is the skill possessed by the worker, usually in the form of qualifications or achieved skills through education and training. This position is championed by human capital theory (Becker 1964; also Dalziel, Chapter 7 in this volume). The second is the skill required to do the job. This position underpins Braverman's (1974) argument that in post-war United States, whilst workers were being upskilled with qualifications, jobs were being deskilled through scientific management and technology. The third position suggests that skills cannot be so neatly and objectively conceived. Instead, we must understand the circumstances by which occupations become socially constructed as skilled.

This third position has been advocated particularly by researchers exploring marginalized, segregated or excluded social groups in the labour market. Most prominently, feminists have argued that men have often organized to exclude women. For men, this exclusion prevents occupational dilution and thereby boosts or maintains their status and pay. Skill is the vehicle for this occupational enclosure (Steinberg 1990). Jobs are sex-typed, with some jobs associated with masculine and some jobs feminine attributes, strength, stamina, and logic for the former and sensitivity, supportiveness, and patience for the latter for example. Such assertions then enable male workers to be able to argue why women can't and shouldn't do their jobs. As Attewell (1990) explains, an occupation seeks to remove itself from market competition either by levering for itself a legal monopoly through the state or by trade union action to create a closed shop. The literature on the social construction of skill turns on a key distinction between education and training—*achieved skill* (with qualification as its proxy)—and *ascribed skill* based on social category. Exclusion of certain social groups from certain jobs can result from blocking their access to achieved skills or from ascribing lack of skill to them. The two exclusionary processes may be linked, as Attewell points out. Moreover, ascription tends to be self-reinforcing: the absence (via exclusion) of a given social group from a given job reinforces the sense that persons of this group are not well suited to the job.

This chapter is about what we term the 'new' social construction of skill. We are not arguing that the old social construction of skill has disappeared. Now recast as 'professionalization projects', some female-dominated occupations such as physiotherapists in the United Kingdom's public health service have recently established occupational enclosure in an attempt to boost their status and pay, with achieved skills again the lever (Anderson and Warhurst 2012). What we are suggesting is that the conditions under which such attempts have thrived in the past, principally the existence of strong labour unions and professions and often in the manufacturing industries, have changed, and with them the social construction of skill.

We argue that in the wealthier countries there have been two shifts: a shift in how skill has been defined and a shift in who has the power to define it. The first, definitional shift has moved skills' centre of gravity towards more informal 'skills' often dubbed 'soft skills'—notably motivation and the ability to interact successfully with others (Moss and Tilly 2001; Grugulis et al. 2004). Thus, larger-scale US employer surveys yield consistent results: employers rank attitude as more important than specific technical skills or academic performance (Bowles et al. 2001). This focus on soft skills is to some extent a consequence of a sectoral shift towards services. It also results from a similar shift in the composition of occupations: technology and offshoring have replaced more routine work processes (such as phone-based menus and offshored call centre work), leaving in place more variable tasks, such as unscripted interactions with customers—the type of jobs that have experienced most relative growth since the 1980s (Deming 2015). Finally, it stems from changes in the skill mix in existing jobs, with some workers, even factory operatives, formally needing to supplement technical competency with social competency through quality circles (requiring interaction skills) for example (Findlay et al. 2000).

Lloyd and Payne (2009) take umbrage at claims that soft skills are skills, arguing that this categorization devalues the concept of skill. Referring to Attewell's (1990) infinite regression problem, they point out that if we accept that workers managing their attitudes are highly skilled, then, suddenly, we are all highly skilled workers. However, nostalgia for a definition of being skilled centred on 'hard' technical and certified abilities and knowhow delivered through apprenticeships in unionized workplaces—a productionist view of skill—ignores the shifts that have happened in the advanced economies since the 1950s.

We have identified what we call the '4Cs' to denote the main actors involved in defining and assessing skill: capital, colleagues, credentialers, and customers. The second shift, in *who* defines skill, places more power in the hands of customers, credentialers, and capital, reducing the influence of colleagues. *Customers* gain sway because they are ever-more important judges of what constitutes a positive service encounter (Korczynski 2009). *Credentialers*, particularly institutions of higher education, have loomed larger as firm-based training programmes have atrophied and worker mobility across employers has heightened (Cappelli et al. 1997; Grubb and Lazerson 2004). *Capital* can use customers' evaluation of service workers to enhance (whilst masking) its control of work processes (Fuller and Smith 1991) but, perhaps more importantly, capital now carries more weight because the fourth C, *colleagues*, has *lost* ground. Several decades ago, in most richer countries, unions and professional associations had more to say about what constitutes skill. Weaker unions and increased corporate and bureaucratic control have transferred more definitional (and dispositive) power to owners—to capital (Burawoy 2010). Of course, whilst their power in relation to capital has waned, colleagues remain an important force.

As a consequence of these shifts in the *definition* of skill and *who has the power to define and assess skill*, the social construction of skill has been restructured in three ways that distinguish it from its older incarnation. First, these changes open the door wider to ascription of skill. This opportunity arises because the growing importance of soft skills privileges more subjective approaches to skill assessment and because, in customer-contact work environments, customers represent another source of subjective evaluation of skills. The second is not a change within the world of skill but in skill's place in larger social systems of allocation and reward. Codes that discriminate *explicitly* on the basis of social categories such as race, ethnicity, gender, and class have been increasingly marginalized, discredited and, in some cases, outlawed in favour of meritocratic codes. Processes of exclusion or sorting based on these categories have not been eliminated but excluders now need to justify their actions with a discourse of merit—which in the case of jobs translates into skills and who is and isn't deemed to be skilled. Thus, socially constructed skill has expanded its terrain to occupy spaces formerly held by explicit categorical hierarchies. The third follows to some extent from the other two: the lines between achieved and ascribed skill are increasingly blurred. Key characteristics now considered as skills, such as attractiveness, articulateness, ability to 'relate well' with customers, co-workers, and managers and so on, are highly dependent on the beholder or the party being related to, and his or her own preferences, biases, and expectations.

This new form of the social construction skill is not novel, and certainly resonates with the old social construction of skill, but it is newly important. The next parts of this chapter make this case by reviewing recent empirical research, primarily US and UK-based, addressing the social construction of skill as it relates to gender, race and ethnicity, and class respectively. In the conclusion, we close with a discussion of issues meriting further research and possible alternative strategies for tackling inequalities resulting from the new social construction of skill.

Gender and Skill

With the rise of services and the relocation of some reproductive labour from the domestic economy to the market economy, 'skills' such as sociability, caring, nurturance, communication, and good customer service have been identified as important. It is women who tend to work in many of these jobs, which are concentrated in the lower-wage service sector, for example in caring and hospitality work. Often the skills necessary for doing these jobs are deemed as natural feminine qualities.

Indeed, Belt et al. (2002, 20–21), based on focus group and interview data from managers in 13 call centres in Ireland, the Netherlands, and the United Kingdom note that 'female labour power is increasing in demand at least in part because women are believed to naturally possess in abundance many of the social skills required by employers in the service-based economy.' Specifically, women were perceived to be more comfortable with the ethos of customer service and particularly skilled at listening and empathizing with customers. In addition they were also assumed to be more tolerant with more difficult customers, and less like to react aggressively to them. Likewise, Woodfield (1998) argues that femininity has become a market requirement as employers actively market a version of femininity emphasizing passivity, servicing and attention to customers' needs.

Interestingly, an exception to the pattern found by Belt et al. (2002) was technical support jobs in computer services call centres. Here technical knowledge, qualifications, experience, and interest in computers were considered more important than communication skills. Moreover, when communication skills were specified in these jobs, the term referred to problem-solving abilities and not to having a 'bubbly personality'. Perhaps even more telling is that Belt et al.'s data demonstrated that some managers believed the workers appropriate for technical support jobs were actually less likely to possess those types of social skills. Not surprisingly men occupy more of these jobs.

Employers, then, are first defining the new skills as social skills, and, second, ascribing (most of) these skills to women. Even normally critical academics concur. Hochschild (1983) for example argues that women are over-represented in jobs requiring emotional labour because women are 'more accomplished managers of feeling' (p. 11) since gender is 'determinant' (p. 20) of the skill required to manage feelings.

Two significant processes follow. First emotional work, caring labour and relationship-building are typically associated with women and mothering. The (faulty) assumption then follows that these jobs do not necessitate achieved skill with complex communication or expert knowledge but instead rely on natural qualities ascribed to women. Second, as a consequence, this ascription then justifies the widely held view that workers should not be paid well for performing this work (England etf al. 2002) as they are not performing skilled work. The gendered composition of these jobs and the nature of the required skills contribute to their characterization as low-skill and low-wage, with limited opportunities for advancement. Survey evidence suggests that soft skills used in service work attract no pay premium (Felstead et al. 2007). Thus whilst demanded by employers, women and their ascribed skills attract no pay or prospects premium for these women.

Guy and Newman (2004) use state-level data to quantify the impact of what they termed the 'conflation of gender and emotional labor' on occupational wages. They present interesting comparisons from Florida in the United States between fruit and vegetable terminal market inspectors (100% male), driving licence examiners (65% female), and family services counsellors (80% female). Of these jobs the two that require high levels of emotional labour—driving licence examiners and family services counsellors—are also the ones women dominate. Driving licence examiners earn the least, whilst fruit and vegetable terminal market inspectors and family services counsellors are compensated at the same level. This equal compensation exists despite the fact that family services counsellors are required to hold a bachelor's degree and have passed a written assessment; whereas fruit and vegetable terminal market inspectors require completion of inspection school and six-months' experience. Guy and Newman's analysis indicates once more that 'the conflation of gender with the requirements of emotional labour, predominately emotional labour that involved caritas, results in work skills and abilities that are taken for granted, not listed as bona fide requirements for the job, and not compensated (p. 296).

Interestingly, Rho (2014) finds evidence that even prior to the employee selection process, the seemingly 'objective' process of online recruiting sorts by gender. Analysing around 150,000 jobs posted by around 25,000 recruiters and searched by over 500,000 job seekers on an employment website, Rho discovered two gendered processes. First, gender stereotypes are reflected in lists of qualifications posted for particular jobs; second, women are less likely to enquire about a job listing stereotypically masculine attributes and are more likely to enquire about a job listing 'feminine' traits—even after controlling for occupation.

Recent work by Glover and Guerrier (2010) found that the growth of 'hybrid' IT jobs—those that combine technical and communication skills—has created new gender segregation in an industry already plagued with low representation of women. Whilst hybrid jobs could offer opportunities for women, they found women concentrated in what they term 'inward hybrid roles' requiring soft skills such as project management, team-building, and empathy with other employees. In contrast, men are concentrated in 'outward hybrid roles' dealing with customers and clients in developing and delivering individualized systems. Outward hybrid jobs are better paying and often lead to advancement, along with opportunities to build networks and social capital. So despite the fact that both types of hybrid jobs require soft skills, the labour market rewards are greater for men than for women.

Similarly, Kelan (2008) has found that even though there may be a market for femininity, the value of possessing that skill is gendered. Her analysis of male and female engineers in information andcommunications technology (ICT) found an increased need for both technical and social/emotional skills. However, how these skills are valued is gendered (2008, 63):

> Whilst men are rewarded for showing feminine gender behaviour when they act emotionally competent, women do not gain extra credit for performing technical competencies, as they form the basis of the job. Whilst the atypical skills women perform, here technical competencies do not have exchange value in this context. Emotional competence, a more atypical skill for men, does have exchange value.

Moreover, although soft skills are considered to be 'feminine qualities', some women, particularly single mothers, can be deemed unskilled. In the United States, welfare and workforce policy reinforce this belief by stressing the need to train welfare and unemployed workers in these skills. For example, the core service of the Workforce Investment Act provides potential workers with 'job readiness skills', with the assumption that the problem is that single mothers are not ready to work. As Korteweg (2003, 455) notes, these 'exercises reflected the belief that women on welfare lacked the "soft skills" or job-related social skills required to find job leads and to overcome the hurdle of a job interview. A lack of hard skills, work-related technical knowledge, and expertise that would require education was not considered problematic.' In the United Kingdom government agencies tasked with finding work for unemployed single mothers make the same assumption: after years of isolation looking after their children solo, these women often lack good social skills. As a consequence, they are difficult to place in service jobs such as supermarkets, even though there is growth in the number of such jobs (Nickson et al. 2004).

Likewise, gender intersects with race and ethnicity, and class to marginalize groups of women within service work and to further challenge assumptions associated with skills. A focus on the gender division of labour in service work can mask differences amongst women, particularly around race and ethnicity. Nakano Glenn (1992) has demonstrated that white women tend to be in service jobs that are in the 'public's eye' and require the most interactions and emotional labour; women of colour are over-represented in 'dirty back-room' jobs, such as maids and kitchen workers. Duffy (2005) succinctly sums up this demographic pattern, noting 'it is where reproductive work is seen to lack the need for emotional skills and relational interaction that women of colour are concentrated. Furthermore, these back-room jobs are even lower paying then those more public reproductive labour occupations in which white women are more concentrated' (2005, 72). Using 2000 US Census data, Duffy empirically tests where groups of women were located in the services. She found that white women were represented at a much higher rate in jobs that required emotional labour and care work, whilst Hispanic women had the exact opposite pattern. These women were more likely to be concentrated in 'back of the house' jobs that did not require high levels of emotion work and interactions. In regard to black women, the pattern is more complicated: high representation in both 'front of the house' and 'back of the house' jobs. Duffy also found higher wages associated with work that has high levels of interaction and emotion skills than with jobs that did not require those skills.

Clearly soft skills are ascribed to some workers and not others. Duffy's work reminds us that understanding the new social construction of skill requires not only awareness of the issues attending the feminization of the workforce but also analytical integration of race and ethnicity.

Race, Ethnicity, and Skill

The distinctions drawn between white women and women of colour extend more generally to racial and ethnic distinctions that operate across genders. Indeed the *racialized* social construction of skill overlaps extensively with racial and ethnic discrimination.

First, despite popular discourses of 'post-racialism' and 'colour-blindness' (Bonilla-Silva 2010), there is ample evidence that discriminatory attitudes continue to impact the labour market. Job segregation and unequal outcomes occur even after controlling for other factors (Tomaskovic-Devey 1993; Huffman and Cohen 2004). Employer hiring studies using matched resumés and/or 'testers' (actors trained to play job applicants with identical qualifications) differing only in race or ethnicity are particularly instructive. Bendick (2007) summarizes the results of ten black-white and six Anglo-Latino comparisons from the United States. Except for one study, the results uniformly show a white/Anglo advantage, ranging from 2 to 38 percentage points (this 'net rate of discrimination' is the difference between the percentage of employers who contacted the white/Anglo and the proportion who contacted the black/Latino applicant). More recent research continues to replicate and extend these findings (e.g. Bendick et al. 2010).

Employer interview research suggests that these effects result in large part from skill ascription by employers. Employers, including those sympathetic to workers of colour, often made a connection between a racial group's soft skills and their culture. In-depth interviews, a substantial minority of US and UK employers state assessments of the relative quality of workers from different racial groups (reviewed in Moss and Tilly 2006; see also Zamudio and Lichter 2008). Such studies found two kinds of employer perceptions of the skills of workers of colour: skill hierarchy (which in the United States generally rate whites and Asians highest, Latinos in between, African Americans at the bottom) and skill fit (seeing particular groups of workers as well suited to particular kinds of jobs—notably, viewing immigrant Latinos as ideal for difficult, low-paid manual work). As with gender, even where immigrant workers of colour were seen as more motivated and therefore well suited to certain jobs, this alignment was associated with lower pay for these jobs (Moss and Tilly 2001). In the studies reviewed by Moss and Tilly (2006), employers not only linked soft skills to culture but often spoke of cultural 'fit' as a major hiring criterion. Though those studies examine hiring practices for entry-level jobs, the same cultural fit in hiring decision also emerges in elite professions in the United States (Rivera 2012) and the United Kingdom (Ashley 2010).

Lest one dismiss these findings because only a minority of employers in interview-based studies expressed negative views based on race or ethnicity, there are several reasons for taking the findings seriously. First, even a minority is sufficient to limit labour market opportunities for people of colour. Second, in Holzer's (1996) large-scale employer survey, *less direct* questions about the skills of racial and ethnic groups yielded *higher rates* of negative assessments, suggesting that many employers censor themselves when asked more direct questions. Third, Pager and Quillian (2005) find that employers are considerably more likely to take discriminatory actions than to state discriminatory attitudes.

In addition, employers in interview-based studies mentioned the growing importance of soft skills, particularly in entry-level and customer-facing jobs—in the same conversations in which many of them rated African American workers worse on soft skills (e.g. Moss and Tilly 2001). Consistent with gender findings, Moss and Tilly (2010), and Waldinger and Lichter (2003) show managers in customer-contact jobs seek a racial-ethnic mix of employees with whom customers will feel comfortable; since Anglo whites outnumber Latinos and blacks and have greater purchasing power, this preoccupation with mix privileges Anglo whites in these jobs. These small-sample interview findings are bolstered by large-sample survey regularities in the United States: about one-third of entry-level employers state that customers, employees, or other employers in their industry prefer to deal with members of their own racial or ethnic group (Holzer 1996); the probability of hiring a black applicant for an entry-level job increases with the proportion of the customer base who are black (Holzer 1996); controlling for the racial composition of the applicant pool, employers are less likely to hire blacks and Latinos for entry-level jobs in suburban locations and are less likely to hire blacks in retail jobs (Holzer and Stoll 2000).

The initial hire is only one point where socially constructed perceptions of skill may translate into discriminatory action. Mong and Roscigno (2010) review research showing that once hired, black men are less likely to be promoted, receive lower job evaluations, and are disproportionately subject to discriminatory firing. They find two sets of processes: exercise of supervisorial discretion (holding black men to a higher performance standard) and harassment.

Moreover, job quality, workplace environment, and mode of supervision themselves tend to elicit particular behavioural responses. We should not be surprised if those working in lousy jobs react with sullen attitudes and low commitment. Thus, soft skills are to some extent endogenous, resulting from the types of jobs where different groups of workers are concentrated or their treatment in those jobs. Employer observations of soft skills may also be endogenous: shared racial predilections can create a self-fulfilling prophecy. For example, McCrate (2006) points out that if black workers are monitored more closely for dishonesty, they are more likely to get caught, reinforcing the stereotype of black dishonesty. More generally, whites are observed serving the public in certain roles, which bolsters the perception that whites are better suited to these roles.

Skill ascription processes also shape racial differences in skill *achievement*. Teachers and other actors in schools base their assessments and expectations of children's abilities in part on ascription, and those assessments and expectations influence children's actual learning so that ascription places a double disadvantage on certain racial groups (Delpit 1995). Figlio (2005), reviewing Florida school records, found that amongst black sibling pairs, a sibling having a more 'black-sounding' name on average scored lower on reading and maths tests and was less likely to receive recommendations for a gifted class than the other sibling. Slaton (2011) shows similar processes are resulting in poorer performance of black university-level engineering students. Once in the workplace, disparate treatment can close off opportunities for learning and mentoring (Feagin 2010).

All of the skill achievement processes noted so far relate to the evaluation and learning of 'hard skills'. But segregated and unequal processes even more strongly shape soft skill acquisition. Soft skills are par excellence an example of habitus that is moulded by upbringing, peer culture and early work experience (Bourdieu 1984). To the extent that a segregated society generates subcultures correlated with racial identity, blacks will typically be less fluent in the dominant, 'white' culture that sets norms and expectations in most employment settings. Here recent immigrants not fluent in the country's language, in contrast, split the difference: they are seen as *more* motivated but (at least in the case of recent immigrants) can be even *more* disconnected from mainstream culture than native people of colour. Workplace sorting of people across jobs can reinforce these processes: for example, giving whites preferential access to public-facing positions helps them develop abilities and experiences suited to these jobs.

So far, this discussion of the racialized social construction of skill has largely omitted mention of the importance of social networks in obtaining and advancing in jobs, despite wide attribution of racial and ethnic labour market inequality to segregated networks (Moss and Tilly 2001; Feagin 2010). Segregated and unequal networks do not in themselves denote the social construction of skill differences. However, network effects can implicate the social construction of skill in two instances: when persons occupying key mediating network nodes ascribe skill in racialized ways and when channels to such mediating nodes are themselves affected by ascribed skill. Royster's (2003) study of young white and black men exiting Baltimore vocational education high schools makes a compelling case for the former. The overwhelmingly white teachers in these schools provide a critical link to employment opportunities through referrals and recommendations to acquaintances in the building trades and other craft occupations. However, the teachers much more commonly aid white students in this way, leaving black students to fend for themselves. Royster's teacher interviews link this pattern to their differing ascriptions of skill and 'promise' to young men who, based on school records, are actually very similar. In workplaces, black managers are far less likely to characterize black workers negatively, and express more empathy for the difficulties blacks face in the labour market (Moss and Tilly 2001).

In the new social construction of skill, workers of colour are deemed less skilled than white workers and consequently experience discrimination. Evidence on racialized ascription of skill fingers hiring managers, co-workers, customers, as well as teachers. The point is not that these groups are particular egregious holders of stereotypes and agents of 'colour-blind racism'; rather, the pervasiveness of such biases makes racialized skill ascription endemic in the labour market and workplaces.

Class and Skill

Whilst there is ample debate and research on gender and skill, and some on race and skill, there is today less focus on class and skill (see Livingstone, Chapter 14 in this volume). Once, class and skill were said to be a forceful if damaging combination. In the early 1970s, Marxist re-interest in work trends led by Braverman (1974) posited that one class, employers, was locked into a struggle to deskill the other class, employees, because of the competitive needs of capitalism. By the 1990s, however, a more complex picture of skill trends was emerging and labour process theory, as it was now called, began to distance itself from skill as the point of analysis, arguing instead that managerial control was the issue (cf. Thompson 1989; Thompson and Smith 2010). If skill was now regarded as an inconvenient distraction by some, others over this time thought the same of class and proclaimed its death, usurped by a mixture of education-driven meritocracy and the displacement of production by consumption (see Goldthorpe 2003 and Bauman 1998, respectively). So pervasive did the omission of class become that even the initial formulation of intersectionality (Crenshaw 1989) included only race and sex in its attempt to explain labour market 'sorting' and discrimination.

The siren voices that proclaimed the death of class have been dampened recently: both the birth of meritocracy and death of work have been exposed as myths (Goldthorpe 2003 and Bradley et al. 2000, respectively). Moreover, research on intersectionality now includes race, sex, and class (Kerner 2012). Whilst there are continuing debates about how to conceive, define, and measure class, 'The salience of class remains in its ability not just to define social relations but also, perhaps, more importantly, to shape outcomes,' Platt (2011, 24) states.

Although these outcomes include skill, and class is now being recovered, analysis of the relationship between class and skill remains limited. Instead, the link between class and skill is regarded as so straightforward that it warrants no analysis; one is read off the other, mediated simply by occupation. Despite suggestions to the contrary, practically the relationship is established through standard occupational classifications (SOC). In these classifications, occupations are hierarchically classified on the basis of educational qualifications.[1] Higher ranked occupations thus have higher achieved skills; lower ranked occupations lower achieved skills. As occupations acquire higher achieved skills, they are bumped up the classification (Elias and Birch 2010). If it is a short conceptual leap from skill to occupational hierarchy, it is a similarly short one from occupational hierarchy to class, with occupational level being one of the main ways by which social classes are conceived. Whilst purporting not to hierachicalize or be related to skill, the UK's National Statistics Socio-economic Classification (NS-SEC, in the process of being rolled out across Europe) is 'rebased' on SOC (cf. Rose and Pevalin 2001; 2010).

It is not just that skill determines occupational entry and level (and so class position), once in work workers in lower-level occupations receive less subsequent education and training. Managerial and professional workers, who already have the highest achieved skill levels, tend to be those who receive most employer-provided development opportunities (Kersley et al. 2006).

As such, class position, through occupational classification, is indicative of achieved skill. The relationship between class and achieved skill is thus seemingly straightforward. Using qualifications as a proxy for skill, and occupation as a proxy for class, the working class exits education less skilled than the middle class. Middle class workers are then more skilled than working class workers as they enter employment, which accounts for their occupational super-ordination, and they continue to acquire more achieved skills as their careers progress. By contrast, the working class receives less opportunity for further skill development once in work so that the working class cumulatively acquires less skill than the middle class over their working lives. This differential

[1] See: http://www.ons.gov.uk/ons/guide-method/classifications/current-standard-classifications/soc2010/soc2010-volume-1-structure-and-descriptions-of-unit-groups/index.html#5.

outcome is regarded as unproblematic as it is, after all, why the working class is defined as working class—having a lower level of achieved skill.

What is problematic is that the middle class continues to benefit disproportionally as what characterizes skill has broadened. Now, not only do the middle class acquire more achieved skill through education and training but, with this broadening, being middle class is ascribed as a skill. This development partly reflects how the characterization of 'skill' has broadened to include both achieved skills—that is, for the most part, qualifications—but also the ascribed 'soft' skills formerly constituent of 'personality' (Grugulis et al. 2004) or 'culture', as we have seen in the case of workers of colour. In part it also reflects the shift to service-dominated economies in which jobs involving face-to-face or voice-to-voice interactions between worker and customer. With these jobs the articulation of education and employment has become loosened (Goldthorpe 2003), and these workers' productivity is aligned with ascribed, not just achieved, skills— with socialization rather than education being the source of skill formation.

These skills are particularly pertinent in what might be regarded, using SOC, as working class jobs—entry-level jobs in retail and hospitality for example. A survey by the United Kingdom's Hospitality Training Foundation (2000) found that the skills most demanded by employers then and in the foreseeable future centred on attitude and appearance. These ascribed skills tend to be associated with the middle class. For waiting staff in a new hotel in Glasgow in the United Kingdom, the company explicitly advertised the jobs in the *Sunday Times* newspaper with its middle class readership (Nickson et al. 2001). Similarly in Cambridge in the United Kingdom, Crang and Martin (1991, 106) found employers avoiding hiring workers from the working class:

> One manager of a fashion retail stores said to us, the residential origins of his employees is an important consideration: none came from the large council estates ... as they were not the 'right type of people' he was looking for. They lacked the 'cultural capital' ... to display and sell the middle-class clothes in the store.

What is also notable here is that, although they are offering putatively working class jobs, employers justify not employing the working class by reference to customer matching, as US employers do with workers of colour. That is, firms' product and labour market strategies are aligned.

Beyond firms' market segmentation strategies, the broader issue is the gentrification of ascribed skill as a result of which many more interactive services jobs require middle classness. This gentrification is most salient in debates about emotional labour and aesthetic labour. In the former, Hochschild notes that different airlines have different styles of service—'girl-next-door' and 'sophisticated' for example—but all are variations of employer-demanded 'middle class sociability' (1983, 97). With aesthetic labour, traces of working classness are erased in managerial proscription and prescription of speech used in the service encounter. Some words in the English language have 'a touch more cultural clout', denoting social hierarchy notes Bragg (2003, 59). Thus in UK fashion retail, one worker explained that you weren't allowed to say 'lovely', you had to say [to customers] that's 'exquisite' (Warhurst and Nickson 2016). 'Exquisite' has Latin (Norman) origins and 'lovely' is Old English (Celtic), denoting upper/middle and working class respectively.

Often this middle classness is hired through the employment of middle class university students, as Dutton et al.'s (2005) research of UK food retail highlights and in which, significantly, the companies in the study had a wide product market base, selling across social classes. The outcome is that the middle class and middle class youth in particular are now colonizing working class jobs and displacing the working class from those jobs (for similar developments in the Netherlands, see Hofman and Steijn 2003).

If just being middle class is now cast as being skilled by employers, the working class can be perceived as therefore suffering a skills deficit, and thereby excluded from services employment opportunities. If, with ascribed skills, skill formation is no longer an outcome of education but, as Goldthorpe (2003) notes, socialization, then responsibility for skills development lies with the family and the blame for workers being unskilled rests with bad parenting (Jones 2011). That attitudes and behaviours, including those related to work, are transmitted inter-generationally from parents to children and that what is transmitted differs by class has long been recognized (e.g. Willis 1977; Bourdieu 1984). What is different now is that responsibility for working class unemployability is shifted onto the working class themselves. Ignoring the economic downturn and an already over-qualified workforce (see Felstead et al., Chapter 16 in this volume), it is now argued that to give their children a chance in the labour market requires attitudinal and behavioural change of parents, and if working class parents cannot provide the right home environment then other agencies will have to provide early years intervention to offer these children the social and emotional literacy that their parents cannot (see Curtis 2008; BBC 2011).

Thus whilst conceptualization of skill has become more complex (see Payne, Chapter 3), the relationship between class and skill still holds constant. The middle and working class are differentiated by different levels of achieved skill and now by different types of ascribed skill. With the ascribed skills of the middle class more favoured by employers in services, just being middles class is now regarded as being better skilled. Employers justify discriminating against the working class by reference to customer preferences. For the 'unskilled' working class, labour market exclusion has become a personal problem and the victims blamed.

Implications of the New Social Construction of Skill

A number of issues and implications arise from this new social construction of skill. To start, as evidence summarized above highlights, increasing reliance on soft skills compounds opportunity for stereotyping, raising a second consequent issue: increased opportunities for discriminatory action in the labour market. Gatta's (2011) qualitative research with small high-end American retailers found that they tended to view basic customer service and the required aesthetic and emotion skills as something the prospective worker had or did not have. Building on Gladwell's (2006) 'blink moment', Gatta found that employers judge the possession of such skills and so make their hiring decisions in the initial few seconds of meeting a perspective employee. The blink moment then has the real potential of reproducing social inequality, as employers can end up relying on cultural capital cues, stereotypes, and prejudices. In many ways the blink moment can be code for race and class bias amongst employers, as we noted above. More concrete signifiers of job suitability—such as work-related certifications or years of experience—are seen as less important in hiring decisions. Interestingly, Gladwell notes that 'blinding' prospective hiring managers and thereby eliminating the blink moment can reduce sex bias in recruitment.

A second implication is that insufficient training provision, public or private, is directed to the problem. In shifting to emphasize ascribed rather than achieved skill, employers' role in its acquisition through training diminishes. Employers step away from training because they understand that the acquisition of ascribed skills and cultural capital takes time, after all childhood socialization, for example, is a long, complex, and uncertain process. Employers still want these skills in their employees but buy rather than train them. Abercrombie and Fitch in the United Staff want staff with a 'preppy look' to align with their customer base and so do not hire ethnic minority job applicants who are deemed to lack the appropriate cultural capital (Smith 2013). Likewise, United Kingdom food retail employers hire already suitably skilled middle class students despite the government wanting these employers to hire unemployed lone parents, for whom entry-level jobs help to gain the skills that they currently lack (Dutton et al. 2005). Rather than train, employers prefer 'plug and play' applicants capable of starting work immediately.

Third, the shift to ascribed skills displaces the solution to the productivity problem that exercises the minds of many wealthy economies' governments. In the past, as Grugulis et al. (2004) note, the productivity problem was attributed to poor industrial relations or personnel management, both of which, of course, involved employers. Now the problem is said to be individual workers and their attitudes and behaviour. Productivity is deemed to be hampered because workers have motivational (Grugulis et al. 2004) or discipline deficits (Lafer 2004) or cannot 'endure monotony' (Lloyd and Payne 2009, 630). As Lloyd and Payne argue, responsibility 'shifts to the individual who must improve their "skills" in order to perform or cope better'. Employer responsibility for bad job design or lousy pay quietly drops off the radar despite evidence that firms with above average job quality have higher productivity (Patterson et al. 1997). Working upstream, the solution to the productivity problem and workers' skill deficits is now, as we have already indicated, laid at the door of parents, preschools, schools, and, increasingly, universities and colleges—anyone but employers.

However, many contributing to this literature raise anew the issue of social and state responsibility for skills development. In an echo of early debates about the social construction of skills, Nickson et al. (2003) advocate training in aesthetic labour, for example, as 'an appeal for equity and pragmatism'. They argue (2003, 11):

> Twenty thousand people are unemployed in Glasgow but there exists 5500 unfilled jobs. Our contention is that a proportion of those jobs are likely to remain unfilled unless long-term unemployed people are equipped with aesthetic skills. Such jobs, such as hospitality, clearly demand employees to affect the appropriate role—required bodily dispositions, adopting 'masks for tasks' or simply 'surface acting', and the unemployed should be aware of this need.

Yet in the same ways that middle class aesthetic labour is embodied, so is poverty. For example, the lack of access of the poor to quality and affordable healthcare leaves physical scars of poverty—poor teeth and skin for example, or even simply the lack of a suit for interviews. Such indicators are difficult to 'mask'. So whilst soft skills training can help blunt the blink moment and help enhance some opportunities, it will not eliminate the potential biases in the blink moment nor will it alter the ways this labour market works.

For this reason it is easy to dismiss remedial actions in soft skills training. However, the racialized character of skill definition, ascription and acquisition point to other ways to overcome current racial and ethnic inequalities. First, it is critical to reduce racial gaps in school quality and academic achievement. Second, soft skill training programmes, which have proliferated in the United States, serve a valuable purpose: when to wear a tie, how to shake hands appropriately, who to call 'sir' and 'ma'am' etc. can be learnt. However, some policy discussions stop at this point, leaving the onus on marginalized groups to learn how to 'code-switch' to the dominant culture. Instead of ending there, we would propose three added policy elements. One is to engage in affirmative action that jump-starts the skill acquisition process by preferentially placing people of colour in roles to which they have historically had limited access so that they can learn soft (and other) skills on the job, pass on what they have learnt to later generations, and serve as gatekeepers less burdened by the stereotypes held by so many whites. A second is to recognize and reward certain currently devalued skills acquired through socialization as valuable *achieved* skills, as proposed by advocates of 'comparable worth' and similar approaches to overcome gendered disparities in wage-setting (England 1992; Hampson and Junor 2010). However, such policies, designed to impede discriminatory impacts, undermine the distinction between ascribed and achieved skill, leaving the door wide open to other forms of discrimination: in this framework, is socialization-based 'middle classness' also to be viewed as an achieved skill worthy of reward? A final—and particularly subversive—policy direction, then, is to press business and society at large to 'explode the code' and become more multicultural, open to a range of models and idioms of interaction (Moss and Tilly 2001).

Concluding Remarks

This chapter has outlined a new social construction of skill increasingly based on skill as *ascribed* rather than simply *achieved*, and within ascribed skills, increasingly based on skills acquired through socialization rather than through education or training. The 'old' social construction of skill argued that, historically, skill was gendered, with men organized through trade unions, boosting or securing their pay, status, and job security by having women ascribed as unskilled and so excluded. Actions to counter this process and outcome still continue (see Hampson and Junor 2010), although often now through the vehicle of professionalization projects (Anderson and Warhurst 2012). With changes to how skill is defined and shifts in the power to define it away from colleagues and towards customers, credentialers, and capital we suggest that a 'new' social construction of skill has emerged.

The social construction of skill constitutes the principal and growing portion of employment discrimination today. We suggest that recent literature on gender, and race and ethnicity, supports this contention, and argue that attention should also now be refocused on class. The processes and outcomes involving sex, race, and class are, however, not homogeneous. Whilst the in-demand soft skills are associated with women and are linked to increased female employment participation through positive discrimination, especially with regard to interactive service work, having these skills has brought no material benefit to women. Conversely, deemed to lack the required soft skills some workers of colour and those from the working class experience negative discrimination and are then excluded from the labour market. However, there are also areas of convergence, as when both women and US immigrant Latinos are steered towards particular subordinate job categories at lower pay levels.

Whilst we have focused on sex, race, and class issues in the new social construction of skill, future research needs spatial sensitivity, particularly with respect to potential national differences. There is a liberal market economy (LME) centricism in current English-language research about soft skills and the importance placed on them when there may be differing views about skill across the richer economies. It seems that in the LMEs, such as the United States, United Kingdom, and Australia, employers more readily accept and even promote ascribed skills as skills (Lafer 2004, Nickson et al. 2005, Hall and van den Broek 2012, respectively). This acceptance seems to have less purchase amongstst employers in the co-ordinated market economies (CMEs). This difference certainly created problems for one of us in comparative research of the retail industries of Sweden, Australia, and the United Kingdom, and which starkly exposed the divide between ascribed and achieved skills.[2] Whilst employers in the United Kingdom and

[2] Some of this research is reported in a special issue of the journal *Economic and Industrial Democracy*, 33(1), 2012.

Australia had no difficulty with questionnaires asking about 'skills' related to emotional and aesthetic labour, Swedish employers did, making the point that to be a skill something had to have a qualification attached to it. It is probably no coincidence that Sweden, as with other CMEs, has more employer-provided training, places greater emphasis on trade-union-influenced technical skills, still tends to make, not just sell, things, and whose workers, historically, tended to avoid employer-led deskilling initiatives (Thompson 1989; Gallie 2007).

A tighter link persists between education and employment in the CMEs than the LMEs. With the exception of the traditional professions such as medicine and law, achieved skills less axiomatically map onto jobs in the LMEs. Graduates in the United Kingdom, for example, are content to narrate their employability profiles through soft skills such as the capacity to 'work independently' and that are transferable across the UK's generic graduate labour market. By contrast, students in the Netherlands enter a labour market with high occupational segmentation and a strong relationship between course content and job destination; achieved skills decide labour market position (Tholen 2013). This tighter link between education and employment holds in the CMEs for both high- and intermediate-level skills.

However, the tight link between education and employment and its reliance upon achieved skill in the CMEs may be lessening. Echoing our point about the shifts underpinning the new social construction of skills, Eichhorst and Marx (2009) suggest that a dualism is emerging in Germany. In this dualism, less unionized routine interactive service work has a logic more resembling that in the LMEs. In terms of skill, employers are investing less in training and relying less on occupation-specific achieved skills and more on generic soft skills such as communication and politeness. As these types of jobs grow numerically, Eichhorst and Marx conclude that 'the standard employment relationship and vocational training which were typical for the German CME shrinks ... established patterns of qualification and work are less relevant', and leaves them to boldly predict 'a gradual transition towards a liberal model' (p. 24). As such, ascribed skills would become an issue in the CMEs too, and the issues that we raise in this chapter about the social construction of skill likewise empirically and analytically salient in these countries.

More generally, the development in Germany accords with our point that the social construction of skill, whether old or new, raises basic questions about not just how skill is analysed but also changes the nature of work and the balance of workplace power. Referring to the gender bias that informed what we have called the 'old' social construction of skill, Acker (1989, 60) noted that dominant groups 'write the rules' that lead to the subordination of other groups in the labour market. With changes to work and shifts in the balance of power, capital now more assuredly writes those rules and shifts responsibility for skill acquisition to workers and credentialers, colleagues lose leverage over skill definition, and customers become a useful tool of capital. Changes in the accepted definition of skill and in who has the ability to define it alter not just conceptual categories but the distribution of rewards and power in the economy and society.

References

Acker, J. (1989) 'Making gender visible', in R. Wallace (ed.), *Feminism and Sociological Theory*, Newbury Park, CA: Sage.

Anderson, P. and Warhurst, C. (2012) 'Workplace Upskilling or Upshifting Sleight of Hand? Physiotherapists and Professionalization in the UK's NHS', mimeo, Centre for Research in Lifelong Learning, Glasgow Caledonian University.

Ashley, L. (2010) 'Making a Difference? The Use (and Abuse) of Diversity Management at the UK's Elite Law Firms', *Work, Employment and Society*, 24(4): 711–727.

Attewell, P. (1990) 'What is Skill?', *Work and Occupations*, 14(4): 422–448.

Bauman, Z. (1998) *Work, Consumerism and the New Poor*, Cambridge: Polity.

BBC (2011) 'Free Parenting Class Trial to Run in England', 16 October. http://www.bbc.co.uk/news/education-15312216?print=true.

Becker, G. (1964) *Human Capital*, Chicago: University of Chicago Press.

Belt, V., Richardson, R., and Webster, J. (2002) 'Women, Social Skill and Interactive Service Work in Telephone Call Centres', *New Technology, Work, and Employment*, 17(1): 20–34.

Bendick, M. (2007) 'Situation Testing for Employment Discrimination in the United States of America', *Horizons Stratégiques*, 5: 6–18.

Bendick, M., Rodriguez, R., and Jayaraman, S. (2010) 'Employment Discrimination in Upscale Restaurants: Evidence from Matched Pair Testing', *Social Science Journal*, 47: 802–818.

Bonilla-Silva, E. (2010) *Racism without Racists*, Lanham, MD: Rowman and Littlefield.

Bourdieu, P. (1984) *Distinction*, London: Routledge.

Bowles, S., Gintis, H., and Osborne, M. (2001) 'The Determinants of Earnings: A Behavioral Approach', *Journal of Economic Literature*, 39(4): 1137–1176.

Bradley, H., Erickson, M., Stephenson, C., and Williams, S. (2000) *Myths at Work*, Cambridge: Polity.

Bragg, M. (2003) *The Adventure of English*, London: Sceptre.

Braverman, H. (1974) *Labor and Monopoly Capital*, New York: Monthly Review Press.

Burawoy, M. (2010) 'From Polanyi to Pollyanna: The False Optimism of Global Labor Studies', *Global Labour Journal*, 1(2): 301–313.

Cappelli, P., Bassi, L., Katz, H., Knoke, D., Osterman, P., and Useem, M. (1997) *Change at Work*, New York: Oxford University Press.

Crang, P. and Martin, R. L. (1991) 'Mrs Thatcher's Vision of the "New Britain" and other Sides of the "Cambridge Phenomenon"', *Environment and Planning D: Society and Space*, 9: 91–116.

Crenshaw, K. (1989) 'Demarginalising the Intersection of Race and Sex: A Black Feminist Critique of Antidiscrimination Doctrine', *University of Chicago Legal Forum*, 139–167.

Curtis, P. (2008) 'State Urged to Help Deprived Children to Communicate', *Guardian*, 2 December: 12.

Delpit, L. (1995) *Other People's Children*, New York: New Press.

Deming, D.J. (2015) 'The Growing Importance of Social Sskills in the Labor Market', NBER Working Paper No.21473, National Bureau of Economic Research, Cambridge, MA. http://www.nber.org/papers/w21473.

Duffy, M. (2005) 'Reproducing Labor Inequalities: Challenges for Feminists Conceptualizing Care at the Intersections of Gender, Race, and Class', *Gender and Society*, 19: 66–82.

Dutton, E., Warhurst, C., Nickson, D., and Lockyer, C. (2005) 'Lone Parents, the New Deal and the Opportunities and Barriers to Retail Employment', *Policy Studies*, 26(1): 85–101.

Eichhorst, W. and Marx, P. (2009) 'From the Dual Apprenticeship System to a Dual Labour Market? The German High-Skill Equilibrium and the Service Economy', *Discussion Paper No.4220*, IZA, Bonn.
Elias, P. and Birch, M. (2010) *SOC2010: The Revision of the Standard Occupational Classification 2000*, Newport: Office for National Statistics.
England, P. (1992) *Comparable Worth: Theories and Evidence*, New York: Aldine de Gruyter.
England, P. Budig, M., and Folbre, N. (2002) 'Wages of Virtue: The Relative Pay of Care Work', *Social Problems*, 49: 455–473.
Feagin, J. R. (2010) *Racist America*, New York: Routledge.
Felstead, A., Gallie, D., and Green, F. (2007) *Skills at Work*, Oxford and Cardiff: ESRC Centre on Skills, Knowledge and Organizational Performance, Universities of Oxford and Cardiff.
Figlio, D. N. (2005) 'Names, Expectations and the Black-White Test Score Gap', National Bureau of Economic Research Working Paper w11195, Cambridge, MA.
Findlay, P., McKinlay A., Marks A., and Thompson, P. (2000) 'In Search of Perfect People: Teamwork and Team Players in the Scottish Spirits Industry', *Human Relations*, 53(12): 1549–1574.
Fuller, L. and Smith, V. (1991) 'Consumers' Reports: Management by Customers in a Changing Economy', *Work, Employment and Society*, 5(1): 1–16.
Gallie, D. (2007) 'The Quality of Working Life in Comparative Perspective', in D. Gallie (ed), *Employment Regimes in Europe and the Quality of Work*, Oxford: Oxford University Press: 205–232.
Gatta, M. (2011) 'In the "Blink" of an Eye: American High-End Small Retail Businesses and the Public Workforce System', in I. Grugulis and O. Bozkurt (eds), *Retail Work*, Palgrave: London: 49–67.
Gladwell, M. (2006) *Blink*, London: Penguin.
Glover, J. and Guerrier, Y. (2010) 'Women in Hybrid Roles in IT Employment: A Return to "Nimble Fingers"?' *Journal of Technology Management and Innovation*, 5(1), 85–94.
Goldthorpe, J. (2003) 'The Myth of Education-Based Meritocracy', *New Economy Series*, London: IPPR.
Grubb, W. N. and Lazerson, M. (2004) *The Education Gospel*, Cambridge, MA: Harvard University Press.
Grugulis, I., Warhurst, C., and Keep, E. (2004) 'What's Happening to "Skill"?', in C. Warhurst, I. Grugulis, and E. Keep (eds), *The Skills That Matter*, London: Palgrave: 1–18.
Guy, M. and Newman, M. (2004) 'Women's Jobs, Men's Jobs: Sex Segregation and Emotional Labor', *Public Administration Review*, 64: 289–298.
Hall, R. and van den Broek, D. (2012) 'Aestheticising Retail Workers: Orientations of Aesthetic Labour in Australian Fashion Retail', *Economic and Industrial Democracy*, 33(1): 85–102.
Hampson, I. and Junor, A. (2010) 'Putting the Process Back in: Rethinking Service Sector Skill', *Work, Employment and Society*, 24(3): 526–545.
Hochschild, A. (1983) *The Managed Heart*, Berkeley: University of California Press.
Hofman, W. and Steijn, A. (2003) 'Students or Lower-Skilled Workers? "Displacement" at the Bottom of the Labour Market', *Higher Education*, 45(2): 127–146.
Holzer, H. J. (1996) *What Employers Want*, New York: Russell Sage Foundation.
Holzer, H. J. and Stoll, M. A. (2000) 'Employer Demand for Welfare Recipients by Race', JCPR Working Paper 197, Northwestern University.
Hospitality Training Foundation (2000) *Skills and Employment Forecasts 2000 for the Hospitality Industry*, London: HtF.

Huffman, M. L. and Cohen, P. N. (2004) 'Racial Wage Inequality: Job Segregation and Devaluation across U.S. Labor Markets', *American Journal of Sociology*, 109: 902–936.

Jones, O. (2011) *Chavs*, London: Verso.

Kelan, E. K. (2008) 'Emotions in a Rational Profession: The Gendering of Skills in ICT Work', *Gender, Work and Organization*, 15(1): 49–71.

Kerner, I. (2012) 'Questions of Intersectionality: Reflections on the Current Debate in German Gender Studies', *European Journal of Women's Studies*, 19(2): 203–218.

Kersley, B., Alpin, C., Forth, J., Bryson, A., Bewley, H., Dix, G., and Oxenbridge, S. (2006) *Inside the Workplace*, London: Routledge.

Korczynski, M. (2009) 'Understanding the Contradictory Lived Experience of Service Work: The Customer-Oriented Bureaucracy', in M. Korczynski and C. L. Macdonald (eds), *Service Work*, New York: Routledge: 73–90.

Korteweg, A. (2003) 'Welfare Reform and the Subject of the Working Mother: Get a Job, a Better Job than a Career', *Theory and Society*, 32: 455–480.

Lafer, G. (2004) 'What is "Skill"? Training for Discipline in the Low-Wage Labour Market', in C. Warhurst, I. Grugulis, and E. Keep (eds), *The Skills That Matter*, London: Palgrave: 109–127.

Lloyd, C. and Payne, J. (2009) 'Full of Sound and Fury, Signifying Nothing': Interrogating New Skill Concepts in Service Work: The View from Two UK Call Centres', *Work, Employment and Society*, 23(4): 617–634.

McCrate, E. (2006) 'Why Racial Stereotyping Doesn't Just Go Away: The Question of Honesty and Work Ethic', mimeo, Departments of Economics and Women's Studies, University of Vermont.

Mong, S. N. and Roscigno, V. J. (2010) 'African American Men and the Experience of Employment Discrimination', *Qualitative Sociology*, 33: 1–21.

Moss, P. and Tilly, C. (2001) *Stories Employers Tell*, New York: Russell Sage Foundation.

Moss, P. and Tilly, C. (2006) 'Learning about Discrimination by Talking to Employers', in W. Rodgers III (ed.), *Handbook on the Economics of Discrimination*, Cheltenham: Edward Elgar: 61–96.

Nakano Glenn, E. (1992) 'From Servitude to Service Work: Historical Continuities in the Racial Division of Paid Reproduction Labor', *Signs*, 18(1): 1–43.

Nickson, D., Warhurst, C., Cullen, A-M., and Watt, A. (2003) 'Bringing in the Excluded? Aesthetic Labour, Skills and Training in the New Economy', *Journal of Education and Work*, 16(2): 185–203.

Nickson, D. Warhurst, C., and Dutton, E. (2005) Importance of Attitude and Appearance in the Service Encounter in Retail and Hospitality', *Managing Service Quality*, 15(2): 195–208.

Nickson, D., Warhurst, C., Witz, A., and Cullen, A-M. (2001) 'The Importance of Being Aesthetic: Work, Employment and Service Organization', in A. Sturdy, I. Grugulis, and H. Willmott (eds), *Customer Service*, London: Palgrave: 170–190.

Nickson, D., Warhurst, C. Lockyer, C., and Dutton, E, (2004) 'Flexible Friends? Lone Parents and Retail Employment', *Employee Relations*, 26(3): 255–273.

Pager, D. and Quillian, L. (2005) 'Walking the talk? What Employers Say Versus What They Do', *American Sociological Review*, 70(3): 355–380.

Patterson, M., West, M., Lawthorn, R., and Nickell, S. (1997) 'Impact of People Management Strategies on Business Performance', *Issues in People Management*, vol. 22. London: Institute of Personnel and Development.

Platt, L. (2011) *Understanding Inequalities*, Cambridge: Polity.

Rho, H. J. (2014) 'Language and Prejudice: The "Invisible Hand" of Gender Segregation in Modern Organizations'. Unpublished mimeo, Sloan School of Management, Massachusetts Institute of Technology, Boston, MA.

Rivera, L. A. (2012) 'Hiring as Cultural Matching: The Case of Elite Professional Service Firms', *American Sociological Review*, 77: 999–1021.

Rose, D. and Pevaline, D. (2001) 'The National Statistics Socio-economic Classification: Unifying Official and Sociological Approaches to the Conceptualisation and Measurement of Social Class', ISER Working Papers no.2001–2004, University of Essex.

Rose, D. and Pevaline, D. (2010) 'Re-basing the NS-SEC on SOC2010: A Report to ONS', University of Essex.

Royster, D. A. (2003) *Race and the Invisible Hand*, Berkeley: University of California Press.

Slaton, A. (2011) *Race, Rigor, and Selectivity in U.S. Engineering*, Cambridge, MA: Harvard University Press.

Smith, M. (2013) 'Abercrombie & Fitch under Fire Again for Cool Kids Comment', *The Guardian Express*, 10 May. http://guardianlv.com.

Steinberg, R. J. (1990) 'Social Construction of Skill: Gender, Power and Comparable Worth', *Work and Occupations*, 17(4): 449–482.

Tholen, G. (2013) 'The Social Construction of Competition for Graduate Jobs: A Comparison between Great Briain and the Netherlands', *Sociology*, 47(2): 267–283.

Thompson, P. (1989) *The Nature of Work*, Basingstoke: Macmillan.

Thompson, P. and Smith, C. (2010) 'Debating Labour Process heory and the Sociology of Work', in P. Thompson and C. Smith (eds), *Working Life*, London: Palgrave.

Tomaskovic-Devey, D. (1993) *Gender and Racial Inequality at Work*, Ithaca, NY: ILR Press.

Waldinger, R., and Lichter, M. (2003) *How the Other Half Works*, Berkeley: University of California Press.

Warhurst, C. and Nickson, D. (2016) *Aesthetic Labour*, London: Sage.

Willis, P. (1977) *Learning to Labour*, Westmead: Saxon House.

Woodfield, R. (1998) 'Working Women and Social Labour', Working Paper in Rusel Forum for Comparative Political Economy, University of Exeter.

Zamudio, M. and Lichter, M. (2008) 'Bad Attitudes and Good Soldiers: Soft Skills as a Code for Tractability in the Hiring of Immigrant Latina/os over Native Blacks in the Hotel Industry', *Social Problems*, 55: 573–589.

CHAPTER 5

MEASURING JOB CONTENT

Skills, Technology, and Management Practices

MICHAEL J. HANDEL

INTRODUCTION

THIRTY years ago, research on the *Dictionary of Occupational Titles* (DOT) transformed the study of job skills and related job characteristics (Spenner 1979; Cain and Treiman 1981). Criticism of the quality of DOT measures and an impasse over how to measure job skill requirements soon followed. Kenneth Spenner observed, 'Our conceptualization and measurement of skill are poor. Unidimensional, undefined concepts, nonmeasures, and indirect measures of skill have not served us well' (1983, 825). More recent reflections express some of the same concerns (Borghans et al. 2001).

Recent debates on work, education, and inequality have brought greater attention to job skill requirements than ever before, but there has been little sustained effort to develop better measures and until recently there remained, in fact, little hard, representative data on what people actually do at work. Researchers have had only a general sense of required skill levels, even less information on different skill dimensions and rates of change, and no well-defined intellectual framework.

This chapter presents a conceptual map of skill domains and a strategy for measuring them called 'explicit scaling'. The goal is to demonstrate the feasibility and validity of a relatively comprehensive yet tractable set of measures. The approach is validated using the first wave of the survey of Skills, Technology, and Management Practices (STAMP), a nationally representative, two-wave panel study.

This chapter reviews the skill debates, introduces explicit scaling, develops a conceptual framework for understanding job skill requirements, and presents evidence on the quality of the STAMP measures derived from the proposed approach.

Theories of the Changing Nature of Jobs

Numerous debates hinge on claims regarding job skill levels and trends without articulating a clear vision for directly measuring them. The long-running debate between deskilling and post-industrial theories is well known (Braverman 1974; Bell 1976; Attewell 1987; Form 1987), but methodological problems hindered progress. The frequent reliance on case studies limited generalizability. There was no way to know if cases selected for study were representative and little consistency in measuring skill requirements across cases, so no convincing profile emerged of the overall job structure or its evolution. Skill changes due to shifts in occupation shares were beyond the scope of the method altogether (Spenner 1983). In response, researchers used standardized measures derived from the DOT, often matched to representative labour force surveys (Spenner 1979; Howell and Wolff 1991). Enthusiasm soon faded as DOT ratings were based on a convenience sample and not updated consistently since the 1960s. Consequently, this debate stalled by the late 1980s amid calls for better data (Cain and Treiman 1981; Attewell 1990; Spenner 1990; Vallas 1990; US Department of Labor 1993, 20).

Quite separately, Bluestone and Harrison discovered the rise in earnings inequality in the United States in the early 1980s. They argued that firms returned to profitability after the economic crises of the late 1970s by squeezing workers: eliminating institutional protections (unions, minimum wages), decreasing employment security (outsourcing, casualisation), and job downgrading (pay/benefit cuts, sweating labour) (Bluestone and Harrison 1982; Harrison and Bluestone 1988; Harrison 1994; see also Graham 1993; Green 2006). Many of these ideas, based on declining worker bargaining power, also remain debated because of measurement problems.

By contrast, Piore and Sabel (1984) argued that the same crises were forcing firms to abandon strategies based on low wages in favour of competing on quality, continuous innovation, and customization. Flexible specialization implied job enrichment, worker autonomy, employee involvement (EI) practices, and Japanese-style quality control techniques. Automation and computers reinforced both skill upgrading and decentralized authority in this view (Zuboff 1988).

Mutually reinforcing relationships between skill, technology, and EI practices contrast with the previous perspective, for which computers increase surveillance and narrow autonomy, with EI either a method for intensifying effort or merely a token gesture (Graham 1993; Vallas 2003).

Representative data addressing these debates are also scarce and key constructs, like self-directed teams, subject to vague or varying definitions. There is no real consensus regarding the prevalence of EI practices, much less the relationships between skills, technology, EI, and the other elements of the flexible specialization and critical paradigms.

In response to Bluestone and Harrison's structural account of inequality growth, mainstream labour economists focused on the spread of computers, arguing new technology raised the relative demand for skill and increased returns to education and other human capital (Katz and Murphy 1992; Autor et al. 1998). This theory of skill-biased technological change is dominant amongst labour economists and favoured by some sociologists (e.g. Fernandez 2001), education researchers, policy analysts, and popular writers.

The exact causal argument relating computers to skills and wages remains unsettled. The wage premium observed for using a computer at work suggested the complexity of computer hardware and software required significant specific training investment (Krueger 1993; Dickerson and Green 2004). Others believe computers demand more general cognitive skills because they increase the information content of work and decentralize problem-solving (Autor et al. 2002; Spitz-Oener 2006), even incorporating the flexible specialization position on EI practices (Bresnahan et al. 2002).

One notable criticism argues that skill upgrading is the secular trend but did not accelerate when inequality grew, pointing to the need for long time series data (Mishel and Bernstein 1998).

There is a large research literature on skill-biased technological change (for reviews, see Handel 2003a, 2004), but its original foundation was very rough proxies for job skill requirements, such as workers' own educational attainment, broad occupation category, or DOT scores. Even today there is no consensus on a conceptual framework and operational measures of workplace cognitive skill requirements. Consistent time series data on skills necessary to test the acceleration hypothesis are even scarcer. Measures of technology are limited mostly to indicator variables for computer use or the value of an industry's computer capital investment, rather than the complexity of computer skills used by workers.[1]

Somewhat independently of the academic research, official reports in several countries expressed doubts about the quality of national education systems, perceiving or fearing a growing mismatch between the skills graduates possess and those required by the new economy.[2] Accelerating demand for cognitive and teamwork skills is taken for granted, reflecting popular versions of the theories discussed above. Reports conclude with a long list of education goals considered essential, but lack credible evidence on the share of jobs requiring different levels or kinds of academic skills.[3]

Also somewhat independent of the preceding, poverty researchers saw the inner-city poor as suffering from a mismatch between their levels of education and the cognitive demands of growing industries and occupations (Wilson 1996; Holzer 1996; Moss and Tilly 2001).

[1] For exceptions using British data, see Dickerson and Green (2004), and Borghans and ter Weel (2004).

[2] See US Department of Labor, Secretary's Commission on Achieving Necessary Skills (1991); HM Treasury 2006; see also Keep and Mayhew (1996); Payne (1999); Krahn and Lowe (1998); McIntosh and Steedman (2000); Haahr et al. (2004).

[3] For a review, including contrary evidence, see Handel (2003b). Education research includes Murnane and Levy (1996) and Rosenbaum and Binder (1997).

Finally, diverse research streams focused on interpersonal job requirements as a new dimension of interest. The growing share of white-collar and service jobs shifts demand away from manual and towards interpersonal skills (Bell 1976; Reich 1991), as does the perceived growing importance of teams within occupations. This may be a further difficulty for low-income minority workers with non-standard cultural capital, communication repertoires, and personal styles (Wilson 1996; Moss and Tilly 2001). Research on gender inequality focuses on emotional and caring labour.[4] Other studies show that jobs in fashionable boutiques, restaurants and bars, consulting, and investment banking require self-presentation work and 'aesthetic labor' (see Payne, Chapter 3).

By contrast, service jobs in fast food and call centres can be highly routinized, with very short-cycle, scripted, and ritualized interactions (Leidner 1993). Both the deskilling and emotional/caring labour perspectives agree that interactional demands can be a new source of job stress distinct from traditional forms of overwork. Nevertheless, as with cognitive skills, there has been limited effort to measure interpersonal job requirements.[5]

The various debates over skills and the changing nature of work suggest that a new approach is needed to address the following substantive questions:

- How many and which jobs require what levels of various skills, computer competencies,[6] and participation in EI practices? In brief, what is the skill profile of the evolving job structure?
- What are the functional and causal relationships between skill requirements, computer use, and EI?
- What are the effects of skills, computers, and EI on wages and other outcomes that define desirable or undesirable jobs (e.g. work intensity, promotion opportunities, layoffs, job satisfaction)?
- What are the trends in skill requirements, technology, and EI practices, their interrelationships, and their effects on the other outcomes mentioned above?

An Explicit Scaling Approach

This paper proposes a method called explicit scaling to address the impasse over the measurement of job skill requirements and related job characteristics that limits progress in the intellectual debates described above. Consider a question from the Quality

[4] See Hochschild (1983); Leidner (1993); Wharton (1999); Steinberg and Figart (1999); Glomb et al. (2004); England (2005).

[5] Exceptions include Steinberg and Figart (1999); Brotheridge and Lee (2003); Glomb et al. (2004); Hampson and Junor (2010).

[6] For convenience, 'computer use' sometimes covers the broader category 'computer and other technology use'.

of Employment Survey asking employees how much they agreed: 'My job requires a high level of skill' (Quinn and Staines 1979). Such measures are relatively common (Karasek 1979; Fields 2002, 72ff.).[7]

Amongst their problems, respondents must decide for themselves what 'skill' means and judge their job's overall level. The question and response options, ranging from 'strongly agree' to 'strongly disagree', contain no objective guidelines. The indefinite referents mean researchers can never be sure what the numerical scores mean in any concrete sense.

The question does not prevent responses based on relative standards rather than an absolute yardstick. Respondents are likely to rate their own job partly in comparison to jobs close to their own rather than using the entire range of jobs in the economy as their frame of reference due to its unfamiliarity. Indeed, job analysis has long wrestled with the problem of obtaining self-ratings based on an objective or common standard to ensure that measures mean the same thing across people and jobs.

The DOT's use of expert job analysts and workplace observations avoided many of the problems associated with self-reporting. Nevertheless, many DOT measures, such as a job's relationship to data, people, and things, also did not correspond to obvious, unambiguous, or concrete concepts, and the different levels of some scales are not even clearly ordinal (Table 5.1, top panel) (US Department of Labor 1991, 3–1). Despite the value labels, the distinctions between different levels of data, people, and things appear rather arbitrary, limiting their interpretability. Further, though the use of job analyst site visits produced relatively consistent scores across jobs, their costliness precluded replication so there is no time series for these scores.

The official replacement for the DOT, the Occupational Information Network (O*NET) database, uses mostly survey self-reports from representative samples of employees instead of trained raters and non-probability sampling used for the DOT (Peterson et al. 1999, 2001; US Department of Labor 2005). O*NET is an impressive effort to develop comprehensive measures of occupational characteristics. However, most O*NET survey items are complex or multi-barrelled, abstract, and vague, producing interpretive difficulties (see Table 5.1, bottom panel). Many O*NET items have moderately strong predictive validity, but the use of rating scales with indefinite referents means one can never be quite sure what O*NET scores actually mean in terms of specific real-world tasks (Handel 2016a). If two occupations require different levels of estimating skills, with one rated 3 and the other 4, one cannot really explain how they differ on this dimension beyond the difference in scores themselves because the scores have no inherent or external meaning. This is also true for standardized factor analytic scores constructed from rating scales and other unit-free measures (e.g. Miller et al. 1980, 176ff.; Spenner 1990, 403). Any effort to understand how much more skill might be involved in current jobs compared to the past will be limited insofar as it is not clear what is being quantified or if the quantification is not a real count or lacks cardinality.

[7] The European Union's quinquennial European Survey of Working Conditions asks: 'Does your main job involve complex tasks' (yes/no). The Household, Income and Labour Dynamics survey, an annual Australian panel, asks level of agreement with the statement: 'My job is complex and difficult.'

Table 5.1 Examples of skill measures

Levels of complexity of jobs' relationship to data, people, and things[a]
(Dictionary of Occupational Titles)

Data	People	Things
0 Synthesizing	0 Mentoring	0 Setting up
1 Coordinating	1 Negotiating	1 Precision working
2 Analysing	2 Instructing	2 Operating, controlling
3 Compiling	3 Supervising	3 Driving, operating
4 Computing	4 Diverting	4 Manipulating
5 Copying	5 Persuading	5 Tending
6 Comparing	6 Speaking, signalling	6 Feeding-off, bearing
	7 Serving	7 Handling
	8 Taking instructions, helping	

Occupational Information Network (O*NET) *(Generalized Work Activities survey)*

5. Estimating the quantifiable characteristics of products, events, or information	Estimating sizes, distances, and quantities; or determining time, costs, resources, or materials needed to perform a work activity

A. How *important* is estimating the quantifiable characteristics of products, events, or information to the performance of your current job?

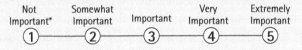

Not Important*	Somewhat Important	Important	Very Important	Extremely Important
1	2	3	4	5

* If you marked 'Not important', skip B below and go on to the next activity.

B. What *level* of estimating the quantifiable characteristics of products, events, or information is needed to perform your current job?

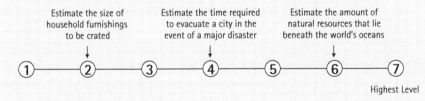

1	2	3	4	5	6	7
	Estimate the size of household furnishings to be crated		Estimate the time required to evacuate a city in the event of a major disaster		Estimate the amount of natural resources that lie beneath the world's oceans	Highest Level

a. DOT codes with higher values indicate lower levels of job complexity.

Job analyses using arbitrary scales are also a problem for studies of mismatch between jobs and workers because it is even more difficult to find measures of workers' estimating skills or factor scores on the same scale to compare directly to job requirements in order to determine match quality.

Explicit scaling seeks to avoid these problems with measures that are objective, concrete, correspond directly to the target of interest, and have absolute meaning. Survey questions refer to specific facts, events, and behaviours, rather than attitudes, evaluations, and holistic judgements, so they have greater external validity. Questions are general enough to encompass diverse work situations, but sufficiently concrete that they have stable meanings across respondents. Response options discriminate a wide range of levels to avoid floor and ceiling effects, and use natural units when possible. Rating scales, vague quantifiers, and factor scores, which have arbitrary metrics and lack specific or objective referents, are a last resort.

Explicit scales are intrinsically desirable because they have definite and easily interpretable meanings compared to measures that are more abstract or vague. Less room for subjective interpretation and self-enhancing biases hopefully also means less measurement error.

On the question of mismatch, for example, a job's educational requirements can be compared easily with a person's own level of educational attainment because both are measured using a common, natural unit. When measures of job and worker characteristics are in non-equivalent units, any analysis of match quality is more or less ad hoc.

Realistically, producing measures that are behaviourally concrete and meaningful in absolute or objective terms is often difficult. Questions that are very precise, referring to occupation-specific skills, for example, may achieve clarity and concreteness at the expense of relevance for most other jobs. Some constructs, such as work intensity, resist explicit scaling because they are complex and differ qualitatively across jobs. Concrete measures of work intensity for pilots, teachers, and assembly-line workers are as diverse as continuous flying hours, class size, and parts worked per hour. Even if a survey had space for a very long inventory of occupation-specific measures, there is no obvious way they could be mapped to a common scale for full-sample analyses due to their incommensurability. This applies to many constructs, such as job autonomy, task variety, and most kinds of occupation-specific skill and training (e.g. operating printing machinery, programming in Perl). When behavioural specificity is incompatible with generality, rating scales may be unavoidable.

Data and Methods

The STAMP survey represents an explicit scaling approach to comprehensive measurement of job skill requirements and related job characteristics. STAMP is a nationally representative, two-wave panel study of employed adults first conducted between October 2004 and January 2006, using standard random-digit-dial telephone survey procedures (n = 2,304). The survey contains approximately 166 unique items on job characteristics, summarised in Table 5.2. This represents the conceptual framework for measuring skills discussed in the next section.

A central goal of explicit scaling is to maximize the clarity and interpretability of items for both respondents and researchers, that is, strong face validity. The corpus of measures should also cover the different facets of constructs reasonably well and avoid floor or ceiling effects in measuring the levels of constructs, that is, content validity (Anastasi 1982). The survey's success in these areas can be judged informally from the descriptions in the next section.

Table 5.2 STAMP survey content (N = number of items)

1. Basic job and organizational information (N = 12)

Occupation, industry, organizational position, organizational and job tenure, union membership, organizational size, organization type

2. Skill and task requirements (N = 60)

Cognitive skills (N = 48)

Mathematics (n = 12)

Reading (n = 8)

Writing (n = 6)

Forms and visual matter (n = 6)

Problem-solving (n = 3)

Education, experience, and training requirements (n = 9)

Skill changes in previous three years (n = 4)

Interpersonal job tasks (n = 8)

Physical job tasks (n = 4)

3. Computer and non-computer technology (N = 49)

Computers (n = 26)

Frequency of use

Use of 14 specific applications

Use of advanced programme features, occupation-specific, and new software

Training times

Complexity of computer skills required

Adequacy of respondents' computer skills

Computer knowledge and experience in prior jobs amongst non-users

Machinery and electronic equipment (n = 18)

Level of machine knowledge needed, training time

Set-up, maintenance, and repair

Automation, equipment and tool programming

Other technology (n = 5)

Telephone, calculator, fax, bar code reader, and medical, scientific, and laboratory equipment

Technological displacement measures

(continued)

Table 5.2 Continued

4. EI practices (N = 18)
Job rotation and cross-training
Pay for skill
Formal quality control programme
Teams activity levels, responsibilities, and decision-making authority
Bonus and stock compensation
5. Autonomy, supervision, and authority (N = 11)
Closeness of supervision, autonomy
Repetitive work
Supervisory responsibilities over others
Decision-making authority over organizational policies
6. Job downgrading (N = 15)
Downsizing and outsourcing
Reductions in pay, and retirement and health benefits
Promotion opportunity, internal labour markets
Workload, pace, and stress
Strike activity
7. Job satisfaction (N = 1)

Criterion validity is assessed formally by comparing means across occupation and education groups and by correlating STAMP skill scores with standard measures of occupational standing and reward expected to be associated with the underlying constructs of interest (occupational prestige, socioeconomic index (SEI) scores, mean occupational wages) (Anastasi 1982, 140ff.).

Construct validity is assessed using several methods of internal consistency (Cronbach's α, principal components analysis, confirmatory factor analysis) (Anastasi 1982, 144ff.; Peterson et al. 1999). Because most STAMP items are dichotomous, nonlinear principal components analysis is used rather than standard PCA (Meulman et al. 2004) and categorical confirmatory factor analysis (CFA) rather than models for continuous measures.[8]

Because many STAMP items were designed to represent a hierarchy of complexity, Mokken scale analysis, a probabilistic form of Guttman scaling, is used to assess

[8] Nonlinear PCA procedures were performed using the CatPCA command in SPSS. Categorical CFA analyses were conducted with Mplus.

construct validity. Classical methods that assume items are parallel are not strictly appropriate for items representing different levels of difficulty (Sijtsma and Molenaar 2002, 55). Mokken scales use Loevinger's coefficient of homogeneity at the item (H_i) and overall scale (H) levels to test whether departures from strictly hierarchical response patterns are sufficiently small that persons and items are consistently orderable. H_i is a measure of item discrimination, somewhat analogous to item–rest correlations in classical item analysis, and H is a measure of overall scalability.[9] These are alternatives to classical measures of a scale's unidimensionality.

Convergent and divergent construct validity are evaluated by examining whether skill measures correlate more strongly with job educational requirements than personal educational attainment, and by comparing correlations between STAMP scales and measures from the DOT and O*NET that represent similar and different constructs.

Finally, measures corresponding more directly to some observable, real-world condition have external or ecological validity because they are more meaningful outside the context of a particular survey instrument than less direct or concrete measures. Verisimilitude, which distinguishes explicit scaling from prior approaches, is a key consideration in judging the quality of the STAMP measures.

Validity And Reliability Of Stamp Measures

Skills

Although the concept of job skill requirements has proven quite contested, it is defined here as technical task demands that are defined by employers as necessary for effective job performance. STAMP divides the skill domain into cognitive, interpersonal, and physical skills following the DOT's data-people-things scheme, which has been validated extensively (Kohn and Schooler 1983; Peterson et al. 1999; Autor et al 2003; Autor and Handel 2009).

Most research focuses on cognitive job skill requirements but faces significant measurement challenges, as discussed above. Covering this domain requires measuring transversal skills that apply to a wide range of jobs, both particular academic skills (e.g. maths, reading, writing) and more general thinking and reasoning demands (e.g. problem-solving). Required level of education captures aspects missed by the others and is an important overall measure.

[9] H_i and H are one minus the ratio of observed to maximum possible Guttman errors, where the latter is the joint distribution of item frequencies based on the item marginals and assuming independence between items. Mokken recommended that all H_i exceed 0.30 and classified H values as indicating weak scalability ($0.30 \leq H < 0.40$), medium scalability ($0.40 \leq H < 0.50$), and strongly scalability ($H \geq 0.50$). He also developed a test of the null hypotheses that $H_i = 0$ and $H = 0$ (Sijtsma and Molenaar 2002, 51ff.; van Schuur 2003, 149). All calculations were performed using the -msp- command in Stata.

More difficult to measure in a comparable fashion across jobs are the diverse occupation- and job-specific skills that are critical for most jobs (e.g. plumbing, computer programming). The only obvious solutions are required prior experience in related jobs and learning time for current job, which can be measured consistently across jobs and correspond closely to human capital concepts.

Maths

Mathematics is relatively well structured into levels of complexity that can be represented by a series of items, from simple counting to the use of calculus and other higher maths (Table 5.3). Respondents report whether they perform each task as a regular part of their jobs (1 = yes). The questions are objective and behaviourally specific yet remain applicable to all occupations and have stable meanings across respondents. Unlike subjective rating scales, they can be related easily to specific aspects of maths curricula and to the personal skill levels of workers and students, which are advantages in investigating skills mismatch.

The top panel of Table 5.3 shows measures of construct validity. Cronbach's α is reasonably large (0.81) and most correlations between individual items with a subscale excluding the item are above 0.50. The first principal component accounts for 63% of the total variance, well above the 30–40% cut-off commonly recommended for a strong dominant factor, and the item loadings are large.

When the items are fit to a Mokken scale, the values of Loevinger's H for the full scale (0.83) and each of the items (>0.70) are all significantly different from zero and show very strong scalability. Indeed, about 91% of all respondents answered the maths items in a strictly cumulative fashion, consistent with the Guttman model. This strongly suggests that the items represent a single hierarchy of skill.

The categorical CFA is more consistent with a two-factor solution distinguishing basic and complex maths (columns 4 and 5). The table shows fully standardized loadings and uses the root mean standard error of approximation (RMSEA) as the overall fit index. The fit is acceptable but the hierarchical quality of the items creates interdependencies amongst the items that makes CFA problematic, so these and similar results should be taken as suggestive.

When the sample is divided into five broad occupation groups, the proportion reporting more complex maths use generally follows a pattern consistent with expectation (see Handel 2016b).[10]

When groups are defined by job education requirements (*job education*) and personal education attainment (*own education*), the maths scales correlate significantly with both criteria but more strongly with job education (≥0.40) than own education (≥0.30), indicating both convergent and divergent validity (Table 5.3).

[10] The occupational groups are upper white-collar (managers, professionals, technical workers), lower white-collar (clerical, sales), upper blue-collar (craft, repair workers), lower blue-collar (operators, labourers), and service workers (health, food, personal, and protective service workers).

Table 5.3 Construct and criterion validity of STAMP maths, reading, and writing task measures

MATHS	Item-rest Correlation	Categorical PCA loading	Mokken Loevinger H_i	CFA standardized Loadings	
Counting	0.42	0.49	1.00	1.02	
Add/subtract	0.50	0.57	0.91	0.97	
Multiply/divide	0.53	0.61	0.88	0.94	
Fractions	0.52	0.62	0.88	0.90	
Algebra (simple)	0.63	0.78	0.90		1.01
Algebra (advanced)	0.53	0.69	0.79		0.93
Geometry/trig	0.52	0.68	0.71		0.87
Statistics	0.54	0.69	0.72		0.89
Calculus	0.42	0.57	0.83		0.91
	Cronbach's α	**Pct. variance**	**Loevinger H**	**RMSEA**	
	0.81	0.63	0.83	0.06	0.06
Correlations					
Job education	0.42	0.41	0.41		
Own education	0.32	0.31	0.31		
READING	**Item-rest Correlation**	**Categorical PCA loading**	**Mokken Loevinger H_i**	**CFA standardized Loadings**	
Any reading	0.30	0.44	1.00	–	
Read one page	0.59	0.75	1.00	–	
Read five pages	0.62	0.77	0.64	0.82	
Trade/news articles	0.60	0.74	0.63	0.85	
Professional articles	0.62	0.75	0.66	0.89	
Books	0.60	0.75	0.61	0.80	
	Cronbach's α	**Pct. variance**	**Loevinger H**	**RMSEA**	
	0.80	0.75	0.68	0.04	
Correlations					
Job education	0.64	0.63	0.59		
Own education	0.51	0.50	0.46		

(continued)

Table 5.3 Continued

WRITING	Item-rest Correlation	Categorical PCA loading	Mokken Loevinger H_i
Any writing	0.30	0.49	1.00
One page	0.51	0.74	1.00
Five pages	0.51	0.75	0.83
Trade/news articles	0.38	0.64	0.70
Books/professional articles	0.32	0.56	0.79
	Cronbach's α	**Pct. variance**	**Loevinger H**
	0.64	0.65	0. 86
Correlations			
Job education	0.61	0.60	0.60
Own education	0.51	0.50	0.50

Reading and Writing

Unfortunately, reading is not as easy to measure on a single difficulty continuum and/or to equate to specific curricular concepts or years of schooling. Unlike mathematics, there are no standard categories available to researchers or survey respondents that capture text complexity in a satisfying way. Educational psychology often uses some combination of average word length and average sentence length. Despite dissatisfactions, no alternative has achieved similar currency (United States Department of Education, National Center for Education Statistics 2001). However, writing can be ranked clearly above reading because it requires skills needed to create as well as interpret text at a given level of complexity (e.g. logically organize and develop ideas) (ACT 2002, 19ff.).

STAMP opted to use a hierarchy of items based on text length at the low end and text complexity in the middle and upper ranges to reflect the varying approaches within education research (Table 5.3, middle panel). It was hoped the items for the middle and upper levels would be well ordered, relatively unambiguous for respondents, and cover the range of text typically used on the job in terms of both qualitative variety and level of difficulty. Reading matter not meant to be read as continuous running text, such as manuals and bills or invoices, were also part of this series but did not scale with the other items. Unfortunately, unexpected issues in question wording also reversed the expected relative frequencies of respondents saying they read work-related books compared to presumably easier reading material (e.g. articles in trade magazines or newspapers).

Nevertheless, the reading scale has reasonable construct validity. Cronbach's α (0.80), variance explained in a non-linear PCA (0.75), and Loevinger's H (0.68), and most measures of item discrimination are high (Table 5.3, middle panel). Large majorities answered the reading items in a strictly cumulative fashion without Guttman errors, whether the scale was constructed assuming books are less difficult than both kinds of articles (71%) or more difficult (65%). Dependencies amongst the items required a trimmed CFA model, which also had good fit (RMSEA = 0.04).

The reading items also have high criterion validity. The proportions of positive responses amongst the five broad occupational groups differed as expected (Handel 2016b). The various scales of reading complexity correlate even more highly with job education (~0.60) and personal education (~0.50) than the maths scales.[11]

The writing items parallel those for reading except that writing professional articles and writing books were collapsed into a single question because few positive responses were anticipated for either task, which was the case.

Whilst the first two columns suggest this scale does not perform as well as the reading scale, the Mokken scale results suggest it performs better (Table 5.3, bottom panel). Reflecting this fact, a very high proportion of respondents answered these items in strictly cumulative fashion (95%). The writing items discriminate amongst complexity levels better than the reading series; the proportion of positive responses drops much more sharply after the second level. Perhaps as a result, various CFA models did not fit well and are not reported.

The correlations between writing tasks and job and own education are similar to those for reading, indicating strong criterion validity (Table 5.3, bottom panel), and writing is more strongly associated with occupational group than reading (Handel 2016b).

Problem-solving

Discussions of the skills crisis often mention the need for problem-solving skills, but typically leave the concept undefined. Problem-solving usually seems to refer to the application of general reasoning ability and common sense to novel or non-routine situations, but sometimes seems stretched to cover non-cognitive dimensions, like willingness to take initiative in novel situations, that is, conscientiousness. The concept of problem-solving used here avoids motivational aspects, such as proactive work orientations.

STAMP operationalizes problem-solving as dealing with new or difficult situations that require thinking for a time about what to do next. Respondents reported how often

[11] The Mokken scale was constructed assuming that books represented a higher level of difficulty than news or journal articles. Cases with Guttmann errors were corrected by arbitrarily assigning values equal to the highest level of self-reported reading task used on the job, with the further restriction that in order for cases with Guttman errors to be coded as reading books the respondents also had to report reading at least one kind of article for their job. The criterion correlations for this scale are somewhat lower than those for the other reading scales. However, if the sample is restricted to cases without Guttman errors the correlations with job education (0.72) and personal education (0.59) would be about 0.10 higher than those using the more conventional scales.

they faced *easy problems*, defined as those that could be solved right away or after getting a little help from others, and *hard problems*, defined as requiring more time and a lot of work to solve. The response options for these items were vague quantifiers (*never, rarely, sometimes, often*), but respondents who dealt with hard problems also reported the number they face in an average week. As a group, the three items measure both frequency and complexity of problem-solving.

The two items dealing with hard problems have high reliability ($\alpha = 0.85$) and account for a large proportion of the variance in a non-linear PCA (0.85).[12] An alternative scale using the two items with vague quantifiers performs a bit better by some measures and worse by others. Correlations with job education (~0.45) and personal education (~0.36) are also strong. In this case, the most behaviourally specific item—number of hard problems per week—may have been difficult for respondents to answer. Nevertheless, the latter is a useful check on the comparability of the vague quantifiers across respondents.

Education, Experience, and Training

Three summary measures eliminate most of any remaining gaps in coverage left by the previous cognitive skill measures:

- level of education needed by the average person to perform the respondent's job (*job education*)
- years of prior experience in related jobs needed by someone with that level of education (*related job experience*)
- length of time needed to learn the job by someone with the required education and experience (*training time*).

All three use objective scales, operationalize important concepts in human capital and other theories, and have intuitive meanings for researchers, policy analysts, practitioners, and laypersons.

By design, job education and personal education are measured on the same scale so they can be compared directly. Mismatch is easily defined, avoiding the problems with the DOT's general educational development (GED) variable, which required judgement or strong estimation assumptions to impute an occupation's required education level to assess match quality with individuals' own education (Berg 1971; Halaby 1994).

A significant problem remaining is accounting for specific skills with measures that are general, parsimonious, and explicit despite the great number and qualitative diversity of occupation- and job-specific skills. Specific skills may appear incommensurate but the labour market rewards them mostly in a common currency and they are too large to be omitted, which would effectively render them the skill equivalent of dark matter.

[12] The number of hard problems was logged after adding a very small number to zero values; both variables were standardized before the scale was constructed.

STAMP uses required experience and training time to capture all non-academic, job-specific skills on an absolute scale. This appears to be the only way to measure the variety of job-specific skill demands on a common basis (Cully et al. 1999, 63).

Data on job education and training times in two waves of the Panel Study of Income Dynamics (1976, 1978) yield test–retest correlation for job stayers of 0.83 (n = 1,356) and 0.60 (n = 1,446), respectively.[13] The corresponding correlations for workers who changed employers and three-digit occupation and industry were 0.51 (n = 228) and 0.22 (n = 257), respectively (Handel 2000, 187f.). This indicates a reasonably high level of consistency for job stayers and a much lower level for job changers, as expected.

Results in Table 5.3 and elsewhere also show that almost all specific skill measures are strongly associated with job education and exceed correlations with personal education, demonstrating criterion, convergent, and divergent validity.

Interpersonal Skills

Job-related interpersonal skills are much less well theorized and well measured than cognitive skill requirements. Even at the most basic level, this domain is weakly conceptualized. This makes it difficult to assess content and construct validity, which require some level of consensus on the elements properly included in the domain.

The literature on interpersonal skills includes communication skills, courtesy and friendliness, service orientation, caring, empathy, counselling, selling skills, persuasion and negotiation, and, less commonly, assertiveness, aggressiveness, and even hostility, at least in adversarial dealings with organizational outsiders (e.g. police, bill collectors, lawyers, businessmen) (Hochschild 1983; US Department of Labor 1991; Hampson and Junor 2010). If dealing with co-workers as well as outsiders were considered, the list would also include leadership, cooperation, teamwork skills, and mentoring skills.

These elements seem qualitatively diverse, rather than different levels of a single trait. Many could be considered ancillary job characteristics, which, whilst often useful, are exercised at the discretion of the employee, rather than job or employer requirements. Often it is not easy to separate interpersonal skills from more purely attitudinal and motivational aspects of work orientations (Moss and Tilly 2001).

On a practical level, survey questions on interpersonal skills produce very high rates of endorsement and low variance if they do not distinguish relations with co-workers from dealings with organizational outsiders, such as customers and clients. Pre-tests show many people respond reflexively that working always requires a positive attitude, willingness to cooperate with others, and so on. Indeed, most managers feel pressure to engage in intensive impression management (Kanter 1977, Morrill 1995; see Riesman et al. 1950 on other-directedness).

To reduce yea-saying biases, STAMP asked a set of relatively specific questions that could apply to relations with organizational insiders or outsiders, as well as several general questions about extended interactions with outsiders only.

[13] 'Job stayers' are respondents with at least two years' job tenure in 1978 and whose reported three-digit occupation and industry were identical across the 1976 and 1978 waves.

The first group included whether jobs require giving people information, counselling, dealing with tense or hostile people, teaching or training, interviewing, and giving formal presentations lasting at least 15 minutes. The questions dealing with outsiders asked if the jobs required contact with customers or the public, frequency of contacts lasting more than 15 minutes, and self-rated importance of such contact for their jobs. Whilst these items attempt to be relatively concrete, substantial room for individual interpretation and yea-saying biases undoubtedly remain.

Caring labour and selling skills were omitted because pre-tests suggested they were relevant only for jobs that could be identified easily from the occupational title. The more generic negotiating, persuading, and influencing skills had the reverse problem. Rather than applying too narrowly, they seemed too open to broad agreement.

Despite these complexities, a single scale showed reasonable levels of overall consistency ($\alpha = 0.72$, variance explained = 0.68, RMSEA = 0.04), and all individual items loaded on the latent construct (Table 5.4).

As expected, a number of items have relatively high levels of endorsement. However, the more specific items on working with the public yield a stronger gradient across occupations in the expected manner.[14] Correlations with education are comparable to those for cognitive skills, though it is not clear that education is appropriate for establishing the criterion validity of interpersonal skills (Table 5.4).

Physical Demands

Physical job requirements are bodily activities usually involving materials, tools, and equipment, corresponding to the final category of the DOT's classification of job tasks as involving data, people, and things.

Simple physical tasks include gross physical exertion (e.g. carrying heavy loads), elementary movements (e.g. sorting mail), use of simple tools or equipment, and machine tending. These are the kinds of tasks assumed to be common in deskilling theory and vanishing rapidly by post-industrial theory.

More complex physical tasks require more training, experience, and background knowledge regarding the properties of physical materials, mechanical processes, and natural laws. Deskilling theory predicts strong declines, but other theories give them less prominence. Unfortunately, specific craft skills are difficult to capture parsimoniously, so this domain is sparser than desirable.

Items on standing and lifting (simple physical tasks) follow principles of explicit scaling using objective yardsticks (bottom panel, Table 5.4). The question on hand-eye coordination and arm steadiness is the only measure of more skilled physical demands beyond whether required education is vocational. A final item uses a subjective rating scale for a more global report of physical demands to capture otherwise unmeasured aspects of this domain.

[14] For example, on an 11-point scale for importance of working with customers, clients, and the public, the mean is 8.8 for upper white-collar workers, 8.3 for lower white-collar workers, 6.9 for service workers, 5.0 for upper blue-collar workers, and 4.2 for lower blue-collar workers.

Table 5.4 Construct and criterion validity of STAMP interpersonal and physical task measures

INTERPERSONAL	Item–rest Correlation	Categorical PCA loading	CFA standard Loading
Information	0.30	0.44	0.81
Counselling	0.43	0.54	0.66
Tense situations	0.34	0.44	0.40
Teach/train	0.37	0.50	0.66
Interview	0.38	0.53	0.74
Presentations	0.43	0.57	0.75
Public contact[a]	0.54	0.80	0.44
Self-rated level[b]	0.54	0.80	0.46
	Cronbach's α	**Pct. variance**	**RMSEA**
	0.72	0.68	0.04
Correlations			
Job education	0.48	0.48	
Own education	0.39	0.40	

PHYSICAL	Item–rest Correlation	Categorical PCA loading	CFA standard Loading
Stand 2 hours	0.56	0.76	0.82
Lift 50 lb	0.57	0.77	0.85
Coordination	0.53	0.73	0.74
Physical demands[c]	0.72	0.87	0.84
	Cronbach's α	**Pct. variance**	**RMSEA**
	0.79	0.80	0.00
Correlations			
Job education	−0.33	−0.34	
Own education	−0.34	−0.34	

Note: The CFA model for interpersonal skills allows 'tense situations' to correlate with 'counselling' and frequency of contact with the public ('public contact'), and allows 'public contact' to correlate with importance of working well with the public ('self-rated level').

a. Six-point scale measuring frequency of contact with people other than co-workers, such as customers, clients, students, or the public (0 = none, 5 = spend at least 15 minutes speaking to non-co-worker more than once a day).

b. Self-rated importance of working well with customers, clients, students, or the public on respondent's job (0 = not important, 11 = extremely important).

c. Self-rated physical demands of job (0 = not all physically demanding, 10 = extremely physically demanding).

Scales using the four items have strong construct validity ($\alpha = 0.79$, variance explained = 0.80, RMSEA = 0.00). The scales correlate negatively with job and personal education (−0.34), as expected. Blue-collar and service workers are much more likely to report their jobs involve physical work. Skilled blue-collar workers are the most likely to say their work requires good eye–hand coordination or a steady hand (Handel 2016b).

Technology

Theories of skill change invariably implicate technology. Yet despite several attempts to develop standardized measures using both nominal classifications and ordinal scales, none has achieved widespread acceptance. Despite its centrality to research on skill and work roles, technology and its various dimensions remain weakly conceptualized.

The concept 'computer literacy', for example, has surprisingly little precise meaning despite its currency amongst both professionals and the general public. Test-makers have failed to develop reliable measures of computer task complexity or computer literacy (ACT 2002; Statistics Canada 2005, 23).

STAMP used 50 questions on computers, automation, and non-computer technology to capture the prevalence of common and important workplace technologies and the levels of skill they require.

Information Technology

Four approaches were used to measure computer task complexity:

- a count of 18 specific software applications and another variable for frequency of computer use;
- five items for higher-level computer tasks (e.g. scientific/engineering calculations) and one for highly routine activity (data entry), to address both post-industrial and deskilling concerns;
- length of computer learning times, a natural metric for skill in human capital theory. Anticipating respondent difficulty recalling time required for learning general computer skills, STAMP asked respondents using job-specific software or learning new programmes in the previous three years how long they needed to learn the most complex such programme; and
- a measure of overall computer task complexity using a subjective rating scale varying from 'very basic' (0) to 'very complex' (10).

Finally, to measure possible computer skill deficits, STAMP asked respondents if they had all the computer skills they needed for their current job and if lack of computer skills had affected their chances of employment, promotion, or pay raise.

A scale combining (1) number of programmes and (4) self-rated complexity of computer tasks has reasonable construct validity (Cronbach's $\alpha = 0.71$, PCA variance explained = 0.77) (Table 5.5). The scale is more highly correlated with job educational requirements (0.43) than own education (0.31), indicating criterion validity. These

Table 5.5 Construct and criterion validity of STAMP computer technology and EI measures

COMPUTERS	Item-scale[b] Correlation	PCA loading	
Applications (#)	0.88	0.71	
Skill level[a]	0.88	0.71	
	Cronbach's α	**Pct. variance**	
	0.71	0.77	
Correlations			
Job education	0.43 (0.56)	0.44 (0.56)	
Own education	0.31 (0.45)	0.32 (0.46)	
EI[c]	**Item-scale Correlation**	**Categorical PCA loading**	**CFA standard Loading**
Job assignment	0.38	0.64	0.59
Task scheduling	0.44	0.73	0.67
Worker scheduling	0.36	0.58	0.54
Changing methods	0.42	0.69	0.60
New equipment	0.40	0.60	0.51
Selecting leader	0.19	0.20	0.26
Quality	0.42	0.52	0.65
Cost, productivity	0.43	0.53	0.65
Cross-communicate	0.31	0.42	0.48
Performance review	0.19	0.24	0.29
	Cronbach's α	**Pct. variance**	**RMSEA**
	0.69	0.67	0.09
Correlations			
Decision-making	0.16		
Autonomy scale	0.14		
Job education	0.10		
Own education	0.13		

Note: Figures in top panel based on computer users only, except those in parentheses, which are based on all respondents.

a. Self-rated complexity of computer skills used on job (0 = very basic, 10 = very complex).

b. Correlations of items with the total scale are presented rather than item–rest correlations because the latter are identical across rows and equal the correlation between the two items (0.55).

c. Statistics based on a sub-sample belonging to teams. Employees in self-reported management positions were ineligible for these items.

calculations are also conservative because they use only the sub-sample of computer users. Using the full sample of users and non-users increases α (0.89) and the correlations with job education (0.56) and own education (0.45) (not shown).

There are clear differences across occupational groups. Upper white-collar workers use 6 applications on average whilst service workers use fewer than 1.5. Much larger proportions of white-collar workers use special software (~60%) compared to blue-collar and service workers (~25%). Upper white-collar workers were the most likely to perform higher-level tasks, such as using spreadsheet formulas, and to have learnt new software in the previous three years (Handel 2016b).

By contrast, the two items on computer skill deficits did not scale with the other items or with one another (α = 0.30). Their correlations with both job and own education are less than 0.10 (not shown).

Non-computer Technology

Technology associated with blue-collar jobs such as heavy machinery and industrial equipment has received even less attention than computers in employee surveys.

Respondents who use heavy machinery other than vehicles were asked 16 questions that addressed sociologists' concerns with deskilling (e.g. machine tending, assembly-line work), traditional craft skills (e.g. machine set-up, maintenance, repair), and newer, high-technology skills (e.g. programmable automation).

Those using equipment introduced in the past three years also reported the time needed to learn the most complex such equipment, providing numerical estimates of both the skill requirements of new technology and the rate of technological change in blue-collar jobs.

All respondents rated the level of mechanical knowledge needed for their jobs (0–10 scale) and whether they required 'a good knowledge of electronics, such as understanding transistors or circuits' (1 = yes).

Finally, to derive estimates of technological displacement, respondents who lost jobs in the previous three years were asked if this was because a machine or computer had replaced them.

Consistent with expectation, the groups most likely to use heavy machinery and industrial equipment are upper blue-collar (65%) and lower blue-collar (46%) workers, whilst the other three occupational groups have very low incidence rates (~10%). The ratings for required level of mechanical knowledge exhibit a similar pattern (Handel 2016b).

Management Practices

Management practices are the third main leg of recent skill debates. This includes EI practices, other aspects of autonomy and control in the workplace, and various aspects of job downgrading.

EI

EI is widely argued to be a significant driver of skill upgrading. Its major elements are relatively well defined: job rotation/cross-training, formal quality programmes, self-directed teams, and supportive training and compensation (e.g. pay for skill, gain-sharing, performance-based pay). STAMP covers all of these dimensions but this section focuses on teams.

To move away from very general questions regarding teams and quality programmes, which may elicit false positive responses (Cully et al. 1999, 42ff.), the questions on team membership include frequency of team meetings and ten questions on specific areas of team authority and responsibilities corresponding to the concept of a self-directed team used in current research (Appelbaum et al. 2000).

The ten team authority items have adequate construct validity using only the subsample of team members for conservative tests ($\alpha = 0.69$, variance explained = 0.67, RMSEA = 0.09) (Table 5.5), but do not form a consistent hierarchy according to a Mokken analysis (not shown).

Somewhat unexpectedly, there is no strong association between the EI measures and occupational group (Handel 2016b). This may reflect relatively uniform diffusion or problems with the questions; current knowledge of EI practices is still too limited to draw strong conclusions. Despite trying to achieve precision, the EI items probably contain significant noise, consistent with other research (Gerhart et al. 2000).

Autonomy, Closeness of Supervision, and Authority

Autonomy–control, authority, and closeness of supervision are related to but distinct from EI and skills.

Autonomy refers to discretion and the ability to work independently, as opposed to working under external control. Psychologists distinguish between employees who can set goals and basic rules, and those who can decide how to meet goals set by others within an existing structure. The former is control over a work situation, or strategic autonomy, and the latter control within a work situation, or operational autonomy (de Jonge 1995, 25f.). Braverman's criticism (1974, 35ff.) of EI practices as a weak substitute for craft autonomy relies implicitly on a similar distinction.

Most measures focus on operational autonomy, such as control over hours of work and break times, the sequence and pacing of job tasks, closeness of supervision, restrictiveness of rules, and task routinization. In contrast, strategic autonomy includes authority to make decisions, direct subordinates, and allocate resources.[15]

There is no objective standard for many of these concepts, and jobs are so diverse that measures of control over work methods are unlikely to be both concrete and widely applicable. Overly general items may be susceptible to self-enhancing biases (Wright 1997; Cully et al. 1999; Handel 2000; Gallie et al. 2004).

STAMP contains four items covering both operational and strategic autonomy: (1) freedom from prescriptive rules and supervisor's instructions, (2) task repetitiveness, (3) closeness of supervision, and (4) policy-making authority.

Construct validity is mixed. Cronbach's α is quite low (0.49), albeit similar to some other autonomy scales (Kalleberg and Lincoln 1988, S136), but the variance explained

15 Examples are Kohn and Schooler (1983, 22ff.); Wright (1985, 316); Kalleberg and Lincoln (1988); de Jonge (1995, 65); Cully et al. (1999, 141f.); Fields (2002).

by the first component of a non-linear PCA is respectable (0.64) and the item loadings are high.

Criterion validity is also mixed. Upper white-collar workers are much more likely to participate in policy-making decisions (44%) than lower white-collar workers, upper blue-collar workers (~20%), and blue-collar and service workers (~15%). Occupational differences for the other three autonomy items are much narrower, but the additive scale using all four items discriminates amongst occupations reasonably well (Handel 2016b).

The scale correlates relatively well with job education (0.43), own education (0.34), and management status (0.39), but not as well with other criteria, such as problem- solving (0.25) and job satisfaction (0.29). The scale's correlation with the employee involvement scale (0.15) is even lower, but may reflect the weaknesses of the EI scale. The evidence suggests it is more reasonable to consider these variables an index rather than a scale. Indeed, the definition of autonomy suggests a variety of concepts rather than a unidimensional trait.

Job Downgrading

Though skill upgrading dominates the discourse on job quality, one cannot ignore the opposing position that explains inequality trends on the basis of worsening job quality (Bluestone and Harrison 1988). If skills are claimed to be more or less important than other dimensions of work, the latter require measurement.

A few standard surveys include questions on non-standard employment arrangements and recent job loss. STAMP also includes factual questions on downsizing, transfer of work outside the establishment (outsourcing), and pay and benefit cuts. Internal labour markets and work intensity are trickier to operationalize as explicit scales but survey questions on personal promotion prospects, organizational promotion policies, and workload, pace, and stress can help address questions regarding the importance of job downgrading versus upskilling.

Further Validity Measures

All scales were also converted to occupational means to compare them with measures from the DOT and O*NET, occupational prestige and SEI scores (Nakao and Treas 1994; Hauser and Warren 1997), and occupational wages (Current Population Survey).

Correlations between STAMP column variables and corresponding DOT and O*NET variables in Tables 5.6 and 5.7 measure the STAMP constructs' convergent validity (in bold), whilst correlations with non-parallel DOT and O*NET variables measure their divergent validity. Correlations between STAMP scales and outcomes like occupational prestige, SEI, and wages measure criterion validity. The final columns of the tables present correlations between DOT and O*NET measures and occupational wages, which can be compared to the STAMP wage correlations in the bottom row of each panel.

STAMP measures have generally strong convergent validity. More than three-quarters of the correlations with parallel DOT and O*NET measures are between 0.65 and 0.92 (mean = 0.72; median = 0.75). Most are also larger than correlations with non-parallel measures in the same column, demonstrating divergent validity.

Table 5.6 Occupation-level correlations between STAMP and alternative measures: skills, autonomy, and authority

	Education	Experience	Training	Maths	Verbal	Problem	(ln) Wage
DOT							
GED	**0.89**	0.46	0.66	0.65	0.90	0.79	0.79
SVP	0.79	**0.65**	**0.70**	0.69	0.83	0.78	0.81
Numerical	0.67	0.54	0.47	**0.64**	0.69	0.66	0.71
Verbal	0.84	0.46	0.57	0.57	**0.88**	0.71	0.74
Data	0.74	0.62	0.61	0.67	0.80	**0.74**	0.76
O*NET							
Education	**0.92**	0.42	0.63	0.54	0.86	0.67	0.77
Experience	0.59	**0.78**	0.56	0.57	0.66	0.66	0.77
Training	0.49	0.52	**0.63**	0.58	0.52	0.57	0.61
OJT	0.52	0.57	**0.66**	0.64	0.54	0.61	0.70
Maths	0.60	0.59	0.51	**0.73**	0.61	0.63	0.72
Verbal	0.86	0.50	0.60	0.55	**0.91**	0.76	0.78
Cognitive	0.87	0.63	0.71	0.64	0.89	**0.82**	0.89
Other							
Occ. prestige	0.88	0.39	0.67	0.61	0.86	0.76	0.79
SEI	0.90	0.37	0.70	0.62	0.85	0.73	0.83
(ln) Wage	0.81	0.71	0.76	0.69	0.83	0.78	

	Index	Autonomy	Decision	Supervision	Repetitive		(ln) Wage
DOT							
DCP	**0.76**	0.46	**0.78**	**−0.50**	−0.53		0.64
REPCON	−0.51	−0.31	−0.38	0.45	**0.42**		−0.53
O*NET							
Autonomy	**0.75**	**0.50**	0.64	−0.49	−0.63		0.69
Management	**0.75**	0.38	**0.75**	**−0.51**	−0.62		0.81
Repetitive	−0.57	−0.32	−0.51	0.37	**0.53**		−0.60
Other							
Occ. prestige	0.56	0.26	0.40	−0.56	−0.53		
SEI	0.58	0.27	0.40	−0.60	−0.55		
(ln) Wage	0.74	0.41	0.61	−0.54	−0.70		

Note: Correlations weighted by sample size within STAMP occupations. Correlations indicating level of convergent validity in bold. The STAMP variable 'Index' is an additive composite of autonomy, decision making, task repetitiveness, and closeness of supervision.

(*continued*)

Table 5.6 Continued

Key for DOT, O*NET, and other variables:

GED = general educational development

SVP = specific vocational preparation

Numerical = numerical aptitude quantile

Verbal = verbal aptitude quantile

Data = workers' relationship to data

Education = required education

Experience = length of related work experience in other jobs

Training = length of employer-provided classroom study

OJT = on-the-job training

Cognitive = general cognitive ability scale combining variables for (1) analytical thinking; (2) critical thinking; (3) complex problem-solving; (4) active learning; (5) analysing data or information; (6) processing information; (7) thinking creatively; (8) updating and using relevant knowledge; (9) deductive reasoning; (10) inductive reasoning; (11) fluency of ideas; and (12) category flexibility (α=0.97)

Maths = scale combining variables for (1) mathematics skills; (2) mathematics knowledge; (3) mathematical reasoning; and (4) number facility (α = 0.92)

Verbal = scale combining variables for (1) reading comprehension; (2) writing skills; (3) writing comprehension; (4) writing ability; (5) knowledge English language rules (spelling, grammar, composition); and (6) frequency of using written letters and memos (α = 0.95)

DCP = temperament suitable to accept responsibility to direct, control, or plan an activity

REPCON = temperament suitable to perform repetitive work or continuously perform same, fixed task

Management = scale combining variables for (1) judgement and decision-making; (2) management of financial resources; (3) management of human resources; (4) knowledge of business administration and management; (5) decision-making and problem-solving; (6) developing objectives and strategies; (7) coaching and developing others; and (8) guiding, directing, and motivating subordinates (α = 0.93)

Autonomy = scale combining variables for (1) freedom to make decisions without supervision and (2) freedom to determine tasks, priorities, or goals (α = 0.89)

Repetitive = time spent making repetitive motions

Occ. Prestige = occupational prestige scores

SEI = socioeconomic index scores

ln (wage) = log mean occupational hourly wages (October 2004–January 2006)

Most STAMP measures also have high predictive criterion validity. Cognitive scales correlate strongly with occupational prestige, SEI, and wages (Table 5.6, top panel). Correlations for autonomy, decision-making, repetitiveness, and closeness of supervision are more mixed but generally high (Table 5.6, bottom panel), as are correlations for interpersonal skills and physical job demands (Table 5.7).

Table 5.7 Occupation-level correlations between STAMP and alternative measures: interpersonal and physical requirements

	Interpersonal	Presentation	Freq	Level		(ln) Wage
DOT						
People	**0.75**	0.62	**0.69**	**0.69**		0.38
O*NET						
People	**0.86**	0.76	0.67	0.69		0.62
Speaking	0.71	**0.79**	0.51	0.56		0.62
Customer/public	0.73	0.47	**0.76**	**0.73**		0.37
Other						
Occ. prestige	0.65	0.71	0.47	0.49		
SEI	0.65	0.74	0.51	0.52		
(ln) Wage	0.63	0.77	0.43	0.42		
	Physical	**Stand**	**Lift**	**Coord**	**Demands**	**(ln) Wage**
DOT						
Dexterity	0.34	0.21	0.32	**0.44**	0.30	−0.28
Effort	**0.83**	**0.62**	**0.78**	0.78	**0.83**	−0.52
O*NET						
Craft skills	0.33	0.25	0.36	0.32	0.29	0.06
Fine motor	0.73	0.51	0.71	**0.72**	0.70	−0.32
Gross physical	**0.91**	**0.84**	**0.79**	0.79	**0.87**	−0.51
Other						
Occ. prestige	−0.42	−0.26	−0.49	−0.32	−0.45	
SEI	−0.47	−0.27	−0.54	−0.39	−0.52	
(ln) Wage	−0.50	−0.41	−0.45	−0.43	−0.53	

Note: Correlations weighted by sample size within STAMP occupations. Correlations indicating level of convergent validity in bold. In the top panel, 'Interpersonal' is the STAMP scale for interpersonal job requirements from Table 5.3. 'Freq' is frequency of contact with people other than co-workers, such as customers and clients. 'Level' is self-rated importance of working well with people other than co-workers. In the bottom panel, 'Physical' is a scale composed of stand, lift, eye–hand coordination, and demands, described in Table 5.3.

(continued)

Table 5.7 Continued

Key for DOT, O*NET, and other variables:

People (DOT): Scale combining (1) workers' relationship to people (People) and (2) temperament for dealing with people beyond giving and receiving instructions (DEPL) ($\alpha = 0.74$)

People (O*NET): Scale combining variables for (1) persuasion; (2) negotiation; (3) speaking skills; (4) instructing skills; (5) service orientation; (6) dealing with angry people; (7) dealing with physically aggressive people; (8) frequency of conflict situations; (9) dealing with external customers or public; (10) frequency of face-to-face discussions; (11) frequency of public speaking; (12) resolving conflicts and negotiating with others; (13) communicating with persons outside organization; (14) performing for or working directly with the public; (15) training and teaching others; (16) interpreting the meaning of information for others; (17) customer and personal service knowledge; (18) education and training knowledge; (19) social orientation; (20) and social perceptiveness ($\alpha = 0.94$)

Speak: Subscale of O*NET people scale, combining variables for (1) speaking skills and (2) frequency of public speaking ($\alpha = 0.70$)

Customer/public: Subscale of O*NET people scale, combining variables for (1) service orientation; (2) dealing with external customers or public and (3) customer and personal service knowledge ($\alpha = 0.86$)

Dexterity: Scale combining (1) workers' relationship to things; (2) finger dexterity; (3) manual dexterity; and (4) motor coordination ($\alpha = 0.85$)

Effort: Scale combining variables for (1) strength, and the sum of responses to the dichotomous variables; (2) climb; (3) stoop; and (4) reach ($\alpha = 0.81$)

Craft skills: Scale combining variables for (1) controlling machines and processes; (2) repairing and maintaining mechanical equipment; (3) repairing and maintaining electronic equipment; (4) equipment maintenance; (5) troubleshooting operating errors; (6) repairing machines; and (7) installing equipment, machines, and wiring ($\alpha = 0.95$)

Fine motor: Scale combining variables for (1) finger dexterity; (2) manual dexterity; (3) arm-hand steadiness; (4) multi-limb coordination; (5) rate control (ability to time movements); (6) operating vehicles, mechanized devices, or equipment; and (7) time spent using hands to handle, control, or feel objects, tools, or controls (α=0.94)

Gross physical: Scale combining variables for (1) handling and moving objects; (2) general physical activities; (3) static strength; (4) dynamic strength; (5) trunk strength; (6) stamina; and time spent (7) sitting; (8) standing; (9) walking; (10) twisting body; (11) kneeling, crouching, stooping, or crawling ($\alpha = 0.98$)

Occ. Prestige = occupational prestige scores

SEI = socioeconomic index scores

ln (wage) = log mean occupational hourly wages (October 2004–January 2006)

Conclusion

Understanding job skill requirements and possible drivers such as new technology and management practices require a clear conceptual framework and direct measures. The various debates that hinge on assumptions regarding skill levels and trends will always remain constrained by speculation in the absence of surveys that ask employees about a wide range of specific skills in concrete detail.

Explicit scaling addresses this problem with objective, behaviourally concrete questions and response options with natural units, rather than rating scales and vague quantifiers. Items and scales using this approach have high validity and reliability and are easily interpreted. By measuring job requirements in ways that can be compared to worker traits, they also facilitate assessment of the congruence or mismatch between people and jobs.

References

ACT (2002) *WorkKeys® Test Descriptions*, Iowa City, IA: ACT.

Anastasi, A. (1982) *Psychological Testing*, New York: Macmillan.

Appelbaum, E., Bailey, T., Berg, P., and A. L. Kalleberg (2000) *Manufacturing Advantage*, Ithaca, NY: ILR Press.

Attewell, P. (1987) 'The Deskilling Controversy', *Work and Occupations*, 14: 323–346.

Attewell, Paul (1990) 'What is Skill?', *Work and Occupations*, 17: 422–447.

Autor, D. H. and Handel, M. J. (2009) 'Putting Tasks to the Test: Human Capital, Job Tasks and Wages'. National Bureau of Economic Research Working Paper #15116, Cambridge, MA.

Autor, D. H., Katz, L. F., and Krueger. A. B. (1998) 'Computing Inequality: Have Computers Changed the Labor Market?', *Quarterly Journal of Economics*, 113: 1169–1213.

Autor, D. H., Levy, F., and Murnane, R. J. (2002) 'Upstairs, Downstairs: Computers and Skills on Two Floors of a Large Bank', *Industrial and Labor Relations Review*, 55: 432–447.

Autor, D. H., Levy, F., and Murnane, R. J. (2003) 'The Skill Content of Recent Technological Change: An Empirical Exploration', *Quarterly Journal of Economics*, 118: 1279–1334.

Bell, D. (1976) *The Coming of Post-Industrial Society*, New York: Basic Books.

Berg, I. (1971) *Education and Jobs*, Boston: Beacon Press.

Bluestone, B. and Harrison, B. (1982) *Deindustrialization of America*, New York: Basic Books.

Borghans, L., Green, F., and Mayhew, K. (2001) 'Skills Measurement and Economic Analysis: An Introduction', *Oxford Economic Papers*, 53: 375–384.

Borghans, L. and ter Weel, B. (2004) 'Are Computer Skills the New Basic Skills? The Returns to Computer, Writing and Math Skills in Britain', *Labour Economics*, 11: 85–98.

Bresnahan, T. F., Brynjolfsson, E., and Hitt, L. M. (2002) 'Information Technology, Workplace Organization, and the Demand for Skilled Labor: Firm-Level Evidence', *Quarterly Journal of Economics*, 17: 339–376.

Brotheridge, C.M. and Lee, R.T. (2003) 'Development and Validation of the Emotional Labour Scale', *Journal of Occupational and Organizational Psychology*, 76: 365–379.

Cain, P. S. and Treiman, D. J. (1981) 'The Dictionary of Occupational Titles as a Source of Occupational Data', *American Sociological Review*, 46: 253–278.

Cully, M., Woodland, S., and O'Reilly, A., et al. (1999) *Britain at Work*, New York: Routledge.

De Jonge, Jan (1995) 'Job Autonomy, Well-Being, and Health: A Study among Dutch Health Care Workers'. PhD thesis, Rijksuniveriteit Limburg, Maastricht, Netherlands.

Dickerson, A. and Green, F. (2004) 'The Growth and Valuation of Computing and Other Generic Skills', *Oxford Economic Papers*, 56: 371–406.

England, P.(2005) 'Emerging Theories of Carework', *Annual Review of Sociology*, 31: 381–399.

Fernandez, R. M. (2001) 'Skill-Biased Technological Change and Wage Inequality: Evidence from a Plant Retooling', *American Journal of Sociology*, 107: 273–320.

Fields, D. L. (2002) *Taking the Measure of Work*, Thousand Oaks, CA: SAGE.

Form, W. (1987) 'On the Degradation of Skills', *Annual Review of Sociology*, 13: 29–47.

Gallie, D., Felstead, A., and Green, F. (2004) 'Changing Patterns of Task Discretion in Britain', *Work, Employment, and Society*, 18: 243–266.

Gerhart, B., Wright, Patrick, M., and McMahan, G. C. (2000) 'Measurement Error in Research on the Human Resources and Firm Performance Relationship: Further Evidence and Analysis', *Personnel Psychology*, 53: 855–872.

Glomb, T. M., Kammeyer-Mueller, J. D., and Rotundo, M. (2004) 'Emotional Labor Demands and Compensating Wage Differentials', *Journal of Applied Psychology*, 89: 700–714.

Graham, L. (1993) 'Inside a Japanese Transplant: A Critical Perspective', *Work and Occupations*, 20: 147–173.

Green, F. (2006) *Demanding Work*, Princeton: Princeton University Press.

Haahr, J. H., Shapiro, H., Sørensen, S., et al. (2004) 'Defining a Strategy for the Direct Assessment of Skills', Danish Technological Institute, Rand and SKOPE.

Halaby, C. N. (1994) 'Overeducation and Skill Mismatch' *Sociology of Education*, 67: 47–59.

Hampson, I. and Junor, A. (2010) 'Putting the Process Back in: Rethinking Service Sector Skill', *Work, Employment and Society*, 24: 526–545.

Handel, M. J. (2000) 'Models of Economic Organization and the New Inequality in the United States'. PhD thesis, Sociology Department, Harvard University.

Handel, M. J. (2003a) 'Implications of Information Technology for Employment, Skills, and Wages: A Review of Recent Research', Arlington, VA: SRI International. http://www.sri.com/policy/csted/reports/sandt/it/.

Handel, M. J. (2003b) 'Skills Mismatch in the Labor Market', *Annual Review of Sociology*, 29: 135–165.

Handel, M. J. (2004) 'Implications of Information Technology for Employment, Skills, and Wages: Findings from Sectoral and Case Study Research'. Arlington, VA: SRI International. http://www.sri.com/policy/csted/reports/sandt/it/.

Handel, M. J. (2016a) 'O*NET: Strengths and Limitations', *Journal of Labour Market Research*, 49: 157–176.

Handel, M. J. (2016b) 'What Do People Do at Work? A Profile of U.S. Jobs from the Survey of Workplace Skills, Technology, and Management Practices (STAMP)', *Journal of Labour Market Research*, 49: 177–197.

Handel, M. J. and Gittleman, M.(2004) 'Is There a Wage Payoff to Innovative Work Practices?', *Industrial Relations*, 43: 67–97.

Harrison, B. (1994) *Lean and Mean*, New York: Basic Books.

Harrison, B. and Bluestone, B. (1988) *The Great U-Turn: Corporate Restructuring and the Polarizing of America*, New York: Basic Books.

Hauser, R. M. and J. R. Warren (1997) 'Socioeconomic Indexes for Occupations: A Review, Update, and Critique', *Sociological Methodology*, 27: 177–298.

HM Treasury (2006) 'Prosperity for All in the Global Economy: World Class Skills', *Leitch Review of Skills Final Report*, London: HM Stationery Office.
Hochschild, A. R. (1983) *The Managed Heart*, Berkeley, CA: University of California Press.
Holzer, H. J. (1996) *What Employers Want*, New York: Russell Sage.
Howell, D. R. and Wolff, E. N. (1991) 'Trends in the Growth and Distribution of Skills in the U.S. Workplace, 1960–1985', Industrial *and Labor Relations Review*, 44: 486–502.
Kalleberg, A. L. and Lincoln, J. R. (1988) 'The Structure of Earnings Inequality in the United States and Japan', *American Journal of Sociology*, 94: S121–S153.
Kanter, R. M. (1977) *Men and* Women *of the Corporation*, New York: Basic Books.
Karasek, R. A. Jr (1979) 'Job Demands, Job Decision Latitude, and Mental Strain: Implications for Job Redesign', *Administrative Science Quarterly*, 24: 285–308.
Katz, L. F. and Murphy, K. M. (1992) 'Changes in Relative Wages, 1963–1987: Supply and Demand Factors', Quarterly *Journal of Economics*, 107: 35–78.
Keep, E. and Mayhew, K. (1996) 'Evaluating the Assumptions that Underlie Training Policy', A. L. Booth and D. J. Snower (eds), *Acquiring Skills*, Cambridge: Cambridge University Press: 305–334.
Kohn, M. L. and Schooler, C. (1983) *Work and Personality*, Norwood, NJ: Ablex.
Krahn, H. and Lowe, G. S. (1998) *Literacy Utilization in Canadian Workplaces*, Ottawa: Statistics Canada.
Krueger, A. B. (1993) 'How Computers Have Changed the Wage Structure: Evidence from Microdata, 1984–1989', *Quarterly Journal of Economics*, 108: 33–61.
Leidner, R. (1993) *Fast Food, Fast Talk*, Berkeley: University of California Press.
McIntosh, S. and Steedman, H. (2000) 'Low Skills: A Problem for Europe', Final Report to DGXII of the European Commission on the NEWSKILLS Programme of Research, Centre for Economic Performance. London School of Economics and Political Science.
Meulman, J. J., Van der Kooij, A. J., and Heiser, W. J. (2004) 'Principal Components Analysis with Nonlinear Optimal Scaling Transformations for Ordinal and Nominal Data', in D. W. Kaplan (ed.), *Handbook of Quantitative Methods in the Social Sciences*, Newbury Park, CA: Sage Publications: 49–70.
Miller, A. R., Treiman, D. J., Cain, Pamela, S., et al. (1980), *Work, Jobs, and Occupations: A Critical Review of the Dictionary of Occupational Titles*, Washington, DC: National Academy Press.
Mishel, L. and Bernstein, J. (1998) 'Technology and the Wage Structure: Has Technology's Impact Accelerated Since the 1970s?', *Research in Labor Economics*, 17: 305–355.
Morrill, C. (1995) *The Executive Way*, Chicago: University of Chicago Press.
Moss, P. I. and Tilly, C. (2001) *Stories Employers Tell*, New York: Russell Sage.
Murnane, R. J. and L.F, Fran (1996) *Teaching the New Basic Skills*, New York: Free Press.
Nakao, K. and Treas, J. (1994) 'Updating Occupational Prestige and Socioeconomic Scores: How the New Measures Measure Up', *Sociological Methodology*, 24: 1–72.
Payne, J. (1999) 'All Things to All People: Changing Perceptions of "Skill" Among Britain's Policy Makers Since the 1950s and Their Implications', SKOPE Research Paper No. 1, Oxford University.
Peterson, N. G., Mumford, M. D., Borman, W. C., Jeanneret, P.R., and Fleishman, E. A. (eds) (1999) *An Occupational Information System for the 21st Century: The Development of O*NET*, Washington, DC: American Psychological Association.

Peterson, N. G., Mumford, M. D., Borman, W. C., and Jeanneret, P. R. (2001) 'Understanding Work Using the Occupational Information Network (O*NET): Implications for Practice and Research', *Personnel Psychology*, 54: 451–492.

Piore, M. J. and Sabel, C. (1984) *The Second Industrial Divide*, New York: Basic Books.

Quinn, R. P. and Staines, G. L. (1979) *The 1977 Quality of Employment Survey*, Ann Arbor: University of Michigan, Institute for Social Research, Survey Research Center.

Riesman, D., Glazer, N., and Denny, R. (1950) *The Lonely Crowd*, New Haven: Yale University Press.

Reich, R. (1991) *The Work of Nations*, New York: A. A. Knopf.

Rosenbaum, J. and Binder, A. (1997) 'Do Employers Really Need More Educated Youth?', *Sociology of Education*, 70: 68–85.

Sijtsma, K. and Molenaar, I. W. (2002) *Introduction to Nonparametric Item Response Theory*, Thousand Oaks, CA: Sage.

Spenner, K. I. (1979) 'Temporal Changes in Work Content', *American Sociological Review*, 44: 968–975.

Spenner, K. I. (1983) 'Deciphering Prometheus: Temporal Change in the Skill Level of Work', *American Sociological Review*, 48: 824–837.

Spenner, K. I. (1990) 'Skill: Meanings, Methods, and Measures', *Work and Occupations*, 17: 399–421.

Spitz-Oener, A. (2006) 'Technical Change, Job Tasks, and Rising Educational Demands: Looking Outside the Wage Structure', *Journal of Labor Economics*, 24: 235–270.

Statistics Canada (2005) 'Measuring Adult Literacy and Life Skills: New Frameworks for Assessment', Ottawa: Statistics Canada.

Steinberg, R. J. and Figart, D. M. (1999) 'Emotional Demands at Work: A Job Content Analysis', *ANNALS of the American Academy of Political and Social Science*, 561: 177–191.

US Department of Education, National Center for Education Statistics by S. White, S. and Clement, J. (2001), 'Assessing the Lexile Framework: Results of a Panel Meeting', NCES 2001–2008, Washington DC.

US Department of Labor. Employment and Training Administration (1991) *The Revised Handbook for Analyzing Jobs*, Washington, DC: GPO.

US Department of Labor. Secretary's Commission on Achieving Necessary Skills (1991) *What Work Requires of Schools: A SCANS Report for America 2000*, Washington, DC: US Deptartment of Labor.

US Department of Labor. Employment and Training Administration (1993) 'The New DOT: A Database of Occupational Titles for the Twenty-First Century', Final Report of the Advisory Panel for the Dictionary of Occupational Titles (APDOT), Washington, DC: US Department of Labor.

US Department of Labor. Employment and Training Administration (2005) 'O*NET Data Collection Program', Office of Management and Budget Clearance Package Supporting Statement and Data Collection Instruments, Washington, DC: US Department of Labor.

Vallas, S. Peter (1990) 'The Concept of Skill: A Critical Review', *Work and Occupations*, 17: 379–398.

Vallas, S. P. (2003) 'Why Teamwork Fails: Obstacles to Workplace Change in Four Manufacturing Plants', *American Sociological Review*, 68: 223–250.

Wharton, A. (1999) 'The Psychosocial Consequences of Emotional Labor', *The ANNALS of the American Academy of Political and Social Science*, 561: 158–176.
Wilson, W. J. (1996) *When Work Disappears*, New York: Knopf.
Wright, E. O. (1985) *Classes*, London: Verso.
Wright, E. O. (1997) 'Rethinking, Once Again, the Concept of Class Structure', in J. R. Hall (ed.), *Reworking Class*, Ithaca, NY: Cornell University Press: 41–72.
Zuboff, S. (1988) *In the Age of the Smart Machine*, New York: Basic Books.

CHAPTER 6

ACCREDITATION AND ASSESSMENT IN VOCATIONAL EDUCATION AND TRAINING

GORDON STANLEY

Introduction

MODERN vocational education and training (VET) has evolved from a long tradition of industry associations and craft guilds which used on-the-job apprenticeship training as the basic model for entry to employment. This traditional approach has undergone major transformation as industries have restructured and economies have changed. Transformation has been driven by ever-changing workplace demands, including the need for retraining existing workers (Carmichael 1993).

In response to these needs a range of institutional structures have been developed to provide for VET. Private providers of vocational training exist alongside public and not-for-profit providers in many countries, and operate in a competitive market to recruit students and compete for government subsidies.

With the current trend to focus on outcomes rather than on how they are achieved, various delivery options are available to providers. Options range from traditional modes to intensive courses run over shorter time periods. To provide customized training meeting specific industry needs, flexible delivery, and 'just-in-time' approaches have become popular. These approaches can deliver students into the workplace quickly and are becoming common when there are skill shortages.

Despite these reforms questions continue to be asked about the quality and work readiness of trainees with many vocational qualifications. In this chapter we will be describing the processes used to regulate and accredit vocational qualifications in the non-university sector. We consider the nature of assessment practised in VET and how it differs from that commonly used in general education. Whilst there are differences across regions in the way vocational training has developed, the dominant influence in recent reform has been from Anglo countries. Additionally, the influence of transnational organizations such as the OECD and the European Union (EU) has led to greater convergence in practice (Field et al. 2009).

Regulation and Accreditation

Today in most countries the approach to regulation of vocational and trade qualifications involves the development of accreditation and registration processes, qualification frameworks, and quality assurance processes. Such processes are typically the responsibility of an agency of government that is independent from the direct management of the government-provider sector. These requirements are there to ensure that all providers meet the appropriate knowledge and skill demands of the industries and occupations where the students will find employment.

Vocational professions such as nursing and engineering generally have their own profession-specific national accreditation processes to ensure achievement of professional competencies and standards. These are incorporated into licence-to-practice requirements for graduates. Often the profession-based processes are endorsed by the regulatory authority as part of the generic requirements for accreditation. In many cases professional standards are becoming common across national borders through interaction between international councils of national professional associations and quality assurance agencies that have a common interest in ensuring the global recognition of equivalent qualifications for practice (Stanley 2012).

Accreditation and registration processes typically require evidence that the provider (referred to as a registered training organization) has the capacity to deliver graduates of VET who meet the standards required by employers or by licensing authorities in the case of registered trades. Such evidence will include details of training infrastructure, qualifications of instructors, course entry requirements, and other requirements considered appropriate for effective outcomes. This evidence is vital to the work of the regulatory authority, which typically would audit such information on a regular basis.

For-profit providers have been quite common in the area of vocational and industry training. Many of the smaller providers select areas where demand is unsatisfied and infrastructure requirements for entry to the market are not excessive. Whilst competition from for-profit providers is seen to be beneficial in providing efficiency pressures on traditional providers, there are issues about whether quality is being compromised.

Especial interest is focused on niche players who are not well capitalized and who tend to be small-scale operators. Given their profit motive and the relatively easy entry price, concerns centre on how adequately they compare in outcomes to the larger and more traditional vocational training institutions. To address such issues, quality audits and quality assurance processes typically play a significant role in the regulatory process for providers. Increasingly such audits are based on a risk analysis and monitoring of performance indicators submitted by the providers.

Qualification Frameworks

In Europe and in many Commonwealth countries qualifications frameworks have been developed to classify levels of qualifications and to define their common standards of achievement. A competence-based approach to standards has been adopted in those countries that have developed qualification frameworks for vocational education. Since their introduction competence-based qualifications have been used primarily for employment purposes such as confirmation of occupational competence, licence to practice, monitoring learner progression, and providing feedback to candidates for future improvement.

Under these frameworks assessments are required to be valid in relation to the learning outcomes against the stated assessment criteria, produce sufficient evidence from learners to enable reliable and consistent judgements to be made about achievement of all the learning outcomes against the stated assessment criteria, be manageable and cost effective, and be accessible (see, for example, Ofqual 2008, 26).

Typically the process of developing qualification frameworks has been at national level, as has occurred in Australia, Hong Kong, New Zealand, and South Africa (Karmel 2010). The most significant project to get an agreed approach to standards across national borders has been attempted by the EU where the common labour market has led to the need for creating better alignment and comparable standards across all levels of education and training.

The European Qualifications Framework for lifelong learning (EQF 2008) represents an important attempt to harmonize education and training in Europe and acknowledges that in modern workplaces ongoing learning and skill development will be required throughout a working career. It is a reference or 'meta-framework' against which individual countries can map their national frameworks in order to articulate equivalences of level between qualifications within the EU.

The EQF brings together in one framework all sectors of education: general, higher, and vocational education. The framework involves generic descriptors across three domains of outcomes for eight levels. The domains describe knowledge, cognitive and practical skills, and responsibility and autonomy (labelled 'competence').

As part of the process of checking the comparability of standards, Lester (2008) reported an attempt to align the England, Wales, and Northern Ireland Qualifications and Credit Framework (QCF) levels to those of the EQF. The findings from the mapping exercises carried out by Lester indicate that, whilst there are legitimate differences in emphasis between the QCF and the EQF, it is possible to demonstrate a consistent relationship between the levels of the two frameworks (Lester 2008, 11).

Contemporary frameworks require vocational qualifications to align with work-related outcomes or competencies at a given standard without specifying the learning programme needed to achieve these outcomes. This approach to training has been adopted in vocational areas ranging from construction, engineering, health and social care, service industries, to business administration and management. These qualifications involve competence-based assessment, essential features of which consist in specification of standards, specification of opportunities to collect sufficient evidence, assessor judgements, learner feedback, and quality assurance.

The basic concepts of competence and competencies involved in policy documents on vocational education are somewhat fuzzy (Stanley 1993). Some years ago it was pointed out that 'perhaps no word has been used more frequently ... with less precision than *competence*' (Grant 1979, 2). The idea of competencies in current approaches to vocational education has been pragmatically developed to focus on knowledge and skills related to specific industry needs. They can be chararacterized 'as complex ability constructs that are context-specific, trainable, and closely related to real life' (Koeppen et al. 2008, 61). Essentially competencies describe activities carried out to the required national occupational standards.

Units of training, usually developed in association with industry skill councils, have assessment criteria that specify the content and range expected of the learner to achieve the learning outcome at the level of the unit. A record is made of evidence from tasks demonstrating achievement of these criteria. Meeting such criteria indicates satisfactory performance of the function covered by the national occupational standard. The type of data and methods of collection used varies across the range of vocational training. The common element is a workplace focus in the evidence collected and judgements made.

Approaches to Assessment

Competencies, standards, and skills are essential elements in the current discussions about education and training outcomes. Clearly it is necessary to understand the evolution of educational assessment and the different models that have characterized traditional education and training regimes. Assessment involves making judgements about performance.

When considering the traditional general education curriculum such judgements are often based on a range of different activities across different subjects. Analysis of written material is commonly used in the humanities: a history essay is designed to allow students to demonstrate subject matter knowledge (the 'facts') as well as reasoning and analysis using higher-order cognitive processes. The sciences add laboratory skills demonstrated in practical work, and the creative and performing arts often involve judgements about bodies of artistic work ranging from painting to dramatic performances.

In considering these examples it needs to be acknowledged that all attempts to make judgements about human capability involve inferences based on sampling of performance. An important issue relates to how we sample the performance we are interested in, and whether or not this represents an appropriate base for the predictive use of the data. The predictive use is critical for all users of the educational assessment. Students need to know that their current ability is being appropriately represented in the assessment. They and others will be making decisions about further study or employment based on the assumption of their ability described by the assessment.

If individuals are said to be competent or to have acquired skills relevant to employment, how well does the assessment model used by educators and trainers deliver to the satisfaction of employers? At the outset it must be pointed out that there are significant differences in the tradition of assessment in general education and in VET. As we have seen, general education has embraced knowledge 'about' or propositional knowledge as well as knowledge of 'how to' or procedural knowledge. General education has often overvalued the former at the expense of the latter, whilst vocational training is seen to have the reverse tendency.

Another important difference in the traditions of assessment relates to the fact that general education has typically rewarded relative performance. The pursuit of excellence in general education has meant developing assessment that sorts people out and identifies those who can perform well. All too often greater weight has been given to the sorting process than the meaning of the outcome. Excellence is recognized by teachers when it occurs, but often the pathway to its achievement is relatively unspecified for students beyond an expectation for them to immerse themselves in the acquisition of knowledge of the subject being studied.

Rather than considering the relative position of the individual with respect to some normative outcome, vocational training in the non-university sector has developed a much greater stress on the meaning of the individual standard of performance, that is, can the person do tasks well enough to meet employer needs? More recent trends in general education driven by the standards and accountability movement have led to an outcome focus and standards-referenced reporting (see Tognolini and Stanley 2007). This may lead to greater convergence in the assessment models used in the two sectors.

Assessment in General Education

In general education student performance has tended to be assessed by examination questions or tasks that provide opportunity for students to demonstrate their knowledge and skills. The assessments generally have been made with implicit norms about proficiency. Student performance is reported in marks or grades where the emphasis is on relative position with respect to average performance. A student who achieves an A grade in history is known to be better than one who received a B grade, but in the traditional reporting mode this is all the information available. The content of the A grade relative to the B grade is aligned to some generic marking rubric, sometimes with rather vaguely implicit criteria. Traversing backwards from the grade reported to an understanding of the content mastered is therefore frequently an opaque process.

Moreover in large-scale examination systems the distribution of grades was usually allocated with respect to a normal curve ('grading on a curve') to ensure consistency of numbers from year to year. Such normative scaling meant that the reported grade was even less clearly related to specific content. These characteristics of traditional reporting of results in general education have not helped end-users who are not part of the academic enterprise. They can get some sense of relative achievement from the grade level, but have no real understanding of the knowledge and skills demonstrated by the recipient to achieve the grade.

One consequence of the traditional stress on relative position and the level of performance of the individual is that students who achieved at lower levels felt like failures and often had no sense of the meaning of their achievement. Their low marks or grades were not informative about what they had actually mastered or what they should do next. A student who was at the bottom range of a highly performing cohort may still have mastered some important knowledge and skills, but the form of reporting results would not necessarily reveal this. The major function of assessment should not be to fail people, but to provide useful information about their current skill level and provide advice about the next step in further skill development. The traditional approach was not very effective in this regard.

In response to the need for greater accountability and better understanding of the outcomes of general education, education systems have moved to being more explicit about the content of academic achievement. In general education this has led to criterion-referenced or standards-referenced reporting (Sadler 1987). Criterion-referenced reporting is the process of giving meaning to student achievement by referencing it to specified outcome criteria (Popham 1978). The main advantage of criterion referencing is that it centres on observation rather than inference about behaviours students have demonstrated. Apart from concerns about the task of record-keeping, the major criticism it has received in general education is that it results in an atomization of the curriculum into behaviours, some of which appear to be relatively trivial in isolation.

In answer to such criticism standards referencing has been developed. Standards referencing builds upon criterion referencing, but instead of referencing achievement to the myriad of behaviours that comprise an examination, course, or unit of study, the achievement is referenced to predetermined standards of performance (MacCann and Stanley 2005). The standards represent more substantial organizers of content than typically encompassed in the behavioural checklists often associated with criterion referencing.

The standards movement in general education makes a distinction between syllabus standards and performance standards. Syllabus standards refer to content areas of knowledge and skills to be developed, and performance standards refer to levels of performance beyond a threshold or minimum level of performance. Typically a number of proficiency levels or grades above the minimum standard are assessed and reported. The oldest framework for reporting in general education the A–E framework usually uses C as a threshold for 'pass' and B and A are for more proficient standards of performance.

Increasingly grades in general education are accompanied by subject-specific or generic statements about the standards achieved by the students achieving each grade. Thus employers and students are provided with information about the typical performance, that is, knowledge and skills demonstrated by someone achieving each grade in each subject reported. This trend in general education has moved reporting closer to the outcome focus that has long been a feature of VET.

Assessment in VET

The traditional training emphasis was on the curriculum with a focus on the outcomes of the learning session. Standards of assessment were derived from job descriptions and training objectives designed to achieve the requirements of the industry. Assessment of competence involved carrying out a test in the training location to find out if the outcomes had been mastered. Such a test may have been written, practical, or oral. Tests often involved tasks that were indirect proxies for workplace events. In this regard the assessment model used in the training arena was not all that different from that used in general education, except that there was a greater emphasis on procedural knowledge in training relative to propositional knowledge.

Over time a major reform of VET occurred with a change from a curriculum-driven process concerned with specification of inputs towards an outcome emphasis on competencies (Carmichael 1993). Five underlying principles guided the reform agenda (see Schwartz et al. 1997):

- a national framework
- competency, not time-based
- demand, not supply-driven
- multiple pathways and flexible delivery
- a commitment to access and equity.

This reform agenda has had a major impact on the traditional technical and further education colleges and other industry training organizations. The move away from a curriculum-driven and time-based process more appropriate to the early school leaver has led to greater flexibility and innovation in delivery. Just-in-time approaches that allow for intensive learning over shorter time periods with assessment when ready are appealing in times of skill shortage and when dealing with adults and retraining of those in the workplace.

However, there are inherent risks in such intensive courses that encourage students to present as soon as possible for assessment. One of the early established principles of experimentally-based learning theory is that distributed practice results in better learning than that which occurs with massed practice (Hilgard 1986; Cepeda et al. 2006). Students who undertake a last-minute 'cram for an exam' may retain enough to pass on the day of the exam, but evidence may soon emerge that their knowledge and skill are not deeply embedded. Moreover, greater time on task is necessary to achieve expertise (Gladwell 2009).

Of course, advocates for the greater flexibility of the new regime can point out successful outcomes and clearly past practice was not always as efficient as it should have been. Nevertheless, the reform agenda generated considerable debate about the nature and definition of competencies and the appropriate approach to ensure students are workplace ready (see Collins 1993). Employers want their employees to be competent in the workplace. How is this want operationalized?

The term 'competence' implies more than just satisfactory performance. There are two aspects to competence that have emerged in the literature on vocational education. The first aspect of competence has centred on the performance of specific workplace skills. Employers want evidence that actual workplace knowledge and skills have been achieved. This has meant a change of emphasis in assessment from the traditional approach to training. From a training perspective competencies relate to the ability to perform activities within an occupation at the minimum standards of competent performance required for that occupation (Fletcher 1991). This emphasis has dominated the emergence of competency-based assessment (CBA).

When the focus is on the individual, the second emphasis has been on seeing competencies as behaviours of the individual related to an effective or superior performance in a job (Boyatzis 1982). This involves consideration of what a person can do and how well they can do it and is in line with the common meaning of competence. Sometimes this has led to a concern for generic skills or personal qualities related to work that may not be narrowly defined in terms of specific activities. The Mayer Key Competencies developed in Australia was one example of this perspective (Mayer 1992). Another is the more recent global interest in employability and twenty-first-century skills.

CBA is the assessment of evidence to judge a person's current abilities against a given set of standards or competencies set by an industry or enterprise to meet industry or enterprise needs. The assessment is designed to measure what a person can do in the workplace rather than what the person knows. It is the emphasis on knowledge-as-action that has characterized this new approach. There is less interest in the process that produces the outcome than in the achievement of the outcome. The approach has been characterized as assessment as learning (Baird et al. 2011).

Competency standards involve specifying competencies related to the needs of the workplace as defined by employers and industry representatives. CBA involves the assessment of skills and knowledge to specific standards and geared to job needs. The competencies assessed embrace the ability to perform a whole range of activities in a specific occupational area, including transferring skills and knowledge to new situations and managing a variety of tasks within a job.

Typically for each industry competencies are developed that include:

- *task* skills: carrying out tasks or specific elements of work such as adjusting and operating equipment and machinery
- *task management* skills: managing a number of different tasks within a job such as planning and organizing day-to-day tasks, balancing conflicting demands
- *contingency management* skills: responding to irregularities and breakdowns in routine, correcting problems, and adopting alternative courses of action
- *job environment management* skills: personal effectiveness, getting on with others in the work context.

The key advantage of assessing competencies in the workplace environment is that it can be seen as a natural task for supervisors and managers as part of their normal role as effective managers. Judgements can be made about all or part of the competency standards as and when the worker is ready. It is claimed that the process leads to a greater commitment of workers to continue using newer or more complex skills and to implement change in work processes. Such assessment can provide ongoing feedback to help identify further developmental needs, and the explicitness of the competency criteria helps both the learner and the assessor and trainer to know what they are aiming for in terms of performance.

The claims for CBA are that it is both valid and reliable (Rutherford 1995). Validity comes from the fact that assessment occurs on the job or as near to it as possible. Hence, the performances assessed are essentially the skills that need to be demonstrated in an everyday work environment. Samples of real work performance remove any ambiguity about requirements. Such directness of the assessment is very appealing to employers who see it delivering assurance about the abilities of their workers. Reliability refers to the consistency of judgements made from one situation to another. It is an important issue in all assessment. The strong claim often made about CBA is that, because CBA competency standards are written so that there is no ambiguity about their meaning, assessors can make consistent and reliable judgements (Rutherford 1995).

Examination systems in general education tend to use moderation measures or independent assessments to estimate directly the extent of reliability of the reported assessment. Such outcome moderation is harder to put into practice in VET. However, variability in judgement between assessors may not be as significant a problem in VET as in general education where small differences in outcome may have significance in high-stakes-selection contexts.

The approach in CBA has been to quality assure the assessment process and to assume consistency of judgement follows from the training of industry assessors and their formal accreditation. For providers of vocational qualifications, a key element has been to have an internal verification process. With respect to English national vocational qualifications (NVQs), for example, the Joint Awarding Body Guidance on Internal Verification of NVQs (2002) states that verification involves sampling assessments, monitoring assessment practice, and standardizing assessment judgements.

Given the range and complexity of vocational education, this emphasis on the front end of assessment procedure is understandable but there are still issues about the outcomes. The claim that CBA avoids the reliability issues that arise more generally in educational assessment needs to be considered. With the assessment tradition developed within the VET sector it is not surprising that there is not a large literature directly relevant to the reliability of vocational assessment outcomes (Johnson 2006).

Assessors in different contexts (candidates, centres) use different sources of evidence yet the same criteria to classify candidates. It is thus necessary for the decisions to be consistent in view of varying evidence when compared to a fixed outcome. Consistency or replication in this context would be that if the candidate were to be judged again, the same judgement should be made based on the evidence provided.

Baartman et al. (2006) point out that traditionally reliability is determined by consistency of measurement over repeated occasions given fixed raters, or in terms of internal consistency measures. They argue that consistency of repeated measures over time does not fit well with the developmental emphasis on shaping performance to converge on the required competency standard. With respect to internal consistency measures they are less appropriate in VET where, instead of multiple test items, whole task performance is commonly used.

They conclude that the traditional statistical procedures used with objective tests to establish reliability are inappropriate for competency assessment and work-placed learning. They assert, 'We should abandon the idea that assessment is an exact science in which a "true score" can be found' (Baartman et al. 2006, 156). Whilst their alternative approach is to develop a framework of quality criteria for competency-assessed programmes, one criterion is *reproducibility of decisions*. By this criterion they focus on the decision made on the basis of evidence accumulated in a programme of competency assessment.

Whilst there is not a large literature on the reliability of vocational assessment outcomes, recent articles suggest the need for further study. Of the UK literature the most recent contributions seem to have come from the Cambridge Assessment Group and work sponsored by The Office of Qualifications and Examinations Regulation (Ofqual) as part of its reliability research programme.

Greatorex and Shannon report that the Joint Awarding Body guidance project found that, in fact, little standardization was carried out. They suggest that the reason centres did not standardize assessment decisions is 'that they think that they are standardizing them by standardizing the assessment process and operationalizing the internal verification system. Indeed centres are unaware that they are not standardizing assessment decisions' (2003, 5). In their own study of assessors of Retail Operations Level 2 they found that assessors believed that following the same procedure would ensure consistent results although in practice their judgements were not always consistent.

Another study by Greatorex addressed the relevance of different types of evidence to consistency of competence judgements and concluded that there was an effect on assessor judgements. She concluded that 'further research is required before we can say precisely which types of evidence affect assessor judgments and in which circumstances' (2005, 162).

As part of the Ofqual-funded reliability research programme, Harth and Hemker (2010) looked at classification consistency in three qualifications in two occupational areas: Level 3 Electrotechnical Services (Electrical Installation—Buildings and Structures), Hairdressing NVQ (several pathways at levels 1, 2, and 3) and the new NVQ Certificate/Diploma in Hairdressing/Barbering/Combined Hair Types (several pathways at QCF levels 1, 2, and 3). The study involved the collection and scoring of centre-devised assessment records from candidate portfolios and of internal verifier reports.

Based on this data they were able to provide procedures estimating the inter-rater agreement, inter-rater reliability, and inter-'item' reliability. Their main findings (Harth and Hemker 2010, 41) were summarized as follows:

- inter-assessor agreement was high (Gower coefficient ranging from 0.90 to 0.99) for electrotechnical services or almost perfect (Gower coefficient ranging from 0.99 to 1.00) for hairdressing
- inter-assessor reliability (Cohen's kappa) was substantial for the electrotechnical pathway (kappa >0.75) and almost perfect for the hairdressing qualifications (kappa >0.95)
- inter-'item' reliability (using a coefficient similar to Cronbach's alpha and Guttman's lambda) could only be estimated for the electrotechnical services and the results showed very high values.

The procedures they used confirmed the possibility of estimating the reliability of these qualifications, although changes would need to be made in the types of records used by assessors and the feedback given to candidates if this were to be carried out routinely. However, they noted that the flexibility required in the structure of these qualifications may prevent these procedures from being applied across all vocational qualifications. They concluded that the existing verification process appears to work effectively in ensuring consistency of decisions and high inter-assessor reliability.

Regulators of VET systems require providers to make assessments that are reliable (Ofqual 2008, 26). However, the practice of VET assessment raises issues about how the requirement of reliable assessment is to be met when common assessment tasks are not common practice. As we have seen, the large number of assessment decisions involved in vocational qualifications and the flexibility afforded in the type of evidence considered make it very difficult to address consistency.

The issue of how to audit assessor consistency has been the subject of discussion in many VET systems. Moderation of assessor decisions is part of the current assessment process in most systems. However, such moderation is based on a sampling methodology and improvement culture rather than as an audit process with independent observations to enable conventional estimate of classification reliability. It is arguable whether or not this is sufficient to guarantee that assessment outcomes are as consistent as should be routinely achievable in practice. One option considered in Australia is statistical moderation, but this would require change to practice (National Quality Council 2009, 13–14)

> Although yet to be pursued at the national level within the VET sector, statistical moderation could be used to ensure that RTO (registered training organisation)

> based assessments are comparable throughout the nation, particularly if grades or marks are to be reported. However, to implement this moderation process, some form of a common assessment task(s) would need to be introduced at a national level in the VET sector (e.g. external exam or standardised assessment tools) to moderate the organisation-based assessments. ... The major benefit of statistical moderation is that it provides the strongest form of quality control over organisation-based assessments. It can also be less expensive to implement and maintain (if paper-based) than external moderation processes. It would however require the introduction of some form of common assessment task(s) at the national level. If the common assessment task was paper-based (as has been typically implemented in other educational sectors due to reduced costs associated with the implementation and scoring procedures), then any adjustments to candidate results would be limited to estimates of candidates' cognitive skills (i.e. knowledge and understanding); and therefore may have limited face and content validity within the VET sector.'

Although considered in the report of the Australian National Quality Council, this option has not received strong support from the VET sector in Australia as an appropriate solution to ensuring increased consistency of assessment. Currently their process is very similar to the quality assurance and external verification-sampling model used in most other systems.

Within the VET sector competency standards are set at a level for satisfactory performance required by industry. The emphasis is on getting all students to the same standard acceptable for practice. Whilst the threshold for the performance standard is set in such a way to encourage skilled performance, typically the emphasis is on attaining the minimum necessary for being able to get employed in the industry. This has led to a perception that performance beyond the standard is not as valued in VET as it should be. However, Schofield and McDonald (2004) argue that the status of a competent result may be devalued by graded assessments.

Clearly, there are some contexts in which it does not make much sense in differentiating performance into proficiency levels: a person can either start up a machine and shut it down, or they cannot. Other skill tasks may involve opportunities for degrees of performance beyond a threshold standard and these differences may be valuable to capture for employers who want higher levels of productivity or efficiency in the people they are hiring.

Many people in the VET area do not like the idea of graded competencies, although, when possible, many training providers make such reports about the students they have assessed. However, as pointed out by Johnson: 'Potentially, the meaning of different grade thresholds might be less transparent than that between competent/not competent if there is lack of understanding about the differences between grades' (2008, 180).

Employability Skills

In considering the outcomes of education and training systems a common concern about the employability of school leavers has emerged. In response to this concern the development of generic employability skills has been a common policy development in a number of OECD countries including Canada, the United Kingdom, New Zealand, Singapore, the Netherlands, France, Germany, and the United States.

Generic employability skills describe the core skills considered necessary for employment and the major groups pushing for such skills have been business groups and employer organizations. There are similarities in the lists of such skills across countries but all have in common an expectation that such skills should be a product of the education and training system. Whilst it appears relatively easy to agree on a list of desirable skills, it is another thing to be confident about how they can be assessed and delivered.

In Canada the Conference Board of Canada (2000) developed Employment Skills 2000+ as a set of skills needed to enter, stay in, and progress in the world of work. Four *fundamental skills* were identified: communicate, manage information, use numbers, think through and solve problems; five *personal management skills*: demonstrate positive attitudes and behaviours, be responsible, be adaptable, learn continuously, and work safely; and two *teamwork skills*: work with others, and participate in projects and tasks.

In Britain key skills are defined as the generic and transferable skills needed by all people to succeed in education and training and work in general. There are six key skills: communication, application of numbers, information technology, working with others, improving own learning, and performance in problem-solving. The first three skills are termed main key skills and are part of the NQF. They are tested by external tests whilst the second set of three wider key skills is verified by portfolios of evidence generated by the candidate (Turner 2002).

As mentioned earlier, the first approach to generic workplace skills was developed by Mayer (1992) and the more recent employability skills framework has built upon this earlier work (ACCI and BCA 2002). The current Australian list of employability skills does not explicitly specify basic skills such as literacy and numeracy as it is assumed that they have been delivered in the general education programme itself and, hence, do not need highlighting as additional skills to be mastered for the purpose of employment readiness. The Australian employability skills framework lists the following set of skills: communication, teamwork, problem-solving, initiative and enterprise, planning and organizing, self-management, learning, and technology skills.

These examples of employability skills have obvious appeal. For example, who would argue against the desirability of communication as a skill that aids employment prospects? The difficulty is in what meaning and, hence, expectation is attached to communication as an outcome for the education system. It would be difficult to specify all forms of communication in the workplace and all contexts in which such skill is applied. Similarly, it is a very difficult task to detail the different levels to which the skill can be developed in all these contexts. Every workplace has its own formal and informal language. Getting agreement about the essential elements of workplace communication skill is not straightforward.

Despite these obvious reactions to the apparently straightforward notion of communication as an important skill for employment, the challenge thrown out to the education community by this push cannot be ignored. There is a perception that the traditional emphasis of the education and training system on learning about and learning to do may not have produced the set of skills needed for socially situated activities such as work and community involvement. Tensions are involved in trying to accommodate the employability communication skills into the general education curriculum. Recent attempts to introduce a variety of text types and communication skills into English syllabuses have not been without considerable controversy.

Clearly, there are difficulties in how these generic employability skills are to be developed and assessed. There are also issues around the relative roles of the general education system and the vocational education system in delivering them as outcomes. In a report for the Australian government, the Allen Consulting Group (2006) recommended for the VET sector an integrated assessment approach. This would involve employability skills being assessed in an integrated manner with technical skills within a qualification and the corresponding units of competency.

Whilst the issue of embedding employability skills into training packages and into the general school curriculum has not been consistently addressed, the policy agenda seems to have shifted somewhat towards an interest in another set of skills referred to as '21st-century skills'. In the United States the National Research Council held a workshop where it was found that across the entire labour market—from high-wage biotechnology scientists and computer sales engineers to low-wage restaurant servers and elder caregivers—five skills appeared to be increasingly valuable: adaptability, complex communication skills, non-routine problem-solving skills, self-management/self-development, and systems thinking (Hilton 2008).

For a follow-up workshop on twenty-first-century skills, these five skills were collapsed into three broad clusters (Koenig 2011, 2):

- *cognitive* skills: non-routine problem-solving, critical thinking, systems thinking
- *interpersonal skills*: complex communication, social skills, teamwork, cultural sensitivity, dealing with diversity
- *intrapersonal skills*: self-management, time management, self-development, self-regulation, adaptability, executive functioning.

In the report (Koenig 2011, 16) on the workshop it was stated that:

> Defining some of the constructs included within the scope of twenty-first-century skills is significantly more challenging than defining more traditional constructs, such as reading comprehension or mathematics and computational skills. One of the challenges is that the definitions tend to be both broad and general. To be useful for test development, the definition needs to be specific so that there can be a shared conception of the construct for use by those writing the assessment questions or preparing the assessment tasks.

Whilst industry groups and policy-makers have welcomed the concept of generic skills, the difficulty of integrating them with a CBA framework is clear. Moreover, despite their appeal, there are real questions about how much some generic skills and capabilities can be developed through instruction. As argued in an earlier debate on generic skills (Stanley 1993, 247):

> One of the difficulties with emphasizing general abilities or generic competencies as educational outcomes is that they may be more dependent on the relative contributions of individual differences which people bring to the task of learning than on the direct outputs of instruction.

Conclusion

Modern VET is a vigorous sector in post-compulsory education. Having a past grounded in traditional industry and technical training, it has been forced to adapt to the challenges of changing employment structures and new workplace requirements. As we have seen, the approach to the accreditation and regulation of providers has involved a strong emphasis on quality improvement and the capacity to deliver outcomes that satisfy industry knowledge and skill requirements.

CBA is the predominant assessment model in contemporary VET systems. CBA has the attraction of explicitness of what is to be assessed but that alone does not guarantee reliability and consistency of assessment. Nevertheless, the focus on a threshold judgement of competence as fitness for employment practice may mean that variability in such judgements may be less significant than if finer gradations of performance were required. Some of the options used in general education for routine moderation of assessment outcomes are not practical and can be seen as inimical to the nature of VET. The front-end focus of training assessors and the requirement for workplace assessment contexts provide practical moves to align assessment with employer needs.

This chapter has considered the prevailing assessment and accreditation systems in VET, especially in the Anglo world (which, in turn, is having a growing influence on a range of international agencies). It has also considered a number of key issues involving skill outcomes associated with such systems. There is, however, a long-standing literature that has questioned the adequacy of CBA systems, despite their usefulness in some industries and occupations (Collins 1993). More recently there have been calls again to shift away from the fragmentation inherent in current CBA systems by moving to structuring skill formation and assessment around a more encompassing notion of capability. This literature is discussed in Chapter 28.

References

ACCI and BCA (2002) 'Employability Skills for the Future', Canberra: DEST.

Allen Consulting Group (2006) 'Assessment and Reporting of Employability Skills Embedded in Training Packages', Report to the Department of Education, Science and Training, Melbourne.

Baartman, L. K. J., Bastiaens, T. J., Kirschner, P. A., and Van der Vleuten, C. P. M. (2006) 'The Wheel of Competency Assessment: Presenting Quality Criteria for Competency Assessment Programs', *Studies in Educational Evaluation*, 32: 153–170.

Baird, J., Béguin, A., Black, P., Pollitt, A., and Stanley, G. (2011) 'The Reliability Programme: Final Report of the Technical Advisory Group', Coventry: Ofqual/11/4825.

Boyatzis, R. (1982) *The Competent Manager: A Model of Effective Performance*, New York: John Wiley.

Carmichael, L. (1993) 'Workplace Imperatives for Education and Competence', in C. Collins (ed), *Competencies: The Competency Debate in Australian Education and Training*, Canberra: Australian College of Education: 15–20.

Cepeda, N. J., Pashler, H., Vul, E., Wixted, J. T., and Rohrer, D. (2006) 'Distributed Practice in Verbal Recall Tasks: A Review and Quantitative Synthesis', *Psychological Bulletin*, 132: 354–380.

Collins, C. (ed) (1993) *Competencies: The Competency Debate in* Australian *Education and Training*, Canberra: Australian College of Education.

Conference Board of Canada (2000) 'Employability skills 2000+'. Available at: www.conference-board.ca/education.

EQF (2008) *The European Qualifications Framework for Lifelong Learning (EQF)*, Brussels: Office for Official Publications of the European Communities.

Field, S., Hoeckel, K., Kis, V., and Kuczera, M. (2009) 'OECD Policy Review of Vocational Education and Training', *Initial report*, OECD, Paris.

Fletcher, S. (1991) *NVQs, Standards and Competence: A Practical Guide for Employers, Managers, and Trainers*, London: Kogan Page.

Gladwell, M. (2009) *Outliers*, London: Penguin.

Grant, G. (1979) 'Implications of Competence-Based Education', in G. Grant (ed.), *On Competence*, San Francisco: Jossey-Bass: 1–16.

Greatorex, J. and Shannon, M. (2003) 'How Can NVQ Assessors' Judgements Be Standardised?', Paper presented at the British Educational Research Association Conference, 11–13 September, Heriot-Watt University, Edinburgh.

Greatorex, J. (2005) 'Assessing the Evidence: Different Types of NVQ Evidence and Their Impact on Reliability and Fairness', *Journal of Vocational Education and Training*, 57(2): 149–164.

Harth, H. and Hemker, B. T. (2010) 'On the Reliability of Results in Vocational Assessment', Ofqual, September.

Hilgard, E. R. (1986) *Theories of Learning*, New York: Appleton-Century-Crofts.

Hilton, M. (Rapporteur) (2008) 'Research on Future Skills Demands: A Workshop Summary', Center for Education, Division of Behavioral and Social Sciences and Education, The National Academies Press, Washington, DC.

Johnson, M. (2006) 'A Review of Vocational Research in the UK 2002–2006: Measurement and Accessibility Issues', *International Journal of Training and Research*, 4(2): 48–71.

Johnson, M. (2008) 'Grading in Competence-Based Qualifications: Is it Desirable and How Might it Affect Validity?', *Journal of Further and Higher Education*, 32(2): 175–184.

Joint Awarding Bodies (2002) *Joint Awarding Bodies Guidance on Verification of NVQs*, London: Department for Education and Skills.

Karmel, T. (2010) 'Vocational Education and Training', in P. Peterson, E. Baker, and B. McGaw (eds), *International Encyclopedia of Education*, 3rd ed., London: Elsevier: 229–239.

Koeppen, K., Hartig, J., Klieme, E., and Leutner, D. (2008) 'Current Issues in Competence Modeling and Assessment', *Zeitschrift für Psychologie*, 216(2): 61–73.

Koenig, J. A. (Rapporteur) (2011) 'Assessing 21st Century Skills: Summary of a Workshop', National Academies Press, Washington, DC.

Lester, S. (2008) 'Linking the Qualifications and Credit Framework Levels to the European Qualifications Framework', Report commissioned by the Qualifications and Curriculum Authority, Taunton, Stan Lester, 23 October.

Mayer, E. (1992) *Putting General Education to Work: The Key Competencies Report*, Melbourne: Australian Education Council.

MacCann, R. G. and Stanley, G. (2005).'The Use of Rasch Modelling to Improve Standards Setting', Practical Assessment Research & Evaluation. Available at: http://pareonline.net.

National Quality Council (2009) 'A Code of Professional Practice for Validation and Moderation'. Available at: www.tvetaustralia.com.au.

Ofqual (2008) 'Regulatory Arrangements for the Qualifications and Credit Framework'. Available at: http://www.ofqual.org.uk/files/Regulatory_arrangements_QCF_August08.pdf.

Popham, W. J. (1978) *Criterion-Referenced Assessment*, New Jersey: Prentice Hall.

Rutherford, P. D. (1995) *Competency Based Assessment*, Melbourne: Pitman.

Sadler, D. R. (1987) 'Specifying and Promulgating Achievement Standards', *Oxford Review of Education*, 13: 191–209.

Schofield, K. and McDonald, R. (2004) *Moving on ... Report of the High Level Review into Training Packages*, Melbourne, Australia: ANTA.

Schwartz, R., McKenzie, P., Hasan, A., and Nexelmann, E. (1997) 'Country Note on Australia for the OECD Transition Review', OECD, Paris.

Stanley, G. (1993) 'The Psychology of Competency-Based Education', in C. Collins (ed), *Competencies: The Competencies Debate in Australian Education and Training*, Canberra: Australian College of Education: 145–153.

Stanley, G. (2012) 'Challenges in the Quest to Create Global Qualifications and Standards are Driving Change in Education Systems', in J. C. Brada, G. Stanley, and W. Bienkowski (eds), *The University in the Age of Globalization: Rankings, Resources and Reforms*, Basingstoke: Palgrave: 145–153.

Tognolini, J. and Stanley, G. (2007) 'Standards-Based Assessment: A Tool and Means to the Development of Human Capital and Capacity Building in Education', *Australian Journal of Education*, 51(2): 129–145.

Turner, D. (2002) *Employability Skills Development in the United Kingdom*, Kensington Park, SA: NCVER.

SECTION II

EDUCATION, TRAINING, AND THE DEVELOPMENT OF WORKFORCE SKILLS

CHAPTER 7

EDUCATION AND QUALIFICATIONS AS SKILLS

PAUL DALZIEL

INTRODUCTION

NATIONAL policy frameworks aimed at raising economic performance and individual well-being typically focus on 'skills' as a key driver. The 2009 report of the UK Commission for Employment and Skills, *Towards Ambition 2020: Skills, Jobs, Growth*, is typical of many similar publications around the world when it advises: 'There is little that is more important than equipping ourselves with the skills we need, for the jobs we need, for the successful businesses of tomorrow' (UKCES 2009, 8). More recently, the Organisation for Economic Cooperation and Development has defined skills as 'the global currency of the 21st century' (OECD 2012, 3):

> Without proper investment in skills, people languish on the margins of society, technological progress does not translate into economic growth, and countries can no longer compete in an increasingly knowledge-based global society. But this 'currency' depreciates as the requirements of labour markets evolve and individuals lose the skills they do not use. Skills do not automatically convert into jobs and growth.

The metaphor of 'investment in skills' comes from the 'human capital' model introduced more than 50 years ago by Jacob Mincer (1958), Theodore Shultz (1961), and Gary Becker (1962, 1964). In this model, economic agents may choose to sacrifice present income in order to engage in education and obtain qualifications. This produces skills that translate into higher future earnings in the labour market, justifying the original sacrifice of income. The Shultz-Becker model has been very powerful in understanding key features of education and qualifications as labour market skills, but has also been subject to significant critiques, some of which have resulted in important extensions. The purpose of this chapter is to provide a critical overview of these developments.

The chapter begins with an introduction of the basic economic model of investment in human capital and the subsequent literature measuring economic returns to education. This is followed in the second section by a discussion of two theories that question the human capital link between education and labour market skills. The first argues that education is a device to signal to potential employers that the individual has high natural abilities whilst the second argues that education sorts workers into different labour markets segmented by wider socio-economic forces. Section 3 considers two more recent developments. The first involves sequential analysis in which the decision-maker learns more about his or her abilities and opportunities as a result of participating in education whilst the second uses a 'skill ecosystem' metaphor to express how educational institutions, students, employers, and policy-makers can combine to sustain a high-skills, high-wage equilibrium or reinforce a low-skills, low-wage equilibrium. The chapter finishes with a brief conclusion in the fourth section.

The Basic Economic Model of Investment in Human Capital

Before the contributions of Mincer, Shultz, and Becker, the term 'capital' in economics generally referred to physical infrastructure, buildings, transport, plant, and machinery that raise the productivity of employed workers. In order to build up its stock of physical capital, a society must forego some consumption, but the reward is greater future consumption opportunities when the new capital increases the productivity of its labour force. Thus, it is commonplace for economists to advise that a higher savings rate invested in physical capital formation will increase a country's economic growth.

Mincer, Shultz, and Becker noticed that the decision by an individual to participate in education has strong similarities to the decision to invest in physical capital. If individuals choose to engage in education, they must forego income that could have been earned in employment during that period and they must pay any direct costs of their studies. At the end of the education period they will have acquired skills (which all three authors termed 'human capital' as a direct analogy to 'physical capital') that will increase their productivity in employment, resulting in a premium above the wages earned by an unskilled worker.

A pictorial representation of the model is shown in Figure 7.1. At the time of the decision, the person's expected income over time, if no education is undertaken, is represented by the dashed line. Investment in education requires some foregone income (the dark shaded area) and some extra study expenses (the light shaded area). The solid line represents the expected income path with the skills produced by the education. The benefit is the higher income after graduation, represented by the vertically shaded area. For the investment in human capital to be justified, the net present value of these future benefits must outweigh the net present value of the foregone income and extra expenses during the education.

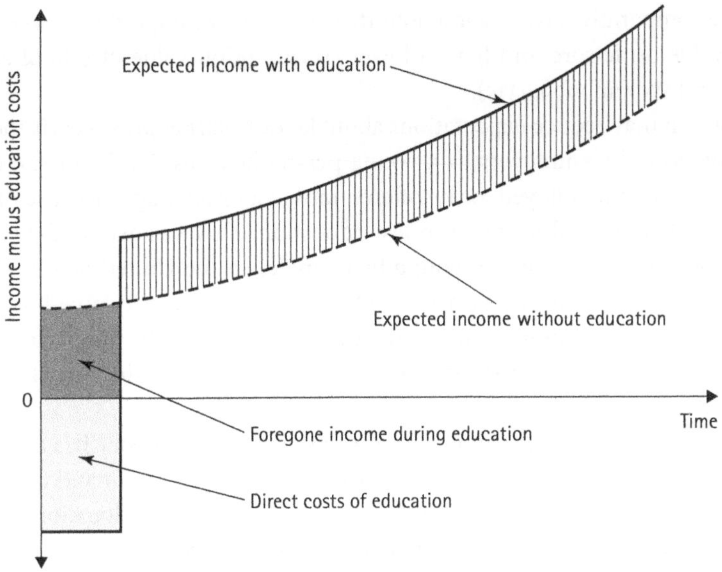

FIGURE 7.1 Costs and benefits of education

The phrase 'net present value' also comes from the literature on investment in physical capital. It recognizes that a decision-maker discounts the value of benefits received some time in the future compared to the value of the same benefit received in the present. The higher the discount rate adopted by the decision-maker, the lower the net present value of future benefits, and so the less likely investment in education.

Thus the model offers explanations for why different people choose different levels of education with significant implications for national economic growth rates (see, for example, the surveys by Harmon et al. 2003; Sianesi and Van Reenen 2003; and Tobias and Li 2004). Different segments of the population may face different costs of education, for example, or may have different financial constraints during the education period of negative income. This second possibility provides part of the economic case in favour of a government-sponsored student loans scheme for post-compulsory education, although the United States evidence suggests that credit constraints do not affect the choice to enrol in post-compulsory education (Keane and Wolpin 2001; Cameron and Taber 2004).

Another explanation is that different individuals may be endowed with different abilities to acquire skills through education or have different expectations about their labour market prospects. Eckstein and Wolpin (1999) is a sophisticated example of this research in which the authors create a sequential model of high school attendance and work decisions to provide insight into factors influencing the decisions of young people to drop out of school. Using US data from the 1979 youth cohort of the National Longitudinal Surveys of Labour Market Experience, the study concludes that 'youths who drop out of high school have different traits from those who graduate—they have lower school ability and/or motivation, they have lower expectations about the rewards from graduation, they have a comparative advantage at jobs that are done by nongraduates, and they place a higher value on leisure and have a lower consumption value of school attendance' (Eckstein and Wolpin 1999, 1335).

A factor that may reduce expectations about labour market prospects is the presence of discrimination by employers. If a young person believes that he or she is likely to spend more time unemployed, or be offered jobs at a lower wage, because of discrimination, then it is rational to invest in less education. This was explored by Keane and Wolpin (2000) in the context of young black males in the United States. They found the relatively low schooling attainments of this group could be explained 'as an optimal response to the combination of discrimination against blacks in wage offers and lower endowments at age 16 of labor market, school, and home production skills' (Wolpin 2000, 643).

One of the most important applications of human capital theory has been its use in econometric studies of the 'returns on education'; indeed, Dickson and Harmon (2011, 1118) observe that 'the estimation of the economic return to education has perhaps been one of the predominant areas of analysis in applied economics for over 50 years.' Following Harmon et al. (2003), consider a person who has s–1 years of education. Another year of education sacrifices the wage paid to a worker with that education, denoted w_{s-1}, and also incurs direct education costs, c_s. Thus the cost to the individual of further education is $(w_{s-1} + c_s)$. After the extra year of education, the individual receives higher wages, $(w_s - w_{s-1})$, for the remainder of their working life. Because these higher wages occur in the future, they must be discounted using a suitable rate of interest, denoted r. The present value of this geometric series for a long working life is approximated by $(w_s - w_{s-1})/r$, which is the benefit of the extra year of education to the individual. The benefit falls as the rate of interest rises whilst there is no impact on the cost; hence there is one interest rate at which benefit equals cost. This equalizing rate of interest, denoted r_s, is the return on the s-th year of education, since it is the interest rate at which the cost of education is just covered by the net present value of future benefits:

$$r_s = \left(w_s - w_{s-1}\right)/\left(w_{s-1} + c_s\right) \quad (1)$$

Conceptually, r_s is very important in the economic analysis of education choices since its value has to be sufficiently high to justify investment in education rather than other consumption and investment opportunities. Hence studies have sought to estimate its value in different contexts. This is not straightforward since in principle there might be different values for c depending on the education chosen and a different value of r_s for each year of education. In practice, some mathematical approximations and simplifying assumptions (for example, that the rate of return is the same for all years of education and for all individuals, and the direct costs of education are negligible compared to wages) produce a relationship known as the Mincer specification, after Mincer (1974):

$$\log\left(w_i\right) = r_e\left(s_i\right) + \delta\left(x_i\right) + \gamma\left(x_i\right)^2 + \mathbf{X}_i\beta + u_i \quad (2)$$

Equation (2) states that an individual's earnings depend on the return to education, r_e, the number of years of education, s_i, on the number of years of work experience, x_i, on a set of individual characteristics of the individual, $\mathbf{X}_i$, and a disturbance term, u_i (δ, γ and β are parameters). Increasingly sophisticated econometric methods have been used on larger and larger datasets to estimate this relationship.

Harmon et al. (2003, 129–131) report the results from a meta-analysis of equation (2) that draws on work by a pan-European Union network of researchers known as PURE (Public Funding and Private Returns to Education), supplemented by some US studies. More than a thousand estimates were generated and produced 'a remarkable similarity in the estimated returns to schooling for a number of possible cuts of the data with an average return of around 6.5% across the majority of countries and model specifications' (Harmon et al. 2003, 130). This average figure of 6.5% suggests that private returns on education are high relative to the returns on other possible investments. The PURE data also suggest other trends in Europe: there are sizeable differences in returns on education in different countries (generally lower in the Nordic countries and higher in the United Kingdom and Ireland); the returns for women are generally higher than for men; and the returns on education generally increased in the 1980s and 1990s (see Long 2010 for a similar finding of these last two trends using US data).

Another feature highlighted by Harmon et al. (2003, 128–129) is that quantile regression can be used to estimate the return on education within different parts of a country's income distribution (see Harmon et al. 2001; Martins and Pereira 2004; Prieto-Rodriguez et al. 2008). These studies consistently find that returns on education are higher for individuals in higher income bands, given their observable characteristics. Reasons suggested for this result include: over-education for some workers in low-skilled and low-paid jobs; a stronger impact of education on high-ability individuals; differences in returns on education for graduates in different fields of study; unmeasured differences in education quality; and differences in endowments of complementary factors such as social or cultural capital. The main policy implication is to suggest that greater investment in education, on its own, may not be an effective public policy for reducing income inequality.

This conclusion is reinforced by another observation: econometric studies of the returns on education using the human capital model generally explain only a small fraction of the variance in earnings. Groshen (1991, 351), for example, presented a table of typical cross-sectional wage regression results in the Current Population Survey of the United States in which the simple Mincer equation explained only 26% of the variance and adding occupation, race, sex, union membership, and industry explained only 51%. The quantile regression analysis of Prieto-Rodriguez et al. (2008) found that wage inequality amongst equally educated people was much more important than wage inequality amongst groups with different levels of education. It is clear that a model relying only on human capital misses most of the determinants of earnings.

The Link between Education and Skills

An essential element in the human capital model is that time spent in education produces skills embodied in the individual that are then demanded by employers willing to pay a wage premium for those skills. That link between education and skills has been challenged by two broad critiques. The first critique argues that the main impact of individual investment in education is to *signal* to potential employers that the individual has higher natural abilities (valuable to the employer) than other candidates for a vacancy. The second argues that labour markets are *segmented* by wider social forces and education is used by employers as a sorting device of workers into these segments. This section considers these alternative explanations in turn.

Signalling Theories of Education

Early signalling theories paid particular attention to an alternative source of labour market skills than college education; namely, on-the-job training (both formal in-house training and informal learning-by-doing). This creates an issue for employers, who want to know at the point of making a job offer whether the candidate is suitable for on-the-job training. Thus Lester Thurow (1972, 68) argued that 'in a labor market based on job competition, the function of education is not to confer skill and therefore increased productivity and higher wages on the worker; it is rather to certify his "trainability" and to confer upon him a certain status by virtue of this certification'. An early summary by Blaug (1976, 846) expressed the theory more fully as follows:

> The employer is therefore faced with a selection problem: given the difficulties of accurately predicting the future performance of job applicants, he is tempted to treat educational qualifications as a screening device to distinguish new workers in terms of ability, achievement motivation, and possibly family origins, that is, in terms of personality traits rather than cognitive skills; cognitive skills are largely acquired by on-the-job training, and employers are therefore fundamentally concerned with selecting job applicants in terms of their trainability.

Michael Spence (1973) introduced the term 'signalling' to describe this theory of labour market behaviour. Spence made the general point that investment in education is costly to the student but these costs may differ in a systematic way with each individual's productive capability. This observation means that an equilibrium can emerge in which 'high-ability' individuals choose a higher level of education than 'low ability' individuals and employers offer better wages to applicants with higher levels of education because they know that extra education signals a higher ability that will make the employee more productive in the firm (for reviews of this substantial literature, see Weiss 1995 and Riley 2001, 459–463).

In Spence's framework, 'trainability' is just one example why higher ability individuals might be more productive, independent of any specific skills they may or may not acquire through education. Similarly, there are a several possible reasons why ability might be negatively correlated with the costs of education. At least since Roy (1951), economists have recognized that individuals choose occupations in which they have a relatively high ability (or 'comparative advantage') based on their endowed talents; see Heckman and Honoré (1990). Further, higher ability individuals find it less time consuming to learn (Zietz and Joshi 2005) and have lower risks of failure (Rochat and Demeulemeester 2001). There is also evidence that they receive a higher return on their investments in education (Weiss 1995, 137; Harmon et al. 2003, 129). Considerations such as these mean that people with higher ability tend to choose more education than people with lower ability and so education can serve as a signalling device.

The signalling model suggests there should be a premium to people who complete a qualification (because of its signalling effect) above the return on the years of education needed to achieve a degree. This has been termed the 'sheepskin effect' and there is a range of studies finding empirical support: see, for example, Belman and Heywood (1991), Jaeger and Page (1996), and Gibson (2000). Further, there is a suggestion that minorities facing labour market discrimination may have a particularly high extra return for completing a qualification (supported in the studies of Belman and Heywood 1991 and Gibson 2000, but not by Jaeger and Page 1996).

The major policy implication of the signalling model is that higher education attainment levels may not be effective in lifting individuals out of poverty or increasing a country's labour productivity. This was the main thrust of Thurow's original article, which concluded that 'massive educational investments are apt to be wasted' and 'reliance on education as the ultimate public policy for curing all problems, economic and social, is unwarranted at best and in all probability ineffective' (Thurow 1972, 81). Instead, higher levels of participation in education generate 'credentialism' or 'credential inflation' (Freeman 1976; Burris 1983; Fuller and Unwin 1999; Wolf 2002; McGuinness 2003).

Labour Market Segmentation

The theories discussed so far have focused on the power of the individual to improve their situation by choosing to invest in education, either to increase their labour market skills or to signal their unobservable ability to potential employers. Another group of theories emphasize the relative powerlessness of individuals, in the face of entrenched socio-economic forces that privilege some groups over others. Following the term used in Cain's (1976) survey, this phenomenon may be discussed under the general title of labour market segmentation (see also Fine 1998, chapters 5–7).

In this approach, education is an institution that reinforces socio-economic privilege. The classic treatment of this possibility was by French sociologist Pierre Bourdieu, who recognized in his studies that children from different social classes obtain systematically different scholastic achievements. He rejected the emphasis of Becker's human capital theory on different abilities and investments in education, arguing instead for an alternative concept that he termed *cultural* capital: 'From the very beginning, a definition of human capital, despite its humanistic connotations, does not move beyond economism and ignores, inter alia, the fact that the scholastic yield from education action depends on the cultural capital previously invested by the family" (Bourdieu 1986, 17). The process of accumulating cultural capital does not begin with entry into the education system, but depends critically on the cultural and economic capital already possessed by the parents (Bourdieu 1986, 25).

Thus, what Becker and others termed *human* capital acquired through participation in formal education was for Bourdieu a particular form of *cultural* capital, which he termed 'institutionalized cultural capital' because of the roles played by the associated system of academic qualifications. Bourdieu's approach has not been accepted by economists; indeed his term 'cultural capital' has not found widespread approval in the profession despite its promotion by David Throsby (1994, 1999, 2001). Nevertheless, whilst not using cultural capital, economists using the human capital model do recognize the importance of family background. Haveman and Wolfe (1995, 1855), for example, summarized the previous literature by suggesting that 'perhaps the most fundamental economic factor [determining children's education choices] is the human capital of parents, typically measured by the number of years of schooling attained'. Gaviria (2002, 331) was blunter: 'If one were to summarize the main message of the massive scientific literature dealing with family influences, a single line would suffice: it pays to choose one's parents.'

Socio-economic forces reinforcing privilege and poverty in segmented labour markets produce persistent inequalities in work conditions and wage rates, regionally, nationally, and internationally. Fine (1998, 120) traces the origins of modern segmented labour market theory to the dual labour market model introduced by Doeringer and Piore (1971), and Reich et al. (1973). In the dual labour market model, the primary sector offers highly skilled, highly paid jobs with secure internal career pathways (the 'internal labour market') involving on-the-job training opportunities, whilst the secondary sector offers casual, low-skilled, low-paid jobs with little chance of training. As argued in Bowles and Gintis (1976), the role of education is to prepare students for the primary or secondary sector depending on social expectations based on race, gender and class (see also Edwards et al. 1975).

Developments of the dual labour market theory, particularly by 'the Cambridge school' centred on the Department of Applied Economics at the University of Cambridge in the United Kingdom, questioned whether the low-paid jobs in the secondary sector are necessarily low-skilled. Craig et al. (1982, 87–88), for example, concluded from their study of the effects of the abolition of wages councils that 'there cannot be any presumption that differences in primary and secondary sector wages reflect differences either in job content or in the skills or productivity potential of the workers employed'. This led to the following conclusion (Craig et al. 1982, 94):

> Not only is the supply of 'good' jobs determined by the industrial structure, independent of the stock of human capabilities, but there is also not the expected

> positive relationship between pay and the skill content of jobs. In fact job content only becomes important in determining pay if it influences the worker's bargaining power (Rubery 1978, 31; Turner 1962). However, bargaining power is not a simple function of job content, and disadvantaged workers can be required to undertake demanding and skilled work without any major improvement in their labour market status and bargaining position.

Fine (1998, chapter 7) offered a Marxist version of segmented labour market theory that took these ideas further. Whilst recognizing the connection between social reproduction (through skills training, for example) and segmented labour markets, Fine cautioned against downplaying processes that undermine differentiation. He argued that it is essential to recognize that labour is mobile across sectors and occupations and so 'labour market *structures* do not arise simply because there is *differentiation* of the work-force' (Fine 1998, 195, emphasis in original). This makes a general theory of labour market segmentation impossible; instead 'labour markets are structured both horizontally and vertically, creating structures that are distinct from one another, that function differently from one another, and such structures are contingent upon the more complex outcome of underlying socio-economic processes and structures' (Fine 1998, 198).

Building on Botwinick (1993), Fine argued that only by understanding the dynamics of competition in market societies can wage-setting, and hence wage inequality, be properly understood (for a summary of Botwinick's model, see Buchanan and Considine 2008, 48–49). Whilst education is a factor, it is second order compared to the dynamics created from competition in capital and product markets. These (and not 'human capital') set the upper and lower limits within which wages are set. Institutions such as unions, employers' wage policies, and publicly defined labour standards then shape directly the jobs that are ultimately defined as 'vacancies' by employers and it is only after these processes have prevailed that education qualifications play their part in either screening workers or signalling to employers the 'quality' of labour.

Two Modern Developments

The theories discussed so far are not necessarily mutually exclusive. Education may signal unobservable abilities to employers, for example, but also provide genuine labour market skills. It is also possible for both processes to take place within a context of strong socio-economic forces producing segmented labour markets, each with its own history and distinctive features. This final section describes two modern developments that recognize these possibilities. The first moves human capital theory away from a single decision made at a particular point of time towards sequential decisions made period after period as the decision-maker learns more about abilities and opportunities. The second development analyses the way in which educational institutions, students, employers, and policy-makers can combine to create 'skill ecosystems' that may sustain a high-skills, high-wage equilibrium or reinforce a low-skills, low-wage equilibrium.

Sequential Decisions and Self-Discovery

The human capital model represented in Figure 7.1 suggests that the decision to invest in education is made at a single point in a person's life, based on a good knowledge of future income prospects with or without a qualification. The theory has often been used in exactly this way, but as early as 1976, Blaug was pointing out that 'the process of investment in schooling followed by investment in job search and post-school training is in effect *a sequential process* of individual decisions, subject at each stage to the constraints of past decisions and the stock of human capital accumulated to date' (Blaug 1976, 839–840, emphasis added). Two approaches are now being used to model sequential decision-making in a human capital framework.

The first approach is the stochastic dynamic programming model introduced by Keane and Wolpin (1997). Belzil (2007, 1076) has described this paper as 'most probably the most important contribution to the empirical schooling literature since Willis and Rosen (1979)'. The model uses US data from the youth cohort of the National Longitudinal Surveys of Labor Market Experience (NLSY). Individuals are assumed to make an education or employment choice every year beginning at age 16, with five alternatives: (1) participating in education; (2) working in a white-collar occupation; (3) working in a blue-collar occupation; (4) working in the military; or (5) engaging in home production. The resulting dynamic programming analysis fits the data well.

The second approach models sequential choice based on just two or three periods but highlights the key idea that students *discover* more about their individual interests and abilities as a result of participating in education. This view of education as helping individuals discover and develop their potential is an old one going back at least to Rousseau (1762). Two mathematical models to incorporate this key idea are by Altonji (1993) and Weiler (1994), both of which incorporate two sequential decisions. In the first decision, individuals choose whether to go on to higher education. During their studies, they discover more about their abilities, their interest in study relative to work, and the costs and benefits of further study. These discoveries inform their second decision, which is whether or not to continue with their initial study plans.

Arcidiacono (2004) develops this idea further in a model with three periods. In the first period, individuals choose either to enter the labour force or go to college. If they choose to go to college, they choose the college quality and their major of study (natural sciences; business; education; and social science/humanities/other). At the end of the first period, the students receive grades that provide them with feedback on their abilities. In the second period, individuals at college decide whether to drop out and enter the labour force or to continue their education for one more period. If the later, they may change their choice of college or major depending on what they have learnt about their abilities. In the third period, the individuals enter the labour force and earn income dependent on their qualifications and abilities.

The model produces an equilibrium in which high-ability students tend to go to high quality colleges and low ability students tend to go to low quality colleges. It therefore has a similarity with the signalling literature, but the important difference is that participation in education also has a real effect on individuals, who discover and develop their abilities as a result of their college years.

This leads to some important implications. As Manski (1989) argued, failure in education is not necessarily a bad outcome if it means a person has learnt more about his or her abilities. Indeed, in an entrepreneurial culture, people should be encouraged to try new things and explore their potential interests and abilities. If they learn in the process that they do not have an ability to do well in a particular course of study, then this is important new information in their personal development that should be used to frame future decisions.

A second implication is that obtaining a qualification without genuine ability is not likely to be a good outcome. The review by Harmon et al. (2003) draws on work by Chevalier (2003) to suggest that much of what appears to be over-qualification in the UK labour force is explained by people having invested in qualifications that do not reflect their genuine abilities (see also Hartog 2000). Once employers discover that the qualifications do not match the expected skills, these workers are passed over for on-the-job training or promotion, and end up in positions that do not require their qualifications with a considerable discount on their life-time earnings (Grubb 1997, 2002).

Skill Ecosystems

Recall the argument made by Fine (1998), drawing on Botwinick's (1993) earlier contribution, that a general theory of labour market segmentation is not possible since every individual labour market is distinctive in its structures and underlying socio-economic processes. A corollary of that argument, strongly recognized by both authors, is that an analysis of a particular labour market must pay attention to the full range of supply-side and demand-side factors that sustain it.

This idea has been extended in recent models that adopt the metaphor of a 'skill ecosystem' to explore how interaction between workers, employers, educators, and policy-makers may contribute to desirable or undesirable outcomes in labour markets (see also Buchanan et al., Chapter 21 in this volume). The metaphor recognizes that different agents in a labour market will adapt to any introduced change; hence relying on just one policy intervention (providing incentives for unemployed workers to participate in training, for example) will not generally be sufficient to produce a more desirable outcome. Instead, policy-makers must pay attention to integrating all components of an ecosystem to foster workforce development (Hall and Lansbury 2006, 587).

An early use of the phrase 'skill ecosystem' was made by David Finegold (1999) in his analysis of the cluster of successful biomedical and computer hardware and software firms in California. He defined a high-skill ecosystem as 'a geographic cluster of organizations (both firms and research institutions) employing staff with advanced, specialized skills in a particular industry and/or technology' (Finegold 1999, 61; see also Crouch et al. 1999).

This idea was adopted and extended by a research team led by John Buchanan commissioned by the NSW Board of Vocational Education and Training in Australia to report on options available for policy-makers to shape linkages between work and skills (Buchanan et al. 2001). In particular, the research group argued that the metaphor could be extended beyond high-skill ecosystems to consider a wide range of competencies: 'Understanding how both "general trends" and "diversity" cohere in practice is best achieved by using the notion of "skill ecosystems"—i.e. clusters of high, intermediate and low level competencies in a particular region or industry shaped by interlocking networks of firms, markets and institutions' (Buchanan et al. 2001, 11). The report identified five key features structuring any regional or sectorial skill ecosystem (2001, 22):

- business settings (eg type of product market, competitive strategies business organization/networks, financial system)
- institutional and policy frameworks (VET and Non-VET)
- modes of engaging labour (e.g. labour hire)
- structure of jobs (e.g. job design, work organization)
- level and type of skill formation (e.g. apprenticeships, informal on-the-job training).

Two pilot programmes were established in Australia to test the skill ecosystem idea; one administered by the NSW Department of Education and Training and one funded by the Queensland Department of Employment and Training. Lessons learnt from these pilots and related policy initiatives are reflected in publications by Buchanan (2006), Windsor and Alcorso (2008), and Buchanan and Jakubauskas (2010, 44–49). Figure 7.2 depicts a high-skill ecosystem. It highlights the four groups of different actors involved, and how each group must be motivated by mutually reinforcing advantages, for the high-skill ecosystem to flourish.

A recent report by the OECD on *Climate Change, Employment, and Local Development, Sydney, Australia* adapted the ecosystem approach to highlight the way in which profits and skills must reinforce each other to produce a sustainable outcome (Miranda et al. 2011). The analysis begins with two diagrams: one adopting the perspective of employers and one adopting the perspective of employees (see Figure 7.3). The analysis of the employers' perspective is a standard production function approach in which employers earn profits (in the classical sense of reward for successful entrepreneurial behaviour) by investing in capital and employing productive workers to take advantage of identified market opportunities. The analysis of the employees' perspective draws on the literature discussed in this chapter. Labour market skills are defined to exist when individual abilities are matched with investment in education to take advantage of employment opportunities.

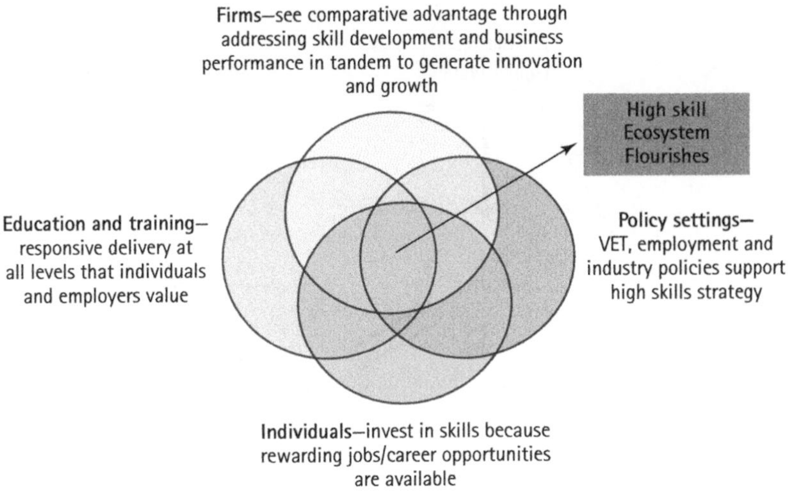

FIGURE 7.2 Depiction of a high-skill ecosystem

Source: Windsor and Alcorso (2008, 5).

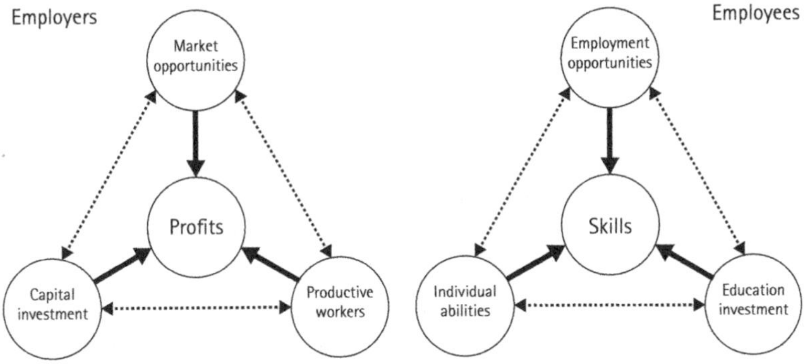

FIGURE 7.3 Perspectives in a skill ecosystem

Source: Dalziel (2010a, 2010b) reproduced from Miranda et al. (2011, 67).

Figure 7.4 brings the two perspectives together into a single ecosystem framework. It recognizes that in order for the employees to be employed as productive workers, they must have skills and in order for employers to offer sustainable employment opportunities, they must generate non-negative profits. Hence the two diagrams are really one, obtained by rotating the right-hand diagram and 'clicking' it into the left-hand diagram to produce the synthesis picture in Figure 7.4.

The OECD report used the framework in Figure 7.4 to analyse skills development in the 'green economy'. It recognized that climate change is creating market opportunities for enterprises that can offer technological solutions to businesses and households wanting to reduce their carbon emissions and energy use. To take advantage of these opportunities, the enterprises must be able to employ trades people who have the appropriate

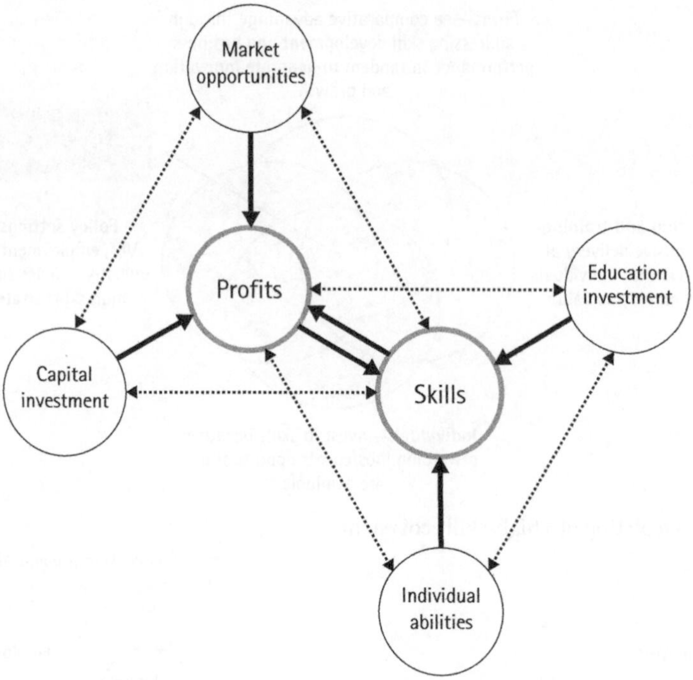

FIGURE 7.4 Skills and profits in a skill ecosystem

Source: Dalziel (2010a,b) reproduced from Miranda et al. (2011, 68).

'green skills' to design, build, sell, and maintain those technologies. Consequently, the Federal Government of Australia has invested millions of dollars to upgrade the ability of Technical and Further Education (TAFE) institutes to offer trades training in industry-defined green skills. This has included funding the acquisition of the latest energy-saving technologies into purpose-built training facilities, so that the education investment by trainees matches the capital investment taking place in businesses.

This was not a matter of the Australian government 'picking winners' for federal support. Rather, it was a matter of recognizing a trend in market opportunities for enterprises and thinking about how government policy could reduce transactions costs that were hampering the development of those opportunities. In particular, the policy sought to facilitate the matching of capital investment with education investment in a way that enhanced mutually reinforcing opportunities for increasing profits and skills. It is a good illustration of how thinking about the skill ecosystem as a whole can lead to good policy design.

Conclusion

This chapter began with recent publications that emphasize investment in skills as a core mechanism for improving social inclusion and economic performance (UKCES 2009;

OECD 2012). The later document specifically warned, however, that 'skills do not automatically convert into jobs and growth' (OECD 2012, 3). The literature surveyed in this chapter addresses some of the reasons why this statement is true. Education and qualifications are essential to the development and demonstration of an individual's skills, but this takes place within a context of powerful (although contested) socio-economic forces that reinforce pathways of privilege and poverty in strongly segmented labour markets. The chapter finished with a discussion of the metaphor of 'skill ecosystems' as a way to frame analysis of integrated policies for improving skill outcomes within this context. The metaphor explains how educational institutions, students, employers, and policy-makers must be motivated by mutually reinforcing advantages for a high-skill ecosystem to flourish (see especially Figure 7.2). It explains how policy must give attention to market opportunities, individual abilities, and the matching of capital investment with education investment (see especially Figure 7.4). This integrated approach to skills development takes us a long way from the individualist approach of the original human capital model introduced by Mincer, Shultz, and Becker half a century ago. Education and qualifications remain important—but they are not usefully conceived as fundamental, independent elements analogous, for example, to the role of technology in physical capital models. Instead, only when the system of formal education and qualifications is located in its broader socio-economic contexts can its role be properly analysed and comprehended.

Acknowledgements

The author acknowledges financial support from the New Zealand Ministry of Business, Innovation, and Employment under Research Programme LINX0603. He is grateful to fellow objective leaders in that project—Jane Higgins, Hazel Phillips, and Karen Vaughan—for many insightful discussions on the theme of this chapter. He thanks John Buchanan for very helpful comments on an earlier draft.

References

Altonji, J. G. (1993) 'The Demand for and Return to Education When Education Outcomes Are Uncertain', *Journal of Labor Economics*, 11(1): 48–83.

Arcidiacono, P. (2004) 'Ability Sorting and the Returns to College Major', *Journal of Econometrics*, 121(1–2): 343–375.

Becker, G. (1962) 'Investment in Human Capital: A Theoretical Analysis', *Journal of Political Economy*, 70(5) (Part 2): 9–49.

Becker, G. (1964) *Human Capital: A Theoretical and Empirical Analysis, with Special Reference to Education*, New York: Columbia University Press.

Belman, D. and Heywood J. S. (1991) 'Sheepskin Effects in the Returns to Education: An Examination of Women and Minorities', *Review of Economics and Statistics*, 73(4): 720–724.

Belzil, C. (2007) 'The Return to Schooling in Structural Dynamic Models: A Survey', *European Economic Review*, 51(5): 1059–1105.

Blaug, M. (1976) 'The Empirical Status of Human Capital Theory: A Slightly Jaundiced Survey', *Journal of Economic Literature*, 14(3): 827–855.

Botwinick, H. I. (1993) *Persistent Inequalities*, Princeton: Princeton University Press.

Bourdieu, P. (1986) 'The Forms of Capital', in J. C. Richardson (ed.), *Handbook of Theory and Research for the Sociology of Education*, 241–258. Westport, CT: Greenwood Publishing Group: 241–258. Translated by R. Nice from the original article published in 1983. Republished and cited from chapter 1, in S. J. Ball (ed.) (2004) *The RoutledgeFarmer Reader in Sociology of Education*, London: RoutledgeFarmer: 15–29.

Bowles, S. and Gintis H. (1976) *Schooling in Capitalist America*, London: Routledge and Kegan Paul.

Buchanan, J. (2006) *From 'Skill Shortages' to Decent Work*, Sydney: NSW Board of Vocational Education and Training.

Buchanan, J. and Considine H. (2008) 'The Significance of Minimum Wages for the Broader Wage-Setting Environment: Understanding the Role and Reach of Australian Awards', in *2008 Minimum Wage Research Forum Proceedings: Volume 1*, Australian Fair Pay Commission Research Report no. 4a/08: 47–62, Sydney: Australian Fair Pay Commission.

Buchanan, J. and Jakubauskas, M. (2010) 'The Political Economy of Work and Skill in Australia: Insights from Recent Applied Research', in J. Bryson (ed.), *Beyond Skill*, London: Palgrave Macmillan: 32–57.

Buchanan, J., Schofield, K., Briggs, K., Considine, G., Hager, G., Hawke, G., Kitay, J., Meagher, G., Macintyre, J., Mounier, J., and Ryan, S. (2001) *Beyond Flexibility*, Sydney: NSW Board of Vocational Education and Training.

Burris, V. (1983) 'The Social and Political Consequences of Overeducation', *American Sociological Review*, 48: 454–467.

Cain, G. G. (1976) 'The Challenge of Segmented Labor Market Theories to Orthodox Theory: A Survey', *Journal of Economic Literature*, 14(4): 1215–1257.

Cameron, S. V. and Taber, C. (2004) 'Estimation of Educational Borrowing Constraints Using Returns to Schooling', *Journal of Political Economy*, 112 (1): 132–182.

Chevalier, A. (2003) 'Measuring Over-education', *Economica*, 70(279): 509–531.

Craig, C., Rubery, J., Tarling, R., and Wilkinson, F. (1982) *Labour Market Structure, Industrial Organisation and Low Pay*, Cambridge: Cambridge University Press.

Crouch, C., Finegold, D., and Sako, M. (1999) *Are Skills the Answer?* Oxford: Oxford University Press.

Dalziel, P. (2010a) 'Developing the Next Generation: Employer-Led Channels for Education Employment Linkages', in J. Bryson (ed.), *Beyond Skill*, London: Palgrave Macmillan: 154–175.

Dalziel, P. (2010b) 'Skills in the Economy and Skill Development for Industry', Presentation to the Industry Training Federation New Zealand Labour Market and Skills Forum, Victoria University of Wellington, 1 September.

Dickson, M. and Harmon, C. (2011) 'Economic Returns to Education: What We Know, What We Don't Know, and Where We Are Going—Some Brief Pointers', *Economics of Education Review*, 30(6): 1115–1117.

Doeringer, P. and Piore, M. (1971) *Internal Labor Markets and Manpower Analysis*, Lexington: Heath Lexington Books.

Eckstein, Z. and Wolpin, K. I. (1999) 'Why Youths Drop Out of High School: The Impact of Preferences, Opportunities, and Abilities', *Econometrica*, 67(6): 1295–1339.

Edwards, R. C., Reich, MM, and Gordon, D. M. (eds) (1975) *Labor Market Segmentation*, Lexington: D. C. Heath.

Fine, B. (1998) *Labour Market Theory*, London: Routledge.

Finegold, D. (1999) 'Creating Self-sustaining, High-skill Ecosystems', *Oxford Review of Economic Policy*, 15(1): 60–81.

Freeman, R. B. (1976) *The Overeducated American*, New York: Academic Press.

Fuller, A. and Unwin, L. (1999) 'Credentialism, National Targets, and the Learning Society: Perspectives on Educational Attainment in the UK Steel Industry', *Journal of Education Policy*, 14(6): 605–617.

Gaviria, A. (2002) 'Intergenerational Mobility, Sibling Inequality and Borrowing Constraints', *Economics of Education Review*, 21(4): 331–340.

Gibson, J. (2000) 'Sheepskin Effects and the Returns to Education in New Zealand: Do They Differ by Ethnic Groups?', *New Zealand Economic Papers*, 34(2): 201–220.

Groshen, E. L. 1991. 'Five Reasons Why Wages Vary Among Employers', *Industrial Relations*, 30(3): 350–381.

Grubb, W. N. (1997) 'The Returns to Education in the Sub-Baccalaureate Labor Market, 1984–1990', *Economics of Education Review*, 16(3): 231–245.

Grubb, W. N. (2002) 'Learning and Earning in the Middle, Part I: National Studies of Pre-Baccalaureate Education', *Economics of Education Review*, 21(4): 299–321.

Hall, R. and Lansbury, R. (2006) 'Skills in Australia: Towards Workforce Development and Sustainable Skill Ecosystems', *Journal of Industrial Relations*, 48(5): 575–592.

Harmon, C., Oosterbeek, H. and Walker, I. (2003) 'The Returns to Education: Microeconomics', *Journal of Economic Surveys*, 17(2): 115–155.

Harmon, C., Walker, I., and Westergaard-Nielsen, N. (eds) (2001) *Education and Earnings in Europe*, Aldershot: Edward Elgar.

Hartog, J. (2000) 'Over-education and Earnings: Where Are We, Where Should We Go?', *Economics of Education Review*, 19(2): 131–147.

Haveman, R. and Wolfe, B. (1995) 'The Determinants of Children's Attainments: A Review of Methods and Findings', *Journal of Economic Literature*, 33(4): 1829–1878.

Heckman, J. J. and Honoré, B. E. (1990) 'The Empirical Content of the Roy Model', *Econometrica*, 58(5): 1121–1149.

Jaeger, D. A. and Page, M. E. (1996) 'Degrees Matter: New Evidence on Sheepskin Effects in the Returns to Education', *Review of Economics and Statistics*, 78(4): 733–740.

Keane, M. P. and Wolpin, K. I. (1997) 'The Career Decisions of Young Men', *Journal of Political Economy*, 105(3): 473–522.

Keane, M. P. and Wolpin, K. I. (2000) 'Eliminating Racial Differences in Schooling Attainment and Labor Market Success', *Journal of Labor Economics*, 18(4): 614–652.

Keane, M. P. and Wolpin, K. I. (2001) 'The Effect of Parental Transfers and Borrowing Constraints on Educational Attainment', *International Economic Review*, 42(4): 1051–1103.

Long, M. C. (2010) 'Changes in the Returns to Education and College Quality', *Economics of Education Review*, 29(3): 338–347.

Manski, C. F. (1989) 'Schooling as Experimentation: A Reappraisal of the Postsecondary Dropout Phenomenon', *Economics of Education Review*, 8(4): 305–312.

Martins, P. S. and Pereira, P. T. (2004) 'Does Education Reduce Wage Inequality? Quantile Regression Evidence from 16 Countries', *Labour Economics*, 11(3): 355–371.

McGuinness, S. (2003) 'Graduate Overeducation as a Sheepskin Effect: Evidence from Northern Ireland', *Applied Economics*, 35(5): 597–608.

Mincer, J. (1958) 'Investment in Human Capital and Personal Income Distribution', *Journal of Political Economy*, 66(4): 281–302.

Mincer, J. (1974) *Schooling, Experience and Earnings*, New York: Columbia University Press.

Miranda, G., Dalziel, P., Estolano, C., Krasnowski, K., and Larcombe, G. (2011) 'Climate Change, Employment and Local Development, Sydney, Australia', OECD Local Economic and Employment Development (LEED) Working Papers, 20112014, OECD, Paris.

OECD (2012) *Better Skills, Better Jobs, Better Lives: A Strategic Approach to Skills Policies*, Paris: OECD.

Prieto-Rodriguez, J., Barros, C. P., and Vieira, J. A. C. (2008) 'What a Quantile Approach Can Tell Us about Returns to Education in Europe', *Education Economics*, 16(4): 391–410.

Reich, M., Gordon, D. M., and Edwards, R. C. (1973) 'A Theory of Labor Market Segmentation', *American Economic Review*, 63(2): 359–365.

Riley, J. (2001) 'Silver Signals: Twenty-five Years of Screening and Signalling', *Journal of Economic Literature*, 34(2): 432–478.

Rochat, D. and Demeulemeester, J.-L. (2001) 'Rational Choice under Unequal Constraints: The Example of Belgian Higher Education', *Economics of Education Review*, 20(1): 15–26.

Rousseau, J.-J. (1762) *Émile*, translated and annotated by A. Bloom, 1991, London: Penguin.

Roy, A. (1951) 'Some Thoughts on the Distribution of Earnings', *Oxford Economic Papers*, 3(2): 135–146.

Rubery, J. (1978) 'Structured Labour Markets, Worker Organisation and Low Pay', *Cambridge Journal of Economics*, 2(1): 17–36.

Shultz, T. W. (1961) 'Investment in Human Capital', *American Economic Review*, 51(1): 1–17.

Sianesi, B. and Van Reenen, J. (2003) 'The Returns to Education: Macroeconomics', *Journal of Economic Surveys*, 17(2): 157–200.

Spence, M. (1973) 'Job Market Signalling', *Quarterly Journal of Economics*, 87 (3): 355–374.

Throsby, D. (1994) 'The Production and Consumption of the Arts: A View of Cultural Economics', *Journal of Economic Literature*, 32(1): 1–29.

Throsby, D. (1999) 'Cultural Capital', *Journal of Cultural Economics*, 23(1): 3–12.

Throsby, D. (2001) *Economics and Culture*, Cambridge: Cambridge University Press.

Thurow, L. (1972) 'Education and Economic Inequality', *The Public Interest*, 28: 66–81.

Tobias, J. L. and Li, M. (2004) 'Returns to Schooling and Bayesian Model Averaging: A Union of Two Literatures', *Journal of Economic Surveys*, 18(2): 153–180.

Turner, H. A. (1962) *Trade Union Growth, Structure and Policy*, London: Allen and Unwin.

UKCES (2009) *Towards Ambition 2020: Skills, Jobs, Growth*, London: UK Commission for Employment and Skills.

Weiler, W. C. (1994) 'Expectations, Undergraduate Debt and the Decision to Attend Graduate School: A Simultaneous Model of Student Choice', *Economics of Education Review*, 13(1): 29–41.

Weiss, A. (1995) 'Human Capital vs. Signalling Explanations of Wages', *Journal of Economic Perspectives*, 9(4): 133–154.

Willis, R. and Rosen, S. (1979) 'Education and Self-selection', *Journal of Political Economy*, 87(5) (Part 2): S7–S35.

Windsor, K. and Alcorso, C. (2008) *Skills in Context: A Guide to the Skill Ecosystem Approach to Workforce Development*, Sydney: NSW Department of Education and Training.

Wolf, A. (2002) *Does Education Matter?* London: Penguin.

Zietz, J. and Joshi, P. (2005) 'Academic Choice Behavior of High School Students: Economic Rationale and Empirical Evidence', Economics *of Education Review*, 24(3): 297–308.

CHAPTER 8

PRE-EMPLOYMENT SKILL FORMATION IN AUSTRALIA AND GERMANY

JOHN POLESEL

Introduction

This chapter seeks to provide a critical analysis of the role that vocational education and training (VET) plays in preparing young people for the labour market in two contrasting systems—Australia and Germany. In Germany, VET occurs mainly in separate secondary schools, within the structure of the 'dual system'. In Australia, it occurs within a scheme of mainly comprehensive high schools, with vocational studies located in the curriculum structures of the senior secondary certificates offered in each state. In Australia, it also occurs, to an extent, in the adult sector VET institutions, and some specialist upper secondary providers, such as trade training centres, which focus on vocational programmes for school-aged youth.

The concepts of education logic and employment logic, as applied to education and training systems (Iannelli and Raffe 2007) and the type of welfare state (Murray and Polesel 2013), whether neocorporatist (coordinated economy) or neoliberal (liberal economy), are used to analyse important differences between the Australian and the German experiences. This allows an examination of the policy imperatives and solutions in each system, and how these are determined by the emphasis that is placed on education or employment and the role of actors within the policy community as well as those outside it—industry, employers' groups, chambers of commerce, trade unions, and epistemic communities—in Australia and Germany. I refer to the work of Bosch and Charest (2008) and the varieties of capitalism approach articulated by Hall and Soskice (2001), who argue that distinctive differences have developed in the way that skills formation is structured and delivered in different nations, and that these differences are related to the forms of capitalism which exist in different systems. I explore these differences and similarities in a comparative transnational context across two systems which may be characterized as adopting different approaches to the welfare state and capitalism—Australia and Germany. These are nations with developed economies characterized by a very high human development rate (UNDP 2011) but quite different education and training systems with different problems and different rates of youth unemployment—8.6% in Germany and 13.8% in Australia.

It is a given that schools have variously been called upon to address a growing range of problems, from building the character of young people to addressing skills shortages and solving unemployment (Malley et al. 2001). The response of The Riots Communities and Victims Panel (2012) to the 2011 youth riots in London, Bristol, Birmingham, and Manchester was that schools did not adequately prepare young people for work, nor, for that matter, sufficiently 'build character in young people' (2012, 7) and it recommended, inter alia, that schools should be fined for failing to teach children properly. By implication, it attributed significant responsibility to the schools for the problems which occurred, despite the fact that youth unemployment in the United Kingdom was above 20% at the time, with significantly higher rates in some of the regions worst affected by the riots.

What is pertinent in the response to the English riots is the view that schools might somehow be responsible for them, or, at the very least, that they might be called upon to prevent them. This, of course, reflects the view I have argued elsewhere (Polesel and Keating 2011), that this burden has fallen largely on secondary schools and has been distributed unequally on different parts of the curriculum, with vocational programmes in particular being asked to address a range of needs not closely linked to the traditional academic mission of secondary schooling (Durkheim 1977). Maynes (1977) has argued that these needs include fostering good work habits in working-class children, whilst Billett (2004) notes that school-based vocational programmes are increasingly expected to meet the needs of industry and government, in addition to their other functions. Recent Australian policy explicitly states that the primary role of vocational education and training 'is to provide people with the skills and knowledge they need to participate fully in the workforce' (Auditor General Victoria 2006, vi).

The instrumental demands currently placed on VET for young people are neither unexpected nor new. School-based vocational training emerged in Australia at the beginning of the twentieth century, at a time when Australia's growing economy had labour shortages in key areas of trades and technology. Government reports (Education Department of Victoria 1973) at that time stated explicitly that state schools were expected to address skills shortages and the need for trained workers. I have argued that these early attempts to introduce vocationally oriented courses into schools met with limited success (Polesel 2007), because students ignored the technical, industrial and agricultural subjects offered in the early prototypes of our state high schools and chose instead subjects which would lead to university. The state schools were seen, understandably, as a means for those students who could not afford private secondary education to go to university.

I have also argued that the culture of secondary schooling, as described so well by Durkheim (1977), at the start of the twentieth century was antithetical to the values and structures required for VET to function effectively in the context of a modern high school. In short, VET was not welcome in the high schools. Its lack of a disciplinary base and history meant it did not have parity of status with the traditional subject-based curriculum. In Germany, this resistance to vocational studies has an even longer history and led, ultimately, to the formation of separate structures of vocational training as early as the 1850s. It led also to the implementation of early tracking (from the age of 11) and highly differentiated schools—an approach which persists, though in somewhat different forms in the different states of the German federal system.

In Australia, these same factors also led to the establishment of separate secondary technical schools; specialized state schools focused on VET, but these have now largely disappeared. The arguments for their establishment, documented in the literature at that time, centred on the belief that the high schools devalued and neglected technical training, and pursued a curriculum designed for university entrance. However, at the time, many policy-makers and officials in the state education departments opposed technical schools. In Victoria, Martin Hansen, the Senior Inspector of Secondary Schools, expressed his fears that the establishment of a separate system of technical schools would lead to social selection, with one group of schools leading middle-class children into university and the professions and another group of schools leading working-class children into factory jobs and trades. He also feared a narrowing of the curriculum and of pedagogical approaches in both sites, with high schools neglecting applied learning and its associated pedagogies, and technical schools neglecting knowledge and general education and culture. In the late 1920s, he led a concerted effort to amalgamate the technical and high schools in Victoria into a comprehensive system of provision. It is instructive that this move failed at the last moment when the governing state Labor Party opposed it, arguing that technical schools represented an important and essential foothold for their working-class constituents in education. The Labor Party, supported by the Technical Division of the Education Department, argued that VET would become marginalized within the system and that technical schools were an important instrument for achieving social mobility and addressing the 'social and economic circumstances' of working-class children (Education Department of Victoria 1973, 643). The debate was bitter and continued for many years, and it was not until the 1980s that the last state system of education in Australia finally abolished its technical schools.

However, arguments about the role of education and training in meeting the needs of governments and the economy have not diminished. The weight that should be given to such a role, compared with the emphasis on general education, represents a debate that has been re-ignited in the recent work of Michael Young (2007). Young argues that competencies delivered in the absence of powerful knowledge represent a betrayal of the working-class children who form the majority of the users of these programmes. Moreover, the evidence that a divided curriculum might be socially selective is not only strong, it is apparent across a range of national systems, even when they have very different approaches to tracking (Bourdieu and Passeron 1977; Ringer 1989; Fini 2007; Benadusi 2007). My own research shows that the social background of VET students in Australian schools is very different from the background of students heading to university (Polesel 2008; Polesel and Clarke 2011).

Furthermore, in Australia, VET continues to struggle to establish a role in secondary schools more generally. Durkheim's view of a secondary school culture which leaves little room for vocational curricula and pedagogies remains relevant, if somewhat less so than at the beginning of the twentieth century. Many parents and students still see it as a second-best option. And many teachers do not believe it is a legitimate part of secondary schooling. VET continues to occupy a lowly place in the status hierarchy of education, regarded as a tool used by government to fix problems, like skills shortages or unemployment.

In Germany, however, half of the secondary school cohort enters VET and it is argued that the explicit and strong links between the training, the qualifications and skills it provides, and the social partners (including trade unions and employers) ensure that transitions from VET to the labour market in systems such as this are effective (Bosch and Charest 2008) and that the status of VET relative to the academic curriculum is high (Iannelli and Raffe 2007).

What Does It Mean to Do a Vocational Programme in School?

One can begin by pointing out that 'doing VET' in an Australian school setting usually means enrolling in one or two VET subjects as part of a broader senior secondary school certificate. This is what Iannelli and Raffe (2007) have characterized as the adoption of an 'education logic', as opposed to what might be described as an 'employment logic' in Germany. In many Australian states, there are limitations imposed by the structure and regulations of the senior certificates on how much VET a student can do, and it is rare for a student to do enough VET to actually get even a very basic VET qualification. I have argued (Polesel 2008) that Australian school-based VET qualifications, although competency-assessed within the framework of the national system of accreditation (the Australian Qualifications Framework), are typically offered at the most basic levels (Certificate I or II). These vocational subjects tend to form only a minor part of a broader suite of general school subjects in which vocational studies and competencies are given little priority. The VET qualifications which arise from these programmes are therefore usually basic or incomplete and rarely provide specific competencies or a 'licence' to practice a particular trade. The education logic of their delivery requires them to adapt and conform to the structures and culture of school subjects. Hall and Soskice (2001) argue that this neoliberal market economy approach, typical of many Anglophone nations, has led to a reliance on market mechanisms rather than training systems to select and train skilled workers. In turn, they argue that this had led to a retreat from policy engagement by industry and trade unions in neoliberal market economies such as the Australian one, with the result that there is little engagement in the design of initial skills formation by industry, little commitment to providing training places (outside the traditional trade apprenticeships), and consequently lowered interest in the skills and qualifications which the VET sector provides.

The limitations which this education logic has imposed on the delivery of VET are confirmed in a report (Phillips 2006) which has criticized VET in Schools (VETiS) for not delivering the basic competencies required by industry, for being too oriented towards graded assessment, and for operating within the constraints of the achievement of academic outcomes. I have made similar criticisms (Polesel 2008) and have presented evidence, based on Victorian destinations data spanning over ten years, that VETiS graduates' destinations have increasingly tended towards university entry, whilst their transitions into post-school vocational providers, including apprenticeship destinations, have declined. Anlezark et al. (2006) have also questioned the efficacy of school-based VET in creating pathways into post-school adult sector VET, arguing that whilst it provides pathways for some boys (for example, into engineering and building trades), it fails to do so for girls and for other groups. Sweet (2000) argues that this phenomenon represents a process of academic drift which may be threatening the pedagogical basis of VETiS programmes.

On the basis of this evidence, it can be argued that the senior certificates in Australia really have remained focused on the subjects which are designed to lead young people into university. At the same time, the proportion of students making a transition to university represents a minority of the cohort. ABS (2011) data report a school completion rate across Australia of approximately 80%. We know from tracking data conducted in two of the larger states, Victoria (DEECD 2011) and Queensland (DET 2011), that just over four in ten of these will go to university. Extrapolating these data to the national cohort suggests that no more than one-third of the cohort will enter university directly upon completion of school. The paradox is clear. Australia has a range of senior secondary certificates which remain focused on university entry, but most students do not go to university.

By way of contrast, the bipartite (or tripartite) structures of secondary education evident in Germany strongly differentiate vocational and academic pathways. Whilst the structures vary somewhat from *Land* to *Land*, differentiation usually begins at the end of primary schooling (at the age of 11), with students tracked into grammar school (*Gymnasium*), a track leading into upper secondary Gymnasium and then to university, or into *Hauptschule*, a basic junior secondary education leading into the upper secondary vocational (*Berufsschule*) track and then to employment. Other tracks, depending on the *Land*, may include a middle-tier school (*Realschule*) which can lead to the dual system or to specialist technical upper secondary schools (*Fachoberschulen*). Finally, there is also a more 'comprehensive' type of school (*Gesamtschule*), common in the east of the country and designed to avoid early tracking.

The main feature which distinguishes the German approach, however, is the *Berufsschule*, or upper secondary dual system, which involves apprenticeship training from the age of 16 in 'dual' locations—the workplace and at school. What also distinguishes the approach, particularly from Australia, is the sheer size of the apprenticeship cohort (approximately half of the secondary school population). This is made possible by the strong neocorporatist alliance of employers, unions, and the state, which results in strong commitment to the provision of training places. Hall and Soskice (2001) have argued that the combination of strong policy engagement by industry, trade unions, and government have created a mutually beneficial dependence on state structures of education and training in the coordinated market economies of nations such as Germany. They argue that this dependence provides a strong incentive for industry to supply apprenticeship places, unlike Australia.

The Culture of Secondary Schooling

Following the 'comprehensivization' of secondary schools in Australia, the delivery of vocational studies has occurred within largely undifferentiated structures of secondary schooling. It has also occurred within the limitations imposed by the senior secondary certificates, cementing the alignment described by Durkheim (1977) between the culture of school and the culture of universities. In Australia, the role of the senior certificates in both preparing young people for university and in selecting them has contributed to the constraints placed upon VET delivery. Ryan (2002) argues that the alienating nature of the curriculum and of schools constitutes a strong argument for applied learning, although he notes the weaknesses associated with delivery of these programmes in traditional school settings. Teachers too have reinforced the message that VET plays a valuable role in managing student diversity, whilst many students express their preference for learning through real-life activities and practical problem-solving (Polesel and Clarke 2011). But despite these positive views, there is significant evidence that VET is not regarded highly in schools. In a case study of a regional high school located in a working-class setting, Polesel and Clarke (2011) present evidence that traditional subjects are given priority in staffing and resourcing, even when most of the students do not go on to university. If there are teacher shortages, maths is given top priority. If a teacher is made permanent, they are allocated to 'proper' subjects—not VET. I would argue that this is a problem of school culture. In the same school, teachers admit that it would be easier to teach the students who want to go to university, even though these represent a minority overall in Australia (and a tiny minority in this particular school).

An older national study conducted with colleagues in 2004 (Polesel et al. 2004) suggested that VET subjects often need to generate funding by charging the students themselves (even in state schools) to cover additional costs for material or resources or external delivery by other providers. The implication seems to be that VET cannot make a legitimate claim on school resources, like science or mathematics, or other traditional disciplines. Given the documented link between socio-economic status and participation in VET, this leads to a situation in which those students most likely to have to pay additional costs for their education are those from the poorest backgrounds. Further to this argument, Clarke (2012) has noted lower levels of participation in school-based VET for the poorest one-fifth of students, a phenomenon which she speculated may be related to weaker family links to the world of work but which may also be related to financial considerations in the selection of subjects.

In Germany, the resistance to vocational studies in the school curriculum has similar origins, but has been largely neutralized by the imposition of very different structures. I have argued (Polesel 2007) that the demands of technical and scientific innovation, as well as a growing middle class in eighteenth century Europe, began to lead to a demand for technological and scientific literacies not traditionally offered in the dominant European grammar school (*Gymnasium*) paradigm. In Germany, this led to the emergence of non-classical grammar schools in the late 1700s, but these were bitterly opposed and largely eliminated by a university strategy designed to disallow their role in university preparation. It would require another century before non-classical grammar schools (teaching, for example modern languages and sciences) were given the mandate to prepare young people for university in Germany. Ringer (1969) argues that the guardians of academic orthodoxy (the 'mandarins') continued to oppose these schools well into the twentieth century. The emergence of vocational training within state-sponsored systemic structures would take even longer in Germany. Whilst well-organized apprenticeship training existed as early as the 1850s, this was delivered by industry or at the local government level. Good (1960) notes that the authorities were reluctant to legislate for vocational training systems or structures at the national level, and it was not until 1938 that Germany implemented a national system of vocational schooling (Mitter 1995).

Having noted this early reluctance to include vocational education within national structures of schooling (a phenomenon evident in many systems other than just Germany and Australia), the bipartite structures of secondary education evident in Germany now are well established and have resisted considerable pressure for reform. Whilst the structures vary somewhat from *Land* to *Land*, they have generally involved a grammar school (*Gymnasium*) track leading to university and a vocational (*Berufsschule*) track leading to employment. The latter is an apprenticeship track, often described as the dual system, as it involves two locations—work and school.

The two main features which distinguish the German dual system from the Australian approach to vocational education, however, are the role of apprenticeships and the sheer size of the vocational cohort (approximately half of the secondary school population). These suggest a removal from, rather than an accommodation to, the academic culture of secondary schooling. Rather than fitting vocational training into the operations and structures of secondary schools which are also required to prepare young people for university, the early separation of young people entering VET from their university-oriented peers into separate schools (in separate locations) obviates the need for the grammar schools (*Gymnasien*) to accommodate the broader range of needs which near-universal secondary participation has created. It could be argued that, unlike Australian schools, German schools are insulated from the conflicting demands of the vocational and academic curricula and the different needs of their associated cohorts, and better able to deal with the specialized needs of the vocational curriculum. Having said this, the technical upper secondary schools (*Fachoberschulen*), represent an attempt to combine aspects of vocational learning with the academic rigours of the *Gymnasium*.

Since they provide a lead in to higher education courses in universities of technical and applied learning, *Fachoberschulen* have shown strong growth in recent years, their graduates growing from 8.6% of all 18–21-year-olds in 1996 to 13.6% in 2006 (Reupold and Tippelt 2011). It might also be asked, however, what the impact of this highly tracked system is on the transition patterns of young people, particularly from the point of view of equity. These questions are asked in the following sections.

Outcomes

Internationally, the effectiveness of VET as a tool for retention has generated only weak evidence in its favour. In Australia, the evidence is similarly mixed. Anlezark et al. (2006) argue that school-based VET confers a small positive effect on retention from Year 10 to Year 11 but a negative one on retention from Year 11 to Year 12. The authors question whether these programmes might be better targeted in the earlier years, as in Germany for example, in order to improve school retention. It might be noted that since the introduction of vocational courses in the upper secondary years of Australian education systems in the 1990s, retention rates have remained stubbornly static, usually falling just under or just above the 80% mark.

Analyses of the outcomes of VET programmes in Australian schools more broadly also provide a mixed report on their efficacy. Given the concerns already raised in this chapter regarding the quality of the training and competencies acquired by young people participating in Australian school-based VET courses, a further consideration is the effectiveness of the transitions to the labour market which graduates from these courses achieve. In the two Australian states which investigate the destinations of school completers, there are significant proportions of completers who enter the labour market directly, without further education or training. In Victoria, this is a transition experienced by just over one-fifth (22.6%) of the school completer cohort (DEECD 2011), whilst in Queensland, it is a little over one-third (35%) of the cohort (DET 2011). Given the stated focus of VET subjects on preparation for work, it is appropriate to ask whether participation in them confers any advantages in this transition over those who have not participated in school-based vocational courses. My research (Polesel 2008) indicates that the kinds of jobs accessed by VET and non-VET graduates over recent years in Victoria are very similar. In both cases, they are largely located in low paid, low-skill occupations, characterized by part-time and casual working conditions. I have argued that 'these types of school-based vocational programmes [do not] confer any material advantage in the types of occupations accessed by school leavers seeking a direct entry to the labour market' (Polesel 2008, 627).

Similar research conducted in Queensland came up with comparable conclusions (DETA 2009). Anlezark et al. (2006) drew similar conclusions in their study, arguing that school-based VET courses need to prepare young people better for entry to work. These arguments resonate with the findings of the English research, which has argued that education and training in England operates within a 'low skill equilibrium' where low-skilled labour produces low-quality goods in an environment of low work satisfaction (Winch and Clarke 2003).

By way of contrast, Germany's is regarded as a highly effective system of training, with close and well-signposted links between qualifications and specific skilled occupations. Iannelli and Raffe's (2007) article would locate Germany in the category of an 'employment logic' system of education and training, with its qualifications closely linked to the needs of industry and consequently highly valued by industry. One of the advantages of the status thus conferred upon training is that the distinction between vocational and general curricula in upper secondary schools 'cannot be reduced to a simple hierarchy of status' (Iannelli and Raffe 2007: 51) as we have seen in the Australian context.

With respect to school completion rates, Reupold and Tippelt (2011) argue that Germany's differentiated system 'which attempts to qualify young people at the educational level that bests suits their capabilities and interests, can result in comparatively high completion rates' (2011, 156). Because of Germany's highly differentiated system, it is difficult to confirm this assertion with a simple or comparable school completion rate. However, ABS data (2012) on the proportion of the 25–34-year-old population with senior secondary education reports a rate of 86% for Germany and 82% for Australia.

Moreover, Hall and Soskice (2001) have argued that in the coordinated market economy approach of Germany, employers can rely on their training systems to generate the highly skilled labour they require, without the need either to export jobs or to import labour to the extent which occurs in the neoliberal economies. These views must be tempered, however, by an acceptance of the system's vulnerabilities. Deissinger (2006) has noted that the effectiveness of the German apprenticeship system is subject to economic conditions as they impact on the ability of industry to offer training places. The *Berufachschule*—full-time vocational school—was in fact established specifically to provide the pre-employment practical training normally received in a work environment, but has been criticized as providing only simulated, school-based training. Lauder et al. (2008) also argue that the impact of globalization and associated 'standardisation of products, processes and people' (2008, 26) is leading some employers and industries to turn away from national training systems and to seek more efficient ways of training their workers, even in the coordinated market economies.

This is a reminder of Young's (2007) argument, that VET, however high its quality may be, cannot compensate for the structure of labour markets or the fact that a youth labour market, such as that of Australia, may be dominated by low-skill jobs. In other words, systems of education and training alone cannot create skilled jobs.

Social Selection

It is important to ask, as Martin Hansen did in Australia in the 1930s, whether tracked provision in schools is socially divisive. It might also be asked whether the different approaches noted in Australia and Germany are better or worse, from the point of view of equity. Recent data indicate that VETiS participation is rising steadily in Australia, with 230,000 upper secondary school students doing at least one vocational subject in 2010 (NCVER 2011). However, this growth has been uneven in terms of schooling sector and the social background of the students. Anlezark et al. (2006) have found that students from family backgrounds with lower education levels are more likely to participate in school-based VET. Using a broader measure of socio-economic status (SES), based on social geography, I found from my own work that students living in urban areas of Melbourne characterized by higher levels of income, housing prices and educational qualifications were less likely to participate in vocational programmes than their peers in poorer areas where the population had lower levels of education (Polesel 2008). The study showed that approximately twice as many students proportionally in the poorest regions of the city participated in school VET, compared with their counterparts in the wealthier suburbs, with VETiS 'most prevalent in the school communities serving the poorest families' (Polesel 2008, 622).

A recent NCVER (National Centre for Vocational Education Research) analysis of school-based VET participation shows that both the highest and the lowest SES quintiles of students are less likely to participate (NCVER Vocstats 2009). This suggests that the most affluent 20% of the student population may be less likely to see a role for VET in their pathways planning, whilst the least affluent 20% (the group most likely to represent the weakest links with the labour market) may not have access, for reasons discussed above. Social segregation, along curriculum lines, and social exclusion from secondary schooling are related phenomena, well documented in many other studies (e.g. Goodson 1993; Teese and Polesel 2003).

There is evidence that the social distribution of VETiS programmes is also related to patterns of public and private education delivery. A recent analysis of Longitudinal Surveys of Australian Youth data (Anlezark et al. 2006) shows that participation is concentrated in government schools rather than in the Catholic or Independent schools. More recent national enrolment data confirm this finding, demonstrating that approximately 40% of upper secondary students in government schools participate in VET, compared with fewer than 30% in Catholic schools and fewer than % in independent schools (NCVER 2011). These findings are also confirmed in a recent NCVER paper (Clarke 2012) which shows the bulk of VET participation amongst low SES students in government schools. Independent schools in Australia, which can charge substantial fees, have a student body boasting higher mean SES levels and lower mean VET enrolments. My own work (Polesel 2008), using data from the state of Victoria, also found a relationship between the average SES of each type of school and the proportion of students doing VET subjects. The independent schools enrolled the wealthiest children and had the lowest participation in VET. Catholic private schools were a little above average in social terms but below average in VET enrolments. Government schools had the lowest proportion of children from wealthy, educated families and the highest proportion in vocational subjects.

These are macro patterns and conceal significant diversity and differences in the way that the VET curriculum is utilized. However, our research indicates that these patterns are reproduced at the school level. In a study we conducted in a working-class school in a regional Australian setting, our research showed that most students in this school were enrolled in VET subjects (Polesel and Clarke 2011). However, even in this setting, dominated by students from low SES backgrounds, the VET subjects were much less likely to be chosen by the few children with university educated fathers.

Social selection is also apparent in the German system. Sweet (2009) notes the very strong relationship in Germany between tracking and SES, and his analysis suggests that this relationship is weaker in the Australian system, supporting a view that Australia is more 'equitable' than Germany. Sweet also links the size of the vocational pathway with equity, suggesting that the greater the relative size of the vocational cohort the lower the level of equity, once again emphasizing Germany's large vocational system and relatively poor performance on the equity measure. The research of Benadusi (2007) highlights Germany as one of the European nations with amongst the highest levels of correlation between educational achievement and socio-economic background, and educational achievement and level of parents' education, although his analysis does not include Australia for comparison. Sweet (2009) further links the early streaming characteristic of the German approach with low levels of tertiary aspiration and low levels of tertiary completion. Blanden et al. (2005) have argued that these phenomena are linked with relatively low rates of intergenerational mobility in Germany. One might, however, balance these rather negative views of equity in the German system with the argument that Germany has one of the lowest Gini coefficients (indicator of inequality) in the world, and a youth unemployment rate about half that of Australia's (8.1%, compared with 13.8%).

What Is the Role of Adult VET Providers for Young People?

Schools, of course, are not the sole providers of VET for young people. The adult vocational sector in Australia, constituting the public technical and further education (TAFE) institutes and a smaller private VET sector, also play a role in the delivery of VET to young people. However, across Australia, the role played by the adult VET sector providers for 15–19 year-olds is relatively limited. Only very small proportions of the total cohort of full-time students are enrolled in adult VET sector institutions, for example, 2.6% of 16-year-olds and 4.9% of 17-year-olds (Census 2011). Nine in ten full-time students aged 17 years are in schools (and 96.5% of 16-year-olds). However, recent Australian policy initiatives now include school completion and qualification targets that include study in non-school providers such as TAFE institutes. Unlike systems such as the English one, where significant proportions of the cohort participate in both vocational and general programmes in the further education college sector, only a small proportion of school-aged young people in Australia use the adult VET sector in this way, with the vast majority of 15–19-year-olds who are in full-time education or training attending school rather than an adult non-school provider (Census 2011).

There are many reasons for these patterns. In part, they are historical and reflect the dominance of the general education curriculum. However, they also reflect a reluctance, or, perhaps, an inability in adult sector providers to cater for the needs of the younger cohort. Wyn et al. (2004) have argued that courses offered in adult VET settings may provide an appropriate option for some school-aged youth, but that a range of conditions, which are not always met in these institutions, would need to be present for them to cater effectively for the majority of younger students. The research literature has identified effective pastoral care, adult settings in which young people are treated with respect and small class sizes as important ways of improving the educational experience of young people in adult VET sector settings (Bradshaw et al. 2001; Wyn et al. 2004). A recent New South Wales study emphasized the need for motivated teachers who enjoy working with young people, strong course and career information, and clearly delineated pathways into the labour market as essential ingredients of TAFE programmes for young people (TAFE Executive Group 2008, 3). In my own work (e.g. Polesel et al. 2004), I have argued that these features are not always evident in courses designed for adult clients and that the range of programmes and support services offered in adult sector institutes, in addition to the experience of the staff, may not always meet the needs of this younger age group. Data collected from interviews with senior TAFE personnel in Victoria suggested that staff did not have the training to deal with young people and their families when problems arose regarding student behaviour. For example, there was a tendency to view the young person as an adult in terms of their legal responsibilities, even when that young person was a minor, leading to situations where inappropriate behaviour on the part of the young person could lead to police involvement rather than a more appropriate response involving the student's parents.

Moreover, the numbers of young persons entering directly into adult VET sector institutions, with or without completing school, are not high. The two annual state-based tracking studies (in Queensland and Victoria) provide good estimates of the transition from school to post-school VET for school completers. In Victoria (DEECD 2011), overall, 18.3% of school completers make the transition to VET. A further 7.9% enter work-based training in the form of apprenticeships or traineeships. Whilst the latter figure (for work-based training) represents a small increase since 2003, when the proportion was 5.7%, the figure for VET represents a sharp drop from 2003 when it was 26.3%. The data also allow an analysis of destinations by SES. They suggest that nearly one-third (32.2%) of students from the lowest SES quartile enter either campus-based VET or work-based training, compared with only 21.8% of those school completers from the highest SES quartile.

The Queensland data (DET 2011) show an even lower proportion entering campus-based adult sector VET (13.1%) but a slightly higher proportion entering work-based training (11.5%). The Queensland data also confirm the social patterns evident in the state of Victoria, with 27.6% of the lowest SES students entering a post-school VET destination, including work-based training, compared with 20.3% of those from the highest SES quartile.

Both surveys suggest that relatively low proportions of school completers enter post-school, campus-based VET—less than one-fifth of the cohort in Victoria and less than one-seventh in Queensland—and that there are strong social patterns in these transitions to VET, with higher SES students much more likely to enter university whilst lower SES students are more likely to enter post-school adult VET institutions. This is similar to the social pattern evident in enrolments in school-based VET and provides further evidence of the social selection associated with vocational programmes.

The extent to which early leavers (non-completers) make a direct transition to VET is more difficult to determine. The only Australian state systematically tracking early leavers into their post-school destinations is Victoria, and there is evidence to suggest that the data are not reliable. The most recent On Track report (DEECD 2011) estimates the proportion of early leavers entering VET as 15.1% of males and 28.4% of females. We may add to this the transition to apprenticeships and traineeships (45.5% of males and 18.1% of females). However, these data are based on a response rate of 34.8% and the authors advise caution in consideration of the data reported for this group. If, as is likely, those students missing from the sample are amongst the more vulnerable in the group, then the proportions reported above may be overstating the strength of the transition to post-school VET for early leavers.

These data suggest that adult VET sector institutions do not currently play a large role in the provision of education and training for young people in Australia. This may increase as there is evidence of growing numbers of TAFE institutes offering dedicated programmes—both vocational and general (senior secondary certificate)—to school-aged youth in various Australian states. Where past research has suggested that TAFE institutes were not funded or trained to deal with the needs of young people (Polesel et al. 2004; Wyn et al. 2004), with reasons including the absence of clear duty of care relationships involving students, parents, and staff, and the inadequacy of courses for a younger clientele, the existence of these programmes suggests that approaches more carefully targeted to the needs of this group may be emerging.

This research suggests that whilst adult VET sector providers are becoming increasingly involved in the delivery of courses for school-aged clients, their role at present is not a large one and is biased towards lower SES populations. Moreover their ability to cater for the needs of school-aged youth has been questioned.

As a footnote to this section, it might be noted that 'hybrid' or 'senior' secondary providers of various kinds have occupied the margins of provision in various guises. Te Riele (2006) has suggested that traditional schooling structures do not meet the needs of some marginalized students and that a more adult setting is more appropriate for some students, particularly those labelled as being 'at risk'. This argument has been supported by many studies over the years (notably Anderson et al. 1980 and Polesel 2002). However, the Year 7–12 (or Year 8–12) secondary school model remains dominant in Australia. The exceptions to this are rare. Some of the publicly funded VET providers (TAFE institutes), for example, have established senior secondary schools within their establishments, offering both the senior secondary certificate and accredited vocational qualifications. Within the school sector itself, a number of states and territories have well-established senior secondary providers, some but not all offering a breadth of subjects which includes vocational studies. Specialist school providers, such as the trade training centres, have also emerged, though their coverage is very limited. There have also been other initiatives in the past, such as the public private partnerships attempted in the Australian technical colleges, which met with little success.

In Germany, there are few opportunities for young people to participate in VET outside the school structures (Polesel et al. 2011). Some transition courses are designed to lead school dropouts back into vocational education, but these are not regarded as being at the same level as the dual system qualifications, which are regarded as equivalent to completing school. Deissinger (2001) argues that vocational qualifications delivered outside of the dual system, including the wholly school-based option and any company-based training, are simply not accepted in the labour market. This may, in fact, be a weakness in an otherwise highly regarded system—a lack of flexibility which denies alternative pathways to the minority not able to adapt to the requirements of the mainstream dual system pathway.

Conclusion

What, then, is the state of pre-employment skill formation for young people in Australia and Germany? This chapter suggests that the neoliberal market economy framework in Australia has led to weak linkages between education and training institutions and employers, trade unions, and other industry organizations. This has led to an 'education logic' being applied to vocational programmes and qualifications, which have struggled to achieve parity of status and to establish a place within the culture of secondary schools. It also argues that social selection remains a problem in the delivery and take-up of school-based vocational education. The documented outcomes of VET programmes suggest that participation in them provides few advantages in the transition to further education and training or directly into the world of work. Moreover, VET is regarded as properly belonging to the adult VET sector providers, with vocational programmes in schools limited to the most basic qualification levels and operating within the constraints of the upper secondary certificates offered in the different states and territories of Australia. At the same time, relatively low proportions of school-aged youth enter adult sector providers for full-time education and training.

By way of contrast, it can be argued that the neocorporatist framework of cooperation between the education and training system, employers, and social partners in Germany has contributed to the establishment of mutually beneficial linkages between these bodies. This has led to the development of well-regarded courses and qualifications which are valued by employers and industry and which facilitate effective transitions for young people leaving school. It has also contributed to a greater parity of status between general and vocational pathways. However, social selection remains a significant concern, as in Australia.

This analysis suggests that there are serious weaknesses in the delivery of school-based vocational programmes in Australia. The evidence suggests that neither meet the needs of employers nor provide the competencies which form one of the major reasons they are offered. However, challenging the quality of VET solely on the basis of poor transitions to the labour market may be missing the point. School-based vocational education cannot lead young people into jobs which do not exist. To suggest this would be to follow the reasoning of the Riots Communities and Victims Panel in England, which held schools responsible for phenomena over which they had no control. Better vocational programmes cannot address youth unemployment nor create skilled jobs for youth.

Having said this, the evidence regarding the deficiencies in the quality of initial skills formation in Australia cannot be ignored. There is no suggestion amongst teachers that VET is not required, but rather that its status should be raised, its quality improved, and its role in creating pathways more carefully considered. There is an onus on schools as institutions to raise the status of VET both in terms of resources and in symbolic terms. In part, this involves changing the expectations surrounding skills formation in schools. A discourse which focuses on addressing skills shortages and which creates an expectation amongst young people that completing these courses will lead to direct entry to skilled jobs is dishonest and harmful. Rather, the role of vocational programmes in creating pathways to post-school VET and to work-based training in apprenticeships needs to emphasized.

This requires a different approach to VET, one which is better integrated with the needs of industry and which is more generously supported by industry. It may require a greater range of providers, better suited to meet the needs of vocational provision and more attuned to the culture of young people. It requires more clearly structured or themed courses which are coherent with a clear curriculum focus, which provide strong general knowledge, and which provide transparent signposted pathways. More controversially, it may mean stronger differentiation of programmes, as is the case in Germany, clearly delineating the pathways into university and the pathways into post-school VET (including apprenticeships). Given the evidence presented regarding social selection, there is an instinctive reluctance to reject this approach. However, the more covert differentiation of pathways and outcomes—disguised under the cover of a 'comprehensive' curriculum, which already occurs—suggests that differentiated pathways need to be exposed and understood before they can be improved.

These suggestions all relate to schools and education systems. However, as we see in Germany, the effectiveness of the system is not the sole responsibility of schools and it is not reasonable to place the onus of reform on schools alone. Poor transitions to the labour market are as much due to the nature of the labour market itself as to the quality of the preparation for it. Evidence from the comparative context of international systems such as the German one suggests that effective training cannot occur without the support of employers and industry. Nations with effective training systems do not succeed solely because of the structures and programmes of the schools. To believe this would lead to the kind of ineffective policy borrowing which would change the structures of education and training provision without putting in place the other elements which contribute to the success of these systems. These include the seamless participation of government, industry, and the social partners which ensure that vocational education is supported financially and that they align with industry needs and standards. Having said this, there is a legitimate debate to be had about the impact of tracking on social selection. The absence of comparable data makes it difficult to assess the impact of early tracking on social selection. Certainly, in both the German and Australian systems, a family's SES is strongly linked to the chances of participating or not participating in VET.

The need to value skills formation for young people requires both symbolic and financial support. It requires support from education providers, from industry, and from the social partners. And finally, it requires an approach to upper secondary education which is not narrowly focused on the sorting and selection mechanisms of universities but on the needs of the full range of young people wishing to complete school in Australia.

References

ABS (Australian Bureau of Statistics) (2012) *Year Book Australia*, Cat. No. 1301.0. Accessed 10 January 2013: http://www.abs.gov.au/ausstats/abs@.nsf/Lookup/by%20Subject/1301.0~2012~Main%20 Features~International%20comparisons~112.

ABS (2011) *Schools Australia*, Cat. No. 4221.0. Available online: http://www.abs.gov.au/ ausstats/abs@.nsf/mf/4221.0.

Anderson, D., Saltet, M., and Vervoorn, A. (1980) *Schools to Grow in: An Evaluation of Senior Secondary Colleges*, Canberra: ANU Press.

Anlezark, A., Karmel, T., and Ong, K. (2006) *Have School Vocational Education and Training Programmes Been Successful?* Adelaide: National Centre for Vocational Education Research.

Auditor General Victoria (2006) *Vocational Education and Training: Meeting the Skill Needs of the Manufacturing Industry*, Melbourne: Victorian Government Printer.

Benadusi, L. (2007) 'Education Equality Indicators in the Nations of the European Union', in R. Teese, S. Lamb, and M. Duru-Bellat (eds), *International Studies in Educational Inequality, Theory and Policy*, Dordrecht: Springer: 155–190.

Billett, S. (2004) 'From your Business to Our Business: Industry and Vocational Education in Australia', *Oxford Review of Education*, 30(1): 13–35.

Blanden, J., Gregg, P., and Machin, S. (2005) 'Educational Inequality and Intergenerational Mobility', in S. Machin and A. Vignoles (eds), *What's the Good of Education?* Princeton: Princeton University Press: 99–114.

Bosch, G. and Charest, J. (2008) 'Vocational Training and the Labour Market in Liberal and Coordinated Economies', *Industrial Relations Journal*, 39(5): 428–447.

Bradshaw, D., Clemans, A., Donovan, C., and Macrae, H. (2001) *Room to Move*, Department of Education Employment and Training, Melbourne.

Bourdieu, P. and Passeron, J.-C. (1977) *Reproduction in Education, Society and Culture*, English ed., London: Sage.

Census (2011) *Australian Census 2011*.

Clarke, K. (2012) *Entry to Vocations: The Efficacy of VET in Schools*, Adelaide: National Centre for Vocational Education Research.

Deissinger, T. (2006) 'The Apprenticeship Crisis in Germany: The National Debate and Implications for Full-time Vocational Education and Training', in L. Mjelde and R. Daly (eds), *Working Knowledge in a Globalising World: From Work to Learning, from Learning to Work*, Bern: Peter Lang: 181–196.

Deissinger (2001) 'Quality Control and Employability: Are the Parameters of VET in Germany's Dual System Facing Severe Challenges?' Paper delivered at AVETRA. http://www.avetra.org.au/abstracts_and_papers_2001/Deissinger_full.pdf.

Department of Education and Early Childhood Development (2011) *The On Track Survey 2011: The Destinations of School Leavers in Victoria*, Melbourne: DEECD.

Department of Education and Training (2011) *Next Step 2011: A Report on the Destinations of Year 12 Completers from 2010 in Queensland*, Brisbane: DET.

Durkheim, E. (1977) *The Evolution of Educational Thought: Lectures on the Formation and Development of Secondary Education in France*, London: Routledge and Kegan Paul.

Education Department of Victoria (1973) *Vision and Realisation: A Centenary History of State Education in Victoria*, Melbourne: The Government Printer.

Education Queensland (2009) *Development of State Secondary Schools*. http://education.qld.gov.au/library/edhistory/state/brief/secondary-1912.html.

Fini, R. (2007) 'Education and Social Selection in Italy', in R. Teese, S. Lamb, and M. Duru-Bellat (eds), *International Studies in Educational Inequality, Theory and Policy*, Dordrecht: Springer: 89–110.

Goodson, I. (1993) *School Subjects and Curriculum Change: Studies in Curriculum History*, London: The Falmer Press, originally published in 1982.

Hall, P. A. and Soskice, D. (2001) 'An Introduction to Varieties of Capitalism', in Hall and Soskice (eds), *Varieties of Capitalism: The Institutional Foundations of Comparative Advantage*, Oxford: Oxford University Press: 1–68.

Iannelli, C. and Raffe, D. (2007) 'Vocational Upper-secondary Education and the Transition from school', *European Sociological Review*, 23(1), 49–63.

Lauder, H., Brown, P., and Ashton, D. (2008) 'Globalization, Skills Formation and the Varieties of Capitalism Approach', *New Political Economy*, 13(1): 19–35.

Malley, J., Keating, J., Robinson, L., and Hawke, G. (2001) *The Quest for a Working Blueprint: Vocational Education and Training in Australian Secondary Schools*, Leabrook: National Centre for Vocational Education Research.

Maynes (1977) *Schooling the Masses: A Comparative Social History of Education in France and Germany*. PhD thesis, University of Michigan, Ann Arbor.

Mitter, W. (1995) 'Continuity and Change: A Basic Question for German Education', in Phillips, D. (ed.), *Education in Germany: Tradition and Reform in Historical Context*, London: Routledge.

Murray, P. and Polesel, J. (2013) 'Pathways and Politics: A Comparative Exploration of Learning Pathways and Transition Systems in Denmark and Australia', *European Journal of Education*, 48(2): 223–246.

NCVER (2011) *Australian Vocational Education and Training Statistics: VET in Schools 2010*, Adelaide: National Centre for Vocational Education Research. http://www.ncver.edu.au/publications/2446.html.

Phillips, K. P. A. (2006) *Improving the Delivery of VET in Schools*, Richmond: K. P. A. Philips.

Polesel, J. (2002) 'Schools for Young Adults: Senior Colleges in Australia', *Australian Journal of Education*, 46(2): 205–221.

Polesel, J. and Helme, S. (2003) *Young Visions Report*, Parkville: The University of Melbourne.

Polesel, J., Helme, S., Davies, M., Teese, R., Nicholas, T., and Vickers, M. (2004) *VET in Schools: A Post-Compulsory Education Perspective*, Adelaide: National Centre for Vocational Education Research.

Polesel, J. (2007) 'The Development of Vocational Programs in Secondary Schools—Victoria and the European Tradition', in R. Teese, S. Lamb, and M. Duru-Bellat (eds), *International Studies in Educational Inequality, Theory and Policy*, 3, Dordrecht: Springer: 151–168.

Polesel, J. (2008) 'Democratising the Curriculum or Training the Children of the Poor: School-based Vocational Training in Australia', *Journal of Education Policy*, 23(6): 615–632.

Polesel, J. and Clarke, K. (2011) 'The Marginalisation of VET in an Australian Secondary School', *Journal of Vocational Education and Training*, 63(4): 525–538.

Polesel, J., Kurantowicz, E. and Nizinska, A. (2011) 'Pathways to Completion for School Dropouts', in S. Lamb, E. Markussen, R. Teese, N. Sandberg, and Polesel, J. (eds), *School Dropout and Completion*, Dordrecht: Springer: 357–367.

Polesel, J. and Volkoff, V. (2009) 'Vocational Studies in School—Does It matter If I'm a Girl and If I'm Poor?', *Educational Practice and Theory*, 31(1), 39–56.

Polesel, J. and Keating, J. (2011) 'School Completion Targets and the "Equivalence" of VET in the Australian Context', *Oxford Review of Education*, 37(3): 367–382.

Reupold, A. and Tippelt, R. (2011) 'Germany's Education System and the Problem of Dropouts: Institutional Segregation and Programme Diversification', in S. Lamb, E. Markussen, R. Teese, N. Sandberg, and J. Polesel (eds), *School Dropout and Completion*, Dordrecht: Springer: 155–171.

Ringer, F. (1969) *The Decline of the German Mandarins: The German Academic Community, 1890–1933*, Cambridge, MA: Harvard University Press.

Ringer, F. (1989) 'On Segmentation in Modern European Educational Systems: The Case of French Secondary Education, 1865–1920', in D. Muller, F. Ringer, and B. Simon (eds), *The Rise of the Modern Educational System*, Cambridge: Cambridge University Press: 53–87.

Ryan, C. (2002) *Individual Returns to Vocational Education and Training Qualifications: Their Implications for Lifelong Learning*, Adelaide: NCVER.

Sweet, R. (2000) 'Retrospective and Prospective Pathway Engineering: Comparative perspectives', Paper delivered at International Career Conference 2000, Perth, Australia, 2–5 April.

Sweet, R. (2009) 'Apprenticeship, Pathways and Career Guidance: A Cautionary Tale', in F. Rauner, E. Smith, U. Hauschildt, and H. Zelloth (eds), *Innovative Apprenticeships: Promoting Successful School-to-Work Transitions, Berlin, LIT*. Proceedings of 3rd INAP Conference, Turin, 17–18 May: 17–34.

TAFE Executive Group (2008) 'Successful Delivery Models for Young People's Participation in TAFE NSW'. Discussion paper, NSW Department of Education and Training.

Teese, R. and Polesel, J. (2003) *Undemocratic Schooling: Equity and Quality in Mass Secondary Education in Australia*, Melbourne: Melbourne University Press.

te Riele, K. (2006) 'Schooling Practices for Marginalized Students—Practice-with-hope, *International Journal of Inclusive Education*, 10(1): 59–74.

The Riots Communities and Victims Panel (2102) *After the Riots*, London: The Riots Communities and Victims Panel.

UNDP (2011) 'International Human Development Indicators', 2011 rankings. http://hdr.undp.org/en/statistics/.

Winch, C. and Clarke, L. (2003) 'Front-loaded' Vocational Education versus Lifelong Learning: A Critique of Current UK Government Policy', *Oxford Review of Education*, 29(2): 239–252.

Wyn, J., Stokes, H., and Tyler, D. (2004) *Stepping Stones: TAFE and ACE Program Development for Early School Leavers*, Adelaide: National Centre for Vocational Education Research.

Young, M. F. (2007) *Bringing Knowledge Back In: From Social Constructivism to Social Realism in the Sociology of Education*, London: Routledge.

CHAPTER 9

SKILL DEVELOPMENT IN MIDDLE-LEVEL OCCUPATIONS

The Role of Apprenticeship Training

ROBERT I. LERMAN

INTRODUCTION

HUMAN resources are central to the performance of every economy. In the short-run, the framing of the skills issue is how best to reduce unemployment. Skill mismatches may hinder the return to full employment and slow economic recovery (Puri 2012). The case of Marlin Steel Wire Products in Baltimore is an example (Weitzman and Harding 2011). In 2011, when the US unemployment rate was over 8%, the company of 30 employees reported that it could not find sufficient qualified workers to maintain high levels of growth. It is hard to blame wages, since Marin offered a compensation package of more than $80,000 per year. Data from a 2011 Manpower Group survey indicated that more than half of employers had difficulty filling jobs and nearly half blame the lack of hard technical job skills. Moreover, the hardest jobs to fill in 2011 were for workers qualified in skilled trades, including machinists and machine operators.

Jobs are the short-run focus, but in the long-run, the central issue is whether a country's human resources are of sufficient quality to promote or even accommodate high rates of economic growth. Although reading, writing, and maths skills and degrees are critical indicators of human capital, so too are competence and mastery in occupational skills and such behavioural skills as listening, communication, problem-solving, and dealing well with superiors and peers (Heckman and Rubinstein 2001; Heckman et al. 2006; Lerman 2008; Almlund et al. 2011). All advanced economies rely on universal primary education to teach verbal and maths literacy. But they differ in how they expect people to learn and use occupational and other workplace skills, especially for intermediate- or middle-level occupations.

In nearly all countries, technical and vocational education and training (TVET) systems play a central role in occupational training. But the governance, timing, delivery, location, and experience of TVET vary widely across and often within countries (OECD 2009). In some countries, the government dominates TVET, whilst others involve private employers extensively. Serious TVET begins by age 14 in some countries and not until a student's late teens and early 20s in other countries. Most TVET programmes focus on initial vocational education but some include continuing vocational education to upgrade the skills of workers already in an occupation (Cedefop 2011a). The duration of TVET programmes ranges from less than a year to over four years. Training systems vary in their use of work-based vs. classroom-based learning. Some countries rely almost exclusively on academic subjects, leaving occupational and firm-based training entirely to employers. The range of occupations within the scope of TVET varies widely as well.

Apprenticeship training is common. Apprenticeships usually involve formal agreements under which employers provide workers with structured work-based learning alongside classroom learning. Apprentices participate in the production process, work with a trainer/mentor, and ultimately gain sufficient occupational mastery to become certified by an external body. The scale of apprenticeship programmes varies widely, reaching 4% of the workforce in Germany and Australia but only 0.2% in the United States.

A critical distinction between apprenticeship and other TVET is the way training positions are created. Vocational schools provide openings based on administrative decisions concerning available teachers, budgets, and potential enrolment. Although administrators take some account of market demands, the schools are largely insulated from the job market. In contrast, apprenticeship slots only arise when employers create them. Because employers invest their own money when providing apprenticeship opportunities, their perception of demand is generally better informed than that of school administrators. But, training positions are pro-cyclical, with too many openings in boom periods and too few during trough periods.

This paper examines the diversity of approaches to apprenticeship and related training for intermediate- or middle-level occupations. We begin by defining and describing middle-skills occupations, largely in terms of education and experience. The next step is to describe skill requirements and alternative approaches to preparing and upgrading the skills of individuals for these occupations. Programmes of academic education and apprenticeship programmes emphasizing work-based learning have often competed for the same space but the full picture reveals significant numbers of complementarities. Third, we consider the evidence on the costs and effectiveness of apprenticeship training in several countries. The final section highlights empirical and policy research results concerning the advantages of apprenticeship training for intermediate-level skills jobs and careers.

What Are Middle-Level Occupations?

Classifying occupations or jobs by skill is complicated because of the multi-dimensional character of skills. The middle of a single distribution (say, by educational attainment) fails to capture the variety of skills required to master specific jobs or occupations. Should the skills required to play professional baseball be considered 'middle-skill' positions even if education beyond high school is not necessary for the position? Are the skills required for a master carpenter in some sense *lower* than those required of elementary school teachers with Batchelor's degrees?

One solution is to employ wages as a proxy for skill. Wages may be viewed as incorporating skill levels along various dimensions together with the market valuation of those skills. Just as home prices reflect housing characteristics, along with 'hedonic prices,' one might argue that wages capture the diverse mix and value of skills required for jobs. However, several problems arise with wages as classifying jobs and occupations by skills. Wages reflect not only skill but also the riskiness, job satisfaction, responsibility, status, and flexibility of jobs and occupations. Skill requirements and expertise required in an occupation may not change but the wage return on the occupation may. Wages sometimes are a reward for tenure on the job; seniority often matters. Wage differences can come about from differences in bargaining power. For example, the pay of a longshoreman depends on the high costs of strikes relative to wage increases. Wages for the same occupation often differ widely across geographic areas, partly because of rent differentials. Finally, classifying occupations by mean wages misses the wide wage variation within detailed occupations.

Autor (2010) ranks detailed occupations by their average wages in a base period. Middle-skill jobs are in occupations in the middle segment of the average wage distribution. This approach indicates that middle-skill occupations are declining rapidly relative to high- and low-skill positions. The reasons include the increased power of computers to automate routine tasks undertaken in middle-skill positions, expanding international trade, declining unionization, and the erosion of the minimum wage. Autor sees a 'hollowing out' of the job market. Goos et al. (2009) find that middle-wage occupations declined as a share of employment in all 16 countries that they studied, mostly offset by a rising share of high-wage occupations.

The Autor approach does not capture the wide distribution of wages within detailed occupations.[1] For all employees and across all occupations, hourly earnings at the 75th percentile of jobs were 2.48 times hourly earnings at the 25th percentile. But, the weighted 75:25 ratio *within* occupations was nearly 1.61, or 65% of the overall ratio. Wages overlap across occupations that do and not require a BA degree. In 2012 annual earnings at the 25th percentile of college occupations (defined as having over half of workers with a BA or higher degree) averaged about $53,500. For occupations where

[1] The figures in this paragraph and the following paragraph come from data drawn from the occupational employment survey. See http://www.bls.gov/oes/current/oes_nat.htm.

only 15–50% of workers have a BA or higher degree, average annual earnings at the 75th percentile of those occupations was nearly as high at about $52,000.[2]

Many occupational positions not requiring a BA involve a considerable amount of work-based learning, experience, and other specialized talents (e.g. salesmanship, responsibility, creativity, and detailed expertise). Sub-BA occupations can generate high wages at the top levels of quality and productivity. For example, wage levels, skill, and status differ markedly between 'cook at a restaurant' and 'chefs and head cooks'. Cooks average only about half the hourly earnings level of chefs. Upgrading cooks to high quality and productivity would allow them to compete with the earnings of many college occupations. Occupations with above average earnings and with a majority of workers without a BA include construction managers, buyers and purchasing agents, lodging managers, appraisers, court reporters, various types of technicians, aircraft mechanics, police officers, supervisors of police, and operators of gas plants.

One scheme for classifying occupations into low-, middle-, and high-skills categories relies on educational attainment and training. According to this classification (Holzer and Lerman 2009), middle-skill jobs still make up roughly half of all employment today, though their share of employment fell from about 55% to 48% between 1986 and 2006. Professional and related occupations rose from 17% in 1986 to more than 20% in 2006 and managerial positions increased from about 12% to 15% of total employment. Low-skill (service) jobs barely increased their share from 15% to 16% of total employment. Several intermediate-level occupations with good wages have increased jobs substantially since 1986; medical therapists increased by 30%, carpenters by 20%, heavy vehicle maintenance specialists by 25%, and heating and air conditioning positions by 21%.

In summary, definitions of intermediate-level jobs vary, depending on whether they use wage, occupation, and educational criteria. Generally, intermediate-level jobs are positions between jobs that require very little training and jobs that require a university degree. They are declining modestly as a share of total jobs, but still represent a large segment of the labour market.

Skills Required for Intermediate-Level Occupations

Whether 'middle-skill' occupations are modestly expanding or contracting, the key questions should be: what are the skills required to perform well in these occupations?

[2] These figures involved merging tables published on the Bureau of Labor Statistics website. The occupation and earnings data come from employer-based surveys under the Occupational Employment Statistics (OES) programme whilst the occupation and education data come from the American Community Survey (ACS) conducted by the US Bureau of the Census. See http://www.bls.gov/emp/ep_table_111.htm and the cross industry employment figures on occupations, http://www.bls.gov/oes/oes_dl.htm.

What are the best approaches to educating and training workers to generate high productivity and high wages in these fields?

In determining the skill requirements for intermediate-level occupations, one must consider the appropriate mix of generic academic skills, specific occupational skills, and generic non-academic skills, such as communication, motivation, and responsibility. Mounier's (2001) classification distinguishes between cognitive, technical, and behavioural skills. Some of all three types of skills are required for nearly all jobs, but the levels of each type of skill vary across occupations.

Occupational and behavioural skills are more significant from the employer perspective than is exposure to upper level academic courses. A survey of a representative sample of US workers (Handel 2007) indicates that only 19% use the skills developed in Algebra I on the job, only 9% use the skills for Algebra II and less than 15% of workers ever write anything five pages or more. This does not imply that jobs not requiring certain academic courses are unskilled. Many occupations viewed as low- or middle-skill require a complex mix of cognitive and social skills (Rose 2004). Upper blue-collar and even lower blue-collar workers must know how to read and create visuals, such as maps, diagrams, floor plans, graphs, or blueprints, skills typically learnt in occupation-specific courses. Workers also report the importance of behavioural skills, including problem-solving and communication, teaching and training other workers, dealing with people in tense situations, supervising other workers, and working well with customers. Mastering these skills is cognitively challenging.

The 1992 Secretary's Commission on Achieving Necessary Skills in the United States confirmed the importance of behavioural skills, including allocating resources (time, money, and facilities), interpersonal skills (such as teamwork, teaching others, leadership), acquiring and using information, understanding systems, and working well with technology. Except for college graduates, non-cognitive skills (measured by indices of locus of control and self-esteem) exert as high an impact on job market outcomes as cognitive skills (word knowledge, paragraph comprehension, arithmetic reasoning, mathematical knowledge, and coding speed as measured by the Armed Forces Vocational Aptitude Battery) (Heckman et al. (2006). Lindqvist and Vestman (2011) analyse data on a representative sample of the Swedish male population matched with education, earnings, and information on cognitive and non-cognitive skills obtained in the military enlistment process through interviews with psychologists. Persistence, social skills, and emotional stability are the non-cognitive/behaviour skills measured and coded from the interview. The study finds that within low to mid ranges of skills, non-cognitive skills exert a higher impact on wages than do cognitive skills.

The sociocultural approach provides some revealing examples of how skills are used in context and how non-academic skills are often developed and used as part of a 'community of practice' (Stasz 2001). Nelsen (1997) points out that workplaces not only require formal knowledge—facts, principles, theories, maths and writing skills—but also informal knowledge—embodied in heuristics, work styles, and contextualized understanding of tools and techniques.

What about occupational skills? Occupational qualifications sometimes fit within a broad framework of national vocational qualifications running from basic to intermediate to advanced levels.[3] In the United Kingdom, the National Vocational Qualification (NVQ) system specifies requirements for proficiency that vary widely across types of occupations and over levels within occupations.[4] The ultimate goal is that employers place a value on attaining a qualification level, giving workers an incentive to learn on the job. Although the system has not worked out very well (e.g. Eraut 2001), NVQs have led to some added training in certain sectors (Cox 2007). In the United States, about one in five workers requires a state licence to practise their occupation, up from less than 5% in the early 1950s (Kleiner 2006). Licensing rules vary widely across states, with many states regulating occupations as varied as alarm contractor, auctioneer, manicurist, and massage therapists.

Often, training colleges—such as US community colleges and for-profit schools—decide themselves (sometimes in consultation with potential employers) what constitutes qualifications in quite detailed occupations, such as domestic air conditioner and furnace installer, medical receptionist, and medical coder.[5] Other standards directly involve employers and government entities.

Occupational standards are critical to well-functioning apprenticeship programmes. Australia has developed the national Training Package (collections of competency standards gathered into qualifications) for all industry areas, whilst previously qualifications were only available in a limited range of occupations and industries (Smith 2012). In Canada, the occupational standards in the Interprovincial Standards Red Seal Program allow for effective harmonization of apprenticeship training and assessment in each province and territory (Miller 2012). The Red Seal Program's standards incorporate essential skills (reading, document use, writing, numeracy, oral communication, thinking, digital technology, and lifelong learning), common occupational skills (that apply to a small range of occupations), and specific occupational skills.[6]

In England, the Sector Skills Councils and their employers design the content of each apprenticeship using the national Apprenticeship Blueprint (Miller 2012). As of 2012, there were 200 operating apprenticeship frameworks and another 118 under development. Employers have considerable flexibility in implementing the standards.

France uses Apprenticeship Training Centres (CFA) to help design and deliver the classroom-based components of apprenticeships, with skill standards often developed by Professional Consultative Committees (Dif 2012). They operate under frameworks established by the National Commission for Vocational Qualifications.

In Switzerland, the Federal Office for Professional Education and Technology, together with cantons, employers, trade associations, and unions participate in framing

[3] For a review of national qualification frameworks in Europe, see Cedefop (2012).

[4] For an overview on NVQ and other qualification systems in the United Kingdom, see material provided by the Qualifications and Learning Authority. http://www.qca.org.uk.

[5] Curricula for certificates in these occupations appear in the catalogue for the Kentucky technical college system. http://kctcs.edu/en/students/programs_and_catalog.aspx.

[6] See the documents linked with http://www.red-seal.ca/tr.1d.2@-eng.jsp?tid=51 for examples.

the occupational standards for about 250 occupations (Hoeckel et al. 2009). The canton vocational education programmes implement and supervise the vocational schools, career guidance, and inspection of participating companies and industry training centres. Professional organizations develop qualifications and exams and help develop apprenticeship places.

In Germany, the 'social partners', including government, employer, and employee representatives, determine occupational standards (Hoeckel and Schwartz 2009). The chambers of commerce advise participating companies, register apprenticeship contracts, examine the suitability of training firms and trainers, and set up and grade final exams.

Skill requirements in apprenticeships include academic courses and structured work-based training aimed at helping apprentices learn and master a range of tasks. They often include general tasks that apply to a family of occupations (say, metalworking) and tasks that apply to a specific occupation (say, tool mechanics or metal construction and shipbuilding).

Overall, occupational standards for apprenticeships extend well beyond the traditional construction crafts. In the United Kingdom, for example, apprenticeships are available within business, administration and law; arts, media, and publishing; health and public services; retail and commercial enterprise; and information technology and communication. Common apprenticeships in Switzerland include information technology specialist, commercial employee, pharmacy assistant, and doctor's assistant. German standards cover over 300 occupations, including lawyer's assistant, bank staff worker, industrial mechanic, industrial manager, retail worker, commercial sales, and computer networking. In nearly all fields, students learn skills in closely related occupations. But some apprenticeship programmes rely on an overall narrow approach to learning. Fuller and Unwin (2006) draw attention to the differences at the firm level between the more narrow 'restrictive' skill development and the broader approach used in 'expansive' work environments.

Apprenticeship and School-Based Approaches to Preparing Workers for Middle-Skill Jobs

Countries have developed various approaches to training workers for intermediate-level occupations. Systems differ with respect to the level and duration of general education, the timing of occupation-specific education and training, and the split between classroom-based and work-based learning. These differences can have important consequences. In articles comparing British and German companies in the same industries, Wagner and colleagues cited the higher vocational qualifications of German workers as giving German firms a productivity advantage (see, for example, Steedman and Wagner 1987; see also Prais 1995). Although discussions of skill preparation systems generally focus on the work-based vs school-based distinction, the quality, depth, and portability of what students or apprentices learn are at least as important.

A common concern about apprenticeship is the portability of skills learnt in occupation-specific programmes. However, as Geel and Backes-Gelner (2009, 3) point out, learning even a highly specific skill can yield benefits outside the narrow occupation:

> For example, an adolescent who wants to become a clockmaker should not necessarily be considered poorly equipped for future labor market requirements, even though his industry is small and shrinking. Rather, he is well equipped because his skill combination is very similar to skill combinations of other occupations in a large and growing skill cluster, which includes, for example, medical technicians or tool makers. Despite a seemingly very narrow and inflexible skill combination in his original occupation, he is nonetheless very flexible and well prepared for future labor market changes due to the sustainability of his acquired skills and his current skill cluster.

To operationalize skill specificity, Geel and Backes-Gelner (2009) and Geel et al. (2011) begin with an insight borrowed from Lazear (2009) that all skills are general in a sense and occupation-specific skills are various mixes of skills. The authors compile the key skills and their importance for nearly 80 occupations. They estimate how skills are grouped within narrow occupations, allowing for skills developed ostensibly for one occupation to become useful in other occupations. It identifies occupational clusters that possess similar skill combinations within a given cluster and different skill combinations between clusters. Next, indices for each narrow occupation measure the extent to which the occupation is relatively portable between occupations within the same cluster and/or relatively portable between the initial occupation and all other occupations. The authors use these indices to determine how portability affects mobility, the wage gains and losses in moving between occupations, and the likelihood that employers will invest in training.

Whilst only 42% of apprentices stay in their initial occupation, nearly two-thirds remain with either the occupation they learnt as an apprentice or another occupation in the cluster using a similar mix of skills. Those trained in occupations with more specific skill sets are most likely to remain in their initial occupation or move to occupations within the same cluster. Apprentices actually increase their wages when moving to another occupation within the same cluster but lose somewhat when moving to another cluster. As Geel et al. (2011) show, employers are especially likely to invest in apprenticeships with the most specific skill sets.

Other strong evidence of the high returns on and transferability of German apprenticeship training comes from Clark and Fahr (2001). The overall rates of return to each year of apprenticeship range from 8–12% for training in firms of 50 workers or more and from about 5.5–6.5% for firms of 2–49 workers. Although transferring to another occupation can offset these gains, the reduction is zero for those who quit and only about 1.7% for those who are displaced from their job and shift to another occupation. There is no penalty from displacement into a somewhat related occupation. Göggel and Zwick (2012) show the net gains or losses from switching employers and occupations differ according to the original training occupation, with apprentices in industrial occupations actually experiencing wage advantages whilst those in commerce, trading, and construction seeing modest losses. Finally, Clark and Fahr (2001) look at workers' views on their current use of skills learnt in apprenticeship training. Not surprisingly, 85% of workers remaining in their training occupation use many or very many of the skills they learnt during apprenticeship. This group constitutes 55% of the sample. But, even amongst the remaining 45%, about two out of five workers reported using many or very many of the skills from their apprenticeship and another 20% used some of the skills. Overall, only 18% of all former apprentices stated they used few or no skills learnt in their apprenticeships.

A key issue is whether the general training in apprenticeships (usually financed by the government and/or students) is taught at a level as high as in comparable subjects in school-based programmes. Some researchers see firm-based apprenticeship training as limiting mobility and adaptability (Hanushek et al. 2011). Yet, academic tracks in US secondary schools and community colleges may have no advantage for mobility. First, a high percentage of students drop out of both academic secondary and community college programmes. Second, many community college programmes are at least as specific as apprenticeship programmes. Many certificate programmes within community colleges are almost entirely devoted to learning a narrow occupational skill, such as courses to become a phlebotomist, child care assistant, and plastics processing worker. Some US school-based programmes in for-profit colleges also offer narrow programmes, such as truck driving, medical assistant, and medical insurance billing and coding. Third, skills often erode when they go unused.

Whilst community college and private for-profit students often take highly specific occupational courses, apprentices take some general, classroom courses. Thus, apprentice electricians learn the principles of science, especially those related to electricity. In most countries, collaboration takes place between vocational schools and apprenticeship programmes. In the United States, apprentices often take their required 'related instruction' in classes at community colleges or for-profit colleges (Lerman 2010). From this perspective, US apprenticeship programmes should be viewed as 'dual' programmes that combine work-based and school-based learning.

In other OECD countries, the mix of school-based vs employer-based programmes used to prepare young people for careers varies widely. Secondary school students in Belgium and Sweden participate at high rates in vocational education but have very low rates of participation in work-based programmes. By contrast, most of the vocational education in Germany, Switzerland, and Denmark revolves around work-based learning, including apprenticeships (Cedefop 2012).

Apprenticeship training limits the gaps between what is learnt at school and how to apply these and other skills in the workplace. An extensive body of research documents the high economic returns for workers that result from employer-led training (Bishop 1997). Transmitting skills to the workplace works well with supervisory support, interactive training, and coaching, gives opportunities to perform what was learnt in training, and keeps the training relevant to jobs (Pellegrino and Hilton 2012). These are common characteristics of apprenticeships. Employer-based training like apprenticeships often leads to higher levels of innovation (Bauernschuster et al. 2009), net gains to firms that train during and soon after the training, and externalities, such as benefits for other employers and for the public when workers are well-trained to avoid the consequences of natural or man-made disasters. Under apprenticeships and other forms of employer-based training, the government generally gains by paying little for the training whilst reaping tax benefits from the increased earnings of workers.

Methodological Issues in Estimating the Costs and Benefits of Apprenticeship Training

Conceptual and practical issues arise in trying to estimate the costs and benefits of apprenticeship training (see also Gambin and Hogarth, Chapter 31). One is the variation in the structure and breadth of 'apprenticeship'. The term encompasses a variety of occupations with varying levels of school-based learning at the secondary and the post-secondary levels, varying amounts of work-based learning, and heterogeneity in general vs occupation-specific training. A second issue is defining the counterfactual, or what would have taken place in the absence of apprenticeships. Even when comparing outcomes of apprenticeship participants and those of non-participants with the same observed characteristics, unobserved differences between groups (such as in the motivation to work or in the mode of learning that is most beneficial) may affect both entry into apprenticeship and post-programme earnings. Another issue is that apprenticeship programmes may work well for some occupations but not others. Generalizing in these contexts is difficult.

Uncertainty adds another twist to estimating benefits and costs. Given uncertainty about the productivity returns from irreversible investments in particular workers, the firm's investment creates a real option. When the training is completed, the firm has the option but not the obligation to hire the trained worker. This option value raises the firm's returns and increases the likelihood that they will invest in training.

Finally, several non-economic outcomes are difficult to quantify but do show some association with vocational education and training. One analysis (Cedefop 2011b) found that technical vocational education (including apprenticeship) is linked to higher confidence and self-esteem, improved health, higher citizen participation, and higher job satisfaction. These relationships hold even after controlling for income. Other studies have indicated that apprenticeships improve youth development (Halpern 2009) and vocational identity (Brown et al. 2007), but it is difficult to quantify the economic value of these social benefits.

ESTIMATES OF COSTS AND BENEFITS FOR WORKERS

Notwithstanding the difficulties, researchers have generated estimates of apprenticeship benefits and costs. The OECD's *Learning for Jobs* (2009) cites a few studies dealing with benefits and costs. One US study examined the government costs as well as the worker and government benefits of three types of TVET—secondary vocational education, post-secondary vocational education (in community colleges) and apprenticeship programmes. Using data on individuals in the State of Washington, Hollenbeck (2008) identified groups that entered employment offices, had the same pre-programme earnings, but had different programme experiences. Absolute and relative gains in earnings from apprenticeship were highest, reaching about $2,000 per month compared to about $1,500 per month amongst participating in occupational programmes in two-year colleges.

A study of apprenticeship in ten US states also documents large and statistically significant earnings gains (Reed et al. 2012). It estimates how the length of participation in an apprenticeship affected earnings, holding constant for pre-enrolment earnings of apprenticeship participants. The estimated impacts are consistently and highly positive. At six years after starting a programme, earnings of the average apprenticeship participant (average duration in an apprenticeship) stood at 1.4 times the earnings of non-participants with the same pre-apprenticeship history. The gains were highly consistent across states. Overall, the study finds that apprenticeship returns nearly $28 in benefits for every dollar of government and worker costs.

Many studies have examined the earnings gains from apprenticeship training in European countries. They generally find high rates of return for the workers, often in the range of 15% (Clark and Fahr 2001; Fersterer et al. 2008; Geel and Backes-Gellner 2009). Clark and Fahr (2001) estimate wage gains in this range (about 6–8% per apprenticeship year with a duration of slightly less than three years). The studies of apprenticeship impacts are generally unable to account for possible selection bias that results from employer's selection of young workers who are more capable than their counterparts in ways that analysts cannot observe.

One recent study of the returns on apprenticeship training in small Austrian firms (Fersterer et al. 2008) overcomes much of the selection problem. It focuses on the interaction between apprenticeship duration and failing firms. A firm going out of business will generally cause a sudden and exogenous end to their apprenticeship training. More generally, the timing of firm failure will affect the duration of apprenticeship training and particular worker experiences. By looking at apprentices who obtained training in failed firms, one can examine a large number of trained workers with varying durations in their apprenticeships. The sample covers small firms, where the closing of the firm is likely to occur most suddenly. The results show a significant wage effect from longer durations of apprenticeship. For a 3–4-year apprenticeship, post-apprenticeship wages end up 12–16% higher than they otherwise would be. Since the worker's costs of participating in an apprenticeship are often minimal, the Austrian study indicates high overall benefits relative to modest costs.

Two Canadian analyses indicate a high wage premium for apprenticeships for men but not for women (Boothby and Drewes 2010; Gunderson and Krashinsky 2012). Apprenticeship completion is the highest educational attainment for only about 7% of Canadian men. However, for this group, earnings are substantially higher than the earnings of those who have only completed secondary school and nearly as high as those who have completed college programmes that are at a level less than a university BA. Overall, the gains for men from apprenticeship training are in the range of 17–20%. Even evaluated after 20 years of experience, apprenticeship training in most occupations yields continuing returns of 12–14%.

One Australian study shows very high rates of return to individuals undertaking TVET. Ryan (2002) finds that a male school leaver who completes a skilled vocational qualification whilst working part-time reaps a return of about 24 %. This gain far exceeds the 3.9% return to a male who works part-time whilst obtaining an associates diploma (two-year college degree). Other researchers have highlighted the benefits of well-structured vocational and apprenticeship systems (Steedman 1993; Acemoglu and Pischke 1999; Ryan 2001; OECD 2010).

A sceptical view of returns to apprenticeship emerges in Hanushek et al. (2011). They argue that vocational education (including apprenticeships) improves employment and earnings outcomes of young people but the advantage erodes to a disadvantage at older ages. The erosion of gains at older ages is said to be clearest in countries that emphasize apprenticeship, such as Denmark, Germany, and Switzerland. Yet, according to the authors' estimates in the paper, the advantage in employment rates linked to vocational education in the apprenticeship countries remains through to approximately the age of 60. Moreover, in the apprenticeship countries, the advantage in employment rates is sizable, providing men with vocational education a 9-percentage point higher employment rate at age 40 and a 4-point advantage at age 50.

Costs and Benefits for Employers

For employers, the net costs depend on the mix of classroom and work-based training, occupation, skill and wage progression, and the productivity of the apprentice whilst learning to master the required skill. Direct costs include apprentice wages, the wages of trainer specialists for the time they oversee apprentices, materials, and the costs of the additional space required for apprenticeships (Wolter and Ryan 2011). The benefits depend on the extent to which apprenticeships save on subsequent hiring and training costs, lower turnover costs, and enhance productivity more than added wage costs. Also valuable is the employer's increased certainty that apprentice graduates know all relevant occupational and firm-specific skills and can work well alongside other skilled workers. In addition, having extra-well-trained workers, such as apprentice graduates, provides firms with a valuable option of expanding production without reducing quality in response to uncertain demand shocks and covering for sudden absences of skilled workers.

The most extensive studies of net costs of apprenticeships deal with German and Swiss employers. One analysis compares results from surveys of 1825 German firms and 1471 Swiss firms that refer to the year 2000 (Muehlemann et al. 2010). The study does not include the costs of school-based learning linked to apprenticeships. The firms' main gross costs are the wages of trainers and the wages of apprentices. The authors calculate gross costs and the benefits to employers derived from the productive contributions of apprentices only during the training period. On average, the gross costs per year amounted to €15,500 for German firms and about €18,000 for Swiss firms. Although Swiss firms spend more than German firms, they derive substantially higher benefits from the value added by apprentices. Swiss firms gain over €19,000 per year, more than double the €8,000 benefits that German firms attribute to the value of production generated by apprentices. For a three-year apprenticeship, Swiss firms recoup the €54,400 cost with benefits of €57,100 whilst German firms experience a €46,600 gross cost but only €24,000 in benefits. Whilst the wages paid to apprentices are higher in Switzerland than in Germany, apprentices are at work for more days per year in Switzerland than they are in Germany (468 vs 415 for a three-year apprenticeship). Further, when at workplaces, Swiss apprentices devote 83% of their time to productive tasks, compared to only 57% amongst German apprentices.

One striking feature of apprenticeships in both countries is how quickly apprentices ascend from taking on unskilled to skilled tasks. In Switzerland, the productivity of apprentices rises from 37% of a skilled worker's level in the first year to 75% in the final year; the increase in Germany is as rapid, increasing from 30% to 68% of a skilled worker's productivity over the apprenticeship period. Still, nearly all German firms with apprenticeships (93%) incur net costs whilst a majority of Swiss firms (60%) more than recoup their costs.

Are the higher in-programme net costs to German firms offset by any advantage after the apprenticeship period? The study indicates retention of apprentices within the firm is much higher in Germany than in Switzerland. Thus, whilst German firms bear much higher net costs than Swiss firms during the apprenticeship period, they reap higher returns during the post-apprenticeship period.

Evidence from the Germany surveys of employers offers some insight into post-programme benefits (Beicht and Ulrich 2005). Recruitment and training cost savings average nearly €6,000 for each skilled worker trained in an apprenticeship and taken on permanently. The report cites other benefits, including reduced errors in placing employees, avoiding excessive costs when the demand for skilled workers cannot be met quickly, and performance advantages favouring internally trained workers who understand company processes over skilled workers recruited from the job market. Taking all of these benefits into account makes the apprenticeship investment into a net gain for employers.

Not all recent studies indicate high net costs of apprenticeships in Germany. For example, Mohrenweiser and Zwick (2009) find that for many occupations, the gains to the firm during the apprenticeship period more than offset the costs. They draw their conclusions by estimating the impact of apprenticeships on company profits. For apprenticeships in trade, commercial, craft, and construction occupations, the estimates show a positive impact on profits. Moreover, the gains come from the higher productivity of apprentices (relative to unskilled or semi-skilled workers) and not from lower wages. Only in manufacturing is the effect on current profits negative, indicating a net cost during the apprenticeship period that is presumably offset by post-programme benefits. In another careful study of German apprenticeships, Rauner et al. (2010) finds that the majority of the 100 firms in the sample recouped their investment in apprenticeships during the training period. The same study finds that most firms experience low net costs or even net benefits from sponsoring apprenticeships. However, the net costs vary widely, with some firms gaining more than €10,000 and other experiencing net costs. High quality apprenticeships have higher gross costs but are much more likely than low quality apprenticeships to help employers recoup their investment during the training period.

An extensive study of Canadian employers sponsored by the Canadian Apprenticeship Forum (2006) estimated employer costs and benefits of four-year apprenticeships in 15 occupations. The study drew on responses from 433 employers. The average gross costs varied widely, ranging from about $78,000 for cooks to $275,000 for construction electricians. Average in-programme benefits—measured as the revenue generated by the apprentices—varied widely as well, ranging from $120,000 for cooks to $338,000 for construction electricians. For all 15 occupations, employers earned a positive return on their apprenticeship investments even without taking account of any post-programme benefits.

In a recent analysis of apprenticeships in the United Kingdom based on eight employers, Hasluck and Hogarth (2010) estimated that the average gross costs were higher than the average benefits during the apprenticeship period in all four industries. The gross costs were only modestly higher than the in-programme benefits in retail and business administration, but much higher in engineering and construction. Still, the authors estimate that employers at least break even during the early post-apprenticeship period, when the contributions to production of apprenticeship graduates are worth more than their wages.

No rigorous studies have estimated costs and benefits for US employers. However, evidence from surveys of over 900 employer sponsors of apprenticeships indicates that the overwhelming majority of sponsors believe their programmes are valuable and involve net gains (Lerman et al. 2009).

Government Costs and Benefits of Apprenticeship and Other Vocational Education

Government outlays per student are believed to be considerably higher for school-based vocational education than for academic education (Psacharopoulos 1993; Middleton 1988; Gill et al. 1999; Klein 2001). Yet, there are strikingly few detailed studies of government spending on vocational education and in many countries the cost differences are modest. A graph prepared by Cedefop (2012) indicates virtually identical expenditures per student in a number of European countries, though it shows that outlays are substantially higher for vocational education than general education in France and Germany. In a study of the Geneva canton of Switzerland as of 1994, government costs per student were about 50% higher in full-time vocational education than in general education but government costs per apprentice were only half the costs of general education (Hanhart and Bossio 1998).

Government costs are lower in apprenticeship programmes than in school-based TVET. Students spend less time in school during apprenticeships. Government spending on equipment is less necessary for apprenticeships because apprentices gain experience with relevant equipment at their work site. Successful dual systems reduce the need for government spending on university education or on second-chance training programmes.

The long-term benefits of apprenticeship accruing to governments are rarely estimated. In the United States, Reed et al. (2012) estimates that federal and state governments spent only about $715 per apprenticeship participant, or only about 7% of the amount governments spend per year on two-year college programmes. Hollenbeck (2008) finds a substantial gap between school-based post-secondary TVET and apprenticeships (about $7,600 vs $2,700) in Washington State.

The long-term benefits of apprenticeship accruing to governments are rarely estimated. Reed et al. projects that over the career of an apprentice, the tax returns are more than $27 for each dollar invested. According to Hollenbeck (2008), the government obtains about 20% of the overall net gains in earnings linked to apprenticeship earnings gains.

Investment in apprenticeship training is substantially larger in countries with large systems, such as Austria, Denmark, Germany, and Switzerland. Their governments are generally convinced that such investment bears fruit in the form of low youth unemployment, improving the school-to-work transition, insuring effective skills options for people who learn best by doing, increasing the share of people with a skill qualification, and improving the climate for manufacturing.

Conclusions

Skilled jobs and careers that do not require a BA or higher degree make up a significant share of employment in modern economies. The jobs range from construction crafts and construction management to skilled manufacturing positions, including machinists and laser welders, to police officers and fire fighters, to sales and purchasing positions, to health technicians and licensed practical nurses, to chefs and floral designers, and to legal secretaries. Although the current number and trend of intermediate-level jobs is subject to debate, new jobs plus replacement openings in these fields will continue to make up 40% or more of all jobs in advanced capitalist countries.

Apprenticeships to train workers for intermediate-level careers work well. Skill development through apprenticeships is closely suited to the needs of employers and the job market, reinforces classroom learning with application in the workplace, involves trainees in the production process, makes for a seamless transition from school to a career, provides trainees with a natural mentoring process, allows trainees to earn wages whilst gaining occupational mastery, applies to a wide range of occupations, requires less government spending than other education and training strategies, and generally raises the quality of the workforce. Countries with robust and well-structured apprenticeship programmes appear to outperform other countries in achieving low youth unemployment, raising the status of skilled and semi-skilled occupations, and maintaining more well-paid manufacturing jobs.

Notwithstanding these advantages, the apprenticeship strategy faces serious critiques. To some, employers have little incentive to create apprenticeships because they bear the costs whilst workers and other employers reap the benefits. It is also suggested that training for an occupation can be wasteful if workers often change careers, and this training may limit the ability of workers to shift to other fields without losing their earning power.

An expanding literature suggests that both arguments lack strong empirical support. Investment in apprenticeship training is often recouped during the training period itself. Most employers in Switzerland and many in Germany experience zero or low net costs (training, material costs, and wages minus the value of the apprentice's production). Reduced turnover and training costs and the certainty that the regular worker will meet skill standards are simply added benefits.

For workers, the skills learnt in apprenticeship are generally portable. Changing occupations within the same cluster of occupations often raises wages and those who leave their training occupations report they frequently use the skills learnt in their apprenticeships. The transferability of these skills should not be surprising since apprenticeships teach a range of tasks and include classroom training.

Most studies find high rates of return on apprenticeships generally; however, researchers have not produced definitive estimates of the relative returns to entering college vs entering apprenticeships. In addition, there are two particularly positive conclusions we can draw from the research: dual work-based and school-based apprenticeship programmes offer a way of diversifying routes to rewarding careers beyond the 'academic only' approach; and expanding apprenticeships can help deal with high youth unemployment, low youth skills, the rise in inequality, and the decline of middle-skill jobs.

The dual work-based and school-based apprenticeship programmes offer a way of diversifying routes to rewarding careers beyond the 'academic only' approach. Expanding apprenticeship can help deal with high youth unemployment, low youth skills, the rise in inequality, and the decline of middle-skill jobs. But it is important to learn more about the relative returns to entering college vs. entering apprenticeships for various subgroups, some of which thrive in college programmes while others would achieve far more in apprenticeship programmes. In addition, added evidence on the returns firms can expect from their investments in apprenticeship is vital for countries to scale up the number of apprenticeship slots employers offer.

The OECD (2009, 2010) has already concluded that apprenticeship training should play a much larger role. Several countries—notably Australia, England, and even France, are already pursuing major efforts to expand apprenticeship. Apprenticeship is taking hold and able to succeed in relatively regulated and unregulated labour markets (Muehlemann et al. 2010). Still, expanding the scope of programmes is challenging in several countries, as is building all the necessary components for a substantial and sustainable apprenticeship system. Success in developing and sustaining a major role for apprenticeship will likely help countries in their quest for a well-trained, productive, well-compensated, satisfied, and adaptable work force.

References

Acemoglu, D. and Pischke, J-S. (1999) 'Beyond Becker: Training in Imperfect Markets', *The Economic Journal*, 109(453): 112–142.

Almlund, M., Duckworth, A. Heckman, J., and Kautz, T. (2011) 'Personality, Psychology, and Economics', in E. Hanushek, S. J. Machin, and L. Woessmann (eds), *Handbook of the Economics of Education*, vol. 4, Amsterdam: Elvesier Press.

Autor, D. (2010) 'The Polarization of Job Opportunities in the U.S. Labour Market: Implications for Employment and Earnings', Washington, DC: The Center for American Progress and the Hamilton Project. http://economics.mit.edu/files/5554.

Bauernschuster, S., Falck, O., and Heblich, S. (2009) 'Training and Innovation', *Journal of Human Capital*, 3(4): 323–353.

Beicht, U. and Ulrich, J. (2005) 'Costs and Benefits of In-company Vocational Training', BWP Special Edition. 2005. http://www.bibb.de/dokumente/pdf/a1_bwp_special-edition_beicht.pdf.

Bishop, J. (1997) 'What We Know about Employer-Provided Training: A Review of the Literature', in S. Polachek (ed), *Research in Labour Economics*, 16, Greenwich, CT, and London: JAI Press: 19–87.

Boothby, D. and Drewes, T. (2010). 'Returns to Apprenticeship in Canada'. Working Paper no. 70, Canadian Labour Market and Skills Researcher Network. http://www.clsrn.econ.ubc.ca/workingpapers/CLSRN%20Working%20Paper%20no.%2070%20-%20Boothby%20and%20Drewes.pdf.

Brown, A., Kirpal, S., and Rauner, F. (eds) (2007) *Identities at Work*, Dordrecht: Springer Press.

Canadian Apprenticeship Forum (2006) 'Apprenticeship: Building a Skilled Workforce for a Strong Bottom Line'. http://www.caf-fca.org/files/access/Return_On_Training_Investment-Employers_report.pdf.

Cedefop (2011a) 'Development of National Qualifications Frameworks in Europe', Working Paper no. 12, Publications Office of the European Union, Luxembourg. http://www.cedefop.europa.eu/EN/Files/6112_en.pdf.

Cedefop (2011b) 'Vocational Education and Training Is Good for You: The Social Benefits of VET for Individuals'. Research Paper no. 17, Luxembourg: Publications Office of the European Union. http://www.cedefop.europa.eu/EN/publications/18440.aspx.

Cedefop (2012) http://www.cedefop.europa.eu/EN/Files/3899-img1-1-graph_11-2008.jpg.

Clark, D. and René F. (2001) 'The Promise of Workplace Training for Non-College-Bound Youth: Theory and Evidence from German Apprenticeship'. IZA Discussion Paper no. 378, Bonn: IZA. http://www.iza.org/en/webcontent/publications/papers/viewAbstract?dp_id=378.

Cox, A. (2007) 'Re-visiting the NVQ Debate: "Bad" Qualifications, Expansive Learning Environments and Prospects for Upskilling Workers', SKOPE Research Paper no. 71. http://www.skope.ox.ac.uk/sites/default/files/Research%20Paper%2071%20Cox.pdf.

Dif, M. (2012) 'France', in E. Smith and R. B. Kemmis (eds), *Possible Futures for the Indian Apprenticeships System Project: Interim Report to the World Bank*, Victoria: University of Ballarat.

Eraut, M. (2001) 'The Role and Use of Vocational Qualifications', *National Institute Economic Review*, 178 (October): 88–98.

Fersterer, J., Pischke, J-S., and Winter-Ebmer, R. (2008) 'Returns to Apprenticeship Training in Austria: Evidence from Failed Firms', *Scandinavian Journal of Economics*, 110(4): 733–753.

Fuller, A. and Unwin, L. (2006) 'Expansive and Restrictive Learning Environments', in K. Evans, P. Hodkinson, H. Rainbird, and L. Unwin (eds), *Improving Workplace Learning*, London: Routledge: 27–48.

Geel, R. and Backes-Gellner, U. (2009) 'Occupational Mobility within and between Skill Clusters: An Empirical Analysis Based on the Skill-Weights Approach', Working Paper no. 47, Swiss Leading House on Economics of Education, Firm Behavior and Training Policies, Swiss Federal Office for Professional Education and Technology, Zurich. http://ideas.repec.org/p/iso/educat/0047.html.

Geel, R., Mure, J., and Backes-Gellner, U. (2011) 'Specificity of Occupational Training and Occupational Mobility: An Empirical Study Based on Lazear's Skill-Weights Approach', *Education Economics*, 19(5): 519–535.

Gill, I. S., Dar, A., and Fluitman, A. (1999) 'Constraints and Innovation in Reforming National Training Systems: Cross-Country Comparisons', *International Journal of Manpower*, 20(7): 405–431.

Göggel, K. and Zwick, T. (2012) 'Heterogeneous Wage Effects of Apprenticeship Training', *Scandinavian Journal of Economics*, 114(3): 756–779.

Goos, M., Manning, A., and Salomons, A. (2009) 'Job Polarization in Europe', *American Economic Review*, 99(2): 58–63.

Gunderson, M. and Krashinsky, H. (2012) 'Returns to Apprenticeship: Analysis Based on the 2006 Census', CLSRN Working Paper 99, Canadian Labour Market and Skills Researcher Network, Vancouver, April.

Halpern, R. (2009) *The Means to Grow up: Reinventing Apprenticeship As a Developmental Support in Adolescence*, New York: Routledge.

Hanhart, S. and Bossio, S. (1998) 'Costs and Benefits of Dual Apprenticeship: Lessons from the Swiss System', *International Labour Review*, 137(4): 483–500.

Handel, M. (2007) 'A New Survey of Workplace Skills, Technology, and Management Practices (STAMP): Background and Descriptive Statistics'. Presented at National Research Council Workshop on Future Skills, Washington, DC, May 23.

Hanushek, E., Wößmann, L., and Zhang, L. (2011) 'General Education, Vocational Education and Labor-Market Outcomes over the Life-Cycle'. NBER Working Paper 17504, Cambridge, MA.

Hasluck, C. and Hogarth, T. (2010) 'The Net Benefits to Employers' Investments in Apprenticeships: Case Study Evidence from the UK', *Canadian Apprenticeship Journal*, 2 (Summer).

Heckman, J., Stixrud, J., and Urzoa, S. (2006) 'The Effect of Cognitive and Non-Cognitive Abilities on Labor Market Outcomes and Social Behavior', *Journal of Labor Economics*, 24(3): 411–482.

Heckman, J. and Rubinstein, Y. (2001) 'The Importance of Noncognitive Skills: Lessons from the GED Testing Program', *American Economic Review*, 91(2): 145–149.

Hoeckel, K. and Schwartz, R. (2009) *A Learning for Jobs Review of Germany*, Paris: OECD.

Hoeckel, K., Field, S., and Grubb, W. N. (2009) *A Learning for Jobs Review of Switzerland*, Paris: OECD.

Hollenbeck, K. (2008) 'State Use of Workforce System Net Impact Estimates and Rates of Return'. Paper presented at the Association for Public Policy Analysis and Management (APPAM) Conference, Los Angeles, California. http://research.upjohn.org/confpapers/1.

Holzer, H. and Lerman, R. (2009) 'The Future of Middle Skills Jobs', Center on Children and Families, CCF Brief 47, Washington, DC: The Brookings Institution.

Klein, S. (2001) 'Financing Vocational Education: A State Policymaker's Guide', Berkeley, California: MPR Associates. http://www.mprinc.com/products/pdf/financing_vocational_education.pdf.

Kleiner, M. (2006) *Licensing Competition: Ensuring Quality or Stifling Competition?*, Kalamazoo, MI: W. E. Upjohn Institute for Employment Research.

Lazear, E. (2009) 'Firm-Specific Human Capital: A Skill-Weights Approach', *Journal of Political Economy*, 117: 914–940.

Lerman, R. (2008) 'Widening the Scope of Standards through Work-Based Learning', 30th Research Conference of the Association for Public Policy and Management, Los Angeles, California, November.

Lerman, R., Eyster, L., and Chambers, K. (2009) 'The Benefits and Challenges of Registered Apprenticeship: The Sponsors' Perspective', Washington, DC: US Department of Labor, Employment and Training Administration. http://www.urban.org/UploadedPDF/411907_registered_apprenticeship.pdf.

Lerman, R. (2010) 'Employer-Led Training: Intensive and Extensive Approaches', in D. Finegold, M. Gatta, H. Salzman, and S. Schurman (eds), *Transforming the U.S. Workforce Development System: Lessons from Research and Practicei*, New York: Labor and Employment Relations Association, Cornell University Press: 153–180.

Lindqvist, E. and Vestman R. (2011) 'The Labor Market Returns to Cognitive and Noncognitive Ability: Evidence from the Swedish Enlistment', *American Economic Journal: Applied Economics*, 3(1): 101–128.

Middleton, J. (1988) 'Changing Patterns in Vocational Education', Policy Research Working Paper Series 26, Washington, DC: The World Bank.

Miller, L. (2012) 'Canada' and 'England', in E. Smith and R. B. Kemmis (eds), *Possible Futures for the Indian Apprenticeships System Project: Interim Report to the World Bank*, Victoria: University of Ballarat.

Mohrenweiser, J. and Zwick, T. (2009) 'Why Do Firms Train Apprentices? The Net Cost Puzzle Reconsidered', *Labour Economics*, 16: 631–637.

Mounier, A. (2001) 'The Three Logics of Skills in French Literature'. BVET Working Paper, Sydney, Australia. http://www.bvet.nsw.gov.au/pdf/threelogics.pdf.

Muehlemann, S., Pfeifer, H., Walden, G., Wenzelmann, H., and Wolter, S. 2010. 'The Financing of Apprenticeship Training in the Light of Labor Market Regulations', *Labour Economics*, 17(5), 799–809.

Nelsen, B. (1997) 'Should Social Skills Be in the Vocational Curriculum? Evidence from the Automotive Repair Field', in A. Lesgold, M. Feuer, and A. Black (eds), *Transitions in Work and Learning: Implications for Assessment*, Washington, DC: National Academy Press: 62–88.

OECD (2009) *Learning for Jobs*, Paris: Organization for Economic Development and Cooperation.

OECD (2010) *Off to a Good Start: Jobs for Youth*, Paris: Organization for Economic Development and Cooperation.

Pellegrino J. W. and Hilton, M. L. (eds) (2012) *Education for Life and Work: Developing Transferable Knowledge and Skills in the 21st Century*. Committee on Defining Deeper Learning and 21st Century Skills, Division on Behavioral and Social Sciences and Education, National Research Council, Washington, DC: National Research Council.

Prais, S. J. (1995) *Productivity, Education, and Training: An International Perspective*, Cambridge: National Institute of Economic and Social Research.

Psacharopoulos, G. (1993) 'Returns to Investment in Education: A Global Update'. Policy Research Working Paper Series: 1067. Washington, DC: The World Bank.

Puri, R. (2012) 'Why the Manufacturing Skills Gap Is Creating New Opportunities', Forbes. http://www.forbes.com/sites/bmoharrisbank/2012/12/19/why-the-manufacturing-skills-gap-is-creating-new-opportunities/.

Rauner, F., Heinemann, L. Piening, D., and Bishoff, R. (2010) 'Costs, Benefits, and Quality of Apprenticeships: A Regional Case Study', in F. Rauner and E. Smith (eds), *Rediscovering Apprenticeship: Research Findings from the International Network on Innovative Apprenticeship*, London: Springer Science + Business Media.

Reed, D., Liu, A. Y-H., Kleinman, R. Mastri, A., Reed, D., Sattar, S., and Ziegler, J. (2012) 'An Effectiveness Assessment and Cost-Benefit Analysis of Registered Apprenticeship in 10 States', Washington, DC: Office of Apprenticeship, US Department of Labor. http://wdr.doleta.gov/research/FullText_Documents/ETAOP_2012_10.pdf.

Rose, M. (2004) *The Mind at Work: Valuing the Intelligence of the American Worker*, New York: Viking Books.

Ryan, C. (2002) 'Individual Returns to Vocational Education and Training Qualifications: Their Implications for Lifelong Learning', National Centre for Vocational Education Research, Kensington Park, Australia.

Ryan, P. (2001) 'The School-to-Work Transition: A Cross National Perspective', *Journal of Economic Literature*, March: 34–92.

Saniter, A. (2012) 'Germany', in E. Smith and R. B. Kemmis (eds), *Possible Futures for the Indian Apprenticeships System Project: Interim Report to the World Bank*, Victoria: University of Ballarat.

Secretary's Commission on Achieving Necessary Skills (1992) *Learning a Living: A Blueprint for High Performance. A SCANS Report for America 2000*, Washington, DC: US Department of Labor.

Smith, E. (2012) 'Australia', in E. Smith and R. B. Kemmis (eds), *Possible Futures for the Indian Apprenticeships System Project: Interim Report to the World Bank*, Victoria: University of Ballarat.

Stasz, C. (2001) 'Assessing Skills for Work: Two Perspectives', *Oxford Economic Papers*, 3: 385–405.

Steedman, H. (1993) 'The Economics of Youth Training in Germany', *The Economic Journal*, 103, (420): 1279–1291.

Steedman, H. and Wagner, K. (1987) 'A Second Look at Productivity, Machinery and Skills in Britain and Germany', *National Institute Economic Review*, 122: 84–96.

Weitzman, H. and Harding, R. (2011) 'Skills gap hobbles US employers', *Financial Times*, 13 December.

Wolter, S. C. and P. Ryan (2011) 'Apprenticeship', in E. A. Hanushek, S. Machin, and L. Wößmann (eds), *Economics of Education*. Vol. 3: *Handbooks in Economics*, Amsterdam: North-Holland: 521–576.

CHAPTER 10

WHAT IS EXPECTED OF HIGHER EDUCATION GRADUATES IN THE TWENTY-FIRST CENTURY?

MARTIN HUMBURG AND ROLF VAN DER VELDEN

Introduction

Expectations of higher education institutions (HEIs) and their graduates have always been high. For centuries, universities have been the place where higher-order knowledge and skills have been developed, refined, and nurtured. Never before, however, have expectations of higher education (HE) and its graduates been so strongly expressed and explicitly defined—in particular by employers.

This chapter examines the skill set graduates are increasingly expected to possess, and the role of HE in developing them. As we focus on graduates, we leave basic skills (like numeracy, literacy, and computer skills) out of the analysis, taking them, in a way, for granted.

We identify six trends which form the basis of the changing role of graduates in economic life. These trends are the knowledge society, increasing uncertainty, the information and technology (ICT) revolution, high performance workplaces, globalization, and the change of the economic structure. By changing the nature and range of tasks graduates are expected to fulfil in today's economy, these trends generate new and intensify traditional skill demands, which we summarize as professional expertise, flexibility, innovation and knowledge management, mobilization of human resources, international orientation, and entrepreneurship.

We introduce these six trends knowing that there is no consensus amongst researchers on how many independent trends there are, let alone how to name and define them. We also recognize that in reality these trends are not isolated but are strongly interlinked, with the information and communication technology (ICT) revolution being the main driver of the others. However, we are convinced that the categorization of trends and resulting skill demands we present here are those most relevant to this chapter. They should be seen as a useful tool to examine what is expected of graduates in the twenty-first century, and what the drivers of these skill demands are.

In the next section we elaborate on the six trends and related skill demands. We then discuss their implications for the role of HE and distil some key insights into how HE can position itself in skill formation today. The chapter ends with some concluding remarks.

The Trends and Related Skills

The Knowledge Society and Professional Expertise

The Knowledge Society

In developed nations, the twentieth century has been marked by a transition from an industrial society, characterized by mass production, to a post-industrial one in which the service sector takes on a prominent role and knowledge becomes a valued form of capital. Bell (1999), who coined the term 'post-industrial society' in the 1970s, emphasizes the role played by theoretical knowledge in this type of society, particularly as the source of innovation. For Bills (2004, 100) 'the primacy of theoretical knowledge, even more than the shift from goods to services, or the computerization of the workplace, or any trend towards meritocratic selection, defines the post-industrial society.' The transition from a fabricating to a knowledge society has been facilitated by two (other) major trends: globalization and rapid technological change. It is now possible to generate and to gather vast amounts of data, process them into relevant information and communicate them to recipients for decision-making. For businesses, knowledge has become a major ingredient in gaining and sustaining competitive advantage (Wickramasinghe and Von Lubitz 2007), and on a more general level this applies to nations, too. The emergence of the knowledge society increases the demand for knowledge workers (Reich 1992), whose tasks are complex, non-repetitive, and non-routine, and can therefore not be replaced by rule-based ICT. The demands on knowledge workers are extensive. Clearly, credentialed and cognitively skilled individuals employed in the most information-intense sectors of society are the winners of these changes (Hage and Powers 1992).

Professional Expertise

In order to prosper in the knowledge society, graduates need to be equipped with the skills necessary to fulfil tasks which are at the heart of knowledge work. This entails: (1) a specific body of knowledge (the knowledge and skills needed to solve occupation-specific problems); (2) the ability to apply expert thinking; and (3) general academic skills (e.g. analytical thinking, reflectiveness, and the ability to see the limitations of one's own discipline).

In contrast to the application of more pragmatic and contextual knowledge, knowledge work entails unstructured decision-making. Unstructured decisions concern important, novel, non-routine problems for which no established procedure exists for how to solve them. Levy (2010) calls 'expert thinking' a collection of specific solution methods which vary with the problem at hand. It does not only entail *a specific body of knowledge* but also the *ability to apply expert thinking*. The time necessary to become an expert in a job is usually estimated to be 5–10 years (Hayes 1981; Ericsson and Crutcher 1990). The important difference between a young professional or recent graduate and an expert is that the expert can deviate from routine solution methods. Here, *broad academic skills*, such as analytical thinking and reflectiveness, help the expert to know when doing so is appropriate. These skills also allow knowledge workers to see the limitations of their own discipline and to take other perspectives into account. This is especially important as a substantial proportion of today's innovations takes place at the cross-section of disciplines and knowledge workers have to successfully work in teams of professionals from different disciplines. A certain amount of interdisciplinary knowledge supports this process.

Increasing Uncertainty and Flexibility

Increasing Uncertainty

It is widely recognized that the last 40 years have seen a significant shift of the risks and costs associated with economic activity from institutional shareholders and their agents to smaller businesses and workers. Whilst some authors interpret this shift as a gradual return to equilibrium after the exceptionally long boom from the late 1940s to the early 1960s,[1] others see over-capacity, intensifying international competition, and excess liquidity at the core of this development (Brenner 2006; Froud et al. 2006). Against this background, two main groups of workers have emerged. On the one hand, there is a highly valued core labour force of knowledge workers who are increasingly employed in flexible and fluidly defined work settings. In these work settings, flexibility is functional and internal. The counterpart of this core labour force is a pool of part-timers, temporary workers, self-employed and high-turnover workers, which has been growing in numbers in most developed economies over the last decades (Castells 1996).

Although flexibility is increasingly demanded by employers, skills related to flexibility, such as the ability to rapidly acquire new knowledge, are not necessarily rewarded. Allen and Van der Velden (2011) show that professional expertise—not flexibility-related skills—is by far the skill that has the strongest positive relationship with earnings

[1] For an overview of interpretations of post-war growth, see Crafts and Toniolo (1996).

and the probability to be employed. If the labour force is indeed composed of a highly valued core of knowledge workers and a pool of flexible 'on-demand' workers, professional expertise seems to be the entry ticket to the core group.

The emergence of a system which combines a core labour force with externally flexible workers is often explained by employers' need to react to economic shocks in highly regulated countries. When wages are rigid, firms hire temporary workers or offer workers fixed-term contracts to hedge market uncertainty (DiPrete et al. 2006).

Schmid (1998) argues that social differentiation and the need to deal with demographic challenges adds to this flexibilization trend. He introduces the term 'transitional' labour market to indicate that the standard biography of education—life-time employment—retirement, has changed towards multiple transitions, e.g. between different employers, from employment back to education, or from labour activity to private activity such as caregiving.

Whilst the state establishes the framework for transitional labour markets, it is the individual workers who have to master these transitions. Consequently, individuals have to be equipped with the skills necessary to master the level of external flexibility that is expected of them or that they think is most appropriate for their preferred work-life balance.

Of course, graduates have a high chance of belonging to the valued core labour force. Moreover, further research has to determine whether flexibility is part of a lifelong boundaryless career (Stone, 2006) or just a temporary phenomenon in the early stages of the career (Allen et al. 2011). At the least, also for graduates becoming a member of this valued core might take a while and therefore they need to be prepared to successfully master periods of increased uncertainty.

Flexibility

The following skills contribute to flexibility: (1) the ability to deal with changes and uncertainty; (2) the ability to learn new things; and (3) employability skills (e.g. the willingness to invest in further education and training and the ability to plan and take responsibility for one's own career).

Above all, individuals need to be *able to deal with changes and uncertainty*. They have to incorporate uncertainty and the need to be flexible into their life plans and personal projects. In addition, flexibility is often equated with general skills such as the *ability to learn new things*. Finally flexible workers are increasingly *responsible for their own employability*. This includes making plans and setting aside time and resources for further training and lifelong learning. Being employable demands a substantial level of transition skills. Although flexicurity—the combination of flexibility and security—is mainly seen as a challenge to be resolved at the national level by introducing appropriate labour market institutions (Schmid 1998; Muffels 2008), successfully mastering the many possible transitions between education and training and employment, different forms of employment, employment and unemployment, labour market activity, and private activity requires substantial knowledge about how the system works.

The ICT Revolution, and Innovation and Knowledge Management

The ICT Revolution

Of the six trends we have identified, technological change is probably the one that is most interlinked with the other trends. Technological change, and especially the predominance of ICT, is the driving force behind the emergence of the knowledge society, it has changed markets and contributes to increased levels of market uncertainty, it facilitates and necessitates the emergence of high performance workplaces, and it is a main driver of globalization and changes in the economic structure.

Hage and Powers (1992) draw a distinction between instruments and other machines which are primarily used in production processes. Whilst instruments increase the number of tasks being performed, most machines simply replace labour. ICT can assume both forms and there is widespread consensus that the introduction of ICT into workplaces is skill biased—that it favours higher-skilled workers. For repetitive, routine tasks—often performed by low- and medium-skilled workers—ICT can be seen as replacing labour. ICT is faster and cheaper than people in performing these tasks. With regard to knowledge work and professional expertise, however, ICT is mostly instrumental and complements labour (Autor et al.2003; Levy 2010). Besides being a complement to (mostly skilled) labour, instruments in the form of upgraded equipment make job tasks more complex (Hage and Powers 1992). The tendency that higher-skilled individuals are better suited to use new technologies is therefore often seen as another source of skill bias (Caroli and Van Reenen 2001; Greenan 2003). Organizations in technology rich environments might prefer highly skilled workers as they have higher digital competence and lower training costs.

According to a competing view, the adoption of new technologies by organizations is not exogenous, but a reaction to a large supply of highly skilled workers. Proponents of the endogenous skill biased technological change hypothesis argue that the expansion of HE in the second half of the twentieth century produced a large stock of highly skilled workers, and that this in turn induced the development of new technologies directed at complementing the highly skilled in order to increase productivity and profits (Acemoglu 1998). A highly skilled workforce may therefore have created its own demand.

Whatever the underlying causal direction of this development, the introduction of ICT has revolutionized the way data and knowledge is generated and diffused. There is today an unprecedented range of resources easily available. In the twenty-first century, the challenge is not to access knowledge, but to manage, integrate, and evaluate it. In this regard, graduates play a crucial role within organizations.

Innovation and Knowledge Management

The ICT revolution does not only impact the skills that are directly related to it, but changes the nature and content of most other skills as well. It is hard to conceive of any professional skill that is not affected by ICT. Also basic skills like literacy or 'soft' skills like communication skills have significantly changed in character due to the ICT revolution. Although we recognize this broad impact of ICT on all types of skills, we will concentrate here on the skills that are more directly related to innovation and knowledge management.

ICT has important implications with regard to the skills necessary to manage knowledge in a way that supports and facilitates innovation. Whereas in the past individuals spent considerable amounts of time searching for scarce information, for the first time in history, the predominance of ICT makes for an abundance of data to be readily accessed. Today's challenges do not lie in information gathering, but in establishing a common understanding of information (Levy 2010). The ability to rapidly separate signals from noise is therefore not novel as a valuable capability in degree, but in type (Dede 2010).

The following skills are important components of innovation and knowledge management: (1) innovative/creative skills (the ability to come up with new ideas or the ability to approach problems from a different angle); (2) network, information and strategic ICT skills; and (3) implementation skills.

Organizations' competitiveness is to a large extent based on their capacity to introduce entirely new products or processes, or to substantially improve existing ones. The availability of knowledge workers with good *innovative and creative skills* who have the ability to come up with new ideas or the ability to approach problems from a different angle is of course a major ingredient. But that is not enough. Processed, well-managed and systematically communicated information is crucial to organizations' innovative capabilities. It has been suggested that organizations' innovative capacity depends on diffusion of knowledge to a broad range of key individuals within them (OECD/Eurostat 2005). Knowledge workers therefore are often assigned the role of receptors and distributors of expert information. This presupposes *information and strategic ICT skills* which allows knowledge workers to search, select and process relevant information that contributes to achieving organizational goals (Van Dijk 2005). In addition, knowledge workers need to possess good *networking skills* as they have to be well connected in order to both receive relevant information as well as to spread this information within the organization.

Of course, making information merely flow through the organization is not yet enough. Ideas, new technology and knowledge also have to be absorbed by the organization. Innovation and knowledge management therefore includes the skills to bring an innovation from the 'drawing board' into the organization. These *implementation skills* relate closely to the strategic-organizational and interpersonal skills that we will discuss in the next section.

The Emergence of High Performance Workplaces and the Mobilization of Human Resources

Emergence of High Performance Workplaces

The centrality of knowledge work and increasing levels of market uncertainty requires organizational changes within firms. It is widely believed that traditional bureaucratic management stifles innovation and is ill-equipped for optimally using the potential of knowledge workers. Organizations which heavily rely on knowledge workers to increase productivity and competitiveness, and which adapt their organizational structure accordingly, have been labelled 'high performance organizations' (OECD 1999). What distinguishes them from other organizations is that the high performance workplaces they design involve a broad range of skills and task variety, the extensive use of teamwork, reduced hierarchical levels, and the delegation of responsibility to individuals and teams (Betcherman 1997). As it becomes increasingly difficult for managers to keep pace with technological developments, an argument in favour of giving knowledge workers more weight within the organization is to better align strategic decisions with the latest innovations. Moreover, flattening hierarchies potentially increases the speed of decisions in the face of market uncertainty.

Organizations which adopt high performance work practices have been found to have higher productivity and better financial performance (e.g. Appelbaum et al. 2000; Bartel 2004; Black and Lynch 2004). High performance organizations engage workers in the broader production process and provide them with comprehensive understandings of organizational goals and priorities (Bills 2004). The organization supplies knowledge workers with the means to attain agreed goals and gives them autonomy with regard to the path to get there.

It is difficult to quantify the extent to which high performance workplaces are ousting traditional workplaces and critics have argued that organizational change towards more flexible firms represent management fads rather than new work practices (Ramsay, 1995). There is, however, some evidence of an upward trend in their diffusion: the proportion of firms adopting new work practices is on the rise (Arnal, Ok and Torres, 2001) and with it the demand for the skills they require.

Mobilization of Human Resources

The emergence of high performance workplaces sets high expectations on the mobilization of human resources. If knowledge workers are required to optimally mobilize their own and others' human capital, they need to have at least the following skills: (1) interpersonal skills (the ability to work in a team, and communicate and cooperate effectively with diverse colleagues and clients; (2) (self-)management skills (the ability to work within budget and time constraints, leadership): and (3) strategic-organizational skills (the ability to act strategically towards the achievement of organizational goals).

The importance of *interpersonal skills* is not unique to the twenty- first century (Dede 2010). It is obvious, however, that the skills demanded of workers in settings characterized by autonomous teams with shared decision-making differ from those of workers in traditional hierarchical work settings. Traditionally, interpersonal skills are the domain of managers, who have to be effective in getting others to achieve the organizational goals without necessarily being experts themselves. In high performance workplaces, however, teams and workers are given responsibilities ranging from production, training, and product innovation to customer relations and marketing. Organizational goals are attained by teams of workers with complementary professional expertise (Karoly 2004). This involves a high degree of information-sharing and communication, and fundamentally increases the worth of collaborative capacity for non-management-level workers and the ability to interact in socially heterogeneous groups (Rychen and Salganik 2003). Working in teams and making shared decisions demands workers to be able to communicate effectively, evaluate their work and the work of others, influence team mates, and to seek advice, information, and support when appropriate. The importance of these skills for professionals in Europe has been documented by Felstead et al. Zhou (2007), Allen (2011), and Miles and Martinez-Fernandez (2011).

A high level of autonomy requires knowledge workers to have good *self-management skills,* like the ability to work within time and budget constraints. Traditionally graduates have also been called upon to exert leadership skills. But instead of the 'traditional' leader, high performance workplaces require knowledge workers to have non-traditional *management skills,* such as the ability to mobilize the capacities of others in the team.

Reduced hierarchical levels open up opportunities for professional development. The work of knowledge workers is outcome oriented and the employer's capacity to monitor the working process is low. It is therefore in the interest of the employer to employ individuals with *strategic-organizational skills,* that is the ability to direct their actions independently towards attaining the organizational goal. High degrees of autonomy must not result in knowledge workers leading a self-centred, isolated working life within organizations. Knowledge workers must know their position in the organization and must be able to link their work to the tasks of others. In high performance workplaces, strategic thinking and being able to set one's task in the greater organizational context become key skills for professional and organizational success.

Globalization and International Orientation

Globalization

Globalization—the strengthening and acceleration of world-wide interconnectedness—has certainly been facilitated by the development of ICT. Never before has an economy had the capacity to work as a unit in real time on a planetary scale (Castells 2000). Globalization affects trade levels, production processes, information flows, and the competitive environment in which organizations operate. Globalization is therefore also related to the emergence of the knowledge society, the implementation of high performance workplaces, as well as the flexibilization of the relationship between employers and employees. At this point, however, we would like to highlight the extent to which globalization increases the demand for graduates with an international orientation.

Globalization is characterized by fast flows of ideas, financial capital, goods, services, and people across national borders. As a result, interaction with people from other cultures and with other linguistic backgrounds becomes more common and is now part of the working life of a substantial proportion of the higher-educated workforce. Around one third of European graduates work in organizations whose scope of operation is international (Pavlin and Svetlik 2011). The same proportion indicates that the ability to speak and write in a foreign language is highly required in their job.

Growing global interdependence is certainly one major driving force behind this development. A substantial proportion of graduates' work nowadays takes place across national borders or involves groups of people with diverse national backgrounds. At the same time, the flattening of hierarchical levels also impacts the number of individuals who work within culturally heterogeneous groups. This is because decentralizing decision-making not only grants groups of professionals more autonomy it also shifts large amounts of communication from higher levels of the hierarchy to the working level. Whereas traditionally the managerial level tended to be the recipient and the distributor of information, today the exchange of information increasingly takes place directly between professionals.

International Orientation

International orientation requires knowledge workers to have: (1) proficiency in foreign languages, and (2) intercultural skills (the ability to work with people from different cultural backgrounds and the ability to adapt to new cultural contexts).

Working and interacting with individuals of different cultural and linguistic backgrounds presupposes an elevated degree of *foreign language skills* and cultural sophistication. Naturally, a pre-condition of any goal-oriented interaction between individuals of diverse national backgrounds is to have a common language foundation. Individuals working in international contexts have to be able to understand spoken messages, to initiate, sustain, and conclude conversations, and to read, understand, and produce texts (European Commission 2007).

Yet even if this pre-condition is fulfilled, working in intercultural settings can suffer significant setbacks when patterns of thought or behaviour of others are misinterpreted. Selling products abroad can fail simply by not adjusting marketing strategies and sometimes the product itself to the particularities of the foreign market (Verluyten 2001). Today's graduates increasingly have to be able to take a step backwards from self-reference and familiar frameworks and adapt to new cultural contexts. These *intercultural skills* include knowing—or at least being aware of—particular cultures of e.g. negotiation, politeness, or decision-making.

The Change of the Economic Structure and Entrepreneurship

The Change of the Economic Structure

Over the last decades deregulation, technological change and globalization have fundamentally changed the competitive environment in which organizations operate and have resulted in an unprecedented growth of the service sector. At the same time, the relative importance of small and medium sized firms has increased substantially. To give an often cited example, between 1970 and 1996, the share of employment of the 500 largest US firms dropped from 20% to 8.5% (Carlsson 1992, 1999). Researchers do not agree whether the growing importance of SMEs is a temporary phenomenon (Brock and Evans 1989) or stems from the superiority of small and medium enterprises with regard to flexibility (Piore and Sabel 1984; Meredith 1987; Carlsson 1989) and innovation (Acs 1992; Audtretsch and Thurik 2000; Carree and Thurik 2003).[2] However, the observed growth in importance of small and medium enterprises for employment in combination with the flattening of hierarchies within firms increases demand for graduates who are comfortable with assuming responsibility and with contributing to the success of the organization through entrepreneurship. Audretsch and Thurik (2000) even point to the centrality of entrepreneurship at the country level. For high-wage countries whose key comparative advantage lies in the generation of knowledge and innovation, entrepreneurship may be one of the main ingredients of global competitiveness. At the firm or within-firm level, entrepreneurship can be understood as 'the discovery, evaluation and exploitation of future goods and services' (Eckhardt and Shane 2003: 336).[3] At the institutional level, entrepreneurship involves 'changing the structure within which economic and other activities take place' (Crouch 2005, 101). The importance of entrepreneurship is therefore not confined to knowledge workers working in the private sector but is also relevant for the work of institutional entrepreneurs in the public sector.

Entrepreneurship

The following skills are important components of entrepreneurship: (1) the ability to identify commercial risks and opportunities; (2) a good sense of cost awareness; and (3) the ability to turn an idea into a successful product.

At the firm level, the trends we identify contribute to the blurring of the boundaries between entrepreneurs managing their own firm and knowledge workers fulfilling central tasks within an organization. Boundaries become blurred because an increasing proportion of the workforce is required to possess entrepreneurial skills and commercial awareness. This refers to the ability to perceive changes in the market and to identify competitors as well as commercial risks and opportunities. It also pertains to the *awareness of the costs* associated with one's activities and costs of decisions. Potentially most importantly, it refers to the ability to recognize the commercial value of an idea and to search for and pursue opportunities to turn them into successful products.

Whenever knowledge workers assume a central role within an organization, they have to be increasingly alert to changes in markets and innovations. This not only includes evaluating how developments affect their own work, but also being able to

[2] The superiority of small and medium enterprises (SMEs) with regard to flexibility and innovation has been challenged by, for example, Weimer (1992) and Parker (2001).

[3] According to Eckhardt and Shane, their definition of entrepreneurship follows Venkataraman (1997).

understand the consequences for the organization as a whole. The higher the degree of autonomy knowledge workers enjoy within the organization the more important their ability to independently contribute to the organization's economic and commercial success. This is true for owners of a firm as well as for employees both in the private and the public sector. It is important to note that the importance of entrepreneurial skills is not confined to the private sector. Globalization does not only result in international competition amongst firms but also between countries and regions. Today, one of governments' main challenges is to create institutions which best unfold creative capacity and innovation and which facilitate economic growth. Against this background, institutional entrepreneurs are actors who purposefully leave existing paths and recombine existing governance mechanisms to create new, innovative institutional environments (Crouch 2005).

Entrepreneurs must certainly possess professional expertise, but it is the combination of professional expertise with the ability to perceive market opportunities which really distinguishes them from other experts. As Lazear (2005, 661) puts it, 'A technical engineer may be superb at creating a new device, but that device may not have any business value. The innovator who succeeds is the one who can come up with something that is not only technically sound but business relevant as well.' Commercially successful products are not necessarily the most innovative ones.

Entrepreneurs are conceptually distinct from self-employed individuals offering some kind of well-established services, such as tax counselling. These individuals do not rely on the broad set of skills crucial to entrepreneurs as they do not need to possess the versatility necessary to perceive market opportunities for new products and identify employees suitable for achieving the (new) firm's objectives (Lazear 2005).

Some Key Issues Concerning the Role of HE

Understanding the different trends on the labour market and its effects on the skills that graduates need to have in order to stay employable is only the first piece of the puzzle. In order to make use of this knowledge, we need to understand the features of HE that enable students to develop these skills. Although prior research (e.g. Allen and Van der Velden 2011) has shown that things such as international experience, work experience, and practical experience during HE can be highly effective in promoting graduate employability, we are still very remote from having a full understanding of the mechanisms that drive skill acquisition in education and how this process of skill formation can be improved (Cunha and Heckman 2007). We will therefore refrain from providing a 'recipe' as to how HEIs should adapt their courses and what actions they should take. Instead we will distil some key insights into how HE can position itself in skill formation today.

Producing an Ideal Mix of Graduates Rather Than an Ideal Graduate

The exposé of skill demands presented in the first part of this chapter seems to suggest that HE should produce graduates who are not only experts in their own field, but at the same time also flexible, innovative, strategic, communicative, internationally oriented, and entrepreneurial. In practice, such 'Jacks-of-all-trades' hardly exist, and most people will have their strong and weak points. Even more important, there is no evidence that employers actually want all these skills to be united in one person. The trends presented in this chapter relate more to the mix of skills that is required on the labour market on an aggregate level, rather than an individual level. This means that choices can and should be made and that students can specialize in one or more of these domains. This specialization will in fact increase overall productivity. We still need to identify what the minimum level of skills is in each domain that is required from each graduate to be employable and to be able to work with other graduates who have complementary skills. These minimum skills will primarily relate to the broad academic skills that are part of the professional expertise, the ICT-related skills and the skills related to an effective mobilization of human resources (strategic-organizational and interpersonal skills).

Making a Good Choice of Which Skills Should Be Developed in HE and Which Not

Even if we agree that some specialization can take place and not every skill needs to be acquired by every student, there will still be more demand for skills than can possibly be developed in education. The following questions are commonly grappled with in all societies where there are growing numbers of students entering HE:

1. *Is HE the most efficient environment to develop a certain skill, or is it more efficiently acquired in one's own time or during firm-based training?*

For many academic skills it is evident that HE is a suitable place in which to develop them. However, this probably does not apply to all the skills we have mentioned. For example, it remains unclear whether entrepreneurial skills are best developed in the environment of a university or whether they can be more efficiently acquired elsewhere. And the same may apply to other skills.

2. *What is the best age to develop a certain skill?*

The typical age range in which students are in HE is between 18– and 25. Some of the skills that we have discussed may be better developed at an earlier or a later stage in their educational career. The acquisition of foreign language skills should typically occur before entering HE, whilst for other skills students need some 'life experience' or 'work experience' to be able to develop them (e.g. strategic-organizational or management skills).

3. *What is the trade-off between developing one skill instead of another skill?*

Sometimes skills can be developed together by choosing the appropriate teaching method and then there is no trade-off. However, in many cases such trade-offs do exist and spending more time on developing one skill will be at the expense of developing another skill. HEIs need to identify where these trade-offs exist and need to balance the long-term benefits of developing each type of skill.

4. *Is the development of a certain skill a prerequisite for the development of other relevant skills?*

Sometimes a certain skill is not directly needed in the labour market or in society, but it is considered important to develop other skills that are directly needed. One can think of basic introduction courses to philosophy that are probably needed in every discipline in order to facilitate the development of academic and professional skills. HEIs need to consider these foundation skills as well when designing their curriculum.

Specialists or Generalists? Do not Underestimate the Importance of Specific Knowledge

In today's fast-changing world, many people think that specific knowledge is no longer as important as it was. The idea seems to be that most specific knowledge can be found on the internet and that teaching specific knowledge is a waste of time as technological developments will soon render this type of knowledge obsolete. It is argued that HE should produce generalists rather than specialists; however, this is a misconception of how people learn and what the role of specific knowledge is. The cognitive science literature contains convincing evidence that solving expert tasks requires content-specific skills and knowledge, and that general skills alone have no practical utility. In the words of the German psychologist Weinert: 'Generally, key competencies cannot adequately compensate for a lack of content-specific competencies' (Weinert 2001, 53). Some researchers even doubt whether truly generic competences exist, and argue that even generic competences (like analytical thinking or communication skills) are context-bound (Perkins and Salomon 1989).

The relevance of specific knowledge is also found in labour market studies (Allen et al. 2011; Allen and Van der Velden 2011). These studies have shown that professional expertise is the most important driver of individuals' labour market success, even if a graduate is working outside his or her own domain. It suggests that professional expertise can be a vehicle for developing general skills. It is therefore important that HE keeps paying attention to the development of professional expertise, by designing programmes which are coherent and lead to a specific body of knowledge.

Striking a Balance between Skills Needed for the Short-term and for the Long-term

One goal of HE is to support students in acquiring the skills that help them make a good start in the labour market. This means that graduates should have acquired some skills that can be instantly deployed in the workplace. On the other hand, HE also needs to equip students with the skills that make them employable in the long-run and enable them to have a good career. Faced with these two goals—providing an entry ticket to the labour market and ensuring long-term employability—HEIs need to strike a balance between broad professional skills and more narrow professional skills. Even if we agree that HE should produce professional experts, there is still a matter of the extent of specialization that should be strived for. The challenge is to strike a fine balance between the two goals and the difficulty is to pin down exactly when the line is crossed. There is today a tendency of HEIs to offer ever more specialized study programmes. This is related to the fact that these institutions compete in a studentmarket and need to differentiate themselves from others. Specialization, however, may decrease graduates' long-term employability. Moreover, for employers the large number of programmes offered in HE prevents transparency and decreases the recognition and credibility of some degrees on the labour market. Overall, HEIs have to take into account that offering study programmes whose focus is too broad or too narrow has major repercussions for the short- or long-term employability of their graduates and the transparency of educational credentials on the labour market.

Curriculum Is Not the Only Driver of Skills Acquisition

The naïve but still popular conception of education is that the curriculum defines what students learn. However, the learning formats used and the way in which HE assesses the students drives the learning process as well. Student-centred methods, like problem-based learning or group work, play an important role in developing many of the so-called twenty-first-century skills (Allen and Van der Velden 2013). Self-directedness is promoted whenever tasks involve working independently, making choices and taking decisions autonomously, and directing one's own learning process. Interactive skills are learnt when working in groups or using negotiation and discussion techniques in tutorials, and reflectiveness is practised when thinking about the relationship between the method (e.g. teamwork) and the results (the group's product) (OECD 2010).

The same applies for the assessment of students. Students learn little from multiple-choice exams where success is more dependent on a student's short-term memory capacity than his or her analytical skills (William, 2010). Paying attention to appropriate forms of assessment is therefore crucial for the development of the six skills this chapter identifies as being increasingly expected from HE graduates in the twenty-first century.

The ICT revolution plays a specific role in this. It does not only generate new ICT-related skill demands, but it also changes education itself. ICT can be turned into a powerful tool to develop relevant skills, by opening up new possibilities in terms of content (e.g. open content), learning environment (e.g. virtual reality systems), teaching resources (e.g. distance teaching), diagnosis (e.g. intelligent tutoring systems), and assessment (e.g. authentic assessment). Many of the challenges HE is facing can only be solved by successfully implementing the plethora of possibilities that ICT offers.

The Need for HE to Become More Internationally Oriented

The world of work has become internationalized to a great extent over the last 25 years and it is likely to continue moving in this direction. If we look at research and science, for example, 25 years ago work was predominantly nationally focused, as was the presentation of research output in national workshops and conferences, and its publication in national journals. Today, the reverse is true. Admittedly, some sectors of the economy are more exposed to internationalization than others, and research might not be a representative example. Yet, it can be regarded a herald for the developments in other areas of the economy. Technology, banking, and manufacturing, to name but a few, have experienced similar processes of internationalization and others are likely to follow.

HE is internationalizing, but not at the speed necessary to keep up with what is happening in the world of work. Graduates who have insufficient knowledge of foreign languages to communicate with others will likely be limited in their professional development and labour market opportunities. Organizations might be able to absorb some of the negative effect of a shortage of people with sufficient international orientation by adjusting their organizational structure, nevertheless, this shortage will likely present constraints on their potential for development and expansion. HEIs should continue to encourage students to undertake parts of their studies or compulsory internships abroad. They should also think about offering more courses—or entire study programmes—in foreign languages.

Summary and Concluding Remarks

In this chapter, we have presented the idea that societal, economic, and organizational trends are changing the work environment of graduates and that this requires purposive actions on the part of HEIs. We have identified six trends which are at the core of the changing role of graduates in economic life. These trends are the knowledge society, increasing uncertainty, the ICT revolution, high performance workplaces, globalization, and the change of the economic structure. By changing the nature and range of tasks graduates are expected to fulfil in today's economy, these trends generate new and intensify traditional skill demands, which we have summarized as professional expertise, flexibility, innovation and knowledge management, mobilization of human resources, international orientation, and entrepreneurship.

These six skills have different components as indicated in Table 10.1.

A key concern which we have tried to convey is the changing demand for and character of the professional expertise developed in HE. In the second part of this chapter, we presented possible implications of these developments for HE. We explored some key

Table 10.1 Six relevant skills and related components

Skills	Components
Professional expertise	Specific body of knowledge
	Ability to apply expert thinking
	General academic skills (e.g. analytical thinking, reflectiveness)
Flexibility	Ability to deal with changes and uncertainty
	Ability to learn new things
	Employability skills (e.g. the willingness to invest in further education and training, and the ability to plan and take responsibility for one's own career)
Innovation and knowledge management	Innovative/creative skills (creativity, curiosity)
	Networking, information, and strategic ICT skills
	Implementation skills
Mobilization of human resources	Interpersonal skills (communication skills, teamwork skills)
	(Self-)management skills (working within budget and time restrictions, leadership)
	Strategic-organizational skills
International orientation	Foreign language skills
	Intercultural skills
Entrepreneurship	Ability to identify commercial risks and opportunities
	Cost awareness
	Ability to turn an idea into a successful product

issues concerning the role of HEIs in skill formation. These issues can be summarized as the need to:

- produce an ideal mix of graduates rather than an ideal graduate;
- spend the scarce resources in HE as effectively and efficiently as possible by making a good choice of which skills should be developed in HE and which not;
- understand that specific knowledge is crucial for developing expertise;
- strike a balance between skills that are needed for the short-term and long-term employability;
- understand that the curriculum is not the only driver of skills acquisition but that teaching methods and assessment are just as important; and
- become more internationally oriented.

Whilst we are able to give a general overview, the key issues and trade-offs we have distilled will, however, differ between countries and, within countries, between types of HEI. The positioning of HEIs in skill formation will depend on the degree to which the labour market they are supplying is exposed to the six trends we identified, the institutional environment they are operating in, and the kind of student flows they are servicing at the international, national, and regional level.[4] Consequently, there will be no standard solution to the trade-offs highlighted above but policy-makers and HEIs need to find their own optimal strategy. The most important concern is that national policy-makers and HEIs are aware of what is expected of graduates in the twenty- first century and define their strategies accordingly.

References

Acemoglu, D. (1998) 'Why Do New Technologies Complement Skills? Directed Technical Change and Wage Inequality', *The Quarterly Journal of Economics*, 113: 1055–1089.

Acs, Z. J. (1992) 'Small Business Economics: A Global Perspective', *Challenge*, 35(6): 38–45.

Allen, J. (2011) 'Mobilization of Human Resources', in J. Allen and R. Van der Velden (eds), *The Flexible Professional in the Knowledge Society: New Challenges for Higher Education*, London: Springer: 139–176.

Allen, J., Pavlin, S., and Van der Velden, R. (eds) (2011) *Competencies and Early Labour Market Careers of Higher Education Graduates in Europe*, Ljubljana: University of Ljubljana, Faculty of Social Sciences.

Allen, J., Coenen, J., and Humburg, M. (2011) 'The Transition and Early Career', in J. Allen, S. Pavlin, and R. Van der Velden (eds), *Competencies and Early Labour Market Careers of Higher Education Graduates in Europe*, Ljubljana: University of Ljubljana, Faculty of Social Sciences: 29–54.

[4] Institutional differences between countries have been extensively analysed with regard to 'elite' versus 'mass' education (Trow 2000), the level and type of educational differentiation (Shavit et al. 2007), the degree of curricula standardization (Allmendinger 1989), and individuals' transition from initial education to the labour market (Müller and Gangl 2003; Van der Velden and Wolbers 2003).

Allen, J. and Van der Velden, R. (2011) *The Flexible Professional in the Knowledge Society: New Challenges for Higher Education*, London: Springer.

Allen, J. and Van der Velden, R. (2013) 'Skills for the 21st Century: Implications for Education', in L. R. Smith (ed.), *Higher Education: Recent Trends, Emerging Issues and Future Outlook*, New York: Nova Science Publishers: 1–40.

Allmendinger, J., (1989) 'Educational Systems and Labour Market Outcomes', *European Sociological Review*, 5: 231–250.

Appelbaum, E., Bailey, T., Berg, P., and Kalleberg, A. L. (2000) *Manufacturing Advantage: Why High-Performance Work Systems Pay Off*, Ithaca, NY: ILR Press.

Arnal, E., Ok, W., and Torres, R. (2001) *Knowledge, Work Organisation and Economic Growth*, OECD Labour Market and Social Policy Occasional Papers, 50, Paris: OECD Publishing.

Audretsch, D. B. and Thurik, A. R. (2000) 'Capitalism and Democracy in the 21st Century: From the Managed to the Entrepreneurial Economy', *Journal of Evolutionary Economics*, 10: 17–34.

Autor. D., Levy, F., and Murnane, R. (2003) 'The Skill Content of Recent Technological Change: An Empirical Exploration', *Quarterly Journal of Economics*, 118(4): 1279–1334.

Bartel, A. P. (2004) 'Human Resource Management and Organizational Performance: Evidence from Retail Banking', *Industrial and Labor Relations Review*, 57(1): 181–202.

Bell, D. (1999) *The Coming of Post-Industrial Society: A Venture in Social Forecasting*, New York: Basic Books.

Betcherman, G. (1997) *Changing Workplace Strategies: Achieving Better Outcomes for Enterprises, Workers and Society*, Ottawa: Government of Canada and OECD.

Bills, D. B. (2004) *The Sociology of Education and Work*, Oxford and Victoria: Blackwell.

Black, S. E. and Lynch, L. M. (2004) 'What's Driving the New Economy: The Benefits of Workplace Innovation', *Economic Journal*, 117: 97–116.

Brenner, R. (2006) *The Economics of Global Turbulence: The Advanced Capitalist Economies from Long Boom to Long Downturn, 1945–2005*, New York: Verso.

Brock, W. A. and Evans, D. S. (1989) 'Small Business Economics', *Small Business Economics*, 1: 7–20.

Carlsson, B. (1989) 'The Evolution of Manufacturing Technology and its Impact on Industrial Structure: An International Study', *Small Business Economics*, 1: 21–37.

Carlsson, B. (1992) 'The Rise of Small Business: Causes and Consequences', in W. J. Adams (ed), *Singular Europe, Economy and Policy of the European Community after 1992*, Ann Arbor, MI: University of Michigan Press: 145–169.

Carlsson, B. (1999) 'Small Business, Entrepreneurship, and Industrial Dynamics', in Z. Acs (ed), *Are Small Firms Important?* Boston/Dordrecht: Kluwer Academic Publishers: 99–110.

Caroli, E. and Van Reenen, J. (2001) 'Skill-Biased Organizational Change: Evidence from a Panel of British and French Establishments', *The Quarterly Journal of Economics*, 116(4): 1449–1492.

Carree, M. A. and Thurik, A. R. (2003) 'The Impact of Entrepreneurship on Economic Growth', in Z. Acs and D. B. Audretsch (eds), *Handbook of Entrepreneurship Research*, Amsterdam: Kluwer Academic Publishers: 437–471.

Castells, M. (1996) 'Enterprises and Jobs: Jobs in the Network Enterprise', Discussion paper for the ILO Enterprise Forum 96. http://www.ilo.org.

Castells, M. (2000) *The Rise of the Network Society*, 2nd ed., Oxford: Blackwell.

Crafts, N. and Toniolo, G. (1996) 'Postwar Growth: An Overview', in N. Crafts, and G. Toniolo (eds), *Economic Growth in Europe since 1945*, Cambridge University Press: Cambridge: 1–37.

Crouch, C. (2005) *Capitalist Diversity and Change: Recombinant Governance and Institutional Entrepreneurs*, Oxford: Oxford University Press.

Cunha, F. and Heckman, J. (2007) 'The Technology of Skill Formation', *American Economic Review*, 97(2): 31–47.
Dede, C. (2010) 'Comparing Frameworks for 21st Century Skills', in J. Bellanca and R. Brandt (eds), *21st Century Skills*, Bloomington: Solution Tree Press: 51–76.
DiPrete, T. A., Goux, D., Maurin, E., and Quesnel-Vallee, A. (2006) 'Work and Pay in Flexible and Regulated Labor Markets: A Generalized Perspective on Institutional Evolution and Inequality Trends in Europe and the US', *Research in Social Stratification and Mobility*, 24: 311–332.
Eckhardt, J. T. and Shane, S. A. (2003) 'Opportunities and Entrepreneurship', *Journal of Management*, 29(3): 333–349.
Ericsson, K. A. and Crutcher, R. J. (1990) 'The Nature of Exceptional Performance', in P. B. Baltes, D. L. Featherman, and R. M. Lerner (eds), *Life-Span Development and Behavior*, Hillsdale, NJ: Lawrence Erlbaum: 118–217.
European Commission (2007) *Key Competences for Lifelong Learning—A European Framework*, Luxembourg: Office for Official Publications of the European Communities.
Felstead, A., Gallie, D., Green, F., and Zhou, Y. (2007) *Skills at Work, 1986 to 2006*, Universities of Oxford and Cardiff, ESRC Centre on Skills, Knowledge and Organisational Performance.
Froud, J., Johal, S., Leaver, A., and Williams, K., *Financialization and Strategy: Narratives and Numbers*, London: Routledge.
Greenan, N. (2003) 'Organizational Change, Technology, Employment and Skills: An Empirical Study of French Manufacturing', *Cambridge Journal of Economics*, 27: 287–316.
Hage, J., and Powers, C. H. (1992) *Post-Industrial Lives: Roles and Relationships in the 21st Century*, Newbury Park: Sage.
Hayes, J. (1981) *The Complete Problem Solver*, Philadelphia: The Franklin Institute Press.
Karoly, L. A. (2004) *The 21st Century at Work: Forces Shaping the Future Workforce and Workplace in the United States*, Santa Monica, CA: RAND Corporation.
Lazear, E. P. (2010) 'Entrepreneurship', *Journal of Labor Economics*, 23(4): 649–680.
Levy, F. (2010) 'How Technology Changes Demands for Human Skills', OECD Education Working Papers 45, Paris.
Meredith, J. (1987) 'The Strategic Advantages of New Manufacturing Technologies for Small Firms', *Strategic Management Journal*, 8: 249–258.
Miles, I. and Martinez-Fernandez, C. (2011) 'Implications for Skills, Employment and Management', in C. Martinez-Fernandez, I. Miles, and T. Weyman (eds), *The Knowledge Economy at Work: Skills and Innovation in Knowledge Intensive Service Activities*, Cheltenham: Edward Elgar: 239–265.
Müller, W. and Gangl, M. (2003) 'The Transition from School to Work: A European Perspective', in W. Müller and M. Gangl (eds), *Transitions from Education to Work in Europe: The Integration of Youth into EU Labour Markets*, Oxford: Oxford University Press: 1–19.
Muffels, R. J. A. (2008) 'Flexibility and Employment Security in Europe: Setting the Scene', in R. J. A. Muffels (ed.), *Flexibility and Employment Security in Europe: Labour Markets in Transition*, Cheltenham: Edward Elgar: 3–30.
OECD (1999) *Economic Outlook*, Paris: OECD Publishing.
OECD/Eurostat (2005) *Oslo Manual: Guidelines for Collecting and Interpreting Innovation Data. The Measurement of Scientific and Technological Activities*, 3rd ed., Paris: OECD Publishing.
OECD (2010) *The Nature of Learning: Using Research to Inspire Practice*, Paris: OECD Publishing.

Parker, R. (2001) 'The Myth of the Entrepreneurial Economy: Employment and Innovation in Small Firms', *Work, Employment and Society*, 15(2): 239–253.

Pavlin, S. and Svetlik, I. (2011) 'The World of Work and the Demand for Competences', in J. Allen, J, S. Pavlin, and R. Van der Velden (eds), *Competencies and Early Labour Market Careers of Higher education Graduates in Europe*, University of Ljubljana: Faculty of Social Sciences: 73–106.

Perkins, D. N. and Salomon, G. *(1989)* 'Are Cognitive Skills Context Bound?', *Educational Researcher*, 18: 16–25.

Piore, M. J. and Sabel, C. F. (1984) *The Second Industrial Divide: Possibilities for Prosperity*, New York: Basic Books.

Ramsay, H. (1996) 'Managing Sceptically: A Critique of Organisational Fashion', in S. R. Clegg and G. Palmer (eds), *The Politics of Management Knowledge*, New York: Russell Sage Foundation: 155–172.

Reich, R. B. (1992) *The Work of Nations: Preparing Ourselves for 21st-Century Capitalism*, New York: Knopf.

Rychen, D. S., and Salganik, L. H. (eds) (2003) *Key Competencies for a Successful Life and a Well-Functioning Society*, Göttingen: Hogrefe and Huber.

Schmid, G. (1998) 'Transitional Labor Markets: A New European Employment Strategy', WZB Discussion Paper FS I 98–206, Berlin: WZB.

Shavit, Y., Arum, R., and Gamoran, A. with Menahem, G. (eds) (2007) *Stratification in Higher Education: A Comparative Study*, Stanford, CA: Stanford University Press.

Stone, K. V. W. (2006) 'Thinking and Doing: The Regulation of Workers' Human Capital in the United States', *Socio-Economic Review*, 4: 121–138.

Trow, M. (2000) 'From Mass Higher Education to Universal Access: The American Advantage', *Minerva*, 37(4): 303–328.

Van der Velden, R. and Wolbers, M. (2003) 'The Integration of Young People into the Labour Market: The Role of Training Systems and Labour Market Regulation', in W. Müller and M. Gangl (eds), *Transitions from Education to Work in Europe: The Integration of Youth into EU Labour Markets*, Oxford: Oxford University Press: 186–211.

Van Dijk, J. (2005) *The Deepening Divide. Inequality in the Information Society*, London: Sage Publications.

Venkataraman, S. (1997) 'The Distinctive Domain of Entrepreneurship Research: An Editor's Perspective', in J. Katz and R. Brockhaus (eds) *Advances in Entrepreneurship, Firm Emergence and Growth*, vol. 3, Greenwich, CT: JAI Press: 119–138.

Verluyten, P. (2001) *Intercultural Communication in Business and Organisations: An Introduction*, Leuven: Leusden; London: Acco.

Weimer, S. (1992) 'Small Firms in Big Subcontracting', in N. Altmann, C. Koehler, and P. Meil (eds), *Technology and Work in German Industry*, London: Routledge: 313–322.

Weinert, F. E. (2001) 'Concept of Competence: A Conceptual Clarification', in D. S. Rychen and L. H. Salganik (eds), *Defining and Selecting Key Competencies*, Göttinge: Hogrefe and Huber: 45–66.

Wickramasinghe, N. and Von Lubitz, D. (2007) *Knowledge-Based Enterprise. Theories and Fundamentals*, Hershey: IGI Publishing.

William, D. (2010) 'The Role of Formative Assessment in Effective Learning Environments', in *The Nature of Learning: Using Research to Inspire Practice*, Paris: OECD Publishing: 135–159.

CHAPTER 11

EMPLOYER-LED IN-WORK TRAINING AND SKILL FORMATION

The Challenges of Multi-Varied and Contingent Phenomena

LORNA UNWIN

Introduction

Skill formation is very much a workplace-based process. As individuals go about their everyday work activities, they have opportunities to develop, refine, and reform their expertise. Those opportunities will present themselves in many different guises, including periods of structured training, accidental encounters with colleagues, which can result in a problem being solved or a new technique being learnt, and the co-development with clients of new products and services. Regardless of the size or type of organization, skill formation takes place as an integral part of the way goods and services are produced. At the same time, however, we know that workplaces vary greatly in terms of the extent to which they create the conditions to facilitate and value skill formation, and distribute the opportunities for structured training throughout the workforce.

The variation in approach to skill formation and training arises because, regardless of whether they are in the private or public sectors, workplaces are nested within a series of overlapping contexts formed by: (a) the characteristics of local, national, and/or global product markets, and economic conditions; and (b) the specific productive systems within which a workplace sits, which might involve minimal or complex layers of ownership and regulatory requirements (see Felstead et al. 2009). In addition, an organization's strategies and arrangements for in-work skill formation and training will also be affected by (and may even be helping to shape) one or more national systems of education and training.

The use of the term 'workplace' in this chapter is admittedly problematic given the enormous diversity of what constitutes a place of work from sections within organizations employing thousands of people to one-person enterprises. Many people are self-employed, many have always worked in the home, and increasing numbers work whilst travelling (see Felstead et al. 2005a). In addition, the term 'employer' provokes multiple interpretations despite its often homogenized use by both researchers and policy-makers. At best, employers are categorized by size and by sector, but even within these categorizations, the term 'employer' is a proxy for an organization. Yet it is important to consider employers as people. Their own motivations for and level of understanding about workforce development are partly governed by the business context, but also their personal experiences of training and skill formation.

Context should not be considered in isolation from the characteristics, aspirations and behaviours of the workforce (see inter alia, Cooke et al. 2011). The dynamism of workplaces as environments in which learning takes place is formed through the interaction of individuals with the way work is organized and managed, the nature of the employment contract including reward and incentive structures, the level of discretion employees have to determine how they work, and the extent to which employees are involved in decision-making (for detailed discussions, see Ashton 2004; Rainbird et al. 2004; Fuller and Unwin 2011). A further way in which workplaces can be differentiated relates to the types and levels of employees' expertise and educational backgrounds, and the extent to which they are segregated by job demarcation. Employee agency can overcome both the inertia inside workplaces and the dehumanizing aspects of what Brown and Scase (1991) call 'poor work' (see also Green 2006; Grugulis and Vincent 2009). Yet when employees no longer feel a sense of pride in their work or the work itself does not generate commitment, their motivation to participate in training or to share their knowledge and skills can quickly seep away (Sennett 2008). They may actively seek to subvert the routines and procedures of their workplaces (see, inter alia, Thompson and Smith 2010). Ultimately, employees' access to and involvement in meaningful training and skill formation will be contingent on 'the power relations which characterise the employment relationship' (Rainbird et al. 2004, 39) and the quality of the job (Warhurst et al. 2012). People matter, whether they are employers or employees, because they both shape and are shaped by the work environment.

This chapter argues, therefore, that we need to take a holistic approach to the study of skill formation and training in workplaces. We need to consider a range of evidence when evaluating and conceptualizing these multi-varied and contingent phenomena. To that end, this chapter regards all forms of work and workplace as spaces engaged in skill formation and in-work training. Throughout human history, there has been a concerted and successful effort to privilege certain forms of expertise (see Livingstone and Sawchuk 2003; Unwin 2009). Key examples include medieval apprentices swearing oaths to keep their masters' secrets, the formation of the 'professions', and the current vogue to categorize some forms of expertise as 'knowledge work' and some jobs as 'unskilled'. Whilst there are clearly different requirements in terms of the type of knowledge and skills involved in the vast range of occupations and job roles, all work demands some form of capability. How that capability is developed and nurtured requires continued concerted collective effort and commitment to create the conditions in which individuals can reach and demonstrate their potential.

This chapter is divided into four further sections. The first discusses how developments in the way skill formation and in-work training are conceptualized profoundly shapes how workplaces are understood as 'learning environments'. The second considers what we can learn from the quantitative evidence gathered through surveys of employers about their attitudes to and investment in in-work training. The third provides illustrations from qualitative research of the ways in which in-work training is organized and experienced. Finally, the concluding section provides some remarks about the need for an increased inter-disciplinary effort to capitalize on the emergence of a more nuanced understanding of the phenomenon of skill formation within workplaces. It is argued, that, despite the complex nature of organizations and of work itself, everyone is affected to some extent by the forces discussed here when seeking to acquire and develop the skills they need for work.

Workplaces as Learning Environments

This section begins with a discussion of the evolving way in which skill formation and in-work training are conceptualized. Since the 1990s and the growing influence of situated, socio-cultural, and socio-material theories of learning, there has been an increasing acceptance that the development of occupational and job-specific expertise was not confined to individuals engaging in episodes of planned training to acquire chunks of codified, stable forms of knowledge and perform set routines (see, inter alia, Billett 1991; Darrah 1996; Engeström 2001; Beckett and Hager 2002; Rainbird et al. 2004; Fenwick and Nerland 2014). In their groundbreaking study of apprenticeship, the anthropologists Jean Lave and Etienne Wenger (1991, 29) argued that 'the mastery of knowledge and skill requires newcomers to move towards full participation in the socio-cultural practices of a community'. These insights challenged the dominance of cognitive and behaviourist theories of learning, which focus on the individual as an isolated acquirer of knowledge and skills and which are central to human capital theory (for a critique, see Guile 2010).

Those methodological individualist theories, however, continue to encourage policy-makers and some economists at the national and supra-national levels to view skill formation, workforce development and, indeed the development of human capital more broadly as a formalized, fixed-time, front-loaded and linear activity resulting in outcomes that can be externally measured (see Brown et al. 2001; Felstead et al. 2005b; Pankhurst 2009; James et al. 2012). This is despite evidence to show that, as Grugulis et al. (2004, 14) have argued, 'the concept of skill has become bigger, broader and much fuzzier round the edges' due to the social and technological changes in producing goods and services in the recent past. Thus, the call for a more sophisticated understanding of the dynamic and complex nature of skill is being aligned with developments in the theorization of skill formation and its role in innovation (see, inter alia, Guile 2010). There is growing recognition that participation with others in the daily practice of work, immersion in the culture, technologies and practices of the workplace, and through shared endeavours such as problem-solving, makes skill formation a situated and relational process.

This means that our understanding of the term 'training' has been expanded to encompass a range of activities from non-formal/informal and experiential types of learning through to formalized events such as lectures and direct instruction. These categorizations of formality and informality have provoked intense debate with some scholars arguing that they are based on a false and outdated dichotomy which privileges one form of learning over another (for a review, see Hager and Halliday 2006). As we will see in the next section, the categorizations cause particular problems for large-scale surveys, which attempt to quantify the scale and nature of training activity and investment. As Clarke (2004, 141) has argued, when training is conceptualized through a 'learning perspective', the goal of human resource development is to 'enhance both the organization's, and the individual's within it, capacity to learn'. By contrast, if training is conceptualized through a 'performance perspective', it is 'concerned with ensuring that learning should be translated into behaviour or performance that is associated with meeting organizational goals'.

A key challenge for socio-cultural theories of workplace learning including the concept of 'communities of practice' is the concern that, if too inwardly focused, they can foster conservatism, complacency, and the reproduction of inequalities (see Hughes et al. 2007). Attempts to unlock the sources of and ingredients that underpin knowledge creation and innovation in the workplace are central to the human desire to make progress. The image of the medieval alchemist trying to turn base metal into gold could be used to represent the contemporary pursuit of the most effective ways to maximize productivity and stay ahead of competitors. Nonaka and Takeuchi (1995) have argued that innovation stems from organizing work to enable employees to expose and share both the tacit and explicit knowledge that rests in them as individuals and in the collective processes of production. Through their research in Japanese car manufacturing plants, they conceptualized innovation as the creation of the new knowledge required to solve problems in the work process and develop new products. Thus it is the internal labour market (ILM) of the workplace that is regarded as the site for innovation and, hence, the formation and continuous development of skills (see also Koike and Inoki 1990).

A criticism of the Japanese ILM approach and its emphasis on company-specific skill formation is that it restricts employee mobility and makes firms vulnerable to external forces (see Maki et al. 2005). From a very different cultural and economic context, the German concept of 'work process knowledge' also focuses on the organization of work and the centrality of problem-solving in what Boreham (2002, 10) refers to as post-Taylorist workplaces:

> The new idea, which the concept of work process knowledge introduced, is that workers need to understand not just the technical system they are operating, but the work process in which they themselves are participating—and creating—by way of operating that system. And this involves reconceptualizing the worker as a member of a much broader system, where knowledge is partly owned by the individual worker and partly by the organization.

It has long been argued that, in the case of young people, the German Dual System of apprenticeship forms a key countervailing force against the limitations of the ILM approach. Apprentices develop company-specific skills (through on-the-job training) and general transferable skills and knowledge (through off-the-job vocational education and training (VET)). These assumptions also underpin variations of the German approach to initial VET in many countries. The German model has been criticized for being slow and bureaucratic in updating both the on- and off-the-job curriculum and for the way the dominance of initial VET has hampered the development of provision for continuing training for existing employees (see inter alia, Walden and Troltsch 2013). It is certainly not the intention to dismiss the dual model of skill formation, but rather to question the once widely accepted assumption that an individual's body of expertise and capability can be divided straightforwardly into job and company-specific skills and general transferable skills. This division arises from two contestable propositions, which stem from human capital theory: (a) that knowledge and skills are commodities—to be invested in, acquired and then transported from one place to another (see Hager and Hodkinson 2009 for a critique); and (b) that workplaces only develop so-called company-specific rather than general skills. As Døving and Nordhaug (2002, 4) argue, this latter proposition is 'too crude to grasp the complexity of competences in firms'.

There is now increasing recognition in the labour economics literature of the benefits of general transferable skills acquired in the workplace (see inter alia Marsden 1987; Stevens 1999; Estevez et al. 2001; Thelen 2004). Indeed, there is important evidence showing that in some sectors, employers cover the costs of the formation of these skills because of the benefits accrued to both the individual enterprise and to the sector as a whole (Acemoglu and Pischke 1999).

The Finnish scholar, Yrjo Engeström (2007, 2011), working within the dialectical tradition of the Russian school of cultural-historical activity theory since the late 1980s, has pioneered the development of more radical approaches using the concepts of co-configuration and social production. He argues that these approaches are more suited to an emerging new type of work involving 'active customer involvement and input' into the configuration of new products and services, collaboration between multiple producers in networks within and between organizations, and 'mutual learning from interactions between the parties' (Engeström 2007, 44). For Engeström, learning, and hence skill formation and reformation in-work is dependent upon the collective need to solve problems and resolve tensions and contradictions in the labour process. This is a very different approach to the traditional conception of training 'in which the contents to be learned are well known ahead of time' and seen to be unproblematic (Engeström 2011, 88).

Re-organizing work in the ways outlined above in order to increase employee involvement', level of discretion and, ultimately, empowerment threatens entrenched attitudes to job hierarchies and boundaries and to industrial relations more broadly.

These ideas also challenge entrenched views about which jobs count and, hence, who should get access to training, which will be discussed in the next section. Two other critical enabling factors have to be considered if workplaces are to create what Fuller and Unwin (2004) have termed 'expansive learning environments': (a) the capacity of and discretion afforded to managers to facilitate in-work training; and (b) the availability of sufficient staff to act in a training role. In relation to the role of managers, Eraut and Hirsch (2007, 34) argue that:

> The manager's role is not to do most of the learning support themselves, but to set the climate, encourage their staff to take on this role as an integral part of their working responsibility and include the facilitation of learning in their management of performance.

In the third section of this chapter, case study research provides an illustration of a company that has placed the pedagogical role of managers at the heart of its approach to in-work training and skill formation. A second case study also reveals how the role of the trainer has to be reconsidered when the workplace itself is recognized as a site for skill formation. Research on the multi-varied meaning of 'training' within workplaces and associated processes such as coaching and mentoring is growing (for a recent study in Japanese organizations, see Matsuo 2014).

Whilst much of the skill formation and innovation literature focuses on the development of capability to enhance the productiveness of the organization (and, at the macro-level, the wider economy), an alternative body of research highlights the role employees play in applying their expertise despite working within structures that mitigate against such agency and initiative. This research brings ideas from labour process theory and the sociology of work together with socio-cultural theories of learning. The following examples illustrate how in-depth case study research can expose a lived reality that interrupts the deterministic assumptions of Braverman's (1974) influential deskilling thesis. In their study of the impact of new computerized systems in the public sector in Ontario, Hennessy and Sawchuk (2003) found that case officers handling the claims of people claiming welfare and disability benefits had developed collective strategies ('work-arounds') to maintain the level of service they believed their clients deserved. Similarly, Fuller et al.'s (2011) study of hospital porters in England showed that despite being on the very bottom rung of the National Health Service job banding, the porters were deploying a much broader range of knowledge and skills than was specified in their very narrowly defined job descriptions. Emerging research into the concept of employee-driven innovation will pose further challenges for the still highly static and often abstracted notions of skill in the contemporary workplace (see Høyrup et al. 2012).

Placing skill formation in context necessarily demanded that greater attention be given to the complex nature of workplaces as learning environments. This in turn has stimulated some inter-disciplinary research and certainly much more awareness of the need to look outside disciplinary silos, notably from the fields of organizational studies, sociology, human resource management, social and economic geography, economics, political science, social anthropology, and education. Such cross-fertilization is important because the shift to the now ubiquitous use of the term 'learning' and away from training, instruction, or indeed education needs to be robustly interrogated. In the United Kingdom, this shift led to the renaming of government agencies responsible for VET policies (e.g. the Further Education Funding Council became the Learning and Skills Council in 2001), and many education and training institutions calling their students and/or trainees 'learners' (Unwin 2012). It has also given further ammunition to the promoters of competence-based vocational qualifications in the United Kingdom and Australia who called into question the value of studying abstract and codified knowledge in off-the-job training settings away from the pressures of the workplace (Hager 2004; Wheelahan 2010; Winch 2010; Brockmann et al. 2011 for critiques). Too much emphasis on learning as a process can deflect attention away from what is actually being learnt.

If we simply conceptualize and measure training as a series of events or count the hours individuals spend in training without asking what was involved and whether the training had any relevance, we are in danger of presuming that any training is worthwhile. Similarly, we cannot rely on case studies alone, even though they provide us with rich accounts of how training is generated, experienced, and organized in the workplace. We need to approach the phenomenon through both a macro- and a micro-lens, and hence, in-work training and skill formation have to be considered from both qualitative and quantitative perspectives. The next section considers what the quantitative evidence tells us about the nature of in-work training in advanced economies.

Access to In-Work Training and Skill Formation

This chapter has argued that the extent and nature of in-work training and skill formation varies because organizations and their workplaces are created from and shaped by different conditions at the macro-, meso-, and micro-levels. The extent to which an 'employer' has control over how much to spend on training, who to train, and to what level, will depend upon many factors. In very large organizations, those decisions will rest with human resource managers hopefully in collaboration with managers throughout the business, though they too will be directed from above, even perhaps by directors in other countries. In smaller organizations, with much simpler structures, those decisions might still be constrained by the need to focus the training budget on meeting the latest government and/or sector-related regulatory requirements as opposed to developing new forms of work organization such as a shift to self-managed teams.

Whilst discussion of the political economy of skills policy and practice from both global and national perspectives will be dealt with elsewhere in this book, the actions and pronouncements of governments and supra-national agencies such as the World Bank, International Monetary Fund, and the European Commission do have an impact on employers' behaviour. At the national level, the use of training levies, tax credits, and requirements for workers in certain occupations to acquire a 'licence to practise' and/or to formally record they are updating their skills as part of, for example, a nationally regulated system of apprenticeship or national skills strategy will all help to stimulate both off-the-job and in-work training (see Campbell 2012). The demand for proof of the quality and safety of products also acts as a powerful driver in, for example, sectors such as automotive and aerospace manufacturing, food and drug processing, and software development. In sectors such as medicine, accountancy, and law, longstanding professional bodies maintain regulatory oversight of individual professionals throughout their careers.

External forces and drivers have an impact, therefore, on the extent of in-work training and skill (re)formation within workplaces. Through their case study research in a range of types of organizations and sectors in the United Kingdom, Felstead et al. (2009, 27) argued that these external forces play a key role in the productive systems within which workplaces are nested. As such, they have an effect on who gets access to training:

> Institutions and groups that exercise high levels of overall control within the structures and stages of productive systems may seek to monopolize or contain key skills and forms of knowledge. As a result, critical organizational competences may be highly concentrated within particular parts of the productive system.

Evidence from international surveys (e.g. the European Continuing Vocational Training Survey, and country-specific surveys such as the United Kingdom's Employer Skills Survey) supports this with consistent findings over many years that individuals with the highest levels of educational attainment prior to entering the workforce and in the highest levels in occupational and organizational structures have greater access to and participate more in formal training than their colleagues. The hidden dangers of an exclusively in-work model of skill formation and training, as discussed in the previous section, can be exposed through large-scale surveys. The OECD's (2013a) survey of 1081 small and medium-sized enterprises (SMEs) in Belgium, Canada, New Zealand, Poland, Turkey, and the United Kingdom found that they were involved in 50% less formal training than large firms across the OECD. The key reason for this was the SMEs' lack of critical mass, which reduced their ability to cover the costs of releasing staff and paying for training costs. The SMEs were, however, engaged in what the OECD term 'knowledge intensive activities', including: interactions with consultants, suppliers or clients; attending conferences and meetings; and internal processes such as quality control. The OECD's report (OECD 2013a, 30) notes, that:

> These activities, however, do not carry formal qualifications or standard training certificates and tend to benefit managers, business owners and the higher educated staff members.

People in temporary and part-time jobs, particularly at the low end of the labour market, also have more limited access to training. Analysis of the Labour Force Survey data for 2007 in Britain revealed that male workers over the age of 50 were significantly less likely to participate in training and to report never having been offered training opportunities (see Canduela et al. 2012). By contrast, however, older women were not as marginalized, possibly due to their increased involvement in sectors and occupations such as health and social care where the requirements for formal training have increased. Canduela et al. (2012, 57) argue that 'The negative stereotyping of older workers', and employers' concern that they will not see a return on their investment, 'may remain powerful influencers of how employers ration access to skills'.

The extent to which older workers lose out to younger recruits and vice-versa is a complex issue (see Tikkanen and Nyhan 2006). From their research on apprenticeship in large UK organizations (1,000 employees or more) in four sectors (engineering, construction, retailing, and information and communications technology (ICT)), Ryan et al. (2006) discovered that apprenticeship was attractive for a range of reasons: (a) it generates loyalty to the company so can help reduce turnover; (b) it allows employers to 'socialize' new recruits and select them for long-term employment; and (c) it enables employers to offer educational and career progression to certain employees so building capacity in the company. However, because the same companies were often more concerned about upgrading the skills of existing employees, apprenticeship 'rarely accounts for a majority of the skilled workforce' (Ryan et al. 2006, 16). The current and seemingly entrenched crisis in youth unemployment across the world coupled with the retreat by employers from apprenticeships and other forms of initial VET programmes in many countries, including the Dual System countries, means that significant numbers of young people will remain excluded from in-work training for long periods adding to the scarring effect of being out of the labour market (see inter alia, Gregg and Tominey 2005).

The results from the OECD's first round of the Programme for the International Assessment of Adult Competencies has also emphasized how newly acquired skills need to be used and refined through use in the workplace (OECD 2013b). Employers need to redesign work to increase the number of tasks that use literacy, numeracy, and ICT skills (see Wolf and Evans 2010). This is particularly important for adults with low educational attainment and in elementary level jobs. The problem is notable for countries such as Canada, England/Northern Ireland, Ireland, Italy, Spain, and the United States.

Data from the United Kingdom's Work Employment Relations Survey (WERS) for 2011 provides findings that would resonate in other countries; for example, organizations classed by the survey as being 'high trainers' are more likely to be unionized and in the public sector (see Wanrooy et al. 2013). In the United Kingdom, the highest training sectors are electricity, financial services, water and gas, health and social work, and education. At the lower end are manufacturing and the hotels and restaurant sectors. As Table 11.1 shows, WERS 2011 found that there has been a reduction in some types of training since the previous survey in 2004, though health and safety still accounted for the highest volume of activity.

The predominance of health and safety is, of course, the most potent signal of how in-work training is still very much driven by the need to meet regulatory targets. The mandatory or non-discretionary training that an employer has to invest in comprises what Felstead and Green (1994) have conceptualized as an organization's 'training floor'. Through research into the impact of the recession that followed the 2008 financial crisis in the United Kingdom, Felstead and Jewson (2014) have built on this earlier conceptualization and proposed the concept of the 'training ceiling'. This enables us to consider the balance between the amount of discretionary and non-discretionary training within an organization. In their interviews with employers, Felstead and Jewson (2014) found that many referred to non-discretionary training as the 'must have' and discretionary training as the 'nice to have'. They note that the latter is the 'most immediately vulnerable in times of economic hardship' (2014, 4).

Table 11.1 Types of training in the United Kingdom

Type of training	2004 (%)	2011 (%)
Health and safety	68	68
Operating new equipment	49	42
Customer service	43	39
Communication	45	38
Quality control	35	37
Team-working	40	36
Computing	43	31
Leadership	29	27
Equal opportunities	20	25
Problem-solving	20	18
Working to deadlines	19	16

Source: Wanrooy et al. (2013).

As was noted in the previous section, discussions of in-work training and skill formation have to grapple with the formal/informal conundrum. International surveys now acknowledge this challenge, but as Felstead et al. (2009, 361) argue in their review of survey methodology, this poses considerable difficulties for the designers of survey questions and, hence, there is an understandable tendency to retreat to more easily measureable types of activity:

> If unprompted, individuals regard training as formal courses and employers view it as an activity they fund and/or initiate. In other words, the question stem gives greater emphasis to deliberative, conscious and planned interventions and is less likely to capture other equally, if not more important, learning activities that arise naturally as part of the work process.

In their analysis of the international evidence on SMEs, Ashton et al. (2008, 5) remind us that, regardless of size or sector, the decision to invest in training '... is a derived demand, or one that emanates from the core business strategy' (see also Keep et al. 2006). They add that, '... it is the product market or business strategy of the company and the way in which it is operationalized through the organization of production factors that are crucial in determining the levels of skill that companies need' (Ashton et al. 2008). Their analysis reasserts the need to problematize what we mean by in-work training and skill formation and how we might seek to capture the richness of the phenomenon. Ashton et al. (2008) argue that their evidence shows that formal training can be poorly organized and of poor quality in just the same way 'informal forms of training, and moreover, informal approaches can be used to develop high levels of skills. Rather than imposing top-down approaches, governments should embrace the value of informal approaches in order to support SMEs. Similarly, in a review of policy and practice in relation to SMEs for the OECD, Stone (2012) argues for more attention to be given to the accommodation of formal training with the demands of work to minimize the time employees need to spend off-the-job.

The continued use of the terms 'formal' and 'informal' reflects an understandable desire by the authors of research and policy reports to find a shorthand means of simplifying complex definitional challenges. In the following section, evidence from qualitative case study research shows, however, that what is often classed as 'informal' can embrace a highly structured approach to in-work training and skill formation. In the second section of this chapter, it was argued that workplaces have the potential to play the key role in skill formation and reformation and, moreover, that people develop their expertise through everyday work. To fulfil that potential, employers have to take a number of steps to create the optimal conditions for learning. Fuller and Unwin's (2004; 2011) framework for analysing workplaces along an 'expansive-restrictive' continuum identifies a range of characteristics that combine to render a workplace an 'expansive learning environment'. Their research across a range of private and public sector organizations provided evidence to show that workplaces are dynamic environments and, as such, they all exhibit both expansive and restrictive characteristics. Some workplaces, however, appear better able to maintain a position towards the expansive end of the continuum despite pressures from within their productive system. For example, in their study of health care assistants in the United Kingdom, Rainbird et al. (2004) used the expansive-restrictive framework to analyse how organizations within the same productive system were positioned at different ends of the continuum.

Employers who get some way towards creating expansive learning environments do so by organizing work to enable employees to make full use of and develop their expertise and by affording them the discretion to make judgements based on that expertise. The role of managers as facilitators of employee development and the cross-fertilization of ideas is a key characteristic (through, for example, providing constructive feedback and involving employees in decision-making) is a key expansive characteristic. Apprentices and trainees are given the time and opportunities they need to develop rather than fast-tracked to become productive workers, and, importantly, apprenticeship is recognized as a route to senior positions. In addition, the involvement of more experienced employees in the nurturing of newcomers helps to generate a shared understanding of the benefits of workforce development for both individuals and the organization.

Those employers who understand how to generate these expansive characteristics are in the minority and, hence, too many organizations sit towards the restrictive end of the continuum. Many large employers in the private sector are inhibited by the pressures of maximizing shareholder value in the short run, whilst public sector employers have to grapple with reducing levels of funding for service delivery. These pressures affect the SMEs in the supply chains and generate high levels of work intensification, which mitigates against the characteristics required to produce expansive environments.

The next section explores the dynamics of in-work training in workplaces that demonstrate some expansive characteristics, whilst also highlighting the pressures that can engender more restrictive behaviour. They are intended to show that a more expansive approach is possible, but that this requires commitment and consistent effort by employers, employees, and other stakeholders and cannot be achieved without a radical reconfiguration of the way work is organized and valued.

Experiences of In-Work Training and Skill Formation

In this section, two illustrations from qualitative case study research in the UK are presented to demonstrate the symbiotic relationship between the everyday process of work and in-work training and skill formation.[1] In addition, the case studies

[1] The illustrations are drawn from case study research funded by the UK's Economic and Social Research Council (grant number: RES 139250110) conducted by the author and colleagues in a research team studying learning and training in a range of workplaces in the United Kingdom from 2003 to 2008. Details of the research and more case studies can be found in Felstead et al. (2009).

can be seen as generative devices for the framing of questions about how employers approach the challenge of skill formation. The first illustration is from software engineering and the second from automotive engineering. The companies involved are positioned in very different productive systems and the case studies focus on employees with contrasting levels of prior educational attainment and types of occupational expertise.

Company A develops software and hardware products and solutions for a wide range of international customers including the US and UK military. Operating at the top end of its product market, it was founded some 30 years ago and employs just over 300 people, the majority of whom are software engineers. The company is organized as an Employee Trust with the profits shared annually by the employees. The amount of profit share is determined through reviews of individual performance. Training and skill formation take place predominantly in-house as part of everyday work including interaction with customers.

On one level, the company's approach to the training of its software engineers resembles a classic apprenticeship. In their first year, new recruits (graduates from top UK universities in a range of subjects) are assigned to a mentor and a manager and begin by learning to write code and the core technologies of the business. This is seen as providing the necessary shared platform of expertise. One engineer described his experience as follows:

> I was put into a team of one, so I was given to a guy who was an experienced techy and someone who had management aspirations and I was given to him to manage initially, and I worked with him on supporting a major customer ... well we had like half a million lines of code to support and that's an awful lot of code ... we'd to produce fixes ... it's quite a challenge. Actually I think it gave me a very good start in the company because it put me immediately in a position where I was very much in the deep end because I didn't really know the ropes ... And I had one guy who was a clear expert to guide me through it and that ... meant that I had to learn to stand on my own two feet quite quickly.

The engineers work in project teams, established for up to nine months at a time and then broken so the members work with different people in order to facilitate innovation. Knowledge and expertise are captured within the teams and two key mechanisms have been established to disseminate this throughout the organization. Firstly, engineers and other members of staff lodge ideas and information gained through everyday problem-solving in 'public folders' on the company's intranet. This relates to Nonaka and Takeuchi's (1995) concept of a cycle of 'knowledge conversion'—tacit knowledge is made explicit then expanded through re-engagement with practice. Secondly, ideas from practice are captured through the company's performance review system, which involves all employees being reviewed by their immediate manager every nine months. New recruits are reviewed every three months. The reviews provide the information on which senior managers base decisions about the annual profit share allocations.

The remarkable element of the skill formation process is that management is regarded as a largely pedagogic function. Once an engineer has mastered the basic technical competences, they are assigned a new recruit to train under the supervision of their team leader and so build up to managing their own team. This enabled team members to feel confident about the shared level of expertise and engendered a strong commitment to viewing everyday tasks as part of a wider shared enterprise. All employees are initially trained in the company's head office building in England, though they may then be placed in its other sites in either the United Kingdom or the United States. This initiation in what one director called the 'mother ship' was central to the socialization of new recruits into the company's values as well as the maintenance of a solid platform of shared technical competences.

The successful reproduction and development of skills through in-work training has served this company well, but the concerns about the adequacy of the 'community of practice' approach discussed in section two of this chapter were posing major challenges as it entered a new phase of its corporate history. Whilst the company has many of the characteristics of an 'expansive' learning environment, the heavy reliance on in-work training and skill formation may no longer be sufficient. The company decided it needed to recruit people with different skills from outside the company who could generate new lines of business. One director summed up the problem they were trying to address:

> We're talking about a lot of propeller heads here you see and they want to know the next exciting technology they're going to be working on … the company is full of engineers, it's very engineering dominated and they tend not to be really interested in business an awful lot, but also it comes from the fact that they've grown up with a company that's always successful, that's always stable, that always makes its targets.

In contrast to company A, the second case study illustration highlights the challenges faced by a company that needed to quickly upskill its production operatives in order to survive in a global wheels' market where competition had rapidly intensified and to meet the demands of a new global quality standard, which requires manufacturers to prove their employees have specific levels of competence. Company B has just over 8,000 employees and is a wholly owned subsidiary of a French company with plants in France, Canada, Spain, and Mexico, and, since 1989, in Northern Ireland. It makes alloy wheels and cylinder heads for five car manufacturers.

In order to tackle the upskilling challenge, the company's training manager and his three full-time trainers decided to map the company's skill sets against a nationally recognized vocational qualification in consultation with the engineering Sector Skills Council. They then trained 95 production operatives to achieve the qualification with further training for 30 of them so they could perform the role of assessors. These 'skills tutors' were then assigned one or more operatives to train on the shopfloor. To support the tutors, the training team developed a 'tutor pack' providing detailed descriptions of shopfloor tasks and associated quality checks. The pack also acted as a catalyst when operatives and assessors reviewed the formers' progress towards achieving the specified competences. Tutors, operatives and specialist engineers were encouraged to add to and update the packs so that they remained 'live' resources. This facilitated shop floor discussions about solutions to technical problems, which were incorporated into the pack and which, in turn, generated what the training manager called a 'shared vocabulary' about the skills needed to meet performance indicators on production targets, quality checks and the reduction of waste. There are similarities here to the way the software company sought to utilize and transform the tacit knowledge of its engineers.

The competence-based strategy enabled the company to identify the gaps in the operatives' skills and knowledge. In addition, the opportunity to gain a nationally recognized qualification was welcomed by many of the operatives. However, as one operative noted, 'there's some … they don't like being told anything … [and] they're just not interested in their jobs'. A production manager provided her own categorization of employees as follows:

> [There are] two different types of individuals, those who are self-starters who want to learn and who will actively seek to learn, and others who say 'well, I've never been given any opportunities' … And actually there is a third level as well, people who are doing a job and have got to a point where they say 'no, I like this level, I like this job, I'm happy here, I don't want to do more'.

The training team's knowledge and understanding of the diversity of employees' attitudes to upskilling had led them to keep the training and associated assessment in-house, even though there was a risk of uneven quality. The training manager explained how this was being tackled for the next stage of the initiative:

> We have some guys who are very, very good and we have some guys who are not so good, and we are currently looking at how we reduce the numbers and … have a smaller group who are more efficient. And … we need to look at additional development … There's all sorts of issues there but we're looking at that because for us it's a moving picture.

Two aspects of this company's approach to workforce development demonstrate how a demand to upskill shop floor production operatives can be a vehicle to achieve wider cross-workforce goals. Firstly, the involvement of operatives and more highly skilled colleagues in the co-configuration of training resources ('tutor packs') acted as a catalyst for greater communication across job boundaries and the sharing of expertise. Secondly, the commitment to providing progression opportunities for the 'skills tutors' expanded the potential of the upskilling initiative from the minimal requirement to prove to the parent company that operatives were competent.

Both case study illustrations provide evidence of how the nature of in-work training and skill formation is shaped by a combination of internal and external forces.

Organizations react differently to these forces due to their histories, cultures, positions in a productive system, and the motivations and values of their owners and employees.

CONCLUSION

Researchers, and to some extent policymakers, have become more aware of the symbiotic relationship between contextual factors, the impact of changes to the organization and nature of work, and the contribution of employee agency in the skill formation process. This has led to efforts to study these phenomena using multi- and interdisciplinary perspectives and methodologies. These efforts need to be supported and valued because there is an understandable tendency for researchers to revert to their disciplinary and methodological comfort zones. In addition, policymakers remain wedded to models of skill formation that focus on the (measurable) individual acquisition of knowledge and skills.

As this chapter has shown, in shifting the spotlight to the workplace as the key site for skill formation, we have to take care to monitor the extent to which all employees are included in and are able and willing to benefit from in-work training. As Cooke et al. (2011, 273) remind us: 'Some workers seem to have tangibly superior working conditions when compared with others, including access to training'. Creating the conditions to facilitate and maximize the benefits than can be accrued for an in-work approach requires considerable energy and commitment from managers as well as the broader workforce. To develop our understanding of the extent to which employers understand and have the expertise to embrace these challenges requires renewed research effort. In particular, attention needs to be given to creating more nuanced categorizations of the term 'employer'. Both quantitative and qualitative studies struggle with this, though the former has a tendency to treat employers as an homogenous group, albeit with some delineation regarding size and sector.

Given the relatively recent awareness of the role of the workplace in skill formation, it is not surprising that employers struggle to make the most of their employees' talents and potential as they themselves may have only experienced restrictive workplace environments. Providing support for employers to create and sustain the conditions that foster learning, rather than presuming they have the capacity to respond to the latest ideas in workforce development has to become a greater priority for policy-makers at all levels. Employers may get this support within their professional and sectoral networks, but SMEs and micro-businesses can be isolated from such networks.

Examining the way in which skill formation takes place as part of everyday work provides the means to reconsider other loosely used categorizations such as 'over-qualified', 'unskilled', 'professional' and 'knowledge worker'. These labels reflect a belief in an individualized, static, and abstracted conceptualization of job-related expertise. Moreover, they reflect the view that the knowledge and skills one gains through an accredited programme of education (in particular a university degree) can be directly equated with expertise required in the workplace. This is not to disparage accredited programmes, but rather to strive for a more sophisticated appreciation of the complex nature of all forms of work.

Given the pressures most workplaces now work under, there is more that public policy could do to acknowledge the considerable journey that many employers need to make to create the conditions required for meaningful workforce development. Regulatory measures such as 'licences to practise' and minimum standards for health and safety provide an important lever, but employers (of all types and sizes) need to learn how to effect more systemic and sustainable change. This requires much more effort from employer associations, sector bodies, and trades unions to develop practical models that reflect the realities of specific contexts. It also requires policy-makers to reconsider their own assumptions about what employers can achieve (and want to achieve) on their own. Employees also need to develop their own understanding of how their workplaces could be key sites for developing and practising their skills. They may have limited scope for influencing the way their work is organized, particularly if they are on 'zero-hour', temporary, or part-time contracts, and/or if they find their employers have little idea of or interest in skill formation. This poses a challenge for trades unions and, again, for public policy. Organizations are wasting talent. As Nora Watson, a 28-year-old staff writer for a publisher of health care literature, said in her interview with the American journalist, Studs Terkel (1974, 521):

> Jobs are not big enough for people. It's not just the assembly line worker whose job is too small for his spirit, you know? A job like mine, if you really put your spirit into it, you would sabotage immediately. You don't dare. So you absent your spirit from it. My mind has been so divorced from my job, except as a source of income, it's really absurd.

References

Acemoglu, D. and Pischke, J. (1999) 'Beyond Becker: Training in Imperfect Labour Markets', *The Economic Journal*, 109(453): 112–142.

Ashton, D., Sung, J., Raddon, A., and Riordan, T. (2008) 'Challenging the Myths about Learning and Training in Small and Medium-Sized Enterprises: Implications for Policy', *Employment Working Paper 1*, ILO, Geneva.

Ashton, D. (2004) 'The Impact of Organisational Structure and Practices on Learning in the Workplace', *International Journal of Training and Development*, 8(1): 43–53.

Beckett, D. and Hager, P. (2002) *Life, Work and Learning*, London: Routledge.

Billett, S. (2001) *Learning in the Workplace*, Crows Nest NSW: Allen & Unwin.

Boreham, N. (2002) 'Work Process Knowledge in Technological and Organizational Development,' in N. Boreham, R. Samurcay, and M. Fischer (eds), *Work Process Knowledge*, London: Routledge: 1–14.

Braverman, H. (1974) *Labour and Monopoly Capital*, New York: Monthly Review Press.

Brockmann, M., Clarke, L., and Winch, C. with Hanf, G., Mehault, P. and, Westerhuis, A. (2011) *Knowledge, Skills and Competence in the European Labour Market*, London: Routledge.

Brown, P. and Scase, R. (1994) *Poor Work*, Milton Keynes: Open University Press.

Brown, P., Green, A., and Lauder H. (2001) *High Skills*, Oxford: Oxford University Press.

Campbell, M. (2012) 'Skills for Prosperity? A Review of OECD and Partner Country Skill Strategies', LLAKES Research Paper 39, Centre for Learning and Life Chances in Knowledge Economies and Societies, Institute of Education, University of London.

Canduela, J., Dutton, M., Johnson, S., Lindsay, C., McQuaid, R.W., and Raeside, R. (2012) 'Ageing, Skills and Participation in Work-Related Training in Britain: Assessing the Position of Older workers', *Work, Employment and Society*, 26(1): 42–60.

Clarke, N. (2004) 'HRD and the Challenges of Assessing Learning in the Workplace', *International Journal of Training and Development*, 18(2): 140–156.

Cooke, G. B., Chowan, J., and Brown, T. (2011) 'Declining versus Participating in Employer-Supported Training in Canada, *International Journal of Training Development*, 15(4): 271–289.

Darrah, C. N. (1996) *Learning and Work*, London: Garland Publishing.

Døving, E. and Nordhaug, O. (2002) 'Learning from Specific Knowledge and Skills: Conceptual Issues and Empirical Results'. Paper to the 3rd European Conference on Organizational Knowledge, Learning and Capabilities, Athens. http://www2.warwick.ac.uk/fac/soc/wbs/conf/olkc/archive/oklc3/papers/id341.pdf.

Engeström, Y. (2001) 'Expansive Learning at Work: Toward an Activity-Theoretical Reconceptualization', *Journal of Education and Work*, 14(1): 133–156.

Engeström, Y. (2007) 'From Communities of Practice to Mycorrhizae', in Hughes, J., Jewson, N., and Unwin, L. (eds) (2007) *Communities of Practice*, London: Routledge: 41–54.

Engeström, Y. (2011) 'Activity Theory and Learning at Work', in M. Malloch, Cairns, L., Evans, K., and O'Connor, B. N. (eds), *The SAGE Handbook of Workplace Learning*, London: SAGE: 86–104.

Eraut, M. and Hirsh, W. (2007) *The Significance of Workplace Learning for Individuals, Groups and Organizations*, SKOPE Monograph 9, Oxford/Cardiff: Universities of Oxford and Cardiff.

Estevez-Abe, M., Iversen, T., and Soskice, D. (2001) 'Social Protection and the Formation of Skills: A Reinterpretation of the Welfare State,' in P. A. Hall and D. Soskice (eds), *Varieties of Capatalism*, Oxford: Oxford University Press: 145–183.

Felstead, A. and Green, F. (1994) 'Training in the Recession', *Work, Employment and Society*, 8(2): 199–219.

Felstead, A. and Jewson, N. (2014) 'Training Floors' and 'Training Ceilings': Metonyms for Understanding Training Trends', *Journal of Vocational Education and Training*, 66(3): 296–310.

Felstead, A., Jewson, N., and Walters, S. (2005a) *Changing Places of Work*, Basingstoke: Palgrave Macmillan.

Felstead, A., Fuller, A., Jewson, N., and Unwin, L. (2009) *Improving Working for Learning*, London Routledge.

Felstead, A., Fuller, A., Unwin, L., Ashton, D., Butler, P., and Lee, T. (2005b) 'Surveying the Scene: Learning Metaphors, Survey Design and the Workplace Context', *Journal of Education and Work*, 18(4): 359–383.

Fenwick, T. and Nerland, M. (eds) (2014) *Reconceptualising Professional Learning*, London: Routledge.

Fuller, A. and Unwin, L. (2004) 'Expansive Learning Environments: Integrating Organizational and Personal Development,' in H. Rainbird, A. Fuller, and A. Munro (eds), *Workplace Learning in Context*, London: Routledge: 126–144.

Fuller, A. and Unwin, L. (2011) 'Workplace Learning and the Organization', in M. Malloch, Cairns, L., Evans, K., and O'Connor, B. N. (eds), *The SAGE Handbook of Workplace Learning*, London: SAGE: 46–59.

Fuller, A., Lawrie, I., and Unwin, L. (2011) 'Learning as a Low-Grade worker: The Case of the Hospital Porter', LLAKES Research Paper 25, Centre for Learning and Life Chances in Knowledge Economies and Societies, Institute of Education, University of London.

Green, F. (2006) *Demanding Work*, Princeton: Princeton University Press.

Gregg, P. and Tominey, E. (2005) 'The Wage Scar from Male Youth Unemployment', *Labour Economics*, 12: 487–509.

Grugulis, I., Warhurst, C., and Keep, E. (2004) 'What's Happening to Skills', in Warhurst, C., Grugulis, I., and Keep, E. (eds), *The Skills That Matter*, London, Palgrave Macmillan: 1–18.

Grugulis I. and Vincent S. (2009) 'Whose Skill Is it Anyway?' *Work, Employment and Society*, 23(4): 597–615.

Guile, D. (2010) *The Learning Challenge of the Knowledge Economy*, Rotterdam: Sense Publishers.

Hager, P. (2004) 'The Competence Affair, or Why Vocational Education and Training Urgently Needs a New Understanding of Learning', *Journal of Training and Development*, 56(3): 409–434.

Hager, P. and Halliday, J. (2006) *Recovering Informal Learning*, Dordrecht: Springer.

Hager, P. and Hodkinson, P. (2009) 'Moving Beyond the Metaphor of Transfer of Learning', *British Educational Research Journal*, 35(4): 619–638.

Hennessy, T. and Sawchuk, P. (2003) 'Worker Responses to Technological Change in the Canadian Public Sector: Issues of Learning and the Labour Process, *Journal of Workplace Learning*, 15(7/8): 319–325.

Hodkinson P., Hodkinson H., Evans K., Kersh N., Fuller A., Unwin, L., and Senker P. (2004) 'The Significance of Personal Biography in Workplace Learning', *Studies in the Education of Adults*, 36(1): 6–24.

Høyrup, S., Bonnafous-Boucher, M., Hasse, C., Lotz, M., and Møller, K. (eds) (2012) *Employee-Driven Innovation*, London: Palgrave Macmillan.

Hughes, J., Jewson, N., and Unwin, L. (eds) (2007) *Communities of Practice*, London: Routledge.

James, L., Guile, D. and Unwin, L. (2012) 'Learning and Innovation in the Knowledge-Based Economy: Beyond Clusters and Qualifications', *Journal of Education and Work*, 26(3): 243–266.

Keep, E., Mayhew, K., and Payne, J. (2006) 'From Skills Revolution to Productivity Miracle—Not as Easy as it Sounds?', *Oxford Review of Economic Policy*, 22(4): 539–559.

Koike, K. and Inoki, T. (eds) (1990) *Skill Formation in Japan and Southeast Asia*, Tokyo: University of Tokyo Press.

Lave, J. and Wenger, E. (1991) *Situated Learning*, Cambridge: Cambridge University Press.

Livingstone, D. and Sawchuk, P. (2003) *Hidden Knowledge*, Toronto: Garamond Press.

Maki, T., Yotsuya, K., and Yagi, T. (2005) 'Economic Growth and the Riskiness of Investment in Firm-Specific Skills', *European Economic Review*, 49: 1033–1049.

Marsden, D. (1986) *The End of Economic Man?* Brighton: Wheatsheaf.

Matsuo, M. (2014) 'Instructional Skills for On-the-job Training and Experiential Llearning: An Empirical Study of Japanese Firms', *International Journal of Training Development*, 18(4): 225–240.

Neirotti, P. and Paolucci, E. (2013) 'Why do Firms Train? Empirical Evidence on the Relationship between Training and Technological and Organizational Change', *International Journal of Training Development*, 17(2): 93–114.

Nonaka, I. and Takeuchi, H. (1995) *The Knowledge Creating Company*, New York: Oxford University Press.
OECD (2013a) *Skills Development and Training in SMEs*, Paris: OECD
OECD (2013b) *Skilled for Life? Key Findings from the Survey of Adult Skills*, Paris: OECD.
Pankhurst, K. V. (2009) 'Elements of an Integrated Theory of Work and Learning', in D. Livingstone (ed), *Education & Jobs*, Toronto: Toronto University Press: 137–155.
Rainbird, H., Munro, A., and Holly, L. (2004) 'The Employment Relationship and Workplace Learning', in H. Rainbird, A. Fuller, and A. Munro (eds), *Workplace Learning in Context*, London: Routledge: 38–53.
Ryan, P., Gospel, H., Lewis, P., and Foreman, J. (2006) *Large Employers and Apprenticeship Training*, London: Chartered Institute of Personnel and Development.
Sennett, R. (2008) *The Craftsman*, New Haven: Yale University Press.
Stevens, M. (1999) 'Human Capital Theory and UK Vocational Training Policy', *Oxford Review of Economic Policy*, 15(1): 16–32.
Stone, I. (2012) *Upgrading Workforce Skills in Small Businesses: Reviewing International Policy and Experience: Report for Workshop on Skills Development for SMEs and Entrepreneurship*, Paris: OECD.
Terkel, S. (1974) *Working*, New York: The New Press.
Thelen, K. (2004) *How Institutions Evolve*, Cambridge: Cambridge University Press.
Thompson, P. and Smith, C. (eds) (2010) *Working life*, London: Palgrave Macmillan.
Tikkanen, T. and Nyhan, B. (eds) (2006) *Promoting Lifelong Learning for Older Workers*, Luxembourg: Office for the Official Publications of the European Communities.
Unwin, L. (2004) 'Growing Beans with Thoreau: Rescuing Skills and Vocational Education from the UK's deficit approach', *Oxford Review of Education*, 30(1): 47–60.
Unwin, L. (2009) *Sensuality, Sustainability and Social Justice: Vocational Education in Changing Times*, London: Institute of Education Publications.
Unwin, L. (2012) 'A Critical Approach to Work: The Contribution of Work-Based Learning to Lifelong Learning', in D. N. Aspin, J. Chapman, K. Evans, and R. Bagnall (eds), *Second International Handbook of Lifelong Learning, Part 2*, Dordecht: Springer: 787–800.
Walden, G. and Troltsch, K. (2013) 'Apprenticeship Training in Germany—Still a Future-Oriented Model of Recruiting Skilled Workers?', in A. Fuller and L. Unwin (eds), *Contemporary Apprenticeship*, London: Routledge: 47–64.
Warhurst, C., Carre, F., Findlay, P., and Tilly, C. (eds) (2012) *Are Bad Jobs Inevitable?* London: Palgrave Macmillan.
Wanrooy, van B., Bewley, H., Bryson, A., Forth, J., Freeth, S., Stokes, L., and Wood, S. (2013) *Employment Relations in the Shadow of Recession*, London: Palgrave Macmillan:
Wheelahan, L. (2010) *Why Knowledge Matters in the Curriculum*, London: Routledge.
Winch, C. (2010) *Dimensions of Expertise*, London: Continuum.
Winch, C. (1998) *The Philosophy of Human Learning*, London: Routledge.
Wolf, A. and Evans, K. (2010) *Improving Literacy at Work*, Abingdon: Routledge.

CHAPTER 12

UNIONS, THE SKILLS AGENDA, AND WORKFORCE DEVELOPMENT

MARK STUART AND TONY HUZZARD

Introduction

The education and personal development of members has been a longstanding interest of trade unions. At the end of the nineteenth century in the United Kingdom, Ruskin College was founded with the specific purpose of offering university-standard education for working-class people so that they could act more effectively on behalf of working-class communities and organizations, including trade unions. The establishment of the Workers Educational Association and the National Council of Labour Colleges also reflected this broad aim. Unions generally supported these forms of educating their members who were largely from working-class backgrounds and rarely, in the early decades of trade unionism at least, had any formal education. Courses at institutions such as Ruskin offered trade unionists a second chance. This historical and yet ongoing belief in the significance of education for trade unionists has in essence been an emancipatory endeavour.

In addition to such general educational concerns, the *definition of skills* has also been an historical concern of unions—and ongoing point of contention with employers—with such definitions shaping both the identity and contours of solidarity of unions, along either occupational, industry, or enterprise lines. This was most notable in the way in which craft unions, such as those in the printing industry, controlled entry into a trade through the regulation of time-served apprenticeships (Cockburn 1991; Stuart 1999). More recently, unions have focused on the more ongoing and changing work-related needs, skills and competencies of members (Streeck 1994; Huzzard 2004), typically articulated by the catch-all rubric of lifelong learning. This partly concerns developing the skills of individual members and partly a leveraging of skills and learning, in the more collective sense, at the workplace. Unions are embracing as a strategic issue what can broadly be understood as a skills agenda (Cooney and Stuart 2012). Exploring the nature of this agenda is the aim of this chapter. In focus are a number of questions. Firstly, and foremost, what is the 'skills agenda', and how is it different to the earlier approaches unions adopted to issues concerning skills? Secondly, why are unions appearing to embrace a skills agenda as a significant strategic issue? Thirdly, what are the different forms that the skills agendas take? Fourthly, what industrial relations arrangements are associated with the pursuit of skills as a strategic issue? And finally, how do we account for the differences between them, particularly within a comparative context?

We argue that the significance of the skills agenda is broadly concomitant with a shift in the labour process beyond mass production into newer trajectories, variously described as post-Fordism, post-industrialism, flexible specialization, and new production concepts. As a consequence, unions increasingly equate their members' learning (and skills) as much with enhancing their employability as with emancipation or entry into a trade (Huzzard 2004). This has gone hand in hand with a strategic reorientation of unions, in response to more challenging bargaining environments and a declining membership base (Stuart 1996).

Where unions have sought to advance learning and skills as core agenda items, this has often been in response to wage restraint and advanced either through workplace partnership or more macro-level social pacts—a process that Buchanan et al.(2004) label 'skills orientated left productivism'. Whilst this can be seen as a common trend across many developed economies, different strategies, trajectories, and outcomes are evident across countries. This is in part shaped by national institutions and legacies, but such structures do not necessarily determine practice. The structures, strategies, and practices of unions are also vitally important factors in shaping, for example, whose interests are served by the learning and skills agenda (i.e. management or employees). This chapter therefore stresses agency and voice throughout.

Unions and the Skills Agenda in Historical Perspective

Trade unions historically have, to some extent, always been defined by their approach towards skills. Unions have organized in different ways between, and within, countries, along craft, industry, and workplace lines and union structures have often reflected their representation of skilled, semi-skilled, or unskilled workers. Cockburn's (1991) seminal study of UK craft print workers, for example, illustrates how for unions the definition of skills was *political*, with close control of apprenticeships a means by which unions restricted access to trade protected, skilled worker status and demarcated the jurisdiction of skilled workers from unskilled workers. Such mechanisms of social closure were typically, and problematically, marked by clear gender divisions, with men's work defined as skilled and women's work as unskilled. Those economies with strong traditions of apprenticeship (such as the United Kingdom and Germany) thus often had labour markets structured by occupational means rather than via internal factors (more prevalent in countries such as Japan and the United States), notionally limiting the opportunities for workers to develop through different roles within companies (Marsden 1999; Martin, Chapter 2, this volume).

Where skills are politically defined they are often contested, in this instance between unions and employers (Stuart 1996). Occupational labour markets rely on strong institutional structures to support their operation, including agreements between employers' associations and unions that cut across groups of firms or an industry. Such structures can break down, as the recent history of apprenticeships in the United Kingdom illustrates. The strict control of apprenticeships that craft unions in the United Kingdom imposed from the 1960s onwards was opposed by employers. In industries such as printing and engineering, from the late 1970s technology was used by management to break established definitions of skills, apprenticeships were restructured, and an increasing emphasis was put on competency-based training and module accreditation. Apprentice numbers declined—in print, for example, from a peak of 3,000 in 1979 to just 100 by the early 1990s (Stuart 1999)—industry-wide agreements broke down as did union influence over skills formation. This did not happen in countries such as Germany, where occupational labour markets were more functionally than task delineated and industrial relations structures were less adversarial. The German apprenticeship system, and with it union influence and involvement over initial vocational training, has proved more adaptable, notably in accommodating employers' demands for increased functional flexibility (Marsden 1999). Attempts to modularize training around narrow competencies have been resisted in favour of redesigned conceptions of occupation (Bosch 2010). However, even within systems such as Germany the pressure on unions to develop new 'skills orientated strategies' has intensified, as debates have emerged around the need for more continued vocational education and training and lifelong learning and concerns over the commitment of employers to traditional apprenticeships (Mahnkof 1992; Trappmann 2012).

Beyond their involvement in apprenticeships, initial training and the structuring of entry into occupational labour markets, unions paid little attention historically to continuing training or wider notions of workforce development. This has been a more recent strategic development. In the United Kingdom, partly in response to their declining influence over apprenticeships and the wider regulation of the training system, a number of unions sought to integrate skills into reassessments of bargaining priorities from the late 1980s. By 1994, one author felt able to claim that 'the training of workers has a high priority on the bargaining agendas of most trade unions' (Taylor 1994, 153), though the evidence suggested otherwise (Stuart 1996). This was exemplified by the following type of joint statement issued by the leaders of the Transport and General Workers Union and the General and Municipal and Boilermakers Union (see Taylor 1994, 155):

> Training is not just the key to economic success. It is the means by which our members can achieve a happier and more successful life. Training should be regarded as an individual right as well as an industrial necessity.

This apparent embrace of the skills agenda was mirrored elsewhere. In Sweden the Metalworkers Union at its Congress in 1985 sought to develop a new strategy against the backdrop of low productivity and major quality problems in manufacturing industry (Johansson and Abrahamsson 2009). The union recognized that large-scale production was being replaced by flexibility and customer adaptation, organizational forms were being more decentralized, and the Fordist production line was being increasingly superseded by automation, smaller work groups and quality circles (Huzzard 2000, 184 ff.). The union's response to this was the now well-known policy of 'good work', which included a new emphasis on training being an integral part of one's work. Importantly, the new policy not only aimed at developing the skills of individual members it also saw this as a means to develop the productive capacities of workplaces more generally (Sandberg et al. 1992).

A similar emphasis on skills and training was also detectable among reformists in the Australian unions around this time (Mathews 1993), although this had a rather stronger corporatist element in that links were forged with the then Labor Government to involve the state. The training reform proposed by the unions sought to increase training expenditure as well as put in place mechanisms to ensure transferability of qualifications. A key mechanism was that of Awards as outcomes of industrial tribunals that demarcated work boundaries and skill requirements with the force of industrial law. Eventually, however, this approach was opposed by the employers in a context of what was seen as 'outmoded interventionism' (Hampson 2004, 73; see also Cooney 2002). Indeed, employer opposition and apathy is seen as a critical factor constraining the furtherance of union-led skills agendas more generally.

Why Unions Get Involved in the New Skills Agenda

The Economic Case for Skills

Disciplinary perspectives offer different rationales for why, whether, and how unions may get involved in a new skills agenda. In simple terms, orthodox human capital theory assumes that the impact of unions will be negative, as unions act to inhibit firms' wage flexibility and may impose seniority rules on the hiring and firing of labour and other restrictive practices (Mincer 1958; Becker 1975). The argument here is that by flattening wage profiles and reducing wage differentials through their bargaining strategies, unions disincentivize their members from seeking to better themselves via skills development, nor will firms be disposed to invest in general training (Booth et al. 2003). Such assumptions have been questioned, with much depending on the perceived incentives for firms to invest in general training and their ability to internalize any gains. An alternative perspective is offered by Freeman and Medoff (1984), who argue that unions have two faces: a market and an institutional face. They argue that the voice unions afford employees has a potential productive benefit for employers. Without voice, workers are more likely to quit in response to workplace grievance. With a voice, workers are likely to trade exit for loyalty and in the process allow firms the time needed to internalize the costs associated with investment in training.

Whilst empirical support is mixed and suggests that the causal impact of unions on training outcomes is complex (Boheim and Booth 2004), numerous studies reveal a positive association between union presence and activity and positive training outcomes for union members. For example, Brunello (2004) reports that countries with higher union densities and stronger employment protection policies exhibit higher levels of training. Likewise, numerous studies of large representative datasets in Britain and Australia report a positive impact of unions on workplace training (Arulampalam and Booth 1998; Heyes and Stuart 1998; Green et al. 1999). For Heyes and Stuart (1998) the key factor is not just union presence per se, but the level of active union involvement in workplace investment decisions, either through formal joint committee structures or collective bargaining arrangements. This lends support to the contention of Streeck (1994) that a strong union presence in the firm, perhaps buttressed by suitable legal underpinnings, might contribute positively to skill formation.

New Production Regimes

Whilst the arguments of Streeck and others that a union role in skill formation need not be negative necessarily, they shed little light on why unions may seek to pursue a new skills agenda. To understand this, contributions from the fields of sociology, management, and employment relations are more useful. A useful starting point here is that of post-Fordist models of change or new production concepts, such as lean or flexible production. The increased focus on workplace skills development from the 1980s onwards has been characterized by fundamental shifts in forms of work organization notably in manufacturing and beyond. Specifically, such shifts have entailed the replacement of mass production by new work forms centred on flexibility, self-reliance, project-based team-working, greater use of technology, and the increasing importance of information and knowledge (Drucker 1993; Barley 1996).

Post-Fordism proposes that there has been a substantial shift not just in the labour process, but also in the nature of macro-level social and economic reproduction linked to the notion of a new, post-modern epoch (Piore and Sabel 1984; Harvey 1989; Mahon 1991; Amin 1994; Rifkin 1995). Others have preferred different labels such as post-industrialism (Bell 1973), late modernism (Giddens 1991) or new production concepts (Kern and Schumann 1984). These labels and the assumptions of periodization that underpin them have been subject to critique. Despite this, the evidence that there have been significant changes to the way in which work is organized over the past two or three decades seems overwhelming. Moreover, a belief in the increased significance of learning and knowledge has been a fundamental factor accounting for unions embracing the skills agenda. This can be seen, for example, in the centrality of the skills agenda to the 'good work' policy of the Swedish metalworkers union. It is also evident in Mathews's (1993) call for a new 'industrial relations of skill formation', based on the policies of the Australian metalworkers' union and the development of workplace competency-based frameworks. Whilst the empirical basis for ideal types of new production regimes is weak, the underlying ideas have proved rather enduring. The conclusions for unions are often rather crudely put. Faced with a changing production model, unions need to develop new strategies and approaches. The traditional adversarial wage bargaining agenda is associated with a declining model of business organization that requires unions to innovate in response to more flexible ways of working. Skills and workforce development offer suitable routes for union innovation. They are also perceived as more amenable to cooperative forms of engagement, or partnership, with employers (Mathews 1993).

The Discourse of Employability

Under post-Fordism, employees are no longer components in relatively stable work systems such as production lines or white-collar bureaucracies. The relative job security and, in some cases, clear career trajectories of the Fordist template are now a distant memory. Neither the state nor the capitalist firm can guarantee the right to secure employment or future promotion. This in turn puts considerable responsibility on individuals to manage their own employability, by regularly updating skills and competencies to comply with market requirements. Previously the state undertook to provide guarantees to protect people in their jobs, and employers had some responsibility to employ people. However, employee rights to employment have now been largely superseded by employee responsibility for their own employability (Huzzard 2004; Greenwood and Stuart 2006).

At the policy level, researchers have detected a clear shift from prioritizing full employment to prioritizing employability (Jacobsson 2004). Consistent with neoliberal ideology, individuals now have to assume responsibility both for their access to the labour market and their survival within it (Thedvall 2004). The effect of this 'employability discourse' (Marks and Huzzard 2010) is clearly evident in union strategies. For example, a campaign by the Swedish Union for Clerical Employees in Industry (then SIF, now Unionen) in 1997, designed to recruit graduate engineers, saw the issue of employability as a central union concern. The union marketed itself as a career development facilitator, and, to reinforce this message, the project coined a new phrase to signify the identity of the union, that of 'career coach'. Noteworthy here was a rather different take on skills and learning to that evident in blue-collar unions. The emphasis was not so much on the skills required for immediate and development needs on the job. Rather, the key response was about supplying coaching services in the context of a potentially boundary spanning career and developing the personal skills required for successfully selling oneself in the external labour market (Huzzard 2004).

Social Settlements and Bargaining Priorities

Even though the basis for post-Fordism as a driver of union change is empirically weak, unions have nonetheless sought to adapt and develop their strategies in response to the supposed 'new times'. Skills and workforce development are often situated in this regard as a response to unfolding social settlements, the limits of traditional bargaining agendas, and as a response to membership decline. The Norwegian Competence Reform, for example, was driven by the peak level Norwegian Confederation of Trade Unions, Landsorganisasjonen (LO), partly as a way of offering something to members experiencing wage restraint (Teige and Stuart 2012). Wage restraint was seen as necessary given the economic conditions of the early 1990s and this prompted new demands, through successive biannual national bargaining rounds, for learning for members to enhance their economic power and employability in the labour market. This resulted in new frameworks for competency development and (prior) skill recognition and a new entitlement for workers to have time away from work for learning. However, the reform was only considered a partial success, due to a mix of worker, union, and employer ambivalence, and tensions over the financing of the new training right (Bowman 2005; Teige and Stuart 2012). In the United Kingdom, the Trades Union Congress (TUC) placed the skills agenda centre stage in its bargaining priorities for the 1990s, a strategy that came to be known as the 'new bargaining agenda' (Stuart 1996). The TUC, in this case, sought to push the development of workplace training committees and an annual entitlement to a number of days' training, again with very little success.

Whilst economic and sociological perspectives offer logics for why unions may engage with skills as a new agenda, they do not address the processes by which unions may engage. Such processes have been considered more systematically in the employment relations literature. Of note here is the issue of social partnership. The idea of partnership is relatively longstanding as it essentially focuses on the interplay of cooperative and conflictual models of engagement that define the employment relationship (Stuart and Martinez Lucio 2005). The precise meaning of partnership is somewhat contested, but has been defined by Cave and Coats (1999) as consisting of six principles: commitment to the success of the organization; recognizing legitimate (stakeholder) interests; a commitment to employment security; a focus on the quality of working life; transparency; and adding value to the firm.

Although these principles are fairly concrete, social partnership is a complex phenomenon and will take on very different forms not least because of national institutional factors (Huzzard et al. 2009). In what the Varieties of Capitalism (VoC) and production regimes literatures (Hall and Soskice 2001) call coordinated market economies (such as Germany and the Scandinavian countries), we would normally expect a much more cooperative and inclusive approach to industrial relations engagement than in the liberal market economies (typified by the United Kingdom and the United States). In the Scandinavian countries, for example, unions have been pursuing policies aligned with partnership for some decades. It has been accepted by the Swedish blue-collar union confederation since the 1950s that rationalization in firms was required to facilitate structural adjustment. Such rationalization had to be accepted by the labour movement, albeit alongside active labour market measures undertaken by the state to maintain full employment (Huzzard 2000).

The spirit of partnership was also evident in the support of the unions for legislation on co-determination in 1977 and its subsequent implementation at the workplace. This has meant that the skills agenda as a priority, to be pursued with local management in partnership forums, has been a logical strategic choice for unions. Similarly, unions in Denmark, Finland, and Germany have been noted as playing a significant role in the direct provision of vocational education and training (VET) themselves (Ok and Tergeist 2003). The German system is often seen as a model case in this regard, with trade unions' role in skill provision institutionalized in the 1969 Law on Vocational Training and their voice represented in key governmental institutes for VET. The Works Constitution Act also gives works councils at German firms formal consultation rights on VET (Mahnkopf 1992; Trappmann 2012).

The partnership idea has more recently evolved around new modes of engagement in relation to company change. In simple terms it follows logically from the rationale of the new bargaining agendas discussed above. Faced with limits around what can be achieved in terms of distributive bargaining, unions have looked for new agenda items, and skills and learning are considered apposite as they appear to have more integrative appeal. Simply put, bargaining concerning agendas such as pay, and terms and conditions, are distributive as one party's gain is another's loss (Walton and McKersie 1965). Bargaining in this sense is a zero sum game. Skills or workforce development, on the other hand, are seen to offer integrative settlements whereby all parties may gain. This affords the opportunity for cooperative engagement between unions and management. This idea is most well developed in Kochan and Osterman's (1994) concept of the mutual gains enterprise. Drawing from case study evidence in the United States, they assert that moving towards human resource strategies based on mutual gains and production systems requires 'significant increases in training and skills' (1994, 30). Such a view sees training and development as key sources of competitive advantage (Pfeffer 1994).

The claims of mutual gains advocates have been subject to intense empirical scrutiny, along with the extent to which skills and workforce development can ever be seen as purely integrative. Points of critique include the following notions:

- mutual gains bargaining might actually be bargaining or mere union capitulation to the interests of management (Kelly 1996);
- partnership is seen to relate to union co-option to management interests and therefore potentially damaging (Taylor and Ramsay 1998);

- little evidence for mutual gains exists, with employees receiving little by way of benefit, or at least any gains being skewed towards the benefit of employers (Guest and Pecchei 2001);
- workforce development is not purely integrative, since skills are often related to wider material outcomes and power at the workplace and can therefore easily become distributive and contested (Stuart 1996, 2001).

The final point raises some important issues about how partnership and partnership processes are understood. Firstly, Huzzard et al. (2004) take a more sophisticated stance on the interplay between integrative and distributive strategies. They do not see the former crowding out the latter, but see a potential relationship organized across a 'partnership space'. Thus unions can 'box' and 'dance', cooperating on 'dancefloors' on skills, whilst bargaining in 'boxing rings' around pay and conditions. Whilst critics often reject this possibility, the idea of boxing and dancing chimes more readily with what unions actually do in practice. Munro and Rainbird (2004), for example, have considered this specifically in relation to skills and learning, by differentiating between *general purpose* partnerships, which are seen as potentially problematic given tensions between integrative and distributive bargaining, and *single purpose* learning partnerships, which are seen as less imbued with such tensions. Indeed, trade union colleagues often talk of 'firewalling' learning and skills from the wider bargaining agenda.

This discussion around partnership raises a number of deeper issues. Firstly, the idea of mutual gains brings the issue of *interests* to the fore, and whether potentially competing interests are compatible. Thus, employers and employees may both be interested in skills and workforce development, but their interests may not be identical (Winterton and Winterton 1994; Stuart 1996): employees will be concerned with improving their wider employability, whilst employers will be concerned with improving employee performance and wider corporate efficiency. As Cooney and Stuart (2012) observe, from the perspective of management, training and skills are seen primarily as a *competition good*, whilst for trade unions they are seen as a *labour market good*. Trade unions, accordingly, often look to advance the skills agenda as a new means of engagement with employers, whilst being mindful that skills policy and practice may have been used in the past to weaken organized labour (notably craft organization) in the labour market and employer control over the organization of work (Braverman 1974; Cockburn 1991). The reconciliation of different interests thus presents a central challenge for unions.

Secondly, whether interests can be jointly mediated may be influenced by wider *institutional factors* and the role played by actors in the bargaining process. Kochan and Osterman (1994), for example, explicitly situated mutual gains as a partnership between capital, labour, and the state. Huzzard et al. (2004) show how this wider institutional complex plays out in different countries (see also Bosch and Charest 2010).

A third, and related, factor is that the *balance of power* between institutional actors is also vitally important. As Kelly (1996) correctly notes, writing with regard to the UK context, it is meaningless to talk of partnership with employers who wish that unions did not exist. Likewise, if unions are unable to leverage any power, then any notion of a balance in partnership becomes meaningless. Institutions again may matter in this sense in terms of equipping unions with rights, voice, and scope for action, but are rarely enough in themselves. Far too often agreements and structures are flouted at workplace level and thereby joint initiatives often suffer implementation failure. Unions need the resources and capacity to be able to exercise their own power: agency matters too. In this regard, Streeck (1994) warns of the danger of cooperation for unions and stresses the need for conflictual cooperation. On the other hand, how interests, institutions, and power play out tends to be framed by different national and historical contexts. It is to this matter that we now turn.

Unions and the New Skills Agenda in Comparative Context

Numerous frameworks exist for understanding the differences in employment systems between capitalist economies. These have been applied quite frequently in relation to skills, if not for the role that unions may play per se. Whilst there are variations in the frameworks offered, they tend to bifurcate between those economies most likely to encourage high-skills or low-skills paths, and those economies where unions may play a greater or lesser role. Widely referenced is the Varieties of Capitalism (VoC) school, which differentiates between market-based and coordinated economies (Hall and Soskice 2001; Gallie 2007). Under the former, which typifies economies such as the United Kingdom, the United States, and Australia, little scope exists for unions to actively participate in the coordination of skill formation investment decisions at the workplace level, with such decisions left to employers and the logic of market forces. This may lead to less than optimal investment decisions for an economy as a whole, because of the perceived market failures inherent to skills formation (Streeck 1989).

Coordinated economies are more institutionally dense with greater levels of labour market regulation and a more central role for unions, as one of the social partners, to play a role in the governance of skills formation. Here the market failures associated with skills are mitigated through longer-term investment horizons. Broadly, the VoC literature sees the liberal market economies as having vocational training and education (VET) systems based on general education, emphasizing the role of tertiary education for socio-economic mobility, life success, and job security. This contrasts with the coordinated market economies whose VET systems generally consist of vocational training systems that emphasize the acquisition of firm or sector specific skills (Hall and Soskice 2001; Bosch and Charest 2010).

There is certainly superficial evidence to support the VoC framework. Differences do exist between countries. Germany and Norway are more regulated and highly coordinated than the United Kingdom and tend to have higher levels of skills investment, notably in terms of intermediate skills, and a greater role for unions. But simplistic categorization comes at the expense of empirical subtlety. Firstly, differences exist between market economies: the United Kingdom is not identical to the United States (see for example Marschall 2012) and Australia, and between coordinated economies, Norway is not the same as Germany, or Denmark, or Sweden. Secondly, the VoC approach tends to only look at established developed economies, though similar demarcations have been applied across Eastern European and European Union Accession countries. In contrast, an alternative model is seen to exist across South-east Asian countries, such as Korea, Singapore, and Malaysia, which are seen to follow a Developmental State approach (Ashton and Green 1996), whereby national systems of skill formation evolve in response to wider economic development strategies, and with very different roles for unions. Thirdly, evidence shows that significant intra-country differences exist within specific models of capitalism (Batt et al. 2009). Recent research by Lloyd and Payne (2013), for example, compares the fitness sector in the United Kingdom and Norway, and finds differences within each country depending on whether organizations are publicly or privately owned. Despite the recognized strength of unions in Norway, they have little leverage or even presence in the Norwegian fitness sector, which in many respects is more market focused than many UK establishments. They assert that analysis of sectoral differences across countries is as important as comparing extant national regimes.

The VoC approach is, of course, not the only model for comparative analysis. Winterton (2007) compares the role of unions in skills and learning across European countries and utilizes a framework based on whether the approach to skills is based on market-led versus regulated, or school versus workplace. He then looks at the union role in term of policy and implementation. Curiously, he finds a union role in all countries, but what exactly that roles amounts to varies significantly in terms of levels of participation in decision-making, issues covered, and outcomes.

In respect of comparative analysis, therefore, we need to refer back to key criteria to guide any evaluation. What type of skills agenda do unions get involved in? At what level does this take place? Which institutions are in play? Whose interests do they serve and in what regard? Bosch and Charest (2010) argue that it is important to look at how skills trajectories link with the wider labour market, and the integration of skills, learning, and workforce development with the wider production system. As they explain, 'One fundamental characteristic in determining the attractiveness of vocational training is the linkage with the labour market, good pay and opportunities for promotion. This linkage remains weak without the close involvement of the social partners' (Bosch and Craest 2010, 23).

Another criterion relates to the specific strategies of unions, with Phillmore (1997), distinguishing between skills capture (exclusive) and inclusive strategies. The latter tend to cover a wider range of workers than the former. How employers engage with unions will also shape the extent to which unions are able to push certain strategies or not, so the potential tensions around partnership and bargaining are ever present. With these issues in mind, the chapter will now explore developments in more detail in the United Kingdom and Sweden.

The Cases of the United Kingdom and Sweden

Whilst Sweden and the United Kingdom may be seen as archetypal examples of market and coordinated economies, the reality is rather different. In many respects the union role in the skills agenda is limited in both countries, though both exhibit examples of partial attempts at experimentation. What this suggests is that although institutional differences have some explanatory purchase, a properly nuanced picture requires an appreciation of the role of agency being exercised in a particular institutional context.

The Union Role in the United Kingdom

In the United Kingdom, the economy has seen three recent phases of union involvement: from 1964 to 1979, formal social partnership via national level Industrial Training Boards, and a key union role in the regulation of apprenticeships; from 1979 to 1997, a period of state exclusion and breakdown of occupational labour markets but with developing union innovation; and from 1997 to date, a new union role in the sphere of workplace learning. The period since 1997 is notable as the union role was explicitly supported by the Labour Government (in office between 1997 and 2010). The government signalled its views on the union role in its Green Paper, *The Learning Age*, which foresaw learning as something that a 'modern' union movement should be engaged in and as a 'natural issue' for partnership between unions and employers (Stuart 2001). These aspirations were subsequently supported by specific policy initiatives. Firstly, from 1998, a Union Learning Fund (ULF) was established, which provided resources to unions to develop new initiatives around workplace learning. By 2008, the 11th annual round of the ULF, more than £100m had been invested. Secondly, from the late 1990s, unions sought to develop a new workplace role to help members engage in learning activities: the *Union Learning Representative* (ULR). ULRs were awarded formal statutory rights from 2003, under the auspices of the 2002 Employment Act. Under these provisions, union members have formal rights to train as ULRs and to conduct their duties as ULRs, and employees have the right, though not necessarily in paid work time, to access a ULR. There is no corresponding requirement of employers to recognize, consult, or negotiate with ULRs (Rainbird and Stuart 2011). Finally, the TUC established an internal department specifically related to union learning activities, *unionlearn*. From 2007, unionlearn took over the administration of the ULF, supported with a grant from government. The specific themes that the ULF has supported have changed over time, but are, notionally at least, determined through dialogue between the TUC and government officials. In its early days the ULF focused on training for and building networks of ULRs, and supporting basic skills needs at the workplace. More recently, with the election of a Centre-Right coalition government, the focus has shifted to extending the 'union learning model' into small and non-unionized firms.

The ULF and ULR initiatives have attracted much interest from unions overseas and can be seen as somewhat novel developments within the market-based and voluntarist British training system, and have been widely evaluated. Critical analysis rightly draws attention to the lack of any corresponding obligations on employers to engage with union-led learning. There has also been a lively debate on the contributions of these initiatives towards union renewal more generally. Assessed in aggregate terms, there is limited evidence that such learning activities have contributed in any statistical sense to union renewal, but neither have any other union renewal strategies. Learning is perhaps best understood as a new agenda item in the wider repertoire of union resources and approaches—as Findlay and Warhurst (2011) put it, 'a new tool in the tool kit'. Unions have been able to draw down the resources of the ULF to support and represent their members, engage employers, where they are open to it, and build new institutions to help embed such activities. Whilst the state naturally imposes some criteria and strictures on how ULF monies can be deployed, typically in relation to governmental training targets, unions have proved well versed in working around this to further their own agendas and their members' interests.

Whilst these new initiatives have not resulted in fundamental changes in direction, or the nature of the national training system, or any general renewal of the union movement, they have been significant in terms of the scale of their development and the new role created for unions within skills agendas at the workplace level. At the time of the early 1990s debate on the new bargaining agenda this was a mere aspiration for unions. By 2008, the largest evaluation of the ULF to date reported that some 22,000 new ULRs had been trained, more than 600,000 learning opportunities had been accessed (by non-union as well as union members), 847 learning centres had been created, and 1,557 employer–union learning agreements established (Stuart et al. 2013). Whilst survey evidence suggests that employers are often positive about engaging with unions and report workplace benefits from union-led learning, unions are keen to ensure that any partnerships with employers are buttressed by formal learning agreements and workplace learning committees, which help to codify the rights of ULRs, the content of learning, and whether employees' time to learn is paid for. Establishing such agreements often requires a degree of union tenacity. But evidence suggests that where unions establish agreements and engage in bargaining around learning, the benefits for their members are more significant (Hoque and Bacon 2011; Stuart et al. 2013). The sustainability of union learning is, however, a key concern. The probability is that union learning is likely to continue as a model in the United Kingdom, notably around the activities of ULRs, but in all likelihood on a reduced level. It will also remain a model very much focused on the basic and incremental learning needs of workers rather than the deeper means by which skills are defined in the labour market or utilized at work.

The Union Role in Sweden

Sweden has a stronger history of macro-level co-determination, with strong peak social partners and sectoral level bargaining. This has not necessarily extended to the pursuit of skills and workforce development as a single issue agenda. Instead, the focus has been on 'good work', which includes learning, skills, and teamwork, thus unions have not had to single out skills as a new agenda item. Indeed, LO considered and rejected the idea of following the United Kingdom's ULR initiative in the early 2000s, largely because there was no perceived need. The centrality of bargaining on learning and skills formation, or to be more precise, 'competence development', had become formally codified in many of the sector level 'process agreements or 'cooperation agreements' reached in the latter part of the 1990s. An example is the Agreement on Industrial Development and Wage Formation (Industry Agreement) first signed by ALMEGA in 1997—a group of employers from engineering, chemicals, and other sectors—and various unions from each of the three union confederations: LO, TCO and SACO.[1]

This Agreement not only covered distributional issues (wages) but also established arenas for social dialogue on the general conditions and prerequisites for distributional bargaining including skills and competence development. A key feature is that skills and competence development would be subject to biannual dialogue by a joint 'Industry Committee'. As well as taxes, research and development, and energy policy, the Agreement committed the Industry Committee to enter dialogue on education, training, and competence development in industry.

There have been similar agreements in other sectors. These include the 1998 agreement in the paper and pulp industry, the 1997 agreement in the state sector and the 1996 agreement covering local authority teachers. These agreements are still in force or have been superseded by other agreements: for example, the 2005 Agreement 'FAS 05' in the health and local government sectors that committed the central parties to 'offer a quality certified education as well as delegated responsibility for the work environment to key groups [in line with the Work Environment Act]' and recognized that 'all co-workers shall have the opportunity to engage in personal and professional development'. Such development, however, was seen as intimately bound up with the need for structural change within the sector and that such changes 'must be followed by changes in co-workers competences ... individual development plans are an important aid here.'

[1] ALMEGA is the Employers' Organisation for the Swedish Service Sector; LO is Swedish blue collar union confederation; TCO is the Swedish white collar union confederation; SACO is the Swedish confederation of Swedish professional association.

However, the 'good work' agenda has itself unravelled in recent years, as Swedish capitalism has become more fragile and workplace restructuring has seen different outcomes in terms of old-style models of team-working and functional flexibility (Greenwood and Randle 2007). Shareholder value has become a more significant consideration for Swedish capitalism and lean production the dominant archetype of work organization in manufacturing and beyond. Nonetheless, a specifically Swedish variant of lean and its associated management concepts is detectable. This variant has been characterized by Johansson and Abrahamsson (2009) as consisting of four basic components: rational flows, integrated product groups, flat organizations, and learning in work—'knowledge transfer, competence development, and learning at work for production personnel are considered important. It is about training for individuals, work teams, but is also a question about organizational changes into a *workplace culture* that can handle rapid changes for example in new production techniques, new products and quality demands' (2000, 777).

It is also important to recognize that the unions themselves have also lacked certain capacities in terms of their ability to leverage the 'good work' agenda in the workplace, suggesting that despite engaging with workplace development issues for nearly three decades, there are still capacity shortages or a deficit in what Levinson (2000) has termed participation skills in Swedish unions today.

Conclusion

The chapter has explored the role that unions can play in shaping the contemporary agenda of skills and workforce development. The nature of this agenda is, in historical terms, quite distinctive. It has been less about involvement in skills policy through the definition or control of occupations, and more about individual employability and strategies of lifelong learning. It has been less about initial training and entry into a trade and more about ongoing learning and continuing vocational training. Part of the reason for this lies in the widely claimed shift to more flexible forms of production, and employment, which place a supposed premium on ongoing development and skills upgrading. A further explanation lies in the challenges facing unions with regard to traditional distributive concerns and the perceived attractiveness of new skills orientated production strategies (Mahnkopf 1992). The skills agenda has thus often been portrayed as a route for unions to develop mutual gains bargaining strategies that appeal to both employers' and their members' interests.

The degree of union success in shaping the new skills agenda has, however, been variable, in terms of both mutual gains and the more specific interests of unions and their members. A notable limitation has been the ability of unions to seriously influence employers' investment decisions, policies, and control of the skills agenda. In the case of the United Kingdom, for example, whilst unions have been at the forefront of new innovation in terms of a workplace role on skills and learning, the rights for ULRs are not accompanied by corresponding responsibilities on employers to engage or negotiate with unions. Critics thus question the ability of unions to develop independent agendas and roles and typically regard partnership-based approaches with regard to skills as an accommodation to employer concerns, designed to meet the immediate and specific business interests of employers or the wider targets of the state.

The question is: how can unions actively shape skills policy rather than accommodate the interests of employers or the state? Much depends on the position of unions in the broader social settlement and the context of industrial relations, but three conclusions can be drawn. Firstly, history shows that skills are not value neutral. Thus whilst skills may offer new routes for union engagement with employers, how skills are defined and deployed may very well transform what appear at first sight to be integrative concerns into distribute conflicts (Stuart 2001). This suggests that unions may be best placed to 'dance' around skills, where they also retain the power to 'box'. This is why unions in the UK are so concerned to 'institutionalize' the new workplace skills agenda within structures such as learning committees and agreements that can operate as functional equivalents of bargaining. It is also why even in highly coordinated systems such as Norway strong sectoral agreements do not impact effectively on employer practice in the absence of strong workplace representation.

Secondly, where unions have been able to retain a central role in the operation of apprenticeship systems, such as Germany, they have actively been able to shape the (re)definition of occupations and the quality of functional skills acquired by workers. This success raises a question of whether unions, more generally, could look to reposition themselves for renewal around modernized notions of craft and occupation. The increased prevalence of occupational licensing in economies such as the United Kingdom and the United States, and to some extent a renewed interest in apprenticeships (Bosch and Charest 2010), suggests such a possibility. However, occupational labour markets are contingent on the type of strong, encompassing, and cooperative institutions that are so lacking in many countries, and, even in economies such as Germany, the shrinking influence of employers' associations and industrial unions threatens the longer-term basis of the occupationally orientated skills model.

A third, and to some extent related, option for unions is to focus less on skills as a 'single issue' concern, but rather as a key component of a wider agenda of 'good work', as in the Swedish case. This takes the focus away from the acquisition of skills per se to their deployment, associated working conditions, and the organization of work. Whilst the evidence suggests that the Swedish 'good work' model is increasingly constrained by the dominance of shareholder value capitalism, it is also the case that single issue skills policy may appear something of a luxury for unions in the aftermath of the recent economic crisis. Union interests have increasingly shifted away from the skills agenda and workforce development to the protection of jobs and conditions; boxing has come more to the fore than dancing. However, if unions can develop new and innovative campaigns and strategies for jobs growth and sustainable high quality employment they may yet have a significant role to play in how skills are situated in future capitalist trajectories.

References

Amin, A. (ed) (1994) *Post-Fordism: A Reader*, Oxford: Blackwell.

Arulampalam, W. and Booth, A. L. (1998) 'Training and Labour Market Flexibility: Is there a Trade-Off?', *British Journal of Industrial Relations*, 36(4): 521–536.

Ashton, D. and Green, F. (1996) *Education, Training and the Global Economy*, London: Edward Elgar.

Barley, S (1996) *The New World of Work*, London: British-North America Committee.

Batt, R., Holman, D., and Holtgrewe, U. (2009) 'The Globalization of Service Work: Comparative Institutional Perspectives on Call Centres', *Industrial and Labor Relations Review*, 62(4): 453–488.

Becker, G. (1975) *Human Capital*, New York: Columbia University Press.

Bell, D. (1973) *The Coming of Post-Industrial Society*, New York: Basic Books.

Boheim, R. and Booth, A. L. (2004) 'Trade Union Presence and Employer-Provided Training in Great Britain', *Industrial Relations*, 43(3): 520–545.

Booth, A. L., Francesconi, M., and Zoega, G. (2003) 'Unions, Work-Related Training and Wages: Evidence for British Men', *Industrial and Labor Relations Review*, 57: 68–91.

Bosch, G. and Charest, J. (2010) *Vocational Training: International Perspectives*, New York: Routledge.

Bowman, J. (2005) 'Employers and the Politics of Sill Formation in a Coordinated Market Economy: Collective Action and Class Conflict in Norway', *Politics and Society*, 33(4): 567–594.

Braverman, H. (1974) *Labor and Monopoly Capital*, New York: Monthly Review Press.

Brunello, G. (2004) 'Labour Market Institutions and the Complementarity between Education and Training in Europe', in D. Checchi, and C. Lucifora (eds), *Education, Training and Labour Market Outcomes in Europe*. New York: Macmillan: 188–210.

Buchanan, J., Watson, I., and Briggs, C. (2004) 'Skill and the Renewal of Labour: The Classicial Wage-Earner Model and Left Productivism in Australia', in C. Warhurst, I. Grugulis, and E. Keep (eds), *The Skills that Matter*, Basingstoke: Palgrave Macmillan: 186–206.

Cave, A. and Coats, D. (1999) 'Partnership: The Challenges and Opportunities', in *Tomorrow's Unions*, London: TUC.

Cockburn, C. (1991) *Brothers: Male Dominance and Technical Change*, London: Pluto Press.

Cooney, R. and Stuart, M. (2012) *Trade Unions and Workplace Training*, New York: Routledge.

Drucker, P. (1993) *Post-Capitalist Society*, Oxford: Butterworth Heinemann.

Findlay, P. and Warhurst, C. (2011) 'Union Learning Funds and Trade Union Revitalization: A New Tool in the Toolkit?', *British Journal of Industrial Relations*, 49(S1): 115–134.

Freeman, R. B. and Medoff, J. L. (1984) *What do Unions do?* New York: Basic Books.

Gallie, D. (2007) 'Production Regimes, Employment Regimes and the Quality of Work', in D. Gallie (ed), *Employment Regimes and the Quality of Work*, Oxford: Oxford University Press.

Giddens, A. (1991) *Modernity and Self-identity*, Cambridge: Polity Press.

Green, F., Machin, S., and Wilkinson, D. (1999) 'Trade Unions and Training: Practices in British Workplaces', *Industrial and Labor Relations Review*, 53(3): 443–462.

Greenwood, I. and Randle, H. (2007) 'Teamwork, Restructuring and Skills in the UK and Sweden', *European Journal of Industrial Relations*, 13(3): 361–377.
Greenwood, I. and Stuart, M. (2006) 'Employability and the Flexible Economy: Some Considerations of the Politics and Contradictions of the European Employment Strategy', in L. E. Alonson and M. Martinez Lucio (eds), *Employment Relations in a Changing Society*, Basingstoke: Palgrave MacMillan: 104–119.
Guest, D. E. and Peccei, R. (2001) 'Partnership at Work: Mutuality and the Balance of Advantage', *British Journal of Industrial Relations*, 39(2): 207–236.
Hall, P. A. and Soskice D. (eds) (2001) *Varieties of Capitalism*, Oxford: Oxford University Press.
Hampson, I. (2004) 'Training Reform in a Weakened State: Australia 1987–2000', in C. Warhurst, I. Grugulis, and E. Keep (eds), *The Skills that Matter*, Basingstoke: Palgrave: 72–90.
Harvey, D. (1989) *The Condition of Postmodernity*, Oxford: Basil Blackwell.
Heyes, J. and Stuart, M. (1998) 'Bargaining for Skills: Trade Unions and Training in the Workplace', *British Journal of Industrial Relations*, 36(3): 459–467.
Hoque, K. and Bacon, N. (2011) 'Assessing the Impact of Union Learning Representatives on Training: Evidence from a Matched Sample of ULRs and Managers', *Work, Employment and Society*, 25(2): 218–233.
Huzzard, T. (2000) *Labouring to Learn: Union Renewal in Swedish Manufacturing*, Umeå: Boréa.
Huzzard, T. (2004) 'Constructing the Competent Individual: Trade Union Roles, Responses and Rhetoric', in C. Garsten and K. Jacobsson (eds), *Learning to be Employable*, Basingstoke: Palgrave: 107–130.
Huzzard, T., Gregory, D., and Scott, R. (eds) (2004) *Strategic Unionism and Partnershp*, Basingstoke: Palgrave.
Jacobsson, K. (2004) 'A European Politics for Employability', in C. Garsten and K. Jacobsson (eds), *Learning to be Employable*, Basingstoke: Palgrave: 42–62.
Johansson, J. and Abrahamsson, L. (2009) 'The Good Work: A Swedish Trade Union Vision in the Shadow of Lean Production', *Applied Ergonomics*, 40: 775–780.
Kelly, J. (1996) 'Union Militancy and Social Partnership', in P. Ackers, C. Smith, and P. Smith (eds), *The New Workplace and Trade Unionism*, London: Routledge, 77–109.
Kern, M. and Schumann, H. (1984) *Das Ende der Arbeitsteilung? Rationalisierung in der industriellen Produktion*, Munich: Beck.
Kochan T. A. and Osterman, P. (1994) *The Mutual Gains Enterprise*, Boston: Harvard University Press.
Levinson, K. (2000) 'Codetermination in Sweden: Myth and Reality', *Economic and Industrial Democracy*, 21(4): 457–473.
Lloyd, C. and Payne, J. (2013) 'Changing Job Roles in the Norwegian and UK Fitness Industry: In Search of National Institutional Effects', *Work, Employment and Society*, 27(1).
Mahnkopf, B. (1991) 'The Skill Modernisation Strategies of German Trade Unions: Their Impact on Efficiency and Equality', *British Journal of Industrial Relations*, 30(1): 59–81.
Mahon, R (1991) 'From Solidaristic Wages to Solidaristic Work: A Post-Fordist Historic Compromise for Sweden?', *Economic and Industrial Democracy*, 12: 295–325.
Marks, A. and Huzzard, T. (2010) 'Employability and the ICT Worker: A Study of Employees in Scottish Small Businesses', *New Technology, Work and Employment*, 25(2): 167–181.
Marsden, D. (1999) *A Theory of Employment Systems*, Oxford: Oxford University Press.
Marschall, D. (2012) 'American Unions and the Institutionalization of Workplace Learning: Innovations for New Work Systems and Labour Movement Renewal', in R. Cooney and

M. Stuart (eds), *Trade Unions and Workplace Training: Issues and International Perspectives*, New York: Routledge: 147–167.

Martinez Lucio, M., Skule, S., Kruse, W., and Trappmann, V. (2007) 'Regulating Skill Formation in Europe: A Comparison of German, Norwegian and Spanish Polices on Transferable Skills', *European Journal of Industrial Relations*, 13(3): 323–340.

Mathews, J. (1993) 'The Industrial Relations of Skill Formation', *International Journal of Human Resource Management*, 4(3): 591–609.

Mincer, J. (1958) 'Investments in Human Capital and Personal Income Distribution', *Journal of Political Economy*, LXVI(4): 281–302.

Munro, A. and Rainbird, H. (2004) 'Opening Doors as well as Banging on Tables: An Assessment of UNISON/Employer Partnerships on Learning in the UK Public Sector', *Industrial Relations Journal*, 35(5): 419–433.

Ok, W. and Tergeist, P. (2003) 'Improving Workers' Skills: Analytical Evidence and the Role of the Social Partners', OECD Social, Employment and Migration Working Papers no. 10, Paris.

Pfeffer, J. (1994) *Competitive Advantage through People*. Boston: Harvard Business School Press.

Phillmore, J. (1997) 'Trade Unions and the National Training Reform Agenda in Australia, 1983–1996', *International Journal of Training and Development*, 1(1): 34–48.

Piore, M. J. and Sabel, C. (1984) *The Second Industrial Divide*, New York: Basic Books.

Rainbird, R. and Stuart, M. (2011) 'The State and the Union Learning Agenda in Britain', *Work, Employment and Society*, 25(2): 202–217.

Rifkin, J. (1995) *The End of Work* New York: Tarcher and Putnam.

Sandberg, Å., Broms, G., Grip, A., Sundström, L., Steen, J., and Ullmark, P. (1992) *Technological Change and Co-determination in Sweden*, Philadelphia: Temple University Press.

Streeck, W. (1989) 'Skills and the Limits of New-Liberalism: The Enterprise of the Future as a Place of Learning', *Work, Employment and Society*, 3(1): 80–104.

Streeck, W. (1994) 'Training and the New Industrial Relations: A Strategic Role for Unions?', in M. Regini (ed), *The Future of Labour Movements*, London: Sage: 250–269.

Stuart, M. (1996) 'The Industrial Relations of Training: A Reconsideration of Training Arrangements', *Industrial Relations Journal*, 27(3): 30–44.

Stuart, M. (1999) 'Skill Formation and Restructuring within the Printing Industry', PhD thesis, University of Leeds.

Stuart, M. (2001) 'Contesting Partnership? Evaluating the Demise of a National Training Agreement', *Journal of Vocational Education and Training*, 53(1): 5–20.

Stuart, M. and Martinez Lucio, M. (2005) *Partnership and the Modernization of Employment Relations*, Abingdon: Routledge.

Stuart, M., Cook, H., Cutter, J., and Winterton, J. (2011) *Evaluation of the Union Learning Fund and unionlearn, Final Report*, London: TUC.

Taylor, P. and Ramsay, H. (1998) 'Unions, Partnership and HRM: Sleeping with the Enemy?', *International Journal of Employment Studies*, 6(2): 115–143.

Taylor, R. (1994) *The Future of the Trade Unions*, London: Andre Deutsch.

Teige, B. K. and Stuart, M. (2012) 'Trade Union Involvement in Lifelong Learning in Norway', in R. Cooney and M. Stuart (eds), *Trade Unions and Workplace Training*, New York: Routledge, 126–144.

Thedvall, R. (2004) 'Do it Yourself: Making up the Self-Employed Individual in the Swedish Public Employment Service', in C. Garsten and K. Jacobsson (eds), *Learning to be Employable*, Basingstoke: Palgrave, 131–151.

Trappmann, V. (2012) 'The Shifting Role of Trade Unions in the German VET System', in R. Cooney and M. Stuart, M. (eds), *Trade Unions and Workplace Training*, New York: Routledge, 101–125.

Walton, R. E, McKersie, R. B (1965) *A Behavioral Theory of Labor Negotiations*, New York: McGraw-Hill.

Winterton, J. (2007) 'Building Social Dialogue over Training and Learning: European and National Developments', *European Journal of Industrial Relations*, 13(3): 281–300.

Winterton, J. and Winterton, R. (1994) *Collective Bargaining and Consultation over Continuing Vocational Training*, Sheffield: Employment Department.

CHAPTER 13

A WORKING LIFETIME OF SKILL AND TRAINING NEEDS

GÜNTHER SCHMID

INTRODUCTION

THIS chapter provides an overview of the key factors that shape individuals skill formation, including the challenges and options. Reference is made throughout the chapter to the growing literature on transitional labour markets (TLMs), which examines the changing links between work and life beyond standard employment relationships. Studies based on TLMs do not rely on simplifying assumptions that commonly underpin analysis and policy concerned with working life: linear conceptions of social and labour flows implicit in the 'standard life cycle' are avoided, and breadwinning-carer conceptions of male and female roles in life are eschewed. Instead, considerable attention is devoted to understanding the diversity of approaches to handling five types of critical transition over the life course: flows to and from work associated with education; raising a family; spells of unemployment or non-employment; retirement; and transitions within paid employment. Understanding diversity also implies the rejection of deregulation as a solution and instead recognizes that transitions involving work are highly structured and profoundly shaped by institutional links between the state, market, and family. The central concern of this tradition is the notion of risk: how are the risks associated with these transitions currently distributed between the state, market, and families? How can risks be redistributed to achieve better outcomes for the economy and fairer outcomes across the population at large?

The chapter starts by clarifying the key problems to be addressed if we are to properly understand the challenges involved in skill formation. It highlights the need for a life course (as opposed to a life cycle) framing of the issue, provides an overview of how labour market restructuring is reshaping the distribution of working life risks, and identifies the critical implications of these developments for training and skills. The second section provides a short overview of the TLM approach, which has both analytical and policy uses, and briefly sketches the main challenges of skill-capacity formation over the life course in Europe. The bulk of the chapter then examines the key issue of how risks associated with investing in the development of individuals' skills capacities are shared. Attention is devoted to insights provided by two different types of perspective: those from economics on the one hand and from behavioural science on the other. The chapter concludes by reflecting on the value of seeing working life as being centrally concerned with lifelong learning using the insights provided by the TLM framework.

Life Courses, Labour Market Restructuring, Changing Skills, and Training Needs

The concept of the life cycle emerged at the end of the nineteenth century. Influenced by the Darwinian theory of evolution and natural selection and by Spencer's socio-biological approach, human life was considered as sequence determined by biological stages of age, kinship relationships, and sexual division of labour between unpaid female and paid male work. The labour market was regarded as a market of labour demand and supply, but implicitly also as a social institution with the underlying assumption that the wage of the male breadwinner should provide decent living standards for the private household (Mortimer and Shanahan 2004; Anxo and Erhel 2006; Anxo et al. 2010). Social anthropology added the idea of transmitting social and economic capital over generations, and psychology saw socialization and personal identity-building as a process of maturation (Erikson 1968; O'Rand and Krecker 1990). As neoclassical economists initially paid little attention to the role of time in individual choices, in the first half of the 1960s Modigliani (1998) developed the theory of life cycle income, stating that risk averse and rational individuals endeavour to smooth their consumption over the life span by saving in their early years and spending their savings when retired.

Despite some modification during the 1980s and 1990s, allowing, for instance, for habits or peer groups playing a role in individual decisions, neoclassical economists continued to perceive time as cyclical and life transitions as following the traditional tripartite sequencing of life, that is, a period of education, followed by the periods of employment, and retirement. This is reflected in the idea of optimal sequencing over the life cycle, whereby people invest as much as possible in education before entering the labour market and then collect the returns of investment over their life course (Heckman 2000).

As it became clear that the life cycle concept failed to explain all the transitions observed over the life span and the growing heterogeneity of life transitions in modern societies, in the late 1960s and early 1970s, sociologists started to develop a broader framework that was eventually labelled the life course approach. Elder et al. (2004) argue that while the life cycle entails some form of natural and normative reproductive and iterative cyclical process, the life course perspective involves an evolutionary approach in that it considers individuals' life transitions as lifelong developments embedded in a social structure. According to this approach, individual life is not lived independently. Transitions in one person's life entail transitions for other people as well. If daughters, for instance, transit early to motherhood, they induce her own mothers' early transition to grandparenthood, with respective repercussions for their roles, responsibilities, and social identities; the new mothers, then, might still think of themselves as children and expect their mothers to help care for their children, whereas the early grandmothers may have to meet the additional constraint of their decision to participate in the labour market. If daughters, however, transit late to motherhood—which, at least in Europe, seems to be becoming the rule rather than the exception—they may find that their mothers are at an age in which they need care themselves rather than being able to provide unpaid care services, a situation which certainly increases the problems related to the so-called rush-hour of life. In addition, extended life expectation and repeated marriages may change the 'natural' three-generation family into a contingent multiple-generation family (Saraceno 2008).

Another empirical backdrop to the life course orientation is the acknowledgment of increasing fractures in employment careers through non-standard forms of employment, in particular part-time work, temporary work (including temp-agency work), casual work, own-account work, and self-employment. For example, the aggregate non-standard employment rate, which comprises all non-standard forms of employment by controlling for overlaps (e.g. part-timers in temporary work or in self-employment), increased in Europe from about 16 per cent (1998) to 18 per cent (2008) for men; and from about 19 per cent (1998) to 25 per cent (2008) for women (Schmid 2011).[1] Such breaks in continuous employment careers creates high risks in social security, in particular in old age, and research shows consistently that these risks apply especially to the low skilled.

Skill formation in early childhood and its development in schools and vocational or academic institutions and during the employment career becomes a crucial element in the overall design of life course insurance. Current labour markets clearly reflect the tremendous unequal distribution of the unemployment risk and the huge differences in employment opportunities according to levels of education. In many European Union member states (EU-MS), the difference in unemployment rates between poorly and highly educated people is three- to fourfold. Even during recessions (as exemplified in 2008/9), highly educated people often face unemployment risks that correspond to the common full employment definition, that is, around 3 to 4 per cent of the corresponding active labour force. Differences in actual market skills (i.e. skills of high demand) cannot fully explain this advantage in the incidence of unemployment; qualification in the form of educational credentials or ascribed competences still seem

1 For the USA, see Kalleberg (2009); for Australia, see Buchanan et al. (2001).

to be one of the best insurance devices against unemployment. Differences in income opportunities between poorly and highly educated people through labour market participation are not less striking. Whereas employment rates in the EU-MS of highly educated people aged 20–64 ranged between 78 and 88 per cent in 2010, those of poorly educated people varied between 29 and 68 per cent; the overall gap in employment rates between poorly (53 per cent) and highly educated (83 per cent) people in EU-27 amounts to 30 percentage points.

Forecasts of skill needs show consistently that the demand for high skills in all occupations will increase further but decline for skilled manual occupations (agricultural, craft and trade workers, machine operators). However, the demand for elementary occupations (labourers) with a medium or high skill background will also increase (Cedefop 2010; European Commission 2012a). In Europe, the working age population, however, started to decline from 2013 onwards, which means that—despite increasing levels of graduates from universities—the demand for high skilled workers is becoming more pressing. Between 2010 and 2020, only the elder cohorts (50–54 and especially 55–64) will grow in numbers, whereas the younger cohorts (especially 15–24) will decline. One consequence of an increasingly older workforce is the risk of skill obsolescence. Enhanced life-long-learning (LLL) policies, therefore, will be crucial in order to keep people employable, to allow them to work longer, and to facilitate career-oriented transitions. LLL for low-skilled workers becomes especially urgent as the polarization between the high and low skilled creates further income inequalities. In addition, all studies on future skill needs emphasize rising levels of 'soft' skills related to the tasks of the so-called knowledge economy. Such skill sets include making complex issues understandable, solving unpredictable problems, making difficult decisions, detecting and closing knowledge gaps, and coping with multiple tasks. These skills are especially needed in the domain of secondary service occupations, namely among lawyers, managers, engineers, and scientific, life science, and health, teaching as well as care professionals.

What are the appropriate responses to these challenges? Improving the ability to predict skill needs is clearly one answer. More fully worked-out answers are supplied in the next section.

Transitional Labour Markets as an Analytical Framework

TLMs concentrate on five critical events over the life course: transitions from education to employment, transitions from one job to another (including changing jobs and working time within firms), transitions between household activities and gainful work, transitions between employment and unemployment, and transitions from employment to invalidity or retirement. Each of these transitions is associated with specific risks. First, the risk of insufficient or eroding income capacity over the life course; second, the risk of income volatility due to fluctuating demand and job-to-job transitions or even the risk of in-work poverty due to low wages; third, the risk of restricted income capacities due to social obligations such as child care or elderly care; fourth, the risk of total wage income loss due to involuntary unemployment; fifth, the risk of reduced or zero income capacity due to disability, chronic illness, or old age (Schmid 2008, 165–212).

The theory of TLMs assumes that specific risks require specific securities. According to the principle of requisite variety in general systems theory, the higher the variety of risk, the higher the variety of social security should be. Due to path dependency, however, labour market institutions often fail to adjust quickly or effectively enough to tackle new risks stemming from the increasing diversity of labour markets. They also often follow a logic different from that required by the new risks or do not recognize the normative or behavioural foundations of social risk management, thereby creating the well-known phenomenon of institutional misfits (Schmid 2008, 2013).

Three general strategies of social risk management can be distinguished: prevention and mitigation of risks, and coping with risks. Prevention directly tackles the causes of risk and should therefore be given priority. However, uncertainty looms large, making prevention impossible. Prevention can also be prohibitively expensive or restrict flexible adjustment. Mitigation and coping strategies, therefore, have to complement prevention.

From the TLM perspective, it does not make sense to protect people against the risk of insufficient or eroding skill capacities through high and long-term unemployment benefits. On the contrary, such generous benefits would damage more than resolve the underlying problem. Equally, in-work-benefits for unemployed youth do not make sense since they perpetuate the lack of skill capacities or social networks. Prevention is therefore the main solution here. To prevent youth unemployment, social risk management must start at kindergarten, in preschools, primary, and secondary schools. Both equal opportunities in elementary and secondary education adapted to a knowledge society and elementary social skills for communication and learning abilities have to be ensured at an early stage of the life course. Learning begets learning (Heckman 2000) and has to be considered as the first anchor for successful risk management in skill formation.

Second, each break in a continuous work career has to be considered as a lost opportunity for taking part in the competitive process of career promotion, above all within internal labour markets. This is the reason why women, in particular, who take parental leave for more than one or two years face considerable promotion and income risks that they will never be able to fully recover later on in their life course (Plantenga and Remey 2005; Romàn 2006; Anxo et al. 2010). According to tournament theory, the key issue when searching for job candidates is not the actual level of productivity but the interpersonal competition between employees. Internal career ladders are climbed by beating the competition at each step, whether this is by a length or by a nose. Unique to tournament structures is the fact that prizes are awarded according to the rank order at the finish, not the absolute performance of the participant. The consequences of not participating can differ considerably and depend on both what part of the race is missed (start, middle, finish), and how many rounds (duration) one fails to attend. So, a second general risk-sharing device is to manage critical transitions over the life course in a way that they smooth career breaks and maintain strong links to the labour market (Lazear and Rosen 1981; Becker and Huselid 1992).

Third, against the neoliberal assumption that individual marginal productivity determines the size and structure of employment, dynamic and sustainable efficiency depends on cooperation of multiple skill-sets. Thus, the suggestion by James Heckman (2000), for instance—that educational or training investment in the elderly workforce would not be beneficial since neither employer nor worker could reap investment returns due to upcoming retirement—is not built on sound theory. Furthermore, even when mature aged workers transit into retirement they still retain links with the labour market because of their purchasing power. Only a trained and competent 'silver generation' worker is able to consume and enjoy high quality goods and services produced in the labour market, in particular goods and services related to IT technologies, apart from the fact that higher education contributes to extending his or her life expectation. Recent research provides robust empirical evidence that training can keep older workers longer in the labour market; older workers who do not receive training on-the-job are more likely to retire than those with training. Even more importantly, the effect of training on labour market participation is higher for poorly educated older workers (Fouarge and Schils 2009; Picchio and van Ours 2011).

As part of the European Employment Strategy (EES), the European Union followed these insights in 2002 by setting precise targets through its Education and Training 2010 Work Programme embedded in the Open Method of Coordination. This work programme clearly emphasized early intervention and advocated five benchmarks to reduce the risk of insufficient skill capacities by 2010: (1) the percentage of low-achieving 15-year-olds in reading literacy should decrease by at least 20 per cent compared with 2000; (2) an EU average of no more than 10 per cent of early school leavers should be achieved; (3) at least 85 per cent of 22-year-olds should have completed upper secondary education; (4) the total number of graduates in mathematics, science, and technology should increase by at least 15 per cent, and the level of respective gender imbalance should decrease compared with 2000; (5) increasing the participation of the adult working age population (25–64 year olds) in LLL to at least 12.5 per cent.

Despite some progress, Europe is still far from showing any clear improvement in competences and education corresponding to the rhetoric of a 'knowledge society'. As the PISA reports of the Organisation for Economic Co-operation and Development show, only a few countries have reached the benchmark of 15.5 per cent of students below proficiency level II in reading comprehension; in many countries, this proportion has even increased. Furthermore, the speed of progress preventing early school leaving was well below the Lisbon goal by 2010. Performance related to the LLL objective was impressive on average; however, the positive Scandinavian bias hides the fact that most other European member states did not reach the target, and low skilled people (those at highest risk of unemployment) often do not profit from continuous education and training measures. As mitigation or coping strategy, the EES rightly set the target that

EU-MS should ensure for youth a training place or a job after six months' unemployment at the latest, and for adult a training place or a job offer after twelve months of unemployment at the latest. However, as high long-term unemployment figures, especially for low skilled people, show, many EU-MS still are far from reaching these targets.

Modest success in preventing strategies and significant failures in mitigating or coping strategies raise questions about the appropriate strategies for equipping and supporting lifelong transitions. How can and should skill-related risks be shared in a fair way between state, market (firms), and families?

Sharing Risks of Investing In Skill Capacities from an Economic Perspective

Life course—as opposed to life cycle—policy suggests applying the principles of social insurance rather than individual savings accounts in the face of sharing risks associated with investment in education and learning. There are a number of economic reasons why the state should become involved in sharing risks and why these matters should not be left solely to individual savings or precautionary measures taken by employers or employees (see, for example, Barr 2004; Chapman and Ryan 2005; Jacobs and van der Ploeg 2006).

The first reason why the state should become involved is related to limited savings. Most people with insufficient earning capacities at the beginning of their life course are not able to compensate for their deficiencies during their life course. Studies investigating the reasons for non-participation in training on the supply side emphasize financial bottlenecks as important determinants, especially among low-skilled people (OECD 2005: 314). On the demand side, vocational education and training costs decrease for employers as employee skills improve through higher learning capacities and lower risks of failing in training courses.

The second reason why the state should help shoulder the risks related to education and lifelong learning is failure of the capital market. The market does not grant credit to those most in need of such measures. High risks of default make banks reluctant to grant study loans to young or mature adults. Unlike a housing loan, an education or training loan has no collateral the bank can sell if the loan recipient defaults on repayment. The result is that banks are not interested in underwriting skill capacity investments unless at least one of two conditions is met: (a) they can offer high interest rates with deterrent effects on prospective applicants; and (b) they are offered securities afforded by assets other than 'human capital'. Prospective investors without sufficient financial resources or property will not be able to invest in education or lifelong learning. This has four important consequences: a loss of talent and, hence, a cost to society as a whole; a loss of opportunity for individuals; deepening inequalities resulting from previous disadvantages related to family background and education; and the perpetuation of intergenerational inequality.

The third argument in favour of risk-sharing by the state is lack of equity. The people who call for investment in education or LLL may have the weakest position in private-household bargaining, even where government-assisted bank loans are an option. Government assistance in such cases is linked to means testing. This approach rests on the assumption that the individuals involved have equal access to household income, a supposition that might not hold for young dependent family members or women in a weak bargaining position. This condition would, in turn, restrict loan access for those family members who value skill capacity investments more than do the family members actually making the decision. Finally, risk aversion is intensified by the high uncertainty of returns for investments in education and in particular LLL (Heckman et al. 2002; Card et al. 2009).

What are the alternatives to government loans? Some countries have experimented with various forms of state subsidized individual training accounts, such as individual development accounts (IDA), individual learning accounts (ILA), and time-saving accounts (TSA) especially earmarked for vocational education and training. It is too early to assess these experiments, but most have been failures. Moral hazard and even fraud terminated some of them (e.g. the British ILA) as they were being implemented. In Sweden (where the idea originated), the schemes have never been implemented due to strong resistance by trade unions. Among various other schemes, individual learning budgets (ILB) that are not dependent on individual contributions and targeted training vouchers or training cheques appear promising in terms of o enhancing the skill capacities of both low skilled workers and SMEs (Cedefop 2009).

The strongest arguments in favour of such accounts are that they counterbalance the often arbitrary political discretion of publicly administrated social insurance, encourage individual responsibility, allow individual ownership and individual choice, and perhaps discourage tax evasion and increase incentives to participate in continuous education. The strongest arguments against are that individual training accounts escalate administrative costs, expose workers to market risks and the risk of poor investment choices, erode the benefit level provided to those with low earnings, undercut the sense of community responsibility and shared concerns that is embodied in social security, entail undesirably wide variation in benefits between members of different cohorts employing the same investment strategy, and by diverting revenues and introducing new risks (Diamond 1999: 21–24; Pearson and Martin 2005).

This balance between the pros and cons justifies a certain degree of scepticism about individual training accounts and raises the question as to whether combining social insurance principles and elements of individual savings would be more beneficial than state-subsidized individual training accounts. Income-contingent loans (ICL) are a possible alternative. In efficiency terms, they are designed explicitly to protect borrowers from excessive risks; in equity terms, they assist access because they have built-in insurance against the inability to repay (Barr 2004). In the TLM language, ICL are both: capacity building as well as consumption smoothing over the life course.

A noteworthy example is Australia's Higher Education Contribution Scheme (HECS), introduced in 1989 and amended in 1997 (Chapman and Ryan 2005). HECS goes beyond risk-pooling, which can be organized privately. It is a public–private risk-sharing device for financing higher education. All students are entitled to a loan regardless of family income. The debts must be repaid only if a stated income threshold is exceeded. The issues of default and moral hazard are effectively resolved by a government guarantee if default occurs and by repayment through the governmental tax authorities. Although the Australian scheme seems to be accepted, it has serious flaws. First, it has had no discernible effect on enlarging the proportion of university students from poor family backgrounds. It may have helped expanding overall university attendance, but it has made only the middle class (and perhaps women) better off without making the poor worse off, thereby violating one of the core principles of justice (Rawls 2001). To improve student access from disadvantaged socio-economic backgrounds more financial support has to be provided. Furthermore, the discretionary measure of fixing an earnings threshold beyond which debts must be repaid creates uncertainty, which is prohibiting the most risk-averse students from low socio-economic background from participating.

As its inventors suggest, ICL could also be used for LLL. Apart from the critical points already mentioned, even more practical problems exist in this field. Most LLL is piecemeal and ad hoc, a characteristic that makes it difficult to attribute precisely the proportion of rising income to these kinds of fuzzy investments. And unlike higher education, which generates overwhelmingly general and transferable skills, continuous vocational education and training produce skills that are more company-specific, less transferable, and therefore riskier. Thus, employers and employees would have to share LLL related risk or the company to shoulder all of it. This probably leads, however, to the breakthrough of the 'Matthew' principle that the people who profit most from company-specific training are those who already have a strong position within the company or who enjoy overall employability on the labour market. Moreover, recent literature shows that company-financed training for skilled workers has many more general traits than is usually assumed (Feuer et al. 1991; Acemoglu and Pischke 1998).

Are there alternatives to state-subsidized individual training accounts? It should be clear by now that one-size-fits-all solutions are ineffective in this complicated area of education and LLL. The case for sharing risks through social insurance does not seem strong. After all, the externalities related to LLL might not be as major as those related to primary, secondary, and higher education, and market failures related to LLL might not be as strong. And risk-sharing between employers and employees should be assumed in many instances. Nonetheless, untapped qualification potential, looming shortages of skilled labour, and disadvantaged groups legitimate state involvement. The involvement of the state can take different forms, and second-best solutions are still available through other forms of collective insurance: dual learning systems, redistributive state investments, drawing rights, and collective agreements.

Dual Learning Systems

All reasoning and evidence on the causes of educational poverty as the backdrop of exclusionary transitions hint at the importance of the educational level received in an early stage of the life course. Life course oriented policy therefore must and can reverse the long-standing repercussions of such early disadvantage. It seems that the basic idea of apprenticeship—learning on the job complemented with generalized and eventually universally acknowledged forms of education—remains one promising solution. It is a strategy that can be implemented in variable forms depending on the institutional pathway of educational system, and in principle at all stages of the life course, thereby reversing the dead-end sequences of first-start failures.

If one looks at good practice cases, one can find this strategy realized in various forms. In addition to the 'dual' character of learning, a common element of this strategy is that the state shares the risk not in the form of cash transfers but in the form of in-kind-transfers, that is, educational services and provision of material and legal infrastructure. According to recent research (Callan et al. 2008), In-kind-transfers seem to be more efficient in equalizing income capacity than cash transfers, especially for the disadvantaged target group.

To mention only two examples: in some German states (*Bundeslaender*), especially in Baden-Wuerttemberg, vocational academies (*Berufsakademien, BA*) offer students with a (vocational) high school degree a dual education and training programme (Berufsakademie 2013). Firms contract young students for three years and offer them a career perspective at the firm in order to raise the expectation horizon of risk-adverse students. Students take alternatively courses for three months at the BA, and three-month training courses in the firm. Firms pay training allowances between €400 and €1,600 that may be complemented by state subsidies. The state shares the costs by financing the BA. Between 80 and 90 per cent of BA-leavers are subsequently taken on by the firm or quickly of disadvantaged a job elsewhere in the labour market. The reliance on vocational tracks, of course, has the disadvantage of narrowing the choice of available jobs—especially from a life course perspective. This disadvantage, however, can be mitigated by the broadening of vocational profiles and by opening access to higher education tracks.

In the United States, a new kind of high school programme known as 'career academy' has proliferated in the past quarter century. The programme concentrates on low-income districts, combines job placement, college preparation and classes beyond vocational trades, from accounting to health care. Career academies offer students experience in the workplace and help them get paid jobs while they pursue standard academic coursework. A recent evaluation found that most participants, especially young men, had—eight years after high school—significantly higher earnings than a control group (Kemple and Willner 2008).

Redistributive State Investments

The state can use its redistributive capacity of taxation to ensure a second chance for people who have been unlucky on the education and training market. This option could be a way of financing periodically targeted programmes for lifting the overall level of knowledge and competence of the disadvantaged.[2] An instructive example is the successful Swedish 'Knowledge Lift' (*kunshaftsliftet*) programme, which spent an annual sum of about €350 million on upgrading the knowledge and competence of low-skilled employees or unemployed persons between 1997 and 2002 (Albrecht et al. 2005).

Drawing Rights

Entitlements to unemployment benefits can be 'activated' as 'social drawing rights' in the form of training vouchers or job subsidies. Supiot (2001) defines such drawing rights as rights built on the notion of people's civil status. These rights relate to the exercise of liberty, so their use also implies individual responsibility, including the acknowledgement of quantitative (financial) and qualitative (social) limits. The quantitative limit in extended risk communities of this sort implies the acceptance of fair co-financing. The qualitative limit implies the acceptance of coordination in using the drawing rights, usually by way of negotiation and mutual agreements, that is, through soft forms of governance. The concept of active labour market policy has already broadened the insurance principle to include those unemployed people who need vocational education or training in order to find a new job. Job subsidies for the unskilled can thereby be interpreted as employability measures. For that target group, learning on a matched job in a company is a functional equivalent of formal training (Dustmann and Meghir 2005). The spiralling need for continuous vocational education and training indicates that the entitlement should be expanded to include vouchers for low-skilled employees if they have accumulated unemployment benefit entitlements for a number of years. Denmark and Sweden have long practised this transformation of unemployment benefits into education-and-training benefits. Finally, short-time work can be considered as a risk-sharing device in favour of maintaining jobs for skilled workers (European Commission 2012a, 21–3).

Collective Agreements

Collective agreements can include individual training or time-saving accounts whereby the state guarantees transferability and liquidity of entitlements and funds. Yet another possibility is an agreement on working-time reductions in the form of investment in which employees agree to use reduced working time for education and training and thereby share the costs with their employers. Here again, the state can enter the game—as is often the case, for instance, in the Netherlands—and enlarge the risk community by the mandatory extension of such collective agreements to all workers in order to prevent cut-throat price competition between companies.

[2] This approach corresponds to Dworkin's (2000) theory of equality (another normative pillar in TLM theory), in which he recommended periodic redistribution to correct for random inequalities in order to make access to resources equal.

Sharing Risks of Investing in Skill Capacities from a Behavioural Perspective

It would be a mistake to consider risk aversion only in economic terms. Prospect theory, or the psychological theory of intuitive beliefs and choices, teaches us that risk aversion is not only a matter of rational choice that can be resolved with the right economic incentives (Kahneman 2011). The way that people perceive risks greatly determines their daily choices, and utility is not only a matter of income maximization but also of cognitive and emotional relationships. The question, therefore, arises as to how risk aversion can be overcome in order to induce people to accept more risks and the increased responsibility that goes with them.

Most people tend towards myopic risk perceptions and underestimate, for instance, the risk of unemployment or large income loss due to the erosion or lack of skills over the life course. Furthermore, losses loom larger than gains in risk perception. Most people prefer small certain gains over large uncertain gains or 'a bird in the hand to two in the bush'. Yet most people are extremely averse to loss. They do not like to give things away even if the prospect of gain is bright; the loss–gain ratio is about two to one. It thus makes a difference in perception whether one frames a risk in terms of loss alternatives or gain alternatives.

Important conclusions for the design of risk-sharing policy can be drawn from these insights. Daniel Bernoulli (1954), one of the founders of probability theory and risk management, gives a clue. As he pointed out, a beggar will not give up begging for a workfare job, for he would lose his ability (or skill capacity) to beg. He has to be offered something more. What could this 'more' be? TLM theory suggests a specific solution to this psychological problem: the extension of the expectation horizon through a set of opportunity structures available in the most critical events during the life course.

The first such pillar in an extension of the expectation horizon is the establishment of new social rights that go beyond employment (Supiot 2001). These social rights are new in content, scope, and nature. They are new in that they cover subjects unfamiliar to industrial wage-earners: rights to education and training, to appropriate working hours, to a family life and to occupational redeployment, retraining or vocational rehabilitation. Their scope is also new since they cover not only 'regular' wage-earners but also the self-employed; the semi-self-employed; and temp-agency, contract and marginal workers. They are new in nature because they often take the form of vouchers or social drawing rights, which allow workers to rely on solidarity within defined and perhaps collectively bargained limits when exercising their new freedoms. These new securities can no longer be seen as being given in exchange for subordination (as in the old employment contract), but as the foundations of a new freedom to act. They can be considered as active social securities, which go hand in hand with worker's initiatives to shoulder the risks of flexible employment relationships instead of restricting them.

The second pillar for extending the expectation horizon consists of stepping stones and bridges for overcoming critical events during the life course. The tendency to overestimate immediate small risks and underestimating distant large risks leads people to perceive the risk of being stuck in the low-wage sector to be greater than the risk of long-term unemployment resulting, say, from being too choosy about the jobs they accept. Active labour market policies, therefore, should not be confined solely to offering jobs and placing individuals in work. Follow-up measures, especially in the form of lifelong learning opportunities, are required for transforming sheer workfare measures into stepping stones to a sustainable job career.

The third pillar in the set of opportunity structures is psychological bridges for overcoming asymmetric risk perception. Acceptance of a risky new job often requires abandonment of familiar certainties, such as confidence in one's own productive capacities or the reliability of social assistance benefits possibly supplemented by a small amount of clandestine employment. Among people from a relatively poor background, the psychological dimension of risk aversion is compounded by the financial dimension, with the former paradoxically sometimes being even more important than the latter, as Bernoulli's beggar has already suggested. Motivation studies have shown that poor people are especially dependent on the sociability of their peer groups. But training and education often imply a change of peer group, particularly when job mobility is required. Hence, it might be advisable to arrange group measures instead of individualized measures in such cases.

Another implication for programme design is to ensure that fall-back positions are always clearly available. It is therefore important for people from financially insecure backgrounds to have the opportunity to try out several jobs without benefits being withdrawn immediately if one option does not immediately lead to success. Trust in such sets of opportunities rules out workfare strategies that rigidly preclude trial and error as a productive job search strategy. For the same reason, the implementation of training measures for these target groups should also avoid the creation of exaggerated expectations, which can be nurtured, say, when a job candidate is required to pass formal examinations.

With respect to tertiary education, the Bologna reform of 1999 (introducing the Bachelor-Master differentiation) will, among other reforms, reduce the risk of choosing the wrong course of study and encourage students to take more demanding courses of study. The flexibility and variety of the new system also allow students to wait in the presence of uncertainty until they feel ready to invest in the next step of their career (Jacobs and van der Ploeg 2006: 555–6).

The fourth pillar for extending the expectation horizon is the establishment and reinforcement of learning communities. Coping with the risks of education and training have demonstrated the importance of uncertainty, including that of family timing, of the needs to care for children, of the skills required by the future training market, and of one's position in the market wage distribution decisions after investment. These kinds of uncertainty defy precise advance calculation of financial contributions and benefits, for the risks occur only in the process of doing. It is therefore necessary to design forms of social contract or 'covenant' that make constant revisions possible in order to recalibrate the balance of costs and benefits. Social insurance against new risks thus requires soft forms of governance that allow learning in the process of implementation (Korver and Schmid 2012).

Working Life as Lifelong Learning: An Overview

Modern labour markets, first of all, are characterized by an increasing variety of employment relationships, reflecting new modes of production due to new technologies and increasing international competition, new forms of work organization and new work–life risks related to social and demographic changes. The EES adopted the concept of 'flexicurity' in response to these new challenges which in the meantime, however, are much contested.[3] It did not deliver enough 'good jobs', so that the European Commission had to acknowledge 'intensified wage polarisation' as the key to understand rising income inequalities and risk of poverty in work (European Commission 2012b: 12). This chapter has therefore argued for a new, high-skill equilibrium of flexibility and security based on the concept of TLM.

Second, LLL is an essential ingredient if not the core of the strategy that builds on the concepts of skill capacity (not on 'human capital') and the life course (not on 'life cycle'). The capability of learning and thereby building up a stock of adaptable skills and competences starts—as learning psychologists emphasize—early in life with emotional skills, in particular with a willingness to engage in trial and error (with possible failures) backed up by the emotional (and, if necessary, actual) support of parents or other peers as devices ensuring effectiveness.

Third, the schooling phase of formal learning provides the basic knowledge and skills that are needed for a person's whole life: the capabilities of language, reading, mathematical and logical abstraction, insights into the laws of nature (including animals, plants, and ecology), complemented by 'soft' or second grade abilities of learning such as problem solving, communication, conflict resolution, detection of knowledge gaps and filling these gaps, and, in some cases, the capability of tolerating ambiguity and persistence in following goals set by oneself or commonly agreed. Learning theory thereby emphasizes that children and young adults not only have different cognitive abilities but also different speeds of learning. Labour market segmentation may start in school if the mobilization of cognitive capacities is cut off through institutional barriers at too early a stage. Furthermore, many children might need a more practical environment before

[3] On the concept of 'flexicurity', see Tros (2004) and Wilthagen and EC (2007); for critical assessments, see Keune and Serrano (2014).

starting with abstract and symbolic work. Bringing the world of work, in one way or the other, into school as early as possible seems to become an important precondition for a successful and sustainable transition from school to work.

Fourth, the transition from school to work is the most critical event for most people's working life careers. Compared to older generations, this process becomes more and more complex and it takes more and more time until it ends in something that can be called a 'regular employment relationship' (e.g. Brzinsky-Fay 2011). A successful management of risks related to this phase is of utmost importance since failures in this phase of the beginning working life will have concomitant scare effects. Initiating, supporting, and monitoring transitional employment opportunities that combine formal education and practical training in various ways and adjusted to individuals' and employers' needs are important new tasks of modern labour market services.

Fifth, as most young adults sooner or later raise families, the successful balancing (mostly unpaid) of family work and gainful labour market work becomes crucial for keeping up sustainable work careers. Navigating young adults through these critical transitions has become even more complicated as the traditional labour division between men and women regarding unpaid (yet socially obligatory) care work is increasingly being replaced by the paradigm of the 'adult worker family' in which both partners (more or less equally) share unpaid care and gainful employment responsibilities. Research provides plenty of evidence that a longer absence from the workplace will lead to severe wage punishment which in the later working life may never be made up. The most important finding is that intermediate part-time work may be the solution but only under the condition that the option to return to full-time is not only theoretically available but also practically realized. Otherwise, the transition from full-time into part-time will be a trap into poverty-in-work and, later on, into poverty-in-old age (Salverda and Mayhew 2009). In the context of skill and training needs, one important and often neglected reason for this is not just reduced earnings during part-time employment (in particular related to marginal jobs), but a reduced availability to take part in the continuous tournaments of allocating jobs.

Sixth, the next critical event in a working life may be unemployment, which calls for intelligent management. It has been shown that this risk now applies to more and more people compared with earlier life cohorts, yet it still is unequally distributed among socio-economic groups. Research provides plenty of evidence that a high education level is the first and most important security device preventing this risk. Furthermore, LLL does much to prevent or—later on—mitigate this risk. Effective labour market services (counselling, matching, subsidizing) to support the transition back to employment are another crucial precondition for coping with unemployment risks. Much neglected are the possibilities of internal adjustment mechanisms for preventing unemployment, in particular the instrument of short-time work (possibly combined with training) and corresponding instruments to ensure only extra the partial loss of income. As learning on the job is so crucial, even part-time work (combined with part-time unemployment benefits) may be a more and more important stepping stone back to 'regular employment' and for reducing long-term unemployment.

Seventh, the transition from employment to retirement is not only increasingly postponed (thereby adjusting to the ageing society) but also increasingly extended through combinations of part-time work and retirement benefits, through combinations of gainful 'regular' work and work for non-profit institutions (that may become, later on, the main work environment) or through a phase of (full-time) employment with easier tasks at lower wages, which may be combined with some kind of wage insurance. Research provides robust evidence that LLL, and in particular continuous on-the-job training, supports the maintenance of jobs for mature aged workers. It is often neglected that developed skill capacities also help people to adjust to a smart way of life after gainful employment, and moreover to be able to consume or utilize the intelligent products produced by the 'knowledge' economy.

References

Acemoglu, D. and Pischke, J.-S. (1998) 'Why Do Firms Train? Theory and Evidence', *Quarterly Journal of Economics*, 113: 993–1014.

Albrecht, J., van den Berg, G. J., and Vroman, S. (2005) 'The Knowledge Lift: The Swedish Adult Education Program That Aimed to Eliminate Low Worker Skill Levels', IZA Discussion Paper No. 1503, Bonn.

Anxo, D. and Erhel, C. (2006) 'Irreversibility of Time, Reversibility of Choices? The Life-Course Foundations of the Transitional Labour Market Approach', *Revue Française de Socio-Economie*, 1: 199–219.

Anxo, D., Bosch, G. and Rubery, J. (2010) 'Shaping the Life Course: a European Perspective', in D. Anxo, G. Bosch, and J. Rubery (eds), *The Welfare State and Life Transitions*, Cheltenham: Edward Elgar, 1–78.

Barr, N. (2004) 'Higher-Education Funding', *Oxford Review of Economic Policy*, 20(2): 264–83.

Becker, B. E. and Huselid, M. A. (1992) 'The Incentive Effects of Tournament Competition Systems', *Administrative Science Quarterly*, 37(2): 336–50.

Bernoulli, D. (1954) 'Exposition of a New Theory on the Measurement of Risk', *Econometrica*, 22: 23–36. Originally published in 1738.

Berufsakademie (2013) http://de.wikipedia.org/wiki/Berufsakademie.

Brzinsky-Fay, C. (2011) *School-to-Work Transitions in International Comparison*, Tampere: Acta Universitatis Tamperensis: 1663.

Buchanan, J. et al. (2001) *Beyond Flexibility: Skills and Work in the Future*, Sidney: Board of Vocational Education and Training (NSW).

Callan, T., T. Smeeding, and P. Tsakoglou (2008) *Short-Run Distributional Effects of Public Education Transfers to Tertiary Students in Seven European Countries*, Bonn: IZA Discussion Paper No. 3557.

Card, D., J. Kluve, and A. Weber (2009) *Active Labor Market Policy Evaluations: A Meta-analysis*, IZA Discussion Paper No. 4002, Bonn.

Cedefop (2009) *Individual Learning Accounts*, Luxembourg: Office for Official Publications of the European Communities.

Cedefop (2010) *Skills Supply and Demand in Europe—Medium-term Forecast up to 2020*, Luxembourg: Publications Office of the European Union.

Chapman, B. and Ryan, C. (2005) 'The Access Implications of Income Contingent Charges for Higher Education: Lessons from Australia', *Economics of Education Review*, 24(5): 491–512.

Diamond, P. A. (ed.) (1999) *Issues in Privatizing Social Security. Report of an Expert Panel of the National Academy of Social Insurance*, Cambridge, MA: The MIT Press.

Dustmann, C. and Meghir, C. (2005) 'Wages, Experience and Seniority', *Review of Economic Studies*, 72: 77–108.

Dworkin, R. (2000) *Sovereign Virtue: The Theory and Practice of Equality*, Cambridge, MA: Harvard University Press.

Elder, G. H. and Kirkpatrick Johnson, M., Crosnoe, R. (2004) 'The Emergence and Development of Life Course Theory'. In *Handbook of the Life Course*, ed. J. T. Mortimer and M. J. Shanahan, 3–19. New York: Springer Science + Business.

Erikson, E. (1968) *Identity: Youth and Crisis*. New York: Norton.

European Commission (EC) (2007) 'Council Conclusions Towards Common Principles of Flexicurity', COM(2007) 359 final, Brussels.

European Commission (EC) (2012a) *New Skills and Jobs in Europe: Pathways towards Full Employment*, Luxembourg: Office for Official Publications of the European Communities (report written by G. Schmid). http://ec.europa.eu/research/social-sciences/pdf/new-skils-and-jobs-in-europe_en.pdf.

European Commission (EC) (2012b) *Employment and Social Developments in Europe 2011*, Luxembourg: Office for Official Publications of the European Communities.

Feuer, M. J., Glick, H. A., and Desai, A. (1991) 'Firm Financed Education and Specific Human Capital: A Test of the Insurance Hypothesis', in D. Stern and J. M. M. Ritsen (eds), *Market Failure in Training?*, Berlin: Springer Verlag, 41–59.

Fouarge, D. and Schils, T. (2009) 'The Effect of Early Retirement Incentives on the Training Participation of Older Workers', *LABOUR*, 23(1): 85–109.

Heckman, J. J. (2000) 'Policies to Foster Human Capital', *Research in Economics*, 54: 3–56.

Heckman, J. J., Heinrich, C., and Smith, J. (2002) 'The Performance of Performance Standards', *Journal of Human Resources*, 37(4): 778–811.

Jacobs, B. and van der Ploeg, F. (2006) 'Guide to Reform of Higher Education: A European Perspective', *Economic Policy*, 47 (July): 537–92.

Kahneman, D. (2011) *Thinking Fast and Slow*, London: Allan Lane (Penguin Books).

Kalleberg, A. L. (2009) 'Precarious Work, Insecure Workers—Employment Relations in Transition', *American Sociological Review*, 74(1): 1–22.

Kemple, J. J. and Willner, C. J. (2008) *Career Academies—Long-term Impacts on Labor Market Outcomes, Educational Attainment, and Transitions to Adulthood*, New York: Manpower Demonstration Research Corporation (MDRC), mimeo (7th evaluation report).

Keune, M. and Serrano, A. (eds) (2014) *Deconstructing Flexicurity: Alternative Perspectives*, Oxford: Routledge Chapman & Hall.

Korver, T. and Schmid, G. (2012) 'Enhancing Transition Capacities and Sustainable Transitions', in J. de Munck, C. Didry, I. Ferreras, and A. Jobert (eds), *Renewing Democratic Deliberation in Europe: The Challenge of Social and Civil Dialogue*, Brussels: Peter Lang, 23–55.

Lazear, E.P. and Rosen, S. (1981) 'Rank-order Tournaments as Optimum Labor Contracts', *Journal of Political Economy*, 81: 841–64.

Modigliani, F. (1988) 'The Role of Intergenerational Transfers and Life-cycle Saving in the Accumulation of Wealth', *Journal of Economic Perspectives*, 2(2): 15–40.

Mortimer, J. T. and Shanahan, M. J. (eds) (2004) *Handbook of the Life Course*, New York: Springer Science + Business.

OECD (2005) *Education at a Glance*, Paris: OECD.

O'Rand, A. and Krecker, M. (1990) 'Concepts of Life Cycle: Their History, Meanings and Uses in the Social Sciences', *Annual Review of Sociology*, 16: 241–62.

Pearson, M. and Martin, J. P. (2005) *Should We Extend the Role of Private Social Expenditure?* IZA Discussion Paper No. 1544, Bonn.

Picchio, M. and van Ours, J. C. (2011) *Retaining through Training: Even for Older Workers*, IZA Discussion Paper No. 5591, Bonn.

Plantenga, J. and Remey, C. (2005) *Reconciliation of Work and Private Life: A Comparative Review of Thirty European Countries*, Luxembourg: Office for Official Publications of the European Communities.

Rawls, J. (2001) *Justice as Fairness—A Restatement*, ed. E. Kelly, Cambridge, MA: The Belknap Press of Harvard University Press.

Román, A. A. (2006) *Deviating from the Standard: Effects on Labor Continuity and Career Patterns*, Amsterdam: Dutch University Press.

Salverda, W. and Mayhew, K. (2009) 'Capitalist Economies and Wage Inequality', *Oxford Review of Economic Policy*, 25(1): 126–54.

Saraceno, C. (ed.) (2008) *Families, Ageing and Social Policy: Intergenerational Solidarity in European Welfare States*, Cheltenham: Edward Elgar.

Schmid, G. (2008) *Full Employment in Europe: Managing Labour Market Transitions and Risks*, Cheltenham: Edward Elgar.

Schmid, G. (2011) 'Non- Standard Employment in Europe: Its Development and Consequences for the European Employment Strategy', *German Policy Studies*, 7(1): 171–210. http://spaef.com/gps.php.

Schmid, G. (2013) 'Sharing Risks of Labour Market Transitions: Towards a System of Employment Insurance', *British Journal of Industrial Relations*. Early view. http://www.guentherschmid.eu/pdf/ Sharing_Risks_BJIR-2013.pdf.

Supiot, A. (2001) *Beyond Employment: Changes in Work and the Future of Labour Law in Europe*, Oxford: Oxford University Press.

Wilthagen, T. and Tros, F. (2004) 'The Concept of 'Flexicurity': A New Approach to Regulating Employment and Labour Markets', *Transfer*, 10(2): 166–86.

SECTION III

SKILLS DEMAND AND DEPLOYMENT

CHAPTER 14

SKILL UNDER-UTILIZATION

D. W. LIVINGSTONE

Introduction

Optimal skill utilization is a general principle on which all can agree. Where skill potential is untapped there is a failure of fulfillment for workers and a failure of effective production for society as a whole (Warhurst and Findlay 2012). Under-utilization can lead to social unrest, inefficient business performance, and wasteful government spending on skill training. Assessing skill under-utilization is becoming increasingly topical as evidence mounts that it may be increasing significantly (e.g. Felstead et al., Chapter 16 in this volume). There are at least two basic challenges in assessing the extent of skill under-utilization in any paid labour force. Firstly, an acceptable definition of skill should be established; secondly, the question of who can use the skill for what purpose should be addressed.

Any set of competencies deemed pertinent to the conduct of work could be identified as relevant skills. For example, consider the following list of competencies now often required at a high level by employers of higher education graduates. These competencies include: use computers/internet; use time efficiently; work productively with others; make meaning clear to others; perform under pressure; coordinate activities; rapidly acquire new knowledge; write reports; come up with ideas/solutions; assert your authority; negotiate effectively; mobilize capacities of others; present to an audience; write/speak in foreign language; as well as analytical thinking, mastery of one's own field or discipline, knowledge of other fields/disciplines, willingness to question ideas, and alertness to new opportunities (Allen and van der Velden 2009: 56). The list could be virtually endless. In addition, in the wake of the greatly increased participation of women in paid labour in the past generation and increasing turbulence of labour markets, various unpaid and previously ignored activities are becoming recognized as pertinent skills for employability (e.g. Smith 2010; Livingstone 2010). What is considered relevant skill varies immensely over time, as well as by type of occupation (see Payne, Chapter 3, and Warhurst et al., Chapter 4, in this volume). In practical terms, relevant dimensions of skill are usually reduced to a few that can be relatively easily measured.

Secondly, assuming agreement on any aspect of skill, gaining agreement on appropriate uses of this skill and assessment of the extent of utilization in capitalist production systems is another matter. There is a basic distinction between the use value and the exchange value of labour in relation to skills (see Livingstone 2004; Sawchuk 2006). The direct producers of commodities may primarily value the quality of what they produce, its social usefulness, as well as accrued monetary benefits; their employers are primarily motivated by the profits beyond monetary costs these commodities bring them in market exchanges. From the employers' standpoint, full skill utilization is the maximum application of workers' effort to ensure the greatest number of units produced and sold in a given time. From hired workers' standpoint, appropriate utilization may involve spending sufficient time and care to ensure high quality of a given finished unit, as well as adequate recuperation to enable maintenance of continuing good quality of work. Effective skill utilization is widely presumed to be closely associated with higher quantitative productivity, but from workers' standpoint lower quantitative productivity with higher quality products and more sustainable labour may often be more effective use of skill. Most of the literature on skill utilization ignores this distinction. But it is implicit in discussions that argue that connections between knowledge and work are mediated by the negotiating powers of those in different social groups (e.g. Grugulis 2003; Warhurst et al. Chapter 4 in this volume). With greater power comes greater influence over what is deemed to count as a skill and the extent to which its use is recognized and rewarded. Workers with little workplace power may be relegated to 'getting a little of our own back' by withholding some of their skill or effort (e.g. Hamper 1991). Full skill utilization from an employer's perspective may equate to being used up and excreted as waste from workers' standpoint (Yates 2011).

Without pretending to resolve these basic challenges, this chapter provides a general overview of the current state of knowledge about the extent of skill under-utilization in paid labour forces in advanced capitalist market economies. Firstly, general theoretical approaches to under-utilization are characterized. Then, conceptual dimensions and measurement issues are discussed. Next, summaries of recent empirical findings on the extent of under-utilization are summarized. Then a brief indication of findings of research on antecedents of under-utilization is presented. Finally, some concluding remarks are made about future prospects for research on this phenomenon.

Theoretical Approaches

Classical economic theories viewed market economies as self-regulating systems that tended towards an overall equilibrium, including a balance between the demand for and the supply of largely homogenous labour. These perspectives have been supplemented by theories that are preoccupied with either labour supply or demand. Human capital theories suggest that greater investment in education will lead to supply-driven economic growth, whilst knowledge-based economy theories assume that knowledge deficits require a more highly educated labour force. Other approaches, including segmented labour market theories and credentialism, focus on institutional and social factors to account for an apparent surplus of workers in relation to comparable jobs. Many current conceptions of the relationship between workers' competencies and job requirements tend to focus on mismatches, and especially these apparent surpluses, as the most problematic aspects of relations between the labour force and the labour market.[1]

The approach of the current author (Livingstone 2004, 2009), which could be termed a historical materialist theory of relations between workers' skills and job requirements, posits that inter-firm competition, conflicts between employers and employees over working conditions, and technological innovation all provoke incessant shifts in the number of enterprises, employees, and types of jobs available. Through technological innovation and workers' learning on the job, increased efficiency leads either to expanded production or to unemployment, in either case modifying the overall demand for labour. Popular demand for general education and specialized training increases cumulatively as people seek more knowledge, different specific skills, and added credentials in order to live and qualify for jobs in such a changing society. In this dynamically changing economy, mismatches are inevitable between employers' aggregate demand and requirements for employees on the one hand, and the aggregate supply and qualifications of job seekers on the other. In advanced capitalist societies with widespread public access to knowledge through such means as the internet and with liberal democratic state regimes that acclaim the right to equal educational opportunity, the dominant tendency has been for the supply of qualified job seekers to exceed the demand for most jobs—a reserve army of labour.

Whilst different explanations for current mismatches between workers' competencies and job requirements abound, the focus of the remainder of this chapter is on assessments of the extent of under-utilization on different dimensions skill and some possible implications.

Conceptual and Measurement Issues

This surplus or gap between workers' capabilities and their job requirements has been called *under-utilization, under-employment, over-qualification, over-education* and several other terms. Scurry and Blenkinsopp (2011, 644) assert that:

> A plethora of definitions and conceptualisations have been developed, with a lack of consistency in the terminology used.... To date the research has tended to remain

[1] For discussions of theories of mismatches between workers' competencies and labour market needs, see Desjardins and Rubenson (2011), Livingstone (2009), McKee-Ryan and Harvey (2011), Scurry and Blenkinsopp (2011), and Felstead et al., Chapter 16 in this volume.

> within disciplinary boundaries, and there have been few attempts to bring together different perspectives and conceptualisations from across the full range of disciplines in which this phenomenon has been studied.

Both Desjardins and Rubenson (2011) and McKee-Ryan and Harvey (2011) have recently attempted to develop interdisciplinary reviews. Without becoming immersed in details of such reviews, it is important to register some orienting conceptual and measurement points.

Firstly, the essential notion is the existence of a significant discrepancy between workers' capacities and the capacities required for their jobs—whether or not the uses of these capacities are deemed appropriate by all involved. Conceptions of under-utilization of workers' capabilities encompass both time-based exclusion *from* employment as well as skill-based under-utilization of capabilities *in* employment (Brown and Pintaldi 2005). Primary *time-based dimensions* are the extent of unemployment (including those actively looking for employment, discouraged workers, and others such as prisoners and retired people who want paid work but are restricted from the labour market), and the extent of involuntarily reduced employment in temporary, part-time jobs. Involuntary temporary employment has clearly been increasing over the past generation (e.g. Bureau of Labor Statistics 2010). Whilst some estimates of under-utilization mix the two concepts, skill under-utilization is quite different. *Skill-based conceptions* of under-utilization refer to the surplus capacities, skills, education, or knowledge that workers bring to the job in comparison with what is needed for the job. There is much dispute over the notions of skills, relevant education, and knowledge. Numerous ways of conceiving dimensions of the gap between employed workers' capabilities and the requirements of their jobs have been suggested (e.g. Kalleberg 2008; McKee-Ryan and Harvey 2011). This review will focus on four relatively straightforward conceptual dimensions of the skill gap between workers' capacities and their job requirements. These dimensions are:

- entry *credential gap* between the training credentials that job entrants bring and those required by employers
- *performance gap* between the performance capability of workers and the performance level actually required to do the job
- *relevance gap* between job holders' field of preparatory training and the body of knowledge needed for the job
- *subjective gap* is the extent to which job holders' personal assessments of their capabilities exceed actual job requirements.

It follows from the previous discussion that skill mismatches are likely to occur in both directions, and that there are likely to be deficits as well as surpluses of skill in relation to job requirements. The focus of this chapter is on skill under-utilization, which is also posited as the dominant tendency by my theoretical perspective. But empirical studies will be canvassed for both tendencies.[2]

There is considerable conflation in the research literature between notions of skills, qualifications, and educational attainments. Skills are the most expansive concept, potentially including a very wide array of competencies, but they have rarely been measured directly and only in very limited terms of literacy and numeracy. Qualifications may include various forms of verification of skills but are usually considered in terms of formal certification. Educational attainments in terms of completion of years and levels of schooling are more readily accessible and often the default measure for empirical studies of competencies. But the narrowness of this measure in terms of workers' actual knowledge should be noted (see Livingstone 2009). In addition, substantial differences have been found between skills and qualifications in the few studies that have been able to measures both (Desjardin and Rubenson 2011; Quintini 2011). Furthermore, when the gap between workers' competencies and job requirements is measured in terms of educational attainments, different measures (e.g. self-assessments, expert analyses of education required) may lead to different outcomes (Vehaest and Omey 2010).

With these provisos, we can summarize the empirical research to date on these four dimensions of skill under-utilization.

Empirical Findings

Relying largely on educational attainment-based measures, the empirical research on job requirements has focused mainly on two distinct dimensions: credential requirements to *get* the job and performance requirements to *do* the job. Brief discussion of these two measures as well as measures of workers' own capabilities is helpful before we review findings about skill under-utilization.

Credential and Performance Requirements

Over the past century higher formal education credentials have increasingly been used by employers as criteria for job entry.[3] These primarily US studies show that by the 1930s, post-secondary credentials had become an important criterion for entry into most professions. With the post-World War II expansion of the public school

[2] Warhurst and Findlay (2012, 5) distinguish 'use of better skills and the better use of skills, with the former crucial to the development of a high skills economy and the latter crucial to realising existing untapped workforce potential'. In these terms, the current focus is on better use of existing skills.

[3] For a summary, see Livingstone (2004, 72–78).

system, post-secondary credentials also began to be commonly required for managerial posts. A high school diploma became the criterion for entry to clerical work after World War I; by the 1990s nearly half of all clerical jobs had post-secondary education entry requirements. In the 1930s, hardly any manual labour jobs required a high school diploma. By the 1990s, high school graduation had become a criterion for entry into even the most 'unskilled' manual jobs. There was a substantial basis for the claim that entry credentials were being inflated beyond the education levels required to perform some jobs.

Once a worker has a job, what level of skill and knowledge does she or he need to perform it? This question is more controversial than those about job entry requirements. The empirical dispute centres on the technical abilities needed to actually do a job and the most suitable measures to estimate these performance abilities. Some researchers have used indirect measures of occupational composition to estimate performance skill requirements. The proportions of managers and professional employees appears to have increased in recent decades whilst the proportions of industrial workers have decreased in many advanced market economies (e.g. Erickson and Goldthorpe 2002; Breen and Luijkx 2004). These changes in occupational distribution have typically been assumed to indicate overall increases in the skill requirements for job performance. However, there have been few comparative historical studies of actual changes in the performance requirements of different occupations.

Direct estimates of technical skill requirements of jobs have often used a general educational development (GED) scale or specific vocational preparation scale. There is a large literature on this topic using different variants of these measures.[4] One of the most thorough reviews of research on skill requirements was undertaken by the US National Research Council in 1999. Drawing on diverse surveys and case studies with varied assumptions, the survey's authors stated that 'It does not appear that work is becoming more routine or less skilled than in the past, but we are unwilling to claim that the reverse is true' (National Research Council 1999, 162–163). They concluded that a skill-upgrading trend was most likely amongst blue-collar industrial workers, with service workers being more diverse, professionals experiencing little change in skill requirements, and evidence about managerial work being almost non-existent. A more recent overview (Handel 2005) concluded that there may have been some gradual increase in educational requirements for jobs but that much better information on the actual skill content of jobs was needed.

Based on all the evidence available, the most sensible conclusion is that during the past generation, in terms of formal education needed, there has probably been an overall *gradual* upgrading of both entry credential and performance requirements for jobs in advanced market economies. Yet this information tells us little about the relationship between individual workers' formal education and their jobs, and less about the relation with their more general knowledge and capacities.

[4] For a review of this literature, see Livingstone (2009).

Measures of Workers' Capabilities: Rapid Growth of Schooling

Empirical estimates of workers' capabilities have also generally been made in terms of levels of formal education attainment. In contrast to the limited evidence for gradual general increase in the skill and education requirements of jobs, evidence of the increasing education attainments of the labour force, both throughout the post-World War II period and since the 1980s, is overwhelming. There is a strong long-term rise in school completion everywhere, with the labour force in virtually all advanced industrial countries now averaging nearly 12 years of schooling (Tahlin 2006; Felstead et al., Chapter 16, this volume). The supply of workers with advanced education has continued to rise quickly in recent decades in most countries. In Britain in the late 1990s, for example, about a third of youth cohorts were completing a higher education, compared with an employed general labour force containing 12% with higher education degrees (Green et al. 2002).

Once again, formal education attainments should not be equated with workers' capabilities. Some recent research demonstrates that formal education attainments and the use of specific abilities are only loosely related (Allen and de Weert 2007). The importance of on-the-job training is increasingly recognized as being central to the development of workers' capabilities to do their jobs, and efforts to measure job-related further education and informal learning activities are now considerable (see Livingstone 2010). Whatever the limitations of the prior measures of workers' capabilities, it is reasonable to conclude that the formal educational qualifications workers bring to the job are substantially greater than in prior generations.

Measures of Skill Under-Utilization

Estimates of relations between workers' capabilities and the requirements of their jobs, or 'skill-based' matching, necessarily focus on those who have jobs. Most studies have combined job holders' self-reports of their formal education attainments with either job analysts' estimates or worker self-assessments of education levels required for the job in order to produce education–job matching profiles. It should be stressed here that much of the variation in the estimated extent of under-utilization has been closely related to the measures used (see Felstead et al., Chapter 16, this volume). For example, McGoldrick and Robst (1996) estimated that over half of the employed labour force in the United States around 1980 was over-qualified according to analysts' estimates of educational requirements, whilst self-assessments found around 30% over-qualified. In addition, a statistical method based on mean levels of education held by workers in given occupations identified even lower levels of under-qualification of 15% or less.[5] Evidently, attention should be paid to the measures used if imputing trends in skill under-utilization.

[5] Such arbitrary statistical measures of mismatch are fairly common in the literature (e.g.Verdugo and Verdugo 1989). Others measure under-utilization in terms of earnings ratios less than one's peers (e.g. Feldman 1996). Such measures are of little use for trend analysis and will not be considered further here.

Credential Gap

Credential match research can be dated back to the late 1940s with the first indications that educational expansion was outstripping workplace demands for qualifications (Harris 1949). With the rapid subsequent increase in post-secondary enrolments, this view became widespread and led to several major studies analysing the extent to which credentials required for job entry were being inflated beyond actual performance requirements (Berg 1970; Collins 1979).

Livingstone's (2004) Canadian surveys between 1982 and 1996 based on workers' self-reports of their educational credentials and employers' job entry credential requirements found credential over-qualification or under-employment remained at around 20% throughout the period. The consistent level of over-qualification during this period of very rapid increases in post-secondary completion and gradual increases in job performance requirements suggests some inflation of entry requirements. In time series surveys of Canadian university graduates, Finnie (2002) found fairly stable levels of credential over-qualification of around 30% in 1982, 1986, and 1990 cohorts, in each instance declining to about 25% after they had been in the labour force for three years. For all Canadian university graduates, Li, Gervais, and Duval (2006) found that over-qualification increased marginally from 18% in 1993 to 19% in 2001 but that the total number of over-qualified workers increased by about a third because of the increasing number of workers who obtained university degrees. A series of Canadian national surveys in 1998, 2004, and 2010, using self-report measures, found that the over-qualification for job entry increased from 27% to 31% whilst under-qualification dropped from 22% to 18% during this period (Livingstone 2010b).

In one of the longer time series available on self-reported credential matching, the British Skills Survey has found that about 30% of the employed labour force were over-qualified in terms of the education needed to get their jobs in 1986 and that this figure had increased to nearly 40% by 2006. Conversely, the proportion defined as under-qualified declined from 18% to 14% during this period (Felstead et al. 2007). However, this decline is not to suggest that these over-qualified workers are not using their relatively high qualifications to enter jobs or that they are not using *some* of their skills at work. Felstead et al. (Chapter 16, this volume) suggest that 'over-qualification' has not stopped individuals using their skills at work; the same could be said for the under-qualified. The point is how effectively their arrays of qualifications and skills are being utilized for job entry and job performance, respectively.

Whilst there are indications of increasing surpluses of credential attainments over entry credential requirements in many of these recent studies, virtually all studies have found that a majority of the labour force have jobs with entry credential requirements matching the credentials they have attained.

Performance Gap

Many of the empirical studies in this field have primarily examined performance matching. Studies of the performance gap remain most controversial. As I have noted elsewhere (Livingstone 2004, 78): 'The dispute has centered on the equivalencies between the technical skills required for job task performance and the amount of schooling needed to ensure that these skills have been acquired.' Felstead et al. (Chapter 16 in this volume) conclude: 'There are no adequate measures of skill stocks that comprehensively cover the diversity of skill concepts, including technical skills at all levels, knowledge, and dispositions.' As itemized in this section, many studies of performance matching use different presumptive measures of skill requirements.

An extensive international assessment was undertaken by Groot and van den Brink (2000) in their review of 25 surveys from an unspecified array of European countries and the United States. These surveys covered a 20-year period and used either expert analyst ratings, worker self-reports, or the more arbitrary statistical criterion of a standard deviation from average years of schooling. Their conclusion was that the overall incidence of over-education, or formal education in excess of job performance requirements, was about 26%. However, estimates in these studies varied from 10% to 42%. 'Under-education', or less schooling than the job required, was of lower incidence in all studies but estimates varied widely from 12% to 33% according to different criteria. The authors also concluded that the incidence of over-education had not changed significantly over this period.

Hartog (2000) compared the results of over a dozen studies, from five countries (the United States, Netherlands, Portugal, Spain, and the United Kingdom) over a similar period using diverse criteria. He concluded that matching occurred about 60% of the time in the European countries with the incidence of over-education increasing and under-education decreasing. Matching was somewhat lower in the United States with over-education following a more irregular pattern.

Handel (2003, 2005) has extensively reviewed more recent US studies. He found that the rapid growth in education attainment of the labour force was beginning to slow down and that job skill requirements may have continued a slower, gradual rise. However, given the varied, insufficient measures of workers' skills and employers' job requirements, there is inadequate research on whether job demands exceed workers' capacities. Handel (2005) concludes that more detailed measures for tracking skill requirement trends with representative samples of workers are needed to understand how worker-job matching is changing.

Vaisey (2006) provides estimates of a longer trend in over-qualification of the US labour force, based on job analyst GED measures. Using data from the annual General Social Survey, he found that over-qualification had increased from about 30% in 1972 to 55% in 2002. Increasing over-qualification is not limited to the young but appears highest in disadvantaged groups including women and non-whites.

Verhaest and Omey (2006) conducted a detailed comparative study of several different self-report and expert-based measures of over-education with the 2001 cohort of Flemish school leavers. Leaving aside measures based on standard deviations from the norm, they found levels of over-education ranging from 26% to over 50%. Expert-based measures were higher than self-reports, and under-education was smaller on all these measures. They found similar patterns in over a dozen international studies, mostly in the 1990s, which had previously used multiple types of measures with the same data. They noted continuing conceptual confusion amongst researchers but concluded that most over-education is built into the system and enduring whilst most under-education is frictional and temporary.

McGuiness (2006) provides the most extensive review to date of both expert-based and self-report measures of over-education, including over 30 international studies ranging from the 1970s to 2000. He notes that 'It is not easy to disentangle the information to derive any discernible patterns.' Omitting measures based on standard deviation statistics as merely arbitrary, both the expert-based and self-report measures in this array of studies average around 25% rates of over-education. McGuiness concludes that the incidence of over-education has remained stable over time and that it is costly to individuals, firms, and the economy.

Tahlin (2006) also offers a recent international review of matching studies. He finds that, depending on the criteria used, between 20% and 40% of all workers appear to have more education than their jobs require but that trends in over-education are very poorly established. He cites long-term Swedish survey data based on worker self-reports which found over-education had increased from 15% of all employees in 1974 to 33% in 2000, with matched workers dropping from 70% to 50% and under-educated workers remaining at about 20%. He goes on to argue that the categories of over-educated, well matched, and under-educated are each diverse in themselves. They include logically necessary, logically possible but not necessary, as well as logically impossible combinations of education and job requirements. As many older workers with only compulsory schooling retire from the labour market, the number of under-educated and matched workers will necessarily fall. Considering the assessment of trends in skill demand and job-worker matches at the micro level, Tahlin (2006) views the state of knowledge as especially weak and suggests that a variety of measures should be used.

Whilst there have been relatively few studies of skill mismatch based on direct measures of skill, the 2003–7 Adult Literacy and Lifeskills Survey provides estimates of the extent of literacy and numeracy mismatch across nine developed countries. Such mismatches are found to be widespread, ranging from around 30% to 40%t for literacy and 35% to over 50% for numeracy. Desjardin and Rubenson (2011, 27) find apparent literacy and numeracy skill deficits in every country but the magnitude of skill surpluses tends to be somewhat larger:

> [T]he reserve of skills, skill surplus or alternatively skill under-utilization pertaining to literacy and numeracy skills also varies substantially by country, ranging from 12–32% and 17–46%, respectively. Whilst a skills surplus is good for growing knowledge economies in the long run, a lack of skill use in the workplace may be problematic in the short run because it exposes workers to the risk of skill loss. High rates of skills surplus signal a need to encourage employers to adapt organizational and work practices which ensure that existing skills are used and not lost over time as a consequence of a lack of use.

In a recent meta-analysis of over-qualification across OECD countries which compiles the findings of a large number of studies over more than 30 years, mixing both expert analyst and self-assessment measures, Quintini (2011, 4) concludes that

> Mismatches between workers' competences and what is required by their job are widespread in OECD countries. Studies that use qualifications as proxies for competences suggest that as many as one in four workers could be over-qualified and as many as one in three could be under-qualified for their job.

A series of Canadian national surveys in 1998, 2004, and 2010 using self-report measures, has found that the over-qualification for performance requirements remained at about 28% through this period, whilst the proportion under-qualified dropped from 20% to 15% (Livingstone 2010b).

In sum, what we can be reasonably sure of at this point, given the persistent measurement controversy, is that mismatches are widespread and that under-utilization of workers' education, qualifications, and skills in their jobs continues to be at least as substantial as under-qualification—and more so on some measures of the performance gap.

Recent studies of the other specified dimensions of under-utilization, namely the relevance gap and the subjective gap, remain much rarer with very little available trend data.

Relevance Gap

Studies of the match between job holders' field of preparatory training and the body of knowledge needed for the job have rarely been published in scholarly journals (see Wolbers 2003). This research has been largely limited to post-secondary graduates and asks for graduates' self-assessments of the extent to which their programmes of study in conventional fields have corresponded with or been relevant to their jobs. The matching found has been closely related to levels and types of formal education. For example, national analyses of Canadian university graduates find that those from more advanced graduate and professional groups, most notably the health sciences, experience better education–job matches, whilst graduates of programmess not linked to development of specific job market skills, such as fine arts and humanities and biology, have consistently lower scores (Finnie 2002; Frenette 2004). Similarly, analyses of field of study match by occupational groups have found that graduates in professional/managerial jobs are twice as likely to have jobs related to their field of study as those in service or blue-collar jobs (Krahn and Bowlby 1999, 35). A 2004 national survey found that around 40% of all employees had jobs closely related to their field of studies and that this figure ranged from about two-thirds of professional employees to only a quarter of industrial workers (Livingstone 2009, 92). Such studies have provided little original insight into education–job matching relations to date.

Subjective Gap

Subjective matching research, and particularly subjective under-employment, gained currency in the 1960s when fears were expressed that growing numbers of university and college graduates who could not find commensurate jobs would become increasingly disenchanted and rebellious. US surveys in 1969 and 1977 found that the number of workers who felt they were not able to fully use their qualifications in the workplace grew from 27% to over 36% (Staines and Quinn 1979). A general question about the extent to which people feel qualified for their jobs found about 22% of Canadian workers expressing feelings of over-qualification in the mid-1990s, with a slight increase to 25% in 2000 (Crompton 2002). A series of Canadian national surveys in 1998, 2004, and 2010 has found subjective feelings of over-qualification increasing from 22% to 30% over this period whilst subjective under-qualification remained at around 5% (Livingstone 2010b). Vaisey's (2006) recent US study, whilst based on GED measures, has found significant links of increasing over-qualification with job dissatisfaction and more critical political attitudes.

The overall weight of research evidence suggests that the formal education required to do available jobs generally has increased more gradually than the education attainments of the employed labour force during the past 40 years. Growing attention to under-utilization, under-employment, over-education, or over-qualification as a problem reflects this trend.

All of the above dimensions of skill under-utilization merit considerable further study. It should also be recalled that the large discrepancies between the number of workers *available for employment* and the lesser number of jobs available for workers—that is the workers who are unemployed, or discouraged from seeking jobs, or who are employed involuntarily in temporary or part-time jobs—represent a very different issue than gaps between the education attainments of the *employed* labour force and the levels their employers require. It is widely recognized by international agencies that these time-based forms of under-utilization present a very serious social problem (see International Labour Organization 1998).[6] However, as the present review of recent empirical research confirms, skill-based mismatches have also been found to be very substantial and persistent. Both types of mismatches have significant negative consequences for individuals, families, and societies (e.g. Kalleberg 2008).

Antecedents of Under-Utilization

Given the mixed measures and findings on education–job matching, there have been relatively few consistent findings on social background factors related to skill under-utilization. There is at least suggestive evidence that each of the following factors related

[6] See Jensen and Slack (2003) and Livingstone (2004) for reviews of research on time-based measures.

to the relative power of different workers has a meaningful association with some measures of under-utilization: age of worker or employment experience; race and immigration status; gender; and class.

Many studies that are focused on self-reported job requirements have found that over-educated workers tend to be younger with lower levels of experience and job tenure (McGuiness 2006). These findings are consistent both with the common-sense notion that we learn from experience and with the increasing recognition of the positive cumulative effect of informal on-the-job training. However, a US time series study, based on the GED scale, infers an apparent recent shift. Vaisey (2006) finds that whilst workers over 55 years of age were only half as likely to be over-educated as workers under 35 in the 1970s, there was little difference between these older and younger cohorts in the 1990s. Both cohorts of workers appear to have become more over-educated. This finding may be explained by considering the increasing formal credential attainments of older cohorts, as well as the use of outdated GED ratings. As the general labour force becomes more highly educated, prospects for over-qualification mount if job requirements do not increase accordingly, and age differences diminish.

Systemic racial discrimination appears to be more persistent in the employment of non-white minorities in most advanced market economies. Higher under-employment rates on several measures continue for blacks and increase for Hispanics in the United States (Jensen and Slack 2002). There is considerable evidence from previous generations that immigrants have generally assimilated well enough into receiving countries' cultures for the second generation to achieve similar employment patterns to other domestic social groups (e.g. Reitz 1998). However, at least for some non-white immigrant groups, there is evidence that the combination of non-white and recent immigrant status has created a more enduring double disadvantage in education–job mismatches (e.g. De Jong and Madamba 2001). A series of Canadian national surveys from 1998 to 2010 has found that recent immigrants, most of whom are non-whites, are significantly more highly under-utilized on several dimensions of capacity–requirement matching (Livingstone 2009).

The under-utilization of women's skills should also be noted here. Although women have come close to parity in labour force participation in some countries, they continue to be over-represented in low-paid, part-time jobs, to do more unpaid housework, and be under-represented in well-paid jobs with greater authority (see Livingstone and Pollock 2004; Bergmann 2005). Some studies of matching have suggested greater over-education of women because of greater restriction to local labour markets, but few significant mismatch patterns have been found in such specifically focused studies to date (e.g. McGuiness 2006).

Class

One factor that has nearly evaded systematic comparative analysis in relation to education–job matching is class (for an explanation, see Warhurst et al., Chapter 4 in this volume). The classical social theorists, Marx and Weber, both identified three types of classes based on ownership of property, specialized forms of labour, and provision of general labour, respectively. They made the case for the intimate relation of these classes to various kinds of economic and social inequalities. Given the accumulating evidence of education–job mismatches, the inattention to relations between classes and mismatches is surely an oversight. Considerable empirical research has focused on the development of some professional occupations and their efforts to construct knowledge fields that would ensure the highest possible degree of control over their own work (see Collins 1979; Derber et al. 1990). However, comparative class analyses of matching are still rare.

Several studies have compared some occupational groups in terms of mismatches. Clogg and Shockey (1984) compared the 'mismatch' (over-education) of occupational groups in the US labour force from 1969 to 1980. Their calculations were based on the proportion of workers whose years of schooling were more than a standard deviation beyond the average for their occupational group. They found managers were the most over-educated and that the general labour occupations of clerical sales and other service workers, as well as craft workers, also showed marked increases in over-education during this period. The authors' noted that their measure was not applicable to professional occupations. Dolton and Vignoles (1996), using a 1986 UK sample of 1980 post-secondary graduates, found persistent over-education generally but with significantly stronger effects on the reduced earnings in clerical jobs than in professional occupations. De Witte and Steijn (2000) found that, for a 1994 Dutch national sample, blue-collar workers had high under-employment, whilst professional workers had low unemployment rates. Using national household census surveys in the United States, Sum and Khatiwada (2010) have analysed involuntary temporary employment rates during the 'great recession' of 2007–9 and found that, whilst under-employment rates increased generally, those in working-class occupations and low income groups had rates as much as 10 times higher than those in professional occupations.

Elliott (2000) examined differences between managers, professional and technical employees, and general labourers in job search processes in a US three-city sample in the early 1990s. Employers/owners were not included because they were deemed outside the labour market and not selling their labour power to others. Managers were more likely to get jobs through others with managerial authority reaching down to them personally rather than through their own active searches. Professional and technical employees relied most on open searches based on formal educational qualifications. General labourers were most likely to get their jobs through active searches using personal contacts, such as family and friends. These findings at least suggest that professional and technical employees are likely to have the closest education–job matches, whereas other personal factors are of relatively greater import in job entry for both managers and general labourers, and may be associated with greater education–job mismatches. The series of national surveys and case studies conducted in Canada by Livingstone and colleagues (2009) distinguished the three basic types of classes, used multiple measures of skill under-utilization, and found persistent inequalities in the extent of under-utilization by economic class: professional employees have lower levels of under-utilization than service workers and industrial workers.

Given the significant findings to date, comparisons by class positions, employment experience, race and immigration status and gender should be included in future studies of under-utilization in order to minimize conflation of basic aspects of workers' power with more specific training and job conditions.

Concluding Remarks

Recent findings on the match between educational attainments and job requirements are typically skewed towards an excess of formal education attainments over the levels of education required for jobs. Some measures of skill match find widespread incidence of both under-utilization and under-qualification. It is reasonably clear that under-utilization, under-employment, over-education or over-qualification has become a persistent problem in the employed labour force of advanced market economies through different phases of business cycles. This situation is more likely to get worse than improve. McKee-Ryan and Harvey (2011, 963) point out that 'Trends consistently point to under-employment becoming more prevalent in the future.' In any case, those workers whose capabilities are deemed to exceed job requirements have garnered more attention in recent studies of worker education–job requirements.

It is also becoming clear that formal education qualifications are partial and often poor indicators of workers' capabilities. However, there has been little theoretical analysis of workplace learning and little empirical research that addresses the actual relationship between workers' learning processes and their job requirements. At least one recent project, including theory development, surveys, and case studies, has attempted to take up these limitations (Livingstone 2009). The most relevant finding is that the labour force is continually engaged in informal learning, primarily learning by experience, the content of which is not necessarily related to a worker's current job. Learning by experience is not closely related to the level of formal schooling, participation in further education courses, or the educational level of job requirements. Whatever the measured level of under-utilization, informal learning is at least as useful as further education for improving job performance. In addition, these studies have found that longer employment experience is linked with lower subjective under-employment; there is little evidence of a shortage of computer skills in relation to job requirements; and, as in prior studies, there are very high levels of under-employment amongst recent immigrants, people of colour, and disabled people. Perhaps most importantly, all workers in these studies were engaged in problem-solving in both paid and unpaid work; they continually acquire and reformulate their cognitive knowledge and abilities, and use them to 'micro-modify' their jobs. However, their opportunities to use their abilities are often severely constrained by lack of discretion in their job tasks and/or organizational decision-making, most notably amongst working-class employees.

In terms of the effects of skill mismatches, over-qualified workers have generally been found to earn less than matched workers and to be less satisfied with their jobs (Quintini 2011). Numerous other effects of under-utilization have been suggested by various studies.[7] The most suggestive of these studies are beginning to detect diminishing negative effects of over-qualification in workplace contexts where labour relations are more democratized (Erdogan and Bauer 2009; Belfield 2010).

These findings should raise serious doubts about the wisdom of policy responses to skill under-utilization that continue to be preoccupied with education and training solutions to economic problems. Advocates of both human capital theory and a knowledge-based economy persist in asserting educational investment as the answer. Indeed, from employers' standpoint, a surplus of skills may continue to be both a short-term and long-term benefit. Some scholars now assert that because over-education has not yet led to social upheaval it is not a significant problem, and that the rapid growth of a formally schooled society has transformed work, a 'kind of mass professionalization' (Baker 2009, 166). At least since Thurow (1975), many researchers of education–economy relations have pointed to enhanced lifelong learning and informal job-related learning as solutions for education–jobs mismatches and sustainable economic development. The onus is increasingly placed on workers' own investment in learning. However, a growing corpus of workplace learning studies, such as those just cited, indicate that workers' rich array of learning activities increasingly exceed current actual job requirements and that people generally are already intently engaged in an 'educational arms race' for credentials.

Of course, education provision can always been improved, and more equitable guidance services for transition between school and paid work can be provided. The current efforts to dismantle state-provided education systems must be strongly resisted as an affront to democratic rights. However, effective policy means of reducing skill under-utilization are more likely to come from the adoption by employers of job designs and organizational practices that permit workers to more fully use *existing* skills (e.g. Warhurst and Findlay 2012; Skills Australia 2012), as well as from public policies that facilitate the redistribution of paid work time, wider recognition of workers' prior learning, incentives for workplace participation, and creation of sustainable green jobs (Livingstone 2004, 2009). Whatever the political tenor of the times, it should be self-evident that skill under-utilization can only be fairly addressed by providing further opportunities for use of these higher skills.

To return to the initial challenges in this chapter, the notion of 'over-education' is absurd from the standpoint of workers and learners in general. Gaining knowledge to cope with the environment is the most inherently human activity and virtually always valuable. It is only in the narrow sense of qualifications in excess of what employers require for specific jobs that the concept is intelligible as wasted investment. In contrast, the notion of 'over-employment' is rarely heard; it is absurd from an employers' standpoint which is committed to maximizing the profit-generating efforts of employees. To

[7] For a review, see McKee-Ryan and Harvey (2011).

many employees, the notion *is* readily intelligible as intensification of work or exploitation. Marx (1967) considered that understanding the way in which unpaid surplus labour is drawn from direct producers reveals the 'innermost secret', the hidden basis of the entire social structure and the relationship of rulers and ruled in all historical modes of production. In the capitalist mode of production, the basic way is the extraction of surplus value from hired labourers. Whilst Marx's labour theory of value has been the subject of much criticism, at least one aspect remains valid. Unless and until a significant portion of the employees most directly exploited by their employers grasp this inequity, and envision and act upon alternative forms of production based on economic democracy and sustainable relations with our environment, the over-employment and high exploitation of their skills is likely to persist. By the same token, the persistence of significant skill under-utilization within the capitalist mode of production continues to generate human resources for creation of such alternative forms of production from within capitalism (e.g. Baiman et al. 2011; Ness and Azzellini 2011).

References

Allen, J. and van der Velden, R. (2009) Report on the Large-scale Graduate Survey: Competencies and Early Labour Market Careers of Higher Education Graduates. Lifelong Learning Program, European Commission, Ljubljana: Faculty of Social Sciences, University of Ljubljana.

Baiman, R., Barclay, B., Hollander, S., Kurban, H., Persky, J., Redmond, E., and Rothenberg, M. (2011) 'A Permanent Jobs Program for the US: Economic Restructuring to Meet Human Needs', *Review of Black Political Economy*, 39(1) (March): 29–41.

Baker, D. (2009) 'The Educational Transformation of Work: Towards a New Synthesis', *Journal of Education and Work*, 22(3):163–191.

Belfield, C. (2010) 'Over-Education: What Influence Does the Workplace Have?', *Economics of Education Review*, 29: 236–245.

Berg, I. (1970) *Education and Jobs: The Great Training Robbery*, New York: Praeger.

Bergmann, B. (2005) *The Economic Emergence of Women*, 2nd ed., New York: Palgrave Macmillan.

Breen, R. and Luijkx, R. (2004) 'Social Mobility in Europe between 1970 and 2000', in R. Breen (ed), *Social Mobility in Europe*, Oxford: Oxford University Press: 37–75.

Brown, G. and Pintaldi, F. A. (2005) 'Multidimensional Approach in the Measurement of Underemployment'. UNECE/ILO/EUROSTAT Seminar on the Quality of Work, Working Paper no. 15. www.unece.org/fileadmin/DAM/stats/documents/2005/05/labour/wp.15.e.pdf.

Bureau of Labor Statistics, United States Department of Labor (2010) 'Employment Situation Summary'. http://www.bls.gov/news.release/empsit.nro.htm.

Clogg, C. and Shockey, J. (1984) 'Mismatch between Occupation and Schooling: A Prevalence Measure, Recent Trends and Demographic Analysis', *Demography*, 21(20): 235–257.

Collins, R. (1979) *The Credential Society: An Historical Sociology of Education and Stratification*, New York: Academic Press.

Crompton, S. (2002) 'I Still Feel Overqualified for My Job', *Canadian Social Trends*, 67 (Winter): 23–26.

de Jong, G. F. and Madamba, A. B. (2001) 'A Double Disadvantage? Minority Group, Immigrant Status, and Underemployment in the United States', *Social Science Quarterly*, 82(1): 117–130.

Derber, C., Schwartz, W., and Magrass, Y. (1990) *Power in the Highest Degree: Professionals and the Rise of a New Mandarin Order*, New York: Oxford University Press.

Desjardins, R. and Rubenson, K. (2011) An Analysis of Skill Mismatch Using Direct Measures of Skills'. *OECD Education Working Papers no. 63*, OECD, Paris.

de Witte, M. and Steijn, B. (2000) 'Automation, Job Content, and Underemployment, *Work, Employment and Society*, 14(2): 245–264.

Dolton, P. and Vignoles A. (2000) 'The Incidence and Effects of Overeducation in the U.K. Graduate Labour Market', *Economics of Education Review*, 19: 179–198.

Elliott, J. R. (2000) 'Class, Race, and Job Matching in Contemporary Urban Labor Markets', *Social Science Quarterly*, 81(4): 1036–1052.

Erdogan, B. and Bauer, T. (2009) 'Perceived Overqualification and Its Outcomes: The Moderating Role of Empowerment', *Journal of Applied Psychology*, 94(2): 557–565.

Felstead, A., Gallie, D., Green, F., and Zhou, Y. (2007) 'Skills at Work in Britain, 1986 to 2006', ESRC Centre on Skills, Knowledge and Organisational Performance, Universities of Oxford and Warwick.

Finnie, R. (2002) 'Early Labour Market Outcomes of Recent Canadian University Graduates by Discipline: A Longitudinal, Cross-Cohort Analysis', Analytical Studies Research Paper 164, Ottawa: Statistics Canada.

Frenette, M. and Morissette, R. (2003) 'Will They Ever Converge? Earnings of Immigrant and Canadian-born Workers over the Last Two Decades', Analytical Studies Branch Research Paper 215, Ottawa: Statistics Canada.

Green, F., McIntosh, S., and Vignoles, A. (2002) 'The Utilization of Education and Skills: Evidence from Britain', *The Manchester School*, 70(6): 792–811.

Groot,W. and van den Brink, H. M.(2000) 'Overeducation in the Labour Market: A Meta-Analysis', *Economics of Education Review*, 19(2): 149–158.

Grugulis, I. (2003) 'Putting Skills to Work: Learning and Employment at the Start of the Century', *Human Resource Management Journal*, 13(2): 3–12.

Hartog, J. (2000) 'Overeducation and Earnings: Where Are We, Where Should We Go?', *Economics of Education Review*, 19(2): 131–147.

Hamper, B. (1991) *Rivethead: Tales from the Assembly Line*, New York: Warner Books.

Handel, M. (2003) 'Skills Mismatch in the Labour Market', *Annual Review of Sociology*, 29: 135–165.

Handel, M. (2005) *Worker Skills and Job Requirements: Is there a Mismatch?* Washington, DC: Economic Policy Institute.

Harris, S. (1949) *The Market for College Graduates*, Cambridge, MA: Harvard University Press.

International Labour Office (ILO) (1998) 'Resolution Concerning the Measurement of Underemployment and Inadequate Employment Situations' (adopted by the Sixteenth International Conference of Labour Statisticians), Geneva: International Labour Office.

Jensen, L. and Slack, T. (2002) 'Race, Ethnicity, and Underemployment in Nonmetropolitan America: A 30-Year Profile', *Rural Sociology*, 67(2): 208–233.

Kalleberg, A. (2008) 'The Mismatched Worker: When People Don't Fit Their Jobs, *Academy of Management Perspectives*, 22(1): 24–40.

Krahn, H. and Bowlby, J. W. (1999) 'Education–Job Skills Match: An Analysis of the 1990 and 1995 National Graduates Surveys', Research Paper no. R-00-1-1E. Applied Research

Branch, Strategic Policy, Human Resources Development Canada and Centre for Education Statistics, Ottawa: Statistics Canada.
Li, C. Gervais, G., and Duval, A. (2006) 'The Dynamics of Overqualification: Canada's Underemployed University Graduates'. Analytical Paper no. 11-621-MIE2006039, Ottawa: Statistics Canada.
Livingstone, D. W. (2004) *The Education-Jobs Gap: Underemployment Or Economic Democracy*, 2nd ed., Toronto: Garamond Press.
Livingstone, D. W. (ed.) (2009) *Education and Jobs: Exploring the Gaps*, Toronto: University of Toronto Press.
Livingstone, D. W. (ed.) (2010a) *Lifelong Learning in Paid and Unpaid Work*, New York: Routledge.
Livingstone, D. W. (2010b) 'The Relationship between Workers' Practical Knowledge and Their Job Requirements: Findings of the 1998, 2004, and 2010 National Surveys of Work and Lifelong Learning', Plenary presentation to the Canadian Society for Training and Development Conference and Trade Show, Metro Toronto Convention Centre.
Livingstone, D. W. and Pollock, K. (2005) 'No Room at the Top: Gender Limits to the "Managerial Revolution"', WALL Working Paper, Centre for the Study of Education and Work, OISE, Toronto: University of Toronto.
Marx, K. (1967 [1894]) *Capital*. Vol. 3: *The Process of Capitalist Production as a Whole*, New York: International Publishers.
McGoldrick, K. and Robst, J. (1996) 'Gender Differences in Overeducation: A Test of the Theory of Differential Over-Qualification', *American Economic Review*, 86(2): 280–284.
McGuiness, S. (2006) 'Overeducation in the Labour Market', *Journal of Economic Surveys*, 20(3): 387–418.
McKee-Ryan, F. and Harvey, J. (2011) '"I have a job, but ...": A Review of Underemployment', *Journal of Management*, 37(4): 962–996.
National Research Council (1999) *The Changing Nature of Work: Implications for Occupational Analysis*, Washington, DC: National Academy Press.
Ness, I. and Azzellini, D. (eds) (2011) *Ours to Master and to Own: Workers' Control from the Commune to the Present*, Chicago: Haymarket Books.
Quintini, G. (2011) 'Right for the Job: Over-Qualified or Under-Skilled?' OECD Social, Employment, and Migration Working Papers, no. 120, Paris: OECD.
Sawchuk, P. H. (2006). 'Use-Value and the Re-Thinking of Skills, Learning and the Labour Process', *Journal of Industrial Relations*, 48(5): 593–617.
Scurry, T. and Blenkinsopp, J. (2011) 'Under-Employment amongst Recent Graduates: A Review of the Literature', *Personnel Review*, 40(5): 643–659.
Skills Australia (2012) *Better Use of Skills, Better Outcomes: A Research Report on Skills Utilisation in Australia*, Canberra: Department of Education, Employment and Workplace Relations.
Smith, V. (2010) 'Enhancing Employability: Human, Cultural, and Social Capital in an Era of Turbulent Unpredictability', *Human Relations*, 63(2): 279–303.
Staines, G. and Quinn, R. (1979) 'American Workers Evaluate the Quality of Their Jobs', *Monthly Labor Review*, 102(1): 3–12.
Sum, A. and I. Khatiwada (2010) 'The Nation's Underemployed in the "Great Recession" of 2007–2009', *Monthly Labor Review*, 133(11): 3–15.
Reitz, J. (1998) *Warmth of the Welcome*, Boulder, CO: Westview Press.
Tåhlin, M. (2006) 'Skill Change and Skill Matching in the Labor Market: A Cross-National Overview'. www2.sofi.su.se/~mta/docs/Skill_change_-_a_cross-national_overview.pdf.

Thurow, L. (1975) *Generating Inequality*, New York: Basic Books.

Vaisey, S. (2006) 'Education and its Discontents: Overqualification in America, 1972–2002', *Social Forces*, 85(2): 835–864.

Verdugo, R. and N. Verdugo (1989) 'The Impact of Surplus Schooling on Earnings', *Journal of Human Resources*, 24(4): 629–643.

Verhaest, D. and Omey, E. (2006) 'Measuring the Incidence of Over- and Undereducation', *Quality and Quantity*, 40(5): 783–803.

Verdugo, R. and Verdugo, N. (1989) 'The Impact of Surplus Schooling on Earnings', *Journal of Human Resources*, 24(4): 629–643.

Warhurst, C. and P. Findlay (2012) 'More Effective Skills Utilisation: Shifting the Terrain of Skills Policy in Scotland'. SKOPE Research Paper no. 107, ESRC Centre on Skills, Knowledge and Organisational Performance, Universities of Oxford and Warwick.

Wolbers, M. H. (2003) 'Job Mismatches and their Labour-Market Effects amongst School-Leavers in Europe', *European Sociological Review*, 19(3): 249–266.

Yates, M. (2011) 'The Human-as-Waste, the Labor Theory of Value and Disposability in Contemporary Capitalism', *Antipode*, 43(5): 1679–1695.

CHAPTER 15

BUSINESS STRATEGIES AND SKILLS

DAVID ASHTON, CAROLINE LLOYD, AND CHRIS WARHURST

INTRODUCTION

ACROSS a wide range of countries skills have been identified as key to economic growth and performance. Concerns over globalization, and the rapid expansion of the Indian and Chinese economies, have heightened the issue of the ability of western economies to compete with low wage countries (see Lauder et al., Chapter 19, this volume). The way to maintain future living standards has centred on encouraging more organizations to forego cost-based competition and move into markets that demand high quality and innovation. To this end, policy-makers have exhorted firms to adopt what is called the 'high road' model of competitive advantage in which workers are viewed as an asset and investment in their skills' upgrade a requirement (Mayhew and Keep 2014). A high-skilled workforce is seen as essential to this end and, as a result, governments across the globe have sought to improve their workforce skill base. The basis of these policies is a belief in the critical link between skill and business strategy, with the latter defined as an organization's competitive logic.[1] A high-skilled workforce is viewed both as a driver of this competitive advantage and one of its outcomes (Lloyd and Payne 2006).

Skills are not just viewed as vital for firms in terms of allowing them to compete in specific markets and improving productivity, they also hold out the promise of intrinsic and extrinsic rewards for individual workers. Jobs that require greater knowledge, and are more complex and varied, provide the potential for a more fulfilling working life compared to jobs which are repetitive, routine, and offer little in the way of interest, challenge, or creativity (Gallie 2010). Higher-skilled jobs are generally better paid, are

[1] For a short discussion of the differences and distinctions between and amongst business strategies and business models, see Storey and Salaman (2008).

more likely to involve learning on the job, and provide access to training and opportunities for progression (see also Holmes, Chapter 17, this volume). Skills provide individuals with some protection against substitutability, thereby offering the potential for greater bargaining power over broader conditions of employment. This mutual gains agenda is one that underpins the current emphasis of governments on high performance working practices (HPWP) or high involvement management practices (HIM), which we outline below.

Over many years, a number of countries have pursued the goal of more high-skilled jobs through raising the qualification levels of the workforce, particularly by expanding higher education. This expansion increases the supply of graduates onto the labour market. The idea behind this supply-side intervention is that a high-skilled workforce will attract businesses that wish to or already do compete on quality and/or innovation, or will encourage existing organizations to make use of these skills and improve performance, including moving into higher-value-added markets (Warhurst and Findlay 2012).

The problem is that there is increasing evidence of growing levels of over-qualification and that economies are not generating enough high-skilled jobs (see Livingstone, Chapter 14, this volume). Some critics of a qualifications-driven economic agenda (e.g. Keep and Mayhew 1999) have argued that changes to the supply of qualifications has limited impact on the way firms operate because business strategy reflects a range of institutional opportunities and constraints, with skills being only a minor player. Many firms have remained competitively successful in European economies, operating with low-skilled jobs producing low-cost products and services—the so-called 'low road' to competitive advantage—and national governments would have difficulty persuading firms to shift up the value chain without there being appropriate consumer demand for more expensive quality or innovation-driven products (Keep 2000).

Underlying these debates are assumptions about the relationship between skills and business strategy, and the direction of causation. Drawing on research typically focused on the private sector, this chapter starts by making an important contextual distinction between skill levels and skill use, how they feature in firm business strategies, and their relevance to governments, employers, and employees. The following section then presents the two key theories of skill and business strategies developed in two distinct but overlapping literatures on management and institutionalism. The subsequent section then focuses on current research that seeks to move debate beyond assumptions of direct relationships between strategy and skill. The conclusion notes the current shift in emphasis in thinking about what underpins any relationship between business strategies and skill, and presents an alternative approach to developing this relationship.

What Are Skill Levels and Skill Use?

Traditionally amongst policy-makers, the term 'skill' has been used to refer to the stock of skills in any one country and, as we saw in the introduction, these stocks have been linked to the performance of economies. However, for reasons we discuss below, these relationships are being questioned. At the level of the firm there is growing awareness that if higher levels of workforce skill are going to impact on performance, then they have to be used, which, as we see in the next section, is linked to employers' business strategies. It is this combination that influences the ways in which employees acquire and use skills, the satisfaction they receive from work, and their levels of reward.

Changes in National Skill Levels

As noted in the introduction, workforce skill levels have come to be seen as crucial for economic growth. The basis of this belief comes from studies conducted in the mid-to -late twentieth century that established a link between education levels and economic growth. From this link it was argued that investments in education would provide countries with a pay-off in terms of higher growth (Lucas 1988; Bassanini and Scarpetta 2001; Warhurst and Thompson 2007). Human capital theory provided the theoretical underpinning explaining why, as individuals invested more in education and training, they received high returns in the labour market and were valued more by employers for their perceived higher productivity. These skill levels were measured primarily by years in education or the level of qualifications achieved by individuals. There is still a belief in UK and international policy circles that qualification levels are one of the most important indicators of workforce skills, hence the concern with international league tables (OECD 2013; UKCES 2014).

One consequence has been that over the last three decades there has been a massive increase in the investments many countries have made in education, with the result that there has been an exponential increase in the proportion of the global workforce with higher levels of education. In the early twenty-first century many countries had graduate numbers in excess of 30% of each new cohort entering the labour market (Brown et al. 2008) and in the case of South Korea the number has reached 80% (Yoon and Lee 2009). As each country has sought to produce more graduates to stimulate economic growth, the increased supply of graduates onto the labour market has outstripped the ability of their economies to generate graduate jobs. The result is rising rates of graduate under-employment (Green and Zhu 2010), which is seemingly structural rather than cyclical (Purcell et al. 2013) and which now threatens to undermine the traditional link between investment in education and training and economic returns that lies at the heart of human capital theory (cf. Gambin and Hogarth, Chapter 31 in this volume).

The Distinction between Skill Levels and Skill Use

Over the last decade researchers have successfully established that skills are a derived demand, stemming from the employment and human resources (HR) practices of the employer. If we are to further our understanding of skills in general, researchers such as

Ashton and Sung (2011) have argued that a distinction needs to be made between skill levels, that refer to the qualifications individuals possess and which provide a measure of the stock of skills, and skill utilization which refers to the ways that employers use skills in the workplace. There is long-standing argument that the workforce's skill level is determined by the type of technology (broadly defined) that firms use. An example is provided by the post-WWII industrialism thesis of Kerr et al. (1960), who posited that the then new and more 'advanced technology' of industrial production required countries that wished to industrialize to improve the skill of their workforces so that they become 'highly qualified' (1960, 56, 44). However, as Braverman (1974) noted, the skill level *of* the workforce needs to be distinguished from the skill used *by* the workforce (for a revisiting and update of this distinction, see Sung and Ashton 2015). This skill utilization is shaped more by the human resource management (HRM) practices and work organization adopted by firms. Warhurst and Findlay (2012) also point out that there is a need to distinguish between 'the better use of existing skills' by employers when they want the job done better and 'the use of better skills' when they change a job to demand higher skills.

One consequence of the shift to examine the use of skills was that the research agenda moved away from a pre-occupation with skills supply and instead focused on opening up the 'black box' of employer behaviour. It was hoped that this incursion would provide further understanding of how employers use skills in the process of production and thereby how skills utilization might be improved. One approach to understanding how employers may have increased the skills of employees came from work on HPWP or HIM. This research focused on examining management practices such as cellular production, job redesign, self-managed work teams, multi-skilling, higher levels of training, greater dissemination of business information, appraisals, and performance related pay. The primary purpose of these practices is to improve organizational performance but in that process they might also increase employees' skills (Ashton and Sung 2002) as employers make use of 'better skills'. In this respect these HR practices could be seen as part of a process of upskilling the workforce.

However, there is another tradition of research that provided an alternative perspective on the ways in which employers structure and use the skills of their labour force, namely the labour process school that emerged from the work of Braverman (1974) and which focused on how employers use technology and organizational practices to de-skill work as an integral part of their attempts to reduce labour costs. A key point in this argument was that workplace skills were linked to the competitive strategies of employers: more precisely, that in order to remain competitive employers were compelled to deskill workers in order to cheapen the costs of production (Knights and Willmott 1988). This claim was hotly contested; for example, as Wood (1989) pointed out at the time, there are two different processes of change operating in the workplace: de-skilling as well as upskilling. In both cases, the debate shifted from one concerned with the level (or stock) of skills amongst the workforce generally to qualitative changes to the skill levels of particular jobs in the workplace—that is whether jobs were being stripped of their skills or whether jobs were having their skills enhanced.

In the advanced economies the evidence for deskilling within manufacturing was mixed. Meanwhile, the relocation of low-skilled jobs in manufacturing to the newly growing Asian economies in the 1980 and 1990s led to ideas that firms in the advanced economies could concentrate on the new knowledge-intensive work (Reich 1991). However, the reality was that whilst some employers produced knowledge-intensive products in high-tech engineering and in the delivery of banking and business services, a large proportion of the new jobs were low-skilled in the growing service industries, as mass production methods were used to transform the delivery of services in areas such as retail and fast food. This transformation of jobs was not just limited to low-skilled service sector jobs. With the growth of Digital Taylorism as opposed to the old Mechanical Taylorism, there was first a trend for intermediate-level jobs to also be routinized, epitomized by call centres (Lloyd et al. 2008), followed by the same process being applied to professional, technical, and administrative work, resulting in similarly reduced skill requirements. Companies are now successfully attempting to capture much of the new technical and professional know-how in new software applications, in both manufacturing and service industries, enabling them to routinize knowledge that was previously in the heads of technical and professional staff. As the process of Digital Taylorism is still in its early phases, there has been little research to examine its impact on employees (Brown et al. 2011; also Lauder et al., Chapter 19 in this volume).

The debate between the two approaches helps clarify the impact of these HPWP/HIM on intermediate- and lower-skilled workers. Case studies have shown how in some companies the extensive use of these practices has led to employees having their skills continually developed, whilst receiving some of the benefits of improved organizational performance in the form of higher-level income, but these examples come from only a minority of workplaces. In other instances employers have used some of these practices to intensify work whilst not delivering any material benefits to their employees (e.g. UKCES 2009; Sung and Ashton 2015), which brings us back to our current concern with the business strategies of employers discussed in the next section.

Outcomes for Employees

Whilst this debate continues, firmer ground exists in terms of current knowledge of the impact of work organization in general on employees' personal development, skills, job satisfaction, and other aspects of their work experience and wellbeing. In the 1980s Kohn and Schooler (1983) established a link over time and across countries between job characteristics and personal development. Specifically, those employees in jobs that allowed self-direction had greater self-confidence and intellectual flexibility than those whose jobs were strictly controlled by others, and who exhibited lower self-confidence and less intellectual flexibility. Moreover, as these studies were longitudinal they were able to show how these differences increased over time. The powerful impact of work design on job satisfaction and skill development was also revealed in the studies pioneered by Hackman and Oldman (1980). They demonstrated how jobs that are 'enriched', in that they provide the workers with the opportunity to exercise discretion in the performance of their tasks, have more variety and responsibility, then provide higher levels of work satisfaction and skill utilization for employees. Conversely, jobs in which the employee has low levels of discretion and where the performance of their tasks is tightly controlled result in low levels of job satisfaction and low-skill utilization—findings that are now well established (Wood et al. 2012).

This evidence does not mean that higher-skilled jobs have no negative aspects. As Green (2002) demonstrated, compared to less-skilled jobs, higher-skilled jobs engender greater enthusiasm but also greater anxiety. Taken together, higher-skilled jobs are associated with greater levels of anxiety, whilst those who have experienced an increase in the skills required in their job are more likely to report a rise in their level of stress than those whose skills are stationary or falling. There is also evidence that specific management practices, such as team-working, can have significant effects on employees' experience of work. Thus Gallie et al. (2009) found that the benefits of teamwork, in terms of both productive potential and employee welfare, are confined to self-directive teams, whilst non-self-directive teams suppress the use of personal initiative and discretion at work.

Where current knowledge is more uncertain is on the impact of bundles of such practices on employees. For example, Boxall and Macky (2009) report evidence from New Zealand of a direct relationship between HIM and job satisfaction, finding that when the employees' experience of knowledge, information, rewards, and power increase, the employment relationship moves in a direction that employees find more satisfying. On the other hand, Wood et al. (2012) report from UK data that whilst job enlargement is linked with increased job satisfaction, HIM is negatively related to job satisfaction. Such discrepancies may be the result of national cultural and institutional differences or forms of measurement used in the research. Clearly further research is needed but one suggestion is that when job enlargement or redesign is linked to the HIM practices in workplaces characterized by high levels of trust, then the workers may receive positive gains across the board. However, where jobs remain tightly defined and HIM practices are imposed, it may lead to little skill development, work intensification, higher levels of stress, and less job satisfaction.

In the area of pay, what was once seen as a straightforward relationship between skill levels and pay, with more highly qualified workers receiving higher pay, is now more open to question. Firstly, with the extension of competence-based qualifications to a larger proportion of employees, there is evidence that most lower-level qualifications have no effect on wages (Dickerson and Vignoles 2007). Secondly, as we noted earlier, with the growth of graduate numbers there is a growing problem of graduate underemployment and there is evidence that the economic returns to graduate qualifications are falling, apart from those who enter the highest level of the labour market (Brown et al. 2008; Purcell et al. 2013).

Finally, whilst more is learnt through ongoing research about the impact of different management practices and business strategies on the skills and experience of different groups of workers, it is important to bear in mind that there are also more general trends that are impacting on the labour force as a whole. The work of Green (2006) has shown that whilst the majority of employees in the United Kingdom now feel they use more skills at work then they did 15 years ago, work effort has been intensified and their influence over their daily work tasks has been diminished. Other research highlights how the range of what is perceived to be skills is broader than it was in the past and that skills are no longer axiomatically aligned with qualifications (Grugulis and Lloyd 2010). Indeed as Grugulis et al. (2004) have pointed out, much of what was once perceived as a worker's personality is now cast by employers as a skill—hard work, diligence, attitude, and self-presentation. In the United States, employers in routine services even regard being drug-free as a skill (Lafer 2004). 'In this case', Lafer argues, '"skill" means nothing more than "whatever employers want"' (2004, 118; see also Warhurst et al., Chapter 4 in this volume). Certainly, this shift in employers' demand for the use of putative 'soft skills' in the workplace is linked to growth in importance of services within the advanced and other economies (see Payne, Chapter 3 in this volume). This evidence serves as a good reminder that studies of skill levels and use at the level of the firm may, if we are not careful, blind us to major societal changes that are transforming the wider labour market.

Theories of Skill and Business Strategies

Despite the centrality of skills to debates on economic performance, there is surprisingly little development of theoretical perspectives on how skills link into business strategy. There are two main strands: the first developed from the management literature and the second from institutional approaches.

The HRM Approach

Within much of the management literature, where skills are considered, skills are regarded as third or fourth level issues. The organization begins with a competitive or business strategy—more specifically a product market strategy and the type of good or service being produced by the firm (Hogarth et al. 2004). From this strategy the firm develops particularly forms of technology and work design, followed by the skills that are needed (see Figure 15.1). There is, therefore, a direct causal relationship asserted from business strategy to skills. The most influential work is Schuler and Jackson's (1987) use of Porter's three models of competitiveness (1980); cost reduction, quality enhancement, and innovation. For each strategy, they identify the appropriate human resource (HR) practices and skill characteristics of the workforce. A cost reduction strategy is said to require minimal levels of training, a quality enhancement strategy should be associated with extensive and continuous training and development

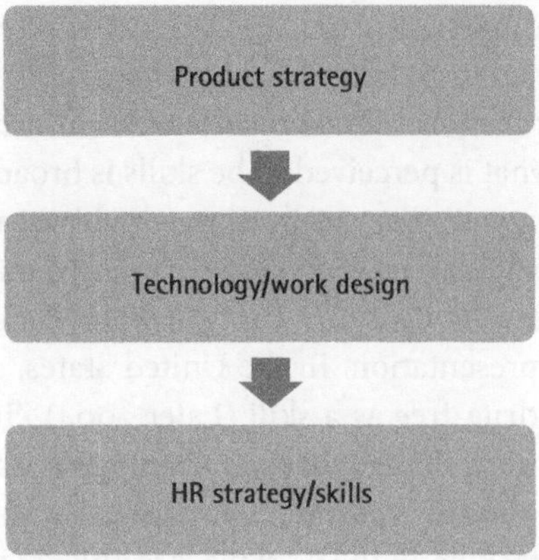

FIGURE 15.1 Skill as a third order issue

of employees and innovation involves highly skilled individuals and the development of a broad range of skills. The skills required are related to the nature of the production process or service delivery found in each type of strategy. Cost reduction is best achieved through designing narrow job tasks and employing low-skilled workers on low pay. Quality enhancement, on the contrary, needs employees to be committed to quality and continuous improvement, therefore flexibility is key alongside having the skills and motivation to participate in ongoing change. In short, organizations start with business development, move on to organizational development (loosely defined) and finally consider any aligning with workforce development needs (Warhurst and Findlay 2012).

Within the management literature sub-field of HRM, much of the research begins from assuming direct links between these three or sometimes two types (omitting the innovation model) of strategy and skills. To produce high quality goods and services requires sophisticated HR policies and practices which include a skilled and well-trained workforce (e.g. Guest 1987; Legge 1995). Similarly other management techniques, such as Total Quality Management (TQM), as well as the HPWP that are outlined above, also proclaim that to produce a 'quality product' requires employees to be better trained (for a discussion, see Rees 1998) and that performance can be improved by enabling workers to undertake more flexible job roles and to take on greater responsibilities (Appelbaum et al. 2000).

There is some evidence that skills do relate positively to product strategy—at least in the United Kingdom (Mason 2004, 45), such that 'some form of correspondence between product market choices and skill requirements' is confirmed. Nevertheless, the links made between business strategy and skills tend to be models about the 'best way' of achieving competitive success rather than about identifying what happens in practice. In other words, they tend to be prescriptive rather than descriptive of practice. There is also little distinction made between being well trained in the range of tasks required, often described as skilled, and levels of skill, i.e. low/intermediate/high, based upon aspects such as knowledge required and years of education/training.

Institutional/Comparative Approaches

Those researchers adopting an institutional perspective shift the primary focus away from the quality/cost dimension within an individual firm towards the broader dimensions of why particular countries tend towards more or less firms adopting particular competitive strategies and related skills profiles. The nature of financial markets, the organization of employers and trade unions, aspects of welfare, employment regulation and the education and training system are seen as interlocking institutions that shape the way companies operate (e.g. Hall and Soskice 2001; Estevez-Abe et al. 2001). Finegold and Soskice (1988) initially developed the idea of different institutional configurations producing a low-skill equilibrium in the United Kingdom and a high-skill equilibrium in countries such as Germany. Long-term relationships, well-developed institutions, and strong regulations encourage firms to adopt a more quality-based strategy producing differentiated goods. Streeck (1997) referred to the German system as providing 'beneficial constraints' that restrict the viability of cost-based strategies. In contrast, the flexibility of the United Kingdom's lightly regulated capital and labour markets makes incremental quality-based approaches more difficult whilst increasing the incentives of cost-based approaches or pursuing a more radical innovative strategy. Certainly many industries in the United Kingdom appear to lean heavily on product strategies that are low-value-adding and rest on having a low-skilled workforce (Mason 2004; UKCES 2010). As such, it is a popular explanation amongst some economic commentators for explaining the relative under-performance, for example, of the United Kingdom compared to Germany (e.g. Hutton 1995). It is also an approach that underpins the economic policy proposals of international development organizations such as the OEDC when they lay out their suggested institutional tools for fixing the problems of low-skill equilibriums (e.g. OECD 2010).

The institutional approach is under-laid by a technical relationship: 'firms producing quality, specialized goods and services require a well-qualified workforce capable of rapid adjustment in the work process and continual product innovation', whereas 'large mass-production manufacturing sector required only a small number of skilled workers and university graduates' (Sorge and Streeck 1988, 21–22). Batch size and 'strategies to translate product demand and variety into batches of components and parts' are identified by Sorge and Streeck (1988, 25) as the main links between the product market and the organization of work and skills. Where batches are smaller, there is a constant need to 'retool, reset, replan, reprogramme, redesign and adapt' (1988, 25), which restricts 'the usefulness of constraining standards and central plans.' The result of these discontinuities is a need for workers with broad and higher levels of skill (see also Steedman and Wagner 1985). By contrast, for large batches it 'pays to concentrate and develop separately a wide range of tasks' (Sorge and Streeck 1988, 24), leading to a more rigid segmentation of work and a polarized distribution of skills.

Although the dominant view is of a direct relationship between product market strategy and skills, the direction of causation is less clear; Sorge and Streeck (1988, 27) refer to it as 'reciprocal causation' as skills supply can also influence the choices open to firms. The availability and type of skills in the labour market can help shape the choices that firms make (see Regini 1997), leading some researchers to argue that a change in the education and training system can push more firms to a quality or innovative competitive pathway (e.g. Soskice 1993). Others, however, insist that the system is interlocked, and that changing one institution will have only a marginal impact on the way firms behave.

These two approaches have different emphases—most obviously one reading off skills from firms' product market strategy, the other reading off skills from firms' institutional embeddedness. Nevertheless, all agree that in higher-quality markets employees within firms will be using higher-level skills than those in cost-based markets. Both approaches have also been largely based upon models developed from research of manufacturing organizations and often, as Mason (2004) has noted, rely on case study research. Stretching the research methodology and industry coverage suggests a more complex even contrary link between business strategy and skills, as the next section outlines.

Moving beyond Direct Relationships between Strategy and Skill

Whilst the general assumption underpinning the two theoretical approaches is of a fairly direct relationship between business strategy and skills, a number of academics have questioned this somewhat deterministic relationship. Criticism, or at least qualification of this assumption, has a number of facets.

A More Complex Relationship?

The first is recognition that the relationship between product market strategy and skills can be fluid. Whilst Mason's (2004) analysis identified an empirical link between strategy and skills, that headline finding has a softer underbelly that is filled with a 'striking amount of within-industry variation' (2004, 44). That is, although there exists a polarization of skills requirements (high vs low) by firm product market strategy (high value-added vs low value-added respectively) within industries, the patterning of firm skill demand is more complex than a straightforward polarization: there can be 'high, medium and low end activities along the product quality spectrum, with associated variation in skill requirements' (2004, 44). He cites the printing and publishing, and specialized retail industries as examples. Whilst Mason confirms a 'correspondence' between the product market strategies of firms and skill requirements, the 'diversity' suggests that the two expected and contrasting outcomes—high- and low-skill equilibria—are too simplistic. Rather, he says, it is better to think of these two outcomes as poles along the spectrum, with firms occupying various positions along this spectrum.

Other research, within another set of literature—that of job quality—suggests that firms' positioning can vary, not just within the same industry but also within the same product market. Metcalf and Dhudwar (2010) reveal that different firms in the same industry and operating in the same product market can have different HR policies and practices—offering, for example, full-time or part-time employment contracts, and changing to offer better, full-time contracts over time. Given the same constraints faced by these firms in this research, this finding raises the possibility of managerial choice rather than simple determinism driven by either product market or institutional embeddedness—a point to which we return below. What is left open in both sets of research is why some firms opt for one position rather than another.

From Manufacturing to Services

Secondly, the two theoretical approaches have been largely based upon models developed from manufacturing organizations. The underpinning assumptions have then been transposed to the service sector, where the main approach is a duality in terms of cost/standardization and quality/differentiation (see Frenkel 2005). Batt (2000) identifies mass-produced services, with standardized services and high volumes where it is rational to automate processes, divide up tasks, and reduce skill levels. For quality service, which requires customization, services need to fit to individual customer demand and offerings are more complex, requiring higher levels of skills for workers (see also Keltner et al. 1999).

This extrapolation from manufacturing to services has been questioned. For example, Eichhorst and Marx (2009, 6) highlight how fewer service firms in Germany offer the same extent of training as manufacturing firms (28% vs 44%). There are a number of possible reasons, they claim, why service firms do not opt for the same skill development model as manufacturing firms. Service work tends to be dominated by female workers, with employers less willing to invest in training for these workers because of fears of labour turnover arising from childcare responsibilities. In addition, people are often part of the product offering and their soft skills are less amenable to technical accreditation. Whilst these explanations are not empirically tested, other research points to the characteristics of some areas of the service sector, such as the hotel industry, where product 'quality' is driven not by the technical content of the product but by the physical landscape and the provision of labour intensive services (see Lloyd et al. 2013).

The types of skill required in services are more varied than in manufacturing. In routine services such as retail, tasks can be Taylorized, made low-skill and so provide little incentive to employers to invest in employee training. What little skills are required tend to be soft skills such as communication and politeness (see also Nickson et al. 2004). These skills are often not trained or employer-, occupation-, or even industry-specific. In more complex services such as the IT and creative industries, Eichhorst and Marx (2009) argue, tertiary education is required. However, the acquired credentials are useful not for their knowledge-base but because they signal possession of more generic skills such as the capacity to learn—important in industries that have radical innovation and need employee flexibility and adaptability. These low- and high-skill industries are therefore 'significantly different to manufacturing' (2009, 8). Nevertheless, Eichhorst and Marx do suggest that some service industries, such as banking, are closer to the 'logic' of manufacturing. These industries are less radical than the IT example but require more firm-specific training than retail. The outcome is training that provides employees with intermediate-level skills. Taking these three types together, Eichhorst and Marx (2009, 8) conclude that 'the service sector exhibits a great deal of heterogeneity in terms of skills, work organization and innovative capacity'. In other words the relationship between business strategy and skill needs found in manufacturing firms is less prevalent amongst service firms and even within services it is varied. Lloyd et al. (2013) go further, arguing that there can be a decoupling of product and labour such that the link between business strategy and skills may not just be 'weaker' but even 'decoupled' in routine services.

Variety within the Service Sector

Thirdly, and related, firms in the service industries seem to mix and match strategies and skills more fluidly. The relatively simple classification of strategy offered by the two HRM and institutional/comparative approaches is considered by other researchers to be too limited to encompass the wide range of businesses operating in the service sector. The most popular approach is to develop a two by two matrix, giving four alternative classifications of types of services that can then be linked to 'appropriate' HR practices, including skill requirements. Heskett et al.'s (1990) typology is based on the extent of service customization and the degree of customer contact, whilst Schmenner (1995) replaces this latter element with the degree of labour intensity and Boxall (2003) with the extent of sustained competitive advantage. In all cases, customization is the common element that provides the potential for higher-level skills. Lashley's (1998) slightly different approach explores the extent to which the service provision is intangible, i.e. the service deliverer is of prime importance rather than the physical environment. As the intangibleness increases, more is required of employees to deliver the service, which, in association with customization, requires a high dependence on skills. The problem with all these types of typologies, however, is that they are better at identifying the extremes, e.g. fast food in one box and lawyers in another (Haskett et al. 1990) than in capturing the complexity and variety of those service operations that fall in-between.

High Value, Low Skills?

Fourthly, questions about the relevance of the approaches to services are now supplemented by questions about the adhesiveness of the approaches even to manufacturing firms. Boxall and Purcell (2008) point out that in manufacturing, cost-based strategies can be pursued both with high-skill and low-skill workers, depending on the extent and the nature of technology required. Alternatively, expertise in certain areas, such as marketing, may enable a high-value-added product to be produced with a relatively low-skill workforce. Wensley (1999) gives the example of Nike, for whom the use of branding can ensure a high price (and thereby high value-added) coexisting alongside a simple production process (for food production similarly, see James and Lloyd 2010).

Whilst high-value-added products may be easier to produce en masse with mainly low-skilled workers, a high specification or customized product may be more difficult. There have been suggestions that technological progress allows 'the possibility that soon it may be feasible to produce high spec by Fordist production (i.e. low-skill) methods' (Keep and Mayhew 1999). Alternatively, organizations may segment their workforce with core operating staff who are skilled and support workers who are not (Boxall and Purcell 2008; Lloyd et al. 2013). The choice of skill profile could be between, firstly, the majority of workers with a broad range of intermediate skills undertaking a wide range of tasks and operate with relative autonomy and, secondly, most workers having limited skills and autonomy carrying out a narrow range of tasks and who are directed and closely supervised by a number of graduates (Mason 1999).

Others have also pointed to a level of indeterminacy in relationships between strategy and skills. In this approach institutional influences are acknowledged but so too is actor agency within these institutions. For example, Thompson et al. (1995, 721) argue 'there is no *necessary* congruence between markets, technologies and particular forms of work design' (emphasis added). They suggest a more nuanced relationship between skills and markets, 'mediated by institutional frameworks, corporate strategic choices and attempts by managers and other actors in the employment relationship to socially construct and attach meanings to the processes involved' (1995, 740). Similarly, Lloyd and Payne (2002) argue that power relations within the firm, in conjunction with wider institutional constraints, play a key role in the development of forms of work organization and skill levels. Even with high quality product strategies, weak trade unions and limited labour market regulations can mean that employers seek to reduce skill levels and job autonomy (see also Gallie 2007). There may be more limitations in how far price competitive organizations can adopt high-skill approaches.

The Role of Managerial Choice

This last point is developed in a fifth criticism that more overtly emphasizes managerial choice. Ashton and Sung (Ashton and Sung 2006; Sung and Ashton 2015) attempt to move the theoretical framing forwards by extending beyond the technical relations of production seen in the dichotomy between mass production and customization. They add the concept of interpersonal relationships which refers to the way people are managed and has a degree of independence from technical relationships. Irrespective of the nature of the product or service, employers can pursue task-focused strategies where there is a high level of control over delivery of specified tasks, and skills are minimized. Alternatively, employers can pursue a people-developed focus in which the aim is to maximize individual contributions, with skills regarded as an important competitive advantage related to issues such as motivation, commitment, and behaviour. The relative autonomy of the two spheres means that a mass production company can use higher skills than anticipated, whereas a differentiated strategy could be associated with a low-skilled workforce. The reasons why one strategy over another is pursued is linked to individual managerial choice, market opportunities within a sector, and the constraints—or lack of them—in relation to regulation and legislation. Hence the complexity, and even contrariness in the business strategy–workforce skill articulation, becomes more comprehendible. These issues, however, raise further questions about how these choices emerge and might be shaped and which are signalled in the concluding remarks below.

Concluding Remarks

Great emphasis has been put on skills as part of firms' business strategies. In particular, a higher-skilled workforce is regarded as a vital component of competitive advantage. In this context the supply of more and better skilled workers has been boosted by governments across the advanced economies in recent decades, supported by the OECD (2010). This high road approach involves business strategies predicated on firms making better use of skills and using better skills. Employees too can benefit from this focus on skills by firms. Empirical evidence reveals, however, that whilst mutual benefits for firms and employees can exist, there remain significant challenges in delivering the types of HPWP/HIM that best capture the ideal.

Part of the problem lies in the slow advance of theory on how skills link to business strategy. The two main and very influential theories both emphasize the importance of a high-skilled workforce, but arrive at that conclusion from different starting points. Both also tend to base their analyses on research of manufacturing. Applying their approaches to service industries reveals more complex and even contrary links between skills and firms' business strategies. As a consequence, the basic tenet of the two main approaches—the deterministic importance of high-skilled workers to perceived best practice business strategy—has been challenged. Pushing beyond this determinism, more recent theorization has sought to appreciate the role of managerial choice in linking skill to business strategy (Sung and Ashton 2015).

Despite continued emphasis on the centrality of skills to improving national performance, there has been a shift in emphasis. The OECD (2010) recognizes that for skills to be embedded in firms' business strategies, and for firms to make the organizational changes that enable that, requires 'patient capital' that allows firms to make medium- and longer-term investments. They also recommend that national governments establish both 'policy instruments' to boost skill utilization and 'area-based partnerships' (OECD 2010, 35) to better match skills supply and demand. Meanwhile employers should likewise think about improving HRM and work organization, and work with trade unions and other intermediaries to help make these improvements. As to this latter suggestion, pre-crisis, Lloyd and Payne (2002, 386) go further, arguing that a 'strengthened labour movement' is needed that is capable of 'imposing a new competitiveness contract on reluctant capital'.

Whether adopting the softer or stronger position, the problem, as Coffield (2004) points out, is that it is not clear where the agency for this change comes from or the length of time required for this change to take effect. Drawing on another set of literature—that of innovation and which draws on Danish research—Warhurst and Findlay (2012) stress the importance of developing eco-systems of actors, structures, and a set of protocols that identifies the responsibilities and resources need to incentivize and enact change. However, this approach still leaves open the question of whether a government, led by a political party or coalition of parties, would be willing and able to act as a catalyst for this sort of policy development. The 'Better Not Cheaper' campaign in North Rhine-Wesfalia in Germany suggests that some governments are willing to do so. Here firms were supported by stakeholders to develop alternative business strategies with attendant organizational and workforce development in order to avoid locally based firms competing on cost with China (for a short overview, see Warhurst and Findlay 2012).

In this respect, Mason (2004) is right to also suggest that more research is needed on how firms develop their strategies, not just those strategies' outcomes. We would agree with this position if it encompasses recognition of the potential for managerial agency within product market or institutional constraints. It might be that firms need help to make the right decisions and rethink their business strategies. Managers are the obvious target group here. However, a distinction needs to be made between senior and middle or operational management. It is the former that have strategic responsibility and who conceive new firm directions; the latter have operational responsibility and execute the plans of senior management. It is the former who need to think 'outside the box' in order 'to grasp new business opportunities and how best to make use of them (Ashton and Sung 2011, 10). They also need help to do so, in part because, certainly in the United Kingdom, they themselves often lack the skills to make the 'right' decisions (Hogarth et al. 2004; Brink 2010) and are 'imprisoned by their historical mental models and assumptions' which make them unwilling or unable 'to think in new ways' (Storey and Salaman 2008, 37). In the case of small firm owner-managers, they also often lack not just the capability but also the capacity to make the right decisions (Warhurst and Findlay 2012). Thus a key issue Storey and Salaman note is what knowledge firms need to allow consideration of a shift up the value chain. Their answer is a change in the strategic level knowledge possessed by the senior management of firms, that is 'the underlying sets of assumptions, beliefs and propositions … [that] underpin decisions on, and discussions about, issues of strategy and organization' (Storey and Salaman 2008, 40–41).

Ashton and Sung (2011) too argue that targeting senior managers is an imperative if firm and national competitiveness is to be raised through business strategy and skill. They posit that it is policy-makers who must find ways to improve senior managers' capabilities and capacities to perceive and act upon new business opportunities or pressing needs. They argue that these managers have, however, proved impervious to exhortation by government and that other means have to be found to bring pressure to bear upon them if they are 'to change their mindset and modify their business strategy' (Ashton and Sung 2011, 13). They suggest regulation might be one option; other options include the carrot of grant awards to firms from government for the introduction of new ways of organization. Whilst Ashton and Sung make their argument based on UK research, it is an argument that has international resonance: the OECD (2013) now advocates a role for government in shaping rather than merely responding to firms' business strategies. Another option would be more and better management education to address skills deficits amongst senior and other managers (see also Warhurst 2015).

At a time when governments are seeking to find ways of influencing firms' business strategies, the challenge is to provide an intellectual framework that will incorporate the insights of the various schools of thought and the developments that have taken place within them. Moving forwards requires a more 'reality congruent' picture of the processes involved in employers' decision-making about the formulation and implementation of business strategy. The aim has to be to shape the context within which employers' decisions are made: to influence the cost-benefit calculations concerning their investments, their decisions about how to compete in the market and the type of products and services they offer, and how they use their resources and organize their work. Doing so means not simply focusing on managers per se but influencing government decisions at the national level about the regulation of labour, the wages firms pay, the training firms deliver, and the role of trades unions in both of these issues. As a starting point, intervention might focus on the sector level. As Sung and Ashton (2015) argue it is at this level that employers make these decisions. It is here that the competitive environment, the major players in terms of other employers and trade unions, and the various regulations, incentives, market opportunities, and constraints come together to form the sector's 'institutional logic' which shapes the employers' dispositions and decision-making processes. Of course such arrangements take time to establish and would differ from one sector and country to another, but offer the possibility of delivering a more effective form of policy implementation in linking business strategy and skill.

References

Appelbaum, E., Bailey, T., Berg, P., and Kalleberg, A. (2000) *Manufacturing Advantage*, Ithaca: Cornell University Press.

Ashton, D. and Sung, J. (2002) *Supporting Workplace Learning for High-Performance Working*, Geneva: ILO.

Ashton, D. and Sung, J. (2006) 'How Competitive Strategy Matters? Understanding the Drivers of Training, Learning and Performance at the Level of the Firm', SKOPE Research Paper no. 66, SKOPE, Universities of Oxford and Warwick.

Ashton, D. and Sung, J. (2011) *Productivity and Skills: Skills in Focus*, Glasgow: Skills Development Scotland.

Bassanini, A and Scarpetta, S. (2001) 'Does Human Capital Matter for Growth in OECD Countries? Evidence from Pooled Mean Group Estimates', *OECD Economics Department Working Papers No. 282, OECD, Paris.*

Batt, R. (2000) 'Strategic Segmentation in Front-Line Services: Matching Customers, Employees and Human Resource Systems', *International Journal of Human Resource Management*, 11(3): 540–561.

Boxall, P. (2003) 'HR Strategy and Competitive Advantage in the Service Sector', *Human Resource Management Journal*, 13(3): 5–20.

Boxall, P. and Macky, K. (2009) 'Research and Theory on High-Performance Work Systems: Progressing the High-Involvement Stream', *Human Resource Management Journal*, 19(1): 3–23.

Braverman, H. (1974) *Labor and Monopoly Capital*, New York: Monthly Review Press.

Brown, P., Lauder, H., and Ashton, D. (2011) *The Global Auction*, New York: Oxford University Press.

Brown, P., Ashton, D., Lauder, H., and Tholen, G. (2008) 'Toward a High-Skilled, Low-Waged, Workforce? A Review of Global Trends in Education, Employment and the Labour Market', SKOPE Monograph no. 10, SKOPE, Universities of Oxford and Cardiff.

Coffield, F. (2004) 'Alternative Routes out of the Low Skills Equilibrium: A Rejoinder to Lloyd and Payne', *Journal of Education Policy*, 19(6): 733–740.

Dickerson, A. and Vignoles, A. (2007) 'The Distribution and Returns to Qualifications in the Sector Skills Councils', SSDA Research Report no. 21, SSDA, Wath-Upon-Dearne: Sector Skills Development Agency.

Eichhorst, W. and Marx, P. (2009) 'From the Dual Apprenticeship System to a Dual Labour Market? The German High-Skill Equilibrium and the Service Economy', Discussion Paper no. 4220, IZA, Berlin.

Estevez-Abe, M. Iverson, T., and Soskice, D. (2001) 'Social Protection and the Formation of Skills: A Reinterpretation of the Welfare State', in P. A. Hall and D. Soskice (eds), *Varieties of Capitalism*, Oxford: Oxford University Press.

Frenkel, S. (2005) 'Service Workers in Search of Decent Work', in S. Ackroyd, R. Batt, P. Thompson, and P. S. Tolbert (eds), *Oxford Handbook of Work and Organization*, Oxford: Oxford University Press.

Gallie, D., Zhou, Y., Felstead, A., and Green, F. (2009) 'Teamwork, Productive Potential and Employee Welfare', SKOPE Research Paper no. 84, SKOPE, Universities of Oxford and Cardiff.

Gambin, L., Hogarth, T., Murphy, L., Spreadbury, K., Warhurst, C., and Winterbotham, M. (2015) *Research to Understand the Extent, Nature and Impact of Skills Mismatches in the Economy*, London: Department for Business Innovation and Skills.

Green, F. (2002) 'High Skills and High Anxiety: Skills Hard Work and Mental Well-Being', SKOPE Research Paper no. 27, Universities of Oxford and Warwick.

Green, F. (2006) *Demanding Work*, Princeton, NJ: Princeton University Press.

Green, F. and Zhou, Y. (2010) 'Overqualification, Job Dissatisfaction, and Increasing Dispersion in the Returns to Graduate Education', *Oxford Economic Papers*, Oxford: Oxford University Press.

Grugulis, I. and Lloyd, C. 2010 'Skill and the Labour Process: The Conditions and Consequences of Change', in P. Thompson and C. Smith (eds), *Working Life*, Basingstoke: Palgrave Macmillan: 91–112.

Grugulis, I., Warhurst, C., and Keep, E. (2004) 'What's Happening to Skill?', in C. Warhurst, E. Keep, and I. Grugulis (eds), *The Skills That Matter*, London: Palgrave: 1–18.

Guest, D. (1987) 'Human Resource Management and Industrial Relations', *Journal of Management Studies*, 24(5): 503–521.

Hackman, J. R. and Oldman, G. R. (1980) *Work Redesign*, Reading, MA: Addison-Wesley.

Hall, P. A. and Soskice, D. (2001) *Varieties of Capitalism*, Oxford: Oxford University Press.

Heskett, J., Earl Sasser, W., and Hart, C. (1990) *Service Breakthroughs: Changing the Rules of the Game*, New York: The Free Press.

Hogarth, T., Adams, L., Daniel, W. W., Lorentzien-White, D., and Shury, J. (2004) *Skills in Scotland: Case Study Report*, Glasgow, Futureskills Scotland.

Hutton, W. (1995) *They State We're In*, London: Jonathan Cape.

James, S. and Lloyd, C. (2008) 'Supply Chain Pressures and Migrant Workers: Deteriorating Job Quality in the UK Food Processing Industry', in C. Lloyd, G. Mason, and K. Mayhew (eds), *Low-Wage Work in the United Kingdom*, New York: Russell Sage Foundation: 211–246.

Keep. E. (2000) *Upskilling Scotland*, New Horizon Reports, Glasgow: University of Strathclyde/ Industrial Society.

Keep, E. and Mayhew, K. (1999) 'The Assessment: Knowledge, Skills and Competitiveness', *Oxford Review of Economic Policy*, 15(1): 1–15.

Keltner, B., Finegold, D., Mason, G., and Wagner, K. (1999) 'Market Segmentation Strategies and Service Sector Productivity', *California Management Review*, 41(4): 84–102.

Kerr, C., Dunlop, J. T., Harbison, F., and Myers, C. A. (1960) *Industrialism and Industrial Man*, Cambridge, MA: Harvard University Press.

Knights, D. and H. Willmott (1988) *New Technology and the Labour Process*, London: Macmillan.

Kohn, M. L. and Schooler, C. (1983) *Work and Personality*, Norwood, NJ: Ablex.

Lafer, G. (2004) 'What is "Skill"? Training for Discipline in the Low-Wage Labour Market', in C. Warhurst, E. Keep, and I. Grugulis (eds), *The Skills That Matter*, London: Palgrave: 109–127.

Lashley, C. (1998) 'Matching the Management of Human Resources to Service Operations', *International Journal of Contemporary Hospitality Management*, 10(1): 24–33.

Legge, K. (1995) *Human Resource Management*, Basingstoke: MacMillan.

Lloyd, C. and Payne, J. (2002) 'On "the Political Economy of Skill": Assessing the Possibilities for a Viable High Skills Project in the UK', *New Political Economy*, 7(3): 367–395.

Lloyd, C., Mason, G., and Meyhew, K. (2008) *Low-Wage Work in the United Kingdom*, New York: Russell Sage Foundation.

Lloyd, C., Warhurst, C., and Dutton, E. (2013) 'The Weakest Link? Product Market Strategies, Skill and Pay in the Hotel Industry', *Work, Employment and Society*, 27(2): 254–271.

Lucas, R. E. (1988) 'On the Mechanics of Economic Development', *Journal of Monetary Economics*, 22, 3–42.

Mason, G. (2004) 'Enterprise Product Strategies and Employer Demand for Skills in Britain: Evidence form the Employer Skill Survey', Research Paper no. 50, SKOPE, Universities of Oxford and Warwick.

Mayhew K. and Keep E. (2014) *Industrial Strategy and the Future of Skills Policy*, London: CIPD.

Metcalf, H. and Dhudwar, A. (2010) *Employers' Role in the Low-Pay/No-ay Cycle*, York: Joseph Rowntree Foundation.

Nickson, D., Warhurst, C., and Dutton, E. (2004) 'Aesthetic Labour and the Policy-Making Agenda: Time for a Re-appraisal of Skills?', Research Paper no. 48, SKOPE, Universities of Oxford and Warwick.

Organisation for Economic Co-operation and Development (OECD) (2010) *Putting in Place Jobs that Last*, Paris: OECD.

Organisation for Economic Co-operation and Development (OECD) (2013) *OECD Skills Outlook 2013—First Results from the Survey of Adult Skills*, Paris: OECD.

Porter, M. (1980) *Competitive Strategy*, New York: Free Press.

Purcell, K., Elias, P., Atfield, G., Behle, H., Ellison, R., and Luchinskaya, D. (2013) 'Transitions into Employment, Further Study and Other Outcomes', Futuretrack Stage 4 Report, Manchester: HECSU/Institute for Employment Research, University of Warwick.

Rees, C. (1998) 'Empowerment through Quality Management: Employee Accounts from Inside a Bank, a Hotel and Two Factories', in C. Mabey, D. Skinner, and T. Clark (eds), *Experiencing Human Resource Management*, London: Sage.

Reich, R. (1991) *The Work of Nations*, New York: Vintage.

Schuler, R. and Jackson, S. (1987) 'Linking Competitive Strategies and Human Resource Management Practices', *Academy of Management Executive*, 1(3): 207–219.

Sorge, A. and Streeck, W. (1988) 'Industrial Relations and Technical Change: The Case for an Extended Perspective', in R. Hyman and W. Streeck (eds), *New Technology and Industrial Relations*, Oxford: Basil Blackwell: 19–47.

Steedman, H. and Wagner, K. (1989) 'Productivity, Machinery and Skills: Clothing Manufacture in Britain and Germany', *National Institute Economic Review*, 128: 40–57.

Storey, J. and Salaman, G. (2008) 'Business Models and Their Implications for Skills', Monograph no. 50, SKOPE, Universities of Oxford and Cardiff.

Streeck, W. (1997) 'Beneficial Constraints: On the Economic Limits of Rational Voluntarism', in J. Rogers Hollingsworth and R. Boyer (eds), *Contemporary Capitalism*, Cambridge: Cambridge University Press: 197–219.

Sung, J. and Ashton, D. N. (2015) *Skills in Business: The Role of Business Strategy, Sectoral Skills Development and Skills Policy*, London: Sage

Thompson, P., Wallace, T., Flecker, J., and Ahlstrand, R. (1995) 'It Ain't What You Do, It's The Way That You Do It: Production Organisation and Skill Utilisation in Commercial Vehicles', *Work, Employment and Society*, 9(4): 719–742.

UK Commission for Employment and Skills (UKCES) (2009) *High Performance Working: A Synthesis of Key Literature*, Wath-upon-Dearne: UKCES.

UK Commission for Employment and Skills (UKCES) (2010) *Ambition 2020: The 2010 Report*, Wath-upon-Dearne: UKCES.

UK Commission for Employment and Skills (UKCES) (2014) *UK Skill Levels and International Competitiveness 2013*, Evidence Report 85, Wath-upon-Dearne: UKCES.

Warhurst, C. (2015) 'Issues to be Considered when Promoting Job Quality', Evidence submitted to the Scottish Parliament Inquiry into Work, Wages and Well-Being in Scotland.

Warhurst, C. and Thompson, P. (2006) 'Mapping Knowledge in Work: Proxies or Practices?', *Work, Employment and Society*, 20(4): 787–800.

Warhurst, C. and Findlay, P. (2012) 'More Effective Skills Utilisation: Shifting the Terrain of Skills Policy in Scotland', SKOPE Research Paper, no. 107, SKOPE Universities of Oxford and Cardiff.

Wood. S. (1989) 'The Transformation of Work?', in S. Wood (ed), *The Transformation of Work?*, London: Unwin.

Wood, S., van Veldhoven, M., Croon, M., and de Menezes, L. M. (2012) 'Enriched Job Design, High Involvement Management and Organizational Performance: The Mediating Roles of Job Satisfaction and Well-Being', *Human Relations*, 65(4): 419–446.

Yoon, J. H. and Lee, B-H. (2009) 'The Transformation of the Government-Led Vocational Training System in Korea', in G. Bosch and J. Charest (eds), *Vocational Training: International Perspectives*, London: Routledge.

CHAPTER 16

MEASURING SKILLS STOCK, JOB SKILLS, AND SKILLS MISMATCH

ALAN FELSTEAD, DUNCAN GALLIE, AND FRANCIS GREEN

Introduction

This chapter presents the different types of international and national skills data currently available, and critically appraises the underlying concepts of skill and the collection techniques used. By these means, the chapter assesses how 'skills' are operationalized in data collection exercises carried out across the world and the relative merits of different measurement approaches (for other reviews, see Felstead 2009 and Green 2013).

This endeavour is not only of academic interest. Governments around the world make substantial investment in education and training to equip citizens with skills to use in and out of work. Great effort is also spent on comparing how nations perform in these respects. The World Economic Forum's *Global Competitiveness Report*, for example, compares 134 countries against more than 110 measures, ten of which are related to the quality of the educational system and the availability of skilled labour. According to its evidence, eight of the ten top skill performers are European countries, with Finland coming top, followed by Sweden and Switzerland. The two non-European countries are Singapore (4th) and Taiwan (10th). The United States and the United Kingdom come outside the top ten, ranked 13th and 16th respectively (Sala-i-Martin 2011, see table 6 of the report). This chapter critically reviews the evidence on which these kinds of international comparisons are made.

The chapter is divided into three substantive sections. The first focuses on measuring the skills stock; that is, the skills held by a given group of individuals. These stocks can be measured for employers, regions, or nations as well as for individuals with different characteristics (see also Holmes, Chapter 17; Smith, Chapter 23; and Gambin and Hogarth, Chapter 31, this volume). The total stock of skills in the working age population can be affected by the relative balance of the inward flow of young people entering the labour market against the outward flow of older workers who leave the labour market by retiring or exit because of ill-health. Today, outflows are much greater than inflows in many parts of the developed world, with significant implications for the availability of skills of those in or available for work (Dunnell 2008; Lutz et al. 2010).

The second section focuses on job skills, that is, the skills required to do a job competently. These vary from job to job with some more complex than others. Complexity varies according to the nature of the work. This includes the abilities and techniques required, the intricacies of the steps involved, and the knowledge of equipment, products, and processes needed for competent performance (Attewell 1990; Spenner 1990; also Handel, Chapter 5). It is important to point out here that there is a significant conceptual difference between labour process definitions of 'deskilling', which refer to reductions of worker autonomy in carrying out work activities and the definition used in this chapter, which refers to a reduction in those ability levels (Felstead et al. 2009; Grugulis and Lloyd 2010). Whilst all jobs are carried out within prescribed rules—whether set by law, occupational standards, or custom and practice—an element of choice/judgement remains. These levels of autonomy are often, but not always, related to job skills (Braverman 1974; Zuboff 1988). If workers do not decide on what tools or methods are needed to accomplish a task and if they cannot schedule what to do and when, they lack control of the labour process, but this lack of control does not necessarily mean that they are low-skilled. Even in these rule-bound circumstances, their jobs may still require them to exercise high-level abilities at interacting, persuading, influencing, and so on. At the same time, it should be noted that these job skills are distinct from what workers themselves bring to the job in terms of their abilities, attitudes, and motivation (Moss and Tilly 1996).

The third section considers mismatches which may occur between the skills stock and job skills. As with the previous two sections, attention focuses on how these mismatches are measured and what international datasets are available for analysts. The chapter ends with a summary of the type of data currently available and some reflections on future research possibilities.

Skills Stock

Implicit in many data collection exercises is a concept of 'skill' found in standard English dictionaries. As a noun, it is 'the ability to do something well', whilst as an adjective, it is 'having or showing the knowledge, ability, or training to perform a certain task or activity well' (Pearall 1998, 1745). When used as a verb, the word refers to a process of movement, which can go up as well as down. So, 'upskilling' refers to the process by which more abilities are acquired, possibly through formal training or informal learning, whilst 'deskilling' refers to the process whereby these abilities are lost through, for example, technological change or lack of use.

Whilst a useful building block, the standard dictionary definition of skill is also problematic in that it does not differentiate levels of performance. Furthermore, it does not recognize the diversity of meanings attached to skill, both in academic discourse and common parlance (Green 2013; also Payne, Chapter 23). There are no adequate measures of skill stocks that comprehensively cover the diversity of skill concepts, including technical skills at all levels, knowledge, and dispositions. The additional measurement challenge is to create a common yardstick which renders skills of different domains commensurate and scalable at the same time as conforming to the methodological norms of reliability and validity (Attewell 1990). Proxies are, therefore, commonly used.

One of the most widely used proxies for measuring the level of skills that people possess is the number of years spent in formal education. It is assumed that through longer exposure times individuals will increase their ability to carry out particular activities. When deployed at work, this enhanced human capital acquired through schooling makes workers more productive and hence increases the economy's output of goods and services. Outside of work, it has been shown that education has a strong impact on social outcomes such as fertility, crime, anti-social behavior, and health. In order to compare educational attainments across countries and quantify the relationship between these economic and social outcomes, data has been collected on the time spent in education and the level of schooling completed. To scale the latter, the most commonly used system is the International Standard Classification of Education (ISCED). This system was created by the United Nations Educational, Scientific and Cultural Organisation (UNESCO) in 1976. It been subject to two revisions: in 1997 and 2011 (UNESCO 2011).

Despite these revisions, the motivation for ISCED remains the same today as it was in 1976. It was recognized then, as now, that the world's education systems vary widely in terms of structure and curricular content. This variation makes it difficult to compare the stock of educated individuals—and by implication the skills stock—across the world. However, by collecting educational data across countries according to a common classification of the level of education completed, this task becomes easier. These 'levels' of education are represented by an ordered set of categories. Each level groups educational programmes according to the learning experiences and the knowledge, skills, and competencies which each programme is designed to impart. The levels therefore represent steps in educational progression. The more advanced the programme, the higher the level of education. The 2011 version of the classification system has nine levels, ranging from pre-primary to doctoral education.

This kind of data can be used to track changes in the stock of skills within countries as well as make comparisons between them. For example, amongst the Organisation for Economic Co-operation and Development (OECD) countries around 30% of 25–64-year-olds have completed tertiary level education (ISCED 5 and above)

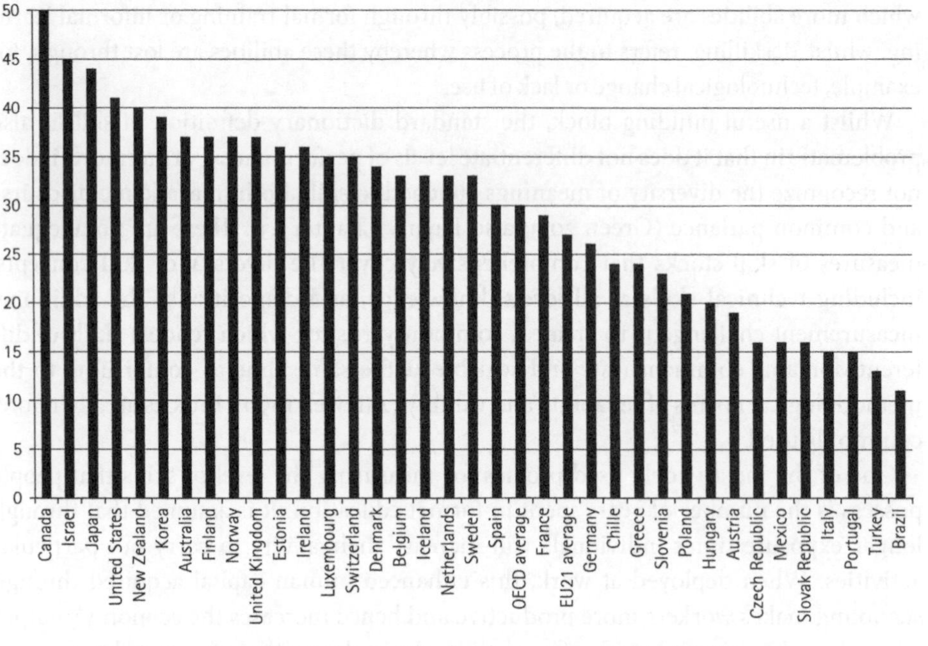

FIGURE 16.1 Proportions educated to tertiary level, 25–64-year-olds, OECD, 2009

Source: OECD (2011a, table A1.4).

(see Figure 16.1). However, some countries are well above the average, whilst others are well below. Four countries—Canada, Israel, Japan, and the United States—have over 40% educated to this level, whilst four countries—Italy, Portugal, Turkey, and Brazil—have around 15% of their 25–64-year-olds educated to tertiary level. The rate of change is also striking. Between 1997 and 2009, for example, the share of tertiary educated workers rose on average by nine percentage points in the OECD, whilst the share of people with less than upper secondary education (ISCED 2 and below) fell by an equivalent amount.

However, there are a number of problems with skills stock data of this type. For example, the number of years spent in each educational level differs between countries and so the time to complete an educational level in one country may not be the same as in other countries. Similarly, the time spent in educational levels even within a single country may change over time, so that one generation's educational level is not the same as another's. Attempts have been made to construct improved measures which take these variations into account. Such calculations are based on the 'percentage of the population who have successfully completed a given level of schooling'—of the type presented in Figure 16.1—adjusted by the 'typical duration of each level of schooling within countries' (Barro and Lee 2001: 542). This means that schooling levels across countries are made equivalent in terms of the number of years taken to complete them.

Even these adjusted figures do not take into account the skills gained by individuals after leaving formal education nor do they take into account the deterioration in the skills they acquired at school through lack of use. A more comprehensive measure of qualifications needs to take account of the qualifications held by individuals regardless of whether they were acquired at school, university, or at work. Such an approach recognizes the importance of work as an additional site of learning where skills can be acquired and certified. It therefore begins to loosen the association of skills with formal (school) education. Government surveys of the labour force collect data of this type routinely and, again, have led to international comparisons. Such comparisons are complex and difficult to carry out. Qualification standards, norms, and scope differ between nations and therefore adjustments need to be made to the raw data.

The desire for international comparability is, however, no longer simply of academic importance. In order to make qualifications across Europe convertible, hence promoting mobility across Europe, national governments were required as of 2008 to map their qualifications onto the European Qualifications Framework. This framework acts as a translation device to make national qualifications more readable across Europe. However, the mapping process has revealed differences in the scope and breadth of the learning required to achieve the same qualification level in different parts of Europe (Brockmann et al. 2011). Researching measures of comparable qualification levels is fraught with difficulties.

Nevertheless, research does exist which attempts to make these adjustments and then make comparisons across the world in terms of equivalent qualification levels. These results have been used, for example, to highlight some of the strengths and weaknesses of the UK system. Its strength lies in the production of graduates—approaching a quarter of the population have qualifications above National Vocational Qualification (NVQ) level 3, a proportion which has more than doubled over the last decade (cf. Figure 16.1). Furthermore, significant progress has been made in raising the qualifications levels of the workforce and stimulating supply over the last ten years, so, compared to other OECD nations, the supply of highly qualified people is predicted to put the UK 10th in the OECD by 2020 (UKCES 2010). However, the UK has proportionately more people with low qualification levels than many of its major comparators and is ranked 18th across the OECD countries on this measure. Five million people have no formal qualifications at all (HM Treasury 2005, 40). The United Kingdom also has a smaller than average proportion of people with intermediate-level qualifications which puts it 20th out of the 30 countries in the OECD (HM Treasury 2005, 43).

An even more significant problem is that whilst ISCED-type data provides a measure of the quantity of schooling, it does not have anything to say about the quality of that provision. Indeed, the evidence suggests that the correlation between the quantity of schooling and its quality is low, particularly at post-compulsory level. Nevertheless, analysis suggests that both average years schooling and measures of schooling quality, such as test scores, are significantly correlated with economic growth (Hanushek and Kimko 2000). This analysis implies that measuring the stock of skills requires data on both the quantity and the quality of the educational input.

There are several reasons why qualifications may not be a good guide to quality. Whilst qualifications data are not exclusively focused on the school system, the connection between qualifications and their use at work can be loose. Furthermore, just as schooling can vary in quality, so too can qualifications, with some easier to acquire than others. Moreover, there are frequent claims of grade inflation with providers under pressure to increase their pass rates or lose business. The reliability of qualifications data is therefore questionable within a single country, let alone between countries and over time.

Direct testing of individuals' abilities is one of the most effective ways of assessing skill levels and avoiding many of these problems. One example of such an approach is the Trends in International Mathematics and Science Study (TIMSS). This is a worldwide research project which began in 1995 and which is repeated every four years with the latest taking place in 2011. It assesses the knowledge and skills of pupils aged 9–10 and 13–14 year olds around the world, and enables researchers to collect extensive background information about the quantity, quality, and content of teaching, and which can be used to make international comparisons. TIMSS 2007 involved approximately 425,000 pupils in 59 countries around the world. The 2011 version of the study includes 62 countries and jurisdictions, and around 500,000 students around the world (Sturman et al. 2012).

A similar exercise has been carried out by the OECD since 2000. It is known as PISA (Programme for International Student Assessment) and is conducted every three years with the latest taking place in 2012. It assesses how far students near the end of compulsory education (at the age of 15) have acquired the knowledge and skills considered essential for full participation in society. In all sweeps of the survey, the domains of reading, mathematical, and scientific literacy are covered. The number of participating countries has grown from 43 in 2000 to 64 in 2012 (OECD, 2010a). Pupils in the Shanghai region of China come top of the list across all three categories with the south-east Asian countries/regions of Singapore, South Korea, and Hong Kong appearing the top six (see Table 16.1). Both the United K and the United States come much lower down the rankings. For maths, American pupils were ranked 31st out of 65, performing significantly below the OECD average. The United Kingdom did a little better; coming about average and ranked 28th.

Aside from ranking countries according to the average test scores that their students achieved, research has also examined how high performance varies by country. Results show just over half (1.7%) as many achieved the highest level in maths in England as across the OECD as a whole (3.1%). This performance compares poorly to the 8.7% of high performers in Flemish Belgium and 7.8% in Switzerland. On a world scale, the picture is even more striking—26.6% achieved the highest level in Shanghai, 15.6% in Singapore and 10.8% in Hong Kong. Even in reading, where the test is thought to favour English-speaking countries, England is at the OECD average, but there are proportionately three times as many high performing readers in New Zealand and twice as many in Australia (Smithers and Robinson 2012: see charts 6.1 and 6.3 within the book).

Test scores can also be used to provide construct validity to other measures of the skills stock such as the use of the completion of particular phases of education as encapsulated in the ISCED system. Research shows, for example, that a substantial proportion of individuals who have little or no education (that is, no higher than ISCED level 2, i.e.

Table 16.1 Reading, maths and science test scores, OECD country rankings, 2009

Rank	Reading	Maths	Science
1	China: Shanghai	China: Shanghai	China: Shanghai
2	South Korea	Singapore	Finland
3	Finland	Hong Kong	Hong Kong
4	Hong Kong	South Korea	Singapore
5	Singapore	Chinese Taipei	Japan
6	Canada	Finland	South Korea
7	New Zealand	Liechtenstein	New Zealand
8	Japan	Switzerland	Canada
9	Australia	Japan	Estonia
10	Netherlands	Canada	Australia

Source: OECD (2010b, figure 1).

no further than lower secondary schooling) are also deemed low skilled according to their TIMSS test scores (Steedman and McIntosh 2001), although outside of this low-skilled group the correlation weakens significantly (Barro and Lee 2001).

Both TIMSS and PISA use standardized tests to rate the performance of school pupils of various ages. They do not focus on adults. This omission is a major drawback for measuring the stock of skills since the two measures generate only a partial picture and ignore the world of work. To provide such a picture, the OECD developed the International Adult Literacy Survey (IALS) in the 1990s (OECD and Statistics Canada 1997). Five European Union (EU) member countries (France, Germany, Ireland, the Netherlands, and Sweden) took part in the first round of the IALS in 1994, as part of a larger programme of surveys that includes non-EU countries. The United Kingdom and Flemish Belgium took part later in Spring 1996, together with Australia and New Zealand. Several other EU member countries joined in a second round in 1998.

IALS tested respondents directly about a limited range of particular skills—'prose', 'document' and 'quantitative' literacy skills—as well as questioning them about the frequency with which these skills were used at work (Blum et al. 2001; McIntosh and Vignoles 2001). The 'prose' tests in the survey were designed to capture the abilities of respondents to extract information from a piece of continuous text such as interpreting instructions on a medicine bottle. Using real world examples, the 'document' skills tests covered the ability of respondents to cope with text such as notices commonly found in restaurants, shops, and workplaces. Respondents' abilities to apply simple arithmetic to numbers embedded in printed materials were also tested with the domain appropriately referred to as 'quantitative' skills. These tests were repeated in the Adult Literacy and

Life Skills survey (ALLS) carried out in 2003, however, only a relatively small number of countries participated, and the exercise has not been repeated in its entirety since then.

The measurement of adult skills was firmly on the agenda with the OECD's launch of the Programme for the International Assessment of Adult Competences (PIAAC). Some 25 countries were initially involved in the first round which took place in 2012. In each country around 5,000 individuals aged 16–65 years old underwent literacy, numeracy, and problem-solving skills tests and also were questioned about the skills they used in and outside of work, such as the home and the community. Some analysis of change over time would be possible for countries which participated in either IALS or ALLS and for which they are comparable questions.

Despite their importance, surveys which test the adult population are expensive and time consuming to administer. The PIAAC survey, for example, took respondents 90–100 minutes to complete and cost participating countries around €23m (OECD 2009). Such surveys also assess work skills in an artificial setting since the tests and interviews take place outside work, in people's homes.

Job Skills

As previously pointed out, the abilities individuals possess—the stock of skills—may or may not be used at work. However, job skills are only found at work; they refer to the demands of the job rather than the capacities individuals possess. A common approach to measuring these skills is to monitor the occupational profile of a country, region, or locality, track change over time, and sometimes make forecasts. Econometric models based on historic data of occupational change, for example, suggest that in the years leading up to 2020 the United Kingdom will experience a 'polarisation of demand for skills, with growth at both top and bottom ends of the skills spectrum' (Wilson and Homenidou 2011, xvii). The translation of occupational change into skill change comes from the fact that 'skills levels' are an integral part of how the Standard Occupational Classification (SOC) system and its international equivalent, the International Standard of Occupational Classification (ISCO), are derived. Both are updated on a regular basis. SOC was revised in 2010 and ISCO in 2008. The nine major groups—the highest level of aggregation in these classification systems—are grouped according to their skill level, as defined by either the level of formal qualifications required for a person to get a particular job or the duration of training and/or work experience normally required for occupational competence (ILO 2007; ONS 2010).

Research which uses occupational change to indicate skill change suggests that job skills have risen over the last decade across Europe and that this rise will continue in the future, albeit at a slighter reduced rate. In Figure 16.2 four occupational skill categories are derived from ISCO data collected across Europe. It shows that 39.8% of workers in 2010 were employed in high-skilled non-manual jobs such as management, professional, or technical work of one kind or another. Ten years earlier the figure was 36.7%

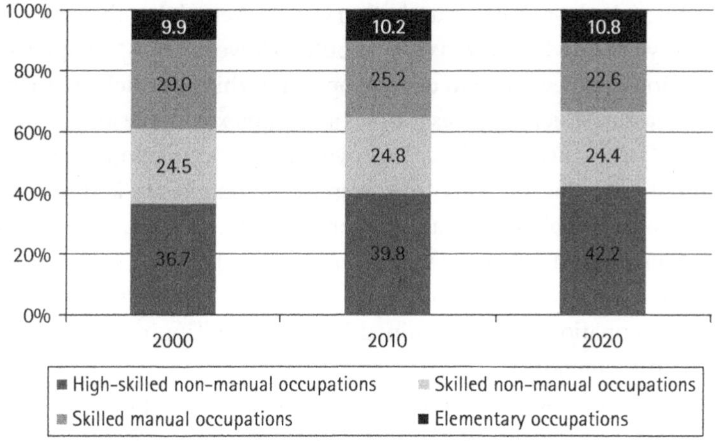

FIGURE 16.2 Past, present, and future job skills, Europe, 2000–2020

Source: Cedefop (2010, figure 22).

and by 2020 it is expected to reach 42.2%. By contrast, skilled manual jobs, such as those in craft and related trades, are forecast to decline—from 29.0% in 2000 to 22.6% in 2020 (see Figure 16.2). These figures suggest that skills are rising amongst non-manual occupations, whilst amongst manual occupations they are falling.

However, comparing occupational structures across countries is not an exact science because the skill content of an occupation in one country may not be the same as that of the same occupation in another country. Furthermore, occupations are coded according to job titles, what equipment is used, and what the job involves. Coding accuracy varies markedly according to the level of detail provided in response to these questions and the coding procedures adopted. Whilst ISCO provides the standard and tries to minimize inter-country data collection and coding variation, measurement differences are likely to remain. Nevertheless, differences may go beyond measurement error. For example, a recent study of 160 occupations across eight European countries suggests that jobs which carry the same title can vary substantially between countries in terms of the skills required to perform them as measured by the importance of and frequency with which tasks are carried out (Tijdens et al. 2011).

Furthermore, analysing skills trends by tracking occupational change alone is hazardous since it fails to pick up changes within categories (Kelleher et al. 1993). A rising proportion of high-level occupations need not necessarily indicate rising skill levels since these occupations may demand lower level skills than in the past. For example, the changing composition of occupations over time has been found to capture no more than half of the changing skill requirements (Green 2012).

Rather than rely on occupational classifications, an alternative approach is to examine the complexity of jobs in detail and then provide an overall rating for each type of job. This was the aim of the US Department of Labor's *Dictionary of Occupational Titles* (DOT), which was first published in 1939. DOT was based on the judgements of inspectors who visited workplaces and observed workers doing their jobs. Thousands of occupations were rated on dozens of attributes. However, most analysts focus on the complexity of jobs as they relate to data, people, and things, which are then combined into a single measure which captures the overall complexity of the job.

The 1991 DOT classified and described over 12,000 occupations, each representing a large group of more specific jobs. This exercise was expensive and time-consuming, leading to calls for simplification and better cost effectiveness. The US Department of Labor responded by replacing DOT with the Occupational Information Network (O*NET) in 1998. This classification focuses on a much smaller number of job titles—around 1,000 occupations were examined in 2010 (see Tippin and Hilton 2010 for a review: www.onetcenter.org).

O*NET is based on the premise that every occupation requires a different mix of knowledge, skills, and abilities, and is performed using a variety of activities and tasks. O*NET measures these distinguishing characteristics using a total of 239 'descriptors'. These are hierarchical measures that are grouped into six domains, which describe the day-to-day aspects of the job and the qualifications and interests of the typical worker. Descriptors are grouped into domains according to how the data are collected. The skills jobs require, for example, are assessed by job analysts according to the importance and level of 35 activities such as communication, use of technology, reading, writing, and critical thinking. The data for other domains comes from self-reported assessments by job incumbents in response to standardized survey questions. The sample sizes are not easy to identify from the publicly released data, but one estimate suggests that the data are based on 40 respondents per descriptor for each occupation.

A major strength of O*NET is that it is updated on a five-year rolling basis, so that by 2013 the information available is a completely refreshed version of that which first appeared in 2008. Feasibility studies have been carried out on how the richness of the US O*NET data could be used to enhance the quality of occupational data held in other countries given the high costs of repeating the O*NET exercise in its entirety. For example, sampling, data collection and analysis costs were recently estimated to be $4.6m per annum (Wilson 2010; Dickerson et al. 2012). Furthermore, in some countries such as Australia, the Czech Republic, New Zealand, China, and Hong Kong the rich description of occupational job skills collected by O*NET has already been used to provide more detailed national skills forecasts (e.g. Esposto 2010; Taylor and Cable 2004). However, it is important to remember that O*NET provides information on job characteristics only at the level of occupations and not at the level of the worker (Autor and Handel 2009). Such a high level of aggregation prevents analysis of within-occupation heterogeneity in task demands which other research suggests can be high.

Smaller scale undertakings have been carried out in other countries; they avoid this drawback by collecting and then releasing individual-level data for subsequent analysis. In Germany, for example, the Qualifications and Careers Survey has been conducted since 1979. To date, it has been administered six times—in 1979, 1985/1986, 1991/1992, 1998/1999, 2005/2006 and 2011/2012. The latest two surveys in the series were funded by the Federal Institute for Vocational Education and Training (BIBB) and carried out with the cooperation of the Federal Institute for Occupational Safety and Health (BAuA). Hence, they are also referred to as the BIBB/BAuA Employment Surveys. Each is a representative cross-section of economically active individuals aged 15 or over living in Germany. Between 20,000 and 35,000 individuals were questioned in each data point (Rohrbach-Schmidt 2009).

Respondents to these surveys were asked about the frequency with which their jobs involved 18 activities or tasks. In 2005/2006 items included: 'measuring, testing, quality control'; 'purchasing, selling'; 'consulting, advising'; and 'organizing, making plans, working out operations'. Respondents were presented with a three-point scale: 'frequently', 'sometimes', and 'never'. Half of these activities have been included in all of the five early surveys with the remainder asked in at least two (Rohrbach-Schmidt and Tiemann 2011).

On a smaller, but more detailed, scale a survey series in Britain has been developed over the last three decades. The series began in 1986 with the Social Change and Economic Life Initiative (SCELI) and then a similar survey—known as Employment in Britain (EIB)—was carried out in 1992 (Penn et al. 1994; Gallie et al. 1998). Building on the skills questions asked of respondents to these employment-focused surveys, the Skills Surveys were launched in 1997 with a specific focus on collecting more skills data than had hitherto been collected in Britain. The survey was repeated in 2001 and 2006 with an enlarged sample size of 7,787 workers aged 20–65 years old. The survey was broadened out slightly in 2012 with more emphasis on the quality of work, although the collection of skills data remains at its core (Ashton et al. 1999; Felstead et al. 2002, 2007, 2013).

By consistently asking questions of job-holders about what they actually do in their work, a picture of skill change has been produced. These surveys focus on what qualifications respondents would need to get their current job, what length of training is needed, how long it takes to learn to do the job, and what activities are important to the job. It is known as the 'job requirements approach'. Based on multiple measures, some of which are illustrated in Figure 16.3, the results show that job skills have been rising in Britain during a 20-year period beginning in 1986.

The proportion of jobs requiring graduate qualifications in Britain is one measure of skill: this doubled from 9.7% to 19.0% between 1986 and 2006. In the same period the number of jobs requiring no qualifications at all fell from 38.4% to 27.9%. Qualification requirements are, however, only one broad measure of skill, and arguably only a loose one. Yet, this same picture of rising requirements is found for two complementary indicators: the amount of learning time required to do the job well, and the cumulative amount of training. The other lines in Figure 16.3 chart the changing use of various generic skills. The indices were obtained by combining responses to ranges of related items grouped into domains (as suggested by factor analyses and indices of internal consistency). It can be seen that there were notable increases in the uses of high levels of literacy skills (reading and writing activities), influence skills (persuading, influencing, instructing) and computing skills (complex or advanced computing activities).

Not all skills activities were moving upwards, however. The main exception was physical skills (activities involving strength and stamina or manual dexterity). Whilst

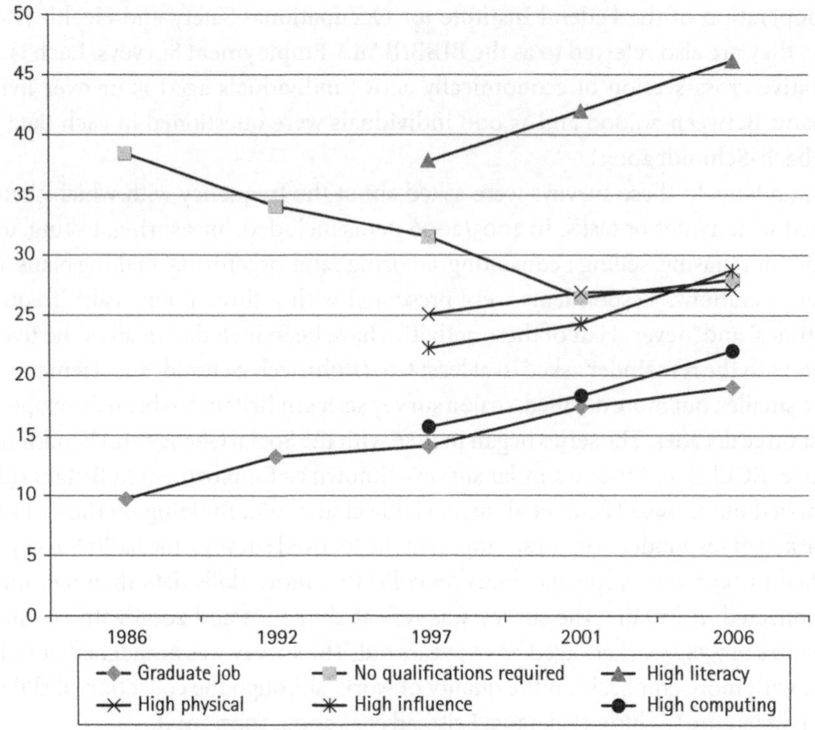

FIGURE 16.3 Job skill requirements, Britain, 1986–2006

Note: Graduate job: degree or better needed to get job. High literacy: reading and writing activities average between 'very important' and 'essential'. High influence: influence/communication activities average between 'very important' and 'essential'. High Computing: computer use at complex or advanced levels.

Source: Green et al. (2012).

the 'knowledge society' paradigm might have led to an expectation of a decline in the use of these skills, the data shows little change—indeed, the change is statistically insignificant either way. Skills moved upwards in other domains (not shown in Figure 16.4) but by smaller albeit significant amounts (Felstead et al. 2007). However, results from the 2012 survey suggest that the changes between 2006 and 2012 are mixed, with most generic and broad skills domains continuing to rise but some remaining stable or declining (Felstead et al. 2013b). Analysis arising from the 2012 survey also tracks how other features of job quality, such as job control, training, work intensification, fear and insecurity at work, and worker wellbeing have changed over time (see Felstead et al. 2013a; Green et al. 2013a,b; Gallie et al. 2013; Inanc et al. 2013).

International data on job skills, however, is much thinner on the ground. Further analysis of PIACC will plug this gap by testing literacy, numeracy, and problem-solving skills as well as questioning respondents about the skills they use in and outside of work. More limited job skills data are collected by other sources such as the European Working Conditions Survey (EWCS) and the European Social Survey (ESS). The ESS asks

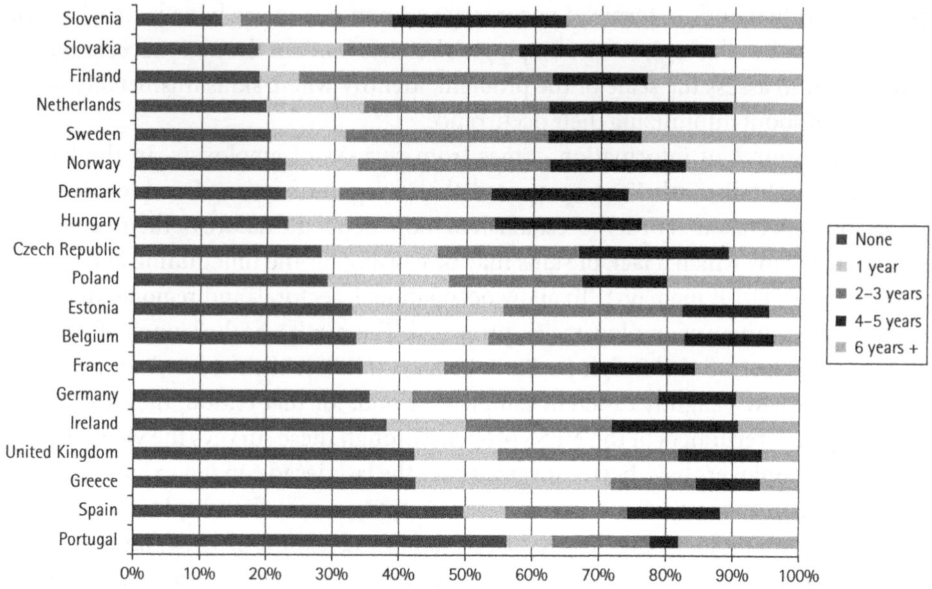

FIGURE 16.4 Post-compulsory educational job requirements, Europe, 2010

Note: Respondents were asked: 'If someone was applying for the job you do now, would they need any education or vocational schooling beyond [the age of national school leaving age or exams]?'. If yes, they were then asked to estimate the number of years of post-compulsory education that would be required.

Source: authors' own calculations.

respondents how many years, if any, a new recruit would need for the job they currently do. It also asks how long it would take for someone with the 'right education and qualifications' to learn to their job reasonably well. These two questions were included in the ESS in 2004 and 2010. Figure 16.4 shows how jobs across Europe vary in terms of their post-compulsory educational requirements. Around half of jobs in Portugal and Spain in 2010, for example, were reported to require no post-compulsory education at all compared to around a fifth of jobs in Sweden, the Netherlands, Finland, Slovakia, and Slovenia. However, data on job skills in the ESS is restricted to these two questions only. Similarly, even though the EWCS has been expanded since it first began in 1990, the fifth version of the survey carried out in 2010 contained only a few questions on job skills. Having said that, they do provide useful insights into the patterns of skills mismatch, which is the focus of the next section.

Skills Mismatch

Given the investments made in enhancing the skills stock—by governments, companies, and individuals—there is considerable interest in minimizing the mismatch between the skills stock and job skills. Misalignments can have negative consequences for the individual both in terms of pecuniary and non-pecuniary benefits (such as job satisfaction and wellbeing), for the employer's business and for the national economy. It is important to assess the scale of the problem, identify where skills mismatches occur and then set about minimizing their occurrence.

One rich source of information comes from surveys of employers. In the United Kingdom, the Skills Task Force proposed that a regular survey of employers' skills needed be undertaken in order to 'establish in more detail the nature of their skill needs and the problems which a lack of skills may be causing for the functioning and growth of companies' (DfEE 1999, 90). To allow occupational, sectoral, and regional disaggregation, a large survey of employers was proposed. The result was the launch of what are referred to as the National Employer Skills Surveys (NESS). The 1999 and 2001 versions of the survey had a slightly different sample base and, for that reason, they are usually treated as the forerunners of the NESS proper. Through these surveys the views of large numbers of employers have been canvassed over the last decade: in 1999 27,000 employers took part; in 2001 a similar number were surveyed; in 2003 the sample was increased to over 72,000 employers; it dropped back to around 27,000 in 2004; and it rose to over 75,000 in 2005, 2007 and 2009 (e.g., Shury et al. 2005, 2006, 2010; Winterbotham et al. 2008). Similar employer surveys were carried out in Wales, Scotland, and Northern Ireland, although with less regularity and correspondingly smaller sample sizes. In 2011 a UK-wide employer survey was completed with around 87,500 employers taking part with plans to repeat the surveys every two years (Davies et al. 2012).

Standard economic theory is based on the principles of demand and supply. Applied to the labour market this translates into the demand for and supply of labour. The result of these two forces is either an equilibrium wage (price) and level of employment (quantity) or if these forces do not operate—for whatever reason—an over-supply or a shortage of labour. Applied to skills this means that the supply of skills may not always be in alignment with employer demand. This may be reflected in skill shortages which arise where employers find it difficult to fill their vacancies with appropriately skilled applicants. Respondents to NESS were therefore asked questions about the incidence and cause of any hard-to-fill vacancies they reported. Despite the low reported level of skill shortage vacancies—affecting just 3–5% of establishments over the last decade—skill shortages frequently make newspaper headlines, especially when they spark large wage rises or hamper business expansion (e.g. Pavia 2006; Marsh 2012). Employers' perceptions of deficiencies in the skills of the existing workforce were more frequently reported. These deficiencies—often referred to as latent skills gaps—affected around one in six establishments and have remained at that level since the survey first began (Davies et al. 2012, appendix A).

Until recently, these employer surveys focused on the deficiencies of current or potential workers and not on whether the skills of the existing workforce were used effectively or not. That type of analysis was left to individual-level surveys. However, the 2011 survey broke new ground and included a question which asked employers how many of their staff they considered to have both qualifications and skills that were more advanced than required for their current job. Across the United Kingdom almost half of all establishments (49%) reported having at least one employee over-qualified and over-skilled—what is sometimes referred to as 'real over-qualification'. This figure equates to just under 4.5 million workers, or 16% of the total UK workforce, and dwarfs estimates for skill shortage vacancies (103,000) and skill gaps (1,490,000), which have been the focus of the NESS surveys since the series began (Davies et al. 2012, 22–46). However, it should also be remembered that this 'real over-qualification' estimate is derived from a single question and is based on employers' knowledge of the qualifications held by workers in their charge.

More precise estimates of skills mismatches are available from individual-level surveys which contain a series of questions about job skills and the skills held by workers themselves. The 'self-declared' method measures the difference between workers' views of what qualifications—used as a proxy for skills—are required to be hired for the job and the qualifications they in fact hold. Those workers with qualifications higher than those required are deemed to be 'over-qualified', whilst those with qualifications lower than required are deemed to be 'under-qualified'. The British Skills Survey data suggests that qualification mismatch has grown over time. The proportion defined as 'over-qualified' has risen from 30.2% in 1992 to 39.5% in 2006 (see Table 16.2).

In order to take the analysis further, responses to questions posed elsewhere in these surveys can be used to examine whether those 'over-qualified' were also unable to use their skills at work effectively. This suggests that 'real over-qualification' (those over-qualified and unable to use their skills at work) has remained unchanged at around 13% over the 1992–2006 period. Instead, most of the growth in 'over-qualification' has not stopped individuals using their skills at work. This suggests that the matching process is working rather better than the unadjusted 'over-qualification' figures would suggest.

Table 16.2 Qualification and skill mismatches, Britain, 1992–2006

	1992	2001	2006
All			
Over-qualified	30.2	35.1	39.5
of which:			
over-qualified & over-skilled	12.9	12.1	13.0
over-qualified but skill matched	17.4	22.9	26.6

Notes: The 'over-qualified' are defined as those workers who have qualifications which exceed the level of qualification required for the job. This group is then sub-divided according to the response given to the question: 'How much of your past experience, skill and abilities can you make use of in your present job?' Those answering 'very little' or 'a little' (and reporting over-qualification) are classified as experiencing 'real over-qualification'. The remainder, that is, those responding 'quite a lot' or 'almost all' are classified as experiencing 'formal over-qualification' (cf. Green and Zhu 2010, 750–752).

Source: authors' own calculations.

Qualification mismatch has received significant attention in recent years (McGuinness 2006). However, despite the extensive literature, international comparisons are rare given the paucity of adequate comparable indicators (which draw on a direct measure of the required education level in each job). One notable exception is a survey carried out in 2001 which indicated that Norway (18%), Italy (17%), and Bulgaria (22%) had lower rates of over-qualification than Germany (37%), Israel (39%), and the United Kingdom (37%) (Dolton and Marcenaro-Gutierrez 2009). Separate country studies, using non-comparable indicators, typically find that over-education is prevalent in upwards of 20% of the population. Data for Germany, which as with Britain are available over time, also indicate, using a consistent measure, that over-qualification amongst male full-time workers has increased from 23% in 1997 to 32% in 2006 (Rohrbach-Schmidt and Tiemann 2011).

An alternative method for measuring over-qualification uses the modal education level of job-holders as an indicator of the qualification requirement in each occupation. However, this method is unsuitable for use in international comparisons since it assumes not only that the qualification requirement is the same for everyone in an occupation but also that the requirement for each occupation is the same in all countries. In our view, this approach stretches the assumptions of the method too far although there are opposing views (see OECD 2011b). Moreover, the modal method inherently hides trends over time in over-qualification; data which is potentially the most revealing.

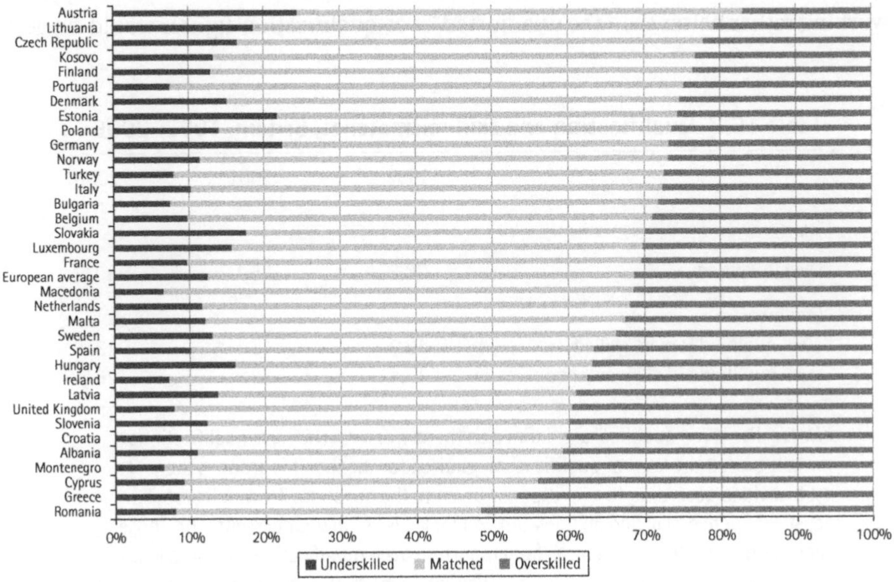

FIGURE 16.5 Self-declared skills matching, Europe, 2010

Note: Respondents were asked to select one of the following alternatives: (a) 'I need further training to cope well with my duties'; (b) 'My present skills correspond well with my duties', and (c) 'I have the skills to cope with more demanding duties'.

Source: Green (2013: table 8A.3).

Comparative individuals' perceptions of skills mismatch, in contrast to education mismatch, are more widely available from the 2010 European Working Conditions Survey (EWCS). Self-declared patterns of 'over-skilling' and 'under-skilling' show that 31.4% of European workers 'have the skills to cope with more demanding duties' ('over-skilled'), whilst 56.1% said that their present skills corresponded well with what their job required ('matched') and 12.5% suggested that they needed 'further training to cope well' with their duties (see Figure 16.5). The figures vary substantially between countries, with Austria showing the lowest proportion (17%) of workers who perceive themselves to be over-skilled and Romania revealing the greatest (52%). Interpretation of subjective skills mismatch questions is an ongoing topic of research, and it is possible that such questions will be superseded when separate data on skills held and skills used will become available.

Conclusion

This chapter has critically reviewed what type of data is currently available on: the stock of skills; what skills jobs require: whether skills supply and demand are misaligned; and if so, to what extent. To summarize, we take each of these three areas in turn. Measures of skills stock are well developed with international data on years of compulsory education, participation rates at various points in the educational cycle, qualification attainment levels, and student test scores. However, the data tend to focus on those in formal education—schools, colleges, and universities. Job skill measures, on the other hand, focus by definition on those in work since they refer to the demands of the job rather than the capacities individuals possess. These data are more difficult and costly to collect. As a result, most job skill measures are carried out at a high level of aggregation. In classification systems, for example, groups of occupations are crudely ordered to reflect the job skills needed by post-holders. However, there have been attempts to measure job complexity by directly asking job-holders about the abilities they are required to exercise at work (e.g. Felstead et al. 2013b). Data on skills mismatch, too, are rare and international comparative data rarer still. The most regularly collected and largest scale data comes from employer-based reports of labour shortages attributable to a lack of available skills and reported skill deficiencies amongst existing workers. More focused individual-level data on skill under-utilization come from surveys of workers but these surveys are less frequently conducted and are based on much smaller sample sizes.

The case for a 'big science' approach in the field of skills is, therefore, a compelling one. It is one which seems to have been accepted with the first round of countries carrying out PIAAC in 2012 and a second round of countries collecting data in 2014. This dataset will provide the basis for a step-change in our understanding of skills stocks, job skills, and skill mismatches across the OECD countries for adult workers. Up until this point, labour market analysts have had to rely on small-scale and piecemeal data collection exercises. This chapter has attempted to review the strengths and weaknesses of the survey tools and concepts which they have developed, and piece together some of main findings which have emerged. In so doing, the chapter has attempted to equip readers with the necessary tools to navigate their own way through the myriad of datasets available and the measures they use.

However, whilst PIAAC offers an important way forward, it is not the last and final word on the subject. Gaps remain in its architecture, which need to be plugged with other data collection exercises. Most notably, it tests skills outside of the work context and whilst it collects data on job skills, it pays relatively little attention to the organization of work and its situation in the productive system. Research on high performance working, for example, suggests that work organization can expand or restrict the use of skills at work (Felstead et al. 2010). To investigate such effects, a useful step forward would be the operationalization of the Measuring the Dynamics of Organisations and Work (MEADOW) initiative, a proposal for a combined survey of employers and employees across countries. The instruments have already been designed and piloted, and are intended to capture work organization, job skills. and other aspects of job quality using a consistent and comparable framework across several countries (MEADOW Consortium 2010). As such it offers an innovative and exciting way of advancing skills research and the data infrastructure needed to investigate how best to enhance skills used at work.

References

Ashton, D., Davies, B., Felstead, A., and Green, F. (1999) *Work Skills in Britain*, Oxford: ESRC Centre on Skills, Knowledge and Organisational Performance.

Attewell, P. (1990) 'What is Skill?', *Work and Occupations*, 17(4): 422–448.

Autor, D. H. and Handel, M. J. (2009) 'Putting Tasks to the Test: Human Capital, Job Tasks and Wages', NBER Working Paper no. 15116, Cambridge, MA: National Bureau of Economic Research.

Barro, R. J. and Lee, J-W. (2001) 'International Data on Educational Attainment: Updates and Implications', *Oxford Economic Papers*, 53(3): 541–563.

Blum, A., Goldstein, H. and Guérin-Pace, F. (2001) 'International Adult Literacy Survey (IALS): An Analysis of International Comparisons of Adult Literacy', *Assessment in Education*, 8(2): 225–246.

Braverman, H. (1974) *Labor and Monopoly Capital*, New York: Monthly Review Press.

Brockmann, M., Clarke, L. and Winch, C. (2011) *Knowledge, Skills and Competence in the European Labour Market: What's in a Vocational Qualification?* London: Routledge.

Cedefop (2010) *Skills Supply and Demand in Europe: Medium-Term Forecast up to 2020*, Luxembourg: Publications Office of the European Union.

Davies, B., Gore, K., Shury, J., Vivian, D., Winterbotham, M. and Constable, S. (2012) 'UK Commission's Employer Skills Survey 2011: UK Results', *Evidence Report 45*, Wath-upon-Dearne: UK Commission for Employment and Skills.

DfEE (1999) Delivering Skills for All: Second Report of the National Skills Task Force, London: Department for Education and Employment.

DfEE and Cabinet Office (1996) 'The Skills Audit Report: A Report from an Interdepartmental Group', Occasional Paper, London: HMSO.

Dickerson, A., Wilson, R., Kik, G., and Dhilton, D. (2012) 'Developing Occupational Skills Profiles for the UK: A Feasibility Study', Evidence Report 44, Wath-upon-Dearne: UK Commission for Employment and Skills.

Dolton, P. and Marcenaro-Gutierrez, O. (2009) 'Overeducation across Europe', in P. Dolton, R. Asplund, and E. Barth, E (eds), *Education and Inequality Across Europe*, Cheltenham: Edward Elgar.

Dunnell, K. (2008) 'Ageing and Mortality in the UK: National Statistician's Annual Article on the Population', *Population Trends*, 134 (Winter): 6–23.

Esposto, A. (2010) 'The Labour Market and the Knowledge Intensification of Australian Jobs: A View to the Future', *International Review of Business Research Papers*, 6(4): 18–29.

Felstead, A. (2009) *Getting Fitter for the Job: Improving the Quality of Labour Market Information Using Individual-Level Surveys*, Report for the UK Commission for Employment and Skills, February, www.wiserd.ac.uk/files/9013/5072/7620/WISERD_WDR_001.pdf

Felstead, A., Gallie, D. and Green, F. (2002) *Work Skills in Britain, 1986–2001*, London: Department for Education and Skills.

Felstead, A., Gallie, D., Green, F. and Zhou, Y. (2007) *Skills at Work in Britain, 1986 to 2006*, Oxford: ESRC Centre on Skills, Knowledge and Organisational Performance.

Felstead, A., Fuller, A., Jewson, N. and Unwin, L. (2009) *Improving Working as Learning*, London: Routledge.

Felstead, A., Gallie, D., Green, F., and Zhou, Y. (2010) 'Employee Involvement, the Quality of Training and the Learning Environment: An Individual-Level Analysis', *International Journal of Human Resource Management*, 21(10): 1667–1688.

Felstead, A., Gallie, D., Green, F., and Inanc, H. (2013a) *Work Intensification in Britain: First Findings from the Skills and Employment Survey 2012*, London: ESRC Centre for Learning and Life Chances in Knowledge Economies and Societies.

Felstead, A., Gallie, D., Green, F., and Inanc, H. (2013b) *Work Skills in Britain: First Findings from the Skills and Employment Survey 2012*, London: ESRC Centre for Learning and Life Chances in Knowledge Economies and Societies.

Gallie, D., White, M., Cheng, Y., and Tomlinson, M. (1998) *Restructuring the Employment Relationship*, Oxford: Clarendon Press.

Gallie, D., Felstead, A., Green, F., and Inanc, H. (2013) *Fear at Work in Britain: First Findings from the Skills and Employment Survey 2012*, London: ESRC Centre for Learning and Life Chances in Knowledge Economies and Societies.

Green, F. (2012) 'Employee Involvement, Technology and Evolution in Job Skills: A Task-Based Analysis', *Industrial and Labor Relations Review*, 65(1): 36–67.

Green, F. (2013) *Skilled Work: An Economic and Social Analysis*, Oxford: Oxford University Press.

Green, F. and Zhou Y. (2010) 'Overqualification, Job Dissatisfaction, and Increasing Dispersion in the Returns to Graduate Education', *Oxford Economic Papers*, 62: 740–763.

Green, F., Felstead, A. and Gallie, D. (2012) 'Skills and Work Organisation in Britain', in F. Green and M. Keese, M (eds), *Job Tasks, Work Skills and the Labour Market*, Paris: Organisation for Economic Co-operation and Development.

Green, F., Felstead, A., Gallie, D., and Inanc, H. (2013a) *Job-Related Well-Being in Britain: First Findings from the Skills and Employment Survey 2012,* London: ESRC Centre for Learning and Life Chances in Knowledge Economies and Societies.

Green, F., Felstead, A., Gallie, D,. and Inanc, H. (2013b) *Training in Britain: First Findings from the Skills and Employment Survey 2012*, London: ESRC Centre for Learning and Life Chances in Knowledge Economies and Societies.

Grugulis, I. and Lloyd, C. (2010) 'Skill and the Labour Process: The Conditions and Consequences of Change', in P. Thompson and C. Smith (eds), *Working Life:* London: Palgrave.

HM Treasury (2005) *Skills in the UK: The Long Term Challenge—Interim Report*, London: HM Treasury.

Hanushek, E. and Kimko, D. (2000) 'Schooling, Labor Force Quality, and the Growth of Nations', *American Economic Review*, 90: 1184–1208.

ILO (2007) *Resolution Concerning Updating the International Standard Classification of Occupations*. www.ilo.org/public/english/bureau/stat/isco/docs/resol08.pdf downloaded 13 July 2012.

Inanc, H., Felstead, A., Gallie, D. and Green, F. (2013) *Job Control in Britain: First Findings from the Skills and Employment Survey 2012*, London: ESRC Centre for Learning and Life Chances in Knowledge Economies and Societies.

Kelleher, M., Scott, P. and Jones, B. (1993) 'Resistant to Change? Some Unexplained Omissions in the 1990 Standard Occupational Classification', *Work, Employment and Society*, 7(3): 437–449.

Lutz, W., Mamolo, M., Scherbov, S., and Sobotka, T. (2010) *European Demographic Datasheet 2010*. www.oeaw.ac.at/vid/datasheet/download/European_Demographic_Data_Sheet_2010.pdf downloaded 15 June 2012.

Marsh, P. (2012) 'Skills Hunt Puts Brake on Growing Businesses', *Financial Times*, 16 July.

McGuinness, S. (2006). 'Overeducation in the Labour Market', *Journal of Economic Surveys*, 20(3): 387–418.

McIntosh, S. and Vignoles, A. (2001) 'Measuring and Assessing the Impact of Basic Skills on Labour Market Outcomes', *Oxford Economic Papers*, 53(3): 453–481.

MEADOW Consortium (2010) 'The MEADOW Guidelines'. Project funded within the 6th Framework Programme of the European Commission's DG Research, Grigny, France. http://www.meadow-project.eu/index.php?/Article-du-site/Guidelines.htm downloaded on 9 September 2012.

Moss, P. and Tilly, C. (1996) '"Soft" Skills and Race: An Investigation of Black Men's Employment Problems', *Work and Occupations*, 23(3): 252–276.

OECD (2009) *PIAAC: Total Budget cost (2008–2013)*, 4th Meeting of BPC, 2–3 April, COM/DELSA/EDU/PIAAC(2009)8, Paris: Organisation for Economic Co-operation and Development.

OECD (2010a) *PISA 2009 at a Glance*, Paris: Organisation for Economic Co-operation and Development.

OECD (2010b) *PISA 2009 Results: Executive Summary*, Paris: Organisation for Economic Co-operation and Development.

OECD (2011a) *Education at a Glance 2011: OECD Indicators*, Paris: Organisation for Economic Co-operation and Development.

OECD (2011b) *OECD Employment Outlook 2011*, Paris: Organisation for Economic Co-operation and Development.

OECD and Statistics Canada (1997) *Literacy, Economy and Society*, Paris: Organisation for Economic Co-operation and Development.

ONS (2010) *Standard Occupational Classification 2010*. Vol. 1: *Structure and Descriptions of Unit Groups*, Basingstoke: Palgrave.

Pavia, W. (2006) 'Work Dries up for City Boys Lured to Plumbing', *The Times*, 3 January.

Pearsall, J. (ed.) (1998) *The New Oxford Dictionary of English*, Oxford: Oxford University Press.

Penn, R., Rose, M., and Rubery, J. (1994) (eds) *Skill and Occupational Change*, Oxford: Oxford University Press.

Rohrbach-Schmidt, D. (2009) *The BIBB/IAB and BIBB/BAuA Surveys of The Working Population on Qualification and Working Conditions in Germany: Data and Methods Manual*, Bonn: Federal Institute for Vocational Education and Training.

Rohrbach-Schmidt, D. and Tiemann, M. (2011) 'Mismatching and Job Tasks in Germany: Rising Over-Qualification through Polarization?', *Empirical Research in Vocational Education and Training*, 1(3): 39–53.

Sala-i-Martin, X. (2011) *The Global Competitiveness Report 2011–2012*, Geneva: World Economic Forum.

Shury, J., Winterbotham, M., Adams, L., and Carter, K. (2005) *National Employers Skills Survey 2004: Main Report*, Coventry: Learning and Skills Council.

Shury, J., Winterbotham, M., Carter, K. and Schäfer, S. (2006) *National Employers Skills Survey 2005: Main Report*, Coventry: Learning and Skills Council.

Shury, J., Winterbotham, M., Davies, B., Oldfield, K., Spilsbury, M., and Constable, S. (2010) *National Employer Skills Survey for England 2009: Key Findings Report*, Wath-upon-Dearne: UK Commission for Employment and Skills.

Smithers, A. and Robinson, P. (2012) *Educating the Higher Able*, London: Sutton Trust.

Spenner, K. I. (1990) 'Skill, Meanings, Methods and Measures', *Work and Occupations*, 17: 399–421.

Steedman, H. and McIntosh, S. (2001) 'Measuring Low Skills in Europe: How Useful Is the ISCED Framework?', *Oxford Economic Papers*, 53(3): 564–581.

Sturman, L., Burge, B., Cook, R., and Weaving, H. (2012) 'TIMSS 2011: Mathematics and Science Achievement', Department for Education Research Brief DFE-RB263, London: Department for Education.

Taylor, P. and Cable, D. (2004) 'Using the Occupational Information Network (O*Net) in New Zealand', *Human Resources*, 9(2): 26–29.

Tijdens, K, De Ruijter, E and De Ruijter, J (2011) 'Inside Occupations: Comparing the Task Descriptions of 160 Occupations across Eight EU Member States'. Paper presented to the 32nd Annual Conference of the International Working Party on Labour Market Segmentation, 11–13 July, Bamberg, Germany.

Tippin, N. T. and Hilton, M. L. (eds) (2010) *A Database for a Changing Economy: Review of the Occupational Information Network (O*NET)*, Washington DC: National Academies Press.

UKCES (2009) *Ambition 2020: World Class Skills and Jobs for the UK*, Wath-upon-Dearne: UK Commission for Employment and Skills.

UKCES (2010) *Skills for Jobs: Today and Tomorrow—The National Strategic Skills Adult for England*. Vol. 2: *The Evidence Report*, Wath-upon-Dearne: UK Commission for Employment and Skills.

UNESCO (2011) 'Revision of the International Standard Classification of Education (ISCED)', United Nations Educational, Scientific and Cultural Organisation, General Conference, 36th Session, Paris: UNESCO.

Wilson, R. A. (2010) 'Lessons from America: A Research and Policy Briefing', *Briefing Paper Series*, Wath-upon-Dearne: UK Commission for Employment and Skills.
Wilson, R. A. and Homenidou, K. (2011) 'Working Futures 2010–2020', Evidence Report 41, Wath-upon-Dearne: UK Commission for Employment and Skills.
Winterbotham, M., Shury, J., Carter, K. and Schäfer, S. (2008) *National Employers Skills Survey 2007: Main Report*, Coventry: Learning and Skills Council.
Zuboff, S. (1988) *In the Age of the Smart Machine*, New York: Basic Books.

SECTION IV

SKILL OUTCOMES

CHAPTER 17

THE INDIVIDUAL BENEFITS OF INVESTING IN SKILLS

CRAIG HOLMES

Introduction

Acquiring skills through education and training is not a costless process. Individuals who participate incur direct monetary costs, such as course fees, non-monetary costs, such as the mental effort that needs to be exerted to complete the course, and indirect costs, such as the earnings that have been forgone whilst studying and learning. In general, individuals are willing to incur these costs because the rewards they receive from completion (or at least those they expect they will receive) are greater.

The rewards may take several forms. For some people, learning may be an enjoyable end in itself. However, when most people invest in their skills, the benefits they expect to receive are those produced when these newly acquired skills are employed in the labour market. These benefits arise because new skills add to an individual's existing human capital. They become more productive in the workplace given the extra capabilities their new skills have generated, and as a result find themselves in greater demand by employers. This gives the individual more options when supplying their labour and, to the extent that there are a limited number of people who also make this investment, makes the individual a scarce and highly valued potential recruit for employers.

The higher productivity of skilled workers and willingness of firms and employers to compete for such individuals, combined with the relative scarcity of the skills they possess, imply two individual labour market benefits from investing in skill—a greater likelihood of finding work, and higher wages once in work. This chapter is concerned with quantifying the size of these benefits in different parts of the world and exploring the methodological challenges faced—and often overlooked—in the huge empirical literature that has attempted to do this.

Many of the skills that an individual might possess, from basic literacy and numeracy to advanced knowledge of foreign languages or computer programming (to give just two examples of high-level skills) comes from formal education in the primary, secondary, and tertiary sectors. Therefore, the chapter starts (in the next section) with a broad description of the earnings and employment prospects of individuals who have completed different levels of formal education across different countries.

However, just looking at raw differences in earnings or the likelihood of employment is not sufficient for measuring the value labour markets attach to different skills, as we do not immediately know the make-up of the groups being compared. The third section, explains the way researchers have estimated skills premia after controlling for all other observable explanatory factors that potentially affect labour market outcomes. For wages, this estimation is known as a Mincerian wage equation after economist Jacob Mincer. Here, I summarize findings from the large literature that has followed, and in some cases adapted, Mincer's methodology.

However, there are a number of important issues linked to the interpretation of the numbers produced. These issues are, in turn, the relationship between levels of education and acquisition of skills, the problem of establishing causation, and the distribution of returns around the average given by estimates of these wage equations. Later sections discuss these issues. This chapter argues that despite efforts to deal with these problems, much is left unresolved, in part because issues around the demand for the available supply of productive skills are largely overlooked.

The majority of what follows draws on research relating to skills developed in the education and training system. Many of these skills are general in the sense that they raise productivity across a number of potential employers, occupations, or industries. Of course, the generality of skills such as being able to speak the native language is greater than the ability to tile bathrooms or argue a legal case in court. However, the common feature is that an employer would be wary of helping towards the cost of such skill investments in case the worker left and took their skills to a rival firm. Hence, general skills are usually produced prior to entering employment and are paid for by individuals or the state. In contrast, firms do pay for training where they feel they can retain the trainee, which is much more likely if the skills produced are only really valuable in that firm. In this final section, I consider the investment in skills that takes place once individuals have entered the workplace.

The final section argues that interpreting such research is very difficult, especially from the perspective of policy-making. Workplace training is often closely linked to the unique arrangements within a firm. Employer-provided training is obviously directed towards producing skills that will be used in work in the future. Government-run or funded training programmes can only be an imperfect substitute for such training unless there is some guarantee that the skills will be used within the jobs that are available. If we believe that the incidence and quality of firm training is too low, it is not simply a case of public investment in programmes. The challenge in this situation is creating both the demand and the supply for skills.

Education, Earnings, and Employment

The now-standard way of thinking about the link between education and training on the one hand, and labour market outcomes on the other is known as human capital theory, which was developed by a number of economists in the 1960s and 1970s.[1] From the point of view of human capital theory, skills developed by education and training increase worker productivity and generate higher wages and better employment prospects owing to the higher value employers will subsequently place on that individual. Evidence from across the world is consistent with this expectation—taking the average across all the developed OECD countries, an individual with educational attainment below International Standard Classification of Education (ISCED) level 3 earns, on average, 23% less than an individual with ISCED level 3 or 4.[2] They are also less likely to be in employment—someone with only lower secondary (ISCED level 2) education is 19% less likely to be employed rather than unemployed or economically inactive than someone with ISCED level 3A.[3] Those with high levels of vocational education (ISCED 5B) earn, on average, 24% more than those at ISCED level 3 or 4 and 11% are more likely to be in employment than someone with upper secondary (ISCED 3A) education only. Finally, those with first and higher degrees (ISCED 5A and 6) earn 65% more on average than workers with level 3 or 4, with employment rates 16% higher than a person with upper secondary education.

Figure 17.1 shows that there is considerable variation across countries within the OECD. For higher education, the Scandinavian countries of Norway, Sweden, and Denmark have the lowest wage gap of around 30–40% above those with ISCED 3–4 level qualification, whilst at the upper end countries like the United Kingdom, Germany and the United States see earnings premia of around 80–90%, and Ireland, Greece, and Hungary show premia in excess of 100%. There is no obvious pattern or correlation between these features and the wage gaps between the low- and middle-educated groups. For example, the three Scandinavian countries see wage premia between these

[1] See, for example, Mincer (1958, 1970), Schultz (1961), and Becker (1962).

[2] The ISCED had, in its 1997 version used in this chapter, seven levels of educational attainment. Level 3 is, broadly speaking, the completion of an upper secondary education. For example, in the United Kingdom the completion of GCSEs or A-Levels would place a student at level 3—the latter is given a higher status within the level due to the progression opportunities it provides to higher study. Level 4 qualifications are post-compulsory but pre-tertiary, such as the final stages of the German vocational education dual system. Individuals below level 3 will typically not have completed compulsory education in most developed countries. Level 5 corresponds to the first stage of tertiary education (such as a bachelor's degree or a higher vocational or professional qualification), while level 6 covers higher degrees such as Master's or PhD qualifications.

[3] ISCED 3 covers all upper secondary education. Level 3A are general education programmes (rather than vocational programmes) which allow access into tertiary education. 3B is the equivalent for vocational programmes, whilst 3C covers shorter programmes at this level that do not provide access to higher education.

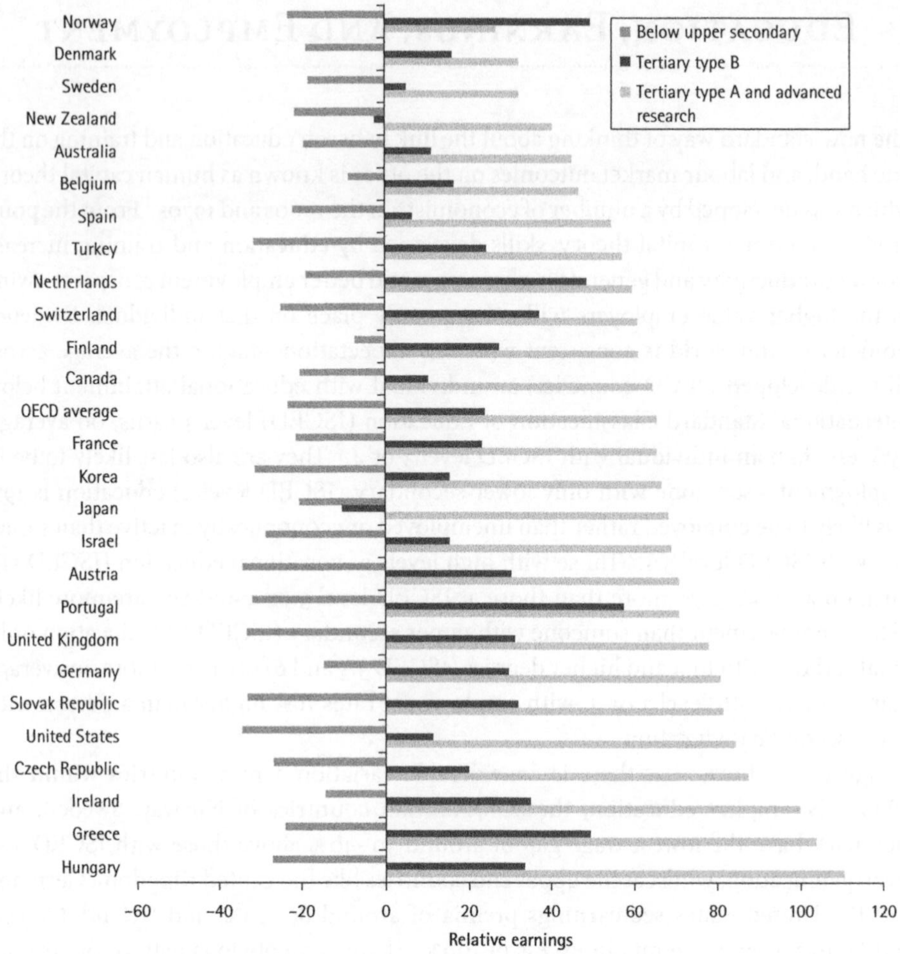

FIGURE 17.1 Earnings differences by level of education and country

Note: Mean earnings relative to ISCED 3 and 4.
Source: OECD.

two groups close to the OECD average, whilst Belgium, Finland, Germany, and Ireland have much smaller labour market penalties for having a low level of education. There as similarly large penalties to having low levels of education in the United States and the United Kingdom as there are in countries with far lower returns to higher qualifications, such as Austria, Korea, and Turkey. Finally, there is little obvious correlation between premia to the two types of tertiary education. The wage benefits of vocationally orientated tertiary education are larger than the academically orientated equivalent in Norway, and are twice as large as the OECD average. Similarly, high premia to vocational higher education are seen in the Netherlands (which has moderate premia to academic higher education) and Portugal (which has high returns on academic education). For most countries where there are high wage premia to completing academic tertiary education, wage benefits for higher vocational education tends to be more moderate, and in the United States, Korea, Israel, and Japan, these benefits are particularly low.

Figure 17.2 shows that wage and employment benefits of investing in education and training do not always go hand-in-hand, which means we always need to consider both when talking about the overall payoff on an investment. Tertiary education graduates in countries such as Germany, Greece, Turkey, and Ireland are over 25% more likely to

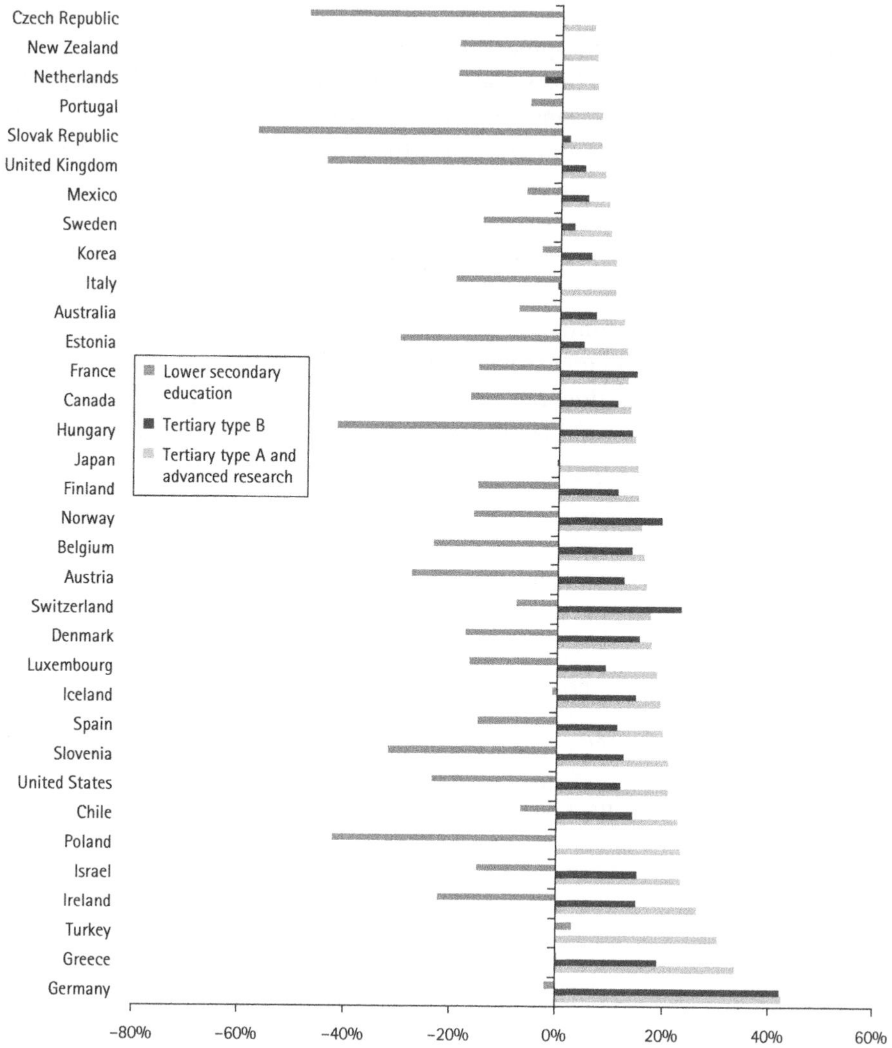

FIGURE 17.2 Employment rate differences by level of education and country

Notes: Employment rates relative to ISCED 3A (upper secondary education). Differences are expressed in relative rather than absolute terms—e.g. if the two employment rates being compared were 80% and 90%, the difference would be 12.5%, not 10 percentage points. Missing data: Tertiary type B—Czech Republic, Poland, Portugal, Turkey; Lower secondary—Japan.

Source: OECD.

be in employment than high school graduates, whereas the differences in the likelihood of finding a job is below 10% in countries such as the Czech Republic, New Zealand, the Netherlands, Portugal, Slovakia, and the United Kingdom. Only a small number of countries demonstrate both large penalties due to low levels of education and large benefits due to high levels of education with respect to employment rates, such as Ireland, the United States, Poland, and Slovenia. Comparing vocational and academic education at the tertiary level, Germany, Switzerland, Norway, and France are amongst the countries where the two pathways have similar employment rewards, whereas the employment benefits of tertiary graduates in places like New Zealand, Japan, and Italy are experienced by those in academic programmes only.

How can we interpret all of this variation? In the human capital model, wages and employment are determined by supply and demand. The premium on skills is connected to their scarcity—some countries might meet the higher demand for skilled workers with a greater supply, which reduces the wage premium placed on those with the skills. To illustrate, Figure 17.3 compares wage premia for tertiary educational attainment with the proportion of the population with those qualifications. There is a negative correlation between supply and wages, although it is not very strong ($r = 0.27$). Moreover, the figure shows a number of countries with high wage premia and low scarcity, and vice versa, which indicates that different supply is not the only relevant factor.

It could be that Figure 17.3 does not compare like for like if different educational systems produce different types and levels of skills (a point that is looked at in the fourth

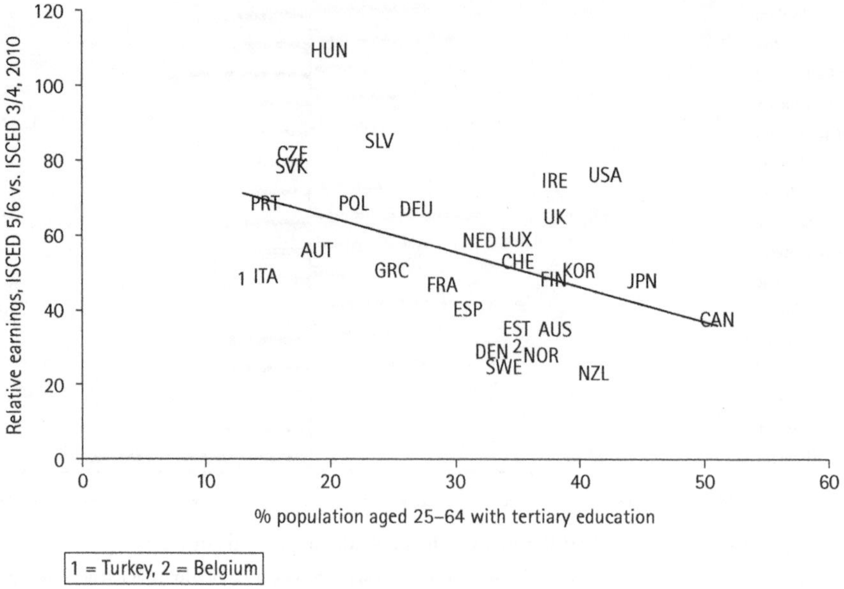

FIGURE 17.3 Relative wages and tertiary education attainment

Note: OECD averages marked on diagram.

Source: OECD (2014).

section). The productivity of a qualified individual also depends on other factors such as investment in capital that is complementary to work. This might explain why returns to education and training are lower in less wealthy developed countries such as Turkey, but it is not a convincing explanation for the lower returns in the Scandinavian countries (or, for that matter, countries such as Belgium or Australia), compared to similarly rich countries such as the United Kingdom and the United States.

Institutional differences across countries that affect wage setting also play a role. For example, the Scandinavian countries and Belgium have high rates of unionization and union wage agreement coverage. Strong unions, particularly those which bargain over the wages of the lower and middle parts of the labour market, tend to reduce wage inequality (Checchi and García Peñalosa 2005), which would be reflected in lower educational earnings premia.[4] Minimum wage policy would also have an impact on wages for lower skilled individuals, placing a floor on the potential size of the gap. Minimum wage critics have argued that such policies trade off higher pay for less productive workers with lower employment rates (Wascher and Neumark 2012), which would contribute to maintaining the overall return to greater educational attainment, although there is little reliably strong evidence of such effects occurring (Schmidt 2013).

Calculating Rates of Return

If the only difference between groups were their levels of educational attainment and, by implication, their skills, then we could easily interpret these relative wages and employment rates as the economic benefit an individual would expect to receive for participating in that programme of study. However, it is typically not the case that education is the only difference between groups, and some of these other differences affect wages as well. As a result, some of the differences in wages might be the result of factors other than education which feature more strongly in one group rather than the other. To deal with this, labour economists tend to use wage regressions, which assume a simple but theoretically plausible relationship between wages and factors that affect wages, and estimates the standalone effect of each one of these on earnings, whilst holding all of the others constant. The challenge is in choosing the right set of factors.

Wage Equation Regression

Mincer (1974) proposed a model in which earnings depend on just two things: education, measured in years of full-time education ('schooling') and labour market

[4] There are a number of channels for this effect to take place, from the union effects on productivity for less educated workers through demands for more training, to solidaristic bargaining principles which pursue more equal wages for all workers covered by negotiations.

experience. In most wage regressions of the form proposed by Mincer, the dependent variable is the natural logarithm of wages (which might be in hourly or annual terms).[5] The model assumes that each year of schooling increases productivity, on average, in a constant fashion—so, for example, going from four to five years of education has the same effect on productivity and wages as going from 11 years to 12. It also assumed that individual productivity continues to increase after the end of full-time education due to investments in on-the-job training but at a diminishing rate as individuals rationally invest less in their skills as they age. This is due to a combination of declining time to enjoy the benefits of this investment and the increases in the size of potential earnings that are lost due to deciding to remain in education and not enter the labour market. Hence, the standard dependent variables are education, experience (which is often approximated using age, less the number of years of completed schooling and the compulsory school starting age) and the square of experience (which we anticipate having a negative effect, capturing the diminishing returns to experience).

An alternative approach is to include variables which indicate attainment of particular levels of education or qualifications. The advantage of this is that is allows for the effect of education on earnings to vary rather than imposing the assumption that an extra year of education, however spent, increases earning potential at a constant rate. However, one practical problem is that many datasets ask for an individual's highest qualification only. The coefficient on a variable indicating, for example, the completion of a post-graduate degree would tell you how much more someone earns on average if they possess such a qualification compared to, say, someone who has completed compulsory secondary education. However, in the time between completing the two qualifications, people may have followed a variety of pathways. Part of the wage premium will capture the other investments in education and training made during this time, although we do not always have the information to work out how much of the wage premium comes from this.

There are many other variables which explain the distribution of wages. Different demographic groups appear to experience systematic gaps in their earnings even after controlling for education and experience differences. Women earn less than men on average, even where the two groups have been highly educated and could be expected to possess equivalent levels of skills. The same can be said for people with equivalent levels of human capital from different ethnic or racial groups. There are numerous possible explanations for these two observations, from deliberate discrimination caused by employer prejudice to differences in human capital not captured by measuring years of schooling or work experience—for example, if schools are of a lower quality in areas with larger ethnic minority

[5] The natural logarithm of wage is used as the dependent variable as it fits the data better for a linear function (i.e. a function that has the form $Y = a + bX + cZ$, where Y is the dependent variable and X and Z are explanatory variables). When log wages are used, the regression coefficients (b and c) approximately capture percentage increases rather than absolute increases in the dependent variable for a change in X and Z, respectively.

populations. It is therefore important to control for these demographic differences as it is likely that part of the raw gap in pay relates to how men and women from different ethnic groups are spread out across levels of education and training. For example, there may be a heavy concentration of black workers, who experience lower pay on average for any level of education and training, in lower attainment groups, which would widen the gap.

Other controls that are commonly included in a wage regression include geographic location (capturing differences in local labour markets other than their supply of skills and human capital) or marital status (as people with families have different priorities and constraints when searching for work). Finally, union status is also often included where those data are available—membership of a union is associated with higher pay compared to an equivalent worker with no union representation. Again, assuming people from these different groups are not randomly allocated across levels of education, the raw differences in pay shown in the second section will partly reflect the effect of some of these other variables.

It is often tempting for econometricians to include as many control variables as possible in their wage regression estimations. Doing so is fine providing the variables in question are exogenous—that is, that whilst different values of these variables help explain and predict outcomes such as wages or employment, these different values are not themselves determined by other variables included in the model. For example, gender is a truly exogenous variable. Being male—everything else being equal—correlates with higher earnings. We can interpret this as an effect of gender on wages because it does not make sense to think about the relationship going in the opposite direction—that is, it is not the case that being male or female is determined by potential labour market earnings.

For other factors, this is perhaps less clear cut. Angrist and Pischke (2008) use occupation as their example of a 'bad control'. It might seem like quite a good idea to control for differences in the types of work people with different levels of education and skills have. Some very well-trained people end up working in jobs which do not require the full extent of their skills, and it would be strange to expect that they would have the same earning potential as similarly qualified individuals in more demanding jobs. However, a person's occupation is also, at least in part, an outcome of the system—where someone has more skills and productive potential than another person, this is reflected in the job that they do. Acquiring skills through education and training could lead to an increase in the number of people entering occupations that require those skills. Therefore, including occupation in a regression downplays the return on education—part of the return on investing in more human capital is the ability to work in higher-paying occupations, now accounted for separately in the regression. The issue of exogenous and endogenous variables is picked up again towards the end of the chapter.

Wage Premia and Rates of Return

The types of wage equations discussed above estimate a wage premium—that is, the average percentage increase in wages associated with one level of education compared to another, whilst holding everything else constant. When educational differences are captured by years of education, it is common to see this referred to as a rate of return. However, calling it this is only correct under certain restrictive assumptions.[6] Moreover, if education attainment levels or qualifications are used, the wage premia estimated cannot be interpreted as rates of return even if these assumptions were to hold—although this does not seem to prevent the terms being used interchangeably in the popular discourse. In most cases, then, it is more accurate to calculate the rate of return of a particular educational investment in the same way a business would when contemplating an investment in new machinery or equipment, i.e. by assessing both the benefits *and* the costs from the moment of purchase onwards. In the case of education and training, the benefits to an individual are those noted previously—an expectation of higher wages and better employment prospects throughout working life—whilst the costs include course fees, forgone earnings, and non-monetary costs like the effort required to study something challenging. Once these have been quantified, we can calculate the expected net present value (NPV) of the investment as follows:[7]

$$NPV = \sum_{t=0}^{T} \frac{E\left(B_t - C_t\right)}{\left(1+r\right)^t}$$

where E(.) indicates we are looking at expectations of values at the time of the decision, B_t and C_t are the benefits and costs at time t, and r is the individual's subjective discount rate—we typically assume future benefits and costs are valued less than those experienced in the present as people dislike have to wait for good things and like being able to delay bad things. For any investment where the costs occur early on and the benefits to the investor are delayed, the NPV to a particular individual depends on their own discount rate. The higher the discount rate, the lower the value placed on future outcomes relative to immediate ones, and consequently, the lower the NPV of the investment. The internal rate of return (IRR) of any investment, including those in skills and training, is defined as the rate at which future benefits would need to be discounted in order for the NPV to be equal to zero, i.e. for the investment to be just worthwhile. For individuals who discount the future at a lower rate than this, the investment has a positive NPV and should be pursued. For individuals with a high discount rate, such an investment would make them worse off and should not be accepted.

Given the assumptions in footnote 6, the IRR and the wage premium on an extra year of educational or training investment becomes the same thing. To see this, let the wage premium arising from the investment be b and suppose earnings before the investment

6 For example, that foregone earnings are the only cost of spending additional time in education and training, and that individuals choose their education and training optimally so that the benefits of further human capital investment at that point are just equal to the cost of doing so.

7 We talk about expected net present value because there is some uncertainty around the realization of the size of the benefits and costs, and the time period over which they will be enjoyed and incurred. For simplicity, these can be thought of as some form of average experience of an individual making the decision to invest in their skills.

are standardized to 1 (so in the first period, the cost is from forgoing these earnings and in all other periods, the benefits are $b \times 1 = b$). Then, the NPV calculation becomes:

$$NPV = -1 + b\sum_{t=0}^{T} \frac{1}{(1+r)^t}$$

The sum of the discount factors for each period in the future can be shown to be approximately equal to $1/r$,[8] which means that NPV will be equal to zero if $b = r$, or if the wage premium equals the IRR.

Overview of Existing Wage Equation Estimates

There would not be sufficient space in this handbook, let alone this chapter, to give a detailed survey of the many estimates of wage equations that have been conducted across different countries, time periods, and available datasets. In this sub-section, I give a brief overview of some recent estimates to illustrate the magnitude of the effects commonly found from a select number of studies. The three studies which give us the broadest range of estimates for the returns on education are two produced for the World Bank (Psacharopoulos and Patrinos 2004, and Montenegro and Patrinos 2014) and the OECD's annual review of educational outcomes (OECD 2014). The three studies have different approaches—the OECD calculates full internal rates of return whilst Montenegro and Patrinos (2014) uses the Mincerian wage premium approach. Psacharopoulos and Patrinos (2004), which surveys existing studies, combine both approaches. Table 17.1 shows a range of the estimates from these studies. The first column, taken from Psacharopoulos and Patrinos (2004), gives what was the most recent estimate at time of publication for the Mincerian wage premium on an additional year of education. As it surveys existing work, the timing of these estimates here varies from 1977 in the case of the France to 1995 in the case of the United States. The second column gives the more recent set of wage premium estimates produced by Montenegro and Patrinos (2014) for an extra year of education—the column gives the range of estimates from years in the period 2000–2010. The final two columns are from the OECD's IRR calculations for participation in and completion of academic and vocational programmes at the levels of ISCED 3–4 (compared to ISCED 2) and ISCED 5 (compared to ISCED 3–4). Almost all of these estimates come from 2010 earnings and employment data, with the exception of Australia (2009), Italy (2008), and Japan (2007).

A few general points can be made from scanning this table. Firstly, there is significant variation in wage premia on years of education between developed countries and in some

[8] This is from a mathematical result called the sum of an infinite geometric series. This is a finite series (as people do not continue to earn for ever) so the approximation is acceptable assuming T is sufficiently large that the discount factor has become close to zero. For example, if $r = 10\%$, the discount factor for $t = 40$ is 0.02, and beyond that it becomes increasingly small.

Table 17.1 Selected wage premia and rates of return

Country	Wage premium, years of education (Psacharopoulos and Patrinos 2004) (%)	Wage premium (Montenegro and Patrinos 2014) (%)	IRR, upper secondvary or post-compulsory education (OECD 2014) (%)	IRR, tertiary education (OECD 2014) (%)
United Kingdom	6.8	7.6–1.9	18.2 (male)	14.3 (male)
			6.7 (female)	12.3 (female)
United States	10.0	11.8–13.8	19.4 (male)	15.4 (male)
			16.7 (female)	12.9 (female)
Australia	8.0	9.8–14.1	19.9 (male)	9.0 (male)
			12.7 (female)	8.9 (female)
France	10.0	8.0–9.2	10.6 (male)	11.4 (male)
			8.1 (female)	10.9 (female)
Germany	7.7	11.0–15.2	7.5 (male)	13.4 (male)
			6.4 (female)	8.5 (female)
Hungary	4.3	11.9–14.7	19.3 (male)	28.5 (male)
			15.8 (female)	24.6 (female)
Italy	2.7	6.4–7.0	8.1 (male)	8.1 (male)
			8.4 (female)	6.9 (female)
Sweden	5.0	4.4–5.7	16.5 (male)	7.4 (male)
			11.5 (female)	7.1 (female)
Japan	13.2	9.9–14.0	–	7.4 (male)
				7.8 (female)
South Korea	13.5	13.2	13.1 (male)	12.8 (male)
			11.3 (female)	11.0 (female)

instances, within a country over time. Secondly, there is no clear pattern between wage premia estimates and full IRR calculations—Sweden, for example, has consistently low wage premia relative to all the other countries included, yet when the full costs, taxation system, and employment prospects are factored in has far higher estimated returns than the Mincerian approach would otherwise suggest. In Germany, the relationship is the other way around—there is a high wage premium from Mincerian estimates but lower rates of return. Secondly, patterns in the difference of returns experienced by men and women vary across countries. In general, the estimates point to lower returns to women than men, but there are some exceptions to this. The size of the gap also varies quite a lot, often only for one level of education—for example, secondary education but not tertiary education in Australia. Thirdly, there is a lot of variation in estimated returns at different levels—while in general it would seem that secondary education is associated with higher returns than tertiary education for both men and women, this is not true in Germany, France, or Italy. This variation in estimated returns exists within countries as well. Table 17.2 shows, just for the case of the United Kingdom, how widely estimated returns to higher education (compared to an individual with two or more A-Levels or their equivalent) have varied, due to differences in time period, dataset, and methodology.

The World Bank studies can help put the experience of these select developed countries in the global context. Looking at the OECD specifically, the estimated wage premium is 7.5%, which is predictably lower than places with lower educational attainment, such as Latin America (12.0%), Asia (9.9%), and Sub-Saharan Africa (11.7%).

Looking at different levels of education, Montenegro and Patrinos find average global wage premia of 10.6%, 7.2%, and 15.2% for primary, secondary, and tertiary education respectively, although these returns tend to be lower where participation is higher. For

Table 17.2 Wage premia and rates of return on higher education in the United Kingdom

Study	Earnings data	Wage premium (%)	IRR (if given) (%)	NPV (£1,000s)
Harkness and Machin (1999)	General Household Survey, 1974–1995	14.2–23.0 (male) 20.5–26.7 (female)		
Blundell et al. (2000)	National Child Development Study, 1991	20.8 (male) 39.1 (female) †	–	–
O'Leary and Sloane (2005)	UK Labour Force Survey, 1994–2002	20.2 (male) 35.5 (female)	–	–
Bratti et al. (2008)	British Cohort Study, 2000	14.6 (male) 17.8 (female) ††	–	–
Walker and Zhou (2008)	UK Labour Force Survey, 1994–2006	18.2 (male) 27.9 (female) †††	–	–
Conlon and Patrignani (2011)	UK Labour Force Survey, 1996–2009	21.1 (male) 26.2 (female)	15.6 (male) 14.8 (female)	121 (male) 82 (female)
Walker and Zhu (2013)	UK Labour Force Survey, 1993–2010	20.5 (male) 26.8 (female)	–	168 (male) 252 (female)

Notes: †—For comparability with the rest of the table, the raw estimate without ability, test score or family background controls are given. Controls reduce the male premium to 17.1% and 36.8%, respectively This is discussed further in section 5. ††—The authors only report the return controlling for ability and family background, although they state that dropping ability measures has no effect on the premia. †††—Authors test for changes in the premium for pre- and post-expansion cohorts and find zero change for men but a 4% increase in the wage premium for women.

example, in the OECD the average returns to primary education are 4.9%, whereas in South Asia and Latin America, average returns are 6.0% and 7.8%, respectively. They also find that wage premia are, in almost all cases, larger for women than for men. As shown in Table 17.1, internal rates of return tend to show the opposite. This again highlights how estimates of the return on education and training can look different based on the choice of methodology—in the case of women and men, there are differences in the pattern of lifecycle earnings, periods of time out of the labour market, and retirement which can all be accounted for in a full IRR calculation, but for which the Mincerian approach may be too restrictive.

Return to Skills

One of the problems with most attempts to investigate the return to investment in skills comes from accurately measuring the skills that a given amount of education produces. Largely due to data availability, the literature has focused on the return to years of schooling or completion of a particular programme or qualification. These act as proxies for the skills which attract rewards in the labour market but they are obviously imperfect. Two people may have different levels of skills if the quality of that education or training were different even if their numbers of years of education or their highest qualification were the same. This problem is particularly large in cross-country comparisons as researchers would have to deal with different curricula, teaching methods, and quality of institutions to fully captures skills differences.

It has become possible in recent years to directly measure the skills possessed by individuals due to the propagation of large scale international tests by organizations such as the OECD of the actual competencies of workers across different countries. Whilst the Programme for International Student Assessment (PISA) attracts more headlines—typically as a measure of various educational systems' relative performance through the maths and science abilities of their 15-year-old children, assessing labour market outcomes requires testing of working age individuals, such as the International Adult Literacy Survey (IALS) and the more recent International Assessment of Adult Competencies (PIAAC).

Hanuschek et al. (2013) use PIAAC to provide the most recent internationally comparable data about the returns to cognitive skills across 22 OECD countries. In this analysis, the authors adapt the standard Mincer earnings equation to replace years of schooling with a measure of individual skill taken from tests of literacy, numeracy, and problem-solving. When included separately, the estimated wage premia were 17.8%, 17.1%, and 14.3% for the three skill groups across all of the countries[9]—literacy,

[9] As scores are standardized in each country, these wage premia can be interpreted as the change in earnings from increasing skill by one standard deviation. To illustrate the size of this marginal effect, if skill were normally distributed, a one standard deviation increase is equivalent to going from the median to the 84th percentile of the distribution, or from the 74th percentile to the 95th.

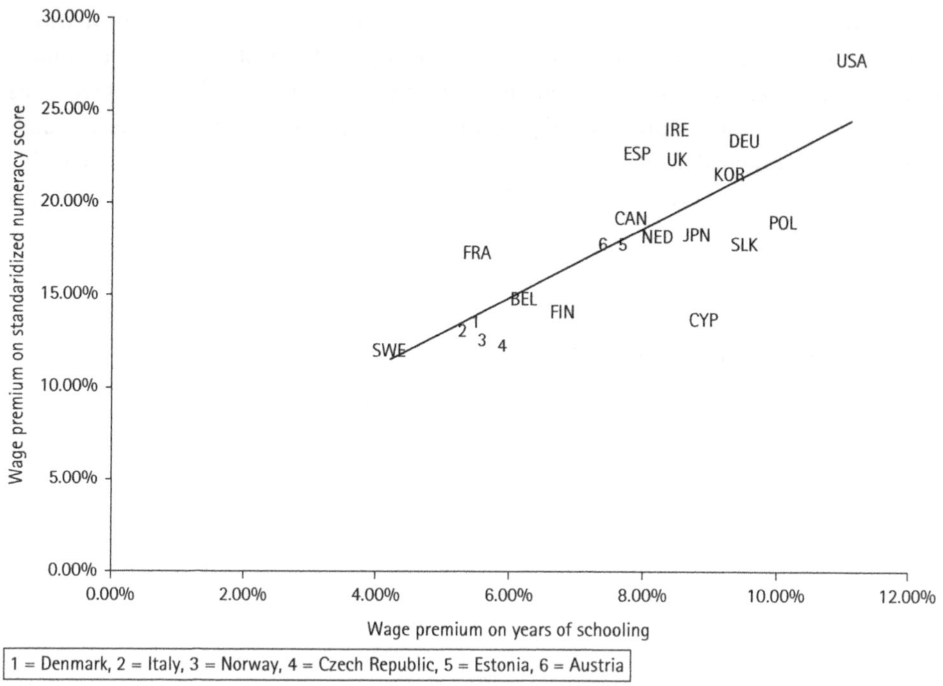

FIGURE 17.4 Returns to schooling and skills

Source: Hanushek et al. (2013).

numeracy, and problem-solving skills are highly correlated so it is unsurprising these effects are similar. However, they are not so correlated that it was not possible to include all three skills in one regression. In this case, the wage premia on each skill category was 7.8%, 7.6%, and 3.7%, respectively.

Figure 17.4 shows the estimated results for each country separately, looking at numeracy skills only. It compares this wage premia to that found in a standard earnings regression using years of schooling. Clearly, the two estimates are connected, although the correlation is not perfect.

The analysis also estimates a wage regression using both numeracy—as the proxy for cognitive skills—and the standard years of education. Including numeracy lowers the estimated returns to years of schooling from 7.5% to around 6% when all countries are included together, but the years of schooling measure remains significant. This could be interpreted as saying that a lot of the return to education isn't about skill differences, and that the amount of education may also be capturing characteristics that employers care about which are typically found amongst the better educated, but which are not produced within education directly. On the other hand, it is possible that the test is not a perfect way of measuring an individual's actual numeracy skills, and that this measurement error lowers the return on skills directly and allocates some of it to years of education. Just as likely is that there are other skills and abilities not captured by just looking at numeracy—for example, creativity or communication skills—which are also rewarded in the labour market. Hence, whilst including direct measures of particular skills gives us a partial insight into what the return on qualifications or the amount of education and training is capturing, it does not give us as unambiguous a conclusion as similar estimates at the macro-level, whereas related research has shown that after controlling for a country's average level of cognitive skills, the effect of average years of education on growth vanishes (Hanushek and Woessmann 2008).

Interpreting Wage Equations: Are They Causal?

The Ability Bias Problem

Returning to the more conventional wage regression approach, perhaps the most substantial problem for labour market researchers is causality. The theory of human capital suggests that investment in education and training increases worker productivity, which raises demand for those workers, which improves wages. In the regression analysis shown in the third section of this chapter, we observe a wage premium for workers with more education and training, holding all other sources of earnings difference constant, which would support the human capital model and indicate the extra productivity gained from investing in skills. However, it is not possible to control for all factors that affect wages, as some things are difficult for a researcher to observe (for example, an individual's self-motivation or their innate talents). This becomes a problem when these characteristics are themselves correlated with educational attainment because those with higher earning potential due to unobservable characteristics tend to invest more in their education. In this case, education ceases to be an exogenous variable (as defined earlier in this chapter) Consequently, the researcher ends up attributing too much of the variation in wages to the educational attainment variable as it captures some of these other unobserved differences in workers.

To illustrate, suppose there are just two levels of ability—high and low—and that education has a constant linear effect that adds to this ability and gives the individual's final productivity (and wage). Imagine education has been randomly assigned—that is, an individual of low ability is as likely to receive a given level of education as someone of high ability. We could collect data on education and wages, and use a Mincerian wage equation to establish the effect of education on wages, as shown in Figure 17.5 (a)—notice the estimated (dashed) line has the same slope as the true relationships.

However, if higher ability individuals complete more education and training than lower ability individuals (i.e. if educational attainment is determined, at least in part, by ability), then any observational data collected would have far fewer points in the top left and bottom right of the diagram, meaning there are just not that many high-ability,

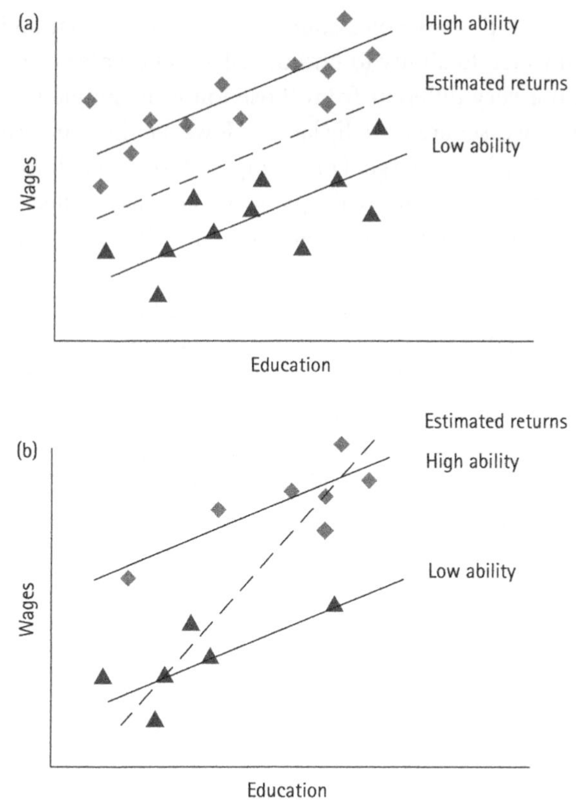

FIGURE 17.5 Ability bias and the return to education. (a) Estimated returns when education is not correlated to unobserved ability. (b) Estimated returns when education is correlated to unobserved ability

low-education or low-ability, high-education types in this labour market. Estimating a wage equation now would look like Figure 17.5(b)—the estimated line has a steeper slope than the true effect of education. This is known in the literature as ability bias and implies that the correlation between education and wages is not entirely causal.[10]

Card (1999) provides a comprehensive survey of the various techniques used to deal with this issue. There are a number of approaches that have been used, for example twin studies (e.g. Ashenfelter and Krueger 1994), instrumental variables (e.g. Angrist and Krueger 1991; Card 1993; Harmon and Walker 1995), and natural experiments. What Card's review suggests is that evidence from twin studies and instrumental variable

[10] Ability bias is a specific example of omitted variable bias. A related problem occurs when focusing on a particular occupation. Entry into an occupation requires having a certain level of competence—a combination of formal education and training, as well as hard-to-measure natural abilities or previous working experiences. Hence, on average, those that have less of the former are likely to have more of the latter. This pushes down the estimated return on education below the true effect that would be found if we were able to compare two groups of otherwise identical individuals.

estimates—which attempt to exploit a source of exogenous variation in schooling that is plausibly unconnected to ability to find the effect on earnings—is that estimates of wage premia are not very different from those found in simple OLS (ordinary least squares), and in many cases are actually larger. However, there are other studies which would imply the ability bias is large. For example, studies which include measures of prior ability have shown significant drops in the estimated effect of education and training on earnings (Blackburn and Neumark 1995; Blundell et al. 2000). Natural experiments concerning the effect of military service drafts or compulsory education laws show mixed results. Angrist and Krueger (1992) find large returns to education resulting from increased participation in education to delay Vietnam military service in the United States; however, Mouganie (2014) does not find such effects for peace-time conscription in France. Oreopolous (2006) analysed the students affected by the 1947 change in the age of compulsory education in the United Kingdom from 14 to 15 and finds a large return to the additional year of schooling possessed by students just after the law was introduced. However, Devereux and Hart (2010) found errors in this study, and using alternative data find a very small effect. This finding is consistent with other studies of similar law changes elsewhere, such as in Germany (Pischke and von Wachter 2008).

Signalling and Screening

The ability bias problem is often conflated with a similar sounding but ultimately separate issue—that education is a signal, rather than a determinant, of an individual's productive potential. In both cases, individuals may differ in their innate talents and abilities. In the problem discussed in the previous section on ability bias, employers are assumed to be rewarding these abilities with higher pay although the econometrician running a wage regression does not see this, and ends up predicting too high a return for human capital investments. It is also possible that employers are not better at discerning the unobservable productivity differences than econometricians are. In this case, more able individuals would want to signal their superior abilities to prospective employers—if they did not, they would end up being paid less than their productivity would deserve. Education and training may serve this signalling role (Spence 1973), assuming that the effort and time-cost required to reach a certain level of educational attainment is greater for less able workers. In this case, more able workers might be able to pursue education that others would not find worthwhile (given the higher costs of completion) imitating. If employers recognize this signal, they would then increase pay to those completing higher levels of education and training. In the educational signalling model, acquiring more education has a causal impact on wages (those with the signal get paid more) but not as much of a causal impact on productivity, which is still, at least in part, dictated by the initial set of talents and abilities.

As a result, many of the approaches to dealing with ability bias do not help distinguish between signalling and human capital explanations of wage premia to education and training. For example, if two twins acquire different levels of education, they will experience different wages in the signalling model, even though they have the same natural ability. The twin with more education will be paid the average productivity of his group, which on average contains more high ability individuals. The signalling model would suggest that one of the twins made a mistake—either the more educated one acquired a signal that was too costly for him, given the rewards or the other twin failed to acquire a signal that would have given them more benefits than its cost—but that is irrelevant for the final distribution of wages.

Similarly, proxying for ability makes no difference on the estimated return to education if employers are unable to see those same test scores. Instead, they base their wages on the signal presented to them at the point of recruitment. Moreover, the simplest version of the signalling model implies that employers have no incentive to seek out more information unless it is free, as wages adjust to reflect the average ability of the groups possessing the signal.[11]

The Distribution of Returns

Much of the debate around the returns to skills, education, and training has centred on the competing ideas of the human capital and the signalling model discussed in the last sub-section (see, for example, Chevalier et al. 2004). However, both of these theories are concerned with what is happening on the supply side of the labour market to determine wages—individual marginal productivity, whether determined by skill investment, prior ability, or a combination of the two is key. This tends to mean less attention is placed on the demand for skills. As Rubery (2006) argues:

> [H]uman capital theory provided a much more benign interpretation of the role of employers in shaping labour market outcomes; it placed the responsibility firmly back on the individual to develop their skills and productivity, with the apparent prospect that organisations would smoothly adjust their employment systems to utilise all new potential productivity on the labour market.

However, firms and employers can affect the productivity of workers– and hence the return to their investments in education and training—through the jobs they design and create, and the skills that are then needed and put to work (see, for example, the job competition model of Thurow 1976). Of course, some jobs will require skills to be developed before recruitment, as in the human capital interpretation of educational wage premia. In other cases, skills may be developed on the job, either through formal training or working experience and more informal learning. Employers may then use educational signals

[11] A more realistic model might suggest that matching particular types of individual to particular jobs is good for employers too, so that it is in their interest to find out individual attributes before hiring.

as indications of suitability for learning the job once hired, and so prospective employers will invest in education to compete against other workers for the available distribution of jobs. As with the pure signalling model, this educational investment can lead to higher wages but not due to a premium paid to skills created through this investment.

Incorporating the demand side of skills has important implications for the discussion of the returns to skill investments. One of these is that once there are sufficient skills produced in the labour market to meet the existing demand, the distribution of wages can be fixed unless something changes on the employers' side—for example, if a new production technology is adopted. Further skill investments beyond that point will tend to lead to under-utilized skills, which by definition do not attract any financial return, and may lower overall returns (including non-monetary returns if they lower the life satisfaction of those who are working below their capabilities). By contrast, both the human capital model and the signalling model do not say anything about the phenomena of over-education because all skills are assumed to be fully utilized.[12] In the human capital model, any alteration in the supply of skills is brought into equilibrium through fluctuations in wages, at least in the short-run, because these skills are now less scarce (relative to the existing amount of capital, equipment, and other factors of production that individuals work with). Similarly, increasing educational participation of lower ability workers in the signalling model reduces wages to that group because the value of the signal has been reduced. In the demand-constrained job competition model, however, there is no wage adjustment mechanism—instead, some educated, trained, and skilled workers lose out and are pushed into finding less demanding, less well-paid work instead.

Recognizing this possibility is important for taking anything meaningful away from the many estimates of the return to education. Firstly, in the human capital model, wage premia can be interpreted as proxies for the greater productivity of skilled workers, and hence social value of skills. Moreover, if these premia do not fluctuate over time, this could be interpreted as saying that demand for these skills is keeping up with their supply, as is the often the case when looking at the returns to a university degree (see, for example, Katz and Murphy 1992 for the United States; and Walker and Zhou 2008, 2013 for the United Kingdom). In the job competition model, it would be more accurate to think about wage premia reflecting the average productivity of the jobs secured by one group compared to another. A constant premium over time, even when the supply

[12] Over-education is meant here to mean people participating in education and training longer than is necessary to perform their job. This is sometimes conflated or confused with other phenomena. For example, a person may have more qualifications than is necessary to acquire a job given the criteria set out by the hiring firm, but their additional abilities and skills may be useful once hired. This obviously depends on the nature of the work. A second phenomenon is where high qualifications are required to even get an interview for a job opening, possibly because prospective employees use educational credentials to compete for jobs and employers formally recognize this to reduce the applicant pool, but where the job requires far fewer skills than candidates possess. This type of situation would fit with our definition of over-education, although workers may not consider themselves over-educated given that their education was a requirement of the job.

of skills is increased, need not mean there is an increasing demand. Instead, individuals with more qualifications find themselves working in a wider array of jobs, but in doing so they push out the less qualified. Consequently, the average wage and productivity of both groups falls, which leads to stable wage differentials and increased levels of over-education.

There will also be different effects on the distribution of returns around the estimated wage premium, which captures the average or expected wage benefit of making the investment. However, in a world with uncertainty, investors, including people investing in their education and skills, care about the spread of returns around this average and the probabilities associated with ending up at different points of this spread. In human capital theory, the distribution of wages for people who have made similar educational and training investments reflects qualitative (and potentially unobserved) differences in either their unobserved abilities, or the quality of the educational institution, or the specific types of skills produced by different courses at the same level. With enough data, this could be added into the calculation, leading to rates of return by subject of study or institution. Over time, the distribution of the return on a particular type of education or training may change if these things alter. This might be because increased provision comes at the expense of teaching quality, for example, or because some courses grow more rapidly than others.[13]

In the job competition model, the distribution of returns changes if the jobs offered by employers change, or if the amount of people with comparable education and training increases. Specifically, if nothing else changes to the structure of jobs, increasing participation extends the distribution at the low end, as people with those qualifications compete for a wider range of jobs from the overall distribution. The distribution will widen even if an expansion of that level of education or training were achieved without compromising the quality of provision or even the mix of skills.

From the perspective of public policy, it is the return to the marginal student rather than the average that is relevant—that is, the student who is on the cusp of participating or not participating. Carneiro et al. (2011) have shown that the marginal returns to expanding US college attendance are far lower than the returns estimated from Mincerian wage equations, even when the return is estimated using sophisticated instrumental variable techniques (see section 5.1). Such a finding is also consistent with some of the natural experiments discussed previously (that aimed to address issues of ability bias) where a policy shift that increases participation produces low or zero returns. Both sets of findings are predicted by the job competition model in which the demand for skills and the structure of jobs are rigid.

[13] For the researcher, the observed distribution might change because the group is becoming more heterogeneous in terms of pre-education abilities, but it should be noted that this is less relevant for the individual concerned, who presumably has some knowledge of their own pre-investment capabilities and considers returns from that starting point.

Workplace Training

Up until this point, this chapter has largely focused on the returns on skills which are, to varying degrees, general, in the sense that they might raise the productivity of workers across a number of potential employers, occupations, or industries. Becker (1962) explained how such skills would be under-provided by employers themselves as they would worry that, once they had made the investment, a different firm would poach the worker. Hence, either workers or the state should pay the cost of general skill investments, largely in primary, secondary, and tertiary education.

However, individuals continue to invest in their skills beyond the formal education and training system. Becker argued that firms will provide training in specific skills—that is, skills which rival firms are unlikely to poach—but workers will likely be given a share in the proceeds of that investment in order to create incentives for them to stay in their current job so that the firm can maximize its own return on its skill investment. In this last section, we consider the return on these sorts of investments.

In theory, the methodological approaches and problems to general education and training discussed previously apply equally to workplace training. In a wage regression, the variable of interest will usually capture participation in some form of training or could measure the amount of time spent in a training programme, which leads to issues about what types and levels of skills are actually being measured. As before, there are issues relating to unobserved differences between participants and non-participants. Those who complete a training programme are unlikely to be a random selection of all potential trainees—they may be more motivated or have other abilities which both improve their future earning potential (even without the training) and make it more likely they participate in and complete training. Hence, simple estimates of the wage premium to training are affected by the same ability biases shown in Figure 17.5.

Unlike general education and training, individuals typically work before and after episodes of firm-based training. As a result, researchers can use panel data to attempt to deal with ability bias. Specifically, if we assume that the unobservable factors which affect wages and are correlated with participation in training do not change over time, then the change in wages before and after training for trainees compared to non-trainees would estimate the true return on the investment.[14] This approach tends to significantly reduce the measured return relative to a naïve regression of participating on wages. For example, Cedefop (2011) finds a significant wage premium across European data for employees who experienced some training in a 12-month period relative to those that do not—for men this was estimated as 9.6% using one data set and 15.5% using another, with 10.2% and 12.4% being equivalent figures for women. Once fixed

[14] The specific technique used here is called fixed effects regression.

effects were used, all estimates reduced and none remained statistically significantly different from zero.

This approach has been popular in the literature and has found significant, positive effects of training on wages (for a survey, see Leuven 2004) To give one example, Blundell et al. (1996) found a cohort of UK males' wages grew by 3.6% between 1981 and 1991 if they had participated in employer-funded on-the-job training. For women, the premium was 4.8%. Moreover, for employer-funded off-the-job training, the premia were 6.6% and 9.6%, respectively. Similarly, Loewenstein and Spletzer (1998), using US panel data, found a 3.5% premium on participating in formal company training. Note that the wage premia captured by these regressions typically are based on a training period that can be measured in weeks rather than years. Frazis and Loewenstein (2005) estimate (for their baseline specification) a wage premium of 4.5% for the median training period of 60 hours. This would imply rates of return that far exceed anything found in formal education—in this example, the authors calculate a rate of return of around 150%.

However, fixed effects regressions will not identify the true effect of training on wages if the unobserved differences between individuals are not the same before and after training (for example, if those who participate in training tend to have faster wage growth already). There is some evidence that this matters. Leuven and Oosterbeek (2008) use a unique survey that can identify those who wanted to participate in training but were unable to due to a random event from within the non-trained control group. This reduces the unobserved differences between those who receive training and those that do not. Doing this reduces the wage premium for participating in a training programme from 12.5% to a statistically insignificant 0.6%.

Some governments, such as that of the United Kingdom, are heavily involved in workplace training due to a concern that currently firms are under-investing, which largely follows from some of the higher estimates of wage returns. Even if these estimates were true—and reasons to worry about them have certainly been advanced in this section—recognizing the role of the demand side of the labour market when interpreting wage premia is as important here as it was for formal education and training. When firms offer training, they are able to match up the programme with the specific skill requirements of the jobs their trainees will ultimately move into. If they do not have greater skill needs that would generate the greater productivity that allows for the payment of higher wages to try to retain those they train, they will not offer training. Hence, unobserved differences in the types of firms offering training to their employees is as important to consider as unobserved differences in individual abilities—so, for example, larger firms with hierarchies of increasingly demanding jobs tend to provide more training (to meet the needs of the different levels) and offer greater wage growth (through internal promotion of those who have sufficient skills to progress). If governments provide or subsidize additional training that firms would otherwise have not provided (as in the case of the UK Train to Gain scheme under the 1997–2010 Labour government), then they rely on something changing about the available jobs and the demand for skills. If it does not, which has been a concern about UK training policies that goes back at least as far as Finegold and Soskice (1988), then little wage return can be expected for participants. It is perhaps no coincidence that the estimate wage premia on the lower level qualifications which tend to accompany such schemes are essentially zero (McIntosh 2006; Conlon et al. 2011).

Conclusion

In principle, the rates of return on education and training are valuable information to have, not only for individuals considering whether or not to participate in a particular programme but also for policy-makers and governments to justify public investment in skills. As a result, there is a huge array of studies which have tried to estimate the rates of return for all sorts of skill investments. This chapter has explained the main approaches employed to generate these estimates and shown that a wide range of return has been found over the past couple of decades, depending on country, level of education, and indeed the methodological choices made by researchers. A lot of effort has gone into dealing with the issue of ability bias, but, as this chapter has explained, no consensus on the size of this bias exists.

Whatever the results, estimates are almost invariably interpreted through the lens of human capital theory, according to which the existence of a wage premium indicates additional productivity due to skill investment. Far too little attention is given to the possibility that the results of these regressions may actually represent a world where skills demands are relatively constant and constrain labour market outcomes so that the main function of education is to allow people to compete for the jobs the labour market is providing. In respect of the issues surveyed in this chapter, much may well be explained through this alternative view. Increased variability in the distribution of returns, coupled with low marginal returns, would certainly be predicted by such a model. An inability to explain returns to education as solely being related to skill differences would also fit. Moreover, this model suggests that ability bias ceases to be the main omitted variable of concern—employer demand for skill and job design is far more relevant.

These requirements should be a concern for individuals wanting to invest in skills. Private rewards do still exist for people who make investments, but they might be lower or more risky that currently assumed. From the perspective of policy-makers, the issue is much greater, as private returns cannot be easily equated to the broader benefits to society. This chapter has argued that when demand for skills does not increase in line with supply, estimated wage premia no longer indicate where further investment could raise productivity or reduce inequalities in the distribution of income as the situation becomes closer to a zero-sum game. It is but a short step to argue that, at present, too much emphasis is placed on producing and reporting on rate of return analyses whenever skills, education, or labour market policy is being discussed. If the notion of rate of return is not to be discarded entirely, at the very least the analyses should be combined with a variety of additional evidence that is relevant to the existing and future demand for skills.

REFERENCES

Angrist, J. and Krueger, A. (1991) *Does Compulsory School Attendance Affect Schooling and Earning?*, *Quarterly Journal of Economics*, 106(4): 979–1014.

Angrist, J. and Krueger, A. (1992) 'Estimating the Payoff to Schooling Using the Vietnam-Era Draft Lottery', NBER Working Paper no. 4067, Cambridge, MA.

Angrist, J. and Pischke, J. (2008), *Mostly Harmless Econometrics*, Princeton, NJ: Princeton University Press.

Ashenfelter, O. and Krueger, A. (1994) 'Estimates of the Economic Return to Schooling from a New Sample of Twins', *American Economic Review*, 84(5): 1157–1173.

Becker, G. (1962) 'Investment in Human Capital: A Theoretical Analysis', *Journal of Political Economy*, 70(5): 9–49.

Blackburn, M. and Neumark, D. (1995) 'Are OLS Estimates of the Return to Schooling Biased Downward? Another Look', *The Review of Economics and Statistics*, 77(2): 217–230.

Blundell, R., Dearden, L., and Meghir, C. (1996) *The Determinants and Effects of Work Related Training in Britain*, London: Institute of Fiscal Studies.

Blundell, R., Dearden, L., Goodman A., and H. Reed (2000) 'The Returns to Higher Education in Britain: Evidence from a British Cohort', *The Economic Journal*, 110: 82–99.

Bratti, M., Naylor, R, and Smith, J. (2008) 'Heterogeneities in the Returns to Degrees: Evidence from the British Cohort Study 1970', working paper no. 2008-40, Department of Economics, Business and Statistics at Università degli Studi di Milano, Milan.

Card, D. (1993) 'Using Geographic Variation in College Proximity to Estimate the Return to Schooling', NBER Working Paper no. 4483, Cambridge, MA.

Card, D. (1999), 'The Causal Effect of Education on Earnings', in O. Ashenfelter and D. Card (eds), *Handbook of Labor Economics*, vol. 3A, Amsterdam: Elsevier: 1801–1856.

Carneiro, P., Heckman, J., and Vytlacil, E. (2011) 'Estimating Marginal Returns to Education', *American Economic Review*, 101(6): 2754–2781.

Checchi, D. and García Peñalosa, C. (2005) 'Labour Shares and the Personal Distribution of Income in the OECD', IZA Discussion Paper no. 1681/2005.

Chevalier, A., Harmon, C., Walker, I., and Zhou, Y. (2004) 'Does Education Raise Productivity or Just Reflect it?', *Economic Journal*, 114: 499–517.

Conlon, G. and Patrignani, P. (2011) 'The Returns on Higher Education Qualifications', BIS research paper no. 45, London: Department of Business, Innovation and Skills.

Conlon, G., Patrignani, P., and Chapman, J. (2011) 'Returns to Intermediate and Low Level Vocational Qualifications', BIS research paper 53, London: Department of Business, Innovation and Skills.

Devereux, P. and Hart, R. (2010) 'Forced to Be Rich? Returns to Compulsory Schooling in Britain', *The Economic Journal*, 120: 1345–1364.

Frazis, H. and Loewenstein, M. (2005), 'Reexamining the Returns to Training: Functional Form, Magnitude, and Interpretation', *Journal of Human Resources*, 15(2): 453–476.

Hanushek, E. and Woessmann, L. (2008) 'The Role of Cognitive Skills in Economic Development', *Journal of Economic Literature*, 46(3): 607–668.
Hanushek, E., Schwerdt, G., Wiederhold, S., and Woessmann, L. (2013), 'Returns to Skills Around the World: Evidence from PIAAC', OECD Education Working Papers, no. 101.
Harkness, S. and Machin, S. (1999) *Graduate Earnings in Britain, 1974–1995*, Department for Employment and Education, Research Report RR95.
Harmon, C. and Walker, I. (1995) 'Estimates of the Economic Return to Schooling for the United Kingdom', *American Economic Review*, 85(5): 1278–1286.
Katz, L. and Murphy, K. (1992) 'Changes in Relative Wages, 1963–1987: Supply and Demand Factors', *The Quarterly Journal of Economics*, 107(1): 35–78.
Leuven, E. (2004) 'A Review of the Wage Returns to Private Sector Training', Paper presented at the joint EC-OECD Seminar on Human Capital and Labour Market Performance, Brussels, 8 December. Accessed online 15 April 2015: http://www.oecd.org/els/emp/34932279.pdf.
Leuven, E. and Oosterbeek, H. (2008) 'An Alternative Approach to Estimate the Wage Returns to Private-Sector Training', *Journal of Applied Econometrics*, 23: 423–434.
Loewenstein, M. and Spletzer, J. (1998) 'Dividing the Costs and Returns to General Training', *Journal of Labor Economics*, 16: 142–171.
McIntosh, S. (2006) 'Further Analysis of the Returns to Academic and Vocational Qualifications', *Oxford Bulletin of Economics and Statistics*, 68(2): 225–251.
Mincer, J. (1958) 'Investment in Human Capital and Personal Income Distribution', *Journal of Political Economy*, 66(4): 281–302.
Mincer, J. (1970) 'The Distribution of Labour Incomes: A Survey with Special Reference to the Human Capital Approach', *Journal of Economic Literature*, 8(1): 1–26.
Mincer, J. (1974) *Schooling, Experience and Earnings*, New York: National Bureau of Economic Research.
Montenegro, C. and Patrinos, H. (2014) 'Comparable Estimates of Returns to Schooling Around the World', Network for International Policies and Cooperation in Education and Training.
Mouganie, P. (2014) 'The Effects of Conscription on Education and Earnings: Regression Discontinuity Evidence', Unpublished working paper. SSRN: http://ssrn.com/abstract=2494651.
Neumark, D., Salas, J. M., and Wascher, W. (2013), 'Revisiting the Minimum Wage-Employment Debate: Throwing Out the Baby with the Bathwater?', NBER Working Paper no. 18681, Cambridge, MA.
O'Leary, N. and Sloane, P. (2005) 'The Return to a University Education in Britain', *National Institute Economic Review*, 193(1): 75–89.
OECD (2014) 'Education at a Glance 2014: OECD Indicators', OECD Publishing
Oreopolous, P. (2006). 'Estimating Average and Local Average Treatment Effects of Education when Compulsory Schooling Laws Really Matter', *American Economic Review*, 96(1): 152–175.
Pischke, J. and von Wachter, T. (2008) 'Zero Returns to Compulsory Schooling in Germany: Evidence and Interpretation', *The Review of Economics and Statistics*, 90(3): 592–598.
Psacharopoulos, G. and Patrinos, H. (2004) 'Returns to Investment in Education: A Further Update', *Education Economics*, 12(2): 111–134.
Rubery, J. (2006) 'Segmentation Theory Thirty Years On'. Paper presented at the 27th conference of the International Working Party on Labour Market Segmentation, 16 September.

Schultz, T. (1961) 'Investment in Human Capital', *American Economic Review*, 51(1): 1–17.
Spence, M, (1973) 'Job Market Signalling', *Quarterly Journal of Economics*, 87(3): 355–374.
Thurow, L. (1976) *Generating Inequality*, London: Macmillan.
Walker, I. and Zhou, Y. (2008) 'The College Wage Premium and the Expansion of Higher Education in the UK', *Scandinavian Journal of Economics*, 110(4): 695–709.
Walker, I. and Zhou, Y. (2013) 'The Impact of University Degrees on the Lifecycle of Earnings: Some Further Analysis', BIS research paper no. 112, London: Department of Business, Innovation and Skills.

CHAPTER 18

THE ECONOMIC AND SOCIAL BENEFITS OF SKILLS

IRENA GRUGULIS, CRAIG HOLMES, AND KEN MAYHEW

Introduction

The returns to individuals from investing in skill are considered in Chapter 17. This chapter is concerned with the wider returns on skills. First we consider their economic benefits. More skilled workers can earn higher wages because they are more productive. However, only under certain conditions do these wages capture all the productivity gains. Some of the benefits accrue to employers in the form of higher profits/lower costs. Thus this chapter begins by examining the literature on the relationship between skills and organizational performance. It then goes on to consider the implications for national income and economic growth, paying particular attention to the likelihood of spillover between firms. One example would be where a trained worker moves to a different firm, taking his skills with him. A second example is related to the drivers of long-term economic growth. New theories of growth rely on there being public benefits to developing skills that affect the output of all firms, including those that train less than others.

The existence of these wider benefits to skills has prompted policymakers to devote significant resources to raising skill levels in the workforce. We discuss the rationale for their policies.

Finally, we consider potentially wider benefits to society from acquiring greater levels of skills—the social returns in terms of health, civic participation, crime, and other non-economic dimensions.

The Returns to the Organization

It ought not to be surprising that, on average, organizations benefit from their investment in training. After all, if they did not, this would suggest extraordinary incompetence on the part of those who run the organizations concerned. A recent analysis (Cedefop 2011) of 62 econometric studies of the relationship between some measure of firm performance and some measure of work-related training confirms this link.[1] The majority of these studies suggest that there is a positive impact on organization performance, although there is a sizeable minority of studies that do not establish such a relationship. A meta-analysis of the 264 estimates of the relationship between training and firm performance found in these studies concludes that training has a positive influence on the economic performance of firms. It finds that this conclusion holds for most measures of performance (the most common one used being productivity), and that evidence of positive effects is least persuasive for profitability and costs. In addition, it finds that positive effects are least likely to be found in non-manufacturing, and that there is some evidence that vocational education and training (VET) impact is greater in larger firms.

Whilst this seems a pretty fair summary of the extant literature, these conclusions bear scrutiny. The first issue is that of lags. Over half the studies covered by Cedefop do not consider the length of time over which the benefits of training might be felt and indeed look at only contemporaneous relationships (see, for example, Barron et al. 1989; Dearden et al. 2000; Black and Lynch 2001; de Kok 2002). It seems reasonable to assume that this would lead to an underestimate of the positive effects of training investments, compared with studies that have included lagged variables (for example, Black and Lynch 1996; Bassi et al. 2001; Conti 2005; Zwick 2006). That said, the Cedefop meta-analysis suggests that whether or not lags are allowed for in the impact of training does not seem to greatly affect the generally positive results.

Secondly, all econometric work in this area encounters the problem of endogeneity of the supposedly independent variable. This would be where the firm's performance directly or indirectly affects the level of VET training, leading to overestimates of the direct causal effect of VET on company performance. For example, a firm might be particularly successful at recruiting highly productive new workers and these workers might tend to participate in more training once hired, meaning that firm success and the incidence of training appear to be correlated, although the connection is not entirely causal.

[1] These studies cover 23 different countries, with some studies covering several countries. The countries most frequently studied are the United States, Germany, France, and the United Kingdom.

A common cause of endogeneity is the omission of relevant variables that also explain differences in firm performance. If there is a correlation between the omitted variable and the training variable, then the estimate of the effect of training will be overstated if the analysis uses standard linear techniques such as ordinary least squares estimation, since it will be 'picking up' the impact of the missing variable. Thus it is critical that sufficient and appropriate 'control' variables are deployed. Typical control variables include occupation and sector (for example, Barron et al. 1989), educational attainment of trainees (for example, Conti 2005), competitiveness of industry and union pressure (Delaney and Huselid 1996), human resources management practices (Delaney and Huselid 1996; Nikandrou et al. 2008), research and development (R&D) intensity (Dearden et al. 2000; Leiponen 2000), and size of firm (for example, de Kok 2002).

For studies that use a panel of firm data, there are techniques that can help control for potential missing variables that are correlated to both performance and training. Some studies use fixed effects models, which assume that the contribution of the unmeasured missing variables is constant for each firm over time. As a result, taking a difference between two time periods removes the omitted variable effect and any potential biases it might create. Of course, this technique does not work as effectively if the unmeasured variable changes over the time period.

Even when all relevant observable variables are included, there may be further problems establishing causality from training to firm performance. For example, a highly profitable firm may decide to use some of its earnings to further train its workforce, meaning that the direction of causation in the model runs in the opposite direction. Again, linear regression techniques will not be able to deal with this. Some studies (for example, Tan and Batra 1996; Addison and Belfield 2008) use instrumental variables to deal with this—these are variables which capture an exogenous change in training that can not be attributed to a change in performance. A large number of studies use non-linear techniques such as the generalized method of moments (see, for example, Ballot et al. 2001; Black and Lynch 2001; or Zwick 2007). The meta-analysis confirms that various methods for correcting potential endogeneity biases reduce the impact of VET but it usually still remains positive.

Finally, there are problems with the quality of the data. Measurement error of the independent variable—defined as a systematic tendency to over- or under-report any of the factors the researcher is interested in—may also cause biases in the estimate of the measured effects. Training statistics are notably flawed and partial. Moreover, there is a real problem with what exactly is meant by training. Historically labour economists talked about training and development. Training itself was characterized as off-the-job and on-the-job. Development was the less easily defined process of 'sitting by Nelly', a process by which supervisors and colleagues taught new members of staff as they actually did the job. Empirical work has been driven by data availability, which generally means that the training variable used has been identifiable training episodes. As a result it is highly likely that most studies fail to capture the full benefits of learning in the workplace.

The literature has a deeper problem relating to its purpose. Many of the studies underlying the Cedefop meta-analysis appear to be more interested in the sign and significance, rather than the magnitude, of any estimated effect of training on firm performance. This then filters through to the headline conclusions of any overview of the literature and in statements made by policymakers. Why is there such an obsession with establishing the apparently obvious? As a point of comparison, consider that there is also a large literature on the returns to physical investment, but this goes far beyond establishing that more often than not there are positive payoffs. It is concerned to establish the precise size of the payoff to any given investment, to compare this with the payoff to alternative investments, and crucially to set such returns against costs and thereby establish criteria for whether or not an investment should proceed. Whilst an estimate along these sorts of lines may be found in some of the training studies, this is not usually the case, and, moreover, such considerations are rarely evident in any overview of the literature on the returns to investment in training. Why? Obviously, measurement and methodological issues such as those described above mean that it is difficult to meaningfully compare studies in terms of the magnitude of the effects of training. Hence, the only solid conclusion taking all these studies as a whole is about the direction, and not the magnitude, of the effect. Is there anything in the literature that produces anything more interesting or useful than the econometric studies? Perhaps this could be found in indications as to how organizations might maximize the benefits of any given training investment, or in whether training attached to qualifications was more useful than training which was not, which is where qualitative work comes into its own. A 2008 study for the OECD (Hoeckel 2008) provides a partial overview of some of this literature, as does a 2004 study for the UK Department of Trade and Industry (Sung and Ashton 2004). Clearly a single piece of qualitative work, often based on a case study approach, is rarely capable of being generalized. Nevertheless, an aggregate of such studies can yield useful information. It is unlikely to yield interesting measures of rates of return or precise quantification of benefits. However, it could give us clues about:

- whether certain forms of training are more or less effective than others
- whether the use of certification/qualifications is effective
- what constrains training activity
- what might maximize the effectiveness of any given quantum of training—accompanying human resources management practices, etc.
- what motivates employers to engage in training activity. For example, it may not be seen directly as a means of improving organizational performance but simply as a defensive measure in the face of health and safety regulations.

Unsurprisingly the evidence with regard to such matters is fragmented and piecemeal. Whilst useful information may emerge from such studies for policymakers in particular sectors in particular countries, this does not amount to a generalizable corpus of evidence. The unfortunate conclusion to be drawn is that research on returns to training by employers is much effort that signifies very little.

The Returns to the National Economy

First, we consider the effect of skills on total productivity of an economy, which in turn affects its national output or income. We then examine the link between investment in skills and the way national output increases over time. Finally, we discuss the 'high-skills vision' espoused by most OECD governments.

Skills and Productivity

The gross domestic product (GDP) of a country measures the amount of goods and services produced. As everything sold generates an income for somebody, this is closely related to national income.[2] The quantity of goods and services an economy can produce depends on the use of different factors of production, such as machinery, land, raw materials, and labour. Skills also enter into this production relationship.

Skills and the Production Function

One way of thinking about this is to treat skills as a stock of human capital in the same way that factory machinery is part of the stock of physical capital. This human capital stock affects the productive capabilities of labour.[3] An increase in the human capital stock, through formal education, in-work training, or informal learning on-the-job, raises the amount produced by a given number of workers. This leads to an increase in the total output and income of the economy.

Formally, the production process can be defined as:

$$Y = A.F(K, L, H)$$

where Y is national output, $F(.)$ is the production relationship that gives the output for a combination of capital (K), labour (L), and human capital (H), and A is referred to as total factor productivity—increases in A scale up production for a given combination of inputs. It is usually thought of as a measure of the level of technological advancement of a particular economy.

Mankiw et al. (1992) assume that equation (1) has a specific functional form known as a Cobb–Douglas function, which is defined as:

$$Y = AK^{\alpha}L^{\beta}H^{\gamma} \qquad (1)$$

[2] It differs when owners of a country's factors of production are from another country, and also when some production is being used to replace worn-out assets.

[3] The human capital stock also includes a number of other factors that are not individual productivity-enhancing skills. These include knowledge, which is shared by everyone, as well as factors such as physical health. The focus here is on productivity-enhancing skills.

where $\alpha + \beta + \gamma = 1$, meaning that this function exhibits constant returns to scale.[4] Therefore, we would expect to see a relationship between national output and some measure of the stock of human capital, in a way similar to the relationship between earnings and individual levels of education and training.

Productivity and Schooling

The stock of human capital is affected by two factors: the productivity-enhancing skills possessed by workers, and the number of workers there are. Thus, we can define $H = hL$, where h is the average skill level of workers. We can also go one step further and posit that this skill level depends on the amount of education and training an individual receives. Conventionally:

$$h = \exp\left(\varphi(s)\right) \tag{2}$$

where s is the average amount of time that the workforce spends acquiring skills, and $\varphi(.)$ is the function that relates these years to the average productivity of workers. In the interest of simplicity, we can assume there is a linear relationship, $\varphi(s) = a + bs$, where b is the rate of return to an additional year of education and training, although more complex relationships are possible (see Card 1999). For example, we could allow for the possibility that post-compulsory education or firm-based training may not increase output at the same rate as early years schooling. Following Bils and Klenow (2000) and Hall and Jones (1999), the effect of schooling, s, on productivity enters equation (2) as an exponential term, to reflect the micro evidence that there is a linear relationship between the natural logarithm of wages (as a proxy for productivity) and years of schooling. Consequently, output per capita can be expressed as:

$$y = \frac{Y}{L} = A\left(\frac{K}{L}\right)^{\alpha} \exp\left(a + bs\right)^{\gamma}$$

Taking natural logarithms of this gives a simple linear relationship between income per capita and schooling:

$$\ln y = \ln A + \alpha \ln k + \gamma\left(a + bs\right) \tag{3}$$

Equation (3) can be thought of as a macro Mincer equation (Heckman and Klenow 1997), analogous to the relationship between individual wages and educational attainment in the famous micro Mincer equation.

The variable, s, would ideally be an internationally comparable measure of the education and training workers have received. In cross-country comparison work, it is often

[4] A production function is said to have constant returns to scale if, when all factors are increased by a fixed proportion, total output increases by the same proportion, for example, where a doubling of all the inputs leads to twice as much output being produced.

proxied by measures of schooling attainment, whilst comparable measures of firm-based training are difficult to find. Figures 18.1 and 18.2 show cross-country comparisons of GDP per capita against two measures of educational attainment for a selection of OECD countries.

These figures show a significant positive relationship between educational attainment and the log of income per capita across countries. They also show considerable variation around this relationship. Countries like Hungary, Poland, and Slovakia have similar levels of output per capita as Mexico and Turkey, despite large differences in educational attainment. Equation (3) suggests that this could be explained by differences in the capital stock per worker across countries. Similarly, differences in total factor productivity, captured by A in equation (3), affect output for a given input of physical capital and skills. As well as differences in the take-up of technology and the distance a particular country is from the frontier of technical progress, institutional factors can increase or decrease the overall productivity of a given combination of inputs. For example, strong and enforceable intellectual property laws allow firms to innovate without fear of having their investments appropriated by rival firms. Similarly, features of both labour and product markets that make them work more or less efficiently can also play a role. Hall and Jones (1999) find that differences in human capital and physical capital explain a relatively small amount of variation in output per worker, suggesting that most of the difference is down to unobservable differences in technology, institutional arrangement, and total factor productivity.

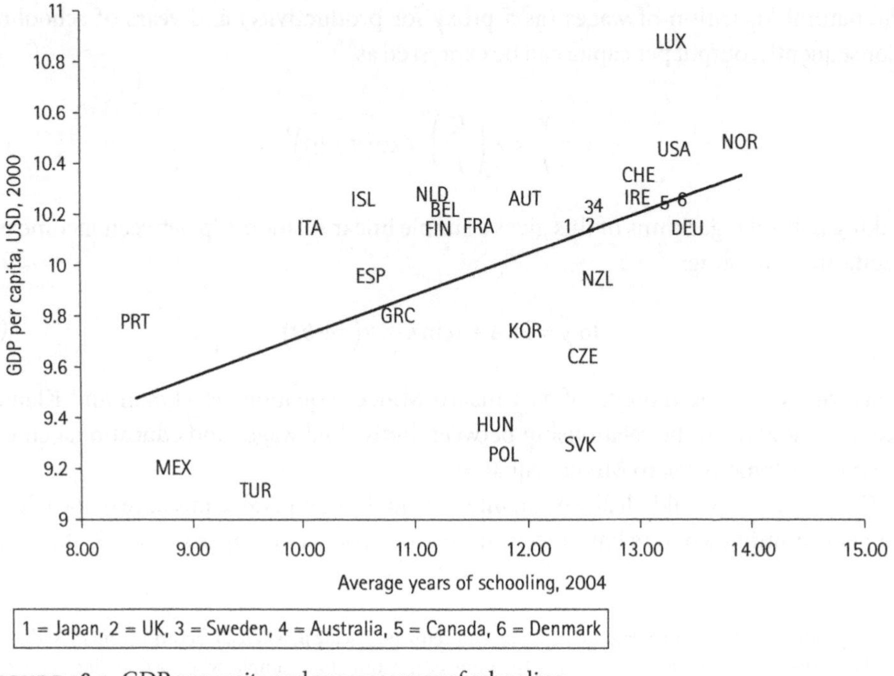

FIGURE 18.1 GDP per capita and average years of schooling

Source: OECD.

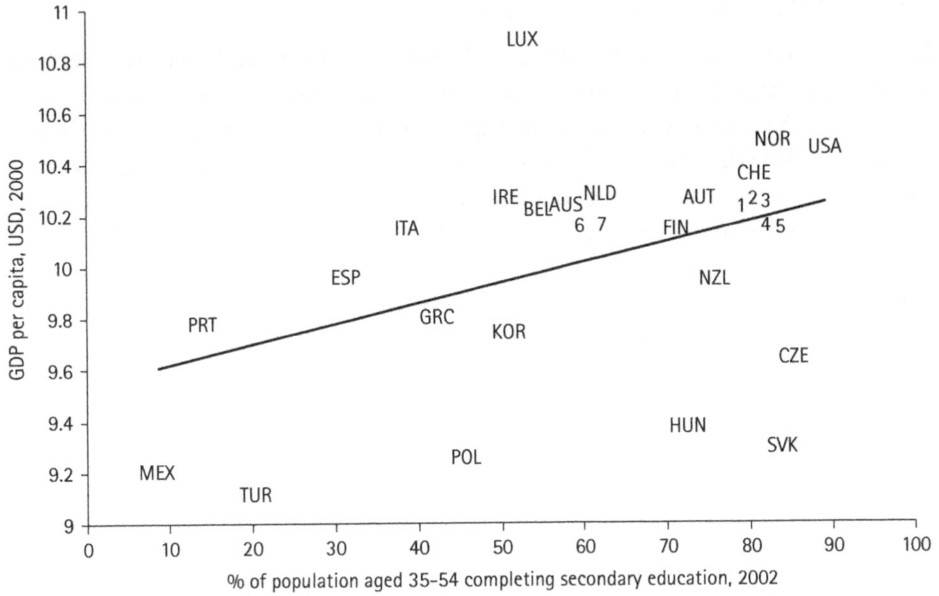

1 = Sweden, 2 = Denmark, 3 = Canada, 4 = Japan, 5 = Germany, 6 = France, 7 = UK
Iceland has been omitted compared to the original

FIGURE 18.2 GDP per capita and proportion of 35–54-year-old population having completed secondary education

Source: OECD.

Two further issues are relevant. Firstly, the approach does not take account of differences in educational quality in producing these skills. If some education and training systems are better than others at producing skills for the same number of years spent in schooling, then part of the residual will include the differences in skills. A second but related issue concerns the type of skills each education and training system produces. The separate elements of an education and training system produce different skills—cognitive skills, such as numeracy and literacy, are developed throughout primary education and secondary education, whereas technical competences in a particular trade largely result from a vocational programme or apprenticeship. Some skills are valuable in certain contexts, for example, language skills are much more important in a small country which relies heavily on exports. Other skills depend on demands created by the structure of the economy and the labour market. Autor et al. (2003) demonstrated that technological progress has shifted demand away from routine occupations (such as semi-skilled manufacturing and administrative jobs) towards non-routine work. Some non-routine jobs (such as professional and management) require greater communication and critical thinking skills, whereas other non-routine jobs (such as cleaner and retail assistant) require low-level manual and customer service skills. As these demands change, the relationship between the amount of education and training, and income per capita, will depend on the VET system's ability to produce the relevant skills to meet labour market demands.

Returns to Schooling: Micro versus Macro

If education and training is generating productivity enhancing skills that are reflected in higher wages, as proposed by human capital theory (for example, Becker 1964), then the estimates of the effects of education on wages from both microeconomic studies should be comparable with the effect of education on output per worker in cross-country macroeconomic estimations, such as the one depicted in Figure 18.1. However, there are a number of sources of divergence. Firstly, wages would need to reflect all additional productivity. This is generally true in a competitive labour market, where the forces of supply and demand ensure that the market price equals the additional output from employing an additional worker, and firms compete away any profits. This may therefore be a good model for self-employed workers, such as tradesmen and consultants, and employees in sectors with lots of small firms. It does not hold in imperfectly competitive labour markets, where part of this additional output becomes higher profits for employers rather than higher wages for workers. In this case, macro estimates (which include all forms of income, not just earned wage income) should exceed micro estimates. There are also issues when pay is set outside of market forces (for example, for public sector employees).

Macro estimates may also be larger than micro estimates if there are any spillovers from those who have acquired some skills to other workers. We will return to these externalities in the next section, as they are central to models of long-run economic growth and human capital investment.

Finally, macro estimates of the returns to schooling may be lower if education and training does not have a *causal* impact on productivity. Specifically, if differences in educational attainment reflect prior ability—as suggested by the signalling model of education (see Spence 1973)—then micro returns will reflect the difference in the average productivity of groups of individuals with similar levels of educational attainment, but at the macro level the average productivity of workers will not be strongly related to the amount of schooling.

Heckman and Klenow (1998) found that estimates of the macroeconomic return to years of education were roughly comparable to those coming from microeconomic estimates, once they had controlled for differences in the level of technology employed. This could be interpreted in two ways: either the theoretical reasons given above as to why macro and micro estimates should diverge are not important, or they are important but cancel each other out.

Skills and Economic Growth

In the previous section we examined at the link between levels of skills and national income at one moment in time. The obvious extension of this is to look at how skills and investing in education and training are related to the *growth* of national output.

The Neoclassical Framework

The starting point for any modern analysis is the neoclassical growth model, usually attributed to Solow (1956). This model takes, as a starting point, a production process similar to that captured by equation (2), with the exception that the original models did not include human capital, so $\alpha + \beta = 1$. In this model, short-term growth can be driven by increases in capital stock. A key feature of the model is that investment in capital depends on saving, which is proportionate to national income. Hence, as incomes rise, saving and investment rise, meaning that new capital is added to the economy. However, since $\alpha < 1$, there are diminishing returns to increases in the capital stock (if the population remains unchanged), which means that the increase in capital has increasingly smaller effects on output.

There is an amount of investment that is required each year to keep the amount of capital per worker constant. This depends on the rate of growth of the labour force and the rate of depreciation of existing capital. As the economy grows, investment becomes increasingly used simply to maintain capital per worker and less is available to increase capital stock. Figure 18.3 demonstrates this.

At the steady state of the model, k^*, investment in new capital is just sufficient to meet replacement requirements, without adding any more capital per worker to the economy. Once at the steady state, growth depends on changes in the exogenous level of technology and total factor productivity, captured by A in equation (1).

Mankiw et al. (1992) introduced a human-capital augmented version of the Solow model, with a production process identical to that shown in equation (1). We showed above that this model predicted that countries that spend more on education should have higher national incomes—therefore, a country that increases the skill level of its workforce should expect to see its national income grow faster during the period when skill levels are increasing. However, the model treats skills identically to physical capital, with diminishing returns to increases in the stock of human capital ($\gamma < 1$). Saving from

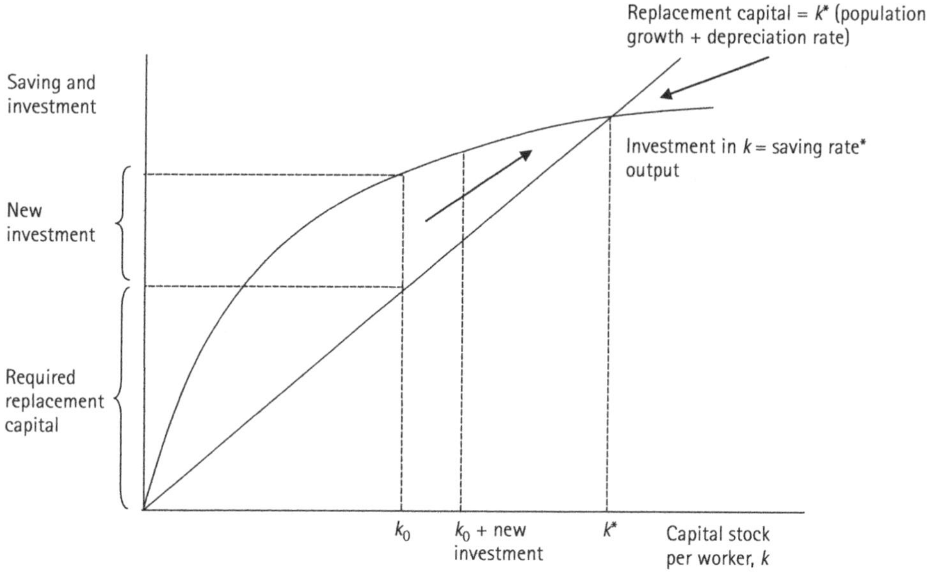

FIGURE 18.3 The Solow growth model

income can be invested in either physical or human capital accumulation. Investment in human capital, through education and training, raises human capital stocks, whilst depreciation (for example, through skills becoming out-of-date, or through retirement of older workers) creates a requirement to replace existing human capital. The steady state occurs where both physical and human capital investment just meets the replacement requirement, similar to the situation shown in Figure 18.3.

Therefore, the Solow model, even if augmented to include productivity-improving skills and human capital, would still suggest that long-term growth rates of national income are not affected by investment in education and training, although short-term changes in output per worker should be related to increasing the supply of skills.

Skills and Human Capital in 'New' Growth Models

In the 1980s, a number of economists proposed models of economic growth that went beyond the Solow model. These developed for a number of reasons (see Romer 1994, for a more in-depth account). One reason was that for long-term growth to depend solely on exogenous technological progress seemed theoretically unsatisfactory. These growth theorists wanted to be able to explain which factors drove improvements in total factor productivity. A second reason was that the Solow model made a number of unsatisfactory predictions about long-term growth patterns. Countries did not appear to converge in growth rates towards the exogenous rate of technological progress as much as anticipated. Countries should grow faster when they are further away from their steady state, whilst, in the long-run, all countries should grow at the rate of technological progress. By contrast, many poor countries grew far more slowly than richer countries, and catch-up has been limited to a number of middle-income nations. To move beyond the neoclassical framework, new growth theories proposed models that emphasize the potential for spillovers and externality effects from investments—although these are the same types of externalities that Heckman and Klenow (1998) found little support for in their study. Lucas's (1988) model of economic growth and human capital is one of the most influential. A number of other models have similar features, but we focus on the Lucas model here since it explicitly mentions the role of human capital and skills. A key assumption of this model is that learning facilitates further learning—more skilled workers are better able to learn by doing once they start working, and may even generate new working knowledge and production process innovations that can be shared by other skilled workers. Therefore, the output of an economy shown in equation (1) can be adjusted as follows to include these spillovers:

$$Y = AK^{\alpha}L^{\beta}H^{\gamma}h^{\delta} \qquad (4)$$

where $\delta < 1$, so that there are spillovers, but that these are subject to diminishing marginal returns to increases in one factor alone. Suppose, for simplicity, that $\delta = \beta$. Output per capita would then be given as:

$$y = \frac{Y}{L} = A\left(\frac{K}{L}\right)^{\alpha} h^{1-\alpha}$$

This means that the production function now exhibits constant returns to scale—if human capital and physical capital per workers double, then output per worker also doubles. Therefore, if we redefine k as a measure of the broad stock of capital (both physical and human), then the production function becomes:

$$y = Ak \tag{5}$$

Therefore the steady state in this model is not one where investment is simply sufficient to meet the replacement needs of the current capital stock, unlike the earlier Solow model. This is because savings, and hence investment per worker, would increase in proportion to the required replacement investment, so the two do not converge and output per worker is able to continue growing in perpetuity. This is shown in Figure 18.4.

These models became known as 'endogenous growth theories'—the rate of growth is generated within the model by the accumulation of factors of production. Increasing the stock of these factors generates higher incomes, which leads to more investment, which again leads to higher incomes, and so on. Therefore, the long-term growth rate of the economy will be the rate at which this broad measure of capital grows.

Physical capital, we can assume, increases in a similar way as before: savings are lent to firms to finance their investments where investment in excess of the replacement requirement leads to new capital formation. Added to the spillover effects of human capital, which eliminate the existence of a steady state, the second important feature is how human capital is accumulated. In the Lucas (1988) model, the human capital

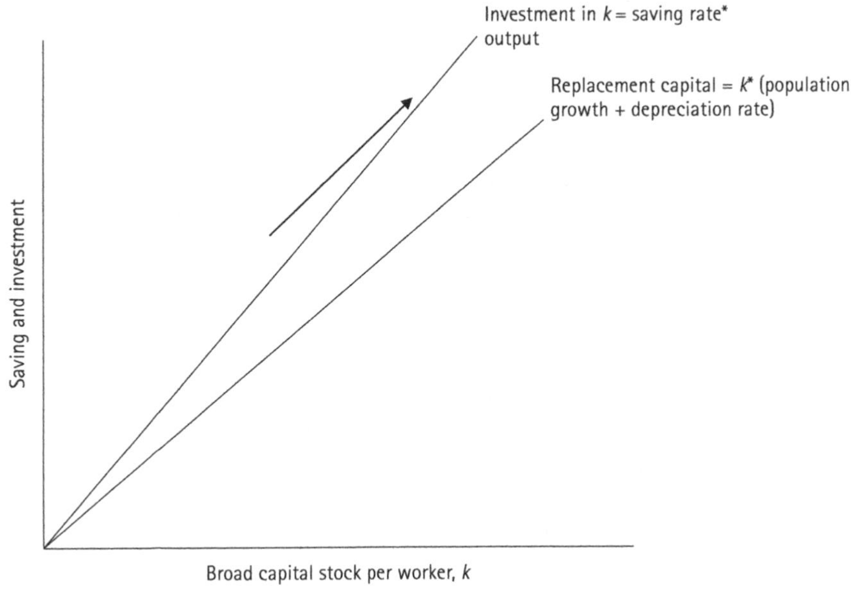

FIGURE 18.4 An endogenous growth model

growth rate is proportionate to the fraction of time spent in education and training activities, so that:

$$\textit{growth rate of } h = \theta(1-u) \tag{6}$$

where u is the proportion of total working time not spent studying and training, and θ is a parameter that captures the maximum growth rate if all time was allocated to education. Notice that this differs from the accumulation process suggested in equation (2), where the growth rate of human capital would depend on the *change* in the average level of schooling, rather than the *level* of education. Equation (6), by contrast, suggests that a year of schooling permanently adds to the human capital stock. In essence, new generations 'inherit' the human capital stock of the retiring generation, and add to it as they themselves pass through education and training. This emphasizes once more the importance of spillovers in these models.

Comparing Models

This assumption may seem strange in the context of skill development. To examine this further, it is useful to draw on Romer's (1986) distinction between rival and non-rival forms of human capital. Rival forms of human capital are those that can only be used by the person who possesses them. They cannot simply be transferred to another individual. If skills are rival, then Mankiw, Romer, and Weil's model would seem like the most appropriate, and economic growth should be related to changes in the stock of human capital. By contrast, knowledge can be a non-rival form of human capital—just because one person knows something does not mean another person cannot benefit from that knowledge. Knowledge is like a public good and can be transferred from one individual to another without the first person giving it up. This is the form of human capital envisioned by endogenous growth theory.

The distinction between rival and non-rival human capital is emphasized in Romer's (1986) model of endogenous growth. The model has similarities to the Lucas model. It generates constant returns to a broad measure of capital, but the spillovers that lead to this arise out of investment in physical capital rather than human capital. Romer argued that as firms invest in new physical capital, knowledge increases along with it.[5] So, for example, installing a new piece of machinery in a factory generates new skills as workers use it and generate new knowledge about how to produce more efficiently. This knowledge is non-rival and can be shared amongst firms that have not made the same physical capital investments. It can also increase without bound and be passed on to future generations through their education, training, and work experience.

Thus, investing in skills that allow for non-rival human capital to be more easily absorbed in the workplace might be necessary. Consequently, numerous authors have placed an emphasis on mathematical and scientific skills as being key to linking schooling with long-term economic growth (Hanuschek and Kimko 2000).

[5] This can be expressed as before in equation (4), but where h is proportionate to K. This then leads to equation (5) as before.

Similarly, in other growth models knowledge is explicitly linked to R&D activities, and long-term growth rates depend on the output of this sector. Therefore, it is important that there are enough workers in the economy with the particular skills to carry out R&D. Again, this draws attention to mathematical and scientific skills, including those generated through higher education. These models also generate growth endogenously, as investment in R&D increases the stock of knowledge, which helps facilitate further advances in a way similar to the human capital accumulation relationship described in equation (6).[6]

The remainder of this section looks at attempts to empirically test the nature of the relationship between economic growth and measures of human capital.

Measuring Skills and Growth

A simple way to evaluate these theories is to look at a cross-country regression of the annual *percentage change* in GDP over a given time period against a measure of the outcomes of the education and training system. The most common way of measuring the latter, given the state of comparable international data, is to deploy average years of schooling completed as a crude proxy for skills. Almost all cross-country studies suggest that these types of measures are related to economic growth rates. However, the neoclassical model predicts that the effect comes from changes in schooling outcomes, whilst endogenous growth theories suggest that it is the initial levels that matter in the long-term. This has been a contentious issue: Benhabib and Spiegel (1994) found support for the latter, whilst Krueger and Lindahl (2001) suggested that the result relied on numerous measurement errors and other biases. Their analysis lends more support to the neoclassical view.

Both these studies treat years of schooling as homogenous across age groups and countries. Using similar specifications to Lindahl and Krueger (2001), Holmes (2013) distinguishes between different levels of schooling and finds that, whilst primary and secondary education are related to growth in various ways (the former by its level, in support of endogenous growth theories; the latter through its change, in support of the neoclassical approach), neither the increase nor the level of higher education has any significant effect on growth.

6 Jones (1999) aptly illustrates this process by referring to the famous Isaac Newton quotation: 'If I have seen further, it was by standing on the shoulders of Giants.' In Romer's (1990) model of R&D, this assumption results in the prediction that economic growth is proportional to the stock of human capital engaged in R&D (rather than changes in the stock). This has some problematic implications as it suggests that, holding everything else constant (including the share of resources allocated towards research), larger countries should grow faster, which is empirically false. Introducing diminishing returns to the existing stock of knowledge, the R&D production function (Jones 1995) removes this prediction and suggests long-term economic growth depends solely on the growth rate of the number of workers engaged in R&D. Consequently, policy levers, such as an increase in the resources allocated to research, only have short-term effects, as diminishing returns to knowledge reduces growth in subsequent periods. Similarly, multi-sector models (for example, Young 1998), where economic growth leads to a widening variety of products, also deal with the scale effects in Romer (1990), but retain the long-term effect of the policy lever (research intensity). Jones (1999) provides a good summary of each class of model.

Hanuschek and Kimko (2000) and Hanuschek and Wossmann (2007) argue that measures of skills and education based on the quantity of schooling are misleading, as differences in the quality of education are important. They construct a measure of labour quality using internationally comparable data on mathematics and science tests. When these are included in growth equation estimations, the role of the quantity measures of schooling (such as the average years of schooling for the working age population) disappears, whilst the quality measure is highly significant. Their quality measures are much more closely related to concepts of productive skills and not the type of human capital envisioned in the endogenous growth models of authors like Lucas.

There is also some evidence that R&D activity is positively associated with growth rates. Holmes (2013) finds a marginally significant effect of the proportion of R&D workers in an economy on growth rates. This finding corroborates other recent studies. For example, Aghion et al. (2009) find that patenting is related to increases in spending on US university degrees, which then generates higher growth. Therefore, higher skills related to science and technology may have a role in boosting economic growth through facilitating innovation.

There are, however, a number of methodological issues in this literature. Holmes (2013) argues that cross-country comparison studies tend to be quite sensitive to the sample analysed. In one example, estimating the same equation over two time periods six years apart changed the significance of the effect of schooling years on growth, even though the variables in each time period were highly correlated. Similarly, missing data means that the countries included in a sample can change based on which control variables are included. For example, comparative schooling data is available for a wide range of countries, whilst international assessment data tends to be found in developed countries only. Therefore, the decision to look at quality over quantity of education and training immediately removes a sizeable number of countries from the estimation.

There are also problems with measurement error, particularly for the explanatory variables. Whilst the quality of data improves with each revision (see Barro and Lee 2010, for details on the most widely used dataset), Holmes (2013) notes that we 'cannot rule out the possibility that mismeasuring the size and importance of tertiary education' is responsible for some of the results mentioned earlier.

One final important question is whether we can be sure that estimated relationships are causal. One concern is that countries may invest in education more if they are growing faster, as governments will have growing tax revenues to spend on these investments, and households will be encouraged to invest more in education given the promise of high and rising future earnings. In other words, the causal relationship runs the other way. Bils and Klenow (2000) found some evidence for this. Furthermore, there may be no causal relationship at all. There may be an omitted variable for which we do not have useful data that influences both national output and education investment decisions. For example, the state of health care may raise output through creating a more productive workforce. A government may decide for political reasons to spend more on all public services, including health and education. In this case, if a proxy for the effectiveness of health care is not included, then education and growth will apparently be correlated in the data.

The Case for Government Intervention

Governments around the world are heavily involved in the production of skills in their countries. At various levels (school, post-compulsory education, and work-based training) there is a presupposition that, if left to their own devices, employers and individuals will provide a socially suboptimal amount of skills. As a consequence, firms will not be as productive as they could be and countries will not grow as quickly as they have potential to. Reflecting this belief, policymakers have welcomed academic work that demonstrates the advantages that training brings to employers and indeed have themselves commissioned much such work. This may explain why so much effort has gone into confirming that employers that train have higher levels of success, as discussed earlier.

There are four types of arguments used to justify government intervention on the grounds of social benefits. These are:

- the externalities argument
- the distributional concerns
- privately suboptimal decisions
- the high-skills vision

Externalities have already been mentioned in the context of economic growth, such that individual skill acquisition has wider, long-term effects on the productivity of the economy. A similar externality argument exists at the level of firm-based training. For skills that are transferable between employers, the social marginal gain will be larger than the private marginal gain as long as there is a positive probability that an employee will leave the firm that trained him for an alternative employer who is not involved in the decision to train or not (Stevens 1999). This is sometimes referred to as a 'poaching' externality.

Governments need to be concerned when private decisions are not socially optimal ones. Private optimal decisions are those where the trainee and/or employer invest up to the point where the private marginal costs of the training just equal the private marginal gains. Equivalently, training is socially optimal where the social marginal costs equal the social marginal gains. When there are externalities the social marginal gains may exceed the private marginal gains, and the government may need to intervene to achieve social optimality.

The second reason for government intervention is distributional. This was, for example, the original motivation behind the UK Labour government's Train to Gain policy. In this particular case there was concern to give a second chance to those adults who had 'lost out' in the formal education system and left the system with few if any qualifications. Subsidies were designed to encourage employers to train such people up to a qualification that would improve their prospects in the labour market at large.

The third motive for government intervention is that individuals and firms are not making choices that are even privately optimal—that is, they fail to invest in skills even up to the point where the private benefits are exhausted. This shortfall would exist even if externalities did not. Two forms of market failure may come into play here: capital market failure and imperfect information. The former implies that to the extent that the individual worker or employer is expected to pay for training, there may not be sufficient access to the necessary funding to do so. The latter implies that she does not have adequate information to make optimal decisions.

The fourth justification for intervention relates to coordination problems between the demand and supply for skill, and is connected with the high-skills vision that most, if not all, OECD governments have espoused. The essence of this is that, in a globalizing world where emergent economies provide ever-increasing competition, the only viable route for a wealthy country that wants to maintain a reasonable distribution of income is to move as much of its production as possible upmarket (Reich 1992). In so doing it tends to avoid competition simply on price and cost, where it is liable to lose, and compete on product niche and quality where price is not so constraining. It is presumed that, for any narrowly defined product, such a move upmarket implies greater skill intensity of the production process. Therefore, whilst the literature on national income and growth described above is concerned with the *volume* of output, the high-skills vision is more concerned with its composition, although this ultimately translates to greater volume of output if the high-skills vision becomes reality and leads to higher growth rates.

Proponents of the high-skills vision presume that as the production of a specific product moves upmarket, then the production process will become more skill intensive. Therefore, it may be that employers and individuals are indeed training optimally for their present needs but if there were significant moves across the economy as a whole towards high specification products and services, then the demand for skills would increase. Thus, depending on the initial stocks of skill, improving the human capital of a nation might well become a necessary condition for achieving the high-skills vision.

Do these justifications for government intervention hold water? The distributional argument is a sustainable one. Subsidies might well be justified as long as the workers concerned really do improve their labour market prospects and as long as the employer receiving the subsidy would not have engaged in the training in any event. These are empirical questions to be asked of any specific scheme. There is certainly also a valid argument that governments should help correct market failures. In terms of capital market failures, this is the justification for the state provision of student loans and other training grants. However, the third justification, which suggests that individuals and employers may make privately suboptimal choices, is potentially problematic since it supposes that policymakers might be better informed about these private benefits than those who receive them. It is possible to produce reasons why this might be the case, for example, where collecting information is costly and complicated, or where widely held perceptions differ from the actual facts—but it would be a mistake to automatically assume these factors were in play. The decision not to acquire more skills is not, in and of itself, a market failure—it only becomes so when there are unrealized social benefits to doing so.

The externalities argument for intervention is the most commonly accepted. However, it should be noted that there are three generic ways of tackling such problems: government intervention, private negotiation, or forming clubs. In the context of training all three are possibilities. Subsidies are one form of government intervention, but there are other options, for example, taxing inadequate trainers. The tax could be seen as a negative subsidy. Private negotiation would in this case take the form of training contracts, whereby the employee would agree to pay back some or all of the costs of training if he left before a specified time interval had elapsed. Forming a club means that the agents who impose externalities on each other become (formally or informally) a single decision-taking unit and thereby 'internalize' the externality. The example of high-technology eco-clusters like Silicon Valley provides a relevant example in the training context. There are lots of small firms there that provide considerable training to their employees and yet seem unconcerned that mobility between firms is frequent. The reason for lack of concern is essentially a 'swings and roundabouts' one. A firm may quickly lose a highly and recently trained employee but easily pick up a replacement from another firm in the area. This is an example of an informal club. Whilst this argument has been readily accepted for examples such as Silicon Valley, there seems to be a reluctance to accept its validity across a broader range of enterprises. This seems to us not necessarily to be justified. In other words, the extent of the unresolved externality problem is an open issue. To the extent that subsidies are used to address the problem, they are being used without any real evidence as to the extent of the problem.

Finally, it should be noted that whilst improving the skills of the workforce is a necessary condition for achieving the aims of a high-skills vision, it is not a sufficient condition. Unless the product strategy and the production process actually change, the extra skills would be unused. This realization has recently led policymakers in OECD countries to place much more emphasis on linking skills policies with what is becoming known as the new industrial policy (Froy 2013). Nevertheless, in some countries there is arguably still a tendency to regard increasing the supply of skills as the magic bullet that will hasten the move to a high-specification, high-value economy. The belief is that increasing supply will generate its own demand. It would simultaneously make workers more demanding about the content of their jobs and at the same time relieve a possible constraint on their employers from moving upmarket. Although this might be a possibility, there is no evidence to suggest that it would be a strong foundation upon which to base policy. Subsidising for possible but uncertain future skill needs could lead to appalling waste of public money.

Similarly, there is the possibility that processes may change in a way that requires less skill. The upskilling assumption is based on a historical image of Fordist manufacturing techniques where mass production meant that skill could often be designed out of many or even most of the jobs involved. The corollary was that as production moved to a concentration on quality and less on standardized products, more jobs would require more skill. Brown et al. (2011) have argued that the digital revolution may be rendering this historical image at least partially outdated, as technological progress has allowed the types of knowledge work that would previously have been considered high-skill to become routinized, standardized, and deskilled.

Thus, the argument for government intervention in employer-based training is a more limited one than is often appreciated, whilst the use of subsidies as the form of intervention is even more dubiously based.

The Non-Economic Returns to Society

The benefits of skills may not be limited to narrowly defined economic outcomes. There is a substantial literature on a wide range of social, health, and other advantages that educated and skilled people enjoy. This section reviews some of this literature and then attempts to explain the links between education and better health, stronger social connections, and reduced likelihood of engaging in criminal activity by considering the influence of a range of factors, including status, access to resources, learning, socialization, and deferred gratification. It goes on to explore whether the benefits ascribed to education can also be attributed to skill.

When non-economic benefits are considered there is a fairly consistent message. The more highly educated people are, the more likely they are to participate in almost any kind of social activity, from outings and dinner parties with friends to sitting on committees and organizing clubs and charities (Helliwell and Putnam 1999; Putnam 2000). Given this, it is probably not surprising that more educated people are also more likely to trust their peers (Brehm and Rahn 1997).

More education is also related to better health at almost every level (Sabates 2009). The better-educated report lower incidences of poor health, depression, or anxiety, are less likely to suffer hypertension or diabetes and, when seriously ill, are less likely to die within five years. In the United States, high school dropouts aged 25–64 have double the mortality rate of those with some college education, to the extent that each additional year in education is estimated to add 0.6 years to an individual's life (Cutler and Lleras-Muney 2006). This longevity is not confined to the United States. Studies from Canada, Israel, Bangladesh, Western and Eastern Europe, Russia, and Korea all confirm that the better educated live longer and healthier lives (Cutler and Lleras-Muney 2006), although some cancers, including breast cancer, do disproportionately affect educated people (Marmot 1994). Nor are the benefits restricted to the individual. Well-educated mothers are less likely to have low birth-weight babies and their babies are less likely to die in the first year of life, with health benefits observable until the age of 42 (Case et al. 2005).

These maternal advantages extend beyond health and into parenting since better-educated mothers are also likely to be better parents (DeGarmo et al. 1999), even if living in poverty, a factor which generally increases the likelihood of problem parenting

(Fox et al. 1995). Educated mothers are more nurturing and better at discipline (Fox et al. 1995), show more constructive parenting, less destructive parenting, and are less likely to report 'difficult' children—actions not observed equally in educated fathers (Simons et al. 1990). Single mothers with low education are likely to have little social support and are more likely to exhibit ineffective parenting techniques (Simons et al. 1993).

Turning to undesirable social activities, there is a negative correlation between education and crime (Ehrlich 1975; Lorchner 2010). Educated people are less likely to be arrested or imprisoned, and prisoners who undertake education programmes are less likely to commit further crimes. In the United States completing high school reduces the risk of incarceration (Lorchner and Moretti 2001) whilst, on the other side of the equation, the prison population is less well educated than are those beyond its confines (Ehrlich 1975), with 19% of US prisoners illiterate and 60% functionally illiterate (Karpowitz and Kenner n.d., 4). Similarly, in the United Kingdom half of all prisoners lack the skills demanded by 96% of jobs (Schuller 2009, 16). There is one exception to this picture according to Groot and van den Brink (2010): whilst education is negatively correlated with almost every other offence, it is positively correlated with the likelihood of tax evasion.

It is, of course, possible that the effect of education is to reduce the risk of detection or capture rather than limit the number of offences (Ehrlich 1975), but most of the evidence suggests that the reduction in offences stems from genuine differences in behaviour (Lorchner and Moretti 2001; Buonanno and Leonida 2009). In Machin et al.'s 2011 study, changing the school-leaving age in the United Kingdom resulted in a reduction in crime levels. These changes to behaviour can also be observed when offenders engage in education. There are a number of educational schemes run for prisoners and those who access them are less likely to commit future crimes, less likely to be rearrested, reconvicted and reincarcerated, as well as more likely to get a job and more likely to earn higher wages (Steurer and Smith 2003; Schuller 2009). Clearly there may be a problem with selection bias here, that a prisoner who chooses to enrol in an educational programme in prison is already taking steps to change their behaviour, but even when random groups of prisoners are assigned to educational programmes positive effects are observable (Steurer and Smith 2003).

Of course, correlations do not necessarily imply causal connections—many of the modes of behaviour described above may be characteristic of the sort of people who seek education rather than the consequence of the education itself. Such causal issues cannot be fully resolved but the nature of some of the relationships can be explained more fully. Here, considering status, financial resources, and the nature of the categories observed, we attempt to explain the reasons behind those links.

Status plays an important role. Education is often described as a positional competition with many of the benefits accruing to those who are successful because they have displaced those on the ladder above them. Such success can have profound social and psychological effects. Those with higher status have the confidence to engage socially because they know they are not at the bottom of the social ladder. On the negative side, unequal societies are characterized by less trust and lower levels of social capital. This also impacts on health. Socially polarized societies have less favourable health outcomes, with those of low status more likely to die young and be unhealthy (Kawachi et al. 1997; Wilkinson and Pickett 2010). In Marmot's (1994) Whitehall studies both mortality rates and sickness absence were linked to civil service rank, with those at the top much healthier and longer-living.

Financial resources are also important. Educational success attracts a wage premium so educated people are more likely to be able to afford better living conditions, access to medical and other care, and a reasonable standard of living in retirement. These are likely to impact on their health, their desire and financial capacity to engage socially, and to remove any economic motivation to commit crime by supplying other, less risky and better-rewarded options.

There is also considerable overlap in the *nature* of the categories being measured. Education involves learning, and learning to learn. It may be, for example, that successful scholars are less likely to die of chronic conditions because they learn about them and make efforts to access better care or adapt their behaviour appropriately. They are certainly more likely to have vaccinations and mammograms than their less well-educated peers as well as smoke and drink less, exercise more, and enjoy a better diet. Although the well-educated report experimenting with illegal drugs *more* frequently, they also give them up more readily. In other words, the better a person is at learning in general, the better they are at learning healthy behaviours or ways of defeating and holding back serious illnesses. This may also explain the links between increasing the minimum school-leaving age in a number of countries (certain US states, the United Kingdom, Sweden, Ireland, and Denmark) and the subsequent improvement in population health (Cutler and Lleras-Muney 2006).

Education also involves participating in society, demonstrating both the willingness and the capacity to be socialized in the way that society currently deems appropriate. So it is no surprise that those who have been successful in this form of social participation in their youth also engage in various other forms of social participation as adults: securing gainful employment and participating in formal and informal social groups. This participation also has health benefits. Parents whose children are highly educated also benefit from an intergenerational peer effect since educated children may persuade their parents to stop smoking (Field 2005 in Cutler and Lleras-Muney 2006). There seems to be a multiplier effect here, with higher levels of social participation supporting healthier and more socially positive behaviours, hence its impact on parenting. This may also help to explain the positive effect of education in prisons, which exists independently of any advantages gaining work or wage premiums, in that it exerts a normalizing effect on prisoners (Karpowitz and Kenner n.d.). The public nature of prisoners' educational programmes is also likely to help socialize participants. As Schuller (2009) observes, most prisoners lose their legitimate social networks. Marriages break up, families are reluctant to stay in touch, and many friends dissociate themselves. Participating in an educational programme sends an extremely positive message to non-criminal contacts and may persuade them to preserve a relationship or assist with job-hunting.

In addition to these direct relationships there may also be separate factors (unobserved variables) that influence success in these areas. One such factor is deferred gratification. People who learn to delay rewards are more likely to spend their time studying, adopt healthy behaviours, and generally invest in activities that will benefit them in the longer-term.

However, important as these factors are, we should be wary of dismissing all of the non-economic benefits related to education as a result of status or resources or social participation or learning and changing behaviours. Even when researchers attempt to control for these factors, education and health are still correlated. Snowdon's (2001) detailed account of the life and health of the School Sisters of Notre Dame—nuns living in a convent where goods were held in common, accommodation was shared, and there was equal access to healthcare—still observes more positive health outcomes for those nuns who entered the order with higher qualifications.

Whilst for individuals there is a clear link between education and social participation, this link works less well in longitudinal societal studies. Although educational participation has risen dramatically over the last few decades, social participation has declined. It may be that, as observed above, this is a positional competition, in which it is the relative, rather than the absolute, levels of education that matter. In this case, increasing overall educational levels has few positive effects, at least for social participation (with Helliwell and Putnam 1999; though contrast Nieet al. 1996).

For these links to operate in the way that they do, context is key. It is not education in isolation that drives the benefits but education as part of a wider social system. This is dramatically illustrated in Rubio's (1997) study of Colombia, where the negative relationship between education and criminal activity identified elsewhere fails to hold true. In Colombia formal education yields a low return on investment, whilst crime is profitable and involves little risk. The rewards for formal education have stagnated whilst those for minor crime have increased considerably. Unsurprisingly, the proportion of convicted criminals with either university or high school education has risen dramatically (see also Mars 1982).

As noted above, the links described in the literature are between *education* and various benefits rather than *skills* as such. Do *skilled* workers also enjoy these positive outcomes? Clearly these categories overlap. High skilled work such as knowledge work usually demands success in education. Doctors, lawyers, accountants, and many other professions require both degrees and professional certification as licences to practice. Investment banks and consultants recruit from the academic elite to secure some of the Ivy League cachet when dealing with clients (Ho 2009), and TV and film production may privilege the middle-class graduates who fit in well with their existing workforce (Grugulis and Stoyanova 2012). In these professions high skills also means high levels of education. In others the link is not so secure. The new professions such as computer programmer or systems analyst demand high skills but do not always use education as a proxy or an entry route.

The position is more complicated when we consider skilled workers. Unlike the professionals described above, credentials here are likely to be vocational and therefore not captured by studies that focus on years in school and certification gained then. There are studies assessing the impact of vocational qualifications on earnings. There is little, however, on the non-economic benefits. Given the reasoning behind the benefits of education—namely, that it offers status, provides access to better-paid work, enhances the ability to learn, improves placing in a positional competition, and socializes individuals into acceptable forms of behaviour—we might speculate that similar advantages would be seen by those with vocational qualifications, but on a smaller scale. Clearly, given the nature of positional competitions, this is uncertain (since not being in the first cohort might itself have a damaging effect), whilst increasing numbers in education and polarized rewards may further disadvantage those with vocational qualifications. Vocational qualifications vary dramatically in both rigour and status (Grugulis 2003; Bosch and Charest 2010). Where vocational training is of high quality, we might expect to see qualification holders enjoying status, earning more and so on. However such benefits are likely to be more fragile than those experienced by people with educational qualifications.

Conclusions

Skill is vital to the success of organizations and of the national economy. There is also evidence that it brings broader non-economic benefits. However, the links between skill and both economic and non-economic gains are complex and not necessarily guaranteed. This complexity is of particular importance when it comes to considering the extent to which governments should intervene. In particular we have argued:

1. Many public training subsidies to employers are hard to justify.
2. Not all increments to training prove economically beneficial. This depends on the training's quality and relevance.
3. Skill utilization is as important as skill acquisition.
4. Policymakers wishing to improve economic performance too often regard skill as the magic bullet. Skills policy needs to be embedded in broader economic development policy.

The returns available to skills, education, and training depend on both the forms such skills, education, and training take *and* the economic and social context.

References

Addison, J. and Belfield, C. (2008) 'Unions, Training and Firm Performance', IZA discussion paper no. 3294.

Aghion, P., Boustan, L., Hoxby, C., and Vandenbussche, V. (2009) 'The Causal Impact of Education on Economic Growth: Evidence from the United States', *Brookings Papers on*

Economic Activity, Spring 2009, Conference Draft. www.brookings.edu/economics/bpea/bpea.aspx.

Autor, D., Levy, F., and Murnane, R. (2003) 'The Skill Content of Recent Technological Change: An Empirical Exploration', *Quarterly Journal of Economics*, 118(4): 1279–1333.

Ballot, G., Fakhfakha, F., and Taymazb, E. (2001) 'Firms' Human Capital, R&D and Performance: A Study on French and Swedish firms', *Labour Economics*, 8(2): 443–62.

Barro, R. and Lee, J. (2010) 'A New Data Set of Educational Attainment in the World, 1950–2010', NBER working paper no. 15902, Cambridge, MA.

Barron, J. M., Black, D., and Loewenstein, M. (1989) 'Job Matching and On-the-Job Training', *Journal of Labor Economics*, 7: 1–19.

Bassi, L., Harrison, P., Ludwig, J., and McMurrer, D. (2001) *Human Capital Investments and Firm Performance*, Washington, DC: Human Capital Dynamics, Inc.

Becker, G. (1964) *Human Capital: A Theoretical Analysis with Special Reference to Education*, Chicago: University of Chicago Press.

Benhabib, J. and Spiegel, M. (1994) 'The Role of Human Capital in Economic Development Evidence from Aggregate Cross-country Data', *Journal of Monetary Economics*, 34(2): 143–173.

Bils, M. and Klenow, P. (2000) 'Does Schooling Cause Growth?', *American Economic Review*, 90(5): 1160–1183.

Black, S. and Lynch, L. (1996) 'Human-capital Investments and Productivity', *American Economic Review*, 86(2): 263–267.

Black, S. and Lynch, L. (2001) 'How to Compete: The Impact of Workplace Practices and Information Technology on Productivity', *Review of Economics and Statistics*, 18(3): 434–445.

Bosch, G. and Charest, J. (2010) 'Vocational Training: International Perspectives', in G. Bosch and J. Charest (eds), *Vocational Training: International Perspectives*, New York and London: Routledge: 1–26.

Brehm, J. and Rahn, W. (1997) 'Individual-level Evidence for the Causes and Consequences of Social Capital', *American Journal of Political Science*, 41(3): 999–1023.

Brown, P., Lauder, H., and Ashton, D. (2011) *The Global Auction: The Broken Promises of Education, Jobs and Incomes*, Oxford: Oxford University Press.

Buonanno, P. and Leonida, L. (2009) 'Non-Market Effects of Education on Crime: Evidence from Italian Regions', *Economics of Education Review*, 28(1): 11–17.

Card, D. (1999) 'The Causal Effect of Education on Earnings', in O. Ashenfelter and D. Card (eds), *Handbook of Labor Economics*, vol. 3A. Amsterdam: Elsevier.

Case, A., Fertig, A., and Paxson, C. (2005) 'The Lasting Impact of Childhood Health and Circumstance', *Journal of Health Economics*, 24(2): 364–389.

Cedefop (2011). 'The Impact of Vocational Education and Training on Company Performance', Research Paper no. 19. Luxembourg: Publications Office of the European Union.

Conti, G. (2005). 'Training, Productivity and Wages in Italy', *Labour Economics*, 12(4): 557–76.

Cutler, D. M. and Lleras-Muney, A. (2006) 'Education and Health: Evaluating Theories and Evidence', National Bureau of Economic Research Working Paper no. 12352, Cambridge, MA.

DeGarmo, D.S., Forgatch, M.S., and Martinez, C.R. (1999) 'Parenting of Divorced Mothers as a Link Between Social Status and Boys' Academic Outcomes: Unpacking the Effects of Socioeconomic Status', *Child Development*, 70(5): 1231–1245.

De Kok, J. (2002) 'The Impact of Firm-Provided Training on Production: Testing For Firm-Size Effects', *International Small Business Journal*, 20(3): 271–295.

Dearden, L., Reed, H., and van Reenen, J. (2000) 'Who Gains When Workers Train? Training and Corporate Productivity in a Panel of British industries', IFS working paper 00/04. London: Institute for Fiscal Studies.

Delaney, J. and Huselid, M. (1996). 'The Impact of Human Resource Management Practices on Perceptions of Organisational Performance', *Academy of Management Journal*, 39: 949–969.

Ehrlich, I. (1975) 'On the Relation Between Education and Crime', in F. T. Juster (ed.), *Education, Income and Human Behaviour*, Washington: National Bureau of Economic Research.

Fox, R. A., Platz, D. L., and Bentley, K. S. (1995) 'Maternal Factors Related to Parenting Practices, Developmental Expectation and Perceptions of Child Behaviour Problems', *Journal of Genetic Psychology*, 156(4): 431–441.

Groot, W. and van den Brink, H. M. (2010) 'The Effects of Education on Crime', *Applied Economics*, 42(3): 279–289.

Grugulis, I. (2003) 'The Contribution of NVQs to the Growth of Skills in the UK', *British Journal of Industrial Relations*, 41(3): 457–475.

Grugulis, I. and Stoyanova, D. (2012) 'Social Capital and Networks in Film and TV: Jobs for the Boys?', *Organization Studies*, 33(10): 1311–31.

Hall, R. and Jones, C. (1999) 'Why Do Some Countries Produce So Much More Output Per Worker Than Others?', *Quarterly Journal of Economics*, 114(1): 83–116.

Hanuschek, E. and Kimko, D. (2000) 'Schooling, Labour Force Quality, and the Growth of Nations', *American Economic Review*, 90: 1184–1208.

Heckman, J. and Klenow, P. (1997) 'Human Capital Policy', University of Chicago working paper.

Helliwell, J. F. and Putnam, R. D. (1999) 'Education and Social Capital' Working Paper 7121, Cambridge, MA: National Bureau of Economic Research.

Ho, K. (2009) *Liquidated: An Ethnography of Wall Street*, Durham: Duke University Press.

Hoeckel, K. (2008) *Costs and Benefits in Vocational Education and Training*, Paris: OECD.

Holmes, C. (2013) 'Has the Expansion of Higher Education Led to Greater Economic Growth?', *National Institute Economic Review*, 224(1), research section: 29–47.

Jones, C. (1995) 'R&D Based Models of Economic Growth', *Journal of Political Economy* 103(4): 759–784.

Jones, C. (1999) 'Growth: With or Without Scale Effects?', *American Economic Review Papers and Proceedings*, 89: 139–144.

Karpowitz, D. and Kenner, M. (n.d.) *Education as Crime Prevention: The Case for Reinstating Pell Grant Eligibility for the Incarcerated*, Annandale-on-Hudson, NY: Bard Prison Initiative.

Kawachi, I., Kennedy, B. P., Lochner, K., and Prothrow-Stith, D. (1997) 'Social Capital, Income Inequality and Mortality', *American Journal of Public Health*, 87(9): 1491–1498.

Leiponen, A. (2000) 'Competencies, Innovation and Profitability of Firms', *Economics of Innovation and New Technology*, 9(1): 1–24.

Lindahl and Krueger, A. (2001) 'Education and Growth: Why and For Whom?', *Quarterly Journal of Economics*, 39(4): 1101–1136.

Lorchner, L. (2010) 'Education and Crime', in P. Peterson, E. Baker, and B. McGaw (eds), *International Encyclopaedia of Education*, 3rd ed., Elsevier Science.

Lorchner, L. and Moretti, E. (2001) 'The Effect of Education on Crime: Evidence from Prison Inmates, Arrests and Self-reports', no. 8605, Cambridge, MA: National Bureau of Economic Research.

Lucas, R. (1988) 'On the Mechanics of Economic Development', *Journal of Monetary Economics*, 22: 3–42.
Machin, S., Marie, O., and Vujic, S. (2011) 'The Crime Reducing Effects of Education', *The Economic Journal*, 121(552): 463–484.
Mankiw, G., Romer, D., and Weil, D. (1992) 'A Contribution to the Empirics on Economic Growth', *Quarterly Journal of Economics*, 107: 407–437.
Marmot, M. (1994) 'Social Differentials in Health within and between Populations', *Daedalus*, 123(4): 197–217.
Mars, G. (1982) *Cheats at Work: An Anthropology of Workplace Crime*, London: Allen and Unwin.
Nie, N. H., Junn, J., and Stehlik-Barry, K. (1996) *Education and Democratic Citizenship in America*, Chicago: University of Chicago Press.
Nikandrou, I., Apospori, E., and Panayotopoulou, L. (2008) 'Training and Firm Performance in Europe: The Impact of National and OrganizationOrganizational Characteristics', *International Journal of Human Resource Management*, 19(11): 2057–2078.
Putnam, R. B. (2000) *Bowling Alone: The Collapse and Revival of American Community*, New York: Simon and Schuster Paperbacks.
Reich, R. (1992) *The Work of Nations: Preparing Ourselves for 21st Century Capitalism*, New York: Vintage.
Romer, P. (1986) 'Increasing Returns and Long Run Economic Growth', *Journal of Political Economy*, 94(5): 1002–1037.
Romer, P. (1990) 'Endogenous Technological Change', *Journal of Political Economy*, 98(5): S71–S102.
Romer, P. (1994) 'The Origins of Endogenous Growth', *Journal of Economic Perspectives*, 8(1): 3–22.
Rubio, M. (1997) 'Perverse Social Capital: Some Evidence from Columbia', *Journal of Economic Issues*, 31(3): 805–816.
Sabates, R. (2009) *The Impact of Lifelong Learning on Poverty Reduction*. Document Number 1, Leicester: National Institute of Adult Continuing Education.
Schuller, T. (2009) *Crime and Lifelong Learning*. Document Number 5, Leicester: National Institute of Adult Continuing Education.
Simons, R. L., Beaman, J., Conger, R. D., and Chao, W. (1993) 'Stress, Support and Antisocial Behaviour Trait as Determinants of Emotional Well-being and Parenting Practices amongst Single Mothers', *Journal of Marriage and Family*, 55(2): 385–398.
Simons, R. L., Whitbeck, L. B., Conger, R. D., et al. (1990) 'Husband and Wife Differences in Determinants of Parenting: A Social Learning and Exchange Model of Parental Behaviour', *Journal of Marriage and Family*, 52(2): 375–392.
Snowdon, D. (2001) *Aging with Grace: The Nun Study and the Science of Old Age: How We Can All Live Longer, Healthier and More Vital Lives*, London: Fourth Estate.
Solow, R. (1956) 'A Contribution to the Theory of Economic Growth', *Quarterly Journal of Economics*, 70(1): 65–94.
Spence, M. (1973) 'Job Market Signaling', *Quarterly Journal of Economics*, 87(3): 355–374.
Steurer, S. and Smith, L. G. (2003) *Education Reduces Crime: Three-State Recidivism Study*, Lanham, MD: Correctional Education Association and Management and Training.
Stevens, M. (1999) 'Human Capital Theory and UK Vocational Training Policy', *Oxford Review of Economic Policy*, 15(1): 16–32.
Sung, J. and Ashton, D. (2005) *High Performance Work Practices: Linking Strategy and Skills to Performance Outcomes*, London: Department of Trade and Industry.

Tan, H. and Batra, G. (1996) 'Enterprise Training in Developing Countries: Incidence, Productivity Effects, and Policy Implications', Washington, DC: World Bank.

Wilkinson, R. and Pickett, K. (2010) *The Spirit Level: Why Equality Is Better for Everyone*, London: Penguin.

Young, A. (1998) 'Growth Without Scale Effects', *Journal of Political Economy*, 106(1): 41–63.

Zwick, T. (2006) 'The Impact of Training Intensity on Establishment Productivity', *Industrial Relations: A Journal of Economy and Society*, 45(1): 26–46.

Zwick, T. (2007) 'Apprenticeship Training in Germany: Investment or Productivity Driven?', *Zeitschrift für Arbeitsmarktforschung*, 40(2/3): 193–204.

SECTION V

DIFFERING SKILL SYSTEMS

The Levels of Determination

CHAPTER 19

THEORIZING SKILL FORMATION IN THE GLOBAL ECONOMY

HUGH LAUDER, PHILLIP BROWN, AND DAVID ASHTON

Introduction

Over the past half century a range of theories has been developed to understand the nature of skill, its development, and its relationship to the economy. These theories have often been competing, with fundamentally different assumptions about the production of skills and their relationship to society. However, recent changes in the nature of economic globalization have raised questions about these theories and their applicability to the present context. In this paper we evaluate the dominant skill formation theories regarding some of their key assumptions and implications for policy. We can distinguish between universal theories of skill formation, (e.g. human capital and skill bias theories) and particularistic theories (Rose 1985), that assume that skill formation is embedded in the institutions and cultures of particular societies (e.g. societal effect and the varieties of capitalism approaches).

It is argued that the universal theories are flawed in several ways, including their capacity for providing policy guidance, because they lead to abstractions that gain no purchase on particular national economies. In contrast, the problem with particularistic theories is that they do not have the capacity to adequately comprehend the impact of global skill formation processes on national systems. With the global economic downturn, a further problem with both theoretical traditions has been brought to the fore: how to create the demand for skilled work. Universal theories assume that a combination of market mechanisms and technology will address this issue, whilst particularistic theories have largely been silent on the question. Given the difficulties with both sets of theories, it is argued that we need to develop a new agenda for skill formation that takes into account some of the insights of the particularistic theories whilst placing them within a model of global skill formation. Such an account also points to the importance of industrial policy in matching the supply of skills to demand.

The chapter first outlines and critiques universal and particularistic theories of skill formation. It then describes the key global changes impacting Western labour markets before relating these trends to theorization of skill formation.

Universal Theories of Skill Formation

This section begins by examining universal theories of human capital and skill bias.

Human Capital Theory

Human capital theory is the most prominent theory of skill formation. The theory states that the better educated a person is, the more productive they are likely to be, for which they will earn a higher income (Becker 1964; Schultz 1971). The theory has three significant assumptions: that it is in the self-interest of individuals to pursue education because it will lead to higher economic returns, which form the basis for aspiration and a sense of progress in society; that education is fundamentally efficient because employers will not hire incompetent people; and that employers will respond to a better educated workforce by investing in new technology to capitalize on the productive potential of a more skilled workforce.

On the basis of these assumptions the theory can be tested through rates of income returns for particular categories of skilled work (Burton-Jones and Spender 2011). It was thought the theory offers universal validation for increasing investment and expansion of mass higher education systems. It has also been given impetus by the rhetoric of the knowledge economy and the idea that technological innovation and new forms of work organization increase the demand for college graduates (Brown et al. 2011).

The apparent strength of human capital theory was that in abstracting relationships from their social context the theory seemed to apply to all societies and hence was assumed to have universal validity. A recent key example of such claims to universality are made by two of the leading proponents of human capital theory, Hanushek and Woessmann (2007) who seek to estimate, for developing countries, long term gross domestic product (GDP) trends from investments in education. However, as we argue below, their research displays the more general failure of human capital theory to attend to the key national particularities that shape the relationship between skills, employment, and incomes, or account for the impact of globalization on national labour markets.

Criticisms of Human Capital Theory

The explanatory structure of human capital theory can at best been seen as primitive (Brown et al. 2001).[1] Notwithstanding the limited view of human motivation, it fails in its own terms both with respect to the assumed relationship between productivity and income and in employers' responses to the supply of educated labour.

The relationship between productivity and income is complex and whilst market economies depend upon some relationship between them, there are clearly significant anomalies. This situation pertains to the so-called knowledge economy. As Alvesson (2001) has noted, with respect to knowledge workers, there is considerable ambiguity in both the qualities that are required for knowledge work, and given the impression management that is often part of their work, and in judgements that are made about them. Nowhere is this ambiguity more clearly demonstrated than in the work of Kahneman (2011), who describes the 'illusion of skill' amongst fund managers because he shows that 'the selection of stocks is more like rolling dice than like playing poker' (2011, 215). When their records are examined over time, the correlation between the fund choices they make and success are not significant. What exists is an industry within which rewards are very high, built, in the case of fund managers, on an illusion.

If there are anomalies with respect to the links between productivity and income, they also exist within employers' strategies: they do not always choose to invest in the technology or skills to upgrade productivity. In terms of the theory, this constitutes another form of market failure. For example, Finegold and Soskice (1988) pointed out that in Britain there was a dual equilibrium economy with low- and high-skill sectors, the former requiring little skilling, whilst the latter required extensive education and skilling. Moreover, despite improved levels of educational qualification, there appears to be a hiatus between education and wages. The proportion of low-waged workers remains stubbornly high in Britain (Salverda and Mayhew 2009) and there is still a debate about whether it is possible to raise the demand for skilled labour in parts of the low-skill sector (Wilson and Hogarth 2003; Keep and Mayhew 2010). Given the persistence of low-wage work in the Anglo-Saxon economies and rising low-wage work in Germany (Bosch 2009), the empirical claim that employers are prepared to invest in the potential productive capacity of workers needs to be heavily qualified. There are explanations for these phenomena, as we show later in the chapter, but they lie outside the structure of human capital theory.

As regards the returns on education, it is helpful to look at those of university graduates. The reason for examining the wages of this group is that the theoretical backdrop to human capital theory in the past two decades has been that of the rhetoric

[1] Orthodox economists will dismiss the criticism of the schematic nature of the explanatory structure providing it enables sound predictions to be made (Friedman 1954).

of the knowledge economy, a key marker of which is graduate labour (Warhurst and Thompson 2006). Becker (2006), buying into the notion of a globalized knowledge economy, argued that we are now on the cusp of the age of human capital. In looking at this issue we need to draw attention to the notion of the graduate premium and the way it can obfuscate important trends when graduate wages are disaggregated. In the OECD countries, it is the case that graduates on average earn more than non-graduates (OECD 2011), but this indicates very little about the labour processes underlying this point. Here, there are several observations worth making. When graduate wages are disaggregated and examined over time in the United States, they have flat-lined for men on wages at the median and 10th percentile since the late 1970s whilst rising for women from a much lower point but still they earn less than men. It is only those at the 90th percentile whose wages have enjoyed a sharp uptick since the late 1980s (Mishel et al. 2009). In Britain, graduate wages flat-lined for all but those at the 90th percentile between 1990 and 2000, and have not increased subsequently (Lauder et al. 2005; Brown et al. 2015.). At the same time, in the United States the wages of non-graduates have declined sharply, thereby contributing to the so-called graduate premium.

These data are not consistent with Becker's (2006) claim that we are entering the age of human capital despite the advent of what many consider a new technological revolution. Our argument is that these trends can only be explained partially within the framework of human capital theory because there is an excess of supply of graduates over demand. Rather, we argue that a more complete explanation needs to take changes in the global labour market and labour processes into account.

To develop this argument we return to Hanushek and Woessmann (2007; also Hanushek et al. 2011). In their 2007 publication these authors seek to establish that the 'quality' of education can make a significant difference to a nation's notional future GDP. In particular, they make the claim that the quality of education, as measured by international tests such as PISA and TIMSS[2] can have a significant influence on future GDP. They calculate that if the educational reforms they recommend were implemented GDP would rise in developing countries by 5%. In 2011, they make more extravagant dollar estimates about how much can be gained by improving education.[3]

Whilst there are many criticisms that can be made of Hanushek and Woessmann's methodology,[4] our focus is on the theory that drives it. A general point is that rates of return depend upon the industrial development path taken. If, for example, the current fates of Ireland and the Republic of Korea are compared, we find that whilst there have

[2] For discussion of these tests, see Felstead et al., Chapter 16, this volume.

[3] They acknowledge a role for institutions, in particular education, and openness to trade. However, their recommendations for education: greater competitiveness and choice, and greater school autonomy and accountability smack more of ideology than of systematic research. See, for example, the OECD evaluation of market competition in education by Waslander et al. (2010).

[4] See, for example, Torrance (2006).

been similarities in their substantial historical investments in higher education, they have radically different growth rates and returns on graduates, based on quite different models of skill formation and economic development (Kim 2000; Field 2002). These differences suggest that the relationships between the state, private enterprise and education systems are crucial to understanding the different outcomes of countries such as Korea and Ireland. Human capital theory has no account of economic development because of its static equilibrium model of the labour market. Furthermore, the assumption made by Hanushek and Woessmann is that educational institutions and cultures have no impact on the way students are taught and socialized and consequently on how their educational experience may impact on innovation and the application of knowledge and skills in the labour market. Yet, different schooling systems approach questions of knowledge, pedagogy, and learning quite differently and this variety appears to impact on the capacity for innovation and the application of skill (Winch et al. 2011). It is for this reason that many countries in East Asia, despite frequently topping the various international educational test league tables, worry about their lack of creativity (Lauder et al. 2012).

Finally, human capital theory, as exemplified by Hanushek and Wasserman (2007), appears to take little account of the global economy. They do have a very limited measure of openness to trade but this measure says nothing of the effects of economic globalization on specific economies. However, in the context of the changes in the global economy that we outline below, it is clear that their strategy of using inductive reasoning to extrapolate from past trends to the future will no longer hold.

Skill Bias Theory

A second and arguably more sophisticated universal approach to skill formation is that of skill bias theory. Skill bias theory makes the universal assumption that the demand for skilled workers will be driven by new technology. Its emphasis on the importance of technology can be seen in precursors such as Kerr et al.'s (1960) view that the technology of modern industry would raise the average skill levels of the workforce, making education 'The handmaiden of industrialism' (1960, 27). On this basis, skill bias theorists argue for a qualified convergence between industrial societies. Here the fundamental proposition is that the general purpose technologies associated with IT is skill biased rather than skill replacing. Its policy significance lies in the support that it has provided and continues to provide for the rapid expansion of university education, whilst assuming that technology will drive the corresponding organizational and economic changes to utilize the skills that graduates acquire.

There are several accounts of skill bias theory. However, the most powerful is that articulated by Acemoglu (2002) who argues that there is an endogenous relationship between new technology and the demand for skilled workers. New technologies are endogenous in that their adoption is a response to incentives; in particular, the increase in the supply of skills will lead to acceleration in the demand for skills. Such a view is consistent with human capital theory in that it also assumes that market mechanisms will ensure that demand will respond to supply.

This approach provides an explanation for the polarization of incomes: where there is an undersupply of skilled labour the *premia* for skilled labour (e.g. graduates) will rise (Goldin and Katz 2008). In the case of the United States, Goldin and Katz argue that the polarization of income is a consequence of a lack of enrolments in four-year college programmes. Economic globalization and the role of international trade are largely ignored. This omission occurs because, whilst they acknowledge that international trade can have an impact on the jobs of low-skilled workers, they assume graduate workers to be immune from global economic processes. The solution therefore is to enable more students to obtain university or college qualifications. In seeking explanations for the relatively low supply of graduates they point to systematic inequalities such as those of social class and ethnicity.

Criticisms of Skill Bias Theory

A major criticism is the propensity to view technology as skill biased rather than skill replacing, assuming that a knowledge economy exists in which new technology will demand an ever higher level of education. However, the historical account of technology in the twentieth century as being skill biased is open to challenge (Braverman 1974; Brown et al. 2011). This optimistic view has a long pedigree (Kerr et al. 1960) and may, in the initial stages of the current technological revolution, have been plausible. However, it is now clear that it is not the processes and effects of the knowledge economy that we are dealing with but those of knowledge capitalism. Moreover, Tate (2001) has noted economic revolutions are revolutions in standardization and for good reason: it is by this means that costs are reduced and profits increased. Hence, what is happening now is the routinization of various aspects of knowledge work (Brown et al. 2011; Brynjolfsson and McAfee 2011). Under these conditions, the idea that new technology has ushered in a skill biased revolution is questionable.

Once it is acknowledged that the supply of educated workers will not create its own demand or indeed that many high-skilled jobs could be substituted for computer routinization or offshored to low cost economies, then universal theories cannot withstand critical scrutiny. A further problem with these theories is that they treat national institutions as empty vessels in that they assume that all forms of education have the same effects on productivity and innovation. However, when the importance of social and historical context it recognized, the universal claims of these theories are once again called into doubt because institutions are structured by the unique political and cultural factors associated with national systems of skill formation (Hansen 2011). What is needed to move forward therefore are alternative theories.

Particularistic Theories of Skill Formation

If there are fundamental problems raised by the universal theories of human capital and skill bias, then a focus on the particular which takes questions of the nature of institutions and related cultures into account may provide the basis for a more adequate explanatory account.

Path-breaking work within the tradition of particularistic theory was undertaken in the 1980s by Maurice et al. (1986). Their societal effect approach revealed significant national differences in skill formation which, they claimed, could only be explained by differences in national institutional configurations. This was a major contribution to knowledge that helped shape research on skills over the next two decades. Its basic assumptions being found in subsequent work on the high skills equilibrium (Finegold and Soskice 1988), the state and skill formation (Ashton and Green 1996) and the varieties of capitalism approaches (Hall and Soskice 2001). By emphasizing an institutional approach, the societal effect approach opened the way to a politics of skill formation since one of the key features of institutions is that they can be shaped and changed by politics (Thelen 2004; Hansen 2011). However, it was only with the advent of the VoC that a more systematic analysis extended the insights of a particularistic approach to the global economy.

VoC

The work of Maurice et al. (1986) foreshadowed the greater interest in different types of capitalism in the aftermath of the collapse of the Berlin Wall. Albert's (1991) path-breaking work was quickly followed by the business systems or VoC approach, pioneered by Whitley (1992) and others. They challenged Kerr's thesis on industrial convergence whilst being consistent with Maurice et al.'s societal effect approach in stressing the crucial role of national institutions and culture in shaping business practices and skill formation. As Whitley observes, difference in national production systems consist of 'mutually interdependent combinations of production techniques, products and markets types, forms of division of labour at the workplace, authority structures, and reward systems' (Whitley 1999, 22).

The recognition that capitalism can be differentiated by unique national configurations of institutions and cultures set the stage for the development of a systematic analysis of national differences and their outcomes. The VoC approach is most closely associated with the work of Hall and Soskice (2001) and their associates, who can be seen as taking forward institutional economics. They provide an integrated theory of the strategies of firms based on distinctive national institutional structures generated by provisional 'solutions' to a series of specific problems that firms in any capitalist economy have to address. These problems are: industrial relations, vocational education and training, corporate governance, inter-firm relations, and the disciplining and motivation of employees. The key point made in VoC theory is that different countries have produced different solutions to these problems thereby generating distinctive national economic institutions and relationships.

A clear example of the VoC approach, with respect to skill formation, is developed by Estevez-Abe et al. (2001). They argue that different ideal-typical economies specialize in the production of predominantly different types of skill. So co-ordinated market economies (CMEs), of which Germany is an example, produce industry-specific skills through the dual system, whereas liberal market economies (LMEs) typically produce general skills because they are more appropriate for low-skilled, low-wage economies for which little specific training is required (see the Chapters 2 and 20 by Martin and Bosch, respectively, this volume).

Given this approach to the production of distinctive skill sets in different ideal-typical economies, how can the VoC approach address the issue of skill formation in relation to the global economy? Hall and Soskice (2001) have responded to this question by applying insights from the law of comparative advantage. So the production of industry-specific skills in CME countries like Germany in, say, engineering, would mean that their companies would not offshore jobs because they would have a greater comparative advantage in the production of goods because of their skilled workforce. In contrast, firms in LMEs, like Britain, will retain jobs in areas where they have greater competitive advantage, such as in financial services, but are more likely to offshore jobs because they have greater expertise in exploiting market structures than less developed nations where they may seek the lower costs of unskilled labour. Finally, firms will engage in institutional arbitrage where they can exploit the advantages of other kinds of economies, for example CMEs to LMEs because the latter have proved more innovative in particular areas. CMEs, like Germany, may utilize the financial services of an LME, such as Britain, because of the latter's greater financial expertise.

Criticisms of the VoC Approach

The VoC approach has engendered considerable debate, rightly so because it has provided a powerful way of understanding both the particularities of national economies and how they might relate to the global economy. However, it is also clear that this approach is flawed for several reasons. Firstly, the rise of highly skilled workers in East Asia and the creation of social technologies of production enable these countries to produce goods and services of a standard comparable to that in both CMEs and LMEs but at a lower cost. This development is as true of middle-range engineering firms in Germany, as it is specialized forms of IT and back-office financial services in the United Kingdom (Lauder et al. 2008). It is only the very high end of engineering in Germany and financial services in the United Kingdom that, for the time being, are not vulnerable to offshoring. It can be argued that the competitive pressures of the global economy have a profound effect on workers' employment conditions. Germany, which is taken as the closest approximation to a CME, exemplifies this issue and it raises the question as to whether we should view national economies in the way assumed by the VoC approach. Thelen (2004) noted the cost pressures of globalized competition on Germany's skill formation some time ago. Perhaps the clearest example of this pressure is that of a leading middle-range engineering transnational company (TNC). In 2005 this company raised the possibility of reducing the apprenticeship for a significant proportion of production workers from three and a half years to two because it no longer considered it necessary to 'overtrain' workers (Lauder et al. 2008). This proposal was a highly significant because it signalled that employers felt sufficiently confident about their TQM and diagnostic systems to dispense with the cost of overtraining workers: the previous method of being able to provide rapid and flexible responses to production line problems (Streeck 1989).

Competitive pressures are now at a point where some of the distinctive features of Germany's CME are under threat (Hassel 2014). Fleckenstein et al. (2011) show that the skills profile of German workers no longer approximates to the view articulated by Estevez-Abe et al. (2001). Rather, there has been a significant rise in both high and low general skills, with some 33% of German workers in low general skilled work. This, perhaps, goes some way to explaining the trends described by Hassel (2014). She documents the decline in the share of employees covered by collective agreements and the varied conditions for workers still under these agreements. At the same time, training in Germany is now far more complex than a singular focus on the vaunted dual system would suggest. Estimates for 2006 show that only 43.5% of the age cohort are in the dual system with a further 39.7% in the 'transition system' and 16.8% in vocational schools.[5] These latter forms of training may lead to transition to the dual system but they may also be indicative that the quality of training associated with the dual system may not be required for work which requires low general skills. Given the rise in low general skilled work in Germany which is also reflected in the estimation that 22% of German workers are in low-wage work (Bosch 2009), how long can extensive training of such workers be afforded, especially when, increasingly, that training is being provided from public money?

Given these trends, the question now is whether what is being characterized by the VoC approach is not so much national economies but rather leading sectors within them. Whilst some theorists have shifted attention from notions of the nation as a unit of analysis to those of a more fragmented nature, such as the sector-based high skills ecosystem (Finegold 1999), the focus within VoC remains firmly on policy changes within the national system. Indeed, the assumption of a relatively closed nation-centred system continues to dominate much of the discussion of skill formation (e.g. Mayer and

[5] Aurtorengruppe Bildungsbereichterstattung (2008), *Bildung in Deutschland, 2006*, Bielefeld: Bertelsmann Stiftung. The transition system provides a varied approach in training both with respect to the time training courses take and to their skill levels.

Solga 2008; Culpepper and Thelen 2008; Bryson 2010). It is not that these authors raise unimportant issues but rather that they are not framed within a new and, as we shall argue, powerful set of global forces that through changes in the labour market threaten the distinctive national arrangements of a CME such as Germany.

Skill Formation Theories and Methodological Nationalism

A major problem with all these theories, universal and particularistic, is that they are committed to methodological nationalism (Wimmer and Glick Schiller 2002), viewing the appropriate level of analysis for skill formation as the nation state. We argue that the appropriate focus should be the interactions between the national and global. This contrast may appear counter-intuitive in relation to universal theories, but whilst both human capital and skill bias theory are capable of taking into account the global level, as we shall suggest, it is the case that they assume that their analyses apply to national economies. This situation is clearly the case in the papers by Hanushek and Woessmann, who do not model the interaction effects between national and global supply and demand for skilled labour. We have noted the same point for skill bias theory: the VoC approach mischaracterizes the paradigm CME, Germany, with respect to skills, whilst failing to take adequate account of the nature of the global labour market. Their analysis is anchored in a version of the law of comparative advantage which no longer holds.

The chapter now turns to analyse some of the key global trends that are impacting Western labour markets irrespective of the type of capitalism in which they are embedded.

Trends in the Global Economy and Their Impact on Labour Markets

Over the past twenty years the institutional conditions within which business strategies are formulated and operationalized have created new global opportunities for transnational companies (TNCs) to compete on both quality and cost with profound consequences for the formation and utilization of skills. In particular, there has been a radical transformation of the processes of production in both the manufacturing sector and the service sector. The exponential growth in computer power together with the availability of programmes designed to rationalize processes and the growth of the internet provide TNCs with options that were not available two decades ago. They can now modularize the production process (Berger 2005) and locate the various components across the globe with the subsequent extension of supply chains. In addition, the growth of the internet has provided the means to reduce transaction costs and to control the process of production from one central location. International standards such as ISO 9000 and others have been developed with associated enforcement systems that now provide companies with a guarantee that the production of goods and services anywhere in the globe will meet specified quality standards. The institutions that regulate world trade such as the World Trade Organization have accepted developing economies into a unified global framework.

These trends represent a change in the global institutional framework for business activities creating the context for the development of global business strategies. It is these business strategies that are enabling TNCs to think globally not only about how to organize production but crucially how to shape and use the skills of their labour force to achieve a competitive advantage in this global context. It has enabled the TNCs to extend their control and capture important aspects of the process of skill formation, leading to what we have termed 'global skills webs'. However, whilst the primary focus is on TNCs, the skilling implications for small and medium-sized enterprises within their supply chains should not be ignored (Ramirez and Rainbird 2011).

There are five trends that can be identified each making an impact on labour markets in the West. These are: the mass production of highly educated labour in the BRICs, particularly in China; the construction of global labour markets through the creation of corporate skill webs; the creation by TNCs of inside-out models of production; the quality-cost revolution in which high-quality goods and services can now be produced in low cost locations; and finally, the routinization of 'knowledge work' through digital Taylorism (Brown et al. 2011).

The Mass Production of Highly Educated Labour in the BRICs

The standard assumption made by economists in the West is that the rising power economies cannot match the innovation systems of Western economies and hence, whilst the West earns a premium through its capacity for innovation, the 'body' work will be undertaken in emerging economies (Rosecrance 1999). This assumption, however, ignores the rise of mass higher education systems beyond the OECD countries and how this is giving TNCs an opportunity to capitalize on the new stock of skills.

There has not only been a 'great doubling' in the size of the global workforce, but a great doubling of university enrolments around the world, reaching close to 140 million by 2007. This expansion of higher education has led to a massive increase in the global supply of highly qualified workers, able to compete on price as well as knowledge. China now has many more students in higher education than the United States and is currently pursuing a 'talent strategy' with a target of increasing the numbers of graduates entering the labour market by an additional 10 million per annum between 2010 and 2020. In India, there were only 27 universities in 1947; by 2006 there were 367 with 13 million students. When countries such as Indonesia, Brazil, and the Russian Federation are added, there is a massive increase in the global supply of highly educated workers. Although, as indicated above, the differences in nature and quality of these higher education systems should be noted.

Although the quality of education will vary in countries experiencing rapid expansion in educational provision, it is nevertheless the case that Asia is also producing more engineers and physical scientists than Europe and North America combined. In both Britain and the United States, home students make up less than half of those undertaking postgraduate degrees in key STEM (science, technology, maths) subjects.

From the perspective of TNCs this development provides a huge new labour market of highly qualified personnel which can be recruited at a fraction of the cost traditionally paid (Brown and Lauder 2010). However, it is increasingly the case that the rise of mass higher education in these societies is now being linked to best practice innovation systems. Where once research and development (R&D) in these countries was confined to the application of products to their markets, now they are undertaking basic research (Brown et al. 2011).

The Construction of Global Labour Markets

TNCs have played a major role in the construction of global labour markets in relation to the utilization of skill. Arguably, the creation of global skill webs has provided an increasing source of competitive advantage and corporate profits. They involve aligning global operations using advances in new technologies, e.g. cloud computing, to create a new global division of labour incorporating well-qualified graduates from the BRICs and other emerging economies. Since these graduates can typically be employed for a much lower price than their counterparts in the West, TNCs are provided with a range of options and possibilities as to how they conduct their relationships with universities, R&D facilities, production units, and supply chains. Clearly there is still much research to be undertaken to fully understand how these global skill webs are constructed and what their implications are for global value chains (Cattaneo et al. 2010) and skill formation (Ramirez and Rainbird 2010). However, there is no doubt that a rapidly developing and far reaching global labour market is emergent which is utilizing high- as well as low-skilled labour.

The Construction of Inside-out Models of Production

Within the developing world new models of 'inside-out' production are being constructed (Brown et al. 2011). Where once it was assumed that a sophisticated infrastructure, including that relating to skill formation, was required for high-quality production, it is now clear that TNCs can set up with minimal levels of infrastructure, so long as they have access to a consistent energy supply, transport logistics, and high-speed internet connectivity. Corporations that operate with this model require well-educated and motivated employees for whom training is provided utilizing modern forms of performance management. These management techniques are combined with the latest technologies to deliver global productivity standards. Inside-out production plants are quick to establish, giving TNCs' great flexibility as to where they invest and enabling them to move to cheaper locations when costs rise. And, as in the German intermediate engineering TNC, they utilize the kinds of TQM and production monitoring systems that enable high-quality production (Lauder et al. 2008).

Inside-out models of production pose a considerable challenge to particularistic theories of skill formation. The latter assume that the production of highly skilled workers requires an infrastructure of societally embedded institutions and traditions of which the institutions and relations of the German dual system may be considered a paradigm case. However, it is clear that high-quality goods and services do not require such a complex infrastructure to produce the skills necessary for these models of production.

This has enabled what may be called the Quality-Cost Revolution.

Competition on the Basis of Quality and Cost

During the 1990s there was a widespread belief that cutting-edge quality goods had to be designed and created in the West due to their superior innovation systems (Reich 1991; Rosecrance 1999). This situation no longer holds, with the exceptions noted above. Moreover, the ambitions of countries such as China and India have motivated them to learn from TNCs, often improving their social technologies as the basis for the development of their own TNCs (Zhang 2003; Simon and Cao 2009). As a result of this transformation, competition in today's global market is now on the basis of quality and cost. It means that companies operating from the older industrial societies are rapidly losing competitive advantage derived from their out-moded innovation systems (Zeng and Williamson 2007).

This transformation has been achieved in remarkably short time. Whereas companies in the 1990s still felt that high-quality goods could only be made in the West, by the first decade of the twenty- first century the same companies were making those same goods in parts of the developing world. In services, this transformation has been even more rapid, facilitated by the fact that many services are 'weightless'. Services such as research, financial analysis, regulatory reporting, accounting, customer services, and invoicing can be transferred across the world.

A key element in the construction of global skill webs has been the development of digital Taylorism.

Digital Taylorism

Today, *digital Taylorism* can be seen as analogous to the introduction of *mechanical Taylorism*, characterized by the Fordist production line, where the knowledge of craft workers was captured by management, codified and re-engineered in the shape of the moving assembly line (Brown et al. 2011). Digital Taylorism involves translating *knowledge work* into *working knowledge* through the extraction, codification, and digitalization of knowledge into software prescripts and templates that can be transmitted and manipulated by others, regardless of location. The result is the standardization of functions and jobs, including an increasing proportion of technical, managerial, and professional roles, which raises fundamental questions about the future of 'knowledge' work. Consequently, employers are not always looking for employees who possess academic knowledge or analytical skills but rather the flexibility to enable them to fit into clearly defined roles that are simplified and codified to enable 'plug-in-and-play' even for highly qualified employees (Markoff 2011).[6] The rapid diffusion of digital Taylorism has become so widespread that Brynjolfsson and McAfee (2011) have argued that it is a significant explanation for jobless growth in the United States.

If the course of digital Taylorism follows that of its precursor Taylorism, then it is likely to be adopted globally, irrespective of the type of economy, because of the competitive pressures that cost-saving routinization exerts. Taylorism, in the inter-war years expanded to manufacturing across all corners of the globe (Merkle 1980), irrespective of particular economic systems: the same may well apply to its digital counterpart.

The Consequences for Theories of Skill Formation

The analysis of the global trends we have presented leads to a fundamental reconsideration of the theoretical merits of the key skill formation theories and their warrant in guiding policy. We examine these implications in relation to universal and particularistic theories in turn.

Universal Theories: Education and Income

Human capital theory's assumed link between graduates' potential greater productivity, jobs and incomes, has significant anomalies and its main empirical propositions

[6] The radical possibilities of digital Taylorism moving up the skills chain are discussed by Garbani and Cecere (2011).

are likely to need qualifying with respect to the West. Whilst there are national factors that are likely to intervene to influence trends in graduate incomes, such as the way national governments respond to the Great Recession, the above analysis points to an unravelling of the relationship between education, employment, and incomes. The outcome will be large numbers of college graduates in jobs that they find less than satisfying and offering much lower incomes than they were led to expect, given the human capital equation of 'learning equals earnings'. Of course, human capital theorists may claim that their theory holds when applied to global labour markets since low wages may be considered a function of an oversupply of skilled labour but at that point we would return to our earlier criticism: the theory provides no guidance as to the industrial trajectory that the West should take to address the potential decline in real terms of graduate incomes.

A similar point can be made to skill bias theorists: from within the confines of their own theory they fail to understand the implications of the technological revolution for the United States and other nation states. This lack of understanding arises because they have ignored the implications of the global reach that new technologies allow, along with the potential to standardize various aspects of 'knowledge' work. As with human capital theorists, the policy recommendation of more education, whilst desirable in its own right, will not address the fundamental problems the West now encounters. Consequently, we need to develop a framework which allows us to relate more loosely integrated national institutions to these global institutional structures.

Particularistic Theories: The Diminishing Role of National Institutions and Cultures?

The development of modern work processes has meant that in both manufacturing and services, the particularistic assumptions of forms of embedded, institutionally based, skill formation systems have increasingly limited application. These modern production techniques enable TNCs to be highly mobile in where they set up and how they construct jobs and utilize skilled labour. In manufacturing, this development is not only about the introduction of robots but of TQM and similar techniques that obviate the need for large numbers of highly skilled production line workers. However, the clearest example of the flexibility that TNCs now have is their use of inside-out models of production. This challenges particularistic theories that focus on how skill formation is embedded in institutions and cultures. We are not arguing that issues of institutional embeddedness are no longer important but may only obtain in niche markets and forms of production.

Equally, the propensity for particularistic theories to view global forces as external/exogenous should be resisted: an error of methodological nationalism. This requires analysis of the 'de-coupled' relationship between the state, education and training, employment, and labour market rewards. For VoC, the challenge is to explain why in so many respects LMEs and CMEs are becoming similar in relation to labour market processes. On the one hand, it is clear, that low-wage work is in part a consequence of institutional factors (Bosch 2009; Salverda and Mayhew 2009). On the other hand, the rise of such work in many economies not normally associated with low skill equilibria (Finegold and Soskice 1988), for example Germany (Salverda and Mayhew 2009), suggests that the introduction of routinized work associated with digital Taylorism may make LME and CMEs equally vulnerable to routinized work and an increasingly large sector of lower skilled work.

The question is whether the forms of coordination and governance in CMEs can survive if their labour market processes are fundamentally changing. If Germany is the citadel of the VoC view of CMEs, then the question is one of how long its dual system with its emphasis on prolonged training, even for low-wage workers, can survive if middle-skilled jobs are being 'hollowed out'.

In the light of these considerations it is clear that there is a strong case for arguing that no current skill formation theory can address the impacts of the global trends that we have outlined. What is needed is a new agenda for research.

The Theoretical and Empirical Challenge: Towards an Agenda for Research and Policy

A new agenda of policy and research is required to understand the interrelationship between the global and the national in processes of skill formation and the policy challenges that they pose. One of the key themes to emerge is the need for a clearer understanding of the relationship between education, skills, jobs, and incomes. The assumption that there is a tightening bond between them is in need of revision. We have outlined a number of interrelated trends that are transforming the relationship between skills, jobs, and incomes. Consequently, many countries will experience a mismatch between education and the demand for skilled labour on the one hand, and jobs and incomes on the other. Future research is therefore needed to examine how these trends are impacting on specific forms of capitalism and industrial sectors.

The Stratification of Knowledge Work

Many of the theories under discussion assume, either implicitly or explicitly, that there is a unity of political interests between national and workers' interests (Brown and Lauder 1996). However, as a result of the global trends we have identified, knowledge work is being stratified with the result that there are at least three forms of potential conflict that can be identified. These relate to the conflicting interests between TNCs and nation states; between knowledge workers and corporate executives engaged in knowledge capture (in both the public and private sector); and between the use of digital Taylorist technologies to create low-waged work and its impact on the skilled workers.

To minimize conflict between nations and TNCs, the aim of national skill formation strategies has been to use skill as a way of raising the incomes of workers. However, it is in the interests of TNCs that they obtain labour at any level of skill at the cheapest cost possible because of pressures of competition. Here the ability to employ inside-out forms of production is the key to their flexibility in the search for lower costs. It is largely for this reason that TNCs have sourced skilled as well as unskilled labour from East Asia rather than utilizing skilled labour in the West. Indeed, even in the West, amongst engineering graduates forms of crowd sourcing are driving down wages with the exception of those working in core labour markets (Newfield 2010). Where TNCs do not extract the most favourable conditions for locating production, they can always move on, as some have from, for example, the East Coast of China to Vietnam.[7] As this example indicates, this conflict applies as much to the former East Asia Tigers and to China, as it does to the West. In the 1990s, Ashton and Green (1996) could identify the underlying national strategies that states in East Asia could adopt to raise skill levels and the incomes of their citizens. Now that is much more difficult, as suggested by the work on skill webs and supply chains by Ashton et al. (2010).

The rise of digital Taylorism signals another kind of conflict between workers' tacit knowledge and the desire of corporations to make that knowledge explicit and hence cheaper—from knowledge work to working knowledge. At root is a power struggle between labour and capital, as employees seek to increase the value and status of their skills and knowledge, at same time that employers want to impose control, reduce labour costs, and increase profits.

This re-stratification of knowledge work raises fundamental research and policy challenges which in the past have been masked by the rhetoric of the knowledge economy and the idea that there is an almost limitless demand for high-skilled workers. One focus is on the fate of the professional and technical middle classes in the face of the global challenges that now confront them. In particular, the role of digital Taylorism as it moves up the skills chain raises a further key question for researchers and policymakers. This question concerns the role of tacit knowledge relating to cultures of innovation. It appears that tacit knowledge can be transferred and translated relatively easily across borders. This diffusion may be the case for TNCs because they have generated an internal culture, or for companies such as those in Silicon Valley that were started by East Asian entrepreneurs which have then relocated elements of their business back to East Asia (Kerr 2008). In these cases national institutions for transferring tacit knowledge have been replaced by the trans-national. However, whilst theorists such as Guile (2010) make a persuasive case for the significance of

[7] For China, the alternative is to encourage investment in the west of the People's Republic that have lower costs.

tacit knowledge, there seem to be few cases empirically where tacit knowledge and culture is able to insulate businesses and workers. In policy terms this issue is crucial because it continues to be assumed that high-skilled innovative work provides a shelter, as well as a premium, for workers.

Another focus is at the other end of the skills ladder. More needs to be known about the effects of standardization and routinization on the rise in low-wage work and the degree to which it will undermine national institutions and forms of coordination, especially those which determine, in part, the wages of workers. There is already a fierce competition for those 'graduate' level jobs that continue to offer good career prospects. College graduates that fail to secure such jobs have become part of a process of 'bumping down' the jobs ladder, leaving young people with few skills in danger of a lifelong employment in low-skilled temporary jobs if not unemployed (Gesthuizen et al. 2011). The re-stratification of knowledge work will also impact on social class, gender, and ethnic divisions in shaping who wins and loses in education, training, and the labour market (Estevez-Abe 2005; Kupfer 2014). Given the position of women in the labour market, where they are consistently underpaid relative to men when they have the same qualifications and when they also undertake work which is may be high skilled but low paid (Kupfer 2014) we need to pay close attention to the trends we have identified in relation to them. This is especially the case in terms of gender for the development of global supply chains, since it is often women that are exploited in these contexts (Dunaway 2013). However, these global trends may affect countries differently and we need to understand more about why this may be the case.

The Role of the State in Skill Formation

The account we have given strongly suggests that market forces are not sufficient in creating either the demand or the coordinating mechanisms for creating skilled work. As a consequence, in the West, as in East Asia, the state has a significant role to play. What is required are forms of industrial policy that can create both the supply and demand for skilled work. Such policy would involve identifying and developing areas of growth within national and global markets. There are many ways in which this can be done (Rodrik 2007; Wade 2012). In turn, industrial policy will determine key elements of skill formation. This is no mean challenge, for in the first instance it means discarding the assumptions underlying the rhetoric of the knowledge economy and changing perceptions and capabilities of government departments and civil servants, in conjunction with business to identify where, in global markets, national action can help provide a competitive advantage (Brown et al. 2010). Nevertheless, we should note the stakes. Given high levels of youth unemployment, including college graduates, in both developed and developing countries, the need to find skilled work for young people is crucial. It is also worth observing that if the criticisms of human capital theory hold, then re-thinking theories of skill formation are as relevant for developing as developed economies. In this respect the inside-out model of production offers some purchase on the development of skilled work in developing economies. Although, as Wade (2012) has noted, attracting TNC investment on its own is of limited use if there are no spillover effects that can aid the broader development of the economy.

However, there are research questions to be raised about the effects of such industrial policies: in particular, whether it is possible, and if so, under what circumstances to develop industrial policies which effectively link strategies for future sector development with skill formation. In this respect comparative studies of economies which have been open to global economic forces whilst seeking to raise the supply and demand for skills would be useful.

Conclusion

In this chapter we have examined the major theories on skill formation and argued that they do not adequately address fundamental changes in the global supply of educated labour and trends in the global division of labour.

Through the development of strategic skill webs, TNCs have been increasingly reducing their dependence on national systems of skill formation. This shift can be seen in terms of their ability to manage corporate skill formation, as they are able to source high-skilled labour from different national locations and speed-up the process of work-related learning, making them less reliant on any individual country for their supply of labour. Crucially, they can now shape those skills and competences to their own requirements within a global context. They now have the ability to rationalize knowledge work and routinize it across the globe (Brown et al. 2011).

Whilst VoC does transcend many of the problems associated with human capital theory it too has failed to recognize the emergence of significant changes in the global transformation of economic activity. This failure is partly because VoC theorists have focused on differences in national economic performance and therefore underplay the wider global context of technological, economic, and social change.

Here we have argued that the combination of the opening of global labour markets, digital Taylorism, and new forms of social and technical control over productive processes lead to fundamental challenges both for theories of skill formation and their implications for policy. As a result, a major re-think of many of the assumptions that currently inform national and transnational policies on skills and skill formation is needed. The trends that inform current understanding of the global economy and the development of corporate skill webs remain in urgent need of further investigation to understand their consequences for individuals, institutions, and nation states.

References

Acemoglu, D. (2002) 'Technical Change, Inequality, and the Labor Market', *Journal of Economic Literature*, XL: 7–72

Albert, M. (1993) *Capitalism against Capitalism*, London: Whurr.

Alvesson, M. (2001) 'Knowledge Work: Ambiguity, Image and Identity', *Human Relations*, 54(7): 863–886.

Ashton, D. and Green, F. (1996) *Education and Training for the Global Economy*, Cheltenham: Edward Elgar.

Ashton, D., Green, F., James, D., and Sung, J. (1999) *Education and Training for Development in East Asia*, London: Routledge.

Ashton, D., Brown, P., and Lauder, H. (2010) 'Skill Webs and International Human Resource Management: Lessons from a Study of the Global Skill Strategies of Transnational Companies', *The International Journal of Human Resource Management*, 21(6): 836–850.

Aurtorengruppe Bildungsbereichterstattung (2008) *Bildung in Deutschland, 2006*, Bielefeld: Bertelsmann, Stiftung.

Becker, G. S. (1964) *Human Capital*, New York: National Bureau of Economic Research.

Becker, G. (2006) 'The Age of Human Capital', in H. Lauder, P. Brown, J. Dillabough, and A. H. Halsey (eds) *Education, Globalization and Social Change*, Oxford: Oxford University Press.

Berger, S. (2005) *How We Compete: What Companies Around the World Are Doing to Make It in the Global Economy*, London: Doubleday.

Bosch, G. (2009) 'Low Wage Work in Five European Countries and the US', *International Labour Review*, 148(4): 337–356.

Braverman, H. (1974) *Labor and Monopoly Capital*, London: Monthly Review Press.

Brown, P. and Lauder, H. (1996) 'Education, Globalization, and Economic Development', *Journal of Education Policy*, 11: 1–24.

Brown, P., Green, A., and Lauder, H. (2001) *High Skills*, Oxford: Oxford University Press.

Brown, P., Ashton, D., and Lauder, H. (2010) 'Skills Are Not Enough: The Globalization of Knowledge and the Future of the UK Economy', PRAXIS no.4, Wath-Upon-Dearne: UK Commission for Employment and Skills.

Brown, P. Lauder, H., and Ashton, D. (2011) *The Global Auction*, New York: Oxford University Press.

Brynjolfsson, E. and McAfee, A. (2011) *Race against the Machine*, London: Digital Frontier Press.

Bryson, J. (ed) (2010) *Beyond Skill*, Basingstoke: Palgrave Macmillan.

Burton-Jones, A. and Spender, J. C. (eds) (2011) *The Oxford Handbook of Human Capital*, Oxford: Oxford University Press.

Cattaneo, O., Gereffi, G., and Staritz., C. (2010) *Global Value Chains in a Post Crisis World*, Washington, DC: The World Bank.

Culpepper, P. D. and Thelen, K, (2008) 'Institutions and Collective Actors in the Provision of Training: Historical and Cross-National Perspectives', in K. Mayer and H. Solga (eds) *Skill Formation*, New York: Cambridge University Press: 21–49.

Dunaway, W. (2013) *Gendered Commodity Chains*, Stanford: Standford University Press.

Estevez-Abe, M. (2005) 'Gender Bias in Skills and Social Policies: The Varieties of Capitalism Perspective on Sex Segregation', *Social Politics: International Studies in Gender, State and Society*, 12(2): 180–215.

Estevez-Abe, M., Iversen, T. and Soskice, D. (2001) 'Social Protection and the Formation of Skills: A Reinterpretation of the Welfare State', in P. A. Hall and D. Soskice (eds) *Varieties of Capitalism*, Oxford: Oxford University Press: 145–183.

Felstead, A., Gallie, D., Green, F., and Zhou, Y. (2007) *Skills at Work, 1988–2006*, SKOPE Monograph, SKOPE, Oxford/Cardiff: Universities of Oxford and Cardiff.

Field, B. (2002) 'The Accidental Tiger', Phd thesis, University of Leicester.

Finegold, D. and Soskice, D. (1988) 'The Failure of British Training: Analysis and Prescription', *Oxford Review of Economic Policy*, 4(3) 21–53.

Finegold, D. (1991) 'Institutional Incentives and Skill Creation: Understanding Decisions that Lead to a High Skill Equilibrium', in P. Ryan (ed.), *International Comparisons of Vocational Education and Training for Intermediate Level Skills*, London: Falmer: 93–116.

Finegold, D. (1999) 'Creating Self-sustaining, High-skill Ecosystems', *Oxford Review of Economic Policy*, 15(1): 60–81.

Fleckenstein, T., Saunders, A., and Seeleib-Kaiser, M. (2011) 'The Dual Transformation of Social Protection and Human Capital: Comparing Great Britain and Germany', *Comparative Political Studies*, 44(12): 1622–1650.

Friedman, M. (1953) 'The Methodology of Positive Economics', *Essays in Positive Economics*, Chicago: Chicago University Press: 1–43.

Garbani, J-P. and Cecere, M. (2011) *IT Infrastructure and Operations: The Next 5 Years*, New York: Forrester.

Gesthuizen, M., Solga, H., and Künster, R. (2011). 'Context Matters: Economic Marginalization of Low-Educated Workers in Cross-National Perspective', *European Sociological Review*, 27(2): 264–280.

Goldin, C. and Katz, L. (2008) *The Race between Education and Technology, Boston,* MA: Harvard University Press.

Green, F. (2006) *Demanding Work*, Princeton: Princeton University Press.

Green, F. and Zhou, Y. (2007) 'Overqualification, Job Dissatisfaction and Increasing Dispersion in the returns to Graduate Education', Manpower Human Resources Lab, Centre for Economic Performance, London School of Economics.

Guilde, D. (2010) *The Learning Challenge of the Knowledge Economy*, Amsterdam: Sense Publishers.

Hall, P. A. and Soskice, D. (eds) (2001) *Varieties of Capitalism*, Oxford: Oxford University Press.

Hansen, H. (2011) 'Rethinking Certification Theory and Educational Development in the US and Germany', *Research in Social Stratification and Mobility*, 29(1), 31–55.

Hanushek, E. and Woessman, L. (2007) *Education, Quality and Economic Growth*, Washington, DC: World Bank.

Hanushek, E., Woessman, L., and Lei Zhang (2011) 'General Education, Vocational Education, and Labour Market Outcomes over the Life Cycle', Discussion Paper IZA DP no. 6083, Institute for the Study of Labour, Bonn.

Hassel, A. (2014) 'The Paradox of Liberalization—Understanding Dualism and the Recovery of the German Political Economy', *British Journal of Industrial Relations*, 52(1): 57–81.

Keep, E. and Payne, J. (2004) 'I Can't Believe It's Not Skill': The Changing Meaning of Skill in the UK Context and Some Implications', in G. Hayward and S. James (eds), *Balancing the Skills Equation*, Bristol: Policy Press: 53–76.

Keep, E. and Mayhew, K. (2010) 'Moving Beyond Skills and a Social and Economic Panacea', *Work, Employment and Society*, 24(3): 565–577.

Kahneman, D. (2011) *Thinking Fast and Slow*, London: Penguin Books.

Kerr, W. (2008) 'Ethnic Scientific Communities and International Technology Diffusion', *The Review of Economics and Statistics*, 90(3): 518–537.

Kerr, C., Dunlop, J. T., Harbison, F. H. and Myers, C. A. (1960) *Industrialism and Industrial Man*, London: Heineman.

Kim, L. and Nelson, R. (2000) *Technology and Learning Innovation: Experience of newly Industrializing Economies*, Cambridge: Cambridge University Press.

Kupfer, A. (2012) 'Towards a Theoretical Framework for the Comparative Understanding of Globalisation, Higher Education, The Labour Market and Inequality', in A. Kupfer (ed.), *Globalisation, Higher Education, the Labour Market and Inequality*, Abingdon: Routledge: 5–28.

Kupfer, A. (2014) 'The Interrelation of Twenty-first Century Education and Work from a Gender Perspective', *International Studies in Sociology of Education*, 24(1): 113–125.

Lauder, H., Brown, P., and Ashton, D. (2008) 'Globalisation, Skill Formation and the Varieties of Capitalism Approach', *New Political Economy*, 13(1): 19–35.

Lauder, H., Young, M., Daniels, H., Balarin, M., and Lowe, J. (2012) 'Introduction: Educating for the Knowledge Economy? Critical Perspectives', in H. Lauder, M. Young, H. Daniels, M. Balarin, and J. Lowe (eds), *Educating for the Knowledge Economy? Critical Perspectives*, London: Routledge.

Markoff, J. (2011) 'Looks Like a Job for an E-Lawyer', *New York Times*, 13 March.

Maurice, M., Sellier, F., and Silvestre, J-J. (1986) *The Social Foundations of Industrial Power*, Boston: MIT Press.

Mayer, K. U. and Solga, H. (2008) *Skill Formation: Interdisciplinary and Cross-National Perspectives*, New York: Cambridge University Press.

Merkle, J. (1980) *Management and Ideology*, Berkeley: University of California Press.

Mishel, L., Bernstein, J., and Shierholz, H. (2009) *The State of Working America, 2008/2009*, Ithaca, NY: Cornell University Press.

Newfield, C. (2012) 'The Structure and Silence of the Cognoariat', in A. Kupfer (ed.), *Globalisation, Higher Education, the Labour market and Inequality*, Abingdon: Routledge.

OECD (2011) *Education at a Glance*, Paris: OECD.

OECD (1977) *Selection and Certification in Education and Employment*, Paris: OECD.

Payne, J. (2000) 'The Changing Meaning of Skill', Issues Paper no.1, SKOPE, Universities of Oxford and Warwick.

Ramirez, P. and Rainbrid, H. (2010) 'Making the Connections: Bringing Skill Formation into Global Value Chain Analysis', *Work, Employment and Society*, 24(4): 699–710.

Reich, R. (1991) *The Work of Nations*, London: Simon and Schuster.

Rodrik, D. (2007) *One Economics Many Recipes*, Princeton: Princeton University Press.

Rose, M. (1985) 'Universalism, Culturalism and the Aix Group: Promise and Problems of a Societal Approach to Economic Institutions', *European Sociological Review*, 1(1): 65–83.

Rosecrance, R. (1999) *The Rise of the Virtual State: Wealth and Power in the Coming Century*, New York: Basic Books.

Salverda, W. and Mayhew, K. (2009) 'Capitalist Economies and Wage Inequality', *Oxford Review of Economic Policy*, 25(1): 126–154.

Schultz, T. W. (1971) *Investment in Human Capital*, New York: Free Press.

Simon, D. F. and Coa, C. (2009) *China's Emerging Technological Edge*, Cambridge: Cambridge University Press.

Streeck, W. (1989) 'Skills and the Limits of Neo-liberalism: The Enterprise of the Future as a Place of Learning', *Work, Employment and Society*, 3(1): 89–104.

Tate, J. (2001) 'National Varieties of Standardization', in P. A. Hall and D. Soskice (eds), *Varieties of Capitalism*, Oxford: Oxford University Press: 442–473.

Thelen, H. (2004) *How Institutions Evolve*, Cambridge: Cambridge University Press.

Torrance, H. (2006) 'Globalizing Empiricism: What If Anything Can Be Learned from International Comparisons of Educational Achievement', in H. Lauder, P. Brown, J. Dillabour, and A. H. Halsey (eds) *Education, Globalization and Social Change*, Oxford: Oxford University Press.

Wade, R., (2012) 'Return of Industrial Policy', *International Review of Applied Economics*, 26(2): 223–239.

Warhurst, C. and Thompson, P. (2006) 'Mapping Knowledge in Work: Proxies or Practices?', *Work, Employment and Society*, 20(4): 787–800.

Waslander, S., Pater, C., and van der Weide, M. (2010) 'Markets in Education: An Analytical Review of Empirical Research on Market Mechanisms in Education', Education Working Papers no.52, Paris: OECD.

Whitley, R. (1999) *Divergent Capitalisms: The Social Structuring and Change of Business Systems*, Oxford: Oxford University Press.

Wilson, R. and Hogarth, T. (eds) (2003) 'Tackling the Low Skills Equilibrium: A Review of Issues and Some New Evidence', Institute for Employment Research, University of Warwick.

Wimmer, A. and Glick Schiller, N (2002) 'Methodological Nationalism and Beyond: Nation-State Building, Migration and the Social Sciences', *Global Networks*, 2(4): 301–334.

Winch, C., Clarke, L., Brockman, M., Hanf, G., Mehaut, P., and Westerhuis, A. (2011) *Knowledge, Skills and Competence in the European Labour Market*, Abingdon: Routledge.

Zhang, M. (2003) 'Transferring Human Resource Management across National Boundaries: The Case of Chinese Multinational Companies in the UK', *Employee Relations*, 25(6): 613–626.

Zheng, M. and Williamson, P. (2007) *Dragons at Your Door: How Chinese Cost Innovation is Disrupting Global Competition*, Boston, MA: Harvard Business School Press.

CHAPTER 20

DIFFERENT NATIONAL SKILL SYSTEMS

GERHARD BOSCH

INTRODUCTION

INTERNATIONAL comparative research shows that, even in countries with similar levels of economic development and similar technologies, products, and services, there are astonishing differences in workers' general and vocational education and training. Thus the Airbus is assembled in Germany, largely by workers who have completed a course of vocational training, whereas in Spain, France, and the United Kingdom the overwhelming majority of workers have acquired their skills over many years on the job (Bremer 2008). Retail staff in Britain, France, and the United States generally undergo just a brief induction period, whereas in Germany they usually complete a two- or three-year apprenticeship (Carré et al. 2010). Nurses in Germany and the Netherlands are mainly trained in specialist nursing schools, whereas in other countries they require a bachelor's degree (Brockmann 2011).

These examples, which are far from exhaustive, show that skills systems are not determined by new technologies or practical constraints specific to individual industries; rather they are social institutions with scope for independent action. The room for manoeuvre they enjoy has four aspects to it. Firstly, comparable skills can be acquired in various ways. International comparisons have revealed a variety of choices, for example between years of learning on the job and formal vocational training or between high-quality vocational training and study at university. Secondly, skills can be acquired at various stages of working life. In some countries, individuals acquire more skills in initial education and training, whilst in others they acquire more in further training or in the workplace. Thirdly, work tasks can be distributed differently, horizontally or vertically. When tasks are equally distributed in a horizontal allocation system, all employees can carry out specialist activities. Conversely, when they are unequally distributed in a vertical allocation system, they are concentrated among a small number of specialists, whilst the others perform routine tasks only. Fourthly, firms can reduce their skill requirements by standardizing tasks and making increased use of technology. All these strategies have a price. Firms that are hierarchically organized and have few specialists can save on training costs but not only lose flexibility and quality but also require more managerial and supervisory staff to instruct and monitor the workforce. The higher cost of investing in a well-trained workforce capable of working independently and taking decisions is often only justified in firms specializing in high-value products and services.

Opinions as to whether skill requirements are reduced with the strategies outlined above diverge considerably. Braverman (1974) and, recently, many supporters of the hourglass economy thesis (Holmes and Mayhew 2012) see a trend towards polarized skill requirements, whilst other commentators foresee skill profiles that vary from country to country (Fernández-Macías 2012). The considerable differences in national education and employment systems and the fact that different countries specialize in different products and services substantiate this argument and give grounds for scepticism towards universal skill forecasts.

Because of high levels of internal differentiation, the numerous institutions and actors involved and the interactions with other national institutions, national education and training systems are not only path-dependent but also unique. Nevertheless, there are considerable structural similarities between groups of countries that can serve as a basis for developing typologies of national skill systems. Most typologies focus on the differences in general and vocational education in upper secondary school, since it is here that the greatest differences between countries are to be observed. However, with increasing investment in young children (Esping-Anderson 2002)—that is in pre-school education, the expansion of university education and the growing importance of education and training for adults—comparative researchers are paying increasing attention to the education and training system as a whole—hence 'skills systems'—with the result that country typologies are becoming more complex.

The country typologies for vocational training can be used to compare the efficiency of different training systems as judged by the criterion of economic success, particularly the integration of young people into employment, and thereby identifying the best training system. As a result, the other effects of training systems tend, on occasions, to be eclipsed. In sociological stratification theories, education and training systems are regarded as key institutions in status allocation and the reproduction of intergenerational social inequality and the expansion of education and training in many countries is not motivated solely by economic considerations but at least as much by the desire of many parents to give their children a head start in the labour market. In more recent research on national skill systems, there has been a tendency to abandon country typologies in favour of individual country studies. One example is the comparison of apprenticeship systems in various countries. These studies have revealed considerable differences between countries that had become submerged when these countries were assigned to a single type but which are fundamental to cross-national studies. Furthermore, skilled workers' increasing mobility across national boundaries and challenging projects such as the introduction of a European qualifications framework have created a surge of interest in comparing the content of training programmes and the acquisition of skills and competences in occupations.

The next section of this chapter outlines the various typologies of national skill systems. The subsequent section describes the research on the differences between national apprenticeship systems, followed by the research on the equivalence of training in occupations. The conclusion raises wider issues that receive less attention is research of national skills systems, such studies such as youth unemployment, work organization, and productivity.

Typologies of Education and Vocational Training Systems

In recent decades, typologies of national education and vocational training systems have been developed from various theoretical standpoints. Sociological research on education has been concerned primarily with the links between social stratification and education systems and has investigated the reproduction of social inequality through different educational pathways. The initial focus was the direct transitions from education into employment; in more recent life course research, however, the time horizon has been stretched to encompass the whole of working life. In education studies, the main concern has been with the various learning cultures and their historical embeddedness. In labour market theories, the connection between labour markets and vocational training is the main area of enquiry. In the tradition of the varieties of capitalism approach, institutional economists have investigated the reciprocal connections between education, production, employment, and welfare systems. In political sciences the main area of enquiry is the influences of the political system, and in particular party structure and voting systems. There are now so many overlaps and crossovers between the typologies in the various disciplines that the boundaries between the disciplines have become fluid. Nevertheless, the continuing differences need to be appreciated, as the following section highlights.

Sociological Stratification Theories

Sociological stratification theories differentiate education systems by the degree of stratification and standardization (Allmendinger 1989; Müller and Shavit 1998). The degree of stratification is an indication of the system's selectiveness. Stratified education systems are organized hierarchically. Pupils are allocated at an early stage to different educational pathways (so-called tracking) that lead to qualifications of different levels and status. Selectiveness is all the greater the fewer people attain the highest level of qualification. The organization of the employment system parallels these educational hierarchies. The various school leaving qualifications feed into different hierarchical levels within firms. Although this link makes transitions into employment easier, it allows little vertical mobility over the course of the working life. In less stratified systems, many young people complete senior high school or even university. In these systems, allocation within the hierarchy takes place more in the employment than in the education system. The less rigid links between the education and employment systems mean that career trajectories are less predetermined, which facilitates vertical mobility. In standardized education systems, the various inputs and outputs, such as teacher training, curricula and leaving qualifications, are uniformly regulated. As a result, firms receive reliable signals from the education system and are able to trust the qualifications obtained by young people leaving the system. In less standardized systems, on the other hand, new recruits have first to be tested by means of entry examinations onto occupations or in the course of an initial training period within firms.

Müller and Shavit (1998) add a third indicator in the shape of what they call occupational specificity. They argue that in countries in which general education predominates, firms assume that young people in practically oriented streams are among the weaker pupils and that they are less likely to succeed in the competition for good jobs. In countries with highly developed occupational labour markets, on the other hand, access to skilled jobs is facilitated by vocational training, so that even high achieving pupils can go down this route.

In a large comparative study of the upper secondary school level of various education systems, a typology of 13 countries from different continents was constructed on the basis of these three criteria. The United States, United Kingdom, and Australia were described as having low levels of stratification and standardization, although they differed in the degree of occupational specificity. Whilst general education dominated in the United States, both the United Kingdom and Australia had intermediate levels of occupational specificity. Germany, Switzerland, and the Netherlands, on the other hand, were described as highly stratified and standardized and also had high levels of occupational specificity (Müller and Shavit 1998).

Differing National Learning Cultures

Underlying national education systems are various guiding principles and learning cultures that are also reflected in the respective educational institutions. Greinert (2004) identifies three basic types of vocational training that emerged following the erosion of artisanal-corporatist vocational training in Europe: the statist-bureaucratic model in France, the dual-corporatist model in Germany, and the liberal market economy in the United Kingdom.

The statist-bureaucratic model essentially comprises a school-based vocational training system regulated by the state. Coordinating supply and demand is the responsibility of state agencies. Since such demand planning cannot go into any great detail, it is most effective when it is carried out on the basis of a limited set of basic occupations. Training is concerned less with current practice than with abstraction and theorizing, even though these principles have no relevance to low-level occupations. The qualifications awarded are academic qualifications and ranked according to the different types of school; they are susceptible to the 'elevator effect' described by Beck (1996). The various courses and programmes have a tendency to move upwards to tertiary level, so that more basic courses have repeatedly to be added at the bottom and the model finds itself in a permanent state of crisis. The system is funded out of the public purse.

The dual-corporatist model is monitored and administered through 'intermediate institutions', such as trade unions, employers' associations, and chambers of commerce, which are public statutory bodies. It is largely separated from the general education system by its independent organizational structure and the legislation governing its functioning. Training is largely provided in firms. Trainees have a contract with a firm but at the same time are enrolled in a vocational training school. Training regulations and standards are developed by the social partners and legitimized by national legislation. The statutory duration of training for a recognized occupation is between two and four years. The costs of training are borne largely by firms, although the vocational training schools are funded by the state.

In the liberal market model, training supply and demand are regulated through the market. The type of skills produced is determined by the assumed needs of the workplace. Training is not particularly standardized, which results in very varied combinations of school-based, firm-based and industry-wide forms of training. Generally recognized examinations and diplomas are the exception. The costs of training are borne by firms or individual trainees.

Greinert (2004) emphasizes the difference between vocational training models and vocational training systems. A 'system' cannot be said to exist unless vocational training has developed as an autonomous societal sub-system with its own nexus of communications, institutional stability, and a self-referential completeness and delineation between itself and the wider environment. In Greinert's view, only the dual-corporatist model fulfils these criteria and can be regarded as an autonomous system. The other two models are shaped by other systems (school and market).

In identifying three ideal types, which are described as occupation, knowledge, and market-oriented respectively, Greinert claims to have pinpointed the building blocks from which the actual vocational training models in European countries are constructed. Even the actual vocational training models in the three reference countries are in fact hybrid types. In each country, elements of the other models can be observed alongside the dominant model: there is the more market-oriented advanced or further training in Germany, the apprenticeship system in France, and the school-based vocational training in the United Kingdom for example.

A further, non-European type of vocational training, which Greinert labels company orientation, is located in large Japanese companies. The emphasis of the training here is less on the technical content than on the social context of the work tasks. An individual's willingness and ability to integrate himself (typically) into a company with unquestioning loyalty is the main priority and is associated with a guarantee of lifelong employment.

The Scandinavian model of egalitarian education that was developed in the post-war period is missing from this analysis. The early allocation of pupils in the first year of secondary education into different types of school and the further stratification in upper secondary education resulting from the segmentation between general academic education for some (higher performing) pupils and vocational training (whether school-based or in the form of apprenticeships) for the rest was regarded as one of the most significant cause of social inequality. Consequently, the different types of school and types of education and training (selective grammar schools, school-based vocational training, and apprenticeships) were abolished in favour of a unitary school-based secondary education. In Denmark, however, unlike in Sweden, the apprenticeship system survived, since the Social-Democratic Party had to govern in coalition and was unable completely to implement its ideas on equality (Wiborg and Cort 2010).

Verdier (2013) is critical of the over-concentration on initial vocational training and identifies five ideal types of lifelong learning regimes. The corporatist system, with its initial vocational training controlled by the social partners, also organizes lifelong learning alongside initial training. The primary objective of further training is higher levels of occupational mastery. The school-based academic regime is characterized by very early selection, with few opportunities to catch up over the course of the working life since further training is largely confined to short-term adjustment measures implemented at company level. In the universalist regime, the training goal is social citizenship and social autonomy. Generous public subsidies give all adults a second chance to undertake vocational training or a higher education course. These opportunities can also be taken up in the 'multi-transitional labour market', in which career interruptions do not leave any significant scar effects, in contrast to the situation in hierarchical internal labour markets with seniority pay, as in France. Verdier further identifies two different market regimes. The first is based on pure market competition, whilst in the second the training markets are indeed private but are regulated. The public regulations lay down quality standards and individuals are offered advice and financial support in the form of vouchers, for example, which can be redeemed in the private training market.

Like Greinert, Verdier's aim in describing the five ideal types is to identify the general building blocks on which the national models are constructed. The three decommodified lifelong learning regimes are strongly aligned with the German, French, and Swedish systems. However, a tendency towards the hybridization of national models can be observed. Thus by including the social partners in the governance of vocational training, France has incorporated elements of the corporatist model into its system. In Germany, the regulated market model is now playing an increasingly important role in further training. In the case of the United Kingdom, Verdier argues that the increased investment in the training of young people (through the New Deal programme of the Blair Labour government) has produced a combination of the universalist model and organized markets in lifelong learning.

Institutionalist Segmentation Theories

Segmentation theory identifies three different ideal types of labour markets, which are directly linked to the type of vocational training (Sengenberger 1987). Firstly, in the unstructured segment of the labour market, employees just have general low-level skills; they are allocated to simple tasks and can be easily substituted. Secondly, entry to occupational labour markets is linked to the acquisition of a recognized vocational diploma. Firms tailor their jobs to the externally defined occupations. In ideal circumstances, workers with vocational qualifications can change jobs without detriment. Occupational labour markets can develop at different skill levels. They range from simple standardized occupations for which only brief training is required via broadly defined, multifunctional occupations in the intermediate segment to highly skilled graduate occupations (lawyers, doctors, etc.). Third, in internal labour markets, skills are acquired within a firm, often during many years of learning on the job as well as through formal training. However, employees are not mobile, either because their skills are very firm-specific or because they are tied to their employer by seniority pay despite having transferable skills.

Rubery and Grimshaw (2003) classify five countries by the dominant labour market type and the form of vocational training regulation (Figure 20.1). In the United States and United Kingdom, there are fairly loosely organized occupational labour markets with the remnants of apprenticeship systems that used to be significantly more extensive. In contrast to the United States, the UK government has made available considerable amounts of funding in an attempt to subsidize firm-based apprenticeships. Otherwise the training system is dominated by a combination of school-based vocational training and usually very short periods of on-the-job learning, the level of which is difficult to assess because of its heterogeneity and lack of standardization. The classification of the other three countries is similar to Greinert's approach, with one fundamental difference. Vocational training is seen less as rooted more in the various forms of work organization than cultural tradition. Consequently, the depreciation in the value of a vocational qualification in the transition from school to work in France is the result not simply of a cultural lack of esteem for vocational training but also of the dominance of internal

	Occupational labour market (OLM)		Germany	
	Features of both OLM and ILM	UK		
Labour market model		US		
	Internal labour market (ILM)		Japan	France
		Market-led	Consensus-led	State-led
		Form of regulation		

FIGURE 20.1 Categorizing national systems of vocational training

Source: Rubery and Grimshaw (2003, 112).

labour markets, in which new entrants, despite their vocational training, begin at the bottom of the job ladder and have to work their way up.

The consensus-led countries produce significantly more intermediate skills than the market-led countries in particular. Rubery and Grimshaw interpret this latter tendency in particular as under-investment in training: in under-developed occupational labour markets, investment in vocational training often does not pay for employees, whilst firms in highly flexible labour markets provide too little training for fear of poaching. However, the shortages of intermediate and lower-level skills are compensated for to some extent by a highly developed university system which in these countries has now become the main source of well-qualified workers.

For Rubery and Grimshaw, the country classification has more of an heuristic function, since it facilitates understanding of national differences at a particular point in time. Reality is dominated by hybrid models that struggle with internal contradictions and also have constantly to adapt to new developments, such as technical change or global competition. As we shall see, an historically systematizing approach of this kind is fundamentally different from the equilibrium models of institutional economics, in which history is suppressed.

Institutional Economics

The typologies of institutional economics seek an economic rationale for the stability of the different training systems, which they find in the link with the employment system. It is assumed that, regardless of their historical origins, institutions survive only if they reduce the risks of investing in training for rational actors.

Referencing Becker (1964), Lynch (1994) distinguishes between general and specific skills. Firms invest less than they may perhaps wish to in general skills that are transferable to other firms, since employees may then change employer. Consequently, firms prefer to invest in specific skills that are not portable and are therefore less risky. Lynch (1994) identifies five alternative answers to the 'complex nature of firms' investment decision' in human capital (1994, 3).

In the first type—the extensive firm-based training in Japan—firms reap the benefit of their investment in training from their employees' high level of commitment and loyalty to the company. Firms' investment risks are minimized by means of a seniority-based pay system. In the second type, the German apprenticeship system, firms are restrained from poaching by moral pressure exerted by the chambers and associations. Furthermore, the investment is divided between trainees and their firms by means of a modest training wage. This approach facilitates investment in qualifications recognized throughout the industry. In the third type, the failure of the market to provide investment in general skills is remedied by public funding, not only for school-based vocational training but also for further training in the event of unemployment, for example. The reference countries here are Norway, Sweden, and the United Kingdom. In the fourth type, the answer to market failure is a levy system of the kind that exists in France and Australia, which distributes training costs among all firms. In the fifth and final type, the state bears the costs of school-based training, whilst firms, in the absence of industry-wide institutions and recognized certificates as is the case in the United States and Canada, confine themselves largely to firm-specific training.

Lynch's classification relates to training systems and not to initial vocational training or to adult learning. This approach points to the difficulties of comparing skill systems across countries. In some countries, initial and further vocational training are clearly separate systems. In other countries, such as Japan, such a delineation makes no sense, since in-firm training takes place over the whole of working life. However, the inadequate differentiation of the training provided in different phases of the working life introduces inaccuracies into Lynch's model. The French training levy that featured prominently in that country's categorization is used mainly to fund further training for employees, whilst the state bears most of the cost of school-based vocational training for young people.

The starting point for Estevez-Abe et al. (2001) is not, as it is for Lynch, firms' investment decisions but those made by individuals. The dichotomous distinction between firm-specific and general skills is supplemented by an intermediate category, namely industry-specific skills, which can be acquired through school-based vocational training or apprenticeships. It is assumed that the investor is a rational agent who expects high returns for his/her investment in training and wishes to avoid uncertainties. Only when job security is high will employees be willing to invest in firm-specific skills, since they stand to lose their investment if they lose their jobs. Moreover, they will not be willing to acquire industry-specific skills unless skilled workers' pay is protected by coordinated wage systems, and good dismissal protection and generous unemployment benefits leave adequate time to search for a job that matches the level of training. Coordinated wage systems also protect firms from poaching, since rates are set outside the firm and competitors cannot offer higher wages. Conversely, when unemployment benefits are low and dismissal protection is weak, employees must reckon on changing their jobs and even their industry frequently and are likely to invest primarily in general skills. Since general skills can be easily transferred to another firm, employees lose interest in campaigning for stronger dismissal protection and better unemployment benefits. Estevez-Abe et al. (2001) start from the assumption that tertiary education mainly provides general skills. This assumption is justified by reference to the English-speaking countries in which there is weak dismissal protection and low levels of unemployment benefit, and university education is not highly specialized.

On this basis, four different skill systems are identified, the reference examples being Denmark, Japan, Germany, and the United States (see Figure 20.2). Germany and Denmark both have a highly developed apprenticeship system and industry-wide collective agreements. In Germany, with its numerous medium-sized and larger firms, investment in industry-specific skills is ensured by means of strong dismissal protection; in Denmark, on the other hand, with its many small firms, the principal mechanism is the particularly generous levels of support for the unemployed. However, many occupations in the German and Danish training systems are in demand not only within

		Employment protection	
		Low	High
Unemployment protection	High	Industry-specific Skills Example: Denmark	Industry-specific skill mix Example: Germany
	Low	General skills Example: United States	Firm-specific skills Example: Japan

FIGURE 20.2 Social protection and predicted skill profiles

Source: Estevez-Abe et al. (2001, 154).

particular industries but also across industries. This situation applies, for example, to electrical, IT, and clerical occupations, so that it is more accurate to speak of occupational rather than industrial specificity.

In the institutionalist typologies, it is assumed that the interactions between national skill systems and the institutions of the employment system and even, in the case of Estevez-Abe et al. (2001), those of the welfare system are solely positive. Lynch (1994) and Estevez-Abe even speak of equilibria. Unlike in neo-classical economics, however, we are not dealing here with a state of equilibrium in a universal market model but rather with very diverse national skill equilibria shaped by institutions. Since firms and employees in this ravelled mesh of institutions have only a slight change of diverging from the national models, the equilibria are regarded as relatively stable. Consequently, change takes place only in accordance with the principles underpinning the system—that is, in a path-dependent way.

However, in focusing on this institutional alignment, such functionalist institutional analyses tend to lose sight of the contradictions and cracks in the systems. Thus the coordinated wage system and unemployment benefits in Germany, for example, have long been under strong deregulatory pressures (Bosch and Weinkopf 2008) and no longer protect skilled workers' wages to the same extent as they used to. In some industries, such as catering, vocational training is being eroded as a result.

The assumption that higher education is always general is also questionable. For certain professions with, in some cases, highly specialized vocational or professional qualifications, universities have always provided high-level 'vocational' training, in medicine, for example. With the expansion of university education and because of the continued high demand for intermediate skills with defined occupational profiles, parts of the vocational training system in many countries, including the United States, Canada, and Australia, have been elevated to bachelor degree level (Bosch and Charest 2010).

Streeck (2012) criticizes the basic efficiency theory assumptions made by Estevez-Abe et al. (2001), according to which unemployment insurance and dismissal protection were the product of a consensus between capital and labour that developed in order to increase productivity and competitiveness (2001, 329). The various national institutional mixes, Streeck argues, can be understood only as the product of class conflicts and political compromises. For example, Streeck sees no plausible reason why US employees with transferable skills should not also be interested in better social protection, which they do not receive because the American trade unions have lost that particular battle.

Streeck's second criticism, levelled at the notions of specific and general skills borrowed from Becker (1994), is equally fundamental. Becker used the distinction in a strictly economic sense in order to understand the effects of worker mobility on investment decisions regardless of the level of the skills and the reasons why they were transferable or not transferable. Becker's terms, which relate only to transferability, are loaded by Estevez-Abe et al. (2001) with assumptions about the level of the skills, with (firm- and industry-) specific skills allocated to the intermediate level and general skills to the tertiary level. Streeck argues that general and specific skills can be found at all levels of qualification. The skills of the simple 'general worker' are transferable, as are those acquired during an academic education in a discipline, such as mathematics, that can be applied in many different fields. Less transferable skills include not only the intermediate skills acquired by Japanese automotive workers, which are tied to the company, but also highly specialized academic skills (such as those acquired by experts in Byzantine history, for example).

Political Science

Iversen and Stephens (2008) extend Estevez-Abe et al.'s welfare-production regime approach with power resource theory, which locates the reasons for the emergence and stabilization of different human capital formation regimes in specific party alignments and electoral systems. The scope of their analyses is not confined to vocational training and higher education but encompasses the entire education and training system, including pre-school education and further training over the life course.

The starting point is the assumption that left-wing governments redistribute income via the taxation system to a greater extent than centre-right governments. As a result, they are also able to invest more in general and specific education and training, which in turn helps to reduce social inequality by improving education and training at the lower end of the skills hierarchy. The scope for action enjoyed by left-wing parties also depends on the dynamics of coalition formation, which is influenced in turn by the electoral system. Iversen and Stephens argue that proportional representation tends to produce centre-left governments and majoritarian systems centre-right governments.

On this basis, three types of human capital formation are identified, which differ from each other most markedly in the expenditure on education and training for the lower third (Figure 20.3). In liberal market economies, represented essentially by the English-speaking countries, centre-right governments predominate. There is only limited redistribution, and public expenditure on education and training is low. Such expenditure is concentrated on primary, secondary, and tertiary education, from which

	Coordinated Market Economies and Proportional Representation		**Liberal Market Economies and Majoritarian**
	Social Democratic	Christian Democratic	Liberal
Day care or preschool	High	Low	Low (but substantial private provision)
Primary and secondary	High	Medium	Medium
Higher education	High??	Medium	Medium (but substantial private component)
Active labor market policy	High	Low	Low
Vocational	High	High	Low

FIGURE 20.3 Expected policy profiles of different worlds of human capital formation

the middle classes benefit considerably. Private expenditure on education, particularly for pre-school and higher education, is high and is regarded as an important means of self-protection in view of the weak social safety net. The lower third of the population has only limited incentives to make an effort at school. And there is virtually no second chance for this group because of the low level of expenditure on active labour market policy. The middle classes have no interest in voting for higher investment for the lower third. Because of the bifurcated skill structure, firms specialize in areas in which they can use low and general skills.

The Christian Democratic model is based on cross-class coalitions. Consequently, it is very difficult to reach a consensus on redistribution via the taxation system and thus the main focus of policy is on income-related and status-protecting social insurance. Expenditure on education is only moderate. Little is invested in pre-school education. Education expenditure is concentrated on primary, secondary, and higher education. Strong dismissal protection and high levels of coverage by collective agreements ensure that workers invest in firm and industry-specific skills. These institutions are geared towards protecting the interests of skilled employees. There is little support for improving the basic education of semi-skilled and unskilled workers, whose interests are largely ignored. Virtually all Western European countries in Continental Europe belong to this model.

In the social democratic model, represented by the Scandinavian countries, left-wing single party governments have been able to use the taxation system to effect a considerable redistribution of wealth. High rates of taxation have made available the funding for above-average levels of public expenditure on early years education and all other stages of education up to lifelong learning for adults, which is delivered through highly developed active labour market policies. In particular, the commitment to equality has ensured high levels of investment in children's education and the highly developed system of school-based vocational training. The OECD literacy study (e.g. OECD 2013) show that the population at the lower end has considerably higher general skills than its counterpart in the other two models. The skill structure is much more compressed, largely because skill levels at the bottom of the hierarchy have been raised. Because of these excellent technical skills and solid basic education, these countries have successfully specialized in high value-added niches.

Differences between Apprenticeship Systems

The strong emphasis on education in the country typologies has led to the considerable differences in apprenticeship systems being neglected. Several studies have now closed this gap. Ryan et al. (2011) compare vocational training in Germany, the United Kingdom, and Switzerland in the retail and mechanical engineering sectors. Country effects dominate in the retail sector. Whilst most sales assistants in Switzerland and Germany complete a two- to three-year apprenticeship, most of their counterparts in the United Kingdom are trained on the job. In the mechanical engineering sector, on the other hand, there is a high-quality apprenticeship system of comparable duration in all three countries, since skilled workers are increasingly required for made-to-order production in this sector. The share of apprentices in the total workforce is virtually the same in all three countries. However, a country effect can be observed in the general skills. General education attainments are lower among British apprentices since a higher share of academically able youngsters go to university; so the supply of good pupils undertaking apprenticeships is lower than in Switzerland and Germany (Ryan et al. 2011).

The differences in the funding of training are interesting. In the United Kingdom, firms are paid considerable subsidies to train apprentices (up to £20,000 for a level 3 apprenticeship in mechanical engineering). However, they have to pay fees for some of the externally provided courses. In Germany and Switzerland, the state funds the vocational training schools that provide the theoretical teaching but firms receive no subsidies. Moreover, firms' economic calculations are determined by apprentices' pay. In general, apprentices' pay is highest in the United Kingdom and lowest in Switzerland, with Germany in between. In the mechanical engineering sector, apprentices' pay in the United Kingdom is 41% of that of a skilled worker, in Germany 29% and in Switzerland only 14%. There are good reasons for these big differences. Since the training in the United Kingdom is less standardized, firms have to compensate for the reduced certainty about training quality by paying higher wages. In Germany and Switzerland, the high training quality standards mean that lower pay is accepted (Ryan et al. 2013).

Since the training period in Switzerland is longer and trainees also perform a higher share of the productive work, training there is largely self-funding. Consequently, Swiss firms encourage mobility after completion of training and are happy to take skilled workers on again after their 'journeyman years'—behaviour characteristic of the ideal type of occupational labour markets. In Germany, on the other hand, apprentice training in most industries gives rise to net costs. Consequently, firms seek to retain trainees once they have passed their final examination in order to amortize the training costs. This practice leads to an overlapping of occupational and internal labour markets. In the United Kingdom as well, most trainees find employment in the mechanical engineering sector, since well-trained workers are scarce in the external labour market.

The study shows that a functioning apprenticeship system is possible even in a country such as Switzerland, with much weaker dismissal protection than in Germany and a higher share of small and medium-sized enterprises with above-average labour turnover. A functional equivalent to the very low rates of apprentice pay found in Switzerland would be a levy system. In Germany, the dual system in the construction industry almost collapsed at the beginning of the 1970s when the numerous small firms stopped training because their skilled workers were being poached. The first two years of training, that is when the share of productive work is still low, are now heavily subsidized by an industry-wide levy system, so that training has once again become attractive (Bosch and Zühlke-Robinet 2003). Similar regulations, introduced in order to compensate for this market failure, can be found in many countries (Bosch and Philips 2003) and in other industries with high skill requirements and high mobility. In Denmark, which has many small firms, firms that train apprentices are compensated for the days trainees spend in vocational school by a levy system (Wiborg and Cort 2010).

The state has other options at its disposal for promoting firm-based training. The right to carry on a trade or profession can be linked to a standardized minimum qualification by means of a licensing arrangement. Such arrangements are often found in occupations in which there is a high degree of risk, such as gas fitter, electrician or plumber. In the liberal market economies, licensing tends to be seen as an obstacle to the proper functioning of the market and is generally applied only to a small number of occupations and even then with low standards (Kleiner 2006). In these counties, however, the professions are well organized and remain protected from the market by their strong links to conservative and liberal parties. In some coordinated market economies, licensing is practised on a larger scale. In Germany, there are 41 nationally standardized occupations that can be practised independently (i.e. on a self-employed basis) only with the relevant vocational qualification and a master tradesman's certificate or at least five years' experience in the occupation in question. Customers benefit from the high quality and prices are kept low by strong inter-firm competition. The state facilitates access to the master tradesman's certificate by awarding grants and loans, so that prices cannot be controlled by barriers to accessing the required qualifications, as they were in the medieval guilds. A second possibility is legislation on public procurement, in which the state makes the award of public contracts dependent on verifiable qualifications and possibly also on adherence to a collective agreement. Philips (2003) shows how, in the United States, apprentice training in the construction industry, funded by a collectively agreed levy, was extended to all public building works by means of prevailing wage laws. A comparison of states with and without prevailing wage laws showed that the use of skilled workers increased productivity and hence reduced building costs. Thirdly, the state can set a good example and oblige its suppliers to provide training, as has been done successfully in London (Evans and Bosch 2012).

Equivalences between Occupations in Different Countries

Because of the increasing international mobility of labour, there is a growing need for comparison of the skills actually acquired and the recognition of training. This comparison generally takes place in individual recognition processes at the request of migrants. To some extent the mutual recognition of qualifications between countries is regulated by agreements or legislation, such as EC Directive 2005/36/EC on the recognition of professional qualifications, which applies to certain regulated professions (doctors, dentists, vets, pharmacists, nurses, midwives, and architects). Similar training standards apply throughout the European Union (EU) for these professions. For the other regulated occupations and professions, an individual examination of the equivalence of the vocational or professional qualification by the appropriate accreditation authority is stipulated. If the contents and duration of the training broadly coincide, then full recognition is granted. If the training contents differ to some degree, then partial recognition can be granted. Applicants can make up for inadequate knowledge by taking an aptitude test or adaptation course.

The European Commission has set itself the ambitious target of making all qualifications within the EU comparable in order to facilitate cross-border mobility.[1] The member states have undertaken to relate their national qualifications to one of the eight reference levels of a grid set out in the European Qualifications Framework. However, the referencing takes place at country level in the respective national qualification frameworks. This method does not necessarily guarantee comparability, since similar occupational titles may conceal differences in training quality; furthermore, national status hierarchies may simply be carried forward regardless of the actual content of the training.

In Germany and Austria, two countries with strong apprenticeship systems, the higher non-university professional qualifications (*Meister*, *Techniker*, and *Fachwirt*, as well as IT specialists) were allocated to levels 6 and 7, which in the rest of Europe are reserved for bachelor's and master's degrees (Nehls 2014). This ranking was highly controversial. The universities and the education ministries of Germany's 16 *Länder*, which are responsible for the universities, argued that these levels should be reserved for

[1] European Qualifications Framework: http://ec.europa.eu/eqf/home_en.htm.

university degrees only, whilst the trade unions and employers' associations argued the case for the equivalence of vocational and university qualifications.

Conclusions

As sources of legitimation for the assignment of social status, education and training systems are more strongly rooted in particular national traditions than other social institutions. Moreover, status differentiation within education systems is stabilized by a corresponding hierarchy of activities in the workplace, such that the early determination of employment trajectories by educational qualifications is often very difficult to rectify through further training for adults. Skill systems do not as yet appear to be converging, although they are constantly being subjected to reforms that have been influenced to some extent by experiences from other countries.

Research has systematized the differences in national skill systems with the aid of country typologies that have their origins in different disciplines but undoubtedly complement each other. Certain elements of skill systems, such as standardized vs market-oriented vocational training, elite school-based vs egalitarian school-based systems, general vs vocational education/training for open labour markets vs on-the-job systems in closed labour markets, are found in all the typologies. The systems are deeply rooted in cultural traditions, although these traditions dissipate quickly if they are not constantly reproduced by strong institutions.

Some of the typologies developed by institutional economists, which are based on the notion of the rational investor, whether that be the employee or the firm, have turned out to be too functionalist. Social institutions do not develop on the basis of a rational consensus; rather, they are the product of compromises, often reached after serious conflicts. In the typologies developed by political scientists, these conflicts and the varying degrees to which interests are taken into account, particularly in the lower segments of the training system, are given prominence. It has also been shown that the economic distinction between general and specific skills facilitates understanding of the economic background of training decisions at the micro-economic level. However, because of its structural blindness to the different levels of general and specific training, this distinction is completely unsuited to macro-level comparisons of different societies.

As a result of the increasing investment in early years education and lifelong learning for adults, today's education and training systems have become more complex. The sub-components of these systems, particularly the newly adapted ones, may certainly be organized around different principles, so that there is an unmistakable trend towards hybridization. Nevertheless, it remains difficult to emulate good experiences from other countries. This difficulty is evident from the many failed attempts to import the German apprenticeship system. What is often missing are the supporting institutions, such as a functioning social partnership, an occupations-based mode of work organization, or a vocational training system with a high reputation among all the relevant societal actors. However, elements of foreign models can be adapted to national structures. In order to learn from other countries, comprehensive information on the characteristics of these models must be available. In revealing the differences between national apprenticeship systems, more recent research has made a necessary contribution in this regard.

In the 1980s, education and training systems with highly developed apprenticeship schemes tended to be negatively viewed, particularly in sociological stratification theories, because of the early tracking they implied. Research has now revealed the positive effects of apprenticeship systems on productivity and innovative forms of work organization, as well as on the school-work transition. However, it should be borne in mind that other countries are producing a good supply of skilled labour by expanding their university systems, so the differences observed could certainly even out.

In the meantime differences remain, and these differences impact on key issues facing European governments but which are less well researched within studies of national skills systems. The most obvious is youth unemployment. The strong scar effects of long-term youth unemployment, i.e. the negative effects on life-time earnings that cannot be overcome, have prompted many countries to revitalize apprentice training. All studies show that countries with apprenticeship systems achieve the best results for the school-work transition. The reasons lie, firstly, in the high-quality training, during which trainees also acquire the increasingly important tacit knowledge that is imparted in the course of their lengthy industrial placements, and in the high degree of congruence between jobs and training. Secondly, apprenticeships tend to mitigate the insider-outside dilemma for young people. Apprentices are employees, and hence insiders, whose interests are defended by works councils and/or trade unions—just like those of the core workforce. Even in times of crisis, the social partners are anxious to recruit new trainees (Bosch 2015). In countries where training is predominantly school-based, it is not only the congruence between jobs and training that is missing but also the tacit knowledge, which adversely affects young people. When this situation is further compounded by strong dismissal protection for insiders, as in Southern Europe, then integration into the labour market becomes difficult. Analysing transitions over a ten-year period in the 1990s in 12 European countries, Müller and Gangl (2009) show that, independently of the economic cycle, young people in countries with strong apprenticeship systems are the quickest to find stable employment. In the liberal market economies of the United Kingdom and Ireland, the labour markets are so flexible that young people are speedily integrated into the labour market after initially high unemployment. It is in the Southern European countries that integration is most protracted; young people here have to contend with many years of high unemployment and unstable employment.

Education and training systems also have demonstrable effects on other key policy issues: work organization and productivity. Several studies have shown that a broadly based vocational training facilitates the delegation of tasks, the establishment of flatter hierarchies, and a reduction in the number of managerial and supervisory staff. Ryan et al. (2011, 14) found that 84% of production workers in the German mechanical engineering industry are skilled workers, compared with 52% in the United Kingdom. This approach has enabled German firms to restrict the share of employees in the bottom layer of management (master craftsmen, technicians, and supervisors) to 4% compared with 11% in the United Kingdom. This finding confirms those of earlier studies (Sorge and Warner 1986; Prais and Wagner 1988).

Given these and the other studies of national skills systems, the interest in education and training systems, and their relative efficiencies, comes as little surprise if they help reveal which achieves better results. Attempts, however, to transpose those better national systems can be fraught. The German and Swiss systems cannot be readily transplanted to countries in which firms are not prepared to invest in training, vocational training has low status, university education is already more than averagely developed, and the social partners are weak. Differences in national skills systems and their outcomes are likely to remain for a while yet therefore and will continue to need to be studied.

References

Allmendinger, J. (1989) 'Educational Systems and Labor Market Outcomes', *European Sociological Review*, 5(3): 231–250.

Beck, U. (1986) *Risikogesellschaft. Auf dem Weg in eine andere Moderne*, Frankfurt a. M.: Suhrkamp.

Becker, G. (1964) *Human Capital*, New York: Columbia University Press.

Bosch, G. (2015) 'The German Welfare State: From an Inclusive to an Exclusive Bismarckian Model', in D. Vaughan-Whitehead (ed.), *The European Social Model in Crisis: Is Europe Losing its Soul?* Cheltenham: Edward Elgar: 175–229.

Bosch, G. and Charest, J. (2010) 'Vocational Training: International Perspectives', in G. Bosch and J. Charest (eds), *Vocational Training: International Perspectives*, New York: Routledge: 1–26.

Bosch, G. and Philips, P. (2003) *Building Chaos*, London: Routledge.

Bosch, G. and Weinkopf, C. (eds) (2008) *Low-Wage Work in Germany*, New York: Russell Sage Foundation.

Bosch, G. and Zühlke-Robinet, K. (2003) 'Germany: The Labor Market in the German Construction Industry', in G. Bosch and P. Philips (eds), *Building Chaos*, London: Routledge: 48–72.

Braverman, H. (1974) *Labor and Monopoly Capital*, New York: Monthly Review Press.

Bremer, R. (2008) 'VET in the European Aircraft and Space Industry', *Journal of European Industrial Training*, 32(2/3): 187–200.

Brockmann, M. (2011) 'Higher Education Qualifications: Convergence and Divergence in Software Engineering and Nursing', in M. Brockmann, L. Clarke, and C. Winch (eds), *Knowledge, Skills and Competence in the European Labour Market*, London: Routledge: 120–135.

Brockmann, M., Clarke, L. and Winch, C. (2013) 'Implementing the EQF: English as Distinct from Continental Bricklaying Qualifications', in L. Deitmer, U. Hauschildt, F. Rauner, and H. Zelloth (eds), *The Architecture of Innovative Apprenticeship*, Dordrecht: Springer International: 122–126.

Carré, F., Tilly, C., Van Klaveren, M., and Voss-Dahm, D. (2010) 'Retail Jobs in Comparative Perspective', in J. Gautié and J. Schmitt (eds), *Low-Wage Work in the Wealthy World*, New York: Russell Sage Foundation: 211–268.

Esping-Andersen, G. (2002) 'A Child-Centred Social Investment Strategy', in G. Esping-Andersen (ed.), *Why we need a New Welfare State*, Oxford: Oxford University Press: 26–67.

Estevez-Abe, M., Iversen T., and Soskice D. (2001) 'Social Protection and the Formation of Skills: A Reinterpretation of the Welfare State', in P. A. Hall and D. Soskice (eds), *Varieties of capitalism*, New York: Oxford University Press: 145–183.

European Commission (2003) *Human Capital in a Global and Knowledge Based Economy*, Luxembourg: European Commission.

Evans, S. and Bosch, G. (2012) 'Apprenticeships in London: Boosting Skills in a City Economy—With Comment on Lessons from Germany', OECD Local Economic and Employment Development (LEED) Working Papers 2012/08, OECD, Paris.

Fernández-Macías, E. (2012) 'Job Polarization in Europe? Changes in the Employment Structure and Job Quality, 1995–2007', *Work and Occupations*, 39(2): 157–182.

Greinert, W.-D. (2004) 'European Vocational Training Systems: Some Thought on the Theoretical Context of their Historical Development', *European Journal of Vocational Training*, 32: 18–25.

Holmes, C. and Mayhew, K. (2012) *The Changing Shape of the UK: Job Market and its Implications for the Bottom Half of Earners*, London: Resolution Foundation.

Iversen, T. and Stephens, J. D. (2008) 'Partisan Politics, the Welfare State, and Three Worlds of Human Capital Formation', *Comparative Political Studies*, 41(4/5): 614.

Kleiner, M. M. (2006) *Licensing Occupations: Ensuring Quality or Restricting Competition?*, Kalamazoo: W. E. Upjohn Institute for Employment Research.

Lynch, L. M. (1994) 'Introduction to "Training and the Private Sector"', in L. M. Lynch (ed), *Training and the Private Sector*, Chicago: University Press of Chicago Press: 1–24.

Müller, W. and Gangl, M. (2009) *Transitions from Education to Work in Europe*, Oxford: Oxford University Press.

Müller, W. and Shavit, Y. (1998) 'The Institutional Embeddedness of the Stratification Process: A Comparative Study of Qualifications and Occupations in Thirteen Countries', in W. Müller and Y. Shavit (eds), *From School to Work*, Oxford: Oxford University Press: 1–48.

Nehls, H. (2014) 'Europäischer und Deutscher Qualifikationsrahmen', *WSI Mitteilungen*, 1: 70–73.

OECD (2013) *OECD Skills Outlook 2013: First Results from the Survey of Adult Skills*, Paris: OECD.

Philips, P. (2003) 'Dual Worlds: The Two Growth Paths in US Construction, in G. Bosch and P. Philips (eds), *Building Chaos*, London: Routledge: 161–187.

Prais, S. J. and Wagner, K. (1988) 'Productivity and Management: The Training of Foremen in Britain and Germany', *National Institute Economic Review*, 23: 34–45.

Rubery, J. and Grimshaw, D. (2003. *The Organisation of Employment*, Houndsmill: Palgrave Macmillan.

Ryan, P., Backes-Gellner, U., Teuber, S., and Wagner, K. (2013) 'Apprentice Pay in Britain, Germany and Switzerland: Institutions, Market Forces, Market Power', *European Journal of Industrial Relations*, 19(3): 201–220.

Ryan, P., Wagner, K., Teuber, S., and Backes-Gellner, U. (2011) 'Financial Aspects of Apprenticeship Training in Germany, Great Britain and Switzerland', *Arbeitspapier 241*, Düsseldorf: Hans Böckler Stiftung.

Sengenberger, W. (1987) *Struktur und Funktionsweise von Arbeitsmärkten*, Frankfurt/New York: Campus Verlag.

Sorge, A. and M. Warner (1986) *Comparative Factory Organisation*, Aldershot: Gower.

Streeck, W. (1992) *Social Institutions and Economic Performance*, London: Sage Publications.

Streeck, W. (2012) 'Skills and Politics: General and Specific', in M. R. Busemeyer and C. Trampusch (eds), *The Political Economy of Collective Skill Formation*, Oxford: Oxford University Press, 317–352.

Verdier, E. (2013) 'Lifelong Learning Regimes versus Vocational Education and Training Systems in Europe: The Growing Hybridisation of National Models', in J. Germen-Janmaat and P. Méhaut (eds), *The Dynamics and Social Outcomes of Education Systems*, Houndmills: Palgrave: 70–93.

Wiborg, S. and Cort, P. (2010) 'The Vocational Education and Training System in Denmark: Innovations and Results', in G. Bosch and J. Charest (eds), *Vocational Training—International Perspectives*, London: Routledge: 84–109.

CHAPTER 21

SKILL ECOSYSTEMS

JOHN BUCHANAN, PAULINE ANDERSON, AND GAIL POWER

INTRODUCTION

SKILL ecosystems are defined as regional or sectoral social formations in which human capability is developed and deployed for productive purposes (Finegold 1999). Their basic elements are business settings and associated business models, institutional/policy frameworks, modes of engaging labour, the structure of jobs, as well as the level of skills and systems for their formation (Buchanan et al. 2001). The defining features of this analytical tradition are a concern with coordination failures (i.e. not just market and/or government failure), a non-linear approach to causal analysis, and a concern with workforce development arrangements at sub- as well as supra-national level.

The recent interest in skill ecosystems represents the latest manifestation of a long-standing tradition of skills analysis: the importance of understanding the context or settings within which skills are developed and used. Researchers working in this tradition explicitly build on labour process theory, comparative political economy, and heterodox labour economics. Its immediate roots lie in critical engagement with mainstream analyses and policies that define most skills issues and problems as essentially side supply related, i.e. as concerning questions of education and training, and the qualifications arising from both. In many countries and amongst international organizations such as the OECD, the 'necessity' to raise education levels or lose out in the modern globalized world has taken on a status approaching that of (an assumed) self-evident truth. Experimentation with skill ecosystem reform has been supported by a small band of policymakers unconvinced or sceptical of this policy orthodoxy. In essence, researchers and policymakers in this tradition seek to understand skills in context, and are concerned with the wider array of determinants associated with workforce development and how this is connected with particular trajectories of social and economic development.

This chapter is structured as follows. It begins with a short account of the analytical and policy origins of this tradition. New knowledge generated by skill ecosystem researchers has tended to come from applied, policy-based research. It is because of this, most attention is devoted to consideration of experiences in three English-speaking countries which have launched an array of initiatives informed—explicitly or implicitly—by the concept in the last two decades: Australia, the United Kingdom, and the United States. An account of the analytical and policy significance of these experiences is provided. Whilst this tradition has generated important analytical insights, the chapter highlights how its lessons for skills policy are more significant.

Analytical and Policy Origins

Understanding the connection between skill and economic development is as old as the discipline of modern political economy. Smith's *Wealth of Nations* (1776) opens with observations about skill levels, work organization, and productivity in the oft-cited example of the pin factory. Since then the topic has been the subject of almost continuous—and often controversial—analytical interest. Whilst Smith noted the empirical benefit of designing work around lower average skill levels, other analytical traditions have examined the benefits of rising skill levels for productivity. In the 1980s a literature emerged that examined the relationship between skills and economic performance at national level. It was especially concerned with what were termed national skill equilibria (e.g. Finegold and Soskice 1988). This literature's major strength was that skills and economic performance were not considered in isolation. It was constellations of policy and practice that were critical. Key variables of interest included the nature of product and labour markets, as well as business organization and management strategy. Its core thesis was simple: countries with what was described as having a high skill equilibrium performed better than low skill equilibrium nations. The policy challenge was clear: high-skill, high-wage economies could only be created where a broad range of initiatives (constituting a different policy mix) achieved widespread and thorough reform. Changes in skills levels alone would be inadequate. This strand in the literature provided another powerful challenge to the 'high skills leads to high growth' narrative.

The skill equilibrium thesis was not without its problems. Prime amongst these problems was the totalizing conception of national economies at the core of the analysis. Entire countries were characterized as being either 'high' or 'low' skill in nature. Longstanding histories of leading and laggard sectors in all nations, however, sat uncomfortably with the central tenet of an all pervasive national skill equilibrium. The notion of skill ecosystems emerged out of reflections on this analytical anomaly. The term was first coined by David Finegold in 1999 and used by Crouch et al. (1999) soon after. This nascent analytical current built on the strengths of the skills equilibria literature about the importance of context, but took seriously the reality of diverse skills clusters within countries. The analogy of distinct 'ecosystems' was used to defined different ensembles of skill existing within and across national boundaries. This analytical category drew thoughtfully on one of the key ideas of the life sciences (i.e. ecology) to capture the often organic and dynamic of relations associated with the skills political-economic development nexus.

Finegold's particular interests were with high-skill ecosystems such as the information technology and bio-technology clusters in California. These clusters were regarded as important potential sources of innovation and growth, not just for regions but for their host nations. If the sources of prosperity were to be understood and promoted, the challenge was not to understand how nations move from a 'low skill' to a 'high skill' equilibrium but, rather, how to understand and support high skill ecosystems. The ecosystems analysed were not just a geographic or sectoral descriptor; for Finegold they constituted a distinct organizational form. Firms came together through intermediaries to pursue initiatives such as improved technical training that were of mutual benefit. Finegold argued, however, that the main way professionals and technicians developed their skills was through informal means such as working with others in their networks to overcome technical challenges. The high skill ecosystem as a distinct organizational form facilitated this mode of knowledge creation and diffusion. As a result, Silicon Valley (and Stanford University) came to constitute the epicentre of innovation in the United States—not only in aerospace and defence related industries but more generally in technology and design sectors.

The academic literature on skill ecosystems is growing but limited (cf. Anderson and Warhurst 2012; Hall 2011; Hall and Lansbury 2006; Payne 2008, 2011). The idea has had greater impact in shaping policy debate and experimentation in Australia and, to a lesser extent, the United Kingdom (especially Scotland). As a matter of practice tacitly informed by these ideas, the United States has also generated a wealth of experience. These developments have attracted the attention of international organizations, especially the OECD (cf. Buchanan et al. 2010; Eddington and Toner 2012; OECD 2012). Whilst the original academic literature on the topic was primarily interested in understanding (and promoting) high skill ecosystems, the policy debates and experimentation in the three countries noted have primarily been concerned with reforming ecosystems associated with workers with low and middle levels of skill (see Buchanan et al. 2001). In Australia and the United Kingdom especially, skill ecosystem analysis has emerged as a distinctive intellectual undercurrent that endeavours to provide a new way of thinking about and reforming what is described in these nations as vocational education and training (VET) and intermediate skills.

Most of this chapter refers to developments in Australia, the United Kingdom, and the United States. This focus is not because these countries offer superior ways of thinking about or nurturing either employment or skills. On the contrary, all three countries have deep problems with their business models and especially their labour markets (cf. Buchanan et al. 2013, 2014). Many other countries have been experimenting with similar types of initiatives, often in different domains of policy and practice. The burgeoning literature on clusters in innovation is one example (cf. Ramstad 2009). We confine our attention to the recent emergence of skill ecosystem approaches to analysis, policy and practice in these countries because the subject matter of clusters and ecological dynamics has explicitly focused on skills and training.

Australia: A Supply-Focused Mainstream Leavened Slightly by an Array of Demand-Side Experiments

Since the mid-1970s Australia's labour market has been transformed. Well-defined occupational and internal labour markets for those workers with intermediate skills have steadily eroded after decades of 'restructuring' (ACIRRT 1999). This transformation has coincided with rising levels of higher education and the total recasting of workforce development for those with intermediate skills (Watson 2003; Buchanan et al. 2004). The key development in skill formation has been the shift to a so-called 'demand driven system'. The older skills regime, especially the apprenticeship system for the skilled trades, was criticized as suffering from 'producer capture'. Teachers in publicly funded technical education colleges were accused of providing skills they thought were important—not what 'industry needed'. To 'teacher-proof' the system, vocational development of people at intermediate level is now defined on the basis of industry determined 'units of competence'. These are highly disaggregated specifications of tasks individuals should be able to perform. It is assumed these can be acquired in any combination any employer deems relevant. To help drive the system, public technical education funding has been recast. Previously block grants were made to longstanding institutes of technical education. Now funds are allocated by competitive funding models and open to other 'registered training organizations'. Increasingly, funding is being allocated by means of 'student entitlements' (i.e. quasi vouchers) to ensure money follows 'demand' and not 'producer preference'.

Whilst the key features of this system are now entrenched, its emergence has not been without controversy. Questions concerning the coherence in skill formation and the quality of the skills offerings have been constant and are rising (OECD 2009). Most importantly, because the system was formally 'demand driven', nearly all attention has focused on supply issues—especially the creation of a 'training market' consisting of thousands of private VET providers. Since the late 1990s, however, the assumption that 'skill demand' is unproblematic and self-evident has been increasingly questioned. What if demand itself is in part, if not *the* major problem with skill formation and use? Whilst a concern with skill ecosystems has not been the central focus of Australian skills policy, the growing interest in demand side aspects of the system has provided the context for considerable interest in the reform of skill ecosystem.

A number of state and national government programmes supporting skill ecosystem reform ran between 2003 and 2011. Over time the object of concern shifted to better 'workforce development'—a term regarded as more accessible but still retaining the central concern with the connection between business and skill development. Most recently 'workforce development' has slipped back to the old concern with boosting the number of people with qualifications. Government funded support to reform demand side problems has all but disappeared in Australia today. Three major programmes collectively supported around 100 different skill ecosystem reform initiatives between 2002 and 2011. Whilst there were some differences between these programmes, there were strong commonalities in how they supported skill ecosystem reform. By and large, all these initiatives:

- were directed at addressing both supply and demand determinants of skills problems and improving business performance as well as outcomes for individuals
- involved interventions directed at changing work organization, employment arrangements and business strategy as well as training design and provision
- typically were funded for less than two years
- were overseen by multi-stakeholder reference groups
- involved engaging one full-time project manager/project officer
- occurred in a diverse range of sectors including: information and communication technology, water, land conservation, horse racing, fruit and vegetable supply chain, defence support industries, forestry, dairy manufacturing, aged care, disability support services, mental health services.

Whilst documentation on these initiatives is limited, four distinct findings of fact about the nature and reform of skill ecosystems can be discerned. The first is that the nature of skill ecosystems and the problems they face are often difficult to define. Understanding skills in context has intuitive appeal. The challenge is clarifying just what it is about 'context' that is problematic. The second is that effective skill ecosystem reform requires leaders with deep knowledge of their domain as well as high-level analytical and political/organizational skills. All evaluations of all Australian programmes identified the crucial role of project coordinators or facilitators. Evesson and Oxenbridge (2013) argue that the key role necessary for success is people who work as 'integrators'. The best occupants of this role appear to be people with deep knowledge of, and who are widely respected in, the domain of interest. Such people are hard to find. The third distinct finding is that establishing social coalitions to achieve skill ecosystem reform is difficult and time consuming. By definition, a skill ecosystem has many components. Only rarely can one part be changed in isolation. Building partnerships between relevant agents is difficult. Key players in a sector or region are often competitors as well as colleagues. Building trust amongst such players takes time and considerable skill. Few of the 100 or so pilot initiatives had either the time or personnel necessary to achieve enduring change. Finally, only rarely do skill ecosystem reform campaigns result in new and better local 'skill equilibriums'. Current funding models do not nourish even successful initiatives. Even if all these matters are successfully addressed, there is no guarantee of initiatives enduring unless, to use Finegold's term, the reformed skill ecosystem is 'nourished'. The absence of such 'nourishment' was noted in the evaluations of all the recent government supported initiatives (cf. Windsor and Alcorso 2008; Eddington and Toner 2012; Evesson and Oxenbridge 2013).

However, a number of autonomous initiatives have emerged from within particular sectors and regions. In these initiatives, local employers have endeavoured to become collectively self-reliant in ensuring workforce development meets their business needs. One of the most sustained of these initiatives occurred in the Australian dairy sector. Farmers in this sector have placed a levy on themselves to resource the development of new workforce capability. This levy supports four pilot studies—two in two dairy farming regions, one in dairy manufacturing and one in services providers (i.e. milk machine mechanics)—to identify how better to configure resources to ensure the industry is able to recruit and develop the labour it needs for the future. In all pilots, whilst training was one aspect of the initiative it was not the sole or even major concern (AWPA 2013). A related initiative amongst the dairy farmers in Victoria's Alpine Valleys is tackling the most challenging issue of all: making it easier for young farmers from non-farming families to enter the industry by way of accessing the capital needed to buy a farm and revitalizing dairy districts. Again this initiative is organized on a collective and not on a farm-by-farm basis, by the farmers and local councils (Bridge 2014). A regionally based initiative has also been emerging in the Narrabri district of northwest New South Wales. Employers from agriculture, construction, and the local council devised a labour demand calendar to help coordinate job offerings, thereby turning seasonally based fragments of jobs into, potentially, a year round offering of employment for local workers. In addition the employer- and community-based 'Make it work' committee promotes a local 'employer of choice' programme to improve the quality of jobs offered more generally in the district. Whilst most of the achievements so far have been modest, in 2013 the initiative became the model that five other districts are now emulating.

New Directions in Skills Planning

Historically, workforce planning has involved making projections about the likely changes in the industry and occupational nature of employment in the future. Whilst modelling techniques vary in sophistication, their underlying assumption has been that past trends can help predict the future. Education and training providers were then informed of the likely demands for their services. Implicit in this was the assumption labour demand should be taken as a given, and those concerned with skills should gear up to meet projected demand. Recognition about the importance of understanding and managing skills in context had a major influence in skills planning at national, sectoral, and regional level in Australia in the period 2008 to 2014.

At the heart of the new approach was noting that the nature of labour demand is far from self-evident. The challenge is not so much to predict specific skill sets which will be needed but rather what capacities and capabilities are best developed now to ensure the country has the capacity to adapt rapidly as circumstances change and, where possible, shape the way jobs are defined. Between 2008 and 2014 the national body responsible for advising on changing skill requirements—the Australian Productivity and Workforce Authority (AWPA, and formerly Skills Australia)—worked on this new approach to problem definition. AWPA oversaw a three-year programme of scenario development and refinement. The scenarios specified plausible but starkly different medium and longer-term futures. The challenge for policy then became how to best equip Australia to navigate the future, no matter which scenario or combination of scenarios prevailed. Similar approaches emerged at state level, especially in South Australia and Western Australia (TASC 2013; DTWD 2013). Most interesting of all is the growth of sometimes quite sophisticated planning practices at regional and local level concerned not just with 'workforce planning—but planning for workforce development' that help identify a wide array factors that need to be monitored and shaped to address skills problems.

These recent experiences must be kept in perspective. They have never been 'system defining'. At best they have constituted a novel undercurrent of policy and practical innovation. Whilst the government-funded pilots spawned a wealth of novel experimentation, little enduring change has been achieved. The autonomous initiatives in particular sectors and regions appear to provide more promising models of change. The defining feature has been groups of employers prepared to share in responsibility for becoming collectively self-reliant in meeting their workforce development needs. These initiatives have survived despite, not because of, current funding models. Unless these ideas mature and begin to reshape funding models to support the development of building adaptive capacity as opposed to issuing *de facto* vouchers for a 'training market', examples of successful and enduring skill ecosystem reform are unlikely to flourish.

United Kingdom (Especially Scotland): Policy in Search of Effective Practice

The United Kingdom comprises what Raffe et al. (1999, 9) best describe as 'four "national" football teams': Scotland, England, Northern Ireland, and Wales. The Scottish education system has been historically held in high esteem (cf. Paterson 2003) and is regarded as one of the 'nation's defining institutions'—producing a distinctive flavour (cf. Davie 1961; Paterson 1997) that has strengthened following devolution in 1999 (Humes and Bryce 2003), notably in post-16 provision (White and Yonwin 2004; Keating 2005; Gallacher 2007). The Scottish Government has been especially eager to realize its ambition of a 'smarter, more successful, Scotland' (Scottish Executive 2001). Futureskills Scotland was established to ensure progression towards this vision, operating as a feed into policymakers, and was an important catalyst in recent skill ecosystem reform. In contrast to Australia, this reform has been a matter of interest at the highest levels of the Scottish Government. Unlike Australia, however, practical experimentation and impact on skills planning has been limited. Employer engagement remains an issue and, whilst there is an unequivocal will to make something happen, the infrastructure necessary to effect actual change is yet to be established. Initiatives associated with the idea, despite these failings, remain a continuing force in the reform of post-compulsory education, most notably in the area of intermediate-level skills and qualifications.

Throughout the 1990s and 2000s, as with the rest of the United Kingdom, Scotland devoted considerable resources to boosting education levels as the primary policy response to the challenges of 'globalization' and the 'new economy' (Anderson and Warhurst 2012). These initiatives largely ignored demand side factors increasingly recognized as the primary generators of most skill problems (e.g. Buchanan et al. 2001; Keep 2002; Warhurst and Findlay 2012). The limits of the supply side strategy were particularly stark in Scotland. Scotland has one of the highest higher education participation rates amongst OECD countries—consistently higher than England and now standing at 56% (SFC 2012, 4)—and yet the prolonged, large-scale injection of more 'knowledge workers' into the labour market has not improved productive performance. A report for Futureskills Scotland (Felstead 2007) was blunt on this matter. It found that despite relative success in producing a highly qualified labour force, 57% of all Scottish jobs demanded fewer than three months' training, 31% did not require any qualifications, job polarization had increased, and over-qualification and skills under-utilization were endemic. The skill content of Scottish jobs was lower than the rest of the United Kingdom and, what is more, had declined over the preceding decade. Stimulating demand and ensuring employers made better use of employee skills, Felstead's report proposed, should be a policy priority. An allied report prepared by Payne (2008) argued that Scottish policymakers could learn from emerging Australian experiences with skill ecosystem reform. UK policymakers, he urged, should emulate this approach because simply boosting the supply of people with higher-level qualifications did not engage the key skills issues such as skills under-utilization, job polarization, and poor training and progression pathways.

In 2007 a new government took office. One of its first activities was to produce a new, distinctly Scottish skills' strategy. *Skills for Scotland: A Lifelong Skills Strategy* (Scottish Government 2007b) unequivocally embraced skills ecosystem thinking, drawing heavily on the work of Payne and a range of related Futureskills Scotland reports:

> Simply adding more skills to the workforce will not secure the full benefit for our economy unless employers and individuals maximize the benefits that they can derive from these skills. Furthermore, how skills interact with the other drivers of productivity, such as capital investment and innovation, is crucial. Equally,

> investment in capital and innovation will be most productive when it is supported by a well-trained workforce. We need to move beyond a focus on meeting the current demand for skills and tackle the issues which underlie and drive demand. We need the skills to facilitate sustainable economic growth but we also need our firms to be ambitious and demanding users of skills. (Scottish Government 2007a, 13)

Skill ecosystems thinking has been badged in Scotland as 'skills utilization' and focuses on developing individuals *and* workplaces in order to increase productivity, improve job satisfaction and stimulate investment and innovation (Scottish Government 2010, 6). The Scottish Government attempted to bring this new approach to life in a number of ways. A new national skills agency for Scotland, Skills Development Scotland, was established. The Scottish Government signed a joint communiqué with the Scottish Trades Union Congress (STUC) committing the parties to pursue the main aims of the new skills strategy (Scottish Government/STUC 2008). To foster communication and strategic cohesion between key partners, the Scottish Government discussed with business leaders and other stakeholders how they could take forward the skills utilization agenda. One of the key outcomes was the establishment of the Skills Utilization Leadership Group, chaired by the Cabinet Secretary.

As a direct result of the work of the Skills Utilization Leadership Group, the Scottish Funding Council called for proposals for skills utilization pilot, exploration or development projects (SFC 2008). Just less than £3m was awarded to 12 projects (SFC 2009, 9–11).[1] Examples of projects included: working with business leaders in the creative industries through their professional body to examine ways in which creative thinking and design processes could be harnessed to improve productivity; working with the Scottish dairy industry to address problems of attracting and retaining staff through workforce development; and a regional college/university knowledge transfer network linked to improving rural business skills.

Important insights into the operation and impact of these pilots were provided in an interim evaluation (Payne 2011). As with the Australian experiences, the short funding time frame of the pilot studies was noted as severely restricting their impact (UKCES 2010; Payne 2011). Evaluation also highlighted problems of programme design and employer engagement. Colleges and/or universities were the lead agents in the pilot reform initiatives; unsurprisingly therefore most projects tended to revert to skill supply/development solutions. Future initiatives, it was proposed, should focus on bringing together a broader range of actors—with employer engagement and job redesign/work reorganization priority areas. As with the evaluations of the Australian experience, the importance of building networks 'in a particular sector, region, or supply chain' and securing key stakeholder engagement were identified as being especially important (Payne 2011, 52). The evaluation did not just identify the need for 'more employer engagement'; it also emphasized the importance of cultivating *appropriate* business

[1] The Scottish Funding Council is the funding body for Scotland's colleges and higher education institutions.

engagement. In particular Payne questioned the benefit of engaging with employers who were neither ambitious nor demanding users of skills, and disinclined to move up the value chain. This last insight has proved to be prescient. Employer engagement has emerged as arguably the most problematic aspect of skill ecosystem reform. The Skills Utilization Leadership Group was disbanded in 2010; employers are still grappling with the term, let alone concept, of 'skill utilization' (Warhurst and Findlay 2012); and any infrastructure to meaningfully engage employers at the local/regional level remains conspicuously absent.

New Directions in Post-Compulsory Education and Intermediate Skills

Engagement with employers has proven difficult but a concern with skill ecosystem reform has remained an ongoing element of the changes in Scotland. A key area of reform has been developing intermediate-level skills for intermediate-level jobs. Beyond the traditional trades there has been limited and, recently, declining public support for quality jobs in this part of the labour market (e.g. Canning and Lang 2004; Gallacher et al. 2004; Anderson 2014). Colleges in Scotland are an important source in middle skill supply but what OECD and other headline data typically fail to reveal is that one- and two-year sub-batchelor's certificates/diplomas (HNCs/HNDs) delivered in colleges account for 40% of Scotland's higher education participation rate (SFC 2012, 13). In the past, these certificates/diplomas provided the middle-level qualifications integral to ecosystems based around intermediate skill levels. Changes in the content of HNCs/HNDs and a policy focus on large-scale articulation to, often less prestigious, universities, has meant that these qualifications are variable and best conceived as on a continuum from vocational to transitional—fulfilling neither function particularly well (cf. Gallacher and Ingram 2012). Meeting middle skill demand in key growth/comparative advantage sectors is also proving problematic. Middle skill demand in the renewables sector is of particular interest. The Scottish Government is committed to become 'the renewables powerhouse of Europe' (Scottish Government 2011a, 8) and the green economy provides more 'decent' jobs at intermediate level than other sectors (Muro et al. 2011).

Reflecting the realization that investment in education and training for middle skilled jobs has lagged, policymakers are now addressing issues associated with these jobs. In 2013 the Scottish Government established *The Commission for Developing Scotland's Young Workforce* (Scottish Government 2013). The Commission is charged with producing a set of recommendations on the future direction of Scottish VET to help ensure that young people develop the requisite skills to move into sustainable, high quality jobs. These recommendations will: focus on the development of high-quality VET in key sectors identified in the Scottish Government's economic strategy as most promising in terms of growth/comparative advantage (e.g. Scottish Government 2011b); provide guidance on how to better engage employers and other key partners; include suggestions on how to improve Modern Apprenticeships; take proper cognizance of post-compulsory education reforms (e.g. Post-16 Education (Scotland) Act of 2013); and make recommendations to support Scotland's evolving regionalization agenda (e.g. Skills Investment Plans, Regional Skills Assessments, Regional Outcome Agreements). Colleges, often regarded as the 'Cinderella Service' (cf. Randle and Brady 1997), have now got a VIP ticket to the regionalization ball and have been clustered/merged into distinct geographic areas. There will be 'a duty on regional college boards and regional boards to consult representatives of local communities and local employers' (Scottish Government 2012b, 10). Regionalization endeavours to improve local and regional decision-making and encourage a 'bottom-up' sectoral skills policy/practice approach to economic, social and workforce development. These developments mean that, by a remarkable coincidence, the indirect end point of workforce development reform in Scotland is very similar to that of Australia's situation where there is growing interest in rethinking the content of intermediate qualifications. Whilst the influence of skill ecosystem on skills planning is not as advanced as in Australia, the experimentation with skill ecosystems in Scotland has contributed to a positive legacy for the forgotten middle skilled jobs.

The United States: Dynamic Innovations on the Margins of a Fragmented System

Skill ecosystems thinking is not immediately discernible in US policy discourse—despite the fact that the term was coined by David Finegold of the United States. On closer inspection, however, an abundance of effective skill ecosystem reform in practice and interesting policy developments are evident; these developments are partly linked to the infrastructure provided in, and a series of initiatives following, the Workforce Investment Act (WIA) of 1998. Non-profit organizations feature prominently in US developments and have been adept in helping the most disadvantaged, often tapping into government funding sources. In contrast to Scotland and Australia, the United States has been comparatively successful in engaging employers and other key stakeholders. Recent promising innovations have a distinct regional/sectoral focus. Yet it is important to view these initiatives in context. Innovations remain a tiny feature of the overall, still fragmented, system of workforce development in the United States. The absence of a national skills policy is problematic and financial cuts have been severe in recent years. Developments in the United States are therefore best understood as effective skill ecosystems practice on the periphery of a system in dire need of sustained funding injections and a coordinated skills policy. Despite such drawbacks many dynamic innovations continue and evolve.

Whilst the United Kingdom was still pursuing skill supply policies, the United States moved to a 'demand-led' workforce development system in the late 1990s—deeming the old system no longer fit for purpose in the context of a rapidly changing global economy. Federal/state/local provision of services was fragmented and ill-equipped to produce the increasing level—and changing nature—of skills required of the new century. The new infrastructure has nurtured considerable innovation and experimentation. Much of this innovation, however, has focused less on large-scale upskilling and more on moving disadvantaged/displaced workers into paid employment, much of it low skilled in nature (Osterman 2007). Low-skilled work/low levels of educational attainment are inextricably linked to America's in-work poverty problem (cf. Osterman and Shulman 2011; Bureau of Labor Statistics 2013). The United States has not kept pace with the demand for higher-level skills since the late 1970s (Autor 2011). Once the world-leading producer of higher education graduates (Freeman 2010), anxiety about the potential oversupply of graduate skills in the early 1970s quickly transferred to anxiety about their undersupply—with an ever-declining US participate rate in comparison to other OECD counties (Schurman and Soares 2010). Higher education non-completion is especially problematic, further exacerbating America's diminishing capacity to innovate in high-tech sectors (Freeman 2010). In response to this situation the Obama Administration declared that 'by 2020, America would once again have the highest proportion of college graduates in the world' (US Department of Education 2012, 1). This ambitious target is in the context of creating more flexible, affordable higher education and training pathways through the life course, linked to industry demand—especially in STEM (science, technology, engineering and mathematics) subject areas.

After its introduction by the Clinton Administration in 1998, The WIA was formally implemented in 2000. WIA is the largest single source of federal funding for workforce development activities. Replacing the Job Training Partnership Act (JTPA), WIA set out to create an infrastructure to 'improve the quality of the workforce, reduce welfare dependency, and enhance the productivity and competitiveness of the Nation' (WIA 1998). This infrastructure, Clagett (2006) explains, was specifically designed to support a demand-led workforce investment system, better coordinate and integrate services for jobseekers and employers and, importantly, transfer powers from federal to state level. This transfer of power increased the potential to respond flexibly to local circumstances.

The Department of Labor administers WIA with funds distributed to states. WIA requires state governors to establish State Workforce Investment Boards, comprising a range of key stakeholders including state labour and business representatives—stipulating that the majority of board members must be drawn from the business community and a chair selected from this group. Governors are also required to identify local workforce investment areas and establish local workforce investment boards (LWIBs), made up of a similar grouping of local stakeholder partners. One-Stop centres/shops are an important mechanism for streamlining and consolidating mandatory services (Blank 2009). One-Stops have been created in all local areas of the United States and boards assigned responsibility for overseeing mandated and other 'desirable' local partners (John J. Heldrich Center for Workforce Development 2002, 5). There are now just fewer than 600 distinct LWIBs and 3,000 One-Stops operating in the United States, and the National Association for Workforce Boards point to the 13,000 volunteer members of the business community serving on LWIBs.

Heinrich et al.'s (2008, 49) non-experimental evaluation of WIA notes a positive net impact 'in almost all states'. The Government Accountability Office (GAO) highlighted 14 initiatives generally regarded as exemplars of innovative practice in employer/WIB collaboration (GAO 2012)—many of which were notably supported by additional employer cash or in-kind support. Employer engagement with One-Stops, however, tends to be primarily around recruiting low-skilled workers (Blank 2009, 8), with private sector employer engagement limited (Cottingham and Besharov 2011). WIA's 'work first' ethos has also meant that issues concerning job quality are often ignored and career progression opportunities limited (Conway and Rademacher 2003). What is more, LWIB employer representatives are not always necessarily the 'best' or most appropriate (Holzer 2011). Edelman et al. (2011) argue that despite such difficulties policy innovation at state level in particular has been 'impressive'. WIA has helped institutionalize the link between workforce development and economic development (Bray et al. 2011). This link has supported federal initiatives such as *Workforce Innovation in Regional Economic Development (WIRED)*, targeting labour market areas in high-growth sectors within and across state borders (US Department of Labor 2008). The final report of the California Innovation Corridor initiative, led by the California Space Authority, underlines the success of the WIRED approach (Conner 2010, 5). Certainly, there is increasing academic and policymaking consensus that sector and/or cluster-based initiatives are delivering fruitful results (cf. Conway and Rademacher 2003; Froy and Giguère 2010; King and Heinrich 2011). This approach can support multi-employer engagement, address job quality issues, map career pathways to middle- and highskilled jobs, join up networks, foster regional and cross-state cooperation, and further align workforce development to economic development, i.e. generally start to address whole skill ecosystems (National Governors Association 2008).

The relatively small size of the US welfare system in comparison to Scotland and Australia may go some way to explain why non-profit initiatives/organizations, especially those supported by charitable foundations, are a prominent feature in US workforce development. The sustained work of non-profits is impressive. Philanthropedia recently spotlighted 16 'outstanding' US workforce development non-profits, including the National Skills Coalition, The Aspen Institute, the Wisconsin Regional Training Partnership, and Year Up. These initiatives/organizations envelop practitioner-based activities, policy/advocacy activities, and research-as-catalysts activities. Some initiatives are directed at system, not just project-based, change. The Annie E. Casey Foundation (AECF), for instance, set up its Jobs Initiative in 1995. It invested $30m dollars supporting disadvantaged families in securing sustainable jobs with career progression paths, concentrating its work in six US cities and aiming for 'system change': 'We care about system change because, whilst innovative employment projects are important, we simply cannot address the needs of thousands of workers and businesses without changing the rules of the game' (Hebert 2010, 6).

Evidence of changing the rules of the game was clear in its Milwaukee Jobs Initiative, which was later incorporated into the Wisconsin Regional Training Partnership. Systemic transformations included the introduction of effective workplace reorganization and adoption of 'high road' strategies in the healthcare, manufacturing, hospitality, and technology sectors—with demonstrable benefits for employers and employees (Hebert et al. 2005). Although the AECF Jobs Initiative has now ended, its legacy is one of sustained system change (AECF 2007). There is no sign, moreover, that the work of a broad range of non-profits in the area of workforce development will wane. However, as many non-profits rely on government funding sources, recent spending cuts following the global economic downturn have come at a time when demand for services has risen (Boris et al. 2010).

Funding Squeeze and Renewed Interest in Middle Skills

A key problem for US workforce development is systemic underfunding (Biroonak and Kaleba 2010). Longer-term trends suggest a further funding squeeze, although the American Reinvestment and Recovery Act of 2009 provided some temporary respite (Decker and Berk 2011). Edelman et al. (2011) note that WIA Governors' Reserves have been disproportionately affected—reserves that allowed for experimentation and innovation. WIA was due to be reauthorized in 2003 but endures only under a Continuing Resolution (King and Heinrich 2011). The revised content of WIA when it is finally reauthorized is not inconsequential.

Notwithstanding impressive innovations at the margins, Jacobs (2013) argues that WIA is inextricably tied to remedial efforts at the low skills segment of the labour market and represents just one facet of a largely fragmented workforce development system which, despite claims to the contrary, is still far from 'demand-led'. Lerman (2010) points to the cost-effectiveness and impressive rate of return to US apprenticeships in comparison to other education/training options offered through WIA. The nature of apprenticeship training, he suggests, renders it an apt, effective vehicle for linking skills investment to business/economic growth. Despite the comparatively low proportion of apprentices in the United States (Steedman 2012), unsurprisingly given past political resistance (e.g. Reich 1998), apprenticeships are now being pushed as one solution to the US middle skills gap (Kochan et al. 2012; Lerman 2013). Indeed there is renewed interest in what Holzer and Lerman (2007) term America's *Forgotten Middle-Skilled Jobs*. Almost half of all US jobs are at middle-skill level and there is a widening middle-skills gap across a range of industrial sectors (Kochan et al. 2012). As part of a broader transformation of Careers and Technical Education (CTE) (US Department of Education 2012), community colleges, much as is happening in Scotland, are being manoeuvred centre stage in the fight to develop the right, and increasingly middle, skills for America's future (GPO 2010; Soares and Steigleder 2012; US Department of Education 2012). Helping to support the Obama Administration's 2020 higher education target, community colleges are seen as key players in addressing STEM demand. Community college fees are cheaper for individuals (an important factor in reducing non-completion rates) and college qualifications have a dual role as labour market 'tickets' and transitional qualifications (US Department of Education 2012). Employers, Osterman (2007, 127) points out, view community colleges in a much more positive light than community employment/training organizations—suggesting that the 'real center of gravity for the adult training system is America's roughly 1,200 community colleges'.

Conclusion: The Importance of the Content as well As the Context of Skill

At the heart of many skills problems is not so much market or government failure but the challenge of coordinating a wide array of practices and arrangements shaping the development and deployment of labour. Historically, education policy has assumed market failure and turned to public provision as a solution. Over time, the limits of government intervention have legitimized calls for market inspired solutions, with policy problems becoming narrowly defined challenges of appropriate 'market design'. Both responses are inadequate. There are more options available for solving problems of political-economic coordination than either 'markets' or 'states' with their allocative mechanisms of 'prices' or 'plans'. As has long been recognized, this binary conception of alternatives mis-specifies profoundly how societies function. These allocative mechanisms are not mutually exclusive; neither are they the only means of coordination. Within markets, enterprises do considerable conscious planning. Wherever possible, governments usually avoid relying on bureaucratic power; instead they work with and endeavour to shape (and not supersede) market operations. Occupational arrangements associated with the professions and recognized trades can provide a third logic of coordinating skill development and use (Freidson 2001).

The skill ecosystem literature and the initiatives associated with their reform are the latest variant of this more nuanced approach to understanding and engaging with reality. Critical to this understanding has been moving beyond the supply side bias that has characterized much analysis and policy concerned with skills in recent decades. In taking demand seriously this tradition is not just concerned with the quantity but also with the changing nature of labour demand. The initial research and policy work on skill ecosystems focused on the necessity of understanding skills in context. Each of the case study country experiences identified necessary but not sufficient conditions for reform to skill contexts required for effective change. In Australia, the autonomous initiatives of dairy farmers and employers in northwest New South Wales seeking greater collective self-reliance in the development and deployment of labour was identified as a key prerequisite to success. In the case of Scotland, strong leadership at the highest levels of government and the social partners was equally promising. The US technical and funding support for reform by organizations such as the Annie E. Casey Foundation provided serious sustained resources for reform. Ironically, all the elements for successful skill ecosystem reform are in existence across the case study countries, but they are not co-located. Without all the elements, co-existing enduring reform is hard to achieve. It is conceivable that the Narrabri employers and Australian dairy sectors could flourish if supported by Scottish-style peak-level political and stakeholder leadership and Annie E. Casey Foundation-style technical support. Given the findings of the literature so far, however, such an alignment of forces is unlikely in Australia, Scotland, or the United States anytime soon. Without such an alignment enduring, effective change will not occur.

This reality points to a deeper limitation of the skill ecosystem approach. Context is not neutral or self-evident as is implied by the 'ecosystem' metaphor taken from the life sciences. Recent experience with skill ecosystem reform in particular has highlighted that the matter of interest is probably more accurately understood as 'skill settlements' between various actors and their interests. When considered in these terms, a host of questions, only implicit when the issue is defined in terms of 'ecosystem', become manifest. What are the defining features of the settlement of interest? Who are the key parties? What is its character in terms of high-, intermediate-, and low-skill work? The foundation scholarly literature in this field focused on 'high skill ecosystems'. The applied literature, on the other hand, has examined attempts to reform arrangements associated with low and intermediate skills. These initiatives have shown starkly that the problem is not just one of modifying essentially healthy ecosystems. Rather, the reforms have hit considerable tacit resistance as they have run up against key features of the current skill settlements in particular sectors and regions—settlements with which many employers and governments are comfortable.

Ultimately, analysis and reform in this tradition will only advance to the extent the skill ecosystem approach engages with the nature and level of the skills nurtured or hindered by the settlements of interest. Most skills problems are not imperfections in an essentially sound context that need only minor remedies. Rather, most arise from the ways skills in demand are defined, used, and developed, and have their roots in the nature of the work concerned. Often the product and service itself needs to change as well as the way it is produced if the underlying 'skill problem' is to solved (Evesson et al. 2009). Traces of this broader way of defining analytical problems and reform agendas are already emerging in the research being undertaken into modern notion of vocation and occupation (e.g. Bretherton 2012; Yu et al. 2012, 2013, Wheelahan, Chapter 30 in this volume). Such new work, giving appropriate weight to the content as well as the context of skill, will inject more depth into the analysis, and more realistic insight guiding the politics, of skill in the future.

References

ACIRRT (1999) *Australia at Work: Just Managing?* Sydney: Prentice Hall.

Annie E. Casey Foundation (2007) *Strengthening Workforce Policy: Applying the Lessons of the Jobs Initiative to Five Key Challenges*, Baltimore: Annie E. Casey Foundation.

Anderson, P. (2014) 'Plus c'est la même chose: Joinery Apprenticeship Arrangements in Scotland', *Journal of Education and Work*, 27(2): 137–160.

Anderson, P. and Warhurst, C. (2012) 'Lost in Translation? Skills Policy and the Shift to Skill Ecosystems', in D. Nash and T. Dolphin (eds), *Complex New World: Translating New Economic Thinking into Public Policy*, London: IPPR: 109–120.

Autor, D. (2011) 'The Polarization of Job Opportunities in the U.S. Labour Market: Implications for Employment and Earnings', *Community Investments*, 23(2): 11–41.

Australian Workforce and Productivity Agency (AWPA) (2013) *Food and Beverage Workforce Study*, Canberra: AWPA. Available at: www.awpa.gov.au/our-work/sector-specific-skill-needs/Pages/Food-and-beverage-workforce.aspx.

Biroonak, A. and Kaleba, K. (2010) *The Bridge to a New Economy: Worker Training Fills the Gap*, Washington, DC: Institute for America's Future/National Skills Coalition.

Blank, D. (2009) 'What the European Social Fund Can Learn from the WIA Experience Overview of the Workforce Investment Act (WIA)'. Paper to the What the European Social Fund Can Learn from the WIA Experience conference, University of Maryland.

Boris, E., de Leon, E., Roeger, K. and Nikolova, M. (2010) *Human Service Nonprofits and Government Collaboration: Findings from the 2010 National Survey of Nonprofit Government Contracting and Grants*, Washington, DC: Urban Institute.

Bray, J., Painter, R. and Rosin, M. (2011) *Developing Human Capital: Meeting the Growing Global Need for a Skilled and Educated Workforce*, New York: McGraw-Hill Research Foundation.

Bretherton, T. (2011) *The Role of VET in Workforce Development: A Story of Conflicting Expectations*, Adelaide: National Centre for Vocational Education Research.

Bridge, P. (2014) 'North East Dairy Regional Growth Plan and Workforce Development Strategy 2014', Bridge Logic Consulting. Available at: www.towong.vic.gov.au/business-investment/local-business-investment/agriculture/images /NE_Dairy_Plan.pdf.

Buchanan J., Schofield K., Briggs C., Considine G., Hager P., Hawke G., Kitay J., Meagher G., Macintyre J., Mounier A., and Ryan S. (2001) *Beyond Flexibility: Skills and Work in the Future*, Sydney: New South Wales Department of Education and Training.

Buchanan, J., Watson, I., and Briggs, C. (2004) 'Skill and the Renewal of Labour: The Classical Wage-Earner Model and Left Productivism in Australia', in C. Warhurst, E. Keep, and I. Grugulis (eds), *The Skills That Matter*, London: Palgrave: 186–206.

Buchanan, J., Scott, L., Yu, S., Schutz, H., and Jakubauskas, M. (2010), *Skills Demand and Utilization: An International Review of Approaches to Measurement and Policy Development*, Workplace Research Centre, University of Sydney. Available at: www.oecd-ilibrary.org/industry-and-services/skills-demand-and-utilization_5km8zddfr2jk-en.

Buchanan, J., Dymski, G., Froud, J., Johal, S., and Williams, K. (2013) 'Unsustainable Employment Portfolios', *Work, Employment and Society*, 27(3): 396–413.

Buchanan, J., Froud, J., Johal, S., Williams, K., and Yu, S. (2014) 'Do the UK and Australia Have Sustainable Business Models?', in M Hauptmeier and M. Vidal (eds), *The Comparative Political Economy of Work and Employment Relations*, Basingstoke: Palgrave MacMillan: 52–72.

Bureau of Labour Statistics (2013) *A Profile of the Working Poor, 2011*, Report 1041. Washington, DC: US Department of Labor.

Canning, R. and Laing, I. (2004) 'Modern Apprenticeships in Scotland', *Journal of Education Policy*, 19(2), 163–177.

Chapple, K. (2005) 'Building Institutions from the Ground Up: Regional Workforce Development Collaborations', Working Paper 2005 – 1, Institute for Urban and Regional Development, University of California, Berkeley, CA.

Chapple, K. (2010) 'Are Best Practices Really Better? Stories from the Workforce Development Frontier', Department of City and Regional Planning, University of California, Berkeley, CA.

Clagett, M. (2006) *Workforce Development in the United States: An Overview.* Washington, DC: National Centre on Education and the Economy.

Conner, V. (2010) Insights and Perspectives from the California Innovation Corridor: High-Wage Job Creation and Retention through Innovative Support, Supply Chain Competitiveness, Talent Development. Final Report prepared for the California Space Authority, Programme Lead California Innovation Corridor WIRED Initiative. California: California Innovation Corridor.

Conway, M. and Rademacher, I. (2003) *Industry-Specific Workforce Development.* Washington, DC: Aspen Institute.

Cottingham, P. and Besharov, D. (2011) 'Introduction [to The Workforce Investment Act]', in D. Besharov and P. Cottingham (eds), *The Workforce Investment Act.* Kalamazoo, MI: W. E. Upjohn Institute for Employment Research: 1–46.

Crouch, C., Finegold. D., and Sako, M. (1999) *Are Skills the Answer?* Oxford: Oxford University Press.

Davie, G. (1961) *The Democratic Intellect: Scotland and Her Universities in the Nineteenth Century.* Edinburgh: University Press.

Decker, P. and Berk, J. (2011) 'Ten Years of the Workforce Investment Act (WIA): Interpreting the Research on WIA and Related Programmes', *Journal of Policy Analysis and Management*, 30(4): 906–926.

Department of Training and Workforce Development (DTWD) (2010) *Skilling WA: A Workforce Development Plan for Western Australia*, Perth. Available at: www.dtwd.wa.gov.au/workforce-dataworkforcedevelopment/skillingWA/Pages/default.aspx.

Eddington, N. and Toner, P. (2012) *Queensland Skill Formation Strategies*, Paris: OECD.

Edelman, P., Holzer, H., Seleznow, E., Van Kleunen, A., and Watson, E. (2011) *State Workforce Policy*, Washington, DC: Georgetown Centre on Poverty, Inequality and Public Policy.

Evesson, J. and Oxenbridge, S. (2013) 'An Evaluation of Lessons Learnt from Projects in the Workforce Innovation Fund', Canberra: Employment Research Australia, Canberra.

Evesson, J., Bretherton, T., Buchanan, J., Rafferty, M. and Considine, G. (2009) 'Understanding Vocational Education and Training, Productivity and Workforce Participation', An Issues Participation', an issues paper, Adelaide: National Centre for Vocational Education Research.

Felstead, A. (2007) *How Smart Are Scottish Jobs? Summary Evidence from the Skills Surveys, 1997 to 2006*, Glasgow: FutureSkills Scotland.

Finegold, D. (1999) 'Creating Self-sustaining, High-skill Ecosystems', *Oxford Review of Economic Policy*, 15(1): 60–81.

Finegold, D. and Soskice, D. (1988) 'The Failure of Training in Britain: Analysis and Prescription', *Oxford Review of Economic Policy*, 4(3): 21–53.

Freeman, R. (2010) 'What Does Global Expansion of Higher Education Mean for the United States?', in C. Clotfelter (ed.), *American Universities in a Global Market*, Chicago: University of Chicago Press: 373–404.

Freidson, E. (2001) *Professionalism: The Third Logic*, Chicago: University of Chicago Press.

Froy, F. and S. Giguère (2010) *Putting in Place Jobs that Last: A Guide to Rebuilding Quality Employment at Local Level*, Paris: OECD.

Gallacher, J. (2007) *The Impact of Devolution on Higher Education in Scotland*, Centre for Research in Lifelong Learning, Glasgow Caledonian University.

Gallacher, J. and Ingram, R. (2012) 'Are Vocational Qualifications Vocational?', in M. Pilz (ed.), *The Future of Vocational Education and Training in a Changing World*, Wiesbaden: Springer: 381–402.

Gallacher, J., Whittaker, S., Crossan, B., and Mills, V. (2004) *Modern Apprenticeships: Improving Completion Rates*. Report commissioned by the Scottish Executive Enterprise, Transport and Lifelong Learning Department, Edinburgh: Scottish Executive. Available at: www.scotland.gov.uk/Resource/Doc/47171/0028784.pdf.

Government Accountability Office (GAO) (2012) *Workforce Investment Act: Innovative Collaborations between Workforce Boards and Employers Helped Meet Local Needs*, Washington, DC: US Government Accountability Office.

Government Printing Office (GPO) (2010) *Establishing a Task Force on Skills for America's Future*, Memorandum of October 4, 2010 (Federal Register vol. 75, no. 195/Friday, October 8, 2010/Presidential Documents). Washington, DC: GPO.

Hall, R. (2011) 'Skills and Skill Formation in Australian Workplaces: Beyond the War for Talent', in M. Baird, K. Hancock, and J. Isaac (eds), *Work and Employment Relations*, Sydney: Federation Press: 78–92.

Hall, R. and Lansbury, R. (2006) 'Skills in Australia: Towards Workforce Development and a Sustainable Skill Ecosystem', *Journal of Industrial Relations*, 48(5): 575–592.

Hebert, S. (2010) *Changing Systems Is Like Moving a Mountain ... and Other Insights from Successful Workforce Leaders*, Baltimore: Annie E. Casey Foundation.

Hebert, S., Parkes, S., and Schneider, G (2005) *A Work in Progress: Case Studies in Changing Local Workforce Development Systems—The Jobs Initiative Final Report Series*, Vol. 1, Baltimore: Annie E. Casey Foundation.

Heinrich, C., Mueser, P., and Troske, K. (2008) *Workforce Investment Act Non-Experimental Net Impact Evaluation*, Final Report, Washington, DC: US Department of Labor.

Holzer, H. (2011) 'Raising Job Quality and Skills for American Workers: Creating More-Effective Education and Workforce Development Systems in the States', Discussion paper 2011-2010, Washington DC: Brookings Institution.

Holzer, H. and Lerman, R. (2007) *America's Forgotten Middle-Skill Jobs*. Washington, DC: Workforce Alliance.

Humes, W. and Bryce, T. (2003) 'The Distinctiveness of Scottish Education', in W. Humes and T. Bryce (eds), *Scottish Education: Post-devolution*, Edinburgh: Edinburgh University Press: 108–118.

Jacobs, E (2013) *Principles for Reforming Workforce Development and Human Capital Policies in the United States*. Washington, DC: Brookings Institution.

John J. Heldrich Center for Workforce Development (2002) *One-Stop Innovations: Leading Change under the WIA One-Stop System*, Final Report. New Jersey: John J. Heldrich Center for Workforce Development, Rutgers, the State University of New Jersey.

Keating, M. (2005) 'Higher Education in Scotland and England after Devolution', *Regional and Federal Studies*, 15(4): 423–435.

Keep, E. (2002) 'The English Vocational Education and Training Policy Debate—Fragile "Technologies" or Opening the "Black Box": Two Competing Visions of Where We Go Next', *Journal of Education and Work*, 15(4): 457–479.

King, C. and Heinrich, C. (2011) 'How Effective Are Workforce Development Programs? Implications for US Workforce Policies.' Paper to the Association for Public Policy Analysis and Management's Fall Research Conference, Washington DC.

Kochan, T., Finegold, D., and Osterman, P. (2012) 'Who Can Fix the "Middle-Skills" Gap?' *Harvard Business Review*, 90: 83–90.

Lerman, R. (2010) *Expanding Apprenticeship A Way to Enhance Skills and Careers*, Washington, DC: Urban Institute.

Lerman, R. (2013) 'Skill Development in Middle Level Occupations: The Role of Apprenticeship Training', *IZA Journal of Labor Policy*, 2(6): 1–20.

Muro, M. Rothwell, J., and Saha, D. (2011) *Sizing the Clean Economy*, Washington, DC: The Brookings Institution.

National Governors Association (1998) Jobs for the Future, Regional Technology Strategies *Working on the Demand Side: Emerging State Practices in Workforce Development*, Washington DC: Center for Best Practices, National Governors' Association.

National Governors Association (2008) *Accelerating State Adoption of Sector Strategies: An Eleven-State Project to Promote Regional Solutions to Worker and Employer Needs*. Washington, DC: Centre for Best Practices, National Governors Association.

National Skills Coalition (2011) *Training Policy in Brief: An Overview of Federal Workforce Development Policies, 2011 Edition*. Washington, DC: National Skills Coalition.

OECD (2012) *Better Skills, Better Jobs, Better Lives: A Strategic Approach to Skills Policies*, Paris: OECD.

OECD/CERI 2009 *Systemic Innovation in the Australian VET System: Country Case Study Report*, Paris: OECD.

Osterman, P. (2007) 'Employment and Training Policies: New Directions for Less-Skilled Adults', in H. Holzer and D. Nightingale (eds), *Reshaping the American Workforce in a Changing Economy*, Washington, DC: Urban Institute: 119–154.

Osterman, P. and Shulman, B. (2011) *Good Jobs America: Making Work Better for Everyone*, New York: Russell Sage Foundation.

Paterson, L. (1997) 'Policy-Making in Scottish Education: A Case of Pragmatic Nationalism', in M. Clark and P. Munn (eds), *Education in Scotland*, London: Routlege: 111–124.

Paterson, L. (2003) *Scottish Education in the Twentieth Century*, Edinburgh: Edinburgh University Press.

Payne, J. (2008) 'Skills in context: What Can the UK Learn from Australia's Skill Ecosystem Projects?', *Policy & Politics*, 36(3): 307–323.

Payne, J. (2011) 'Scotland's Skills Utilisation Programme: An Interim Evaluation', SKOPE Research Paper no. 101, Universities of Oxford and Cardiff.

Raffe, D., Brannan K, Croxford, L., and Martin, C. (1999) 'Comparing England, Scotland, Wales and Northern Ireland: The Case for "Home Internationals" in Comparative Research', *Comparative Education*, 35:1, 9–25.

Ramstad, E. (2009) 'Expanding Innovation System and Policy: An Organisational Perspective', *Policy Studies*, 30(5): 533–553.

Randle, K. and Brady, N. (1997) 'Managerialism and Professionalism in the "Cinderella Service", *Journal of Vocational Education & Training*, 49(1): 121–139.

Reich, R. (1998) *Locked in the Cabinet*, New York: Vintage Books.

Schurman, S. and Soares, L. (2010) 'Connecting the Dots: Creating a Postsecondary Education System for the 21st-Century Workforce', in D. Finegold, M. Gatta, H. Salzman and S. Schurman (eds), *Transforming the US Workforce Development System*, Illinois: Labor and Employment Relations Association: 125–151.

Scottish Executive (2001) *A Smart Successful Scotland: Ambitious for the Enterprise Networks*. Edinburgh: Scottish Executive.

Scottish Funding Council (SFC) (2008) *Skills Utilisation: Call for Proposals*, SFC/49/2008. Edinburgh: Scottish Funding Council.

Scottish Funding Council (SFC) (2009) *Skills Utilisation projects: Progress Report*, SC/09/35. Edinburgh: Scottish Funding Council.

Scottish Funding Council (SFC) (2012) *Participation Rates for Entrants to Scottish Higher Education. Statistics Theme and Subtheme: Education and Training*, Edinburgh: Scottish Funding Council.

Scottish Government (2007a) *Skills for Scotland: A Lifelong Learning Strategy*, Edinburgh: Scottish Government.

Scottish Government (2007b) *The Government Economic Strategy*, Edinburgh: Scottish Government.

Scottish Government (2010) *Skills Utilisation Cross-Sectoral Communications and Learning Network: Partners' Guide*, Edinburgh: Scottish Government.

Scottish Government (2011a) *2020 Routemap for Renewable Energy in Scotland*, Edinburgh: Scottish Government.

Scottish Government (2011b) *The Government Economic Strategy*, Edinburgh: Scottish Government.

Scottish Government (2012a) *Action for Jobs—Supporting Young Scots into Work: Scotland's Youth Employment Strategy*, Edinburgh: Scottish Government.

Scottish Government (2012b) *Reinvigorating College Governance: The Scottish Government Response to the Report of the Review of Further Education Governance in Scotland*, Edinburgh: Scottish Government.

Scottish Government (2013) *Commission for Developing Scotland's Young Workforce: Interim Report*, Edinburgh: Scottish Government.

Scottish Government/STUC (2008) *Skills Utilization—Joint Communiqué from the Scottish Government and the STUC*. Available at: www.scotland.gov.uk/Topics/Education/skills-strategy/making-skills-work/utilization/STUC.

Smith, A. (1776 [1976]) *An Inquiry into the Nature and Causes of the Wealth of Nations*, Vol. 1, Oxford: Oxford University Press.

Soares, L. and Steigleder, S. (2012) *Building a Technically Skilled Workforce*, Washington, DC: Centre for American Progress.

Steedman, H. (2012) *Overview of Apprenticeship Systems and Issues: ILO Contribution to the G20 Task Force on Employment*, Geneva: International Labour Organization.

Training and Skills Commission of South Australia (TASC) (2013) 'Skills for Jobs. The Training and Skills Commission Five Year Workforce Development Plan', Adelaide. Available at: www.tasc.sa.gov.au/.../Skills%20for%20Jobs%20five-year%20plan/Skills.

US Department of Education (2012) *Investing in America's Future: A Blueprint for Transforming Career and Technical Education*. Washington, DC: US Department of Education.

US Department of Labor (2008) *Workforce Innovation in Regional Economic Development Combined Regions*. Washington, DC: US Department of Labor.

UK Commission for Employment and Skills (UKCES) (2010) *High Performance Working: A Policy Review*, evidence report 18, Wath-upon-Dearne: UKCES.

Warhurst, C. and Findlay, P. (2012) 'More Effective Skills Utilisation: Shifting the Terrain of Skills Policy in Scotland', SKOPE Research Paper no.107, Universities of Oxford and Cardiff.

Watson, I., Briggs, C., Campbell, I., and Buchanan, J. (2003) *Fragmented Futures*, Sydney: Federation Press.

White, I. and Yonwin, J. (2004) 'Devolution in Scotland', Standard Note SN/PC/3000. House of Commons, London.

Windsor, K. (2007) *Skill Ecosystem National Project: Mid-term Evaluation Report*, Sydney: New South Wales Department of Education and Training/[Federal] Department of Education, Science, and Technology.

Windsor, K and Alcorso, C. (2008) *Skills in Context: A Guide to the Skill Ecosystem Approach to Workforce Development*, Sydney: New South Wales Department of Education and Training.

Yu, S., Bretherton, T., Schutz, J., and Buchanan, J. (2012) 'Vocational Trajectories within the Australian Labour Market', National Centre for Vocational Education Research Research Paper, Adelaide. Available at: www.ncver.edu.au/publications/2557.html.

Yu, S, Bretherton, T, and Buchanan, J (2013) *Defining Vocational Streams: Insights from the Engineering, Finance, Agriculture and Care Sectors*, National Centre for Vocational Education Research Report, Adelaide. Available at: www.ncver.edu.au/publications/2667.html.

CHAPTER 22

EMPLOYMENT SYSTEMS, SKILLS, AND KNOWLEDGE

ALICE LAM AND DAVID MARSDEN

INTRODUCTION

LEARNING-BY-DOING and the accumulation of practical experience whilst in employment provide a large proportion of the skills and knowledge used in all the advanced economies. As a result, employment systems, which encompass the organization of work, career patterns, and the learning opportunities they provide, shape the skills and practical knowledge that workers and managers bring to their jobs. Conventional wisdom has classified the structures within which these evolve into three generic types: organizational internal labour markets (ILMs), occupational or professional labour markets (OLMs), and general or sometimes 'secondary' labour markets (see Robinson 1970; Doeringer and Piore 1971; Eyraud et al. 1990). Although initially useful, this categorization was built against the background of 'managerial capitalism', with a focus on large industrial firms, and at a time when union agreements often set the tone also for non-union firms (Foulkes 1980).

Much has changed since then. In the United States, the 'patient capital' of managerial capitalism has given way to a more 'footloose' form of capital as a result of changes in company finance placing its associated employment practices under great strain (Lazonick and O'Sullivan 1996). The rise of 'Japanese management' and its associated long-term human resource policies have not only challenged the large bureaucratic ILMs analysed in Doeringer and Piore's (1971) classic study of employment practices in US manufacturing but also offers a different relationship between workers' and managers' skills and knowledge, and a different distribution of knowledge within the firm (Cole 1994). A third challenge to the accepted view of skills within ILMs arises from the new ways of managing the distribution of skills and knowledge between firms as illustrated by high-tech clusters of firms, such as in Silicon Valley, and in project-based work (Camuffo 2002). Finally, many writers have argued that the present stage of globalization generates greater competition on quality because firms' participation in the trade in tasks along global value chains has to meet the quality standards required of the whole chain (Ericksson 2010; Sutton 2012). These changes have affected both the large-firm ILMs of the United States and Japan, and the institutionalized occupational labour markets for intermediate and professional skills as in Germany. These developments have led many firms to focus on tasks where there is alignment between their capabilities and their employment practices, and for other tasks, to look outside to external suppliers and collaborative ventures, causing their employment practices to become less inclusive than in the past (e.g. Cappelli 1999; Grimshaw et al. 2001; Appay and Jeffrys 2009).

This chapter begins by looking at structures of workplace knowledge and skill development within different types of employment systems as these are the foundations of firms' capabilities. It then looks at the governance problems created by different knowledge structures within a three-way relationship between workers, managers, and investors, building on Aoki's (2010) argument that they will only adopt a particular governance framework for their cooperation if it protects their respective interests. It then moves on to look at a number of innovative developments in employment systems and their skills, and how these appear to address a number of changes in economic organization that have come about since the classic works on the theory of skills in internal and occupational labour markets, and hopefully sheds some light on their apparent erosion.

Work Organization and the Distribution of Job Knowledge from Learning-By-Doing

Learning-by-doing provides a major component of workforce skills in any economy. It applies both to passing on the *stock* of existing job knowledge to newly hired workers and to the *flow* of new knowledge that arises from solving work-related problems (Koike and Inoki 1991). Mincer (1974) provided one of the earliest quantitative estimates of the value of post-educational experience, based on the argument that the rise in employees' earnings after labour market entry reflected their increasing value to employers, which he attributed to work experience. He found that, in the United States in the late 1950s, experience accounted for roughly half of workers' human capital stock for highly educated workers, and even more for those with low levels of education. Earnings relate to the returns that accrue to workers. However, employers also invest heavily in training, and so might expect returns of their own: one estimate for Britain put it at about 3% of gross domestic product per year (Ryan 1991). The national training systems, time periods, and methods of estimating are different, but taken together they give an idea of the large scale of investments in in-work learning in modern economies.

Given the magnitude of these investments, it is logical that there should be a close relationship between the organization of the jobs that give rise to learning-by-doing, and the nature and distribution of skills and knowledge within the firm. We propose to approach this relationship first by looking at the cognitive structures of knowledge and skills, and then at their governance.

Cognitive and Skill Dimensions

The workplace knowledge that underpins workers' skills comprises two dimensions: its *mode of expression*, whether it is explicit or tacit; and its *locus*, whether held by individuals or groups (Lam 2000). Explicit knowledge is codified whereas tacit knowledge is not—as Polanyi (1967) wrote: 'we know more than we can say'. Explicit knowledge can be transmitted by the written word and conveyed by manuals and formal instruction. Tacit knowledge is usually passed person to person by demonstration and story-telling (Brown and Duguid 1991; Orr 1996).

The *locus* of such knowledge in organizations may be encapsulated within individual workers or distributed within groups or teams. In all organizations there is a division of labour with regard to knowledge. The key difference is how far employees can function independently in their jobs as opposed to needing to draw interactively on the knowledge of other employees. Professional and craft workers often work independently because they have the necessary knowledge to produce the outputs required of them. On the other hand, knowledge can also be distributed within a group or team such that key tasks require multiple contributions from different group members.

Lam (2000) applies these two dimensions to identify four different types of work-related knowledge. These different knowledge types can be described briefly as follows:

- 'Embrained' (explicit-individual): knowledge derived from formal and theoretical training, encapsulated in the 'brains' of individual knowing experts;
- 'Encoded' (explicit-group): knowledge encoded in the organizational routines and written procedures applied in white or blue collar work;
- 'Embodied' (tacit-individual): individual action-oriented knowledge heavily reliant on practical experience;
- 'Embedded' (tacit-group): the collective form of tacit knowledge embedded in the group because of shared norms, mutual adjustment within flexible work roles, and group problem-solving activities which cause new knowledge to be distributed within the group.

The cells in Figure 22.1 show additionally the four types of organization structures that can be aligned with them (Mintzberg 1979, 2009). The bureaucratic structures rely upon coordination by standardization be it of professional or management-designed work roles. In contrast, adhocracy relies upon coordination by mutual adjustment between flexible work roles. Management may also coordinate by specifying either the *outputs* or the *inputs* it requires: relying upon workers' expert knowledge, as in professional bureaucracy and operating adhocracy, or by taking control of the work process,

		Locus of knowledge	
		Individual	Group
Mode of expression of knowledge	Explicit	*Embrained* *(Professional bureaucracy)*	*Encoded* *(Machine bureaucracy)*
	Tacit	*Embodied* *(Operating adhocracy)*	*Embedded* *(Administrative adhocracy, 'J-form' organisation)*

FIGURE 22.1 Knowledge types

as in machine bureaucracy, such as Taylorist systems, and in administrative adhocracy, such as in 'Japanese-form' work organization.

Learning and Sharing of Knowledge/Skills between Workers and Substitutability

In practice, few jobs involve exclusively either explicit or tacit knowledge. As Mincer argued, formal education and experience are complements, although their proportions vary greatly across jobs. Their distribution among co-workers and between workers and managers, and how they evolve also varies greatly, and has an important effect on the bargaining relationships. Consider the types of relationship among co-workers and managers shown in Figure 22.2. They illustrate different settings in which the job-related problems may give rise to problem-solving and learning opportunities. In the first, work has been organized into a set of work posts, with individual workers assigned to each one and coordinated by their line-manager. In the second, the co-workers function as a team, although still coordinated by their manager, and in the latter two, the manager is part of the team, respectively with overlapping and integrated roles.

In all four cases, the emergence of learning opportunities and tacit knowledge arise on the job (Koike and Inoki 1991). However, their scope and distribution differ greatly. In the first, tacit knowledge grows around the margins of each individual work post. As management has the coordinating role even at job level, increases in workers' job knowledge will be confined to problems that arise in their individual work, whereas anything that affects relations between work posts will fall to management. Maurice et al. (1982) observed how semi-skilled French production workers had to stand aside whilst managers and

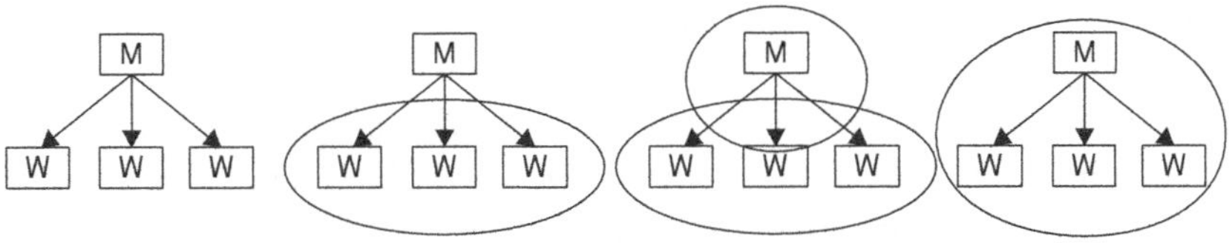

FIGURE 22.2 Management–work group configurations and on-the-job learning

technicians fixed problems for them. Any new knowledge that resulted from that process would, in the first instance, reside within the managerial hierarchy. They contrasted this situation with that in Germany where, whilst still responsible for individual jobs, workers started from a higher level of intermediate skills, which meant that management could delegate more problem-solving tasks to them, albeit within the same hierarchical structure. In the second example in Figure 22.2, co-workers function as a team, working flexibly, so that all develop an understanding of their co-workers' jobs and how they are connected. In this case, co-workers are in a position to deal with problems that arise from how their jobs articulate and can develop a more holistic understanding of their work process. In the final two examples, the management function is integrated increasingly into the team which enables more sophisticated problem-solving, spanning both technical and coordination issues, for example, in the J-form and operating adhocracy structures respectively. This time, as tacit knowledge develops, it is distributed not just horizontally among co-workers as in the previous example but also vertically. This distribution enables more sophisticated problem-solving and skill development, but it also creates greater inter-dependency between managers and workers as neither group has a monopoly of the knowledge required for linking together different parts of the production process.

Organizational knowledge evolves over time as the organization's environment and needs change. Codifying tacit knowledge requires time and resources, so that in practice even the most formalized organizations rely a good deal on tacit knowledge and skills. This means that the organizational structures around which tacit knowledge evolves, such as those in Figure 22.2, will strongly influence the supply of labour with the requisite skills and knowledge. It is widely recognized that tacit knowledge is 'sticky': best communicated by person-to-person contact. In the hierarchical work post example (Figure 22.2), new workers can acquire the requisite skills either by their own experience on the job, or from co-workers who are willing to share their knowledge. This method of training is popular because it is simple and cheap so long as new trainees remain modest in number.

The greater the span of tacit knowledge the more it provides a tool for solving job-related problems but it also places a premium on the quality of cooperation among co-workers and with management. In the co-worker team (Figure 22.2), tacit knowledge can develop within the team as a result of their more integrated problem-solving activities, giving the team a potential information advantage over management. It also creates a stronger basis on which work groups can cooperate with management compared with the previous model. The experience of cooperation among team members, their shared knowledge, and their control over its transmission to new members mean that in a conflict, in the last resort, management would have to replace a whole team as well as its stock of tacit knowledge. In the final two cases in Figure 22.2, management is actively involved in joint problem-solving, as 'player managers'. The greater scope of the activity considerably enhances its value to the organization but, at the same time, blurs the distinction between the tacit knowledge of workers and of management. It is in this sense that Aoki (2010) refers to the skill and knowledge assets of workers and management as 'fused': neither party can substitute an outsider for the other.

Finally, we return to professional skills. Experience is also an important complement to formal educational qualifications, and although many such workers may be engaged in jobs that approximate to the hierarchical model with individual rather than team responsibilities, there is an important difference. The market price for professional skills will reflect the level of productivity when they are fully utilized, so that employers have good reason to align job demands with the range of knowledge of these workers. If workers move between similar jobs in different organizations, then the tacit skills they build up will tend to be of similar nature and thus of use to a variety of employers. Two consequences follow: professional workers retain a viable outside option as both their formal qualification and their experience remain transferable; and employers retain the possibility to recruit replacements externally. In contrast, the firm-specific hierarchical model involves usually narrow and idiosyncratic skills which lack transferability, but because of the limited amount of training, they can also be replaced with relatively short training times from outside. Thus, in both cases, the knowledge assets of the workers can be quite quickly replaced from outside but workers' bargaining power differs greatly owing to the difference in their outside options.

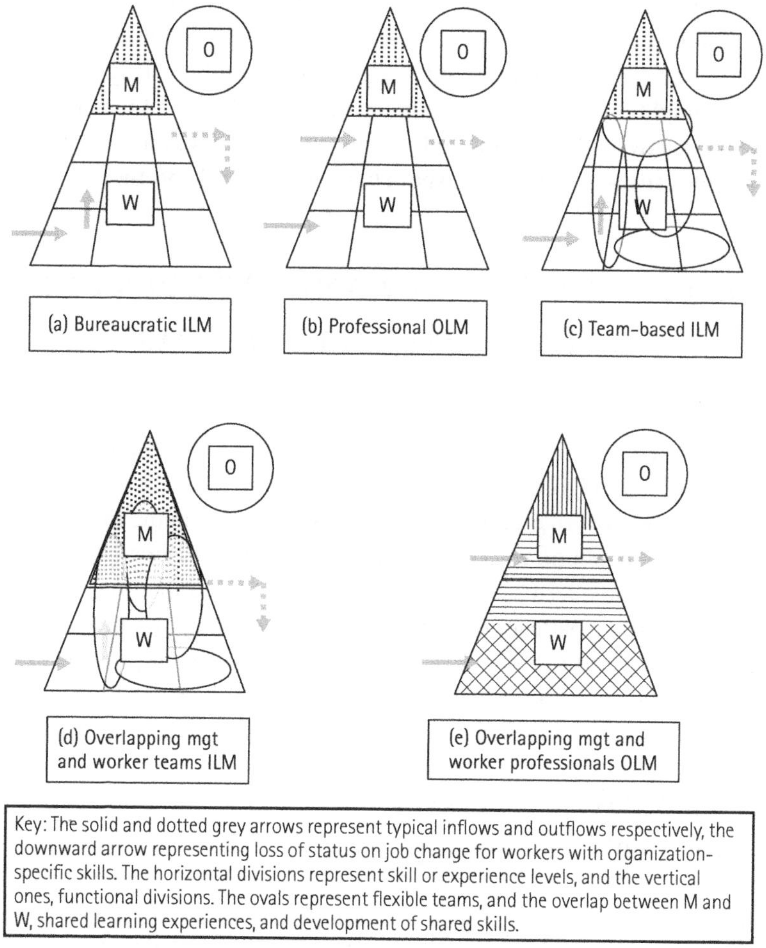
O
M
W
(a) Bureaucratic ILM
(b) Professional OLM
(c) Team-based ILM
(d) Overlapping mgt and worker teams ILM
(e) Overlapping mgt and worker professionals OLM
Key: The solid and dotted grey arrows represent typical inflows and outflows respectively, the downward arrow representing loss of status on job change for workers with organization-specific skills. The horizontal divisions represent skill or experience levels, and the vertical ones, functional divisions. The ovals represent flexible teams, and the overlap between M and W, shared learning experiences, and development of shared skills.

FIGURE 22.3 Different configurations of ILMs and OLMs and employee, manager, and owner relationships

From the above, a number of different configurations of employment systems can be identified. Figure 22.3 shows the three key actors, workers (W), managers (M) and investors or owners (O). Managers are shown at the apex of the pyramid and the workers are divided horizontally by level of skill and, in some cases, vertically by function. The arrows represent typical entry and exit points: the bureaucratic ILM recruiting predominantly at the base of the skill hierarchy, and upgrading subsequently, and the occupational or professional model recruiting directly from outside. The ovals within the triangles represent different possible team configurations that may cross skill and functional boundaries. The traditional US large-firm ILM, as in Doeringer and Piore's model and in Aoki's 'A-firm', is case (a). Versions of Aoki's 'J-firm', with its flexible cross-skill and cross-functional working are represented by cases (c) and (d). The former involves the more 'lean' version in which teams come under stronger management control, whereas the latter provides a richer joint-learning model with overlapping management and worker roles and skills. Lorenz and Valeyre (2005) and Holm et al. (2010) using European data also distinguish team-working into 'lean' and 'learning' versions. The traditional German and British occupational models, with their scope for direct external recruitment at the level of skill required, are shown in case (b). The final case (e) bears some resemblance to the occupational model, except that managers' and workers' skills and knowledge overlap considerably, as they might do in professional service firms. Workers' and managers' skills and knowledge are relatively discrete in the first three cases, whereas in the latter two, joint problem-solving causes them to overlap both in their stock and how they co-evolve.

Skills and Governance Structures of Employment Systems

Suitable governance structures are needed to facilitate the development of workplace skills and knowledge. Figure 22.3 illustrates alternative configurations of skills and knowledge, and the governance problems associated with them. In this section, we consider first how the boundaries of each party's work obligations can be established, and then look, in simple terms, at how they can be enforced in a manner that is self-sustaining. The resulting patterns of work systems will be found to mirror those types of knowledge discussed in the previous section. It also considers the position of investors. It starts by looking at governance in firm ILMs and then looks at occupational markets.

Management–Worker Governance and the Employment Relationship

The employment relationship is flexible, enabling management to hire labour, and only after the contract has been agreed, to determine employees' detailed task obligations.

To varying degrees, this applies to all the models shown in Figure 22.3. Such open-endedness gives employers great flexibility (Simon 1951), but without limits to management's authority to direct work, employees are exposed to abuse. As Williamson (1975) has shown, it would be impractical to specify the content of an employment contract by means of a detailed inventory of tasks, hence the importance of mostly unwritten work rules and conventions that are readily understood by employees and their line-managers to establish the limits of managerial authority over work assignments. These rules and conventions enable workers and their managers to identify the boundaries of jobs and possible breaches to the arrangement. They are the foundations on which governance structures have to build.

The work rules that delimit managerial authority need to be both *enforceable* by ordinary employees and their line-managers, and *efficient* at aligning the employer's job demands with workers' skills (Marsden 1999). Broadly speaking, the enforceability criterion focuses on either the tasks that make up a worker's job or on the function within which the job is integrated. For the efficiency criterion, aligning job demands and skills can be achieved either by taking the job demands as given, for example by technology or organizational design, and shaping workers' skills accordingly; or, in the reverse direction, starting from workers' skills, and adapting job demands. Lazear (1995) described the first as the 'production approach', and Sengenberger (1987) identified the second as the 'training approach'. Figure 22.4 cross-tabulates these two approaches, generating four types of governance arrangements that are congruent with Lam's typology of knowledge types (Figure 22.1). The training approach is associated with the individual dimension of knowledge because skills are packaged so as to enable workers to move from one organization to another, as with the professional and expert skills of professional bureaucracy and operating adhocracy. The production approach is associated with the group or organizational dimension because skills belong to groups that are formed around administrative routines and technologies and by and large are specific to each organization. In such an environment, even when jobs emphasize individual accountability for performance such as in Taylorist work systems, there is a real sense in which the skills are an attribute of the job rather than the individual employee.

		Efficiency criterion	
		Training approach	Production approach
Enforceability criterion	Task-focused	*Embrained* (*Professional bureaucracy*)	*Encoded* (*Machine bureaucracy*)
	Function-focused	*Embodied* (*Operating adhocracy*)	*Embedded* (*Administrative adhocracy, 'J-form' organization*)

FIGURE 22.4 Four approaches to monitoring work obligations

Source: Adapted from Marsden (1999).

Turning to enforceability, it is easier to codify the tasks of individual workers engaged in relatively independent roles than when there is a good deal of mutual adjustment between flexible work roles. In 'machine bureaucracy', with Taylorist work design in the factory and office, work tasks and job contents have a high degree of codification. Detailed job classifications provide one means for management to standardize jobs and reduce job idiosyncrasy. As suggested earlier, tacit knowledge grows around the edges of such jobs but is also limited by their narrow scope. Professional bureaucracy, in both white and blue collar occupations, is similar except that the skills are standardized across firms so that workers may move freely between employers whilst remaining within the same occupation. Whereas machine bureaucracy standardizes jobs around the organization's own internal principles, professional bureaucracy does so around externally given qualifications. This contrast echoes that between the group and individual focus of knowledge, the group following internal organizational principles and the individual following skills that are portable between organizations. Based on flexible work roles, the two adhocratic forms derive enforceability not from individual tasks but from the more abstract concept of the function within which mutual adjustment takes place. Thus a team of scientists might focus on a particular research outcome, and a team of workers operate flexibly within their designated work area of a production system.

Work systems underpinned by these rules are partly self-sustaining because they benefit both parties, and partly maintained by potential sanctions to ensure fair dealing. Termination, and use of the quit and dismissal threats are the ultimate sanctions in any continuous economic relationship, such as employment, should either party fall short on its side of the bargain. They may be supplemented with lesser sanctions and with use of voice (Hirschman 1970). Because of their informal nature, work rules rely heavily on each party's readiness to punish breaches by the other. Drawing on evolutionary game theory, the use of such informal rules to identify job boundaries can be part of a self-sustaining process of cooperation provided that the costs of conflict exceed the potential gains and provided that both parties are equally willing to hold the line against encroachments by the other (Bowles 2005; Marsden 2013). Factors that increase the cost of conflict include joint investments in organization-specific training and knowledge that are lost in the event of quits and dismissals.

This process can be undermined if either party fails to punish breaches systematically, which might happen if the costs of conflict become asymmetrical. For example, high local unemployment may discourage workers from punishing breaches, and inversely, recruitment and retention difficulties may discourage management. In such cases, the weaker party may respond by withdrawing from activities that enhance skills and by reduced 'give-and-take' within the employment relationship. Workers might insist on narrower interpretations of their jobs and greater use of seniority for which breaches are easier to detect and generally lead to smaller gains. Indeed, Doeringer and Piore (1971) identified seniority rules for established job ladders as providing the necessary job security for workers to invest in (narrow) firm-specific skills within the classical north American ILMs.

Strongly developed teams may make flexible work organization more robust in a number of ways, and so support more stable management–worker governance within the employment relationship. On the one hand, teams of workers are harder to replace than single employees, especially when knowledge is diffused within teams. On the other, teams can also enable management to use peer pressures for more consistent performance (Kandel and Lazear 1992). This mixture of reduced dismissal threat and improved work discipline potentially enables teams to provide a useful channel for employee voice with management and so enrich the palet of graduated responses to breach, thus enabling a greater degree of balance between workers and management.

Governance and Investors

One of the challenges posed by the growth of knowledge-intensive activities identified by Aoki (2010) concerns changes in relationships with investors. The hierarchical design of the conventional firm, he argues, works well for the bureaucratic ILM model but comes under increasing strain as worker and manager skills and knowledge become more integrated. Such integration can be found in strong forms of the 'J-firm' and in emerging patterns of project-based organization for example in the high technology and creative sectors. Aoki argues that it increases the risk of a coalition between workers and managers against investors, and unless it can be resolved by a suitable governance mechanism, investors will hold back.

The core of his argument concerns the value derived from control over use of the physical assets provided by investors. In conventional hierarchical firms, this lies in the hands of managers. They are the brokers between the other two stakeholders, and benefit from important information asymmetries. They specialize in commercial and coordination activities, whereas workers focus on the technical aspects of their jobs under management direction. Investors take the residual income, profits, after payment of all costs including contractual payments to managers and workers. Drawing on Hart (1995), Aoki shows that this is an effective form of organizational 'self-governance' as he puts it, provided that investors can discipline managers' activities in both the commercial and internal coordination spheres. In this model, coordination depends upon management's power vis-à-vis workers, which in turn depends upon how easily workers can be replaced externally. The problem for the investors is to judge how far cooperative policies with the workforce deliver business results as opposed to giving management and workers a quiet life. If the investors can easily identify a breach they can apply the usual incentive mechanisms such as linking managers' pay to market performance, dismissal, and hostile takeovers. The more productivity depends upon substantial levels of firm-specific skills and knowledge, the harder it is to identify breach using conventional financial indictors and the harder it is for investors to take corrective action.

The first three types in Figure 22.3 are variants of the conventional hierarchical model although they differ in important respects. The bureaucratic ILM model represents the first. One interpretation of the erosion of large-firm ILMs of US industry since the 1960s arises if we consider Doeringer and Piore's (1971) theory about the growth of firm-specific skills and seniority-based job rights alongside Lazonick and O'Sullivan's (1996) observation of the transition from a situation of dispersed to more coordinated shareholder voice from the 1960s. Under the dispersed ownership of preceding decades a model of training and workforce skills underpinned by seniority rules had grown up that brought workers and management together at the expense of shareholder returns, arguably by over-extending a rigid model of firm-specific skills. Stronger shareholder voice in subsequent years then contested this relationship, pulling management back into its role as agent of the shareholders, and putting a brake on further development of this kind of ILM. The question Aoki asks then is how far can ILMs based on more flexible team models develop whilst satisfying all three parties? He argues that it depends upon a change from extensive to intensive monitoring of management policies and performance by investors, and from an 'arm's length' to a 'relational' approach. He argues that historically this function was carried out by the main bank system in Japan. In Germany, where many large firms also built strong ILMs on an occupational system to be examined shortly, bank finance together with supervisory boards have played a similar role. Thus, where the distribution of knowledge and skills brings management and a significant part of the workforce together, his argument is that extensive, arm's length monitoring is less efficient than intensive, relational monitoring. Looking across a wider range of European countries, Lorenz and Valeyre (2005) identify two types of team-working, 'lean', management-directed teams, and 'learning' teams in which workers have a good deal of scope for problem-solving activities. The lean model appears to be associated with stronger unilateral management control, and the learning model more with greater institutional joint-regulation (Holm et al. 2010).

Finally, how has the three-actor model adapted to the emergence of networks of small and medium-sized firms which have been very dynamic in the knowledge-intensive and creative industries? In many such firms, the distribution of knowledge and skills is such that there is no clear boundary between the roles of management and expert workers, and neither can easily substitute for the other. Under the conventional governance model, the resulting scope for manager-employee coalitions would be unattractive for investors who might then form a coalition against them. Aoki argues that a different governance system has emerged in which teams of workers and managers with a good commercial project compete for funding from venture capitalists. He presents this process as a tournament in which those bidding for funds have to reveal the detail of their business plans, and agree milestones for results and how gains are to be shared, thus overcoming some of the informational asymmetries in this kind of work that weaken the hierarchical model. As will be seen shortly, this model fits well with the labour market conditions found in these industries.

Governance Structures for Occupational Skills

Although employed in both the hierarchical and the networked models, occupational skills require separate treatment because they improve the worker's outside option in this three-partner governance relationship. Becker (1975) made a fundamental distinction between payment mechanisms for on-the-job training that give rise to transferable skills and those where the skills are firm-specific. Transferability means that trainees can quit taking the employer's investment with them once their training is complete. This is not the case for skills which have little value to other employers. As a result, employers will invest in firm-specific but not in transferable skills. The latter course would create a 'free-rider' problem as competitor employers could poach instead of training skilled labour. Although Becker's theory identifies some critical problems of training policy, there has been much debate as to whether, in practice, the picture is as 'black and white' as he supposed. For example, employers can use other policies to retain their skilled workers so that investment in training is more secure (Franz and Sockice 1995; Stevens 1998; Acemoglu and Pischke 1999). In practice, many employers spend considerable sums on developing transferable skills. Nevertheless, fear of poaching by other employers is widely believed to be a major discouragement for firms wishing to provide such training.

Sometimes employer collective action and industrial governance arrangements can facilitate employer investment in transferable skills. According to Olson (1971) collective action can overcome free-rider problems if the group benefits from a strong coordinating body, or alternatively it comprises a small clique of powerful members. In a Norwegian study of employer-funded training for transferable skills, Johansen (2000) found that employers' ability to coordinate conformed to Olson's theory. Employer-funded transferable skill systems developed when sectors benefited from employer coordination, and when they were dominated by a clique of large firms. The sector which could not resolve the collective action problem on account of its dispersed membership and lack of a coordinating body, engineering, had great difficulty in establishing a system of transferable skills. Observers of job training for transferable skills in Germany attribute much of the success of small and medium-sized engineering firms in this sphere to employer-led coordinating bodies (Streeck 1989; Drexel 1993). Large firms, on the other hand, benefit partly from forming small cliques within their sectors, and partly from a system of industrial governance (Franz and Soskice 1995; Backes-Gellner et al. 1997). One element is industry wage bargaining, which limits the opportunities to use pay to poach those workers trained elsewhere. The other concerns the system of co-determination involving workers, management, and investors, which facilitates intensive monitoring of management policies and performance. In the case of training, these institutions also provide workers with some assurance that the skills to which they are contributing will have a viable external market.

To conclude this section, Aoki describes these models as 'self-governance' because he is concerned with the forms that the three stakeholders would adopt voluntarily as a framework for their collaboration. For this to happen, each must feel that its interests are sufficiently protected. Otherwise, it will not collaborate or it will seek an alternative model. If there is a poor match between the governance system and the configuration of skills and knowledge, then one can expect that one or other will gradually be abandoned over time, as appears in the case of the North American large-firm ILMs discussed earlier. Likewise, in Japan and Germany, there is much debate about a realignment of skill and governance systems confining long-term employment commitments to employees whose skills and knowledge are essential to the business (for example, Thelen 2004; Streeck 2009; Aoki 2010; Marsden 2015).

ILMs and Inter-Organizational Linkages

Recent years have witnessed several innovative forms of managing skills and knowledge which provide an alternative to the traditional models of ILMs and OLMs. They are suggestive of possible future lines of development of theory on skills and labour market structures, and also take account of the interests of investors.

Project-based Work and the 'Modular' Approach

Industrial districts comprising clusters of small firms in related activities have long thrived (Marshall 1920; Piore and Sabel 1984; Bellandi 1986). The small firm networks and project-based work of Silicon Valley, Hollywood and other industrial districts elsewhere have been extensively studied. On the labour market side, this research emphasizes the high worker mobility between firms and between projects, and the resulting fast communication of new, and especially tacit, knowledge across organizations (Saxenian 1996). A key part has been played by occupational communities of practice (CoP), that is, mostly informal groups of workers with a particular expertise who recognize each other's competence and reputation. Because of this recognition, they are willing to join together in project teams or in small firms in the belief that their collaboration will be fruitful. In many such activities, most of the members are highly qualified and there is often no clear division between the expertise of the entrepreneur and that of the other members.

On the financial side, Aoki (2010) has argued that the base for such activities is provided by a modular organization of activity, combined with tournaments for funds from venture capitalists. Modular organization enables firms to combine extensive knowledge sharing about basic principles and common platforms, whilst retaining key areas of expertise which enable them to compete with other similar firms. The 'black box' of knowledge within the firm can be integrated within a wider production process by specifying requirements at the interface between different modules. Thus firms might use a common platform to which they all contribute, but retain a specific area or service for their own operations. To finance module development, and bigger collaborative projects, they engage in competitive bidding for venture capital funding which protects investor interests by enabling them to select the best managed proposals.

On the employment side, many writers have argued that CoPs provide an alternative incentive framework to that of large firms. CoPs encapsulate a collective memory of how well and fairly individual members have performed in the past, through their reputation. They derive their effectiveness from the social bonds that bind them together, whether they be the local communities that underpinned the northern Italian industrial districts (Piore and Sabel 1984) or the shared educational backgrounds and places of socialization of Silicon Valley (Saxenian 1996) and the media industry (Sydow 2002; Baumann 2003). They are built on 'weak ties' such as those based on shared past educational and work experiences (Granovetter 1974).

How do workers gain entry into these more fluid and less structured communities, and what happens to the training and quality control functions of selection into traditionally organized ILMs and OLMs? In some occupations, these institutionally regulated entry paths have eroded in recent years as employment on a more transient project basis has spread, for example, in some knowledge-intensive activities in the media, new technology and research. There, one-off production is common, and has required an organizational adaptation towards more transient structures. In many activities in the creative sectors, the development of a new product, be it a film, a piece of software, or a research project often requires an intensive input of time and resources, whereas its subsequent reproduction is relatively easy and cheap, hence the problems of intellectual and artistic copyright (Baumann 2003). In comparison with traditional manufacturing organizations, project-based organization is less dependent on permanent structures, and so lacks the basis both for well-developed ILMs, and for employer investment in transferable skills.

A potential solution that has emerged in some activities in Britain might be described as 'extended entry tournaments' in which aspirant members of an occupation compete for peer recognition as full members of an occupational community. In traditionally structured occupations, they would have competed for entry into the firms that provided the best ILMs or the highest quality occupational training places. If they failed there, they would move down the queue, and in a relatively short time would have either found a suitable employer, or reconciled themselves to a different occupation. In the less structured case, owing to the ambiguity of signals of successful entry, aspirant members may be tempted to persist for much longer. Because income levels tend to be low during this stage, they often draw on family economic resources for support (Sutton Trust 2006; Eikhof and Warhurst 2013). During this time, they take on commissions and short-term work for contacts and experience, hoping for the 'break' that will bring peer recognition and entry into the occupation.

One reason why this appears to be an economically viable form of labour market organization can be found in Aoki's analysis. In knowledge-intensive activities, the boundary between the knowledge and skills of creative workers and their managers is fuzzy, and they may join forces to compete for funds from investors. Established members of an occupational community need to know whether their aspirant collaborators will produce work of the right quality, and will work well with their colleagues. In a study of legal partnerships, Landers et al. (1996) argued that a tournament process was at work in which aspirants demonstrate their acceptance of occupational norms is by

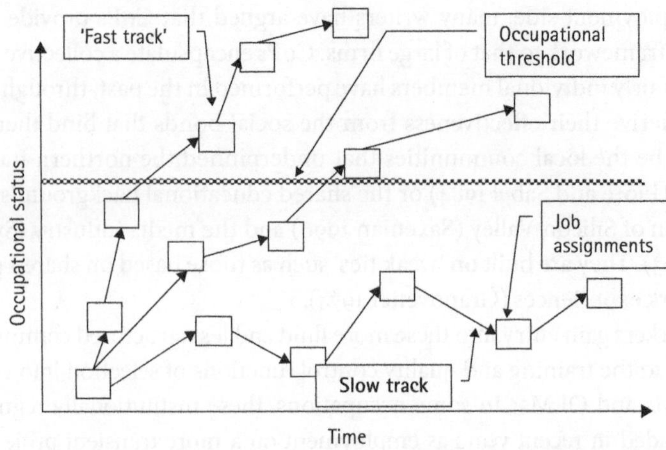

FIGURE 22.5 Career tracks for an unstructured occupational entry for a given cohort

working very long hours. In less structured occupations, willingness to work in unstable and low-paid conditions whilst the quality of your work is being established—'waiting for the break'—provides a similar mechanism.

Figure 22.5 provides a stylized representation of the entry process into an occupation where there is little pre-established structure in the entry segment, and aspirants have to find work assignments, represented by the small boxes that bring them relevant experience, network contacts, and help them build up their career portfolios and reputations. It shows three possible career paths linking successive jobs or work assignments through which aspirant members might progress. These paths are known only *ex post*, and during their careers, aspirants know only about their past and present jobs. Progression is not always upwards. The next job may be better or worse than the current one, and aspirants do not know in advance whether their career is fast or slow track. The fuzzy grey line represents the threshold of peer recognition as a full member of the occupational community. Unlike in occupations with structured entry paths, there is no clear signal and no clear map, and aspirants may end up trapped outside the occupation but having left it too late to change orientation. These people have many of the skills needed within the occupation, and so may add to the competition for work.

In such tournaments, aspirants are under strong pressure to assume the costs of training and building up their work experience and contacts, which creates scope for increased rewards for those who succeed in becoming members, boosting the attractiveness of entering the tournament. If they lack the funds themselves, they may draw support from their families who sustain them through years of work on a low income. The outcome is a form of social selection (Sutton Trust 2006; Eikhof and Warhurst 2013). Firms benefit from their reduced training costs when employees bear more of the cost of gaining experience, and they also benefit from employees' apparent willingness to remain in the occupation's outer orbit long after their prospects of entry have declined. Such savings are likely to offset the pay cost of the small minority at the top.

Thus, in the less structured labour markets of the knowledge-intensive and creative industries, the overlapping of skills and knowledge of those with the managerial and worker functions, combined with the transient nature of projects, two problems appear to have called forth two institutional innovations. The first concerns the tournaments for funding which protect investor interests; and the second, the tournaments for peer recognition within a community of practice, which regulate the relationships between established and non-established members of the community.

Skills, Subcontracting, and Voice Relationships

A nother type of innovation concerns the management of skill inputs across organizational boundaries using voice relationships to ensure supplier skill inputs are of the appropriate quality, and co-evolve according to the buyer's needs. In former decades, these activities might have been encompassed within a single organizational ILM.

A traditional way of thinking about make-or-buy decisions, and thus whether a group of workers would be included within an organization's ILM, has been to emphasize the bargaining dimension, and thus to focus on product specification and price, and to ensure that the buyer is never dependent on a single supplier. Should the buyer organization take direct control of the physical and cognitive assets of the supplier or should it continue to contract externally? If we follow Sutton's argument, mentioned in the Introduction, about quality along supply chains, then it might seem that the buyer firm should simply take control when skills and knowledge are such important contributors to quality, and thus potential sources of informational asymmetry. Although this approach may prevent one kind of hold-up, threatening to switch to another buyer, it leaves another, namely that the workers and managers of the supplier unit collude, using their superior knowledge, to negotiate a better deal for themselves. Given that the buyer firm now owns its former supplier, it is harder for it to extricate itself from the relationship. As Gibbons (2001) argues, if one focuses exclusively on explicit contractual rights, then the problem of quality in a supply chain can seem intractable. However, forms of relational contracting open up a wider range of possibilities.

In a series of studies of buyer–supplier relations among Japanese and US firms, Helper and Sako (1995) illustrate the importance of 'voice' in long-term contractor relationships where supplier and buyer mutually adapt their skills and knowledge. The ownership of physical assets remains distinct but voice creates possibilities for a richer collaboration in the development of employee skills and of organizational capabilities in the supplier firms. In long-term voice relationships exit remains the option of last resort but joint skill and product development create opportunities for both parties to monitor each other's behaviour, and to signal to the other if they feel conditions are tipping unfairly one way or the other. Commitment, or 'loyalty', as Hirschman (1970) described it, is valuable to both parties because it motivates effective voice and so facilitates collaborative production. Such relational contracting may be more valuable in some cases than in others. In particular it offers an alternative solution where worker and manager skills and knowledge in the supplier unit create scope for them to collude against the buyer unit whether it uses open-market contracting or integration into a single organization's internal labour market.

Overlapping Internal Labour Markets

The third example concerns organizations that need to mobilize different capabilities in combination for a particular activity, and yet these capabilities fit best into different types of employment systems. The five models of employment systems shown in Figure 22.3 treated organizations implicitly as focusing on a homogeneous set of capabilities and related skill resources. What happens if organizations need to combine two types of resources that are each best suited to a different model of employment system and governance structure? For example, what happens if the conditions which favour basic research conflict with those that favour commercialization, as might occur with the development of a new drug?

One solution is illustrated by Lam's (2007) study of university–industry joint research ventures (Figure 22.6). These joint ventures sought to deal with the tension between two contrasted capabilities, one focused on discipline-based theoretical knowledge and the other on knowledge in commercial application. In terms of the models in Figure 22.3 above, one might think of the university as characterized by model (e), with a great deal of knowledge overlap between those in managerial and non-managerial positions, and with investors placed at arm's length. In the private firm, management has more clearly defined authority to determine the content of employees' work, and to relate this directly to its business objectives. The past experience of the firms highlighted the difficulty for them to run research operations. In previous decades, they had alternated between internalizing and externalizing their research functions. Internalization had been associated with the development

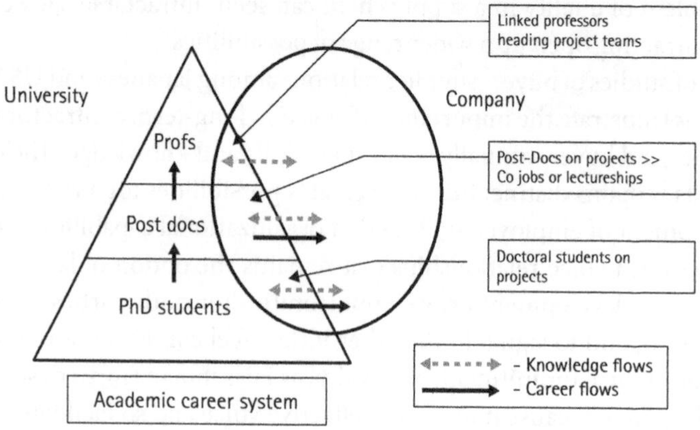

FIGURE 22.6 Project-based overlapping internal labour markets

Source: Based on Lam (2007).

of narrow research agendas and a slowness to respond to new scientific advances, whereas externalization had meant that firms lost their ability to assess the latest research developments and appreciate their commercial significance.

To address these limitations, a number of knowledge-intensive firms had engaged in collaborations with major research universities. Unlike the firms' previous internal research staff, university researchers compete to stay at the cutting edge of new developments in their field: access to research funds and journals depends upon being first to publish. At the same time, academics also have wide-ranging knowledge networks among their peers which they maintain by publication, conference presentations, and general scientific interchange. Academic science places new knowledge in the public domain, and this brings reputation, promotion, and access to research funds. Commercial science depends upon establishing property rights over new knowledge and its applications so that it can generate marketable products.

By collaborating with a research university, the firm can gain access to cutting-edge and pre-publication knowledge, and it is guided to the best scientists by the university's academic standing and the reputation of its researchers. The university stands to gain research funding. However, a suitable framework is needed if this collaboration is to work, and in particular if the bridge between academic and applied research is to be crossed. The solution identified in Lam's case studies was to construct a form of 'overlapping ILM' with knowledge, personnel and funding exchanges between the two organizations. The firms would provide funding for basic research relevant to their commercial needs, and they would deal with its commercial application. The university would provide the mechanisms of peer review in publication and promotion necessary for the quality control of the scientists' work. The academic career system provides the rewards and incentives for the academic scientists involved. At the same time, by recruiting a number of former doctoral students and post-doctoral researchers, the collaborating firms can build up their internal capacity to absorb and evaluate new knowledge so that they can draw out the best commercial opportunities. By organizing collaboration on a project basis, or by means of a series of projects, the academics retain a long-term career system, and the firms avoid becoming locked into paths of research that may cease to be commercially useful to them. In this way, the overlapping ILM helps to overcome some of the drawbacks of both the internalization and externalization strategies.

Societal Dimension and Conclusion

This chapter has outlined the implications for learning-by-doing and the accumulation of practical experience and skill in the context of organizational change. So far, the argument has been abstracted from societal influences on employment systems and skills. This link is explored historically by Martin, Chapter 2 in this volume. Here, the analysis suggests a number of ways in which societal influences may affect the current operation of employment systems. They could be thought of as coming from two principal directions: the nature of skills and knowledge that employees bring to the labour market from educational systems; and the way societal institutions affect the operation and choice of governance arrangements for skills and knowledge.

Educational systems clearly play an important role as they determine the platform on which experiential learning-by-doing can build. Does the educational and vocational training system encourage firm-based internal labour markets or does it support inter-firm occupational markets? The initial Franco-German study by the Aix group showed the influence of the labour market entry skills of French and German workers on firms' choice between the internal and the occupational models (Maurice et al. 1982). On the governance side, Johansen's study of Norwegian employer-based training showed that the capacity for collective action was a key factor in the development of employer-funded transferable skills. In particular, the existence or otherwise of strong employer coordinating bodies in different economies has been a major influence on the success of systems of occupational skills. An interesting development in the United States has been that occupational licensing has expanded in step with the decline in unionization and joint union-management-regulated ILMs (Kleiner and Krueger 2010). The precise causes of this change are not fully known but one possibility is that if employers are less willing to engage in skill formation within ILMs, occupational skills provide an alternative route. If employees are to acquire these skills in sufficient numbers, they need a regulatory framework to ensure they can earn a return on their investment. Licensing is one method. On the other hand, for non-transferable skills a critical support is given by employment protection rules, whose strength varies considerably among OECD countries. Earlier in this chapter, it was argued that employees need some form of protection against bad faith dismissal threats if they are to invest in non-transferable experience. Otherwise, employers would face either reduced availability of such skills or reluctance on the part of employees to accept flexible, team-based working, and the associated skill and knowledge benefits.

This chapter has sought to provide a partial review of the direction of travel of thinking on employment systems, skills, knowledge, and labour market organization, and to draw a link with the research on the changing competitive and funding environment in which firms operate. Sutton's (2012) work on globalization and its impact on competition on quality offers a useful counterweight to the arguments about a 'race to the bottom' which would see the dismantling of ILMs as part of a cost reduction strategy by western employers. This chapter has sought to provide a means of understanding how and why they might be refocusing rather than wholly dismantling them, something borne out by the resilience of the proportion of long-term jobs in the advanced industrial economies documented by the ILO (2003) and regularly shown in the OECD's Statview data on job tenures in different countries.

References

Acemoglu D, and Pischke J-S. (1999) 'Beyond Becker: Training in Imperfect Labour Markets', *Economic Journal*, 109(453): 112–142.

Aoki, M. (2010) *Corporations in Evolving Diversity*, Oxford: Oxford University Press.

Appay, B. and Jeffrys, S. (eds) (2009) *Restructurations, précarisation, valeurs*. Toulouse: Editions Octares.

Backes-Gellner, U. (1996) *Betriebliche Bildungs- und Wettbewerbsstrategien im deutsch-britischen Vergleich*. Mering: Rainer Hampp Verlag.

Backes-Gellner, U., Frick, B., and Sadowski, D. (1997) 'Codetermination and Personnel Policies of German Firms: The Influence of Works Councils on Turnover and Further Training', *International Journal of Human Resource Management*, 8:(3): 328–347.

Baumann, A. (2003) 'Path-Dependency or Convergence? The Emergence of Labour Market Institutions in the Media Production Industries of the UK and Germany'. PhD thesis, European University Institute, Florence.

Becker, G. S. (1975) *Human Capital: A Theoretical and Empirical Analysis, with Special Reference to Education*, Chicago: University of Chicago Press.

Bellandi, M. (1986) 'The Marshallian Industrial District'. Working Paper # 42, Dipartimento di Scienze Economiche, Universita degli Studi di Firenze, Florence.

Bowles, S. (2004) *Microeconomics: Behavior, Institutions and Evolution*, Princeton/New York: Russell Sage Foundation/Princeton University Press.

Brown, J. S. and Duguid, P. (1991) 'Organizational Learning and Communities-of-practice: Toward a Unified View of Working, Learning, and Innovation', *Organization Science*, 2(1): 40–57.

Camuffo, A.(2002) 'The Changing Nature of Internal Labor Markets', *Journal of Management and Governance*, 6: 281–294.

Cappelli, P. (1999) 'Career Jobs are Dead', *California Management Review*, 42(1): 146–167.

Cole, R. (1994) 'Different Quality Paradigms and Their Implications for Organisational Learning', in M. Aoki and R. Dore R (eds), *The Japanese Firm*, Oxford: Oxford University Press: 66–83.

Doeringer P. B, and Piore M. J. (1971) *Internal Labor Markets and Manpower Analysis*, Lexington, MA: Heath.

Drexel I. (1993) *Das Ende des Facharbeiteraufstiegs?* Frankfurt: Campus Verlag.

Eikhof, D. and Warhurst, C. (2013) 'The Promised Land? Why Social Inequalities are Systemic to the Creative Industries', *Employee Relations*, 35(5): 495–508.

Ericksson, T. (2010) Labour Market Outcomes on Internationalisation: What Have We Learnt from Analysis of Microdata on Firms and Their Employees?, in D. Marsden and F. Rycx (eds), *Wage Structures, Employment Adjustments and Globalization*, Basingstoke: Palgrave Macmillan: 221–243.

Eyraud, F, Marsden, D., and Silvestre, J-J. (1990) 'Occupational and Internal Labour Markets in Britain and France', *International Labour Review*, 129(4): 501–517.

Foulkes F. (1980) *Personnel Policies of Large Nonunion Companies*, Englewood Cliffs, NJ: Prentice-Hall.

Franz, W, and Soskice, D. (1995) 'The German Apprenticeship System', in Buttler F., Franz, W., Schettkat, R., and Soskice D. (eds), *Institutional Frameworks and Labour Market Performance*, London: Routledge.

Gibbons, R. (2001) 'Firms (and Other Relationships)', in P. di Maggio (ed.), *The Twenty-first-century Firm*, Princeton: Princeton University Press.

Granovetter, M. (1974) *Getting a Job*, Cambridge, MA: Harvard University Press.

Grimshaw D., Ward, K. G., Rubery, J., and Beynon, H. (2001) 'Organisations and the Transformation of the Internal Labour Market in the UK', *Work, Employment & Society*, 15(1): 25–54.

Hart, O. (1995) *Firms, Contracts and Financial Structure*, Oxford: Oxford University Press.

Helper, S. and Sako, M. (1995) 'Supplier Relations in Japan and the United States: Are They Converging?', *Sloan Management Review*, 36(3): 77–84.

Hirschman, A.O. (1970) *Exit, Voice and Loyalty*, Cambridge, MA: Harvard University Press.

Holm, J. R., Lorenz. E., Lundvall, B-Å., and Valeyre, A. (2010) 'Organizational Learning and Systems of Labor Market Regulation in Europe', *Industrial and Corporate Change*, 19(4): 1141–1173.

ILO (2003) 'Job Stability in Industrialized Countries Remains Surprisingly Strong'. http://www.ilo.org/global/About_the_ILO/Media_and_public_information/Feature_stories/lang--en/WCMS_075624/index.htm#.

Johansen, L-H. (2000) 'Transferable Training and the Collective Action Problem for Employers: An Analysis of Further Education and Training in Four Norwegian Industries'. PhD thesis, London School of Economics, University of London.

Kandel, E. and Lazear, E. P. (1992) 'Peer Pressure and Partnerships', *The Journal of Political Economy*, 100(4): 801–817.

Kleiner, M. M. and Krueger, A. B. (2010) 'The Prevalence and Effects of Occupational Licensing', *British Journal of Industrial Relations*, 48(4): 676–687.

Koike, K. and Inoki, T. (eds) (1990) *Skill Formation in Japan and Southeast Asia*, Tokyo: University of Tokyo Press.

Lam, A. (2000) 'Tacit Knowledge, Organizational Learning and Societal Institutions: A Integrated Approach', *Organization Studies*, 21(3): 487–513.

Lam, A. (2007) 'Knowledge Networks and Careers: Academic Scientists in Industry-University Links', *Journal of Management Studies*, 44(6): 993–1016.

Landers R., Rebitzer, J, and Taylor, L. (1996) 'Human Resources Practices and the Demographic Transformation of Professional Labour Markets', in Osterman P. (ed), *Broken Ladders*, New York: Oxford University Press: 215–245.

Lazear E. (1995) *Personnel Economics*, Cambridge, MA: MIT Press.

Lazonick, W. and O'Sullivan, M. (1996) 'Organization, Finance and International Competition', *Industrial and Corporate Change*, 5(1): 1–49.

Lorenz, E. and Valeyre, A. (2005) 'Organisational Innovation, Human Resource Management and Labour Market Structure: A Comparaison of the EU-15', *Journal of Industrial Relations*, 47(4): 424–442.

Marsden, D. (1999) *A Theory of Employment Systems*, Oxford: Oxford University Press.

Marsden, D. (2011) 'The Growth of Extended "Entry Tournaments" and the Decline of Institutionalised Occupational Labour Markets in Britain', in Lee, S. and McCann, D. (eds), *Regulating for Decent Work*, Basingstoke: ILO, Geneva/Palgrave: 91–122.

Marsden, D. (2013) 'Job Flexibility and the Employment Relationship', Centre for Economic Performance Working Paper no. 1974, London School of Economics.

Marsden D. (2015) 'The Future of the German Industrial Relations Model', *Journal for Labour Market Research / Zeitschrift für Arbeitsmarktforschung* (ZAFO), August, 48(2): 169–187.

Marshall, A. (1920) *Principles of Economics*, London: Macmillan.

Maurice M., Sellier F., and Silvestre J.-J. (1982) *Politique d'éducation et organisation industrielle en France et en Allemagne*, Paris: Presses Universitaires de France.

Mincer, J. (1974) *Schooling, Experience and Earnings*, New York: National Bureau of Economic Research.

Mintzberg, H. (1979) *The Structuring of Organisations*, Englewood Cliffs, NJ: Prentice-Hall

Mintzberg, H. (2009) *Managing*, Harlow: Financial Times Prentice Hall.

Olson, M. (1971) *The Logic of Collective Action*, Cambridge, MA: Harvard University Press.
Orr, J. E. (1996) *Talking about Machines*, Ithaca, NY: ILR Press.
Piore, M. J. and Sabel C. F. (1984) *The Second Industrial Divide*, New York: Basic Books.
Polanyi, M. (1967) *The Tacit Dimension*, New York: Doubleday Anchor.
Robinson, D. (ed) (1970) *Local Labour Markets and Wage Structures*, London: Gower.
Ryan, P. (1991) 'How Much Do Employers Spend on Training? An Assessment of the "Training in Britain" Estimates', *Human Resource Management Journal*, 1(4): 55–76.
Saxenian A. (1996) 'Beyond Boundaries: Open Labor Markets and Learning in Silicon Valley', in M. Arthur and D. Rousseau (eds), *The Boundaryless Career*, New York: Oxford University Press.
Sengenberger, W. (1987) *Struktur und Funktionsweise von Arbeitsmärkten: die Bundesrepublik Deutschland im internationalen Vergleich*, Frankfurt: Campus Verlag.
Simon, H. A. (1951) 'A Formal Theory of the Employment Relationship', *Econometrica*, 19(3): 293–305.
Streeck, W. (1989) 'Skills and the Limits of Neo-Liberalism: The Enterprise of the Future as a Place of Learning', *Work, Employment and Society*, 3: 89–104.
Streeck, W. (2009) *Re-forming Capitalism, Oxford*: Oxford University Press.
Sutton Trust (2006) *The Educational Backgrounds of Leading Journalists*, London: The Sutton Trust.
Sutton, J. (2012) *Competing in Capabilities*, Oxford: Oxford University Press.
Sydow, J. and Staber, U. (2002) 'The Institutional Embeddedness of Project Networks: The Case of Content Production in German Television', *Regional Studies*, 36(3): 215–227.
Williamson, O. E. (1975) *Markets and Hierarchies*, New York: Free Press.

SECTION VI

DIFFERING SKILL SYSTEMS

The Dynamics of Development in a Global Economy

CHAPTER 23

SKILL DEMANDS AND DEVELOPMENTS IN THE ADVANCED ECONOMIES

CAROLINE SMITH

INTRODUCTION

WHILST skills are increasingly seen as a global currency (OECD 2012a), determining the actual and anticipated skills demands of employers and individuals are key challenges for policymakers and an area of ongoing interest for academics. Like many other aspects of debates around skills (Grugulis and Lloyd 2010), issues of skills demand are highly contested and complex.

In academic debates since the 1960s there have been a range of views about how to define and measure skills and whether we are witnessing an increase in the skills requirements in a 'knowledge economy' or whether deskilling is actually taking place. The shift from manufacturing to services has challenged the conceptualization of skills, with an increasing focus on 'soft' skills; both academics and policymakers are focusing on the importance of 'employability' skills, deriving from real and perceived employer needs, intensified by the problematic job markets that followed the global financial crisis (GFC) of 2008. Encouraging employability skills is also a strategy to bridge a growing gap between 'skill haves' and 'skill have-nots,' as the latter risk being left behind in the knowledge economy. The orthodoxy has emerged among OECD policymakers that increasing skills is one of the key factors required to enhance economic competitiveness and productivity.

Evidence suggests that the qualifications of the workforce, a common proxy for skills, are increasing in most of the advanced economies as well as many emerging economies. Anticipating employer demand for skills through forecasting is used in many advanced economies to assist in planning for future skills needs, which in turn inform skills policy development. Most modelling shows that demand for higher level skills is increasing, although there are different views about what is happening to lower- level and middle-level jobs, and whether the growth in job demand has been keeping pace with the growth in skills supply. It seems clear that employers have responded to the huge increase in the supply of graduates by raising their expectations of employee skills, particularly at the point of hire.

Whilst focusing on improving skill levels, advanced economies continue to take very different paths to skill development. Skills development in the coordinated market economies (CMEs) of northern Europe, Japan, and Korea is often institutionally based and codified through social partnership agreements within a framework established by the state (Soskice 1999). In contrast, the Liberal Market Economies (LMEs) which include the Anglo-Saxon economies and Ireland, give management the prerogative regarding skill development, with little coordination between companies, unions often excluded, and limited state intervention in skill development outside of the formal education system.

However, academics and policymakers have increasingly argued that skills alone will not result in a 'productivity miracle,' highlighting a need to consider how skills are used in the workplace (Keep et al. 2006, 547). Without employer strategies that create high-skill jobs and foster innovation, there is a risk that the return on investment in skills will be low. Whilst CMEs have long sought to link skills and innovation policy, the policy tools available are not always palatable particularly in the LMEs, or indeed guaranteed of success. In LMEs, the voice of employees has been less likely to be embedded in policy and practice, although trade unions are increasingly seeking involvement in training issues (see Stuart and Huzzard, Chapter 12, this volume).

The sections that follow consider academic debates about the demand for skills, as well as government expectations about skills and how these have been influenced by academic discussions. This is followed by data on trends and forecasting of skills development. How and where policy and practice positions are formulated will be considered for CMEs and LMEs, as well as the shifting policy positions and policy interventions. The chapter concludes with a commentary on these debates, trends, and interventions.

Back to the Future and Back Again: Academic Debates about Government and Employer Demand for Skills

Academic debates about the trajectory of skills over the past 50 years have shifted between assumptions of upskilling and deskilling. In the high growth, high employment economy of the 1960s, there was a general consensus that the quality of jobs and skills levels were both improving as technology replaced many unskilled jobs (Grugulis et al. 2004). However, this relative consensus broke down in the 1970s. Braverman (1974) argued that technology increased the separation of thought and execution, with an inevitable decrease in the skills of the worker and increase in management control.

Braverman's work was influential, but his focus on deskilling and control was seen as overly deterministic. Employers have choices, and may 'reskill, recombine tasks or widen workers discretion and responsibility' (Thompson 1990, 100). Despite the critiques, many subsequent writers, from a labour process perspective, broadly supported Braverman's approach. Some empirical evidence for this theory appeared in the United States in the mid-1970s, when the supply of university graduates appeared to outstrip demand, leading to a decrease in the wage premium (Freeman 1976). Whilst this work was briefly influential (e.g. Smith and Welch 1978), the trend was soon reversed, as graduate jobs and wages grew notably in the decades that followed, along with increasing returns for post-secondary education (Carnevale et al. 2012).

The upskilling thesis held sway in the 1980s and early 1990s in the form of the knowledge economy. The central argument is that knowledge workers require ever higher levels of skill and are able to deploy these skills at work. As a result they are assumed to have choice and a strong position in the labour market. In a *network society*, a 'highly skilled, creative and increasingly autonomous labour force becomes the fundamental source of productivity and competitiveness' (Castells 1996, 40). Robert Reich (1991), Secretary of Labor in the Clinton administration, identified three types of workers in the new economy: symbiotic analysts, routine production workers, and personal service workers. Symbiotic analysts, who deal with information and symbols for a living, were well educated and could expect to be even more advantaged in the new economy. These approaches have been described as a 'new upskilling thesis', which was linked to the emergence of information technology (Lloyd and Grugulis 2010, 91).

Once again, however, concerns over deskilling emerged, this time with a greater focus on the growing services sector. Ritzer (1998) argued that standardization of processes following the fast food model was occurring in the 'McDonaldization' of society, which also resulted in a degradation of skills. In a similar vein, debates about call centre employment focused on the 'Taylorization' of white collar work (Taylor and Bain 1999). However, this literature recognizes a variety of skill levels across call centre employment (Frenkel et al. 1998). The influence of information and communication technology (ICT) on skills continues to be a source of interest and debate. Elliott (see Chapter 26 in this volume) argues that up to 82% of current jobs, including many intermediate- and higher-skilled jobs, are at risk of being obsolete by 2030 through adoption of ICT.

Debates about deskilling are often centred on developments in the United Kingdom and the United States. In considering the skills trajectory more broadly across the advanced economies, employers appear more willing to offer training and higher-skilled opportunities (Grugulis et al. 2004).

The concept of the knowledge economy and its requirements for more and better skills tends also to mask differences in the attainment of skill levels by workers, as well as polarization of skill levels by jobs. Those without post-school qualifications are less likely to participate in the labour force (see for example Keating et al. 2012), and also face barriers to accessing further skills development. Availability of time, resources, and work-life issues all tend to be greater constraints to training participation for workers in lower paid, lower skill occupations (Pocock et al. 2011). A greater focus on the lower skilled, including pathways to higher-skilled jobs, is important to ensure that those with lower skills are not increasingly left behind.

Traditional notions of skill have been associated with craft and manual occupations (Payne 2000). The skills required in manufacturing environments are based primarily on technical knowledge. In these jobs the interface is with products, processes, and machines as well as colleagues, but capacity for interaction with clients or customers has not been part of the required skills mix. The shift from manufacturing to services industries has led to a changing emphasis in skill requirements from technical know-how to considering personal characteristics, attributes, or behaviours as skills (Keep and Mayhew 1999; Bolton 2004; Grugulis et al. 2004). However, whilst technical skills in craft occupations have traditionally been well rewarded, this is not necessarily the case for soft skills in the service sector. Given the growth in the services sector and the tendency towards lower pay, there has been a significant amount of academic debate about the value of service work. The interaction with customers in a variety of contexts has been described as 'emotional labour' (Hochschild 1983). Rather than being low skilled, the service worker is a 'multi-skilled emotion manager' who should be valued accordingly (Hochschild 1983). Service work therefore may be low paid and low status, but may not be low skilled (Korcynski 2005, 7). For a full discussion on the changing nature of how skills are defined and skills in the service sector see Warhurst et al., Chapter 4 in this volume).

Changes in the world economy mean that knowledge workers in the advanced economies are not guaranteed a high-skill, high-wage path. The knowledge economy debates assumed that advanced economies would compete on skills whilst emerging economies would compete on price (Brown et al. 2008). However, the increasing education levels of emerging economies and strategies of multinational companies to conduct professional services work offshore mean that 'knowledge workers' in the advanced countries face growing challenges in the labour market (Brown et al. 2008; Sako, Chapter 28 in this volume). Whilst wages for tertiary graduates are holding at this point, there is a 'global auction for jobs' that provides employers with international sources of labour willing to provide an ever lower price (Brown et al. 2010). If this continues, the debates over the stock of skills and their value in the advanced economies will become even more complex.

Skilling for a Better Economy and Society: Government Expectations about Skills

Despite the continuing academic debates, there is a growing consensus among governments around the world that 'skills are the global currency of the 21st century'

(OECD 2012, 1). This is increasingly the case in both advanced and emerging economies. Indeed 'virtually all national governments in both developed and emerging economies view the upgrading of skills as key to economic competitiveness, social justice and a cohesive society' (Brown et al. 2008, 1).

The value of increased skills has also been articulated in intergovernmental statements. For example, the G20 Training Strategy states, 'ultimately, each country's prosperity depends on how many of its people are in work and how productive they are, which in turn rests on the skills they have and how effectively those skills are used. Skills are the foundation of decent work' (International Labour Office 2011, 1). The OECD Skills Strategy highlights the importance of skills in the twenty-first century and advises governments on how to identify strengths and weaknesses and benchmark against other countries (OECD 2012b).

A key challenge for national governments is trying to ensure skills supply matches current and future skills demand. This incorporates efforts to identify the skills required and strategies to achieve them. When skill mismatches occur and take time to resolve, there are significant costs to individuals, enterprises and societies (Cedefop 2010). Among the range of possible skills mismatches are skills shortages, which can impact wages, quality and output (Richardson 2007), along with over-skilling, which for the individuals involved may mean lower pay rates and low job satisfaction (Mavromaras et al. 2011).

Governments tend to focus on measurable skills outcomes, targets, and accreditation (Grugulis et al. 2004). This focus on qualifications as a proxy for skills tends to underestimate the important role that informal learning plays in achieving social and economic goals. There is evidence that informal learning is linked to productivity (Fuller et al. 2003), and social inclusion (Hodkinson et al. 2003).

There is a paradox in the upskilling agenda of governments given the ongoing repercussions for employment of the GFC. For example, many people with higher-level skills in the United States have lost their jobs and are struggling to find work (Gatta and Finegold 2010). In Europe, it is expected that the supply of highly qualified workers will rise faster than demand in the short term (Cedefop 2012b). And even in rapidly growing economies like China and India, the expansion in the supply of graduates has been far more rapid than the growth in high-skill jobs (Liu and Finegold, Chapter 25 this volume). This highlights the importance of seeing skills as part of broader economic development, employment, and innovation policies.

The changing nature of the modern workplace increasingly requires education systems to deliver graduates who are adaptable, flexible, and also have technical proficiency (US National Academy of Sciences 1995). This has been described as a need for 'hybrid' (Palmer 1990), or 'T-shaped' workers (*Gazelle Global* 2012), who have the right balance between soft skills and technical skills to meet employer demand. Developing these skills can pose a particular challenge for countries such as Australia and the United Kingdom, whose vocational training systems are based on technical competencies, although there are efforts underway to incorporate soft skills. For example, Australia has embedded employability skills in training packages which incorporate industry endorsed national standards for the vocational training system (Australian

Government 2013). The United Kingdom has used a similar approach through General National Vocational Qualifications, although these are generally not viewed as having worked well. Countries such as the Netherlands and Germany already have embedded knowledge-based definitions of competency (Buchanan et al. 2010).

In the higher education (HE) sector, there are ongoing efforts to incorporate work-integrated learning into programmes so that graduates have employability skills. This approach is being implemented in the United States, for example through the professional science master's (PSM) degrees that have been developed in conjunction with industry. PSM degrees allow students to pursue two years of academic training in science or mathematics, whilst simultaneously developing workplace skills through a professional component including business and communications (PSM 2013). Similar interdisciplinary degrees are being considered in countries such as the United Kingdom, Singapore, and Australia and are likely to develop further over time.

What Do the Data Tell Us? Trends and Forecasting of Skills Development

Countries across the OECD have increasingly higher skilled populations as younger people in particular are becoming more highly educated. People aged 35–44 are more likely to hold a post-secondary qualification than people aged 45 and over in all OECD countries (OECD 2012). As Figure 23.1 shows, the increase in tertiary education has been

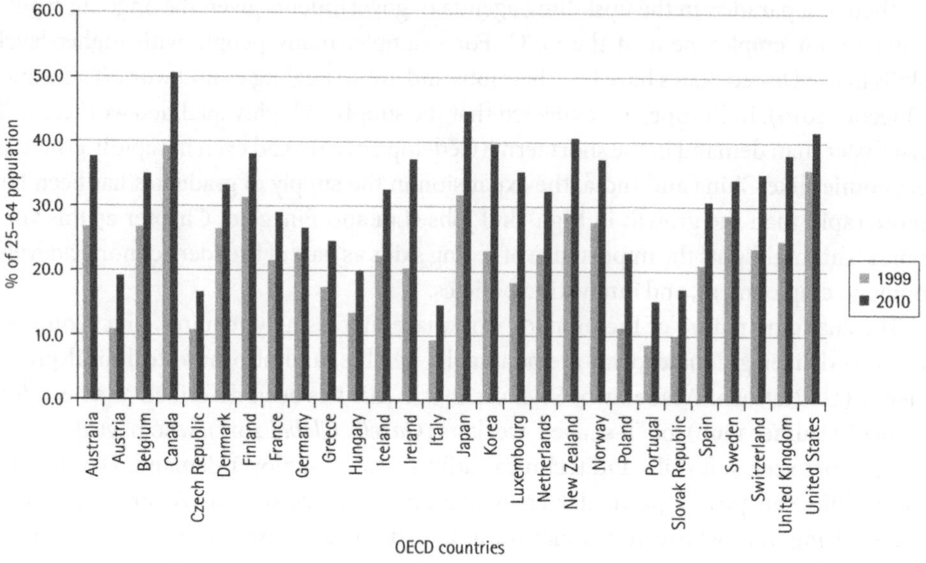

FIGURE 23.1 Population that has attained tertiary qualifications, OECD, 1999 and 2010

Source: OECD (2009, table A1.4; 2012b, table A1.3a).

very rapid in many countries, for example, almost doubling in South Korea, Luxemburg, and Ireland between 1999 and 2010. The recent economic troubles of Ireland and Japan suggest that a high level of skills does not necessarily equate to a strong economy. This point is also demonstrated by the case of Scotland, which despite having higher education levels than other parts of the United Kingdom, lags behind in economic performance (Scottish Government 2007).

There are also countries where growth in tertiary level education for 25–64 year olds has been comparatively slow, most noticeably in the United States and Germany. Whilst growth is still positive, this raises the question of whether increasing skills levels are inevitable, and also illustrates the influence of local circumstances in skills supply.

To assist in policy development, many governments undertake or commission forecasts of future skills needs. Given the complexity of skills forecasting, forecasters 'use simplified proxies for the complex reality' (Richardson and Tan 2008, 171). Approaches used vary within and between countries, but many modellers forecast future employment by industry and occupation and then derive skills demand (Richardson and Tan 2008). Other techniques include focusing on skills rather than qualifications (see, for example, Lowry et al. 2008).

Whilst future projections can assist governments in planning for future skills demands, it is difficult to forecast into the future with any degree of certainty, particularly at a detailed level (Richardson and Tan 2008). As modelling tends to rely on past trends that are extrapolated into the future, changes that impact the labour market such as technology and globalization also impact the accuracy of forecasting (Richardson and Teese 2008). A further limitation is the capability to incorporate qualitative, as well as quantitative, changes in the nature of work into modelling approaches (Watson 2011). The variation in projections supports the need for 'bottom-up' approaches that take account of local differences in projecting skills (Richardson and Tan 2008).

Projections of skill requirements suggest an increase in job opportunities for those with higher skill levels. For example, 27 European countries are projected to see a 20% increase in jobs requiring high level qualifications, and a similar decrease in the proportion of jobs requiring low level qualifications. However, jobs requiring medium-level qualifications are projected to continue to provide the most opportunities, at just under half of all employment (Cedefop 2012a).

The US Bureau of Labour Statistics (BLS) forecasts that jobs typically requiring post-secondary education will grow fastest from 2010–20 (Bureau of Labour Statistics 2012). However BLS forecasts have been argued to under-estimate skills demand because they incorporate changes in educational demand from changes in employment composition but not changing educational requirements within occupations. This risks underinvestment in skills development (Carnevale et al. 2010).

In the United Kingdom, there is a projected expansion in managerial and professional professions to 2020 as well as growth at the lower-skilled end of the labour market such as personal services. Significant declines are expected in skilled and semi-skilled manual roles, and administrative and secretarial occupations (UKCES 2011). This hollowing out of middle-level jobs has been described as 'the hourglass' or barbell economy (University Alliance 2012).

To help manage uncertainty and minimize the risks associated with longer-term projections, the former Australian Workforce and Productivity Agency (AWPA) adopted a scenario approach that involves considering a range of plausible futures. In its work to develop a 2013 national workforce development strategy, AWPA developed four scenarios that were then modelled to provide a number of different projections for Australia's skills and workforce to 2025. Issues in common across the scenarios were considered to be relatively certain to occur and able to be planned for. The four scenarios—The Long Boom, Smart Recovery, Terms of Trade Shock, and Ring of Fire—all had in common increasing demand for higher-level skills, an ageing population, the growing importance of Asia, and increasing take-up of technology. Differences between the scenarios, such as industry structure, were considered to be more uncertain and require flexible responses (AWPA 2012).

The How and the Where ... Employer Engagement in Skills Acquisition in the Advanced Economies

Whilst there is relative consensus in public policy terms about the importance of skills, the institutions, and policies to stimulate employer engagement and investment in skills acquisition differ quite significantly between the advanced economies. This is because national approaches to skills are the result of the historical dynamics between labour markets, education and training systems, and how they have evolved over time in context of institutional, social, and political structures and cultures (Keating 2009). However, there are some areas of similarity within, but also between, LMEs and CMEs.

Broad patterns can be identified within LMEs and CMEs in relation to institutional support for skills development and the domain in which skills formation strategies are developed—national, regional/sectoral and the workplace. Indeed, 'most countries apply different forms of financial and non-financial incentives and regulatory measures to promote adult participation in education and training and to encourage a shared responsibility between individuals and employers' (Cedefop 2012c, 1).

Sectoral training funds (STFs) exist in Singapore (Sung and Raddon, Chapter 24 in this volume) and a number of European countries to increase skills investment. Though they are governed in different ways, STFs tend to be funded through a levy on wages, and are managed by employers and employees. They therefore require good cooperation between unions and employer organizations (Cedefop 2008). In most European countries payback clauses are in place, which are designed to reduce the real or perceived risk to employers that employees leave soon after they are trained. Payback clauses are governed through a range of mechanisms, including national labour codes, sector or workplace agreements (Cedefop 2012).

Collective bargaining plays an important role in skills development in CMEs, with agreements between unions and employer organizations at a number of different levels. In France, employers and unions exert considerable influence over training policy through social dialogue at the national and sectoral level (Le Deist and Winterton 2012). In Sweden, a national agreement sets out a framework for cooperation, and agreements for vocational training are set at the sectoral level along with pay and working time (EIRO 2013a). National level agreements in Norway are supplemented by negotiations and agreements at the enterprise level (EIRO 2013b). In Denmark, collective bargaining occurs at multiple levels within a framework of 'centralized decentralization'. Most of the collective bargaining on training and lifelong learning occurs within sectoral agreements (EIRO 2013c).

Institutions such as collective bargaining and works councils, underpinned by legislative requirements, can also be the domain in which dialogue occurs over how work is organized, including responses to changes in technology or restructuring. These arrangements, most common in CMEs, include rights to information, consultation, and co-determination, the latter sometimes meaning a right of veto. For example, in Austria there is a requirement for consultation with the works council on planned structural changes or reorganization programmes. In Germany, co-determination rights include the participation in a 'social plan' in the event of a substantial change to the enterprise. There are some areas where companies cannot proceed without approval of the works council, including the principles underlying company suggestion schemes for improvements. Information and consultation arrangements on these matters do exist in some LMEs, but these are generally voluntary (Arrigo and Casale 2010).

The social partnership approach to governance of skills has weakened in several countries over the past two decades (Keating 2009). Whilst protections for workers remain strong, the proportion of workers covered by collective agreements has declined as a share of overall employment in Germany, Japan, and Italy in the period 1960–2010 (Schmitt and Mitukiewicz 2012). There has traditionally been a focus in Germany on initial vocational training through the dual system, and whilst the majority continue to pursue apprenticeships, the system has been under strain for more than a decade. Continuing vocational training has become more important, but despite the strong tradition of cooperation between unions and employer organizations, this is an area that is now largely influenced by employers (Trappmann 2012). Collective bargaining coverage has remained steady or increased slightly over this period in many other CMEs (Schmitt and Mitukiewicz 2012).

In contrast to the institutional focus of skills formation within CMEs, LMEs have weaker institutional structures and a much stronger focus on company-driven workplace training (Cooney and Stuart 2012). There has been almost universal decline in collective bargaining coverage in LMEs between 1960–2010 (Schmitt and Mitukiewicz 2012). Skills development is largely left to management, with the absence of frameworks to regulate skills development (Cooney and Stewart 2012). There is also a higher expectation that individuals will pay for enhancing their own skills.

In line with the increasing focus on the importance of skills, continuing training is of increasing interest to trade unions in some countries (Cooney and Stuart 2012). In the United Kingdom, Union Learning Representatives (ULRs) were established in the mid-1990s as a new form of workplace union representative, with a core focus on increasing access to skills training for workers (Stuart and Huzzard, Chapter 12, this volume). The role of the ULR focuses on supporting skills acquisition, but does not extend to issues of skills utilization such as job design (Green 2010). This initiative received significant public funding from 1997 through the Union Learning Fund. ULRs have focused on supporting workers with poor literacy and numeracy skills, but are now also in place across the UK union movement in a variety of job roles including professions. Evaluations of the impact of these initiatives have identified increased organizational performance and improved trust relations between management and unions (Stuart et al. 2010). The ULR model has been replicated in a number of different countries, from LMEs, such as New Zealand, to CMEs, such as Finland and Sweden.

LMEs tend to focus on market-based approaches to encourage skills investment, but may intervene in areas of market failure. Market approaches generally combine the use of financial and other mechanisms to stimulate demand for skills by employers and workers, often alongside devolution of authority for decisions to training providers (Keating 2009) or industry bodies. These strategies have been used in the United Kingdom and Australia, although in more recent times the UK government has shifted away from funding employer training. The US workforce development system largely leaves responsibility for skills investment to employers and individuals. This has been argued as risking underinvestment in skills that will leave the United States at a disadvantage with no national workforce development strategy in place (Gatta and Finegold 2010).

Unions and employers do, to some degree, play a role in sectoral and sub-national institutional arrangements in the LMEs (Sung 2006). LMEs such as Australia, the United Kingdom, New Zealand, and Canada have all established sectoral training councils. Whilst generally involving both employers and unions, the focus is on employer engagement as a mechanism to increase employer ownership, investment, and provision of training.

Some LMEs have put in place measures to regulate aspects of skills formation; for example, a training levy is in place in Quebec, Canada, similar to Singapore's STF. Such a levy had been introduced in the mid-1960s in the United Kingdom and mid-1990s in Australia, though both were later repealed (Charest 2012). In the United Kingdom, other legislative measures include the statutory underpinning of ULRs and an employee Right to Request training. However, these approaches are often fluid; for example, in Australia training was included in industrial and occupational awards but is no longer part of the award system.

Despite these structural differences, there are some common emerging themes and broad patterns identifiable in CMEs and LMEs. These include: partial integration of vocational and general education in secondary schools; increased access to recognition of prior learning; establishment of national qualification frameworks; the increasing adoption of competency-based approaches to vocational education; and the use of industry-led sector agencies to develop training standards (Keating 2009).

Changing Terrain ... Shifting Skills Policy Positions and Interventions from Supply to Demand

Whilst the value of skills is increasingly recognized, it is also becoming apparent that skills on their own are not enough. This applies to skills policy and its relationship to innovation and economic development, as well linking skills to productivity at the enterprise level. A range of academic critiques have outlined the constraints of focusing only on skills supply, making the case for a broader approach that links skills with industry and economic policy. As stated by Keep et al. (2006, 547)

> putting the skills cart before the economic development horse may produce rather limited results. If enough public money is expended, we can have a skills revolution, without it necessarily achieving much in the way of a productivity miracle'.

There are signs that change is occurring.[1] There is notable activity at the local level, as illustrated through the OECD Local Economic and Employment Development (LEED). Some US states have identified priority industries and linked economic and workforce development strategies to reinvigorate local economies. However, shifting the focus from skills formation to skills utilization is a significant policy challenge.

At the enterprise level, there is limited evidence that having better-skilled workers encourages employers to create jobs that utilize these workers' skills effectively (Warhurst and Findlay 2012). Further, many employees are not able to deploy their full productive potential, for example, more than 40% of Australians identify as either moderately or severely over-skilled (Mavromaras et al. 2007).

The concept of skills utilization goes to the heart of 'the way in which work and jobs are organised and the ways in which organizations use and deploy skills ... [which are] critical for ensuring that high skilled jobs are created' (Hall and Lansbury 2006, 583).

[1] www.industry.gov.au, accessed 12 February 2014.

However, market models implemented by many LME governments demonstrate reluctance to interfere in issues such as choice of business model, competitive strategy, work organization, job redesign, and employee relations, which are more difficult to achieve than expanding educational provision or providing employer subsidies (Keep et al. 2006).

In this context, the policy challenge is how to influence change in how employers organize work. Warhurst and Findlay (2012) identify three broad options. The first is government regulation, for example through levies or licences to practice. However, even if regulatory approaches can increase skill levels, this does not necessarily translate into influencing organizational design or how skills are used. The second option is exhortation by governments for employers to change their behaviour, for example, through sharing best practices. Identifying and sharing the benefits to employers may provide some leverage in those organizations where there is an alignment with their interests. However, this approach may be limited in its influence, particularly as many employers perceive more effective skills utilization 'as a policy solution to a problem that does not exist' (2012, 5). Collective approaches involving employers, unions, and other stakeholders is a third option to change work organization and improve how skills are used. This is an approach that would be more likely in CMEs, noting that increased skills utilization and productivity in firms does not automatically translate into better wages and working conditions (Froy et al. 2012).

The concepts of ability, motivation, and opportunity recognize the importance of employees as an agent in this process (Appelbaum et al. 2000). They also provide an important conceptual bridge between skills development and deployment. The supply of skills can help ensure ability, so that employees have the required skills. Sufficient motivation is required to deploy that ability, for example job security and/or a share in rewards of innovation and productivity gains. Finally, employers also shape the opportunity for employees to deploy their skills through the design of jobs (Warhurst and Findlay 2012).

Whilst there are examples in particular LME workplaces of unions and employers working together on these issues, this approach is not found systematically in LMEs. In Australia during the 1980s, unions were involved in bargaining over skills in the context of structural adjustment. In New Zealand in the mid-2000s, the Engineering, Printing and Manufacturing Union (EPMU) and the Dairy Workers Union (DWU) established the Centre for High Performance Work. The aim was to ensure workplace efforts to improve productivity would benefit workers as well as employers (Centre for High Performance Work 2008). In the United Kingdom, policy documents on skills utilization tend to acknowledge the presence of unions but 'place them rather on the sidelines of the whole strategy' (Green 2010, 16). This is despite the role that UK unions, particularly the Scottish Trades Union Congress (STUC) have played in putting skills utilization on the policy agenda (Green 2011). With these rare exceptions, there is little evidence that LME governments are actively seeking to promote social partnership as a key mechanism for better use of skills.

Government funding is a fourth potential lever for change that may be more palatable in LMEs, and is a practice used in a number of CMEs. The Scottish government has been a leader in this area, establishing a number of action research projects aimed at exploring the potential contribution of universities and colleges to improve workplace skills utilization (Payne 2011). Another approach is for funding to be made available for both skills development and skills utilization strategies as part of the one programme. The Irish Workplace Innovation Fund sought to improve innovation and performance, including support for building employee capacity for change and redesigning work arrangements (Buchanan et al. 2010). And Australia's former advisory body to the federal Skills Minister, AWPA, recommended changing a key employer training programme, the National Workforce Development Fund, to make funding available for workforce development activities that maximize the use of employee skills and complement training activity (AWPA 2013).

These approaches have had a longer history in a number of European CMEs, where 'state-sponsored workplace development programmes have emerged in pursuit of enhanced productivity and improvements in the quality of working life' (Keep et al. 2006, 544). In Belgium, the Flemish government entered into a pact with the unions and employers to address quality of work, the organization of work, and careers (Buchanan et al. 2010). Issues considered include workload, task variety, and autonomy.

Programmes have been in place in Germany and the Nordic countries for the last three decades to boost organizational innovation and with it, the demand for high-skilled workers (Ramstad 2009). For example, Vinnova is Sweden's innovation agency, whose mission is to promote sustainable growth by improving the conditions for innovation and funding needs driven research.[2] Vinnova includes a focus on renewal of management and work organization with the goal of new or improved working methods and organizational solutions (Eurofound 2012). In Germany, the Fraunhofer Institute for Systems and Innovation Research investigates the scientific, economic, ecological, social, organizational, legal, and political framework conditions for generating innovations and their implications.[3]

The Finnish Workplace Development Programme is a prime success story—it seeks to build institutional capacity by bringing together a range of partners (including employer organizations and trade unions) with an interest in establishing 'learning networks' aimed at sharing knowledge and experience (Keep et al. 2006). In a study of 312 Finnish workplaces, reforms to work processes, teamwork, management, networking, and job rotation were positively related to performance (Ramstad 2005, cited in Ramstad 2009, 535).

With increased policy interest in skills utilization from LMEs, the favoured strategies are within a market framework, focusing on exhortation of employers and some

[2] innova.gov.se/en/About-VINNOVA, accessed 3 June 2013.

[3] http://www.isi.fraunhofer.de, accessed 3 June 2013.

leveraging of government funding. The use of government funding is also a longer-term strategy used in some CMEs.

Conclusion

Whilst skills development is often viewed as a 'win-win', the issue is complex and contested. The mechanisms for matching skills supply and skills demand are many and varied. There are, however, broad patterns within LMEs and CMEs, as well as some similarities between LMEs and CMEs. Therefore a strict delineation between the skills formation strategies of LMEs and CMEs is not entirely accurate. Changes to policy over time also mean that approaches to skills formation are fluid, within the context of historical institutional arrangements.

Academic discourse has vigorously debated whether technology and globalization drive upskilling or deskilling of jobs. In reality, there has probably been a mix of both. The shift from manufacturing to service industries has broadened the definition of skill so 'soft' skills have more of a focus. Soft skills are what employers appear to increasingly demand but are less willing to pay for.

Whilst it is generally expected that high skills will be well rewarded, globalization means that skilled workers in the advanced economies may need to compete with equally skilled workers in emerging economies. A key current and future policy question is will there be enough high-skilled jobs available across the advanced economies? And will the wage premium for high skills remain? These issues highlight the policy challenge of linking skills with employment strategies and economic development.

The stock of skills in the advanced economies is increasing but at different rates. Is the notion of a continually upward skills trajectory realistic? What strategies should be in place at the lower end of the skills spectrum to enable an upskilling agenda to be successfully implemented? If what we are seeing is a polarization of skills, will we also witness increasingly polarized societies based on skills and income?

Given the emerging global consensus of the value of skills, if all countries are striving toward a high-skill economy, what is the comparative advantage for individual countries? It may be the ability to deploy the skills of the workforce that becomes a key factor in countries maximizing their potential. Another factor may be the capacity—and willingness—to identify and support the key subsectors that have all the elements needed to be world-class in innovation, skills demand, and supply.

With the focus on social partnership and a longer-term commitment to linking skills, innovation, and economic development, CMEs have a broader approach to insuring a payoff from skills investment. LMEs are recognizing the need to influence skills utilization, but within a market-based framework there is less appetite for government intervention. In the years to come it will be interesting to see how successful these strategies are and the directions in which policy develops.

References

Appelbaum, E., Kalleberg, A. L., and Berg, P. (2000) *Manufacturing Advantage*, Ithaca: Cornell University Press.

Arrigo, G., and Casale, G. (2010) *A Comparative Overview of Terms and Notions on Employee Participation*, Labour Administration and Inspection Programme, Working Document no. 8, International Labour Organization, Geneva, February.

Australian Government (2013) www.employability skills.training.com.au, accessed 22 March 2013.

Australian Workforce and Productivity Agency (AWPA) (2013), *Future Focus: 2013 National Workforce Development Strategy*, Canberra: Commonwealth of Australia.

Australian Workforce and Productivity Agency (AWPA) (2012), 'Future Focus: Australia's Skills and Workforce Development Needs', Discussion Paper, Commonwealth of Australia.

Bolton, S. (2004) 'Conceptual Confusions: Emotion Work as Skilled Work', in C. Warhurst, I. Grugulis, and E. Keep (eds), *The Skills That Matter*, London: Palgrave Macmillan: 19–37.

Braverman, H. (1974) *Labor and Monopoly Capital*, London: Monthly Review Press.

Brown, G. (2009) 'Changes to the Machinery of Government', Media release 5 June. http://webarchive.nationalarchives.gov.uk/20090706064025/http://www.number10.gov.uk/Page19525, accessed 28 March 2013.

Brown, P., Lauder, H., and Aston, D. (2010) *The Global Auction*, New York: Oxford University Press.

Brown, P., Ashton, D., Lauder, H., and Tholen, G. (2008) *Towards a High-skilled, Low-waged Workforce? A Review of Global Trends in Education, Employment and the Labour Market*, Monograph no. 10, Centre of Skills, Knowledge and Organizational Performance (SKOPE), Cardiff and Oxford Universities.

Buchanan, J., Scott, L., Yu, S., Schultz, H., and Jakubauskas, M. (2010) 'Skills Demand and Utilisation: An International Review of Approaches to Measurement and Policy Development', OECD Local Economic and Employment Development (LEED) Working Papers, 2010/04, OECD, Paris.

Bureau of Labour Statistics (2012) *Employment projections: 2010-2020 summary*, Economic News Release, 1 February.

Carnevale, A. P., Jayasundera, T., and Hudson, A. R. (2012), *Five Ways That Pay: Careers and Technical Education Along the Way to the B.A.*, Georgetown University Public Policy Institute, September.

Carnevale, A. P., Smith, N. and Stroll, J. (2010) *Help Wanted: Projections of Jobs and Education Requirements through 2018*, Georgetown University, Center on Education and the Workforce.

Castells, M. (1996) *The Rise of the Network Society*, Cambridge, MA: Blackwell Publishers.

Centre for High Performance Work (2008) *Building High Performance Workplaces: The Union Approach*, Handbook for Union Members, Auckland: Centre for High Performance Work.

Charest, J. (2012) 'Moving beyond the Rhetoric? Unions and Training in Canada: Challenges and Policy Perspective', in R. Cooney and M. Stuart, M. (eds), *Trade Unions and Workplace Training*, London: Routledge: 59–76.

Cooney, R. and Stuart, M. (2012) *Trade Unions and Workplace Training*, London: Routledge.

Eurofound (2012) *Work Organization and Innovation*, Annexes, Dublin: Eurofound.

European Industrial Relations Observatory Online (2013a) Denmark: Industrial Relations Profile. http://www.eurofound.europa.eu/eiro/country/denmark_4.htm, accessed 13 March 2013.

European Industrial Relations Observatory Online (2013b) Norway: Industrial Relations Profile. http://www.eurofound.europa.eu/eiro/country/norway_4.htm, accessed 13 March.
European Industrial Relations Observatory Online (2013c) Sweden: Industrial Relations Profile. http://www.eurofound.europa.eu/eiro/country/sweden_4.htm, accessed 13 March.
European Centre for the Development of Vocational Training (Cedefop) (2012a) Skills Forecast—Employment Trends. http://www.cedefop.europa.eu/EN/about-cedefop/projects/forecasting-skill-demand-and-supply/skills-forecasts/main-results.aspx?CountryID=31&case=ETBQ, accessed 19 October 2012.
European Centre for the Development of Vocational Training (Cedefop) (2012b), 'Europe's Skills Challenge: Lagging Skill Demand Increases Risks of Mismatch', Briefing Note, Luxembourg, Publications Office of the European Communities.
European Centre for the Development of Vocational Training (Cedefop) (2012c) 'Payback Clauses in Europe: Supporting Company Investment in Training', Cedefop Research Paper no. 23, Luxembourg, Publications Office of the European Communities.
European Centre for the Development of Vocational Training (Cedefop) (2010) *The Skill Matching Challenge: Analysing Skill Mismatch and Policy Implications*, Luxembourg, Publications Office of the European Communities.
European Centre for the Development of Vocational Training (Cedefop) (2008), 'Sectoral training funds In Europe', *Cedefop Panorama Series* no. 156, Luxembourg, Publications Office of the European Communities.
Finegold, D. (1993) 'Breaking out of the Low Skills Equilibrium', *Education Economics*, 1(1): 77–83.
Finegold, D. and Soskice, D. (1988) 'The Failure of Training in Britain: Analysis and Prescription', *Oxford Review of Economic Policy*, 4(3): 21–53.
Frenkel, S., Korczynski, M., Shire, K., and Tam, M (1998), 'Beyond Bureaucracy? Work Organization in Call Centres', *International Journal of Human Resource Management*, 9(6): 957–979.
Froy, F., Giguere, S., and Meghnagi, M. (2012) 'Skills for Competitiveness: A Synthesis Report', OECD Local Economic and Employment Development (LEED) Working Papers, no. 9, Paris.
Fuller, A., Ashton, D., Felstead, A., Unwin, L., Walters, S., and Quin, M. (2003) *The Impact of Informal Learning at Work on Business Productivity*, DTI Research Report, London DTI.
Gatta, M. and Finegold, D (2010) 'Introduction: Meeting America's Skills Challenge', in D. Finegold, M. Gatta, H. Salzman, and S. Schurman (eds), *Transforming the US Workforce Development System: Lessons from Research and Practice*, Washington, DC: Labor and Employment Relations Association Series: 1–17.
Gazelle Global (2012) 'Enterprising Futures: The Changing Landscape and New Possibilities for Further Education', March.
Green, F. (2010) 'Unions and Skills Utilisation', Unionlearn Research Paper no. 11, November.
Green, F. (2009) 'Job Quality in Britain', United Kingdom Commission on Employment and Skills, *Praxis*, 1 (November): 10.
Grugulis, I. and Lloyd, C. (2010) 'Skills and the Labour Process: The Conditions and Consequence of Change', in P. Thompson and C. Smith (eds), *Working Life*, London: Palgrave: 91–112.
Grugulis, I., Warhurst, C., and Keep, E. (2004) 'What's Happening to Skill?', in C. Warhurst I. Grugulis, and E. Keep (eds), *The Skills that Matter*, Basingstoke: Palgrave Macmillan: 1–19.
Hochschild, A. R. (1983) *The Managed Heart*, Berkeley: University of California Press.
Hodkinson, P., Colley, H., and Malcolm J. (2003) 'The Interrelationships Between Informal and Formal Learning, *Journal of Workplace Learning*, 15: 7–8.

International Labour Office (2011) *A Skilled Workforce for Strong, Sustainable and Balanced Growth: A G20 Training Strategy*', Geneva: International Labour Office.

Keating, J. (2009) 'Matching Supply of and Demand for Skills: International Perspectives', *Australian Bulletin of Labour*, 35(6): 528–560.

Keep, E., and Mayhew, K. (2010) 'Moving Beyond Skills as a Social and Economic Panacea', *Work, Employment and Society*, 24(3): 265–577.

Keep, E., Mayhew, K., and Payne, J. (2006) 'From Skills Revolution to Productivity Miracle—Not as Easy as it Sounds?', *Oxford Review of Economic Policy*, 22: 4.

Korczynski, M. (2005) 'Skills in Service Work: An Overview', *Human Resource Management Journal*, 15: 2.

Le Deist, F. and Winterton, J. (2012) 'Trade Unions and Workplace Training in France', in R. Cooney, and M. Stuart (eds), *Trade Unions and Workplace Training*, London: Routledge Research in Employment Relations, Routledge: 77–100.

Lowry, D., Molloy, S., and McGlennon, S. (2008) 'Future Skill Needs: Projections and Employers' Views', *Australian Bulletin of Labour*, 34: 2.

Mavromaras, K., McGuinness, S., Richardson, S., Sloane P., and Wei, Z. (2011) *Over-skilling and Job Satisfaction in the Australian Labour Force*, Adelaide: National Centre for Vocational Education Research.

National Academy of Sciences and National Academy of Engineering, Institute of Medicine (1995) *Reshaping the Graduate Education of Scientists and Engineers*, Washington, DC: Committee on Science, Engineering and Public Policy.

OECD (2009) *Education at a Glance 2009: OECD Insights*, Paris: OECD Publishing.

OECD (2000) *Literacy in the Information Age: Final Report of the International Adult Literacy Survey*, Paris/Vancouver: OECD/Statistics Canada.

OECD (2012a) *OECD Skills Strategy: Better Skills, Better Jobs, Better Lives: A Strategic Approach to Skills Policies*, Paris: OECD Publishing.

OECD (2012b) *Education at a Glance: Highlights*, Paris: OECD Publishing.

Palmer, C. (1990) "Hybrids': A Critical Force in the Application of Information Technology in the Nineties', *Journal of Information Technology*, 5: 232–235.

Payne, J. (2011) 'Scotland's Skills Utilisation Programme: An Interim Evaluation', SKOPE Research Paper no. 101, Cardiff, June.

Payne, J. (2010) 'Skill Utilisation: Towards a Measurement and Evaluation Framework', SKOPE Research Paper no. 93, SKOPE, Cardiff: Cardiff University.

Payne, J. (2000) 'The Unbearable Lightness of Skill: The Changing Meaning of Skill in UK Policy Discourses and Some Implications for Education and Training', *Journal of Education Policy*, 15(3): 353–369.

Pocock, B., Skinner, N., McMahon, C., and Pritchard, S. (2011) *Work, Life and VET Participation amongst Lower-paid Workers*, Monograph Series, 05/ 2011, London: National Centre for Vocational Education and Research (NCVER).

Professional Science Masters (PSM) (2016) http://www.sciencemasters.com/about.

Reich, R. (1991) *The Work of Nations*, London: Knopf Doubleday.

Richardson, S. (2007) *What is a Skills Shortage?* London: National Centre for Vocational Education Research (NCVER).

Richardson, S. and Tan, Y. (2008) 'Forecasting Future Demands: What We Can and Cannot Know', *Australian Bulletin of Labour*, 34: 2.

Richardson, S. and Teese, R. (2008) *A Well-Skilled Future*, Adelaide: National Centre for Vocational Education Research.

Ritzer, G. (1993) *The McDonaldization of Society*, London: Sage.

Schmitt, J. and Mitukiewicz, A. (2012) '*Politics Matter: Changes in Union Organisation Rates in Rich Countries, 1960–2010*', *Industrial Relations Journal*, 43: 3.

Scottish Government (2007) *Skills for Scotland: A Lifelong Skills Strategy*, Edinburgh: Scottish Government.

Skills Australia (2010) *Australian Workforce Futures: A National Workforce Development Strategy*, Canberra: Commonwealth of Australia.

Smith, A. and Billett, S. (2003) 'Making Employers Pay: How Do They Do It Overseas?', AVETRA. http://www.avetra.org.au/abstracts_and_papers_2003/refereed/SmithA.pdf.

Smith, J. P. and Welch, F. (1978) 'The Overeducated American? A Review Article', New York: RAND Corporation.

Soskice, D. (1999) 'Divergent Production Regimes: Coordinated and Uncoordinated Market Economies in the 1980s and 1990s', in H. Kitschelt P. Lange, G. Marks, and J. D. Stephens (eds), *Continuity and Change in Contemporary Capitalism*, Cambridge: Cambridge University Press: 101–134.

Stuart, M., Cook, H., Cutter, J., and Winterton, J. (2010) *Assessing the Impact of Union Learning and the Union Learning Fund: Union and Employer Perspectives*, Centre for Employment Relations Innovation and Change, Leeds University Business School, Policy Report no. 4.

Sung, J., Raddon, A., & Ashton, D. (2006) *Skills Abroad: A Comparative Assessment of International Policy Approaches to Skills Leading to the Development of Policy Recommendations in the UK*, Sector Skills Development Agency, Research Report 16, Wath-upon-Dearne, South Yorkshire.

Taylor, P. and Bain, P. (1999) '"An Assembly Line in the Head": Work and Employee Relations in the Call Centre', *Industrial Relations Journal*, 30: 2.

Thompson, P. (1990) 'Crawling from the Wreckage: The Labour Process and the Politics of Production', in D. Knights and H. Willmott (eds), *Labour Process Theory*, London: MacMillan: 95–124.

Trappmann, V. (2012) 'The Shifting Role of Trade Unions in the German VET System', in R. Cooney and M. Stuart (eds), *Trade Unions and Workplace Training*, New York: Routledge Research in Employment Relations, Routledge: 103–125.

United Kingdom Commission for Employment and Skills (UKCES) (2011) *Working Futures 2010–2020*, Executive Summary 41, December, London: UKCES.

United Kingdom Department of Business, Innovation and Skills (2012), *Business Plan 2012–2015*. https://www.gov.uk/government/uploads/system/uploads/attachment_data/file/31961/12-p58a-bis-2012-business-plan-annexes.pdf, accessed 11 March 2013.

University Alliance (2012) *The Way We'll Work: Labour Market Trends and Preparing for the Hourglass*, London: Universities Alliance.

Warhurst, C., Grugulis, I., and Keep, E. (eds) (2004) *The Skills That Matter*, London: Palgrave Macmillan.

Warhurst, C., and Findlay, P. (2012) 'More Effective Skills Utilisation: Shifting the Terrain of Skills Policy in Scotland', SKOPE: Research Paper no. 107 (January), Cardiff University.

Watson, I. (2011) 'Modelling of Future Skills Demand: The Implications for Skills Planning in NSW', Background Research for the NSW Strategic Skills Plan 2011–15, Board of Vocational and Education and Training (BVET), NSW Department of Education and Training.

CHAPTER 24

APPROACHES TO SKILLS IN THE ASIAN DEVELOPMENTAL STATES

JOHNNY SUNG AND ARWEN RADDON

INTRODUCTION

THIS chapter reviews the emergence and distinctiveness of the 'developmental state' approach to building national skills systems, making reference to South Korea and Singapore specifically, though some comparisons are also made with Japan and Taiwan. By contrasting South Korea with Singapore, we can see that the developmental state is not a rigidly prescribed model, but a general approach that combines the state taking a strong lead in shaping economic development with the market continuing to play an important role. We will identify the key characteristics that were present in the period of the development state-led industrial take-off, and how these characteristics started to wane as industrialization begins to mature.

Proponents of the developmental state model argue that neo-classic economists cannot fully explain the sources of economic development in these Asian 'high performance' countries. Furthermore, in order to understand the role of the skills formation systems in these countries, one has to understand the relationship between the developmental state and economic development, and how various institutions and national systems become 'subordinate' to a set of economic priorities. As such, national skills formation forms an important means to meet long-term economic objectives.

The first part of the chapter examines the emergence of the developmental state model as a powerful alternative explanation to the neo-classical school. Whilst stressing the pivotal role of government policymakers in the rapid growth of the Asian Tigers, the developmental state approach also recognizes the powerful role of global markets. By examining the interplay between the state and market, one opens up a very different interpretation of what explains the formation of national skills systems and what underpins their changes over time. The usual explanations of market failure or social cost-benefit analysis are no longer adequate. Proponents of the developmental state model argue that the strategic behaviour of the developmental state vis-à-vis national economic development is the main explanation of national skills formation. As such, there are four common features that underpin most developmental states: a national vision, an efficient bureaucracy, a global value-chain focus, and coordinating capital and labour—which we will explore in detail.

In the second part of the chapter, we use the cases of South Korea and Singapore to illustrate the relationship between national skills formation and the developmental state's broader economic strategy. We conclude the second part by making an assessment of how well the developmental state model has stood up against the test of time and its current challenges.

Theories of the Developmental State

The publication of *The East Asian Miracle* by the World Bank in 1993 re-ignited an age-old debate in development economics and social sciences in general—what is the role of the state (Amsden 1994; Huff 1995; Ashton et al. 2002)? Indeed, the debate continues today (Chang 1998, 2002, 2003, 2006, 2011). As development economics took centre stage in mainstream social science theory and comparative policy analysis in the immediate post-war period, the 'state' was considered an out-dated concept and state intervention was always viewed with a negative lens (Skocpol 1985). However, the state's position 'improved' by the early 1980s: 'an actor that, although obviously influenced by the society surrounding it, also shapes social and political processes' (Evans et al. 1985, vii).

In Europe, post-war reconstruction also led to a strong focus on building social and political structures that aim to overcome the shortcomings of the market with greater state coordination. This led to increasing recognition of the role of the state, as well as the recognition of different forms of capitalism. Hall and Soskice (2001) argue that there are essentially two types of capitalist economies: liberal market economies and coordinated market economies. Some took this distinction further—Chang (1994) argues that it is questionable whether there is ever such a thing as a pure market. By implication, there is always a role for the state. The question is then: 'What useful role can the state play?'.

Key in the early formulation of the developmental state model was criticism of neo-classical development economics' view that growth and economic development were synonymous. This lack of differentiation was unable to fully account for the diverse patterns of national economic development as well as their outcomes (e.g. Johnson 1982; Amsden 1989, 1994; Sung 2006). By distinguishing economic development from growth, with the former containing social and political goals, e.g. nation-building, improved environment, poverty reduction, and so on, the developmental state model made a radical attempt to provide an alternative explanation for the source of economic development and the critical role of the state.

Like conventional neo-classical economics, the input of labour and capital is regarded as crucial. However, unlike neo-classical economics, the developmental state model identifies a different set of relationships between the state and labour, and likewise between the state and capital. Market mechanisms (including capital accumulation) remain a linchpin in the developmental state model, but are no longer the sole driving force for economic development. Instead, the state's developmental vision forms a key driver that 'subordinates' the role of labour and capital. This approach to economic development has a major impact on the way in which national skills formation systems are designed.

An Alternative to Neo-classical Development Theory

At the core of the classical approach to economic development was the view that the market, if left to function fully, would inherently create national growth (Stiglitz 1996), confining government intervention to dealing with 'market failure' (Friedman and Friedman 1980). The neo-classical growth model relies heavily on the simple mechanics of comparative advantage and free market to support 'free trade'. The problem with this assumption is that some nations have little comparative advantage—what should they do? Some may suggest that there are always 'people' as a form of 'comparative advantage'. Often this argument assumes a static 'resource endowment' view, that there will always be 'low-skilled' trading partners and 'high-skilled' trading partners, such as countries good at producing cotton trading with countries good at making computers.

The problem with this static view about the world is that it comes into severe conflict, not so much with opposing theories, but with reality itself. Would countries (and the people within) be content with the 'natural endowments' they have or would they naturally be seeking something better (whatever 'better' means)? What do we do with countries that have few endowments other than 'cheap labour'? An attractive element of the developmental state model is its argument that comparative advantage is not static; indeed, it may even be 'creatable'. As such, there could be a useful role for the state, especially when one does not want to wait for things to happen by chance.

Thus the developmental state model argues that, whilst neo-classical growth and trade models might have been useful for explaining early industrializing countries, the rather static and restricted view is irrelevant to many so-called late industrializers. Amsden (1989, 3) argues that an important source of economic development for South Korea (also Japan, Taiwan, and Singapore) is the 'learning effect', which enabled the 'late developers' to transform their economies more strategically and at a much faster rate, compared with the industrialized nations before them—i.e. the need to copy, analyse, learn, and improve from what earlier industrializers have done.

This is not equivalent to arguing that early developers did not learn. Rather, late developers can accelerate the learning process by coordinating resources and activities accordingly. Thus, some of the learning effect of the late developers would depend on the mobilization of workers and their willingness to take up increasingly complex knowledge and skills, perhaps at a much quicker pace than occurred with early developers (i.e. within rather than across generations). Thus, Ashton et al. (1999 and 2002) argue that the developmental state's national skills formation system tends to take a strategic supporting role to fulfil the skills needs of the different stages of industrialization.

State or Market: A Mutually Exclusive Choice?

Japan's economic rise in the 1970s and the 'miracle' of the 'Asian Tigers' suggested that there were different paths to economic development than those indicated by classical theory. All of the Asian Tigers except Hong Kong had a significant state-led development trajectory. Equally, persistently 'underdeveloped' economies were not responding to incentives, whether in the form of natural endowment or foreign direct investment, in the manner predicted by conventional theory.

The World Bank (1993) began to argue that these high-performing Asian nations had adopted market-friendly policies and would intervene only in cases of market failure. However, this did not fully reflect the actions and the extent of strategic involvement of these states, prompting a number of critiques. For example, Amsden (1994) noted a number of areas—such as the creation of conglomerates in South Korea or the creation of new industries in Singapore—that the World Bank's report seemed to have conveniently overlooked in order to support its argument for a market focus. Chang (2011) even equates the view that the Asian rapid economic progress was built on the neo-classical market model with the belief that actors in Hong Kong kung-fu movies can actually fly—the problem is that we, the viewers, choose to ignore the wires supporting the actors.

Much negativity relating to the role of the state comes from the assumption that 'bureaucracies' are inherently inefficient. Statists argue, however, that since there are varieties of capitalism, there are also varieties of bureaucracy. It is more important to examine what makes an efficient bureaucracy that avoids 'state failure'. Rueschemeyer and Evans (1985, 50) identify certain core elements that can facilitate intervention. Firstly, following Weber is a large and far-reaching bureaucratic form of state organization that facilitates administration and which is supported by factors such as:

> cohesion ... differentiation and insulation from its environment, unambiguous location of decision making and channels of authority, and internal features fostering instrumental rationality and activism.

At the same time, the bureaucracy must create a shared sense of direction by 'inculcat[ing] shared assumptions and expectations' and may require substantial time before it is fully effective as an organization (1985, 51). However, for the bureaucracy to make effective interventions to support economic transformation there must be a strategic link between the structures of the bureaucracy and those of the market (Schein 1996). Indeed, fundamental to the neo-statist approach to economic development is a focus on the ways in which the state actively cooperates with the market in order to bring about economic development.

In his analysis of Japan, Johnson (1982) argues that state intervention can be both positive and strategic by 'setting national (economic and social) priorities, the use of strategic economic policies (e.g. industrial, investment, and trade policies), and making collaborative arrangements between the state, capital and labour' (Sung 2006, 15). Whilst Johnson's (1999, 32) account of the 'capitalist developmental state' may not seem radical today, at the time it was regarded as 'heresy' amongst his neo-classical, mainstream contemporaries (Johnson 1999; Clemons 2010). His aim was to demonstrate the different types of capitalism that could co-exist, moving away from the obsession in the 1970s with comparing the efficacy and economic efficiency of the US-style market model and Soviet-style central planning.

Johnson's early identification of the developmental state nevertheless had some gaps. Wade (1990) observed that the main difference between the Asian developmental states and other developing countries in the 1970s and 1980s was that the former systematically channelled some of the surplus into higher value-added areas of production or 'key industries' that often required higher skills, whilst the latter failed to transform their economies and societies because of systemic leakage (e.g. corruption and re-investible resources going elsewhere). The balance here was to constantly maintain a critical mass of capital accumulation that had a focus on national development and, at the same time, keep sufficient incentive for the private sector to expand. Wade further argued that the developmental state was fully aware of the existence of a global value chain. Not only would the state need to enable industries to fully engage in international competition, the state would make an assessment about future positions in the global value chain, and provide additional market signals and 'market guidance' to induce structural change (Wade 1990, 27).

In effect, Wade recognized that within the context of comparative economic development, states are actually in competition with each other, which most non-statist analysts would find hard to recognize. However, the logic behind Wade's argument is that, by carefully managing the mix of state role and entrepreneurial activities, the state is in effect part of creating national competitive advantage.

The above discussion thus points to four characteristics of the developmental state: (a) an efficient and 'insulated' bureaucracy (free from the influence of capital and labour) to support; (b) a national vision that requires; (c) the systematic coordination of capital and labour for making progress along; and (d) the global value chain. The combined effect of the four elements shapes the emphases and goals of the national skills formation system. At the policy level, these four characteristics also lead to the heavy reliance on the use of industrial policy.

The Use of Industrial Policy

In Western governments, the use of 'industrial policy' is often seen as 'awkward', because of the free market political ideology. When used, industrial policy tends to be regulatory, information-based and administrative. In contrast, Asian developmental states have been labelled Japan Inc., Korea Inc., Singapore Inc. (Chang 2003; Wall Street Journal 2012, 2013), reflecting the very close relationship between the state and business delivering the developmental state objectives. The resulting institutional arrangement therefore tends to focus on the creation of international competitiveness and long-term structural change, with the state acting as the leading strategist and catalyst, coordinating relevant resources for long-term competitiveness. For example, both Amsden (1990) and Wade (1990) document the linkages between state support and the necessary requirement of performance from those industries that received such support. It has been widely reported that deliberate incentive systems such as tax and credit subsidies were provided to export-oriented industries by the state during the period of building up an export-oriented industrial base. In the early stages of industrial take-off, the cost of borrowing in Japan, South Korea, and Taiwan was found to be cheaper for export industries than for those producing for domestic consumption. Output targets were often set in exchange for further cheap credit and import licences for raw materials (Amsden 1989; Wade 1990; Woo 1991).

Industrial policy is used to influence the 'prerequisites of success.' In much of the developmental state analysis, the workers are assumed to be one of the two critical factors to get developmental state policies into action, as labour-intensive industries were often the first stage of industrialization. However, whilst much has been written about the national incentives for business to bring inward investment, and how the state deals with economic surplus, very little is written about how workers or ordinary citizens buy into the process of state-led development, especially amongst the early developmental state analyses (Myrdal 1953, 1957; Frank 1967, 1978; Cardoso and Faletto 1979; Evans 1979; Wallerstein 1979, 1997; Johnson 1982; Amsden 1989, 1990; Rodan 1989; Wade 1990).

Later research on the development state moved away from the sole focus on industrial policy. Sung (2006) developed a complementary concept of the 'developmental worker' to demonstrate the use of societal stake-holding. Not only is it a means for distributing tangible benefits of economic development, it is also a process of binding citizens to a long-term state-citizen partnership in order to deliver developmental state objectives. In most developmental state models, what appears on the surface to be an economic project for international competitiveness ends up also featuring various social projects leading to nation-building. This development increases in complexity in line with the need to adapt to competing demands from workers, social institutions, and the aspirations of new generations. Whilst most developmental states have done well in moving up the global value chain, not all of them have been successful in meeting the new demands of today's better-educated and financially better-off generations of workers.

The end result is a general decline in the ability of developmental states to maintain their old approaches to economic development.

Skills Formation in South Korea and Singapore

We now contrast two Asian countries that have taken very different approaches to implementing the developmental state model: South Korea and Singapore. South Korea went through a long period of import-substitution policy by fostering its domestic enterprises. In contrast, Singapore has retained its open policy throughout its economic development stages. Thus, multinational corporations have been (and remain) the main source of Singapore's economic development. Whilst both developmental states have been hugely involved in the direction of their economic development, the different emphases of their industrial policies also gave rise to very different approaches to skills formation, which have been crucial to the support of the developmental state strategy. As will be seen in these cases, the developmental state model is not a skills formation model, but an economic development model that has important implications for the role that skill formation plays in society and how it is organized/used as a tool.

South Korea as a Developmental State

The South Korean industrialization strategy largely and purposely followed the Japanese 'Meiji' industrial revolution approach. However, since the Asian Financial Crisis of 1997–8, it is seen to have shifted from a developmental state to a somewhat more neo-liberal approach, due to the need for International Monetary Fund (IMF) financing that was tied to economic restructuring along neo-classical lines. Nevertheless, South Korea's economic history since the 1970s provides a useful example of the developmental state in action. It also raises some interesting questions about future opportunities for sustained, significant growth for a 'post-developmental state' (Park 2007, 426).

In 1960 South Korea was still a predominantly agrarian society with a gross domestic product (GDP) per capita at one twelfth of that of the United States. By 2011, South Korea's GDP per capita was roughly half that of the United States (US$32,100), following a period of very rapid industrialization. However, what was the context for adopting the developmental state strategy? Much has been written about the political turmoil in Korea in the 30 years running up to the subsequent annexation by Japan's colonial empire in 1905 (Jansen 1989; Duus 1995). Japanese annexation led to widespread abuse, exploitation, and the establishment of a police state (McKenzie 1920). Shortly after attaining independence from Japan in 1945, Korea was plunged into crisis by the outbreak of civil war in 1950. In effect, between 1880 and 1954, the country experienced a long period of instability and social upheaval. When the Korean War ended and American aid started to pour in for reconstruction, the country was ready for nation-building: the classic precondition of becoming a developmental state (Amsden 1989).

General Park Chung Hee's autocratic leadership in the 1960s provided a conducive environment for the developmental state model, involving a high level of state intervention, and a heavy focus on rapidly building the economy as a means of resisting the spread of communism (Kohli 2004, 88):

> authoritarian apex that minimised intra-elite division, a variety of top-down institutions that incorporated major social groups, and a commitment to promoting capitalist growth

Park drew on the legacy of colonial Japanese structures, organizational practices, and a militaristic approach to rapidly construct a 'cohesive and purposeful' state with economic development at the core (Amsden 1985; Rueschemeyer and Evans 1985; Kohli 2004). Kohli (2004) notes that, whilst deploying a civil service that was highly educated and committed, Park provided the leadership, setting clear priorities and high standards for the bureaucracy to achieve. This level of coordination and leadership remains a major emphasis in current public policy (World Bank 2013a).

Early developmental state effort emerged as a 'guided' capitalist economy. Supported by key state institutions such as the Economic Planning Board (EPB), the Ministry of Trade and Industry, and the South Korean Central Bank, the South Korean developmental state model was launched as part of the five-year economic plan in 1962 with the objective of creating an 'independent economy' (Chang 2006, 75). Whilst high rates of growth were achieved during many of the plans which ran from 1962 to 1996, they were discontinued after the economic crisis of 1997. The planning model meant that once the EPB published the broad plan, interventions at departmental level were very important, with sectoral economic strategies being developed by the respective ministries and departments in order to achieve the national plan (Amsden 1989). In addition to planning, 'credit control, manipulation of the foreign trade regime, licensing of technology transfers, and control of labour and education policies' were tools for industrial policy (Kohli 2004, 107–108). The emphasis in the early stages of industrialization was not on 'high skills,' but using the education system to mass produce a disciplined workforce that was suitable for industrialization or the requirements of the productive system.

Economic Development via the Chaebol and Impact on Skills Formation

Whilst fostering private enterprise, the state invested heavily in carefully chosen companies in target sectors with large, preferential loans to accelerate indigenous growth and protection from foreign competition. The end result was a handful of large, family-controlled and powerful conglomerates known as the *Chaebol* (Park 2002, 339). The focus on developing the *Chaebol* as the main engine for economic development meant that the national pre-employment training system played a 'supportive' role (Yoon and Lee 2009). Namely, having a workforce that has a strong general education foundation and is highly committed to the national project was the key.

The dominance of the *Chaebol* meant that the conglomerates produced the firm-specific skills they needed via their in-house systems. Through the sub-contracting system, they also influenced the skills in the supply chain, which was made up mostly of small- and medium-sized enterprises (SMEs). Thus, much of the emphasis of national education and training tended to be general or generic in nature, preparing the basic skills and knowledge that workers need to enter employment. The instrumental use of labour as a tool towards economic development meant that public policy towards labour was primarily to ensure that workers were highly 'controlled and disciplined' (Kohli 2004, 98 citing Jang et al. 1989). For example, Park's regime adopted the Japanese model of *sampo* industrial relations—rigid and top-down—under the Korea Central Intelligence Agency, with the aim of supressing labour activity. Also, following Japan, unions were company-based and relatively distanced from workers. Indeed, Kohli (2004, 98) argues that the achievement of rapid economic growth was often at the cost of workers, being sustained by 'long hours of work and relatively low wages'. Women—thought to be willing to work for longer hours and lower pay—made up a large proportion of the frontline workforce in the *Chaebol*. For example, in textiles and electronics in the 1970s, 70% and 60%, respectively, of workers were women (Kohli 2004 citing Jang et al. 1989).

Typical for most of the developmental states at this early stage of industrialization, policymakers exercised a high level of control over education and particularly the technical training system (Ashton 2011). In the 1950s, much of the South Korean education system was private- rather than state-funded. In order to align skills needs and supply with industrial policy the state took a more strategic approach to education and training policy. It focused on linking supply with the skills required by industrialization, expanding participation in general education and particularly increasing vocational education to grow technical skills. The first National Plan (1962–6) introduced the Industrial Education Promotion Act (1963). The Act promoted basic levels of training for low-skill workers. Vocational education was heavily promoted in all subsequent plans to support the expanding industrial sector, with a shift from basic through secondary to higher levels of technical and vocational education and training. By 1970 vocational education catered for almost half the school cohort (Ashton 2011). Indeed, some argue that the strategic emphasis of vocational education in the succession of National Plans meant that it had become a vehicle to engage individuals in the national economic project (Chang 2006).

Education and training policy shifted as the *Chaebol* grew. In the late 1960s, the strategy focused on moving towards heavy industry. To foster development of more specific technical skills, the state introduced a levy to promote in-house company training. The focus shifted again later in the early 1990s to a more knowledge-based economy; tertiary education grew rapidly to ensure an appropriate supply of skills to support the next round of industrial restructuring. During these periods, public provision of education and training was heavily geared towards supporting the *Chaebol*, as they accounted for two-thirds of industrial production and half of overall employment (Amsden 1989). All this shows a general pattern of increasing skills complexity, value content and the need to match labour supply with the skills demanded by industry. This 'matching' process did not happen in the way standard economics would predict, namely that the state would make high skills available in quantities and subsequently business would invest in the new industries to take advantage of the skills. Instead, both the skills supply and incentives for new investment were coordinated in successive National Plans: new skills supply and new industry development became parallel activities. However, as the *Chaebol* tended to be favoured by graduates and more qualified workers, SMEs were somewhat poorly catered for (Lauder 1999).

Unions historically had very little say in matters such as education and training, in keeping with firms' oppressive approach towards workforce discipline (Chang 2009). Indeed, it was not until the late 1990s that industrial relations became less employer-centric, as a result of a government review of labour law in 1996 following industrial conflict, and the IMF's demand for less domestic protection in return for IMF financial assistance following the crisis. Increasing democratic union membership at the workplace gave workers a role in negotiating education and training matters, leading to better provision of internal labour markets for blue-collar workers (Ashton 2011). Until the early 2000s, the *Chaebol* offered a job for life and skill formation (deepening) largely through on-the-job training within the company (Park 2007). However, since the crisis of 1997 and de-regulation, *Chaebol* now tend to take on skilled employees rather than those new to the labour market. De-regulation also led to much higher use of temporary workers who no longer benefit from the same skills development available to regular *Chaebol* employees. Training of younger and less experienced workers has fallen largely to SMEs, which have a poor record of skills investment. Thus the 'post-developmental state' role has included government taking on a much greater role in training, to cope with the subsequent market failure (Park 2007, 426).

In summary, South Korea's chosen path of the developmental state strategy, relying on the *Chaebol* for rapid economic development, had a profound effect on skills formation. Not only is the state's skills supply policy still heavily influenced by the needs of the *Chaebol*, the state's skills intervention was mostly confined to initial training, leaving skill-deepening and re-skilling to the *Chaebol*. As other enterprises did not feature in the plans, they were often left out of public provision as well as the financial incentives. With the shift towards de-regulation and accompanying declining state influence over capital (Park 2007), combined with the reduced role that the *Chaebol* are playing in skill development, the state has been forced to play a more direct role in training and retraining of adult workers and to seek new solutions to the problems of graduate unemployment and underemployment. These patterns contrast sharply with Singapore's experience.

Singapore as a Developmental State

As with South Korea, Singapore was a developing country in the 1960s with low levels of economic development. The colonial territory was mainly an entrepôt and British military base. In 1960 it had a GDP per capita slightly higher than that of South Korea (US$2,250). By 2011 after four decades of sustained economic development, Singapore's GDP per head was slightly below that of the United States.[1] Unlike South Korea, Singapore is a very young country by any standards, having gained independence in 1965. Singapore's drive for economic development was shaped by conditions after the Second World War. Here, we briefly summarize the well-documented events that shaped the emergence of the developmental state following independence (Sung, 2006).

Before the 1950s, it was difficult to speak of the 'Singapore nation'. Singapore was a 'transitory territory' for migrants, especially the Chinese, who moved around Southeast Asia looking for economic opportunities, but their ultimate intention was to make enough money and return home (Cheng 1991). However, when the Communist Party took over China in 1949, all this changed. Fewer Chinese could come out of communist China, and of those who managed to get out, few would return (Turnbull 1989). From the 1950s onwards, the previously transient population began to take root, making Singapore their permanent home.

During this period, Singapore struggled to become economically viable, being too dependent on import-export trade and servicing the British bases. The risk of high unemployment was always in the background (Chan 1971). However, Singapore did have a plan. In 1957 the People's Action Party (PAP), led by Lee Kuan Yew, began self-government. The PAP saw huge opportunity within the Malaysian Federation for trading commodities and basic foodstuffs that moved through Singapore to different parts of the region (Cheng 1991). The economic strategy was to create a 'common market', bringing manufacturing jobs to Singapore and selling products to West Malaysia—Singapore's traditional trading hinterland. Events turned out rather differently, and an unexpected exit from the Malaysian Federation in 1965 meant that the 'common market' strategy would never materialize.[2] Meanwhile, unemployment worsened, with some 25,000 young people joining the labour market annually whilst new jobs were created at a rate of only 5,000 per annum. In 1967 further trouble lay ahead when the British government announced that it was withdrawing its Navy early, closing its base by 1971. Not only would that mean a loss of national income of around 20%, but 18,000 additional jobs had to be found in order to absorb the direct and indirect job losses as a result of the base closure.

[1] Using the 'purchasing power parity' calculation (PPP), the GDP per capita figure for Singapore (US$60,500) in 2011 would be significantly higher than that of the United States.

[2] For the details of the political differences between the dominant United Malay National Organization (UMNO) and the PAP within the Federation, leading to the separation, see Drydale (1984) and Turnbull (1989).

Parallel to these economic events, communal riots broke out in 1964 and 1969, with widespread racial tension throughout the period. In addition, industrial strikes were rife, and communist supporters often used these strikes as a 'front' to create political and social unrest. Between 1960 and 1967, there were 389 industrial disputes recorded. Whilst industrial strikes continued, the image for potential inward investors deteriorated and the chance for Singapore to industrialize was severely weakened (Vasil 1992).

Against this socio-political and economic context, the PAP resorted to 'pragmatic government'. In 1962 Lee Kuan Yew stressed that:

> We had to intervene ... the problem of resettling our population and trying to make a more cohesive society. We never took a vote. Had we asked people in Kampong Kembangan [Malay Village] whether they wanted to be resettled, the answer must be no. ... [To] ask the Hainanese ... Would you like to have a Malay as your neighbour? The answer is no. We decided that we are going to make a nation, we can't have a race riot every now and then ... People talk about consultation, top-down and bottom-up. These are theories, yardsticks worked out by western political scientists who have never been presented the raw, unpleasant, unmanageable facts of making something out of nothing. If we took a poll, we would have never had National Service. I simply decided, 'Introduce it.' It was necessary. After a while, everybody understood it was necessary. (Han et al. 1998: 133)

Obviously, pragmatism alone cannot create legitimacy and support from the populace. The PAP government knew that real economic progress would be needed to strengthen the developmental state's legitimacy. Thus, 'state performance' in tackling economic crises and national emergencies created immense political leverage for the PAP, rallying popular and political support in the decades to come (Sung 2006).

Economic Stages and Skills Formation

Singapore has transitioned through a number of economic development stages since independence. As the economic structure progressed through each stage, national skills formation policy was also re-focused towards new industrial needs. Many skilled occupations were subject to planning to ensure that supply would meet demand. Much of this planning was (and still is) influenced by the inward investment secured by the work of the Economic Development Board (EDB), whose sole purpose was to create employment in Singapore through offering attractive packages to Western multinational corporations (MNCs). Three key economic stages can be observed.

Low-cost and Labour-intensive Manufacturing (late 1960s–1970s)

The cumulative effects of riots, strikes, rising unemployment and British military base closure in the 1960s hastened Singapore's decision to industrialize (Chiang 1998; Omar 2007). Whilst most developing countries in the 1960s were embarking upon the import-substitution strategy for industrialization, the Singapore government aimed to create jobs by attracting MNCs to relocate their production base to Singapore (Lim 2009).

The PAP requested United Nations (UN) assistance. Albert Winsemius, who led the UN team, advised the setting up of the EDB in 1961 (Low 1993; Ashton et al. 1999). Following his further advice, the government sought a toehold in light manufacturing, such as textiles, toys and wigs (Ngiam 2011), as well as attracting more capital-intensive industries such as petroleum, iron, and steel (EDB 2011a). The government often used significant incentives to attract MNCs (Rodan 1985; Hughes 1993). As well as ensuring there was good infrastructure and locations for MNCs, including building manufacturing plants in advance of demand, Singapore sought to demonstrate the presence of a disciplined and suitably skilled workforce and competitive labour costs (World Bank 2013b).

As the major focus was on light manufacturing, this meant that the economy was primarily low-wage and labour-intensive, making basic literacy and numeracy amongst the workers a vital early task. As a result, the core focus for skills policy and intervention was providing universal, basic general and technical education to the next generation of workers (Chiang 1998; Tan 2007; Ngiam 2011). There was a huge programme to build new technical and vocational schools, developing highly sought-after graduates trained in trades where demand was identified (Chiang 1998). The system expanded rapidly from 1,379 students in just two vocational and technical schools in 1961 to 19,747 students by 1967 (Chiang 1998). Technical skills were also integrated into the general education curriculum.

Capital-intensive Stage (mid-1970s–1980s)

By the early 1970s, a tight labour market quickly emerged, with MNCs continuing to relocate to Singapore. The government set out ambitious plans to move up the value chain through industrial restructuring. The 1970 Economic Expansion Incentives (Amendment) Act gave greater incentives to promote capital-intensive industry when new projects are negotiated. By the mid-1970s, Singapore's electronics industry was taking off and diversification encouraged significant development in industries such as petrochemicals. The Vocational and Industrial Training Board (VITB) was formed to better coordinate the training for rising numbers of technical workers.

Despite the effort to promote vocational and technical training, worker shortages were common and dropout rates in technical education were high. The 'Goh Report' of 1979, the first national education review, strengthened the system in two areas: (a) reducing 'drop-out' by improving the pathways for the technical stream; and (b) providing an additional year in secondary education for less academic students. By tackling dropout, the reform was to ensure that there would be more vocationally trained workers in the system.

In the early-1980s, with tripartite involvement, a suite of national adult education and training or post-compulsory programmes were developed, such as the Basic Education for Skills Training (BEST) programme, for workers who those who had no qualifications but had basic maths and English. The concern at the time was that a significant proportion of the Singapore workforce was educated in the 1950s and 1960s. Many of them only finished primary education, if that, creating a 'bottleneck' for upskilling and industrial upgrading. Also, to support workplace training, S$24 million was invested (1983–7) from the Skills Development Fund (SDF) (Singapore Government 1989c). The SDF (established in 1979) is a levy based on wages below a certain level, therefore penalizing low-paid and low-skilled jobs.

Later programmes focused on bringing workers up to secondary level and developing skills to support the growing service sector. By 1992, 78% of the targeted workers (225,000) had gone through BEST, whilst 42% of the targeted workers (122,000) had gone through the Worker Improvement through Secondary Education (WISE) programme (ITE 1993). Both BEST and WISE were, in effect, 'second chance' programmes on a national scale, facilitating re-deployment of the workforce via the process of skills upgrading.

Knowledge-intensive Stage (1990s–present day)

By 1990, Singapore achieved Newly Industrialized Economy status, as one of the 'Asian Tigers'. Ever ambitious, the Strategic Economic Plan of 1991 aimed for Singapore to reach advanced economic and developed country status by 2030—a goal that was met much sooner than planned.

The 1991 plan sought to move the economy further up the value chain to become 'investment-driven' and 'knowledge-intensive'. Thirteen industrial clusters were identified as ways to provide national competitive advantage. Equally, Singaporean companies were encouraged to move out into the Asia Pacific region to form an external economy (or 'regionalization'). This would enable Singapore not only to take advantage of cheaper labour in the nearby less-developed countries, but also to become the 'hub' of the region's drive for economic growth. 'Singapore Incorporated' was to become 'Singapore International Incorporated' (Low et al. 1993). At the same time, to 'catch-up' with advanced economies, the government identified further skills upgrading in three areas: (a) basic/core skills required for effective participation in an advanced industrial society; (b) enhancement of intermediate-level technical skills; and (c) expansion of higher education (HE). The second national education review of 1991 reformed not just primary but secondary and post-secondary education and the pathways amongst them (World Bank 2013b).

Up until the 1990s, HE participation rates were closely managed to avoid any oversupply of skills. However, the 2000s saw some new developments in this area. After decades of focusing heavily on science, technology, engineering and maths (STEM) areas, there was promotion of creative education in order to support a new industrial policy to diversify the economy. In 2012 a review identified a need to expand HE further. Around 27% of the Primary 1 cohort currently enters local universities, set to expand to 40% by 2020 with a particular emphasis on 'applied' degrees (Lee 2012; World Bank 2013a,b).

In order to up-skill the whole workforce, as well as strengthening vocational learning, attention was also directed at creating a comprehensive national qualifications system. In 2003, the Singapore Workforce Development Agency (WDA) was established to develop the national Workforce Skill Qualifications System (WSQ) supporting competence-based training in all the major industry sectors. It took a number of years for WSQ to develop but by 2012, 30 sectors were covered.

Whilst the skills system has long been characterized by a strong demand-led focus, with the development of WSQ in the 2000s, which involved industry and unions providing input into competency standards, public training under the WDA moved closer to meeting employer skills demands in the workplace. The developmental state now has increased access to the skills content of the workplace and can influence the quality of the provision. Generous incentives are provided under SDF funding and a Lifelong Learning Endowment Fund in order to maximize participation and employer and employee engagement.

The various stages of industrial development in Singapore show that, under the developmental state, national skills formation plays an explicit role in supporting national economic development, whilst industrial policy, as well as providing direction, acts like 'glue' that binds all the supporting structures together (i.e. preferential land use, loans, fiscal advantage, housing location for workers, education and training) with a sense of purpose.

Conclusion

We can draw two broad conclusions from this comparison of developmental state models. Firstly, as much as there is a role for the state, the market (i.e. capital, entrepreneurialism, and competition) is an equally important mechanism for economic development to take place. The developmental state model provides a framework to bring forth a rich set of explanations of economic development. For our current purposes, we can see that national skills formation systems may not be the pure consequences of education and training policy. In the developmental state, education and training are a vehicle to achieve long-term economic and social development.

Secondly, the developmental state model must evolve over time if it is to continue to thrive. As significant economic progress was achieved in South Korea and Singapore, it also brought new challenges. Some of these challenges have actually weakened the ability of the state to maintain the developmental state model. For example, the immense power of the *Chaebol* also meant that South Korea has relatively few start-ups. If successful cases emerge, the *Chaebol* simply snap them up and absorb them into the conglomerate. The ever-greater concentration of economic activities in the *Chaebol* means that whilst the *Chaelbol* was useful for national economic development in the past, the state is no longer in the driving seat in terms of future developmental agendas.

The majority of young South Koreans are highly educated these days. Some 82% of high-school leavers go on to university. They, and their parents, have high expectations.

However, the *Chaebol* model was not created to absorb these vast armies of graduates. Once the *Chaebol* cherry-pick the best, many graduates face the prospect of working in the SME sector or in services, with most of their jobs being low-paid. It is therefore not surprising that in 2011, graduates constituted over a third of Korea's unemployed and just under a third of the six million casual workforce who on average earned $1,170 per month (*Economist* 2011). The South Korean state is no longer as 'insulated' from the pressure of capital and workers as it once was. Indeed, after the IMF managed to force the developmental state to de-regulate, the state relinquished even more control over the market.

Likewise, the very successful developmental state in Singapore is facing huge challenges from the next round of 'late developers'. Whilst some of its industries have moved on to the knowledge-intensive and high value-added territories, manufacturing is still a significant contributor to GDP and faces intense competition from China and India as well as other countries in the region. Knowledge-intensive industries tend not to create as many jobs as manufacturing. Thus the transition from manufacturing to the knowledge sector has been slow. Meanwhile, with Singapore's open economy, globalization has also reduced the state's ability to be 'insulated' from the pressure of global capital (i.e. the need to deregulate) and the temptation to sustain manufacturing and other low-pay jobs through cheap imported labour. Along with a sense that Singapore's approach has shifted more towards the classic market mechanism, or 'market fundamentalism', these factors have been blamed as the sources of growing inequality and political pluralism in today's society (Bhaskaran et al. 2012).

Whilst not being exhaustive in assessing the current positions of the Asian developmental states, it would seem that the golden era of the developmental state model was closely tied to the conditions of the three decades prior to intense globalization. Of the four characteristics of the developmental state, most of them—e.g. the efficient bureaucracy, global value-chain transition, and surplus re-investment—still work well today. However, the one characteristic that has been severely eroded is the state's ability to 'lead' capital and labour. In today's highly globalized environment, where capital is also very mobile, committing MNCs (or conglomerates) to long-term projects is increasingly difficult. People, many of whom are highly educated, are mobile too. As the developmental state model weakens, the links amongst the role of the state, national skills formation, and economic development may likewise dilute. It is possible that national skills formation may shift towards meeting individual aspirations instead of national economic priorities in the 'post-industrialization' era.

References

Amsden, A. (1989) *Asia's Next Giant: South Korea and Late Industrialisation*, New York: Oxford University Press.

Amsden, A. and Chu, W. W. (2003) *Beyond Late Development: Taiwan's Upgrading Policies*, Cambridge, MA: MIT Press.

Amsden, A., Kochanowicz, J., and Taylor, L. (1994) *The Market Meets Its Match: Restructuring the Economies of Eastern Europe*, Cambridge, MA: Harvard University Press.

Ashton, D. (2011) 'Lessons from the East Asian and European Experience for Skills Development in African Countries', Unpublished Paper for the African Center for Economic Transformation (ACET), Accra, Ghana.

Amsden, A. (1989) *Asia's Next Giant: South Korea and Late Industrialisation*, New York: Oxford University Press.

Ashton, D., Green, F., Sung, J. and James, D. (2002) 'The Evolution of Education and Training Strategies in Singapore, Taiwan, and S. Korea: A Development Model of Skill Formation', *Journal of Education and Work*, 15(1): 5–30.

Bhaskaran, M., Ho, S. C., Low, D., Tan, K. S., Vadaketh, S., and Keong, Y. L. (2012) *Inequality and the Need for a New Social Compact, Singapore Perspectives 2012, Singapore Inclusive: Bridging Divides*, Singapore: Institute of Policy Studies (IPS), Lee Kuan Yew School of Public Policy.

Cardoso, F. H. and Faletto, E. (1979) *Dependency and Development in Latin America*, Berkeley: University of California Press.

Chan, H. C. (1971) *Singapore: The Politics of Survival, 1965–1967*, Singapore: Oxford University Press.

Chang, H-J. (1994) *The Political Economy of Industrial Policy*, London and Basingstoke: Macmillan.

Chang, H-J. (1998) 'Korea: The Misunderstood Crisis', *World Development*, 26(8): 1555–1561.

Chang, H-J. (1998) 'Breaking the Mould: An Institutionalist Political Economy Alternative to the Neo-Liberal Theory of the Market and the State', *Cambridge Journal of Economics*, 26: 539–559.

Chang, H-J. (2003) *Kicking Away the Ladder: Development Strategy in Historical Perspective*, London: Anthem Press.

Chang, H-J. (2006) *The East Asian Development Experience: The Miracle, The Crisis and the Future*, London: Zed Book.

Chang, H-J. (2011) *23 Things They Don't Tell You about Capitalism*, New York: Bloomsbury Press.

Cheng, S. H. (1991) 'Economic Change and Industrialisation', in E. C. T. Chew and E. Lee (eds), *A History of Singapore*, Singapore: Oxford University Press: 182–215.

Chiang, M. (1998) *From Economic Debacle to Economic Miracle: The History and Development of Technical Education in Singapore*, Singapore: Ministry of Education with Times Editions.

Chua, M. H. (2013) 'Commentary: Punggol East By-election was a Tipping Point', *The Straits Times*, 27 January. http://www.straitstimes.com/the-big-story/punggol-east-election/story/commentary-punggol-east-election-was-tipping-point-2013012.

Clemons, S. (2010) 'The Impact Today and Tomorrow of Chalmers Johnson', *Washington Note*, 21 November. http://www.thewashingtonnote.com/archives/2010/11/the_impact_toda/.

Drydale, J. (1984) *Singapore: Struggle for Success*, Singapore: Times Books International.

Duus, P. (1995) *The Abacus and the Sword: The Japanese Penetration of Korea, 1895–1910*, California: University of California Press.

Economist (2011) 'Education in South Korea: Glutted with Graduates', 3 Nov. http://www.economist.com/blogs/banyan/2011/11/education-south-korea.

EDB (2011) 'The 1980s: The Era of Capital-intensive and High-technology Industries', retrieved May. Singapore: Economic Development Board. http://www.edb.gov.sg/edb/sg/en_uk/index/about_edb/our_history/the_1980s.html.

Evans, P. (1979) *Dependent Development: The Alliance of Multinational, State and Local Capital in Brazil*, Princeton: Princeton University Press.

Evans, P., Rueschemeyer, D., and Skocpol, T. (1985) (eds) *Bringing the State Back In*, Cambridge: Cambridge University Press.

Frank, A. G. (1967) *Capitalism and Underdevelopment in Latin America*, New York: Monthly Review Press.

Frank, A. G. (1969) *Latin America: Underdevelopment or Revolution: Essays in the Development of Underdevelopment and the Immediate Enemy*, New York: Monthly Review Press.

Frank, A. G. (1978) *Dependent Accumulation and Underdevelopment*, New York: Macmillan.

Friedman, M. and Friedman, R. (1980) *Free to Choose: A Personal Statement*, New York: Harcourt Brace Jovanovich.

Hall and Soskice (2001) *Varieties of Capitalism*, Oxford: Oxford University Press.

Han, F. W., Fernandez, W., and Tan, S. (1998) *Lee Kuan Yew: The Man and His Ideas*, Singapore: Singapore Press Holdings.

Huff, W. G. (1995) 'The Developmental State, Government, and Singapore's Economic Development since 1960', *World Development*, 23(8): 1421–1438.

Hughes, H. (1993) 'An External View', in L. Low, M. H. Toh, T. W. Soon, K. Y. Tan, and H. Hughes (eds), *Challenge and Response: Thirty Years of the Economic Development Board*, Singapore: Times Academic Press: 1–25.

ITE (1993) *Institute of Technical Education, Annual Report 92–93*, Singapore: Institute of Technical Education.

Jansen, M. B. (1989) *The Cambridge History of Japan. Vol. 5: The Nineteenth Century*, Cambridge: Cambridge University Press.

Johnson, C. (1982) *MITI and the Japanese Miracle: The Growth of Industrial Policy, 1925–1975*, Stanford: Stanford University Press.

Johnson, C. (1999) 'The Developmental State: Odyssey of a Concept', in M. Woo-Cummings (ed.), *The Developmental State*, Cornell: Cornell University Press: 32–60.

Johnson, C. (2000) *Blowback*, New York: Henry Holt.

Kohli, A. (2004) *State-Directed Development*, Cambridge: Cambridge University Press.

Lauder, H. (1999) 'Competitiveness and the Problems of Low Skills Equilibria: A Comparative Analysis', *Journal of Education and Work*, 12(3): 281–294.

Lee, H. L. (2012) 'A Home With Hope and Heart', Prime Minister Lee Hsien Loong's Speech in English, Sunday 26 August at University Cultural Centre, National Day Rally. http://www.channelnewsasia.com/annex/ND2012_PMLEE_ENGTEXT.pdf.

Lee, J-W. (2004) 'Lessons from the Korean Financial Crisis', in C. Harvie, H-H. Lee, and J. Oh (eds), *Post-Crisis Policies, Issues and Prospects*, Cheltenham: Edward Elgar: 11–21.

Lim, F. C. B. (2009) 'Education Hub at a Crossroads: The Development of Quality Assurance as a Competitive Tool for Singapore's Private Tertiary Education', *Quality Assurance in Education*, 17(1): 79–94.

Low, L. (1993) 'The Economic Development Board', in L. Low, M. H. Toh, T. W. Soon, K. Y. Tan, and H. Hughes (eds), *Challenge and Response: Thirty Years of the Economic Development Board*, Singapore: Times Academic Press: 61–120.

Low, L., Heng, T. M., and Wong, S. T. (1991) *Economics of Education and Manpower: Issues and Politics in Singapore*, Singapore: McGraw-Hill.

McKenzie, F. A. (1920) *Korea's Fight for Freedom*, New York: Fleming H. Revell Company.

Myrdal, G. (1953) *The Political Element in the Development of Economic Theory*, London: Routledge. https://www.amazon.com/Political-Element-Development-Economic-Theory/dp/0887388272.

Myrdal, G. (1957) *Economic Theory and Underdeveloped Regions*, London: Duckworth.

Ngiam, T. D. (2011) *Dynamics of the Singapore Success Story: Insights by Ngiam Tong Dow*, introduced and edited by Dr Zhang Zhibin, Singapore: Cengage Learning.

Omar, M. (2007) 'British Withdrawal from Singapore', *Singapore Infopedia*. Accessed May 2011, http://infopedia.nl.sg/articles/SIP_1001_2009-02-10.html.

Park, I. (2007) 'The Labour Market, Skill Formation and Training in the 'Post-Developmental' State: The Example of South Korea', *Journal of Education and Work*, 20(5): 417–435.

Park, J. H. (2002) 'The East Asian Model of Economic Development and Developing Countries', *Journal of Developing Societies*, 18(4): 330–353.

Rodan, G. (1985) 'Singapore's "Second Industrial Revolution": State Intervention and Foreign Investment', ASEAN-Australia Economic Papers no. 18, ASEAN-Australia Joint Research Project, Kuala Lumpur and Canberra: ASEAN.

Rodan, G. (1989) *The Political Economy of Singapore's Industrialisation*, Selangor: Forum Enterprise.

Rueschemeyer, D. and Evans, P. (1985) 'The State and Economic Transformation', in P. Evans, D. Rueschemeyer and T. Skocpol (eds), *Bringing the State Back In*, Cambridge: Cambridge University Press: 44–77.

Skocpol, T. (1985) 'Bringing the State Back In: Current Research', in P. Evans, D. Rueschemeyer and T. Skocpol (eds), *Bringing the State Back In*, Cambridge: Cambridge University Press: 3–37.

Stiglitz, J. E. (1996) *Whither Socialism?*, Cambridge, MA: MIT Press.

Sung, J. (2006) *Explaining the Economic Success of Singapore: The Developmental Worker as the Missing Link*, Cheltenham and Massachusetts: Edward Elgar.

Tan, J. (2007) 'Schooling in Singapore', in G. A. Postiglione and J. Tan (eds) *Going to School in East Asia*, Westport, CT: Greenwood Press: 301–319.

Turnbull, C. M. (1989) *A History of Singapore, 1819–1988*, Singapore: Oxford University Press.

Vasil, R. (2000) *Governing Singapore*, Australia: Allen & Unwin.

Wade, R. (1990) *Governing the Market*, Princeton: Princeton University Press.

Wall Street Journal (2012) 'Singapore Inc. Needs a Rethink', 16 January. http://blogs.wsj.com/searealtime/2012/01/16/singapore-inc-needs-a-rethink-economists-say/.

Wall Street Journal (2013) 'Abenomics is No Cure-All for Japan Inc.,' 7 February. http://online.wsj.com/article/SB10001424127887324590904578289372938981756.html.

Wallerstein, I. (1978) 'World-system Analysis: Theoretical and Interpretive Issues', in Kaplan B. B. (ed), *Social Change in the Capitalist World Economy*, Beverly Hills, CA: Sage: 219–235.

Wallerstein, I. (1979) *The Capitalist World Economy*, Cambridge: Cambridge University Press.

Wallerstein, I. (1997a) 'The Rise and Future Demise of World-systems Analysis', Fernand Braudel Center Working Paper, Binghamton University. http://fbc.binghamton.edu/iwwsa-r&.htm.

Wallerstein, I. (1997b) 'The Rise of East Asia: The World-system in the Twenty-first Century' Fernand Braudel Center Working Paper, Binghamton University. http://fbc.binghamton.edu/iwrise.htm.

Woo, J. E. (1991) *Race to the Swift: State and Finance in Korean Industrialisation*, New York: Columbia University Press.

World Bank (1993) *The East Asian Miracle*, New York: Oxford University Press.

World Bank (2013a) *South Korea Workforce Development, SABER Multiyear Country Report*, Washington: World Bank.

World Bank (2013b) *Singapore Workforce Development, SABER Multiyear Country Report*, Washington: World Bank.

Yoon, J. H. and Lee B-H. (2009) 'The Transformation of the Government-led Vocational Training System in Korea', in Bosch, G. and J. Charest (eds), *Vocational Training*, London: Routledge: 163–186.

CHAPTER 25

EMERGING ECONOMIC POWERS

The Transformation of the Skills Systems in China and India

MINGWEI LIU AND DAVID FINEGOLD

INTRODUCTION

As the world's two most populous nations, China and India together will account for roughly one third of the world's workforce in the coming decades. Though sometimes called 'the factory of the world' and 'the back office of the world,' China and India are no longer confined to competing on low labour costs, but increasingly participate in a wide range of high-skill sectors from computer programming and semiconductors to biotechnology and legal services. A 2010 survey of human resources (HR) heads for the world's leading corporations suggested that most of their future hiring would be in emerging economies (with China and India topping the list at 40% and 29% growth respectively); these rapidly growing economies generate the majority of these firms' sales growth and have the most talent available (IBM 2010, 15).

How the workforce in China and India is educated and trained therefore has tremendous impact on the competitiveness of the two countries and the 'global talent pool' (Levin Institute 2005). Whilst skill development in OECD nations has been widely studied (e.g. Crouch et al. 1999), few systematic efforts have been taken to examine education, training, and skill formation in China and India. To date, the limited research on skill issues in China and India has focused on the large and rapidly growing supply of scientists and engineers that these two Asian giants are producing and the impact of this talented workforce on the global economy (e.g. Gereffi et al. 2008; Wadhwa et al. 2009). There has been little research, however, on the rapidly evolving skill development systems of China and India, particularly their efforts at major skill-upgrading.

This chapter aims to provide a brief, comparative review and analysis of skill formation in these two countries.

China and India are making major efforts to move their economies from generally low-skills equilibria to develop more high-skills sectors and employment. However, both countries face great challenges in making this transition, including areas of both skills shortage and surplus imbalance, and large segments of the workforce and employers that remain trapped in low-skills equilibria. Moreover, despite many similar goals, the trajectories of skill development of the two countries are shaped by different sets of political, socioeconomic, institutional, cultural, demographic, and organizational factors. Consequently, whilst facing some similar challenges, China and India are evolving very different skill formation and demand models, with some complementary strengths and weaknesses.

Skill Development in China

For many observers, China's economic miracle of the past several decades can be attributed primarily to the huge supply of cheap, low-skilled labour that enabled it to dominate the low-cost manufacturing in the world market. Until recently China may be largely viewed as a stable low-skills equilibrium in which employers pursue low-cost, low-value-added, labour-intensive manufacturing and service strategies requiring only a low-skilled workforce. Although China's high-technology exports have rapidly increased in the past decade, the vast majority of these exports are from the IT hardware industry which is dominated by foreign-owned enterprises, considerably less R&D-intensive than its counterpart in developed countries, not innovative in terms of novel-product creation, and dependent on imported high-value components for high-volume assembly (OECD 2006, 2008; Breznitz and Murphree 2011). Even the largest high-tech exporter in China, Foxconn, a Taiwanese supplier to the World IT giants such as Apple, Intel, and Dell, heavily depends on exploitation of rural unskilled labour for its competiveness which has been widely publicized and criticized within and outside China.

On the supply side, China has had to confront the historical legacy of a poorly developed education and training (ET) system. According to the Ministry of Human Resources and Social Security (MHRSS) (2011), despite several decades of intensive investment, by the end of 2010, 76.1% of China's labour force still had junior secondary schooling or less and only 10.09% had received tertiary education. The low skill-levels of Chinese workers have hindered China's economic development and greatly affected productivity—China's overall labour productivity is lower than that of not only advanced industrial countries, but also some developing Asian nations such as Thailand, Malaysia, and the Philippines (it is a little higher than Indian labour productivity, however) (Asian Productivity Organization 2008).

As China has emerged as the world's second largest economy, it has recognized the significant drawbacks and unsustainability of the low-road economic development model. The vulnerability of China's, low-skill, export-driven growth model (i.e. sharp decrease of exports and layoffs of millions of factory workers) became particularly apparent during the 2008–9 global financial crisis. The Chinese government is determined to upgrade China's industrial structure and shift its development focus from low-end manufacturing to higher end, more innovative sectors where a well-educated, highly skilled workforce is a necessity.

Move towards a Higher Skills Equilibrium

Since the 1980s, China has launched numerous policy initiatives and made huge investments to reform and develop its ET system. First, within a short period, China has successfully universalized nine-year compulsory education, implementing free primary and junior secondary school education (with all tuition and miscellaneous fees waived) nationwide starting in the fall of 2008.[1] The following data are illustrative of the achievements. The net primary school enrolment rate in China rose from 93.0% in 1980 to 99.7% in 2010, whilst the average years of schooling in the population 15 and over increased from 5.3 years in 1982 to more than 8.7 years, the equivalent of a junior secondary school education, by 2008 (Wang 2009; MOE 2012; Xin and Kang 2012). As China has achieved near universal secondary education, a second wave of education reform beginning in 1999 has focused on fostering students' innovative spirit and practical abilities.

At the same time, China has also taken measures to develop its vocational education (VE) system. In 1996 China enacted the Vocational Education Law which provides a legal framework for the development of VE in China and enabled new providers to enter the VE market along with state-run institutions. The improved status of VE and rapidly increasing input of private funding into VE institutions have contributed to significant expansion of Chinese VE in recent years. According to the Ministry of Education (MOE) statistics, the number of secondary vocational schools and total enrolments increased from 6,374 and 6,757,000 in 1980 to 14,401 and 21,951,700 in 2009, of which private schools and their enrolments accounted for 22.2% and 14.5% respectively; and the number of tertiary vocational colleges and total enrolments increased from 114 and 72,449 in 1990 to 1,071 and 6,314,723 in 2009. As many of their graduates have intermediate or even advanced level vocational qualifications, VE institutions have become a key source of supply of China's skilled and semi-skilled workers. The quality of China's VE and instructors has also gradually improved (Pan et al. 2007).

[1] Students still need to pay for services, such as special programmes and tutoring, and various expenses such as books and school suits, which are much more than tuition. In addition, students who want to enter good schools or who are not eligible for local school enrolment due to their non-local household registration status often need to make a big lump sum payment to get enrolled.

Perhaps the most notable educational development is the reform and expansion of Chinese higher education (HE) since the 1980s. Under the socialist planned economy, Chinese HE was centrally controlled, segmented, and overspecialized. With the progress of market-oriented economic reform, Chinese HE has become more decentralized, diverse, and increasingly marketized: local governments and HE institutions have been granted more autonomy; free HE for elite students has changed to mass HE with a fee-charging system; the graduate job assignment system has been replaced by a free graduate labour market; private HE institutions have emerged and grown quickly; and universities have taken on multiple functions including research, teaching, business, and social services (Bai 2006).

In 1999 the state decided to further expand HE as a way to meet surging domestic demand from the rising middle and upper classes. As a result, the number of HE institutions (including both four-year universities and three-year colleges) and total enrolments of HE sharply increased from 1,071 and 4,085,874 (or 10.5% of the 18–22 age population) in 1999 to 2,358 and 22,317,929 (or 26.5% of the 18–22 age population) in 2010 (MOE statistics). A particular focus has been on building world-class Chinese universities through the 211 Programme, the 985 Programme, and more recently the 2011 Programme, three large, ambitious, government-funded schemes. Alongside this huge domestic growth, China has seen a large increase in the number of students obtaining a degree abroad. According to the MOE statistics, 339,700 Chinese students studied abroad in 2011 (an increase of 19% compared to 2010), amongst whom 24,900 were sponsored by the state and other organizations. More recently, as competition for admission to top-ranked foreign universities has intensified, a growing number of Chinese students are going abroad for high school to further enhance their English skills.

To try to stem this flow of students abroad as well as attract more international students to China and stimulate innovation amongst their national universities, the government has authorized new joint-venture English-language campuses between the world's top research universities. The first international joint-venture campus, the University of Nottingham Ningbo, was established in 2004, and the list is growing with more and more leading US and UK universities such as Berkeley, Liverpool, the University of London, and New York University joining the club. The number of foreign students and the percentage in HE degree programmes increased from 44,711 and 25.67% in 1999 to 292,611 and 40.61% in 2011. In addition, 25,687 (or 8.78%) foreign students received Chinese government scholarships in 2011, an increase of 14.73% compared to just a year earlier (MOE statistics). The state has also introduced various policies to attract overseas talent including both Chinese and foreigners to work in Chinese universities, research institutes, and enterprises or to establish their own business in China, such as granting special permits for entering and leaving the country, generous government subsidies and start-up funds, tax reductions or exemptions, favourable import regulations, and priority employment for spouses and educational enrolment for children (OECD 2008). As a result, an increasing number of overseas Chinese students, scientists, and engineers have returned to China since the late 1990s. In 2011, 186,200

Chinese students returned to China after study abroad, an increase of more than 38% in just one year (MOE statistics).

The great expansion of HE has significantly enlarged China's talent pool. According to the national population census, the population with degrees increased from 0.62% in 1982 to 8.93% in 2010. China has also recently surpassed the United States as the world's top producer of PhDs, awarding 48,987 doctorates in 2010 (MOE statistics). In particular, China's science and engineering sector has significantly benefited from the rapid expansion of HE, which has provided an increasing supply of scientists and engineers. In 2008 China's science and technology sector employed 46 million people, of whom 20 million had a bachelor's degree or above, which gave China the world's largest graduate science and technology workforce (Ministry of Science and Technology (MOST) statistics). Moreover, the number of scientists and engineers per 10,000 workers more than doubled between 1991 and 2008, increasing from 20 to 43 (MOST 2010).

In addition to the reform and development of the formal education system, China has made efforts to improve workplace training through introducing a range of regulations with regard to training providers, contents, intensity, funding, and so on (Cooke 2005). Despite their weak and uneven enforcement, these regulations have provided impetus for enterprise training. In particular, two major state-driven training initiatives, i.e. occupational training combined with a requirement that workers must obtain a vocational qualification certificate prior to entering many skilled and semi-skilled occupations, have significantly promoted enterprise training (Cooke 2005). A survey of IT professionals in 2009 found that 52.3% of the respondents had received internal training provided by their enterprises (Li et al. 2011).

In addition, given that unskilled or semi-skilled rural-to-urban migrant workers have become a major source of labour supply in China, the Chinese state started to provide pre-employment skill training to migrant workers in 2003. According to the MHRSS, 7.04 million (person-time) migrant workers received government-provided skill training in 2010. All of these efforts in workplace training have been facilitated by the mushrooming private training institutions. In 2010 there were 20,144 private training agencies in China with 10,052,775 graduates, 52.4% of whom obtained certain vocational or professional qualification certificates (MHRSS 2011).

Due to severe shortages of high-quality managers, both the Chinese government and enterprises have also made great efforts to improve management ET, including sending managers overseas to receive training, promoting local management training institutions, and cooperating with international training institutions or foreign enterprises in China in providing customized management training (Wang and Wang 2006; Au et al. 2008; Warner and Goodall 2009; Li et al. 2011). Joint and international Executive MBA programmes have also been allowed to operate in China and more than 60 universities have been accredited by the MOE to offer Executive MBA programmes.

On the demand side, Chinese national state and provincial/city governments have taken a number of strategic policy initiatives to develop high-tech, higher-skill industries. Firstly, China has carried out various programmes to support basic research that is critical to building the country's long-term innovation capability, but which struggles to attract private-sector investment. These initiatives include the National Science Foundation programmes, the National Basic Research Programme (i.e. the 973 Programme), the reform of public research institutions, and programmes to attract and develop top researchers such as the Yangtze River Scholars Programme and the Chinese Academy of Science Hundred Talents Programme. In addition, China has a wide range of initiatives to support technology innovation and commercialization, and the establishment of high-tech parks and incubators.[2] The priority of technology innovation and industrial upgrading, according to China's 12th Five-Year Plan, is given to seven 'strategic emerging industries': new-generation information technology, energy-saving and environment protection, new energy, biology, high-end equipment manufacturing, new materials, and new-energy cars. In addition, the Industrial Transformation and Upgrading Plan (2011–15) includes supports for the raw materials, consumer products, electronics, national defence, and manufacturing-related service sectors. Following the central government's lead, local governments have also established preferential policies to support technology innovation and industrial upgrading.

China's state-led investments to 'leapfrog' from a low-skill to innovation-driven economy are impressive. China's real R&D spending has increased about 20% annually since 2000 and China's share of the global R&D reached 12% in 2009 overtaking Japan as the second largest R&D investor globally (National Science Board 2012). Although the R&D spending/gross domestic product ratio of China remains relatively low, at 1.83% in 2011, it had more than doubled from 0.8% in 1999 (National Bureau of Statistics 2012). China's R&D output in terms of scientific publications and patents has also grown very fast. According to the Royal Society (2011), China's share of world scientific publications rose from 4.4% during 1993–2003 to 10.2% during 2004–8; China has overtaken the United Kingdom as the second leading producer of research publications; and the quality of Chinese scientific publications has also been improved, as seen from the increase of China's citation count from virtually nil to a 4% global share. Chinese scientific publications are particularly strong in material science, analytical chemistry, rice genomics, and stem-cell biology, and China has surpassed the United States as the top publishing country in nanotechnology (Bhattacharya and Bhati 2011). Published applications from China's patent office grew at an average 16.7% annually from 171,000 in 2006 to about 314,000 in 2010 and surpassed the United States and Japan as the world's top patent filer in 2011. In addition, China has actively participated in the creation and adoption of technical standards to gain early-mover advantage in emerging technologies (Bhattacharya and Bhati 2011).

[2] These initiatives include the High Technology R&D Programme (i.e. the 863 Programme), the National Key Technology R&D Programme, various programmes for the development of new products such as the National New Product Programme, the Spark Programme, the Science and Technology Achievement Dissemination Programme, and a large number of S&T industrial parks, university science parks, and technology business incubators under the Torch Programme as new infrastructures to encourage industry-science relationships.

Thanks to this intensive research investment, China has emerged as one of the top five global R&D leaders in high-tech industries such as clean energy, satellite and spacecraft, commercial aircraft, electric cars, supercomputers, and life sciences, and is rapidly catching up in some others, such as high-speed rail and information and communication technology (Ernst 2011). With the significant development of China's R&D and high-tech industries, an increasing number of Chinese innovative enterprises such as Huawei, TCL, and Lenovo have acquired global visibility and market presence. And some Chinese enterprises have formed joint ventures with enterprises in the United States to accelerate development and international commercialization (Friedman 2011). In addition, internet and technology-based enterprises, such as Ali Baba and Baidu, have experienced explosive development, partly owing to the huge government investment in the development of science and technology parks and incubators (OECD 2008).

Obviously great efforts have been made by the Chinese state in skill development, including not only redressing the externalities or capital market failures but also planning, coordinating, and fostering the demand and supply of high skills. Looking ahead, China has set up a goal of becoming an 'innovation-oriented,' learning society and great power of HR in its Mid- and Long-Term Plans for Science and Technology Development and Education Reform and Development. According to the former plan, by 2020, China will spend 2.5% of its GDP in R&D, raise the contribution of technological advance to economic growth to more than 60%, and reduce its dependence on imported technology to no more than 30%. According to the latter, by 2020, China will largely universalize preschool education; further strengthen nine-year compulsory education; universalize high school education with the net enrolment rate reaching 90%; further expand HE with the net enrolment reaching 40%; increase the average years of education of the major working-age population to 11.2; and double the population with HE qualifications from 2009. These objectives draw a bright picture for China's skill development. In particular, in a few high-tech, innovative sectors, such as satellite and spacecraft, clean technology, and electric cars, China may be able to reach a high-skills equilibrium. However, as we explore in the next section, these impressive numbers may mask some of the major challenges still facing China's skill development system.

Major Issues Facing China's ET System

Despite China's significant achievements in enhancing skill formation in the past three decades, the Chinese ET system faces great challenges at every level in its ongoing efforts to move towards a higher-skill economy.

To begin with, although legally nine-years of compulsory education has been universalized, inequality of access to and the uneven quality of compulsory education remain great obstacles for upgrading the skills of disadvantaged groups. This is especially true in rural areas where educational development has significantly lagged behind that of urban areas due to much less investment and poorer quality facilities and teachers (Wang 2003). Two problems are particularly worth noting. The first is a high percentage of rural students dropping out of compulsory education especially at the stage of junior secondary schools. An investigation of more than 130 rural junior secondary schools in six inland provinces revealed that in many of these schools the student drop-out rate was higher than 20%, with the highest reaching 81% (Wang 2003). Various factors account for the high rural student drop-out rates: Firstly, China's exam-oriented education system puts students under intense pressure and causes many who feel they are unlikely to succeed to lose interest in learning. Secondly, the idea of 'education is useless' has become popular in rural areas in recent years due to the unemployment and underemployment of a large number of college graduates, especially those who lack connections in cities. Thirdly, most rural families are still very poor. Even with free tuition, many families, especially those having several children, either cannot afford other school costs or want their children to earn an income early, leading to high drop-out rates of poor students. Finally, there have been large-scale closures and mergers of rural primary and secondary schools in recent years driven by the demographic decline (see page 541), with the number of rural primary schools dropping 52.1% between 2000 and 2010 (MOE statistics); this has increased rural families' costs such as transportation and dormitory expenses, resulted in many safety issues and inconvenience during students' daily long trips to schools, and increased student–teacher ratios, all of which add additional challenges in retaining rural students (Ma 2009).

The second problem is the poor quality of compulsory education received by the huge population of children of migrant workers, of which 58 million are left behind in the countryside with grandparents or other relatives and 19 million remain in the cities with their parents (China Labor Bulletin 2009). Those left behind often see their parents only once a year; with little help and supervision, they tend to have poorer academic performance and more behavioral problems than their peers (China Labor Bulletin 2009). Those who stay with their parents in cities, however, often have a difficulty enrolling in local public schools due to China's household registration system that excludes rural migrants from urban social welfare and the education system (Branigan 2010). Given the low income of migrant workers, they cannot afford to send their children to private schools. A large number of migrant workers' children end up in special schools for migrants, which often operate illegally, have extremely poor facilities and quality, and are frequently shut down by government. And about 6% of migrant children have never attended school (Branigan 2010).

These problems become even more severe when it comes to the stage of high school education which is neither free nor compulsory. Most cities, especially Beijing and Shanghai, either do not allow or impose great barriers on migrant workers' children gaining access to quality public high schools, to preserve preferences given to registered urban children in preparing for college entrance exams. In addition to the huge rural-urban gap, inequality in primary and secondary education exists within each region: those with power, money, or strong social connections can have their children admitted to well-funded key public schools with the best teachers and facilities, whilst disadvantaged groups can only send their children to poorly financed, low-quality normal schools.

Another pervasive problem in China's compulsory and secondary education, despite reform efforts, is the ongoing emphasis on rote learning and examination performance at the expense of other important aspects of development such as creative thinking, personality, and social skills. As exam results remain the single most important evaluation criterion of students, teachers, and schools, schools often form key classes by assigning students with better academic performance to better teachers to improve their chances on various entrance examinations. In addition to the intense pressure that such exams impose, their narrow focus has a deep impact on the skill formation of the Chinese workforce: lack of soft skills, a frequent complaint by employers.

VE in China also faces significant challenges. Although the number of VE graduates has grown rapidly in recent years, the quality of these graduates is still unsatisfactory (Li and Sheldon 2011). Due to the cultural bias against VE in China, the sector has been particularly underfunded by the government and only students with the lowest academic achievement choose to follow this route. VE students do not receive a government subsidy like those in general HE. Many vocational colleges and schools lack technical facilities and qualified teachers to carry out the necessary training especially practical training (Pan et al. 2007). Moreover, most vocational school teachers are not specialized in what they teach and are over-burdened as the growth in teachers has failed to keep pace with expanded student numbers and changing technology and industry needs (Cooke 2005). The curriculum of vocational colleges and schools tends to focus on theory rather than practical skills (Cooke 2005). The MOE's repeated efforts to strengthen the linkages between industry demands and courses offered in vocational institutions, have failed because few private-sector actors respond to or cooperate with these government efforts.

HE has been better off in terms of government financial support. However, its rapid expansion since 1999 has resulted in decreasing per-college-student expenditure and therefore a crisis of financial resources, especially for those 'non-key' universities and colleges (Simon and Cao 2009).[3] As a result, the quality of Chinese college graduates varies greatly. The rapid expansion of HE has also made it difficult for many universities and colleges to sustain their key facilities such as classrooms, laboratories and libraries (Bai 2006), and caused a sharp rise in the average student–teacher ratio across HE institutions from 6.8:1 in 1992 to 17.3:1 in 2009 (MOE Statistics). In addition, the overall quality of faculty members has not kept pace with the quantitative expansion of HE. As of 2006 only 10% of faculty members in Chinese universities had a doctoral degree (Simon and Cao 2009). The curriculum of universities and colleges also tends to be narrowly designed and delivered, and is often out of date (Hennock 2012; Meng 2005; Ren et al. 2011). Rote learning still dominates Chinese HE, and engaged student discussion

[3] Although the growth of Chinese HE started in the early 1990s, the pace had been slow until 1999 when the national HE expansion policy took effect.

is rare. Whilst political and ideological education is still a significant part of the HE curriculum, creative thinking, entrepreneurship, and interpersonal and intercultural skills are largely missing from the pedagogy or curriculum of HE institutions (Hennock 2012; Simon and Cao 2009). The patchy and unsustainable involvement of enterprises in HE (including vocational HE) has further reduced the practical elements in the curriculum and resulted in few opportunities for students to gain hands-on experience and problem-solving skills (Simon and Cao 2009; Li and Sheldon 2011; Ren et al. 2011; Hennock 2012).

Whilst students who make it into undergraduate or graduate programmes may have worked hard to be admitted, many of them lose interest or motivation to learn after admission. Firstly, it is relatively easy to graduate from college, and few students have failed due to unsatisfactory performance; in 2011 the failure rate of college students was under 1% (MOE statistics). Secondly, students must choose their subject before entering college, and it is extremely difficult for students to change their majors or transfer to another HE institution if they lose interest in their speciality. Thirdly, the narrowly designed and outdated HE curriculum mentioned earlier significantly lowers student interest and motivation to learn; the Mycos (2013) national survey of college graduates found that 6% overall, and 21% of tertiary VE graduates, reported that their courses did not raise their interest in learning. Fourthly, working hard in college may not make much difference when it comes to securing a good job. A national survey of college graduates in 2010 found that the top 20% of academic performers made about 10% less on their first jobs than the 80% of mediocre ones. But graduates from the top 20% of richest families or families with at least one parent being a government official had a first job wage premium of 25% and 18% respectively (Li et al. 2012). Some of the top gradates may have lower earnings due to attending graduate school and their first job wages may not reflect life-time earnings, but the significant wage gaps caused by family resources and *guanxi* (i.e. connections) may discourage the majority of students educational efforts.

Another challenge since the early 2000s is the rising unemployment of college graduates. The MOE statistics suggest that employment rates of graduates have declined as the supply of HE graduates has increased dramatically, but still more than 70% of graduates have been able to find jobs by each September over the last decade. However, the official data are questionable as many graduates have been 'employed on paper' without their knowledge (Tan 2009). The incentive to inflate these numbers has been high since 2002, when MOE set the 70% employment target; colleges which fail to meet it risk being downsized or even closed down (Li et al. 2008; Burkitt 2011).[4] Interestingly, according to both the MOE statistics and surveys by Mycos, a private consulting company which has conducted nation-wide online surveys of graduates since 2007, half a year after graduation the employment rate seems to significantly increase, reaching around 90% (Mycos, 2009–13). Although a 10% unemployment rate for new college graduates compares

[4] The latest plan of MOE, announced in 2011, was to downsize or cut those university majors in which the employment rate of graduates falls below 60% for two consecutive years.

favourably with many OECD nations since 2008, it is troubling given the severe shortages of skills identified earlier. Moreover, the sharp increase in the employment rate between September and December each year may be at the price of declining quality of employment, as graduates without work are forced to lower their job expectations, accepting whatever jobs are available. Some become members of 'ant tribes,' who have low-paid, contingent jobs and crowd together in China's largest cities (Lian 2009, 2010). Others have stable and well-paid jobs (mostly in government and public institutions), but are over-qualified for the work they're performing. In addition, a significant percentage of graduates have jobs that do not match their speciality. According to Mycos (2011), the overall employment-speciality match rate of HE graduates was merely 64% in 2010, which suggests a large waste of skills.

The high levels of unemployment and underemployment of HE graduates may be caused by the problems of China's HE system, as well as several socioeconomic and cultural factors. On the demand side, China's current economic and work structures may not be able to provide enough jobs for the rapidly increasing number of HE graduates. The engine of China's economic development has been the labour-intensive, export-oriented manufacturing sector, which needs a huge number of production workers, both skilled and non-skilled, but far fewer professionals and office staff. Although the service sector has grown very fast, most jobs are in low-end service industries which do not require college education.

On the supply side, despite the employment challenges, Chinese culture highly values education. People with more education or higher academic degrees gain higher respect and have a better chance of getting good jobs. The 'diploma worship' in Chinese society, together with fierce competition in the graduate labour market, has led to higher bars for many types of jobs. As a result, it is not uncommon for even low-end administrative jobs to require candidates to have HE degrees, which contributes to over-education or waste of skills. In particular, in the government sector and public institutions where jobs are stable and linked with high social status, entry standards tend to be very high.

The programmes and pedagogy of Chinese HE institutions have been slow to respond to changing labour market demands, contributing to high levels of graduate unemployment, underemployment, and speciality-employment mismatch. The state's central planning of HE programmes and its decisions on HE expansion are often made without taking full account of China's economic structure and changing market demand for skills (Bai 2006). Moreover, the rigid two-line (i.e. the Party line and the administrative line) governance of HE institutions formed under the planned economy has not significantly changed (Bai 2006). Although there have been moves towards decentralization, granting HE institutions more autonomy and encouraging new models through joint ventures with foreign universities, the state still centrally controls enrolment size and approves all degree programmes. Thus, Chinese universities find it hard to quickly adapt their programmes and curriculum to changing market demands, and cannot always be sure whether proposals for new programmes will gain state approval (Zhou 2005).

Faced with recent declines in government support and student numbers as the one-child generation reaches university age, however, many second- and third-tier universities and vocational colleges have attempted to create new 'hot programmes' to attract students and tuition income. Whilst setting up 'hot programmes' may suggest an improving market orientation of HE institutions, two factors make it problematic. Firstly, as HE institutions are insensitive to market dynamics (see discussion above), they are often not able to identify genuinely 'hot skills' with robust future market demands. In addition, because of the delays in gaining approval for new programmes, many 'hot programmes' become 'cold' in the labour market by the time students graduate. Even those 'hot programmes' that are correctly identified and established quickly often are unable to provide high-quality curriculum and training to students. The increasing number of poor quality 'hot programmes' has not only resulted in high unemployment of their graduates, but also led to surplus of these 'hot skills' in general affecting employment opportunities of top programme graduates. For example, in 2010 only 13% of the legal-studies graduates of China University of Political Science and Law, a top university specializing in law in China, found law-related jobs (Ren 2011).

In addition, Chinese universities and colleges lack the capacity to provide effective career services to students. A survey of college graduates seeking jobs in Shenyang, for example, found that 60% of the respondents had not received any career advice from their universities or colleges (Meng 2005).

Whilst the Chinese education system has various deficits, workplace training is even more problematic. Although the state has enacted a number of laws and regulations to institutionalize enterprise-based training, weak enforcement and lack of supervision have greatly reduced the effectiveness of these efforts. In particular, most enterprises do not have sufficient training funds. Whilst the state requires enterprises to spend 1.5% of total wages on training, a significant percentage of enterprises do not have any training funds at all (ACFTU 2006). Even in high-tech industries, training investments have been far from adequate (Li et al. 2011). In enterprises that have sufficient training funds, however, training tends to be nominal and in many cases only a small portion of funds are used for workers' skill training (Chen et al. 2009). The low intensity of workplace training may be due to enterprises overlooking the importance of training, their focus on cost control, and the lack of independent employee representation in the Chinese workplace. In addition, high levels of employee turnover and poaching make enterprises that do want to invest in training hesitate; the national average employee turnover rate in 2011 was as high as 26.8%, with the manufacturing sector reaching 35.6% (Ma 2012). And a survey of three industrial parks found that 80% of enterprises experienced employee poaching in the past year (Li and Sheldon 2011). Therefore, enterprises that need skilled workers may rely on the external labour market rather than train employees internally.

On the employee side, due to China's suppressive industrial relations system, independent labour unions are not allowed, and staff and workers' congresses either do not exist or have limited power; thus even workers who may desire workplace skill training may not have an effective way to influence managerial training policies. Given that most enterprises are unwilling to train workers, especially migrant workers, the government has taken initiatives to provide skill training to rural migrants. However, only a small percentage of migrant workers have received government-sponsored training, and such training has been highly formalistic and ineffective (Ge 2005; Guo 2006).

On the demand side, several structural and institutional constraints reduce the need for high-skilled employees in Chinese enterprises. Firstly, although high-tech industries have experienced significant development in recent years, low- and medium-end manufacturing and service sectors are still the back bone of China's economy. Therefore, it is not surprising that most Chinese enterprises do not feel the need for high-skilled labour. Secondly, the prevailing Taylorist work organization further reduces the demand for skills in even capital-intensive, high-end manufacturing enterprises. Thirdly, the government's concern to promote stability by maintaining high levels of economic growth and employment, has led to industrial policies that provide significant incentives, such as tax reductions and export subsidies, for the development of labour-intensive industries that may suppress the demand for high-skilled labour. Fourthly, two deficiencies of the innovation system, i.e. weak intellectual property protection and inefficient government investment in R&D (in both industries and HE institutions) caused by bureaucracy, a focus on short-term political objectives, and rampant corruption, may greatly discourage novel-product innovation and therefore lower the demand for high-skilled labour. Fifthly, the state-controlled financial system makes it very difficult for the private, innovative sector to get loans from the state-owned banks who favour still mainly state-owned and politically-connected enterprises (Herd et al. 2010). Finally, corporate governance in both the state and private sector tends to maximize short-term profits, whilst discouraging long-term investments in R&D and skill development.

China's problematic ET system is further challenged by the demographic changes which, to a large extent, are the product of the one-child policy introduced in the late 1970s. According to the US Census Bureau, China's total fertility rate (a measure of births per woman per lifetime) is currently down to 1.5, more than 30% lower than the level required for long-term population stability. Although China has recently eased the restrictions on two-child families, the working-age population is set to decline by about 1% a year between 2016 and 2030 (Eberstadt 2011). Moreover, China's labour force is rapidly ageing. The cohort in their 20s will shrink by over 75 million, or 35%, between 2010 and 2030, whilst the 55–64 age group is projected to grow by 80 million, or over 60% (Eberstadt 2011). These demographic changes may significantly reduce economic growth, tighten labour markets, and affect the survival of a large number of education institutions. As noted earlier, in rural areas the declining school-age population has already resulted in large-scale school closures and mergers. Many education providers in urban areas are facing the same fate. According to the MOE statistics, the number of students taking the college entrance exams declined from 10.5 million in 2008 to 9 million in 2012. And it is reported that, in 2011, colleges had 42,000 surplus places. Given these pressure, HE institutions are likely to consolidate in the next ten years (Yang 2012).

Skill Development in India

India's education and training system provides a fascinating comparison with China's. Like China, it has a huge population (the only other nation with over one billion people) that is demanding greater access to ET and a government trying to move the economy from a low-skill equilibrium to compete in higher-skill sectors. And similar to China, it faces challenges with corruption and the poor responsiveness of its public education institutions to shifting market demands. But beneath these high-level similarities, India exhibits stark contrasts with China that suggest a paradox to resolve: on the one hand, the evidence suggests India has had far less success than China in upgrading the skills of the majority of its population. And yet, whilst much of China's competitive advantage remains heavily concentrated in low value-added manufacturing sectors, India has emerged as a world-leader in more high-skill service sectors. The remainder of this chapter will unravel this paradox, showing both the challenges India's skill system faces and how it has been able to overcome these in certain high-skill niches.

In contrast with China's rapidly ageing population, India has both the opportunities and challenges that come with its 'demographic dividend'—550 million young people under the age of 25. This huge supply of human capital could produce a major growth advantage for India in the coming decades if the nation is able to develop its young talent to compete effectively in today's global economy. Failure to meet the rising expectations of these young people for good education and employment, however, risks alienating a generation that could add to the civic and political unrest India is already experiencing in a number of states.

Major Challenges Facing India's ET System

India faces significant challenges at every level of its ET system. The problem begins at birth, with the limited supports for early childhood education. Despite the major increases in national wealth that rapid economic growth has brought over the last two decades, a majority of Indian children are still growing up in villages or poor areas in cities, raised by parents who have had little formal education themselves and struggle to make a living in the informal economy, which accounts for over 85% of India's employment.

The problem continues when children begin compulsory schooling. Primary and secondary education is largely a state responsibility in India, and there is huge variation in how well different states meet this responsibility; a few states, such as Kerala, have literacy rates of over 90%, whilst in other states, such as Bihar, fewer than half of each age cohort complete lower secondary education and average literacy is under 64% (Government of India 2009). Most government schools suffer from a lack of accountability and a poorly motivated teaching workforce, with chronically high absenteeism of 25% or more amongst teachers in rural areas (Kremer 2005). As a consequence, state schools perform poorly compared to even the least resourced and lowest performing private-sector counterparts (Pandey 2013), and their counterparts in other nations; when two Indian states took part in the OECD's 2009 PISA study comparing educational attainment of 15-year-olds, they finished next to last amongst all nations, two standard deviations below the OECD average (OECD 2010; Vishnoi 2011). Even poor families are increasingly opting out of the public education system, with nearly half devoting most of their disposable income to send their children to private schools (Tooley 2009; Pandey 2013).

A key consequence of the poorly performing state school system is that a low percentage of India's young people continue on to upper secondary education. India suffers in comparison not just to the OECD nations and emerging economic powers like China, but also to other developing nations such as Mexico, Paraguay, and Thailand. The Indian Government sought to greatly expand education participation rates in 2009 with the passage of Right to Education Act, which for the first time made access to primary and lower secondary education a constitutional right for all Indian children. But the implementation of the Act has been uneven and in some cases instead made the situation worse as new regulations focusing on educational inputs—i.e. size of playgrounds and classrooms, qualifications of teachers—have adversely impacted low-cost private schools serving the poor that have inferior facilities but strong educational results (Pandey 2013).

For young people not continuing in general education after compulsory schooling, many countries offer an alternative vocational education and training (VET) path to provide young people with a set of occupational skills to enter the labour market. In India, however, the VET path is extremely under-developed, with only 3% of the population taking part in formal VET through the Industrial Training Institutes (ITIs), polytechnics, or other training providers and another 8% participating in informal training, which typically consists of working alongside a parent or worker in some trade to learn their skills on-the-job (NSS 2007). Two main reasons for the low participation in ITI programmes are firstly that manual work, even if linked to a high wage, is seen as lower status than office work; and secondly, that the ITIs have historically had only weak ties with local employers. This is reflected in the high unemployment rates of ITI graduates that persist even whilst many manufacturing and IT sectors struggle to find workers with the requisite skills (NSS 2007). In some sectors, such as information technology, the private sector has responded to fill this skills gap. NIIT, for example, has grown to be one of the world's five largest training companies, providing a wide range of training courses leading to recognized certification in computer programming and other IT skills.

One area where India has made great progress in the last decade is expanding its HE capacity to meet rapidly rising demand. There has been a huge increase in the number of private colleges approved by AICTE (the All India Council for Technical Education that accredits technical and management HE institutions), with the number of engineering programmes doubling between 2005 and 2010, and a near doubling of the number of management degrees. They have emerged to fill the market demand for business and engineering degrees unmet by the public HE system. State colleges and universities, which account for over 90% of all public undergraduate education, have suffered from lack of resources (caused by very low tuition fees and limited growth in government funding), chronic faculty shortages, limited institutional autonomy, and lack of research, which has historically occurred in separate government institutes. The problem, however, is the low quality of the education provided at many of these new colleges—whilst officially not-for-profit, most of these colleges are run effectively as lucrative businesses. Concerns about these institutions include their small size (the median college has under 500 students), corruption and lack of transparency, and the poor caliber of faculty (Umarji 2013); over 180 business schools alone failed in 2012 because the poor employment record of their graduates meant they were unable to attract new students. A range of studies by the McKinsey Global Institute and industry associations suggest that only 20–25% of India's engineering graduates and an even smaller percentage of arts graduates (5–10%) are considered employable by top Indian or multinational corporations (Hyderabad India Online 2013). Whilst more comprehensive research is needed on HE quality, the fact that companies like Infosys put all 20,000+ of their new engineering graduate hires through an intensive 16-week classroom training programme before they begin working suggests that there is significant room for improvement in the educational foundation that these HE institutions provide.

Explaining India's Success: The '3Es'

Despite these significant issues at each stage of its ET system, India has been very successful in creating a human-capital driven, global services business model that many other developing economies—Malaysia, the Phillipines, Eastern Europe, Africa—have sought to emulate. First in IT, call centres, and routine business services, and more recently in healthcare, biopharma, financial and legal services, India has been able to generate millions of new jobs by attracting foreign investment and creating its own rapidly growing service enterprises by offering talented young people at a low price (Brown et al. 2010). Perhaps no firm better illustrates this shift in global labour than IBM, which has dramatically expanded its Indian workforce, as it made the shift from an advanced manufacturer to a global services company. Within a span of just five years (2003–8), it expanded its workforce in India ten-fold, from 10,000 to over 100,000, as India surpassed the United States as its largest employment location (Lohr 2007).

As the wages of graduates have risen significantly in the major Indian cities, India has moved forward from this low-cost, high-skill model of attracting foreign direct investment to create new jobs in a variety of ways. Firstly, it has given birth to its own large companies, as firms like Infosys, Wipro, and Tata Consulting Services have created hundreds of thousands of jobs to compete with firms like IBM and Accenture. Secondly, existing firms, both Indian and multinational companies (MNCs), have moved up the value-chain, shifting from more routine work to R&D and providing comprehensive outsourcing services to multinational organizations. Thirdly, the model that worked well in IT and business processes has been replicated in other knowledge-intensive sectors, such as biopharma (Finegold et al. 2009), legal services (Sako, Chapter 28 in this volume), and even healthcare, once seen as a quintessentially local service. And finally, there have been second-order effects as the rapid growth in the Indian middle class (estimated at over 250 million people), made possible by their success as a provider of knowledge services has, in turn, fuelled demand for higher-quality goods and services, which is driving the creation of new jobs in manufacturing, healthcare, and HE.

How has India overcome its ET system's weaknesses to create this talent-driven services model? The success can be traced to three factors—the 3Es—enabled by a globally connected IT infrastructure: (1) a fiercely competitive, meritocratic national Examination system that motivates the brightest, hardest-working individuals amongst its huge youth population to study hard to qualify for a university place; (2) a set of Elite educational institutions—the IITS, IIMs (Indian Institutes of Technology and Management) and some of the top federal universities—which provide a good quality, heavily subsidized education that is affordable to all those who qualify for places, and (3) English language proficiency, which gives Indian graduates a significant advantage over their peers in other large Asian economic powers such as China and South Korea in competition for global service employment. These three advantages of the Indian system have been reinforced by a fourth E—Ex-patriates—the large supply of talent that was educated and worked in the West, but now sees opportunities to return to create, lead, and invest in new businesses that leverage India's large supply of low-cost graduates to serve a range of global markets.

Whilst the low-cost, talent-driven strategy for offshored services has helped drive India's relatively high growth rates over the last two decades, it is important to recognize that the drivers of company location decisions can shift quite rapidly. The combination of rapidly rising labour costs, particularly in the major cities, and relatively high rates of inflation, combined with the emergence of new competitors with similar models—e.g. Eastern Europe, the Phillipines, Vietnam, and Thailand—have reduced India's labour arbitrage advantage (Brown et al. 2010). Sustaining the success of this strategy thus appears to depend both on whether Indian companies and MNCs locating there can continue to move up the value-chain into higher value-added service and manufacturing markets, and whether the Modi government can be more successful than its predecessor in improving the quality of ET provision on offer for the majority of the population that is willing to invest its time and money in improving their human capital.

Discussion: Common and Contrasting Challenges and Opportunities

This chapter has highlighted a number of the issues that Chinese and Indian policymakers must address if they are to continue the impressive strides they have made in upgrading their skills systems and economies over the coming decade. As we will highlight in this conclusion, some of the challenges are quite similar in the world's two most populous nations, and in other cases they approach them from a very different starting point.

Providing a Strong Educational Foundation for Vulnerable Groups

In China and India, the vast rural population, either staying in the countryside or 'floating' in cities, face great obstacles to accessing high-quality education, sometimes even during the compulsory phase of schooling. Both countries have seen a huge inward migration to the cities in search of economic opportunity, and vulnerable groups in urban areas, such as children from families of unemployed, laid-off and low-wage workers, have a very low chance to be admitted by high-quality primary and secondary schools. China has made far greater strides than India, however, in raising literacy levels by insuring that those remaining in the villages receive a solid educational foundation, while India is struggling to implement the new Right to Education Act. And whilst both nations have dramatically expanded their HE sectors, the rising costs of attending college since the late 1990s have excluded a larger number of young people from rural and urban poor families. Given the huge size of the low-skilled and informal sector workforce, providing better education opportunities to those disadvantaged groups and their children remains one of the key challenges facing both nations.

Corruption and Rising Inequality

Whilst economic liberalization has brought major increases in living standards and economic opportunities to both nations, it has been accompanied by widespread corruption and a sharp growth in inequality that has undermined the confidence of citizens in the government, and fairness of the government and education systems. In China, although there has been increasing private involvement in primary, secondary, and vocational education, the education system is still dominated by the authoritarian state. The unchecked power of government in education administration and resource allocation has resulted in corruption in almost every corner of the education system. Likewise in India, it is often bribes and/or connections, rather than performance, that helps determine who is selected for civil service teaching positions, helping to explain the problem of chronic teacher absenteeism in rural schools. A consequence of the widespread corruption is rising inequality between the powerful or rich and normal people in terms of access to high-quality education. To develop a high-skilled workforce, both nations must take measures to ensure education equity and fairness, which, however, is not easy without profound political reform.

Skills Mismatch: Quantity over Quality

Both China and India have been far more successful in expanding the size of their education systems and the number of young people receiving degrees and qualifications than they have been in improving the quality of the education and training on offer. Indeed, because the highest-quality universities have been understandably reluctant to grow significantly, most of the expansion has occurred in lower-quality new institutions. Because these institutions receive little or no government subsidy compared to top universities, they charge individuals more to attend than their higher-rated counterparts, but young people who fall short in the highly competitive national entrance exams are still willing to pay because they have few alternatives.

In addition, most education and training institutions still rely on rote memorization, rather than more engaging pedagogy with a focus on critical thinking, problem-solving, and communication skills. And they have relatively weak links with employers and highly bureaucratic systems for adapting the curriculum, so that what they are teaching is often poorly matched with the needs of today's global labour markets. As a result, many families invest their life savings to provide their children with educational opportunities only to find that they are unemployed or underemployed when they graduate. This problem has been exacerbated in the last decade as the rate of increase in the supply of graduates has outstripped the increases in demand for high-skilled workers and professionals. Both governments are initiating reforms that would give employers a greater voice and involvement in shaping skills provision.

Raising Employer Skill Demands

Employer demands for high skills are still very low in both China and India. In China this is mainly caused by several structural and institutional constraints including the dominance of low-end manufacturing and service industries, government industrial policies that encourage exports of labour-intensive products, and deficiencies in the innovation system, the financial system, and corporate governance. As these constraints touch many aspects of the Chinese capitalism, raising employer skill demands may need systematic reform of the Chinese political economy. India faces similar systemic challenges, but starts from an even lower base of skill demands, with far more limited success in building higher value-added manufacturing than China—for example, 41% of

India's job growth in the last decade was in low-skill construction compared with 16% in China (McKinsey Global Institute 2012, 6).

Contrasting Paths

Demographics

Whilst China and India have shared the challenge of educating the world's two largest populations of young people over the last few decades, their demographic futures offer perhaps the starkest contrast between the two countries. India's 550 million young people will only become a 'demographic dividend,' producing sustained high levels of economic growth, if it is able to reform its skills system in time to offer them high-quality education and job opportunities; it faces growing unrest from a disenfranchised generation if it cannot. Conversely, China has already begun the gradual adjustment process precipitated by the one-child generation, closing rural schools and lower quality VET providers. Over the coming decade its HE system and employers will face similar adjustments, as they prepare for a sharp drop in the number of school graduates. This offers several major advantages to China's skill system: pushing up HE participation rates still further, as institutions compete to attract students from a smaller cohort; continuing to push up wages, job quality, and productivity, as employers can no longer rely on an unlimited supply of cheap, reserve labour; and providing large private investment for skills, as parents and grandparents concentrate their savings on providing every educational opportunity to their sole heirs. China, however, also needs to cope with the economic and social challenges from what is known as the 'little emperors and empresses:' greatly raised expectations, slowing economic growth, and the costs of coping with a rapidly ageing population. Even with the easing of the one-child policy, most experts predict only a limited increase in the birth rate, as China, in this next growth phase, seems likely to mirror its neighbours in South Korea and Japan where birth rates are now far below replacement levels despite government incentives, rather than restrictions on having children.

Role of the State

Although the state has been critical for skill formation in both China and India, its role differs in the two countries. The Chinese state still follows the legacy of the socialist command economy intervening heavily the skill formation system. On the one hand, state intervention has been the key factor driving China's skill development towards a high-skills equilibrium. Through its numerous policy initiatives, massive investments, detailed planning and extensive coordination, the state has significantly increased the demand for and supply of high skills, particularly in a few high-technology sectors. On the other hand, however, the Chinese state has failed to develop a set of institutions that are favourable to a high-skills ecosystem such as the innovation system, the financial system, and the industrial relations system. India faces many similar structural challenges, but its huge democratic state has been far less efficient in mobilizing resources to upgrade the educational infrastructure. The Singh government had an ambitious education reform agenda, but was unable to get most of it passed through a divided parliament from 2004 to 2014. It remains to be seen whether the Modi administration can bring about badly needed reforms.

Secondary Education

One of the starkest contrasts between India and China is China's much greater success in achieving near universal literacy and numeracy, and insuring that the vast majority of its young people are now completing secondary education. In 2011 China's literacy rate amongst the population aged 15 years and above reached 94.79%; and amongst the 20.3 million students admitted to primary schools in 1999, 13.3 million (or 65.5%) graduated from high schools or equivalent secondary vocational schools in 2011 (NBS 2012). Although India passed landmark legislation in 2009 providing for the first time a constitutional right to education for all of its young people, this right currently only extends to age 14, and even then, the country remains far from making this right a reality. Projections suggest that unless the government can substantially raise participation India is facing a shortage of 45 million workers with secondary education, alongside a surplus of 27 million low-skilled workers by 2030 (McKinsey Global Institute 2012).

Research Universities

Both nations recognize that the innovations and high-quality graduates and faculty produced by world-class research universities are vital if they are to be competitive in higher-skill markets. China has been investing very heavily to upgrade the research capabilities of its top universities, with impressive results in terms of expanding PhD programmes, top-tier international publications, and increases in patentable new discoveries (although the value of many of these patents has yet to be proven). Through the 2011 scheme, it is seeking to concentrate investment in a group of top universities to help them improve innovation capacity and move into the top tier of global university rankings. India has fared poorly by comparison, with growing, but still far more limited resources for research, with most of it still conducted in separate government institutes that are poorly connected to the needs of the economy and fail to produce the next generation of faculty that India desperately requires to increase its HE capacity.

Internationalization of HE

One of the key elements in China's strategy for improving the quality of its HE system is enticing many of the world's leading research universities (Yale, Chicago, UC Berkeley, NYU, Liverpool) to create joint-venture, English-language campuses in China with their Chinese peers. Local and regional governments are offering free land and construction, start-up operating subsidies, and research grants to attract these universities to China. In return, they hope to: retain more of the Chinese students now going abroad for their degrees; attract more students from around the world to study in China; and promote innovation among Chinese universities by closely studying and then diffusing the best practices of these joint-venture campuses to other institutions, as they have done in many of their industries. Conversely, in India, foreign universities have been prohibited from operating, with the Singh government's reform efforts failing in parliament. Even if it had passed, it is unclear whether the law would have had the desired effect for attracting high-quality universities, as it requires universities to post an $11 million bond to create a campus, rather than offering a generous package of incentives, as is occurring in China.

References

All China Federation of Trade Unions (2006) *Report on Enterprises' Education and Training Funds and Their Uses*, Beijing: All China Federation of Trade Unions.

Asian Productivity Organization (2008) *APO Productivity Databook 2008*, Beijing: Asian Productivity Organization.

Au, A. K. M., Altman, Y., and Roussel, J. (2008) 'Employee Training Needs and Perceived Value of Training in the Pearl River Delta of China: A Human Capital Development Approach,' *European Journal of Industrial Training*, 32(1): 19–32.

Bai, L. (2006) 'Graduate Unemployment: Dilemmas and Challenges in China's Move to Mass Higher Education', *The China Quarterly*, 185: 128–144.

Bhattacharya, S. and Bhati, M. (2011) 'China's Emergence as a Global Nanotech Player: Lessons for Countries in Transition', *China Report*, 47(4): 243–262.

Branigan, T. (2010) 'Millions of Chinese Rural Migrants Denied Education for their Children', *The Guardian*, 14 March.

Breznitz, D. and Murphree, M. (2011) *Run of the Red Queen: Government, Innovation, Globalization, and Economic Growth in China*. New Haven: Yale University Press.

Brown, Phillip, Lauder, Hugh, and Ashton, David (2010). *The Global Auction: The Broken Promises of Education, Jobs and Incomes*, Oxford: Oxford University Press.

Burkitt, L. (2011) 'China to Cancel College Majors That Don't Pay', *Wall Street Journal*. http://blogs.wsj.com/chinarealtime/2011/11/23/china-to-cancel-colleg.

Chen, Kuiwei, Feng Gao, Xin Chen, and Shu Yang (2009) 'Report on Chinese Enterprise Training', *Vocational and Technical Training*, 30: 59–67.

China Labor Bulletin (2009) 'The Children of Migrant Workers in China'. http://www.clb.org.hk/en/node/100460#part2_heading06.

Cooke, F. L. (2005) 'Vocational and Enterprise Training in China: Policy, Practice, and Prospect', *Journal of the Asia Pacific Economy*, 10(1): 26–55.

Crouch, C., Finegold, D., and Sako, M. (1999) *Are Skills the Answer? The Political Economy of Skill Creation in Advanced Industrial Societies*, Oxford: Oxford University Press.

Eberstadt, N. (2011) 'The Demographic Risks to China's Long-Term Economic Outlook', Swiss Re Center for Global Dialogue. http://cgd.swissre.com/global_dialogue/topics/ageing_longevity/Demographic_risks_to_China.html.

Ernst, D. (2011) 'China's Innovation Policy is a Wake-Up Call for America', *Asia Pacific Issues*, Analysis from the East-West Center no. 100.

Finegold, David, Erhardt, Nicholas, and Sako, Mari. (2009) 'Offshoring Knowledge Work: How Far Can It Go? Evidence from Drug R&D', in K. Carettas (ed.), *Outsourcing Economics, Management, and Risks*, Hauppauge, NY: Nova Publishers: 1–14.

Friedman, J. S. (2011) 'How Chinese Innovation is Changing Green Technology', *Foreign Affairs*, 13 December.

Ge, F. (2005) 'Analysis of Current Situation of Vocational Training of Rural Labor Force in Guangdong and Policy Suggestions', *South Countryside*, 1: 47–50.

Gereffi, G., Wadhwa, V., Rissing, B., and Ong, R. (2008) 'Getting the Numbers Right: International Engineering Education in the United States, China, and India', *Journal of Engineering Education*, 97(1): 13–25.

Government of India (2009) *India 2009: A Reference Manual*, New Delhi: Government of India: 225.

Guo, J. (2006) 'Migrant Workers' Skill Training: What Is the Solution?', *Education and Occupation*, 19: 80.

Hennock, M. (2012) 'In the Wake of China's Quickening Economy, Universities Struggle to Keep Pace', *The Chronicle of Higher Education*, 22 April. http://chronicle.com/article/Chinas-Universities-Struggle/131610/?key.

Herd, R., Hill, S., and Pigott, C. (2010) *China's Financial Sector Reforms*, Paris: OECD.

Hyderabad India Online (2013) 'Lack of Employable Talent in Today's Indian Graduates'. http://hyderabad-india-online.com/2013/03/lack-of-employable-talent-graduates/.

IBM (2010) *Working Beyond Borders: Insights from the Global Chief Human Resource Officer Study*. Somers, NY: IBM Institute for Business Value. http://www-935.ibm.com/services/c-suite/chro/study/.

Kremer, Michael, Chaudhury, Nazmul, Rogers, Halsey, F., Muralidharan, Karthik, and Hammer, Jeffrey (2005) 'Teacher Absence in India: A Snapshot', *Journal of the European Economic Association*, 2–3 (March): 658–667.

Levin Institute (2005) 'The Evolving Global Talent Pool: Issues, Challenges, and Strategic Implications', Conference Report, New York: Levin Institute.

Li, F., Morgan, J., and Ding, X (2008) 'The Expansion of Higher Education, Employment and Over-Education in China', *International Journal of Educational Development*, 28: 687–697.

Li, Hongbin, Lingsheng Meng, Xinzheng Shi, Binzhen Wu, and Yang Wang (2012) *Report on Chinese College Graduates*, Beijing: Tsinghua University.

Li, Y. and Sheldon, P. (2011) 'Skill Shortages', in P. Shelton, S. Kim, Y. Li, and Warner, M. (eds), *China's Changing Workplace*, London: Routledge: 129–143.

Li, Y., Sheldon., and Sun, J. (2011) 'Education, Training, and Skills', in P. Shelton, S. Kim, Y. Li, and M. Warner (eds), *China's Changing Workplace*, London: Routledge: 111–128.

Lian, S. (ed) (2009) *Ant Tribes: Investigation of the Village of College Graduates*, Nanning, China: Guangxi Normal University Press.

Lian, S. (2010) *Ant Tribes II*, Beijing: China CITIC Press.

Ma, K. (2012) 'Survey Found Persistent High Employee Turnover; 75% of the Enterprises Were Going to Raise Wages', China Business News, 4 May. http://finance.sina.com.cn/leadership/xcqs/20120504/081611984325.shtml.

Ma, Y. (2009) 'Why Did Rural Students Drop-Out Rates Increase after School Restructuring?', *Xinhua Net*, 10 November. http://news.xinhuanet.com/focus/2009-11/10/content_12392723_1.htm.

McKinsey Global Institute (2012) *The World at Work: Jobs, Pay and Skills for 3.5 Billion People*, June, New York: McKinsey & Co.: 10.

Meng, Q. (2005) 'Examination of the Seven Deep-Rooted Problems of Graduate Unemployment', *Guangming Daily*, 7 January. http://www.syrc.com.cn/viewpoint/info.php?lid=1013.

Ministry of Education (2012) 'Education Statistics 2010'. http://www.moe.edu.cn/publicfiles/business/htmlfiles/moe/s6200/index.html.

Ministry of Human Resources and Social Security (2011) *China Labour Statistics Yearbook 2010*, Beijing: China Statistics Press.

Ministry of Science and Technology (2010) http://www.most.gov.cn/eng/.

Mycos (2009–13) *Report on Employment of College Graduates in China*, Beijing: Social Sciences Academic Press.

National Bureau of Statistics (2012) *China Statistics Yearbook 2011*, Beijing: China Statistics Press.

National Science Board (2012) *Science and Engineering Indicators 2012*. http://www.nsf.gov/statistics/seind12/.

NSS (2007) 'Status of Vocational Education and Training in India', 20045, NSS 61st round, New Delhi.

OECD (2006) *Information Technology Outlook 2006*, Paris: OECD.

OECD (2008) *OECD Reviews of Innovation Policy: China*, Paris: OECD.

OECD (2010) *PISA Results 2009: What Students Know and Can Do*, Paris: OECD.

Pan, Chenguang, Meng Li, and Wei Lou (2007) 'Development and Challenges of China's Vocational and Technical Education: A Survey of 32 Vocational Schools and Colleges in China', *The Chinese Journal of Population Science*, 2: 52–60.

Pandey, A. (2013) 'Sharp Decline in Education Standard Across Country: Study', 18 January, New Delhi: NDTV. http://www.ndtv.com/article/india/sharp-decline-in-education-standard-across-country-study-319042.

Ren, S., Zhu, Y., and Warner, M. (2011) 'Human Resources, Higher Education Reform and Employment Opportunities for University Graduates in the People's Republic of China', *The International Journal of Human Resource Management*, 22(16): 3429–3446.

Ren, W. (2011) 'Hot Majors in the Past Meet Employment Difficulty', *Jinhua Evening*, 6 July. http://www.jhnews.com.cn/jhwb/2011-07/06/content_1680172.htm.

Simon, D. and Cao, C. (2009) *China's Emerging Technological Edge: Assessing the Role of High-End Talent*, Cambridge: Cambridge University Press.

Tan, R. (2009) 'Universities Fabricate Employment Agreements for Graduates; "Being Employed" Becomes A Popular Term', *Nandu Daily*, 17 July. http://news.sina.com.cn/s/2009-07-17/045418238644.shtml.

The Royal Society (2011) *Knowledge, Networks and Nations: Global Scientific Collaboration in the 21st Century*, London: The Royal Society.

Tooley, J. (2009) *The Beautiful Tree*, Washington, DC: The Cato Institute.

Umarji, V.(2013) 'MBA in India: 90 Percent of Graduates Unemployable', *Business Standard*, 31 January. http://www.rediff.com/getahead/slide-show/slide-show-1-career-only-10-percent-mbas-employable/20130131.htm.
Vishnoi, Anubhuti. 2011. 'Indian schools dwarfed in global ratings programme,' Indian Express, 21 December. http://archive.indianexpress.com/news/indian-schools-dwarfed-in-global-ratings-programmeme/890091/.
Wadhwa, V., Saxenian, A. L., Freeman, R. B., and Gereffi, G. (2009) 'America's Loss is the World's Gain: America's New Immigrant Entrepreneurs, Part 4. Available at SSRN: http://ssrn.com/abstract=1348616.
Wang, B. (2009) *Thirty Years of Reform in China's Education: Basic Education*, Beijing: Beijing Normal University Press.
Wang, D. (2003) 'Compulsory Education in China Rural Area: Current Situation, Problems and Solutions', Working Paper Series no.35, Institute of Population and Labour Economics, Chinese Academy of Social Sciences.
Wang, J. and Wang, G. (2006) 'Exploring National Human Resource Development: A Case of China Management Development in a Transitioning Context', *Human Resource Development Review*, 5(2): 176–201.
Wang, J. (2003) *Research on the Problem of Students Dropping Out of Rural Junior High Schools*, Changchun: Northeastern University Press.
Warner, M. and Goodall K. (eds) (2009) *Management Training and Development in China: Educating Managers in a Globalized Economy*, Abingdon: Routledge.
Xin, T. and Kang, C. (2012) 'Qualitative Advances of China's Basic Education Since Reform and Opening Up: A Brief Review', *Chinese Education and Society*, 45(1): 42–50.
Yang, C. (2012) 'The Number of National College Entrance Exam Takers Decreased 1.4 Million in 4 Years; Some Higher Education Institutions May be Closed in the Next 10 Years', China Broadcast Net, 5 June. http://china.cnr.cn/xwwgf/201206/t20120605_509812424.shtml.
Zhou, Y. (2005) 'On the Structure of Undergraduate Programs of General Higher Education Institutes', *Journal of Southwestern University for Nationalities*, 11: 363–365.

SECTION VII

CURRENT CHALLENGES

CHAPTER 26

PROJECTING THE IMPACT OF INFORMATION TECHNOLOGY ON WORK AND SKILLS IN THE 2030S

STUART W. ELLIOTT

Introduction

Analysts typically gather information about changes in skill demand by looking at measures of the skills used in different jobs and tracking how the skills used have been changing, either within jobs or across a mix of jobs in the economy. This is a reasonable strategy for describing past changes and it provides a way of projecting changes in skill demand into the near future, since it is often plausible to think that recent trends will continue. Unfortunately, this approach to projecting changes in skill demand provides no way of detecting possible major shifts beyond the near future, which is precisely the aspect of the future that it might be most helpful to know something about.

In contrast to the typical approach, this chapter provides a way of thinking systematically about possible future shifts in skill demand before they occur. The approach is focused on possible future skill demand shifts that are likely to arise from one important source—the growing capabilities of information technology (IT). IT is notable as a potential source for disruptive changes to skill demand for two reasons. Firstly, when considered broadly to include information, communications, and robotics technology, IT includes research on reproducing the full range of human abilities, with implications for skill demand across all occupations. Secondly, the strong trends in increased power and decreased cost in computing provide a continuing opportunity to transform expensive and slow IT capabilities developed in research settings into cheap and fast applications in commercial settings. Moore's Law—the longstanding trend of processor development showing a doubling of processing power every 18 months—is a well-known characterization of this steady advance, which is mirrored in other aspects of IT development. Such change in the raw power of the technology can result in transformational changes in IT capabilities over a period of a decade or two.

This chapter analyses possible IT-driven changes in skill demand by reviewing the computer science research literature through the lens of human work skills. The rationale for this approach is that it is possible to see the demonstration of IT capabilities in the research literature before they are widely applied throughout the economy, thus providing a way of projecting important future shifts in skill demand before they occur.

This projection will necessarily be rough. In particular, knowing that an innovation exists in the research literature does not tell us how long it will take before it is widely applied. We know from the literature on the diffusion of innovations that new technologies often take several decades to diffuse (Mansfield 1989; Rogers 1995). In addition to the time it takes for information about an innovation to spread, it can also take substantial time to refine the innovation, figure out how to incorporate it into work processes, and make the necessary investments to bring about those changes (David 1990). Although there are a number of examples of IT innovations that have diffused quickly—such as social media websites like Facebook and tablet computers like the iPad—there are also numerous examples of legacy business processes that have taken substantial time to be computerized. Particularly when technologies relate to complex business structures—such as enterprise resource planning systems—it can take a long time for businesses to make the necessary changes to adopt them. Even for consumers, the adoption of new uses of technology—like electronic billing—can be slow if it requires changes in established habits.

The analysis in this chapter should be viewed as providing a guide to IT capabilities that could be broadly applied over a period of several decades. Given the roughness in the timeline, the title of the chapter refers loosely to projections to the '2030s.' In addition, the analysis itself reflects the rough timeline by taking the shortcut of ignoring the question of cost. The shortcut can partly be justified by the expectation that IT costs will continue to decline substantially in the future, as they have in the past. Therefore, as a first approximation, it seems reasonable to ignore the question of current costs and to focus primarily on defining the capabilities that IT has achieved. However, a more specific timeline would need a refined analysis that considered what constraints costs impose.

The analysis uses the US Department of Labor's database on occupational characteristics—O*NET—to define the set of human skills that are broadly relevant to work and to provide a way to contrast different levels of those skills. This taxonomy of skills and skill levels is then used to interpret the IT capabilities described in the research literature in terms that can be related to the human skills required by different occupations. The IT capabilities currently demonstrated by research systems are then used to identify tasks and occupations where IT could substantially replace workers over the next few decades. Finally, the extent of employment in those vulnerable occupations provides a high-level picture of the pressures that IT is likely to place on the workforce over this period.

The analysis is conservative in focusing on IT capabilities that have already been demonstrated in the research literature. Of course, we know that substantial applied research will be required to apply these demonstrated capabilities to the many different settings where such skills are currently used throughout the economy. However, we already understand enough about the basic capabilities to know that fundamental additional breakthroughs are not required. Although there will certainly also be new breakthroughs over the next few decades that develop new levels of IT capabilities that are not yet in the literature, the chapter does not attempt to predict such changes.

The purpose of the analysis is to identify shifts in skill demand across the workforce that will result as current IT capabilities are applied to current occupations where they can reproduce the full bundle of required skills. Those particular bundles of skills will likely be performed by IT in the future, rather than by workers. To stay employed, the workers themselves will need to switch to different bundles of skills—requiring capabilities that IT still lacks. That change will happen partly by expanding employment in current occupations that IT cannot perform, partly by reinventing current occupations to use different bundles of skills, and partly by inventing new occupations that currently do not exist. Of course, some workers may also leave the labour force, either voluntarily or involuntarily. The analysis in this chapter does not address the mix of occupational changes that will take place, but instead focuses on understanding the portion of the workforce that will be forced to change their skills or stop working in response and where those workers are currently located.

Current Ability Requirements of the US Workforce

The O*NET database includes information about most of the occupations classified within the Standard Occupational Classification (SOC) (Peterson et al. 1995, chapter 1).[1] Data are collected from job incumbents and occupation experts in an ongoing process that populated the database in a series of waves and successively provides revised information about all occupations, including any new occupations added to the occupational taxonomy. Over the past ten years, data have been collected about all occupations included in the database, with about half having been updated a second time.

The analysis in this chapter uses the Abilities set of descriptors from O*NET. This set is defined to reflect 'enduring attributes of the individual that influence performance,' which are described in a sufficiently general way that we can compare them to corresponding IT abilities that are described in the computer science research literature. The entire set of descriptors for Abilities includes 52 scales. For many of these

[1] If data were available, it would be useful to carry out this analysis globally. Most of the information on the O*NET programme has been drawn from the project's website at http://www.onetcenter.org/.

Table 26.1 Distribution of current employment across ability groups

Ability level	Language group (%)	Reasoning group (%)	Vision group (%)	Movement group (%)
1	0.0	0.0	0.3	2.6
2	0.4	1.5	23.2	26.6
3	17.8	45.1	61.8	51.1
4	64.5	42.8	14.5	18.9
5	15.9	10.2	0.2	0.4
6	1.3	0.5	0.0	0.3
7	0.0	0.0	0.0	0.0

scales—such as the four abilities related to strength or the ability related to number facility—a cursory consideration suggests that technology already surpasses human abilities. The current analysis focuses on 22 ability scales where humans are still clearly superior to technology. These 22 abilities are placed into four groups—language, reasoning, vision, and movement—for comparison to projects in the computer science literature.

For collecting information about the different ability scales from job incumbents and occupation experts, the O*NET questionnaires use 7-point scales with three anchoring tasks provided for each ability (Peterson et al. 1995, 10–22). In most cases, the three anchoring tasks are at levels 2, 4, and 6.

To aggregate the separate ability scales within each of the four groups, the analysis uses the maximum rating across the separate scales. The maximum is used rather than the average because IT would usually need to be capable of the full set abilities in the group to be able to carry out the associated tasks. Thus a job requiring a low level of written comprehension but a high level of oral expression is rated as requiring a high level of language ability. After taking the maximum, the rating for each ability group for each occupation is rounded to the nearest whole number.

Table 26.1 shows the distribution of civilian employment across the seven ability levels for the four different ability groups.[2] Most employment is concentrated in just three levels of difficulty, rather than the full seven levels on the scales. For language and reasoning most employment occurs in levels 3–5, whereas for vision and movement most

[2] The analysis uses O*NET Production 16.0 database from 2011, which covers 857 occupations. The O*NET data are linked to employment data by occupation for 2010, downloaded from the BLS at http://data.bls.gov/oes/. The occupations in the O*NET database cover occupations representing 94.4% of civilian employment. For occupations omitted from O*NET, the ability levels are estimated from the nearest cluster of similar occupations by taking the maximum rating across the cluster for each ability group.

Table 26.2 Distribution of current employment across joint language-reasoning (LR) and vision-movement (VM) ability groups

	VM = 1	VM = 2	VM = 3	VM = 4	VM = 5	VM = 6	VM = 7
LR = 1	0.0%	0.0%	0.0%	0.0%	0.0%	0.0%	0.0%
LR = 2	0.0%	0.0%	0.0%	0.4%	0.0%	0.0%	0.0%
LR = 3	0.0%	2.4%	9.1%	5.4%	0.0%	0.0%	0.0%
LR = 4	0.0%	5.0%	**47.5%**	**11.8%**	0.3%	0.2%	0.0%
LR = 5	0.0%	0.5%	7.8%	7.6%	0.3%	0.0%	0.0%
LR = 6	0.0%	0.1%	0.8%	0.5%	0.0%	0.1%	0.0%
LR = 7	0.0%	0.0%	0.0%	0.0%	0.0%	0.0%	0.0%

employment occurs in levels 2–4. Only a small portion of employment requires abilities at level 6, the level typically associated with the high anchor on the ability scales.

To provide a rough picture of the distribution of employment across the full set of abilities, Table 26.2 aggregates the four ability groups into two, combining language and reasoning abilities together into a single group and similarly combining vision and movement abilities. The aggregation is performed by taking the maximum across the two groups in each pair. This table also shows the percentage of current employment in occupations requiring each combination of language-reasoning (LR) abilities and vision-movement (VM) abilities. Table 26.2 suggests that substantial automation of current employment is likely to require progress on both LR and VM abilities since most jobs—at least as currently designed—involve some use of abilities across all four major groups.

IT Capabilities in the Current Research Literature

To conduct the literature review of current IT capabilities, recent articles from *AI Magazine* and *IEEE Robotics & Automation Magazine* were used to provide concrete examples of systems in the research literature in computer science. The articles in both of these journals are technical without being so detailed as to be difficult for a non-specialist to understand. A review of the titles and abstracts for the articles published between 2003 and 2012 produced a set of articles that collectively addresses each of the four ability groups. The articles were analysed separately for the earlier and later periods (2003–7, 2008–12) to identify areas where there have been notable recent changes in the nature of IT skill levels.

The literature review was designed to find a set of articles within each of the four ability areas that give concrete examples of current IT capabilities that can be compared to the anchoring tasks of the O*NET ability questionnaires. The ten-year review produced 40 articles that describe IT systems at the appropriate level of detail, 22 in the earlier period and 18 in the later period. The articles are listed in Table 26.3.

The remainder of this section discusses the four ability groups in turn. The section for each group begins by describing the anchoring tasks on the O*NET ability questionnaires and the contrasts among the different ability levels. This is followed by a synthetic description of the IT capabilities drawn from the systems in Table 26.3 and then a tentative suggestion about the O*NET ability level that corresponds to these abilities.

IT Language Capabilities

There are four O*NET scales in the language group, related to listening, reading, speaking, and writing.[3] The meaning of the scales is straightforward, with two related to understanding, two related to expression, two related to oral language and two related to written language.

The O*NET technical manual (Peterson et al. 1995, appendix G) provides general descriptions at the low and high ends of the ability scales that are intended to capture the contrasts in difficulty represented on each scale. On all four scales, the basic contrast is between language involving simple and complex ideas. For some of the scales, there are elaborations of this contrast, with the low end involving short sentences and common words and the high end involving detailed sentences, clear organization, and unusual words.

At the low end of the anchoring tasks, the language involves a single word or phrase, such as a street sign, or a few sentences, such as a television commercial or a brief request to a customer service representative. At the high end, the language anchoring tasks involve extended and advanced material, such as a lecture or book in a technical area. Between these extremes, the medium level involves language corresponding to a page or two of material, such as an apartment lease, a recommendation letter, or a set of multi-step instructions. Although length is not always accompanied by complexity, the contrasts in the anchoring tasks make use of a common relationship between length and the difficulty of understanding or structuring language.

The IT systems listed in Table 26.3 include seven that involve some aspect of language use in the earlier period (*abfklmn*) and eight in the later period (*qstuxyMN*).[4] The systems span the four language scales of O*NET, with nine involving written comprehension

[3] The O*NET scales are for oral comprehension, written comprehension, oral expression, and written expression.

[4] Italicized letters in parentheses refer to the 40 different systems in Table 26.3. Lower-case letters correspond to systems from *AI Magazine* and upper-case letters correspond to systems from *IEEE Robotics & Automation Magazine.*

Table 26.3 Capabilities of IT systems

AI Magazine: 2003–2007

(*a*) Aggour et al. (2006) 'Automating the Underwriting of Insurance Applications', 27(3): 36–50.

(*b*) Barbuceanu et al. (2004) 'Building Agents to Serve Customers', 25(3): 47–60.

(*c*) Buchanan and Livingston (2004) 'Toward Automated Discovery in the Biological Sciences', 25(1): 69–84.

(*d*) Cheetham and Goebel (2007) 'Appliance Call Center: A Successful Mixed-initiative Case Study', 28(2): 89–100.

(*e*) Forbus and Hinrichs (2006) 'Companion Cognitive Systems: A Step toward Human-level AI', 27(2): 83–95.

(*f*) Friedland et al. (2004) 'Project Halo: Towards a Digital Aristotle', 25(4): 29–48.

(*g*) Gopal et al. (2006) 'TEXTAL: Crystallographic Protein Model Building Using AI and Pattern Recognition', 27(3): 15–24.

(*h*) Jarvis et al. (2005) 'Identifying Terrorist Activity with AI Plan Recognition Technology', 26(3): 73–81.

(*i*) Lima et al. (2005) 'RoboCup 2004 Competitions and Symposium: A Small Kick for Robots, a Giant Score for Science', 26(2): 36–61.

(*j*) Myers et al. (2007) 'An Intelligent Personal Assistant for Task and Time Management', 28(2): 47–61.

(*k*) Nagel (2004) 'Steps Toward a Cognitive Vision System', 25(2): 31–50.

(*l*) Rychtyckyj (2007) 'Machine Translation for Manufacturing: A Case Study at Ford Motor Company', 28(3): 31–43.

(*m*) Simmons et al. (2003) 'GRACE: An Autonomous Robot for the AAAI Robot Challenge', 24(2): 51–72.

(*n*) Swartout et al. (2006) 'Toward Virtual Humans', 27(2): 96–108.

(*o*) Thrun (2006) 'A Personal Account on the Development of Stanley, the Robot that Won the DARPA Grand Challenge', 27(4): 69–82.

AI Magazine: 2008–2012

(*p*) Anderson et al. (2011) 'Report on the AAAI 2010 Robot Exhibition', 32(3): 109–118.

(*q*) Brodley et al. (2012) 'Challenges and Opportunities in Applied Machine Learning', 33(1): 11–24.

(*r*) Chun (2008) 'An AI Framework for the Automatic Assessment of e-government Forms', 29(1): 52–64.

(*s*) Ernandes et al. (2008) 'A Web-based Agent Challenges Human Experts on Crosswords', 29(1): 77–90.

(*t*) Ferrucci et al. (2010) 'Building Watson: An Overview of the DeepQA Project', 31(3): 59–79.

(*u*) Leuski and Traum (2011) 'NPCEditor: Creating Virtual Human Dialogue Using Information Retrieval Techniques', 32(2): 42–56.

(*v*) Menendez and Paillet (2008) 'Fish Inspection System Using a Parallel Neural Network Chip and the Image Knowledge Builder Application', 29(1): 21–28.

(*w*) Rassbach et al. (2011) 'Providing Decision Support for Cosmogenic Isotope Dating', 32(2): 69–78.

(*continued*)

Table 26.3 Continued

(*x*) Simmons et al. (2011) 'Believable Robot Characters', 32(4): 39–52.
(*y*) Tunstall-Pedoe (2010) 'True Knowledge: Open-domain Question Answering Using Structured Knowledge and Inference', 31(3): 80–92.
(*z*) Urmson et al. (2009) 'Autonomous Driving in Traffic: Boss and the Urban Challenge', 30(2): 17–28.
IEEE Robotics & Automation Magazine: 2003–2007
(*A*) Acosta et al. (2003) 'Ping-pong Player Prototype', 10(4): 44–52.
(*B*) Durrant-Whyte et al. (2007) 'An Autonomous Straddle Carrier for Movement of Shipping Containers: From Research to Operational Autonomous Systems', 14(3): 14–23.
(*C*) Graf et al. (2004) 'Mobile Robot Assistants', 11(2): 67–77.
(*D*) Kelly et al. (2007) 'An Infrastructure-free Automated Guided Vehicle based on Computer Vision: An Effort to Make an Industrial Robot Vehicle that Can Operate Without Supporting Infrastructure', 14(3): 24–34.
(*E*) Munich et al. (2006) 'SIFT-ing through Features with ViPR', 13(3): 72–77.
(*F*) Sanz et al. (2005) 'Grasping the Not-so-obvious: Vision- based Object Handling for Industrial Applications', 12(3): 44–52.
(*G*) Van Leeuwen and Groen (2005) 'Vehicle Detection with a Mobile Camera: Spotting Midrange, Distant, and Passing Cars', 12(1): 37–43.
IEEE Robotics & Automation Magazine: 2008–2012
(*H*) Chitta et al. (2012) 'Mobile Manipulation in Unstructured Environments: Perception, Planning and Execution', 19(2): 58–71.
(*I*) Dietrich et al. (2012) 'Reactive Whole-body Control: Dynamic Mobile Manipulation Using a Large Number of Actuated Degrees of Freedom', 19(2): 20–33.
(*J*) Kobers and Peters (2010) 'Imitation and Reinforcement Learning', 17(2): 55–62.
(*K*) Kröger et al. (2008) 'A Manipulator Plays Jenga', 15(3): 79–84.
(*L*) Salvini et al. (2011) 'The Robot DustCart', 18(1): 59–67.
(*M*) Stückler et al. (2012) 'RoboCup@Home: Demonstrating Everyday Manipulation Skills in RoboCup@Home', 19(2): 34–42.
(*N*) Tenorth et al. (2011) 'Web-enabled Robots', 18(2): 58–68.

(*ablqstxyN*), six involving written expression (*bfklty*), five involving oral comprehension (*bmnuM*), and five involving oral expression (*bmnux*).

The systems involve a diverse range of tasks. In the earlier period, the tasks include detecting problematic text in an insurance application (*a*), providing customer service for both sales and repairs (*b*), explaining the answers to chemistry questions in an advanced high school test (*f*), describing the movement of cars in a video of a traffic intersection (*k*), translating car assembly instructions (*l*), asking for help in finding the registration booth at a conference (*m*), giving a conference talk that includes questions from the audience (*m*), and role-playing with students in a training simulation about how a military officer should handle a car accident with a civilian (*n*). In the later period, the tasks include screening medical articles for inclusion in a systematic research review (*q*), solving crossword puzzles with web searches (*s*), answering Jeopardy questions with trick language cues across a large range of topics (*t*), answering questions from museum visitors (*u*), talking with people about directions and the weather (*x*), answering written questions with web searches (*y*), following speech commands to locate and retrieve drinks and laundry in a room (*M*), and using website searches to find information to carry out a novel task (*N*). Five of the systems have been applied commercially (*abluy*).

Thirteen of the systems that use language integrate that ability with one or more of the other three ability groups (*abfkmnqstxyMN*). In all cases the integration involves reasoning, in five it involves vision (*kmxMN*), and in three it involves movement (*mMN*). The integration of different ability groups in these systems indicates that the understanding of appropriate techniques has progressed far enough that it is possible for a single research group to combine techniques for several different ability groups rather than focusing on the challenges of a single ability group alone. This has important implications for the capacity of computers to take over significant portions of human occupations, since the O*NET analysis indicates that most jobs require significant levels of all four ability groups (Table 26.2).

The length and complexity of the language these systems can work with is closest to the medium level of the anchoring tasks: the systems are beyond language use at the word or couple-sentence level but fall far short of language use at the lecture or book level. Although several systems suggest some language use beyond the medium level, their performance is limited. For example, although the system that gave a conference talk (*m*) was able to flexibly answer questions without repeating material in-depth that had already been given, the system did not independently develop the overall structure of its talk.

In addition to length and complexity corresponding to a page or two, some of the medium-level anchoring tasks—giving directions to a lost motorist and writing a job recommendation—involve adjusting language to the needs of the person who is being communicated with and the requirements of the situation. Several systems exhibited this kind of sensitivity, including the ability of the conference talk system to monitor its points and not repeat them (*m*) and the ability of the training simulation to reason about emotion in order to choose appropriate language and understand imprecise language (*n*).

One difference between the earlier and later articles is the range of topics that are addressed by the different systems. In the earlier articles, all of the systems are focused on language use within a single topic area. For example, the training simulation has a speech recognition vocabulary of hundreds of words, a vocabulary for language generation of a thousand words, and an understanding of 40 tasks and 150 properties of the world (*n*). This constraint to a limited topic area is seen in some of the articles in the later period (*ux*), but there are four systems that attempt to deal with an unlimited range of topics by tapping into a range of source material available on the web (*styN*). Although the language anchoring tasks do not highlight the need to cover a broader range of topics at higher levels of language ability, it is clear that all humans who use language are able to do so around a large number of topics.

The review of the systems in Table 26.3 suggests that current IT language capabilities demonstrated in the research literature are at the medium level of difficulty of the O*NET scales. Tentatively, we will say that IT language capabilities are at level 4.

IT Reasoning Capabilities

There are six O*NET scales in the reasoning group. These involve recognizing that a problem exists, applying general rules to solve a problem, and developing new rules or conclusions.[5]

As with the language abilities, the basic contrast between the low and high ends of the reasoning scales is between reasoning involving simple or common ideas on the one hand and complex or unusual ideas on the other (Peterson et al. 1995, appendix G). Although there is a separate scale for originality that specifically focuses on the ability to develop 'unusual,' 'clever,' or 'creative' ideas, the higher ends of the other reasoning scales involve applying or developing rules where the result may well be novel. In addition to the more general scales for deductive and inductive reasoning, there are also separate scales for mathematical reasoning and spatial reasoning.

At the low end of the anchoring tasks, the reasoning involves simple one- or two-step inferences, such as recognizing that a lamp will not work if it is unplugged, realizing that a stalled car can coast downhill, or calculating the cost of ten oranges from their price. In many cases, the low end reasoning tasks are ones that would be classified as 'common sense.' At the high end, the reasoning involves problems with many features and requiring many inference steps, such as diagnosing a disease, designing an aircraft wing, simulating a spacecraft landing, or planning a chess move. The high end anchoring tasks are drawn from domains that are recognized as requiring specialized knowledge and expertise, such as engineering, medicine, and chess. Between the extremes, the medium-level tasks involve a mix of common sense reasoning and more specialized expertise, such as calculating profits, identifying a crime suspect, or following a diagram to assemble a cabinet.

The IT systems in Table 26.3 include 11 articles in the earlier period that involve some aspect of reasoning (*abcdefghjno*) and ten in the later period (*qrstwxyzMN*). The systems span the six reasoning scales, with five involving the recognition that a problem

[5] The O*NET scales are for originality, problem sensitivity, deductive reasoning, inductive reasoning, mathematical reasoning, and visualization.

exists (*ahjrM*), essentially all involving the application of general rules to solve a problem, three involving the development of novel rules or conclusions (*cgw*), two involving mathematical reasoning (*bf*), and eight involving spatial reasoning (*egmowzMN*). As noted in the previous section on language, a number of these systems integrate reasoning and language abilities (*abfmnqstxyMN*). In addition, there are six systems that integrate reasoning with vision or movement (*moxzMN*).

In the articles from the early period, the tasks addressed include making underwriting decisions about long-term care insurance (*a*), providing customer service for both sales and repairs (*b*), developing new hypotheses about good conditions for growing crystals and for recovering from medical disability (*c*), helping diagnose appliance problems (*d*), providing useful analogies for solving problems in qualitative physics and in military tactical games (*e*), providing answers and explanations to chemistry questions in an advanced high school test (*f*), developing novel atomic models for electron density maps of proteins (*g*), identifying patterns of potentially suspicious facts that could indicate a terrorist plan (*h*), resolving problems related to scheduling and project coordination (*j*), role-playing with students in a training simulation about how a military officer should handle a car accident with a civilian (*n*), and driving a vehicle on different road types (*o*). In the later period, the tasks include screening medical articles for inclusion in a systematic research review (*q*), processing government forms related to immigration and marriage (*r*), solving crossword puzzles (*s*), playing Jeopardy (*t*), answering questions from museum visitors (*u*), analysing geological landform data to determine age (*w*), talking with people about directions and the weather (*x*), answering questions with web searches (*y*), driving a vehicle in traffic and on roads with unexpected obstacles (*z*), solving problems with directions that contain missing or erroneous information (*M*), and using websites to find information for carrying out novel tasks (*N*). Nine of the systems have been applied commercially (*abcdgruwy*).

One of the striking aspects of the reasoning systems is their ability to produce high levels of performance. For example, the systems in Table 26.3 make insurance underwriting decisions about easy cases and provide guidance to underwriters about more difficult ones (*a*), produce novel hypotheses about growing crystals that are sufficiently promising to merit further investigation (*c*), substantially improve the ability of call centre representatives to diagnose appliance problems (*d*), achieve scores on a chemistry exam comparable to the mean score for advanced high school students (*f*), produce initial atomic models for proteins that substantially reduce the time for experts to develop refined models (*g*), substitute for medical researchers in screening articles for inclusion in a systematic research review (*q*), solve crossword puzzles at an expert level (*s*), play Jeopardy at an expert level (*t*), and analyse geological landform data at an expert level (*w*). This evidence of performance suggests reasoning at the higher level on the O*NET scales that involve a high level of specialized knowledge and expertise.

It is important to note, however, that the common sense reasoning typical of the lower levels of the O*NET reasoning scales has been surprisingly difficult for computers to perform in many cases. The explanation seems to be that the knowledge required for common sense is very large but is easily overlooked because everyone shares it. Many of the reasoning systems in Table 26.3 rely on knowledge encoded in hundreds or thousands of rules, properties, or cases, whereas the necessary knowledge base for common sense appears to involve millions of elements learned over a lifetime (Lenat 1995). It is only recently that computer systems have been successfully developed that can use large amounts of information from the web across an unlimited number of topics to reproduce more flexible and wide-ranging reasoning that begins to resemble human common sense. For the articles in the earlier period in Table 26.3, many of the IT systems suggest computer capabilities that can reason within narrow areas of specialized expertise at the high level of the O*NET scales but that cannot reason using the common sense required at the low and medium levels of the O*NET scales. However, the systems in the later period that are able to reason using a vast amount of information harvested from the web are able to begin to produce the more common sense reasoning required by the low and medium levels.

The review of the systems in Table 26.3 suggests that current IT reasoning capabilities demonstrated in the research literature are at the high level of difficulty of the O*NET scales. Tentatively, we will say that IT reasoning capabilities are at level 6.

IT Vision Capabilities

There are four O*NET scales in the vision group. These involve recognizing objects and different features of those objects, including their position in space.[6]

The basic contrast in the level of difficulty between the low- and high-level anchoring tasks varies somewhat across the different scales, relating to the complexity of the object that is identified, the complexity of the background against which the object is recognized, or the complexity of features that need to be evaluated (Peterson et al. 1995, appendix G).[7] This complexity can make an object hard to identify—because its own visual pattern is difficult or because other objects occlude or are similar to it—or can make it necessary to focus on precise or subtle features. In two cases, the scales specifically mention speed; although this is a relevant constraint for rating human ability levels, it is less important to consider for this review of IT capabilities because expected future increases in processing power should eliminate any speed constraints shown by current systems.

The low end vision anchoring tasks involve simple patterns and uncluttered environments, such as identifying the zip code on a letter or judging the relative distances

[6] The O*NET scales are for speed of closure, flexibility of closure, perceptual speed, and depth perception.

[7] The two 'closure' scales refer to perception more generally and the low end anchoring tasks are auditory rather than visual.

of cars in traffic. The high end anchoring tasks involve difficult patterns and distracting environments, such as identifying camouflaged tanks from a high-speed plane or the precise location for throwing a football. Between these extremes, the medium level uses tasks such as making sense out of strange handwriting or looking for a golf ball in the rough. While the low and medium levels suggest visual tasks encountered in everyday life for many people, the high level suggests visual tasks that reflect some specialized expertise.

The IT systems in Table 26.3 include 11 in the earlier period that involve vision (*ikmoABCDEFG*) and 11 in the later period (*pvxzHIJKLMN*). All 22 of the systems involve identifying objects, ranging from balls, robots, chess pieces, fish, pallets, lettuce, and blocks in simplified environments (*ipvADFJK*), to cars, roads, registration booths, elevators, hallways, people, and various other objects in naturalistic environments (*kmoxzBCEGHILMN*). All of the systems also involve recognizing features of the identified objects, particularly their location and movement.

In the earlier articles, the tasks of the systems include locating a soccer ball and other soccer players (*i*), identifying cars and their movements in a video of a traffic intersection (*k*), finding the registration booth, an elevator, and several rooms at a conference (*m*), identifying drivable surfaces and obstacles for an autonomous car (*o*), determining the location of a ping-pong ball (*A*), guiding autonomous vehicles to move shipping containers (*B*), identifying people, balls, and obstacles in a crowded museum (*C*), locating pallets in a factory (*D*), recognizing objects in cluttered environments (*E*), guiding a robot to grasp irregularly shaped objects like lettuce (*F*), and identifying vehicles on a road to provide driver assistance (*G*). In the later articles, the tasks include recognizing chess pieces by location (*p*), identifying types of fish (*v*), recognizing the presence of nearby people (*x*), identifying the movements of other vehicles for an autonomous car (*z*), locating, identifying and grasping objects in a cluttered environment (*H*), moving around a cluttered environment without collisions (*I*), learning to play ball-and-cup (*J*), building block towers in the game of Jenga (*K*), navigating public streets and avoiding obstacles to collect trash (*L*), navigating unknown spaces, identifying people, and locating drinks and laundry in an apartment (*M*), and using websites to find visual information for carrying out novel tasks such as making pancakes from a package mix (*N*). All but three of the systems involve integration with either movement (*imopzABCDFHIJKLMN*) or language (*kmxMN*). Five of the systems have been deployed commercially (*vBCEF*).

The systems in Table 26.3 present a range of visual ability levels. A number of them address visual tasks with relatively simple shapes and uncluttered environments (*ipvADFJK*) that correspond to the low end anchoring tasks. However, even more of the systems use vision to find objects in naturalistic environments where there are visual distractions and the target objects may be partially occluded (*kmoxzBCEGHILMN*). By introducing the complexity of more naturalistic environments, the visual tasks addressed by these systems correspond more to the medium level anchoring tasks. Tentatively we will say that IT vision capabilities are at level 4.

IT Movement Capabilities

There are eight O*NET scales in the movement group. These involve spatial orientation, coordination of various body parts, control of a movement or a piece of equipment, and overall body equilibrium.[8]

The basic contrast in the level of difficulty between the low and high ends of the movement scales is specified in somewhat different ways across the different types of control (Peterson et al. 1995, appendix G). For spatial orientation, the difference in difficulty appears in whether the environment is unchanging or changing, with a changing environment requiring repeated adjustments to one's sense of orientation. For the four coordination scales, the difference in difficulty appears between rough and precise levels of movement and the number of body parts that need to be coordinated, as well as the speed of the coordination required. For the two control scales, the difference in difficulty appears in whether adjustments are required a few times or repeatedly and whether they are rough or precise. For the equilibrium scale, the difference in difficulty appears in whether balance is maintained against one or many forces of instability, with the latter presumably requiring more adjustments. Generalizing over these four different types of scales, movement difficulty involves adjustments that are more frequent and more precise and that involve more body parts.

At the low end of the movement scales, the anchoring tasks require only a few steps and these can be fairly rough, such as locating a room from a map, putting coins in a parking meter, adjusting a light with a dimmer switch, or balancing on a ladder. At the high end, the anchoring tasks require repeated and precise adjustments, such as navigating a ship using just the sun and stars, assembling a watch, drilling a tooth, or walking on beams in a high-rise construction site. Between these extremes, the medium level uses such example tasks as walking through a darkened room without hitting anything, operating a forklift in a warehouse, keeping up with a car that changes speed, and walking on ice across a pond.

The systems in Table 26.3 include eight in the earlier period that involve movement (*imoABCDF*) and nine in the later period (*pzHIJKLMN*). All 17 systems involve spatial orientation, coordination, and control. Only one of the systems involves body equilibrium (*i*). For the early period, the tasks of the systems include walking (*i*), kicking a ball (*i*), passing a ball between two robots (*i*), moving down a hallway (*m*), following a map to locate a meeting room in a hotel (*m*), using an elevator (*m*), driving a car in the desert (*o*), playing ping pong (*A*), autonomously moving shipping containers (*B*), navigating around people and pursuing objects in a crowded museum (*C*), moving pallets autonomously in a factory (*D*), and grasping irregularly shaped objects like lettuce (*F*). For the later period, the tasks include moving chess pieces (*p*), driving a car in traffic (*z*), grasping objects in a cluttered environment (*H*), moving around a cluttered environment without collisions (*I*), learning to play ball-and-cup (*J*), building block towers in

[8] The O*NET scales are for spatial orientation, manual dexterity, finger dexterity, control precision, multilimb coordination, rate control, gross body coordination, and gross body equilibrium.

the game of Jenga (*K*), navigating public streets and avoiding obstacles to collect trash (*L*), retrieving and delivering drinks and laundry in an apartment (*M*), and using the web to figure out how to make pancakes from a package mix (*N*). All 17 systems involve integration with vision and three involve integration with language (*mMN*). Three of the systems are being used commercially (*BCF*).

The review of the systems in Table 26.3 suggests that current IT movement capabilities are roughly at the medium level of the O*NET scale. In particular, a number of the systems involve autonomous vehicles moving in complex surroundings that require continuous adjustments to react to obstacles, as well as to people and vehicles that are moving themselves (*imozBCDILM*). Since these systems correspond to two of the anchoring tasks provided for the medium level, we will tentatively say that IT movement capabilities are at level 4.

Employment Implications of IT Capabilities in the Research Literature

The research literature review of IT capabilities tentatively suggests that current systems show ability levels roughly corresponding to level 4 on the O*NET scales for language, vision, and movement abilities, and level 6 for reasoning abilities. The employment analyses in Tables 26.1 and 26.2 show that most employment is in occupations requiring ability levels from 3 to 5 for language and reasoning and from 2 to 4 for vision and movement. As a result, the tentative findings of the literature review imply that IT capabilities that have been demonstrated in research settings could provide the reasoning, vision, and movement skills required in most current jobs; only for language skill does the analysis suggest that a substantial number of current jobs have skill requirements that clearly outstrip the IT capabilities demonstrated in the research literature.

The tentative skill levels assigned to the different IT capabilities can be used to identify the occupations where the workforce is vulnerable to complete displacement by the substitution of IT for human workers. Specifically, workers are vulnerable to being displaced by IT in those occupations where current required ability levels for all four ability groups are at or below current IT capabilities. Table 26.4 provides the percentage of total employment for each of the major civilian SOC occupational groups, along with the employment-weighted average ability levels within each group, and the percentage of employment that is potentially vulnerable to complete displacement as current IT capabilities from the research literature are broadly applied. Given the results of the literature review, in most cases it is the level of language ability required that determines whether or not an occupation is identified as potentially vulnerable to displacement. Overall, the analysis suggests that *occupations representing 82 percent of current employment will be potentially vulnerable to displacement by IT over the*

Table 26.4 Ability ratings and vulnerability to displacement by major occupational group

Major occupational group	% of total employment	Average ability ratings L	R	V	M	% vulnerable
11-0000 Management	4.8	4	4	3	2	68
13-0000 Business and financial operations	4.8	4	4	3	2	43
15-0000 Computer and mathematical science	2.7	4	4	3	3	58
17-0000 Architecture and engineering	1.8	5	4	4	3	36
19-0000 Life, physical, and social science	0.8	5	5	4	3	28
21-0000 Community and social services	1.5	4	4	3	2	46
23-0000 Legal	0.8	5	4	3	2	36
25-0000 Education, training, and library	6.6	5	4	3	2	48
27-0000 Arts, design, entertainment, sports, and media	1.3	4	4	3	3	69
29-0000 Healthcare practitioners and technical	5.9	5	5	4	4	38
31-0000 Healthcare support	3.1	4	4	3	3	100
33-0000 Protective service	2.5	4	4	3	3	95
35-0000 Food preparation and serving related	8.7	3	3	2	3	100
37-0000 Building and grounds cleaning and maintenance	3.3	3	3	2	3	100
39-0000 Personal care and service	2.8	4	3	3	3	100
41-0000 Sales and related	10.6	4	3	2	2	89
43-0000 Office and administrative support	16.7	4	3	3	2	100
45-0000 Farming, fishing, and forestry	0.3	3	3	3	4	100
47-0000 Construction and extraction	3.9	4	3	3	4	100
49-0000 Installation, maintenance, and repair	3.9	4	4	3	4	97
51-0000 Production	6.5	4	3	3	3	94
53-0000 Transportation and material moving	6.7	3	3	3	4	99
Total	100.0					82

next few decades. Obviously the figures in Table 26.4 are only suggestive, since they are based on an initial review of the research literature that should be substantially refined.

The level of change suggested in Table 26.4 would be unprecedented in terms of speed, but it is not unprecedented in terms of scale. Between the early 1800s and the 1970s, a comparable portion of employment was displaced from agriculture to other sectors. And for a number of decades recently, manufacturing has seen high levels of productivity and steadily decreasing employment as new production technologies have been applied. Although it seems implausible that all of the jobs in any of the sectors in Table 26.4 would be completely eliminated over a couple decades, we have seen previous examples where sectors or occupations have shown large declines in employment.

It is important to note, however, that the analysis says nothing directly about the level of occupational change per se over the next few decades. Occupations are used in the analysis only as a way to obtain information about the mix of skill levels being used for the different groups of abilities throughout the economy. The analysis specifically identifies occupations where human workers could be displaced with the application of demonstrated IT capabilities based on the *current* levels of skills used in those occupations. However, it is possible that the opportunities offered by new technologies will allow many of these occupations to be redefined with higher skills levels that will still require human workers. Thus, in principle, it is possible that the distribution of occupations could look much the same in several decades as it does in Table 26.4; on the other hand, it is also possible that the distribution of occupations could look far different, possibly with substantial growth in new occupations that do not currently exist. In either case—whatever the mix of occupational titles—the implication of the analysis is that the skill mix of the workforce in several decades is likely to be substantially different from the skill mix of the current workforce because of the displacement pressure from IT.

It is also important to note that the analysis says nothing directly about the level of unemployment over the next several decades. In principle, it may be possible to move workers smoothly from jobs that IT could now perform to jobs that IT could not yet perform. However, the level of adjustment that this is likely to require will be challenging because it could result in major displacement of workers in many occupations and require substantial increases in skills for those who need to retrain.

Conclusion

The analysis in this chapter is based on a limited review of the research literature about IT capabilities with a coarse grouping of the different skills that are used at work. It would clearly be possible to expand the analysis to include a wider range of research literature, a finer grained consideration of different skills, and a more rigorous process for deriving ratings of the different computer skill levels. In a sense, the analysis in this chapter might be viewed only as a proof of concept for the more in-depth analysis that needs to be carried out. A more refined analysis would provide a much better understanding of the relation between current IT capabilities and the skill levels used in different occupations throughout the economy.

Of course, a more refined analysis of the technology alone would not provide a clear-cut projection of the number of jobs that are likely to be displaced by IT over the next few decades. In addition to the basic capabilities that IT has demonstrated in research settings, there are a host of specific challenges for any particular job that would need to be solved to apply IT successfully and there are industry-specific issues related to competition and investment that will influence the way these applications unfold. Not least, the question of cost—which was ignored in the current analysis—will clearly play a role in determining where and when IT is applied. The jobs facing displacement pressures will not necessarily be displaced in a deterministic way over this period; however, it is reasonable to expect that a number of jobs that face such pressure will indeed be replaced by IT over the next few decades.

While this chapter has focused on the prospects for fully displacing workers, it is important to remember that IT can also complement workers in many ways. For example, although word processing software has largely replaced typists, it is currently used by administrative assistants in a complementary way to perform more complicated organizational tasks. In a wide range of tasks where IT can provide some but not all of the necessary skills, it is often productive for humans and IT to work together, with the workers providing whichever skills that IT cannot yet provide. However, while acknowledgeing that there will be many cases where workers and IT can play complementary roles, for those tasks where IT comes close to the full range of necessary skills it seems more likely that it will be used as a substitute for workers, not as a complement. Table 26.4 suggests that the pressure for IT to substitute for workers is likely to be quite strong over the next few decades.

It is also important to remember that basic IT capabilities will continue to advance. The chapter did not speculate about new skill levels that further basic research may make possible. However, certainly such breakthroughs will take place. Even across the ten-year period spanned by the articles reviewed for this chapter there were interesting advances. In particular, the IT language and reasoning capabilities advanced from systems that only worked within single topic areas to systems that addressed a much larger number of topic areas. Across all of the ability groups, we should expect IT capabilities to improve in the coming years, further increasing the pool of occupations that are subject to pressures to replace human workers with IT.

As IT provides growing pressure on a widening pool of tasks and abilities over the next few decades, society will need to grapple with a full range of policy responses. As currently demonstrated IT capabilities are applied throughout the economy, workers in a number of jobs are likely to be displaced and will need to acquire new skills, particularly the higher-level language skills which computers have not yet demonstrated and that are used in many of the professional occupations. Workers without these skills will have an increasingly difficult time finding work, worsening the economic inequality we are already experiencing.

Further advances in IT capabilities will exacerbate the problem, whilst allowing even greater levels of productivity growth. By the 2030s, there will likely be pressure to displace humans from a majority of jobs, which will have serious implications for the entire structure of our economy and society, raising questions about inequality and the future of work. IT is not yet at that point, but this is a challenge we will need to face in the coming decades.

Acknowledgements

This chapter is a revised version of a paper prepared for the Workshop on Research Evidence Related to Future Skill Demands, Center for Education, National Research Council, 31 May–1 June, 2007. Workshop comments from Ken Spenner and other participants are gratefully acknowledged, as well as early support from the Russell Sage Foundation and the Alfred P. Sloan Foundation.

References

David, P. A. (1990) 'The Dynamo and the Computer: An Historical Perspective on the Modern Productivity Paradox', *AEA Papers and Proceedings*, 80(2): 355–361.

Lenat, D. B. (1995) 'Cyc: A Large-scale Investment in Knowledge Infrastructure', *Communications of the ACM*, 38(11).

Mansfield, E. (1989) 'The Diffusion of Industrial Robots in Japan and the United States', *Research Policy*, 18: 183–192.

Peterson, N. G., Mumford, M. D., Borman, W. C. Jeanneret, P. R., and Fleishman, E. A. (1995) *Development of Prototype Occupational Information Network (O*NET) Content Model*, Utah: Department of Workforce Services.

Rogers, E. (1995) *Diffusion of Innovations*, 4th ed., New York: Free Press.

CHAPTER 27

INTERNATIONAL SKILL FLOWS AND MIGRATION

JAMES WICKHAM

INTRODUCTION

PUBLIC discussion on migration is largely about unskilled migration. At least in Western Europe, understandings of migration are shaped by the mass immigration of the immediate post World War II decades—the *Gastarbeiter* experience. These were the years when migrants from Europe's periphery and former colonies streamed into the rich European core: migrants took jobs in construction, in the expanding public services, and in the 'Fordist' mass production industries such as the car industry.

Since the 1970s, migration into Europe has been shaped more by family reunification or the flight from poverty or war. Migration flows have become more diverse in terms of both origin and destination (Castles and Miller 2009). Throughout these changes the image of the migrant as poor and unskilled has remained. Equally, in countries such as Ireland, where the historical experience of emigration is part of national self-understanding, emigration is understood in terms of the forced migration of the poor: the 'coffin ships' of the Famine years in which one million desperate people left the country—many to die en route. Likewise, whilst the United States was a nation formed through immigration, current debates are dominated by a focus on illegal, largely unskilled immigrants from Central America. Yet such images are not the whole story. Some migrants have always been skilled, but today migration is increasingly the movement of skilled people.

After a brief historical overview of skilled migration, this chapter begins by outlining current accounts of skilled migration in terms of available statistics. Subsequent sections show how skilled migration is best considered a form of mobility, shaped by changes in both economic organization and individual aspirations. Skilled migration has often unexpected consequences for the sending countries, the receiving countries, and for the migrants themselves. Affluent countries increasingly compete for the 'best and brightest', but paradoxically perhaps, this can exacerbate existing problems.

History

Much pre-industrial voluntary migration was skilled migration. In the medieval Mediterranean world, port cities contained 'colonies' of merchants, such as the Venetians and Genoese in Constantinople until its conquest in 1453. Similarly, artisan craftsmen and skilled workers in the luxury trades often lived and worked far from their birthplaces. In the early modern period, mercantilist states attempted to entice skilled craft workers into their territory to develop new industries, so that Catholic France's expulsion of the Huguenots was welcomed as an opportunity by rival monarchs.

Nineteenth century industrialisation created unprecedented demand for unskilled labour in the new industrial cities. Increasingly this was met by long distance migration: from Ireland to Britain, from Polish territories to Germany. However, these new industries also created new skill demands, whether for craft occupations such as 'mechanics' or for the developing occupations such as engineers or doctors which required more theoretical knowledge. Very rapidly however, these needs were met from within the national labour market. Industrialisation in the heartlands of Western Europe occurred very largely within the national economies: new skills were made, not imported.

By contrast, expansion beyond Europe created new skilled migration flows of artisan craftworkers and qualified professionals. This was especially the case for emigration from Britain, the sheer scale of which is usually ignored. From 1870 onwards, over 100,000 emigrants left *England* every year; compared to Irish emigrants, British emigrants were more likely to be skilled and/or educated. This mass movement was only partly because of the British Empire. During the nineteenth century the main destination was the United States, where skilled British migrants probably comprised the most important contribution of immigration to the US economy (Richards 2004, 212). It was only after 1900 that the United States was outweighed by the imperial destinations—Canada, Australia, New Zealand, and South Africa. Even though most such emigrants were potential settlers, British emigration seems to have been unusual for its high return rate: between 1860 and 1914 at least 40% of all English and Welsh emigrants returned, giving a total figure of over 2 million (Richards 2004, 169). At the same time the administration of the Empire itself required engineers, doctors and a growing plethora of professional occupations, in particular missionaries. For such groups, a lengthy sojourn in the colonies with eventual retirement back 'home' became a normal middle-class career (Darwin 2009, 98).

This British emigration both to the United States and the dominions continued well into the second half of the twentieth century, although unnoticed by contemporary sociology. Whilst subsidized emigration to Australia included many relatively unskilled people, this mass movement included both skilled manual workers and a growing number of qualified professionals. The emigration created one of the world's largest—and least noticed—diasporas (Sriskandarajah and Drew 2006), a movement without parallel from any other European country. It is the context for the continued and distinctive levels of skilled emigration from the United Kingdom today.

Statistical Simplifications and Complicated Mobilities

The term 'immigrant' has many different meanings. One deceptively simple definition, as used by the United Nations, is anyone who has been living for more than a year in a country different to their birthplace. This definition includes many, such as students or expatriates, who in some countries would not be considered immigrants. Furthermore, in this definition 'immigrant' is uncoupled from citizenship, the importance of which also varies between countries. In Europe, for example, citizenship has been less important than permanent residence, since this is usually the basis for access to employment and social rights. Recently, however, many European countries have begun to stress the rights and duties of citizenship itself, symbolized by American-style citizenship ceremonies for newly naturalized immigrants (Joppke 2010).

The United Nations definition of immigrant also ignores ethnicity, although in many countries 'immigrant' is often synonymous with membership of an ethnic minority: an 'immigrant' may be the child or even grandchild of someone who immigrated decades earlier. If the analytical concern is with the inflow of *new* skills, then immigrants are usefully treated as people who have entered the country as adults, rather than as ethnic minorities, even though they may well be the descendants of previous immigrants.

Unsurprisingly, the definition of 'skill' and hence of 'skilled migration' also varies. 'Skilled' can refer to current occupation or to previously acquired educational and training qualifications. If 'highly skilled' is restricted purely to science and technology workers, one starting point for classification is the standard statistical science and technology classifications developed within the Frascati and Canberra Manuals (Mahroum 2000). The 'highly skilled' do not necessarily work in the specific sector with which their skill is usually identified. An obvious case is information technology (IT) professionals, many of whom are not employed in the IT sector; Khadria (2001) suggested that this is part of a wider movement away from specific to 'generic' skills amongst skilled migrants. Skills are also often not recognized or under-valued in the destination country, so that many skilled immigrants initially work below their level of qualification (e.g. Chiswick et al. 2005).

The mobile highly skilled include more than those involved directly in S&T. One obvious wider definition would include those with professional qualifications such as medical practitioners. This is compatible with the usual assumption that highly skilled migrants have clearly defined qualifications for which there is an immediately identifiable demand. However, this excludes not only skilled building craft workers—who usually have more transportable qualifications and better pay than many university graduates—but also many other skilled occupations (e.g. musicians and artists) where formal qualifications are hardly decisive. Equally, such a definition can even exclude many managers and entrepreneurs. Thus policy discussion of the 'mobile highly skilled' refers to specific *occupations*: university students, health workers (nurses as well as doctors), information-technology (IT) specialists, researchers, business executives and managers, and intra-company transfers (OECD 2002, 2). In the last decade there has been a growing awareness of 'middling migration': migrants with more intermediate and/or less occupationally specific qualifications, including young graduates in non-graduate jobs (Conradson and Latham 2005).

Discussion of skilled migration can now make use of internationally comparable OECD data (OECD 2008; Widmaier and Dumont 2011) based on national census results, which show the growing absolute and relative importance of skilled migration. Around 2000, 7.5% of the population of OECD countries was foreign born and thus 'immigrants' by the United Nations (UN) definition. By 2005/6 this had increased to 10.8%. Within this immigrant population the proportion with tertiary education is increasing, so in many OECD countries recent immigrants are better educated than earlier arrivals. In the United Kingdom, 44.2% of those immigrants already in the country for more than ten years had a tertiary degree but this had risen to 51.7% amongst those who arrived in the last decade. There has been a similar trend in Canada and Australia, but not in the United States.

Overall immigrants are now better educated than the native population: 28.2% of immigrants in the OECD had tertiary education compared to 20.9% of the indigenous population. Especially in countries such as Australia and Canada, immigrants' field of study is disproportionately in science and engineering, largely because the immigration policies of such countries prioritize these areas.

The OECD data is also the best source that sees migrants as emigrants rather than immigrants. A starting point is the size of the different national expatriate populations: the total number of those born in a particular country who now reside elsewhere. Unsurprisingly, the country with the largest absolute number of 'expatriates' in 2000 was Mexico, with its 'diaspora' of 8.3 million concentrated in the United States. More surprisingly, the third largest diaspora in absolute terms was from Britain, with 3.2 million born in Britain now living elsewhere.

In sending countries, a key concern is the extent of the 'brain drain'—the migration rate amongst the most highly skilled. With rising rates of participation in higher education (HE), the pool of such potential emigrants is rising both absolutely and as a proportion of the population. In sub-Saharan Africa, the fast increase in HE participation has meant both a rise in the absolute number of skilled emigrants and a fall in the skilled emigration rate. In fact in most less developed countries the actual rates of high skilled migration are relatively low. High rates occur largely in few countries with small populations such as Zambia and some Caribbean islands. The emigration of health professionals from less developed countries is often seen as an especially iniquitous form of brain drain. Indeed, the OECD data show that there are some countries with an expatriation rate of health professionals of more than 50% (meaning that over half of all the health professionals from that country are now working abroad). Education in the Philippines specializes in training nurses for export, so that the 110,000 emigrant nurses born in the Philippines now amount for 15% of the total immigrant health workforce within the OECD (OECD 2008, 175).

Concern over the brain drain from less developed countries has detracted from the importance of skilled emigration from some 'developed' countries. Here the United States is distinctive for its relatively low level of emigration, with a total of only 0.8 million American-born workers living abroad. From a historical perspective the American 'empire' of the late twentieth century was unusual in the extent to which, unlike its British predecessor, its citizens did *not* spread across the globe (Ferguson 2005). Although immigration to the United States remains disproportionately unskilled, it is also the case that the United States is the major beneficiary from skilled migration, with a net gain of 7.8 million migrants with tertiary education. Although the vast majority of these have come from outside the OECD, the United States has a net gain of 0.9 million tertiary educated migrants from the EU15. Especially important within this have been British migrants. Indeed, at the turn of the century Britain remained the country with the largest absolute number of expatriates (1.1 million) with tertiary education, another indication of how much skilled migration occurs under the radar.

From Migration to Mobility? Forms of Skilled Labour Flows

Lurking behind the UN definition of immigrant is the assumption that an immigrant moves from one country to another in order to find work and then settles there: the 'move-work-settle' model (Fitzgerald and Hardy 2010). Table 27. 1 presents a simple continuum of forms of migration. At the one extreme are the natives, those living in the same country as they were born; at the other extreme are the immigrants, those born outside the country in which they have now permanently settled. As the International Organization for Migration notes, between these two poles there are intermediate cases, such as long-term temporary migration and circulation migration (Krieger 2004, 9). Arguably these intermediary situations are now numerically the most important forms of migration.

However, the continuum does not capture many contemporary movements which are becoming more important. Sometimes movement between country of origin and country of destination is so frequent that migration has turned into commuting or

Table 27.1 The migration continuum

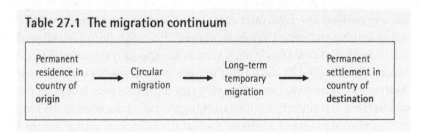

Permanent residence in country of origin	→	Circular migration	→	Long-term temporary migration	→	Permanent settlement in country of destination

co-residence. Migrants, like long-settled residents, may travel onwards from their new base for short trips for business or pleasure. And finally, households may have several 'homes' spread across different countries.

Contemporary transport technologies have made such journeys dramatically easier. Turkish German journalist Hatice Akyün describes her family's annual three-day-long car journey 'home' from Duisburg to Anatolia in the 1980s (Akyün 2007). Thirty years later, during the Celtic Tiger boom, most Polish emigrants in Ireland would have travelled 'home' several times a year on flights lasting only three hours (Krings et al. 2013). And in the financial services, executives travel continuously between London and New York ('NYLON').

By the start of the twenty-first century, the diversity of forms of migration was accelerating. It is now over a decade since a leading migration researcher called for a 'new map' of migration (King 2002). In a classification of forms of short-term skilled migration, Salt (1997) identified 12 different categories of 'temporary highly skilled migrants, ranging from 'corporate transferees' to 'entertainers, sportspeople, and artists'. In similar vein, Mahroum (2000) identified five main groups, each comprising both a particular occupational group and a particular mode of travel. For example, 'Academics and scientists' are 'pilgrims', their mobility inherent in their commitment to the intrinsically universalistic nature of education and especially science (see also Meyer et al. 2001). Crucially the numbers of these different groups has been rising for some time.

Migration and mobility thus overlap. As early as 1998 the International Organization for Migration was suggesting that movement from Eastern to Western Europe should be considered as 'mobility' not migration. The European Union itself has been making agreements entitled 'Mobility Partnerships' with countries with which it wishes to regulate migration. Whilst physical movement as opposed to migration, as such, has long been neglected within sociology, recently there has been a veritable 'mobility turn' exemplified by the work of John Urry (2000) and journals such as *Mobilities*.

Especially for skilled migrants, one simple differentiation is between permanent settlers and those who are merely sojourning. Equally, the multiple occupations and variable earning power of skilled immigrants suggests a basic differentiation between those whose earnings start around the median income of the receiving country and those at the top its income distribution. This produces a four cell classification in terms of duration (visitors versus settlers) and of earnings (experts versus stars), which will be used in several subsequent sections of the chapter (see Table 27. 2).

Table 27.2 Typology of skilled migrants

Duration	Earnings level	
	Experts (above average)	*Stars (top decile)*
Visitors (<5 years)		
Settlers (>5 years)		

Motivations for Mobility: Firms

The trading companies of the European empires, such as the British East India Company, not only created flows of goods, they also generated movements of skilled people, sending merchants and administrators to their 'factories' at the other side of the globe. Although in the twentieth century multinational companies such as Ford created global production systems, these generated surprisingly limited flows of managers and specialist professionals. The classical mid-twentieth century multinational company was owned and headquartered in one country, with units in countries around the world that were staffed predominantly from local labour markets.

Today, however, global transnational companies attempt to generate a unified corporate culture just as they create global brands for their products and services: the working culture of Google is (nearly) similar in Dublin and in the United States. One consequence is the increased flow of managers and skilled professionals across national borders within global companies. Such movements range from traditional expatriation through short-term assignments to the multiple forms of business travel (Salt 2010). Whilst only long-term expatriation involves the long-term move of the primary residence that has been taken to define migration, these are all ways in which firms move people around in order to achieve a series of objectives, ranging from control and cohesion to building trust with clients and the movement of skill and knowledge within the firm (Bozkurt and Mohr 2011). Intra-firm mobility builds the corporate culture, whilst conversely a shared corporate culture facilitates intra-firm transfers.

Large firms increasingly operate across global (or better perhaps transnational) markets rather than as distinct units within national markets. There is also a shift towards project-based organizations, with teams working across national boundaries and interacting continually with clients. Mobility varies also by industrial sector. Traditional expatriate postings are common in extractive industries, whilst in high end financial services frequent movement ties together a few key centres such as London and New York. In the software industry, managers and professionals are often highly mobile. Members of project teams travel to clients' sites to install and maintain new systems; executives travel the globe to market products; even small companies will often have development projects in different international locations (Wickham and Vecchi 2010). Such forms of mobility are therefore both accentuated and facilitated by electronic forms of communication that increasingly enable work to be at least partially disconnected from any one physical workplace (Kesselring and Vogl 2010).

In many countries, the software industry has become particularly dependent on skilled immigrant labour. US software firms have actively recruited workers on immigrant visas, thus creating essentially a two-tiered labour market within the US IT sector (Salzman et al. 2013). At the same time, it also generates new flows of skilled labour through outsourcing and offshoring. For example, UK companies began by recruiting Indian software workers to the United Kingdom before then 'exporting' them back to staff call centres in India (Millar and Salt 2007).

Finally, recruitment agencies have played an important role in facilitating international markets. Recruitment companies do not simply mediate between potential employees and potential employers, they actively 'mobilize' new sources of labour. This involves not just international companies but also specialist agencies with associates in turn linked to ethnic networks who are especially important at the low-high skill area of the labour market especially in body shops (Xiang 2001).

Motivations for Mobility: Individuals

Skilled migrants' motivations are as varied as skilled migrants themselves. Indeed, migrants who move just for higher salaries form a limiting case. Those who move to a foreign country for a high salary—European expatriates working in the Gulf are an oft-cited example (e.g. Harvey and Groutsis 2012)—resemble the 'target earners' amongst unskilled migrants. Like Polish workers on German building sites, they put up with unpleasant conditions because what matters is the pay they will receive relative to what they could earn at home. New forms of circular migration amongst skilled migrants are also based on economic motives. After the 2008 crash in Ireland, qualified and skilled workers predominated amongst the 'mortgage navvies' travelling to Britain to work for the week in order to pay their mortgage on the family home in Ireland. More generally, there is some limited economic evidence that high skill immigrants are more attracted to countries with relatively unequal income distributions (Minns 2005; also Reich 1993) and/or low levels of personal taxation (Liebig and Sousa-Poza 2005).

However, other reasons are involved, starting with longer-term career strategies. Amongst academics and researchers, a period abroad has become a valuable part of the CV, especially for those from the poorer areas of Europe (Guth 2008; Ackers 2008). Whereas low skill immigrants are clustered in low prestige jobs, in academe the higher the prestige of the university, the higher the number of foreigners on the staff (e.g. Mahroum 2001). If the migrant then returns home, this time at the top has an impact on his or her salary, and this is not just true amongst academics. For some time now, Irish returning emigrants have secured an 'emigration premium', earning more than those who merely stayed behind (Barrett and O'Connell 2001). For the young and the educated, especially at the start of their career, notions of self-development and self-realization are also crucial (Krings et al. 2013).

Research on the new professionals or the new 'service class' has stressed the importance of quality of life as determinants of location. According to Florida (2004), the 'creative class', which putatively amounts to about 20% of the population, tends to move to cities that provide a tolerant and attractive environment. The buzz of the city, the quality of the conversation, and the level of cultural facilities are all motivators. Quality of life means different things to different people. On the one hand ethnic diversity is widely recognized as itself an attraction and European Union (EU) citizens who are members of ethnic minorities are beginning to move towards the more tolerant countries. For example, journalistic reports suggest that skilled French nationals of Maghrebi extraction now find London more congenial than Paris. On the other hand, an outdoor lifestyle—as in Australia or Canada—is seen as especially attractive to Irish and British people with qualifications.

Finally, there is the importance of personal relations. Whereas in the past intra-EU migrants had a lower level of education than the population of their destination country, the reverse in now the case: 'EU movers are now a positively selected population in terms of education' (Recchi 2008, 208). The *European Internal Movers Survey* reports that only 25.2% of movers moved for 'work opportunities' and 24% for 'quality of life' but fully 29.7% for 'family and love' (cited in Recchi 2008, 217). Quality of life migrants are not just retirees, but often in the middle of the life-cycle. An extreme example would be those Britons who have abandoned conventional careers in Britain to find a more congenial way of supporting themselves by running a business in rural France (Benson 2010). Nonetheless, the evidence suggests that overall, whilst intra-EU migrants may move for non-economic reasons, such migrants are the better qualified and/or employed in highly skilled jobs.

Consequences for Sending Countries

The term 'brain drain' suggests that skilled emigration is a loss for the emigrants' country of origin, where the home country bears all the costs of their education, but receives none of the benefits. The term seems to have been first used to describe the outflow of scientists from Britain to the United States after World War II, but as a public policy issue now refers in particular to developing countries especially in Africa.

Contemporary research suggests that both short-term and long-term skilled migration can involve mutual gain for both sending and receiving countries (Portes 2009). Short-term migrants can gain skills and knowledge which they bring back to their country of origin when they return. Whilst poor countries can often not afford to develop sufficient high-quality educational institutions to meet domestic demand, their governments have been open to subsidizing their students on the assumption that they will bring back skills and knowledge when they return. However, especially in relatively democratic societies, ensuring that this actually happens is not always easy. When the People's Republic of China began to send students to study in the West the government considered this worthwhile if only 90% returned. In fact, the return rate has been probably closer to 25% and even lower amongst the most talented (Cao 2008).

Paradoxically, however, this is not necessarily a policy failure. Increasingly long-term and even permanent emigrants use their success to support their country of origin. Ethnic professional associations and wealthy individuals fund philanthropic initiatives back home. This has been well documented for Indians in the United States (e.g. Kapur 2010), but a dramatic example is the contribution of Atlantic Philanthropies, created by Irish-American Chuck Feeney, in funding the expansion of HE in Ireland. Ethnic organizations based on skilled migrants have the social and economic resources to influence policy towards their home country. When Italy was a country of mass unskilled emigration in the late nineteenth century, Italy abroad was a crucial national resource for Italian foreign policy (Choate 2008). Today emigrant countries are again developing what could be called 'diaspora policies' but, like the Indian Ministry of Overseas Indian Affairs, focus especially on their skilled emigrants.

Skilled emigration has often led to a new form of ethnic entrepreneurship. Increasingly skilled immigrants working in high-tech industry and services create their own companies, sometimes because they believe they are under-valued by their employers. In Silicon Valley, formal and informal ethnic associations amongst Israeli, Chinese, and Indian professionals also function to support start-ups. These companies in turn use their local knowledge to set up new companies back home. Such transfers were at the origins of the Taiwanese electronics manufacturing and, more recently, the Indian software and business process outsourcing industries; they have made a major contribution to the rapid growth of the Chinese high-tech industry (Saxenian 2006). Even if they do not actually return home, members of these ethnic diasporas transfer ideas and knowledge as well as remittances from the country of destination (Williams 2007; Kapur 2011).

In this way, brain drain can become brain circulation, as skilled emigrants transfer knowledge, technology, and entrepreneurial resources. However, not all skilled emigration generates these benefits. Firstly, these entrepreneurial developments require that the home country has some market liberalization, relatively established property rights and relatively low levels of corruption. Secondly, not all forms of knowledge translate into these forms of innovation: the nature of their discipline means that software engineers are more likely to create their own business than medical students.

High levels of skilled emigration may reduce public support for the public funding of HE in the country of origin: it gives a new twist to the debate on the private versus public returns to education. Unless skilled emigration gives demonstrable public benefits, it is unclear why the state should bestow scarce resources on those who will leave the country. Conversely, if the financial returns to HE are increased by emigration, those in the country of origin will be more ready to pay for it. In the Philippines with one of the highest rates of skilled emigration, almost all tertiary education is privately run. More generally, econometric analysis suggests that a higher proportion of skilled emigrants within the total emigrant flow is linked to a lower level of public expenditure on HE. Thus whilst mass unskilled immigration challenges the welfare state in the destination countries, skilled emigration may undermine public facilities in the countries of origin (Boeri et al. 2011).

Consequences for Receiving Countries

In economic terms short-term and cyclical skilled immigration should reduce skill shortages, whilst long-term and permanent skilled immigration should also increase the receiving country's stock of human capital. Econometric analysis confirms that the positive impact of immigration on overall employment and on investment increases as the proportion of skilled immigrants rises within the total immigrant flow (Boeri et al. 2011, 125). Equally, popular hostility to immigration reduces as the proportion of skilled immigrants rises.

Institutional variation between societies can explain the extent to which countries rely on importing skilled labour to tackle skill shortages (Devitt 2011). The Varieties of Capitalism (VoC) tradition differentiates between liberal market economies (LME) and co-ordinated market economies (CME). The United Kingdom, along with Ireland, is taken as exemplifying the former, Germany the latter (Hall and Soskice 2001). Within an LME vocational education is relatively underdeveloped, an extensive HE system focuses on generalist skills and job tenure, especially for skilled employees, is relatively short. The CME is the mirror image of this: extensive vocational education generates highly developed occupational skills, there is relatively low participation in third level education which itself has a strong technological element, and employees, including managerial and professional staff, have high levels of job tenure.

These factors help explain why both the United Kingdom and Ireland rely so heavily on the importation of skilled labour. Thus, although Ireland has attracted foreign direct investment because of its allegedly skilled labour force, the Irish software industry has for more than a decade depended on the continual import of skilled workers (Wickham and Bruff 2008). By contrast, the German software industry has also lobbied for increased skilled immigration, but German firms tend to be much less likely to recruit skilled immigrants. At an aggregate level in both the United Kingdom and Ireland, immigrants with third level education are over-represented compared to the native-born population, whereas in Germany immigrants are disproportionately unskilled (OECD 2011). At firm level, Winkelmann (2002) has shown that, compared to German firms in the same sector, UK firms are particularly likely to recruit higher skill labour from abroad. Thus the institutional context of the LME encourages firms (and society as a whole) to buy skills on the international market rather than making them at home.

A few studies examine the power of lobby groups to open or close the national labour market in specific sectors. Working within a VoC framework, Cerna (2009) suggested that the greater power of unions within CMEs explains why Germany and Sweden have been slower to import skilled labour than the United Kingdom and Ireland. Noting that 'labour market demands are not automatically translated into immigration flows', Money and Falstrom (2006) explain why, when in the United States in the 1990s there was a perceived shortage of both IT workers and registered nurses, only the former were granted large numbers of entry visas. Because the IT industry is geographically concentrated (especially in Silicon Valley), it could mobilize political support in a way that was not possible for medical employers dispersed across the United States. Lobby groups can also create demand for skilled immigration. Thus the success of medical pressure groups in limiting medical school intake in the United Kingdom and Ireland generates frequent shortages of medical staff, which in turn ensures the need to import foreign-trained doctors in these countries (Devitt 2011; Quinn and Gusciute 2013, 13). Skilled

Table 27.3 Consequences of skilled immigration

Intended duration	Earnings level	
	Experts (>€60k, <€150k)	*Superstars (>€150k)*
Visitors (<5 years)	Reduce inequality by depressing higher salaries (increased supply)	Increase inequality by expanding 'winner takes all' labour markets
Settlers (>5 years)	Potential citizenship contribution	Luxury ghettoes

immigration may reduce incentives for effective national education policies, as has been documented for UK training policy (House of Lords 2008, 31; Ruhs and Anderson 2010, 313).

Conventional economic theory would predict that skilled immigration reduces inequality because it increases competition at the upper end of the income distribution. Such arguments ignore the extent to which skilled labour markets may be segmented, so that the importation of large numbers of IT 'guestworkers' to the United States has little impact on the domestic IT labour market (Salzman et al. 2013). At the top end of the income distribution governments are making tax changes to attract highly skilled professionals and managers and in particular to facilitate those recruited through intra-company transfers. For example, in London recent immigrants from high wage countries are disproportionately concentrated in the upper quintile of the income distribution (Gordon et al. 2007). More difficult to document is the indirect effect: high salaries for such 'guestworkers' and other international managers may in turn raise the aspirations of their indigenous colleagues, thus adding a further twist to the apparently insatiable salary demands of those at the top of corporate structures. At least in the London case, opening the national labour markets to unskilled immigration has depressed wages in the bottom of the distribution, whilst increased high skill immigration has raised salaries at the upper end of the distribution. Table 27.3 suggests the different implications for receiving countries for skilled immigrants classified by their length of stay and their level of earnings.

Consequences for Individuals

Skilled migrants are often taken as exemplifying a benign cosmopolitanism, disconnected from narrow-minded nationalistic particularities. However, in one of the first accounts of the mobility of contemporary skilled professionals Reich (1999) describes those who can now choose where to live and work as 'indifferent cosmopolitans'. Such migrants may have an instrumental relationship to citizenship. An ethnographic account of affluent circular migrants between Hong Kong and Vancouver (Ong 2003) reported that such 'ethnicized cosmopolitan citizenship' generates a tenuous relationship to local institutions. For circular migrants and for members of ethnic diasporas—or simply for the bi-located affluent with homes in several countries—citizenship may be a flag of convenience rather than true membership of a local community. These newer forms of mobility/migration may involve less moral commitment to the 'new' country than traditional forms of permanent settlement. Without more empirical research this must, however, remain conjecture.

Within the EU it is increasingly the skilled and the affluent who take advantage of European citizens' rights to live and work in any member state. Europeans now share common rights and even potentially a common identity. Unsurprisingly, those who have lived in more than one EU member state are especially likely to consider themselves 'European', though usually this is in addition to national identity rather than a replacement for it Intriguingly, intra-European migrants tend to be more politically aware than those without any such mobility experience, but also rather less likely to participate in political activity (Muxel 2009). Even for Europeans moving within Europe, mobility does seem to involve a certain disengagement.

Rather clearer is the impact of some forms of skilled migration on gender relations. According to a German study of highly mobile professionals and managers, men are more likely than women to be frequent travellers. Predictably, those women who are mobile tend to be single and/or childless, whilst mobile men tend to be married to women who have 'traditional' female roles (Kesselring and Vogl 2010). Amongst French professionals living and working in London married couples tend to assume traditional gender roles, with the woman essentially following the male's career. This does, however, have the paradoxical consequence that social integration into British society is achieved largely by women through their involvement in neighbourhood and school-related activities (Ryan and Mulholland 2013). In terms of gender therefore, migration can involve new constraints.

Policies

For more than a decade government policies in most OECD countries have shifted towards selective migration: attempting to attract (wanted) skilled immigrants whilst keeping out (unwanted) unskilled immigrants. The strategy was expressed in French President Sarkozy's demand for 'immigration choisie' instead of 'immigration subie'.

Australia and Canada operate points-based systems of immigration: potential immigrants are awarded points for attributes such as qualifications and English language competence. Above a certain level of points the applicants gain entry. A points-based system aims at increasing the available human capital within the destination country; it runs the risk that once in the country immigrants will find that their qualifications are actually underused or not even recognized. Since 2008 the United Kingdom has operated a points-based system for potential immigrants from outside the EU and the United Kingdom is often held up as a model for other European countries (Menz 2009).

A points-based system is driven by the characteristics of the employee. The alternative is an employer-based system. The employer applies for the visa and the immigrants are essentially tied to the job for which they entered the country, and their stay may be limited. Such visa systems can involve some form of 'labour market testing' by which the employer confirms that no indigenous applicants are available to fill the post. Thus the H1B visa is the main entry route for skilled immigrants to the United States. H1B applicants are required to have a bachelor's degree or the equivalent, but they enter the United States because they are sponsored by a specific employer. Nonetheless, during their stay such immigrants are entitled to apply for permanent residency (the 'Green Card'). Significantly, for all the rhetoric of encouraging skilled immigration, the European 'Blue Card' actually involves no right nor even a route to permanent residency. In our terminology, employer-driven policies are essentially aimed at 'visitors', whilst points-based systems are concerned with 'settlers'.

Table 27.4 shows how migration policy can be divided into *hard* and *soft* modes: the former depending on law, the latter on non-judiciable instruments. Table 27.4 also differentiates between policies that are *focused*, i.e. exclusively concerned with immigrants, and those that are *contextual*, i.e. those that concern others as well as immigrants. Normal discussion of immigration policy is concerned with the top left cell of the table: hard and focused policies such as border control, visa regulation etc. However, focused hard policies also include specific tax policies that vary by the type of skilled immigrant. Using again the terminology of Table 27.3, 'visiting superstars' such as the foreign executives of multinational companies in Ireland can benefit from special tax exemptions for children's education, etc. (Quinn and Gusciute 2013), whilst rather different schemes attempt to entice wealthy individuals and entrepreneurs to settle in a country (Table 27.4).

Table 27.4 Policies for attracting skilled migrants

		Breadth	
		Focused	*Contextual*
Mode	*Hard*	Border control: visas, work permits ...	Labour market regulation and employment protection legislation (EPL)
		Access to citizenship	Taxation
		Access to social rights and social services	Equal opportunities and anti-discrimination legislation and enforcement
		Taxation exemptions	
	Soft	National image ('national brand')	Ethnic diversity and tolerance employment quality
			Quality of life

However, a country wishing to attract skilled immigrants also needs to be concerned with other issues. Immigrants may well make decisions based on the quality of life or the atmosphere of the workplace (Boyle 2006; Krings et al. 2013). There is also spillover from one policy area to another. For example, German hostility towards ethnic minorities and (unskilled) immigrants was highlighted by the 'Kinder statt Inder' saga and clearly made Germany an unattractive destination for the 'visiting experts' that the country so dramatically failed to attract.

Conclusion

Today, there are more skilled migrants than ever before. These new streams are changing the nature of migration. Not only are migrants different, but the boundary between migration and other forms of mobility is more difficult to draw. These shifts have been driven by some quite specific features of contemporary globalization. Large firms have operated on a global scale for decades, but today more activities within firms are organized globally, or at least transnationally. Firms both deploy their existing skilled labour across countries and recruit from an international market. Like any market, this new labour market does not simply exist, it is created and maintained by social actors—firms, recruiting companies, and even national governments. Equally, the skilled themselves do not simply utilize an existing market, they consolidate it and expand it by their deliberate choice of mobility.

For the better educated and relatively privileged across the world, the growth of skilled mobility is something to celebrate: the larger market expands their options. Equally, skilled immigration appears positive for the privileged countries in the world. Discussion of the negative effects of the brain drain has concentrated almost entirely on the deleterious consequences for poor sending countries. Yet these effects are by no means universal. Especially the shift from permanent migration to shorter-term mobility has meant that 'losing' the best and brightest can turn out not to be a loss at all. At the same time, the more negative aspects of skilled labour immigration for the rich countries are only now beginning to be noticed. The importation of 'visiting experts' to the United States shows how labour immigration can be part of a firm strategy that refuses to take any responsibility for training and retaining domestic skilled labour. It is often assumed that immigration contributes to the diversity and vibrancy of cities (e.g. Florida 2004). However, the importation of skilled labour with little commitment to the host country may further stimulate the disconnection of the relatively privileged population from civic involvement. As the controversy over a possible 'mansion tax' in the United Kingdom has shown, visiting celebrities can weaken the tax base and further exacerbate social inequality. It is salutary to consider whether and to what extent the expansion of skilled labour migration may also be part of the dark side of globalization.

References

Ackers, L. and Gill, B. (2008) *Moving People and Knowledge: Scientific Mobility in an Enlarging European Union*, London: Edward Elgar.

Akyün, H. (2007) *Einmal Hans mit Scharfer Soße: Leben in Zwei Welten*, Munich: Goldmann.

Benson, M. (2010) 'The Context and Trajectory of Lifestyle Migration: The Case of British Residents of Southwest France', *European Societies*, 12(1): 45–64.

Boyle, M. (2006) 'Culture in the Rise of Tiger Economies: Scottish Expatriates in Dublin and the 'Creative Class' Thesis', *International Journal of Urban and Regional Research*, 30(2): 403–426.

Bozkurt, Ö. and Mohr, A. T. (2011) 'Forms of Cross-Border Mobility and Social Capital in Multinational Enterprises', *Human Resource Management Journal*, 21(2): 138–155.

Cao, C. (2008) 'China's Brain Drain at the High End: Why Government Policies Have Failed to Attract First-rate Academics to Return', *Asian Population Studies*, 4(3): 331–345.

Castles, S. and Miller, M. J. 2009. *The Age of Migration: International Population Movements in the Modern World*, Basingstoke: Macmillan.

Cerna, L. (2009) 'The Varieties of High-Skilled Immigration Policies: Coalitions and Policy Outputs in Advanced Industrial Countries', *Journal of European Public Policy*, 16(1) 144–161.

Chiswick, B. R., Lee, Y. W., and Miller, P. W. (2005) 'A Longitudinal Analysis of Immigrant Occupational Mobility: A Test of the Immigrant Assimilation Hypothesis', *International Migration Review*, 39(2): 332–353.

Choate, M. I. (2008) *Emigrant Nation: The Making of Italy Abroad*, Cambridge, MA: Harvard University Press.

Conradson, D. and Latham, A. (2005) 'Transnational Urbanism: Attending to Everyday Practices and Mobilities', *Journal of Ethnic and Migration Studies*, 31(2): 227–233.

Darwin, J. (2009) *The Empire Project: The Rise and Fall of the British World System 1830–1970*, Cambridge: Cambridge University Press.

Devitt, C. (2011) 'Varieties of Capitalism, Variation in Labour Immigration', *Journal of Ethnic and Migration Studies*, 37(4): 579–596.

Ferguson, N. (2005) *Colossus: The Rise and Fall of the American Empire*, London: Penguin Press.

Fitzgerald, I. and Hardy, J. (2010) '"Thinking outside the box"? Trade Union Organizing Strategies and Polish Migrant Workers in the United Kingdom', *British Journal of Industrial Relation*, 48(1): 131–150.

Florida, R. L. (2004) *The Rise of the Creative Class: And How It's Transforming Work, Leisure, Community and Everyday Life*, New York: Basic Books.

Gordon, I., Travers, T., and Whitehead, C. (2007) *The Impact of Recent Immigration on the London Economy*, London: London School of Economics for City of London.

Guth, J. (2008) 'The Opening of Borders and Scientific Mobility: The Impact of EU Enlargement on the Movement of Early Career Scientists', *Higher Education in Europe*, 33(4): 395–410.

Harvey, W. and Groutsis, D. (2012) 'Skilled Migrants in the Middle East: Definitions, Mobility and Integration', *International Journal of Business and Globalisation*, 12(4): 438–453.

House of Lords (2008) *The Economic Impact of Immigration*, Vol. 1, Select Committee on Economic Affairs, 1st Report of Session 2007–08, April.

Joppke, C. (2010) 'The Inevitable Lightening of Citizenship', *European Journal of Sociology*, 51(1): 9–32.

Kapur, D. (2010) *Diaspora, Development and Democracy: The Domestic Impact of International Migration from India*, Princeton, NJ: Princeton University Press.

Kesselring, S. and Vogl, G. (2010) *Betriebliche Mobilitätsregime: die sozialen Kosten mobiler Arbeit*, Berlin: Edition Sigma.

Khadria, B. (2001) 'Shifting Paradigms of Globalisation: The Twenty-first Century Transition towards Generics in Skilled Migration from India', *International Migration*, 39(5): 45–71.

King, R. (2002) 'Towards a New Map of European Migration', *International Journal of Population Geography* 8(2): 89–106.

Krieger, H. (2004) *Migration Trends in an Enlarged Europe*, European Foundation for the Improvement of Living and Working Conditions, Luxembourg: Office for Official Publications of the European Communities.

Krings, T., Moriarty, E., Wickham, J., Bobek A., and Salamońska, J. (2013) *New Mobilities in Europe: Polish Migration to Ireland Post-2004*, Manchester: Manchester University Press.

Liebig, T. and Sousa-Poza, A. (2005) 'Taxation, Ethnic Ties and the Location Choice of Highly Skilled Immigrants', OECD Social, Employment and Migration Working Papers, DELSA/ELSA/WD/SEM(2005)3.

Mahroum, S. (2000) 'High Skilled Globetrotters: Mapping the International Migration of Human Capital', *R&D Management*, 30 (1): 23–32.

Menz, G. (2009) *The Political Economy of Managed Migration: Non-State Actors, Europeanization and the Politics of Designing Migration Policies*, Oxford: Oxford University Press.

Meyer, J.-B., Kaplan, D., and Charum, J. (2001) 'Scientific Nomadism and the New Geopolitics of Knowledge', *International Social Science Journal*, 53(168): 309–321.

Millar, J. and Salt, J. (2007) 'In Whose Interests? IT Migration in an Interconnected World Economy', *Population, Space and Place*, 13(1): 41–58.

Millar, J. and Salt, J. (2008) 'Portfolios of Mobility: The Movement of Expertise in Transnational Corporations in Two Sectors: Aerospace and Extractive Industries', *Global Networks*, 8(1): 25–50.

Minns, C. (2005) 'Immigration Policy and the Skills of Irish Immigrants: Evidence and Implications', IIIS Discussion Paper no. 68, Trinity College Dublin.

Muxel, A. (2009) 'EU Movers and Politics: Towards a Fully-Fledged European Citizenship?', in E. Recchi and A. Favell (eds), *Pioneers of European Integration*, Cheltenham: Edward Elgar: 156–178.

OECD (2008) *A Profile of Immigrant Populations in the 21st Century: Data from OECD Countries*, Paris: OECD.

Ong, A. (2003) 'Techno-Migrants in the Network Economy', in U. Beck, N. Sznaider, and R. Winter (eds), *Global America? The Cultural Consequences of Globalization*, Liverpool: Liverpool University Press: 153–173.

Quinn, E. and Gusciute, E. (2013) *Attracting Highly Qualified and Qualified Third Country Nationals: Ireland*, Dublin: Economic and Social Research Institute.

Recchi, E. (2008) 'Cross-State Mobility in the EU: Trends, Puzzles and Consequences', *European Societies*, 10(2): 197–224.

Reich, R. (1993) *The Work of Nations: Preparing Ourselves for 21st Century Capitalism*, 2nd ed., London: A. A. Knopf.

Richards, E. (2004) *Britannia's Children: Emigration from England, Scotland and Wales since 1600*, London: Hambledon Continuum.

Ruhs, M. and Anderson, B. (2010) *Who Needs Migrant Workers? Labour Shortages, Immigration, and Public Policy*, Oxford: Oxford University Press.

Salt, J. (1997) 'International Movements of the Highly Skilled', OECD Social, Employment and Migration Working Papers, no. 3, OECD.

Salt, J. (2010) 'Business Travel and Portfolios of Mobility within Global Companies', in J. Beaverstock, B. Derudder, and J. Faulconbridge (eds), *International Business Travel in the Global Economy*, Guildford: Ashgate Publishing: 107–124.

Salzman, H., Kuehn, D., and B. Lindsay Lowell (2013) 'Guestworkers in the High- Skill US Labor Market: An Analysis of Supply, Employment and Wage Trends', Economic Policy Briefing Paper #359, Washington, DC: Economic Policy Institute.

Saxenian, A-L. (2006) *The New Argonauts: Regional Advantage in a Global Economy*, London: Harvard University Press.

Sriskandarajah, D. and Drew, C. (2006) *Brits Abroad: Mapping the Scale and Nature of British Emmigration*, London: Institute for Public Policy Research.

Urry, J. (2000) *Sociology Beyond Societies: Mobilities for the Twenty-First Century*, London: Routledge.

Wickham, J. and Bruff, I. (2008) 'Skill Shortages Are Not Always What They Seem: Migration and the Irish Software Industry', *New Technology, Work and Employment*, 23(1–2): 30–43.

Wickham, J. and Vecchi, A. (2010) 'Hierarchies in the Air: Varieties of Business Travel', in J. Beaverstock, B. Derudder, and J. Faulconbridge (eds), *International Business Travel in the Global Economy*, Guildford: Ashgate Publishing: 125–143.

Widmaier, S. and Dumont, J-C. (2011) 'Are Recent Immigrants Different? A New Profile of Immigrants in the OECD Based on DIOC 2005/06', OECD Social, Employment and Migration Working Papers no.126, Directorate for Employment, Labour and Social Affairs: OECD.

Williams, A. (2007) 'Listen To Me, Learn With Me: International Migration and Knowledge Transfer', *British Journal of Industrial Relations*, 45(2): 361–382.

Winkelman, R. (2002) 'Why Do Firms Recruit Internationally? Results from the IZA International Employer Survey 2000', *International Mobility of the Highly Skilled*, Paris: OECD: 133–150.

Xiang, B. (2001) 'Structuration of Indian Information Technology Professionals' Migration to Australia: An Ethnographic Study', *International Migration*, 39(5): 73–90.

CHAPTER 28

PROFESSIONAL SKILLS

Impact of Comparative Political Economy

MARI SAKO

This chapter analyses the significance of professions and professional training in the contemporary debate about skills. Skills are of inherent value to people who possess them, but much of the public policy debate over the decades has focused on their contribution to job creation and the international competitiveness of nations. In the twenty-first century, this debate touches a wider portfolio of skills than in the past as global value chains spread from manufacturing to a variety of professional services. The phenomenon of offshoring has given rise to studies on the global mobility of jobs, resulting in a finding that more educated workers hold somewhat more offshoreable jobs (Blinder 2009; Blinder and Krueger 2009). That is, higher levels of education and professional skill attainment are no longer an insurance against job losses caused by international competition from lower cost locations. If such jobs are now subject to a 'global auction' (Brown et al. 2011), in what ways might the nature of professional skills and training change in different parts of the world? This question can be answered fully, only if we conduct a comparative institutional analysis of professional skill formation. This chapter develops a political economy framework to enable such analysis.

Doctors, lawyers, accountants, financial analysts, engineers, and research scientists are professionals of growing importance in the knowledge economy. Professionals are a subset of white-collar workers, as articulated by Mills, who made a distinction between 'free professionals' amongst the old middle class, and 'salaried professionals' amongst the new middle class (Mills 1951 (2002)). In the early part of the twentieth century, professionals of both types constituted no more than 5% of the total labour force in the United States. By 2000 'professional and related occupations' accounted for 18.4% of workers, and grew to 22.2% by 2010 (see Table 28.1 for international comparisons). Similarly, in Britain, professionals constituted around 4% of the total employed in the 1920s and 1930s (Larson 1977), growing to 11.7% by 2001, and to 14.0% by 2010. By 2010 professionals and associated professionals accounted for 28.1% of employment in Britain.

Table 28.1 Occupational composition of employment 2010

	Legislators, senior officials and managers	Professionals	Technicians and associated professionals	Clerks	Service workers; shop and market sales workers	Skilled agricultural and fishery workers	Craft and related trades workers	Plant and machine operators and assemblers	Elementary occupations
JAPAN	2.6	15.8		20.5	26.7	3.9	29.6		
USA	15.1	22.2		13.0	28.8	0.7	20.3		–
BRITAIN	15.3	15.2	12.9	12.6	17.6	1.2	8.5	5.9	10.2
GERMANY	5.8	15.2	21.9	11.9	12.4	1.8	14.4	6.7	8.2
FRANCE	8.8	14.2	18.9	11.5	13.1	3.6	10.9	8.3	9.6
SWEDEN	5.6	19.8	21.5	8.0	18.4	2.0	9.6	9.0	5.7

Note: Occupational classification based on ISCO-88.

Sources:

ILO LABORSTA (http://laborsta.ilo.org/)

Japan:Labour Force Survey 2011

Europe:Eurostat Database(http://epp.eurostat.ec.europa.eu/).

Besides the growing numerical significance of professionals, an increasing proportion of professional work crosses national borders, via international migration, activities of multinational corporations, and offshoring. Consequently, we would expect the skills debate, on how investment in skills contributes to the international competitiveness of nations, to incorporate professional skills. Yet to date, this has not happened in an analytically satisfactory manner. In spite of occupational change from industrial to professional skills, the existing discussion of the political economy of skill formation has been heavily influenced by the system constructed for industrial workers in manufacturing.

A failure to examine the character of professional skills with sufficient care as the economy moves towards services has been pointed out before (Iverson 2005; Riain 2011; Thelen 2012). But no scholar has yet to correct this failure by addressing the following questions:

- In what ways must the existing comparative political economy typologies be modified as skills in question shift from a primary focus on intermediate skills to include professional skills?
- How similar or different are the national institutions that matter for the skill formation system for professional skills as compared to those for industrial skill formation?
- In what ways do the skill formation systems and qualifications for professionals carrying the same title differ across different countries?

This chapter is structured as follows. The first section reviews the main disciplinary frameworks for analysing the education and training of professionals. The second section develops a comparative political economy typology for categorizing *varieties of professional skill formation systems*. The industrial logic that pervades the existing frameworks needs to be modified if professional skills are to be examined by political economists interested in skills and training. The rest of the chapter discusses specific forces that are transforming the nature of professionals, and explores their implications for professional skills and training: the third section focuses on offshoring and digital technology, and the fourth section on the changing models for legitimizing professions. The chapter concludes by identifying key avenues for future research.

Disciplinary Traditions for Studying Professionals

The development of professional workers has received distinctive analytical treatment from several major disciplines: sociology, labour economics, and comparative political

Table 28.2 Major studies on (or with implications for) professional skills

Discipline	Authors	Key findings and implications
Sociology	Carr-Saunders and Wilson (1933) Parsons (1939) Mills (1951) Gouldner (1957) Larson (1977) Freidson (1970, 2001) Krause (1996) Abbott (1988)	• Professions are as much about power and status in society, as about skills and expertise. • Professionalization involves claiming the right to control one's own work, closure via licensing or certification, and higher social status • Professions exist in an eco-system in which each profession vies against each other to defend one's own jurisdictional boundary
Labour economics	Autor et al. (2003) Levy and Murnane (2004) Kleiner (2006) Forth et al. (2011) Greenwood et al. (2005) Mason and Nohara (2010)	• Computer technology is a substitute for 'rule-based' tasks, a complement for 'judgement-based' tasks. Professional tasks tend to be of the latter type. • Occupational licensing leads to restricted supply of labour and wage premiums. • Internal labour markets facilitate the management of professionals in hierarchy
Comparative political economy	Hall and Soskice (1990) Crouch et al. (1999) Thelen (2004) Busemeyer and Trampusch (2011) Krause (1996) Larson (1977) Svensson and Evetts (2010)	• The state and national institutions in labour market (e.g. professional associations, occupational licensing) influence the mode of skill formation and certification • Liberal market economies (LMEs) demand more professional skills than coordinated market economies (CMEs)

economy. This section reviews and integrates the key insights from these disciplines to advance the study of professional skill formation. Table 28.2 summarizes key points from each discipline.

In sociology, scholars have studied the profession as a unit of analysis in relation to social structure (Parsons 1939). For example, Gouldner listed 'commitment to professional skills and values' as a component in latent social identities (Gouldner 1957). A sociological ideal-type of profession incorporates two dimensions: a cognitive one centred on the body of knowledge and skills that professionals apply in their work, and a normative one covering their service orientation and distinctive ethics which justify the privilege and social status granted to them by society (Larson 1977). Larson links the two dimensions thus: 'professionalization is an attempt to translate one order of scarce resources—special knowledge and skills—into another—social and economic rewards' (p. xvii).

What makes a profession distinct from other occupations are the following: the right to control one's own work, rendering 'outside' evaluation illegitimate and intolerable (Freidson 1970); the mechanisms for controlling the market for expertise via guild-like associations (Krause 1996); and the collective process of upward social mobility by claiming higher social status, including the use of the legitimizing force of universities that certify professional competence (Larson 1977; Freidson 2001). Detailed descriptive analysis of various professions (notably Carr-Saunders and Wilson 1933 (1964)) gave way to a more functionalist analysis of the ecological system of professions (Abbott 1988). In the latter, Abbott studied exogenous and endogenous forces that have led contiguous professionals and semi-professionals to defend their jurisdictional boundaries. But these studies continued to give greater attention to the issue of power, control, and status than to the nature of knowledge, expertise, and skills in the professionalization process. Consequently, the question of 'what do professionals do?' is answered not so much with respect to the content of their skills and expertise, but with respect to their latent roles, social status, and the dominant model that legitimizes privileges granted to professions.

A different kind of scholarship, led by economists interested in the impact of computer technology on skills, has developed a typology that sheds light on the substantive nature of professional skills. Building on cognitive and behavioral sciences, Levy and Murnane (2004) draw a distinction between 'rule-based' tasks (for which information processing can be fully described in rules) and 'pattern recognition' tasks. In the latter, rule-based solutions are not possible, and people solve problems through case-based reasoning, a type of pattern recognition, constructing analogies between the new problem and past problems. Computers change the task composition of human work. They substitute for workers carrying out routine 'rule-based' tasks, whilst they complement workers carrying out non-routine problem-solving tasks (Autor et al. 2003). This task-based model of skills has the advantage of enabling the analysis of how the balance of routine vs non-routine tasks change within occupations over time. This avoids the blanket application of 'digital Taylorism' to describe the trend towards standardization in some professional jobs (Brown et al. 2011). The disadvantage of the task-based approach, however, is that these scholars, unlike sociologists, take little interest in how the packaging of tasks into a professional role is mediated by societal and institutional factors.

Next, labour economists and human capital theorists have much to say about professionals from two angles: economic consequences of the monopoly face of occupational closure, and the nature of internal labour markets (ILM) (Osterman 1984). Economists have found that occupational licensing and certification have a restrictive impact on the supply of professional labour, and cause wage and price premiums to a varying degree (Friedman and Kuznets 1954; Kleiner 2000, 2006; Forth et al. 2011). Applying human capital theory, rewarding tenure with a wage premium in ILMs is considered important for controlling professionals in employment contracts (Mason and Nohara 2010).

Firms overcome the difficulty of managing and directing highly skilled professionals by creating incentives for professionals to stay on within the same firm (Greenwood et al. 2005).

For example, in a law firm context, the so-called 'up-or-out system' (in which one either makes it to partner or is asked to depart) and the 'lockstep' compensation system (in which profits are divided on the basis of seniority) are necessary to regulate knowledge assets when property rights over them are difficult to enforce (Rebitzer and Taylor 2007). In a similar vein, Gilson and Mnookin use portfolio theory to explain the existence of large law firms as a means of diversifying risk from human capital investment and the persistence of the 'lockstep' mode of splitting profits as the optimal mode of distributing gains from such diversification (Gilson and Mnookin 1985). Equally important is the use of 'tournament' theory to explain the incentives for promotion built into the up-or-out career development system for lawyers (Galanter and Palay 1990; Galanter and Henderson 2008). These studies, however, are de-contextualized with respect to the political economy in which skill formation takes place. Consequently, we do not have a systematic way of comparing how differences in labour market institutions and the state lead to different types of professional skill formation.

We could conduct such comparisons via an institutional analysis of political economies. This field has been a fertile ground for cultivating excellent research on the formation of skills and its impact on national competitiveness. Many of these studies, however, have focused on intermediate skills in industrial society (Crouch et al. 1999; Finegold and Soskice 1988; Streeck and Yamamura 2001; Thelen 2004; Busemeyer and Trampusch 2012). This focus has been justified in terms of the sheer number of workers with intermediate skills in advanced economies, and their significance in determining the international competitiveness of export-oriented manufacturing sectors.

Professionals, being neither labour nor capital, occupy an ill-fitting position in a political economy framework such as Varieties of Capitalism (Hall and Soskice 2001). Professionals possess highly portable skills, and even those working in managerial hierarchies are likely to be more mobile between firms in a liberal market economy (LME) than in a coordinated market economy (CME). LMEs, as compared to CMEs, also create greater demand for professional skills due to higher levels of corporate activities such as M&A, divestments, and litigation to defend corporate transactions (Sako 2013). However, to date, professional skill formation has not been analysed systematically with explicit reference to the sort of institutions that matter, namely professional associations rather than labour unions, universities and professional schools rather than apprenticeships and vocational schools, and the state that administers occupational licensing. Comparative historical studies of professions have given due attention to these institutions (Krause 1996; Larson 1977; Svensson and Evetts 2010), but have not made much headway with linking them to contemporary debates on skills.

To summarize, sociologists have advanced our understanding of the profession in relation to social structure, but their focus evades analysing the nature of professional skills. Labour economists have shed light on the nature of ILMs to nurture professional skills and the monopoly effect of occupational closure. But they are not interested in the political economy context that defines professional occupational roles. The political economy scholars have made great advances in comparing the institutional bases for skill formation in capitalist economies. But they are preoccupied with an industrial logic that focuses on labour market institutions such as apprenticeships, labour unions. and collective bargaining.

Varieties of Professional Skill Formation Systems

How can we best define what are professionals and professional skills? Professionals are experts who create and institutionalize knowledge. They also tend to provide services that constitute a public good, and societal infrastructure, such as public health and law. However, beyond these, it is easy to be led astray by the rich diversity of institutional arrangements with historical legacy that defy a universal definition of professionals. Evidently, who is included in the category of professionals differ over time (Wilensky 1964) and across geographies, with the notions of self-regulated professions in Britain (Carr-Saunders and Wilson 1933 (1964)), *Beruf* in Germany (Streeck 2012), and *senmonshoku* or *'puro'* in Japan (Dore and Sako 1989).[1] We therefore need to develop a typology of professional skill formation that can accommodate a variety of traditions, including Anglo-Saxon and Continental ones (Svensson and Evetts 2010).

Three dimensions, namely mode of training, required qualification, and standards enforcement, capture varieties in professional skill formation. Firstly, some professions require practical training, as in residency for medical doctors where supervised practice is needed before they are deemed fully qualified. In such cases professional knowledge is a combination of theoretical and practical knowing, which is often difficult to codify fully. Secondly, some professions require a licence to practice legally, whilst others merely require a certificate, which is a formal recognition of the level of competence achieved (Kleiner 2000). Thirdly, ethical and performance standards are enforced in different ways. Self-regulated professionals believe that only members of their profession have the competence and appropriate ethics to enforce these standards, insisting that outsiders—lay members—cannot properly supervise their activities.

Table 28.3 classifies professionals according to these dimensions. Classical professionals such as doctors and lawyers, have all three characteristics: the requirement for practical training, licence to practice, and the within-profession enforcement of standards. However, they come in two types: *independent professionals* have powerful associations which license and enforce standards, whereas *state-sponsored professionals* are beholden to the state agencies to grant licences and enforce standards.

Organizational professionals such as engineers and specialists in finance, marketing, or human resources do not require practical training; in general, do not require a

[1] This section is based largely on Sako (2013).

Table 28.3 Typology of professional skill formation

	Independent professionals	State-sponsored professionals	Organizational professionals	Knowledge professionals
Education and practical training	Formal 'training contract'	Higher education at university	Higher education and on-the-job training	Higher education
Licence to practice?	Yes, by professional association and the state	Yes, by state agencies	No, certification only	No, certification only
Who enforces standards and ethical code?	Professional association and the state	The state	Employers and clients	Collegial
Examples	Doctors Lawyers Accountants	Doctors Lawyers Accountants	Functional specialists, e.g. engineering, marketing, finance	Research scientists

licence to practice; and have standards enforced by employers and clients. In contemporary advanced industrialized countries, professionals are organizational in the sense of being subject to managerial hierarchy (Reed 1996). However, organizational professionals remain experts who advise, rather than managers who command, hence the importance of upholding the distinction between staff and line in bureaucratic organizations (Simon 1954; Etzioni 1959). The move to professionalize general managers via the Masters in Business Administration (MBA) is widespread in certain parts of the world (Khurana 2007). Also, some functional specialists in organizations may become general managers. However, general managers per se (and corporate leaders such as CEOs) are line managers who are not professionals in the current schema.

Knowledge professionals such as research scientists do not have formalized practical training, use certification rather than licensing, and exercise collegial enforcement of standards. Most knowledge professionals are based at educational institutions, for whom there is little distance between theory and practice. For the other three types of professionals, however, a gap may arise between the research-driven frontier theoretical knowledge on the one hand and the technical know-how updating that takes place through continuing professional education classes (Adler et al. 2008).

We can relate the four types of professionals to the notion of guild power articulated by Krause, which consists of control over four domains, namely association, the workplace, the market, and the state (Krause 1996). Independent professionals retain power in all four domains, state-sponsored professionals retain control in all but one (the state), and organizational professionals have lost control with respect to the workplace and the market in particular. This typology is also related to the five different governance mechanisms for intermediate skill formation: market, hierarchy, state, association, and community (in an industrial district for example) (Crouch et al. 1999). Here, organizational professionals come under hierarchical governance and knowledge professionals under community governance, whilst state-sponsored professionals are governed by the state and independent professionals by associational principles.

In any national political economy, the professional skill formation system reflects the intermediate skill formation system to an extent, so that a strong central state, if it exists, is likely to intervene more directly in both systems. But the two systems—in intermediate skills and professional skills—do not necessarily rely on the same set of institutions. In particular, professional associations loom large to govern professional skills, in contrast to employers' associations or labour unions for intermediate skills. Also, occupational licensing is a more significant labour market institution for professional skills than collective bargaining (Kleiner 2000).[2]

To summarize, a political economy framework for analysing professional skills is essential because professions are tied to status and power, as well as to skill and function. The professionalization of skills is therefore about both (a) the cognitive aspect of developing a body of knowledge and expertise, and (b) linking the cognitive aspect to a normative dimension by use of social status and prestige. The four-way typology of professional skills elaborated in this section builds on the sociological foundation of studying professions, whilst being sensitive to the comparative political economists' perspective that acknowledges differences in normative framing of professionals from country to country.

Impacts of Offshoring And Technology

Having outlined a framework for comparing professional skills across political economies, we are now ready to ask a central question of contemporary relevance: how will professionals fare in a more open global economy when they cross national borders via migration or face greater international competition via international trade in professional services? This section and the next aim to shed light on the specific challenges professionals face in the current phase of globalization, and how they might respond by modifying skill content and knowledge base, and/or the sources of legitimacy for their status. This section focuses on the impact of offshoring and digital technology on professional tasks. The next section analyses the impact of globalization on various models for legitimizing professionals' power and status in society.

A comparison with manufacturing highlights the challenges professionals face in responding to the offshoreability and routinization of jobs. Offshoring in manufacturing, in the form of sourcing components and contract assembly from around the world,

[2] Kleiner (2000) notes that occupational licensing affects approximately 18% of US workers, which is more than either the minimum wage (which affects 10% of workers) or unionization (covering no more than 15% of the workforce).

began in the middle of the twentieth century. But offshoring in services—particularly in professional services—is a relatively recent phenomenon, dating from the 1990s. Trading at a distance requires the routinization and standardization of tasks. In manufacturing, modern technology was applied to this end first before offshoring became prevalent (Sturgeon 2002; Gereffi et al. 2005; Thun 2010). In professional services, offshoring is on the rise at the same time that task routinization is spreading. In many cases, offshoring is a trigger to routinize tasks in professional jobs. In professional services, offshoring is equivalent to turning an employment contract into a sales contract (Simon 1951).[3] This contractual shift, to an extent, necessitates codifying things that had been implicit prior to the shift.

Types of Professional Services Offshored

Offshoring is the migration of productive economic activity and the associated employment from a home country—normally a developed nation such as the United States—to low-cost countries such as India and China. Every business firm (or public sector organization) makes two separate decisions, one concerning the boundary of the organization and the other concerning the location of its activities. Firstly, outsourcing involves the option to 'buy' rather than 'make' inputs or services in-house. Secondly, offshoring occurs when firms move production overseas. Offshoring may take the form of outsourcing to an independent supplier, or 'captive offshoring' undertaken by a subsidiary.

What types of professional services are offshored? One statistical indicator of offshoring is imports (i.e. payment for services rendered overseas). UNCTAD, in its 2011 World Investment Report, estimated that services outsourcing exports were in the range of \$90–100 billion in 2009, although the figure could be as high as \$380 billion if intra-firm trading was taken into account (UNCTAD 2011, 137). In 'computer and information services', the major exporters include the European Union (EU) (with Ireland taking a lead), the United States, India, and China, with India and China sustaining a trade surplus (indicating that they are net offshoring destinations) whilst the United States had a trade deficit of \$5.6 billion in 2009 (see Figure 28.1). In 'business, professional and technical services', by contrast, the United States and the EU have trade surpluses in many subcategories, including 'legal, accounting, management, and public relations' (see Figure 28.2).

The offshoring research network survey of 253 US companies at Duke University reveals that by 2006, the most common type of functional category offshored by US firms was information technology (IT) services, followed by product development and administrative services (see Figure 28.3) (Lewin et al. 2009). Using the global value chain framework, Gereffi and his colleagues have examined specific mechanisms

[3] I thank John Forth for this insight.

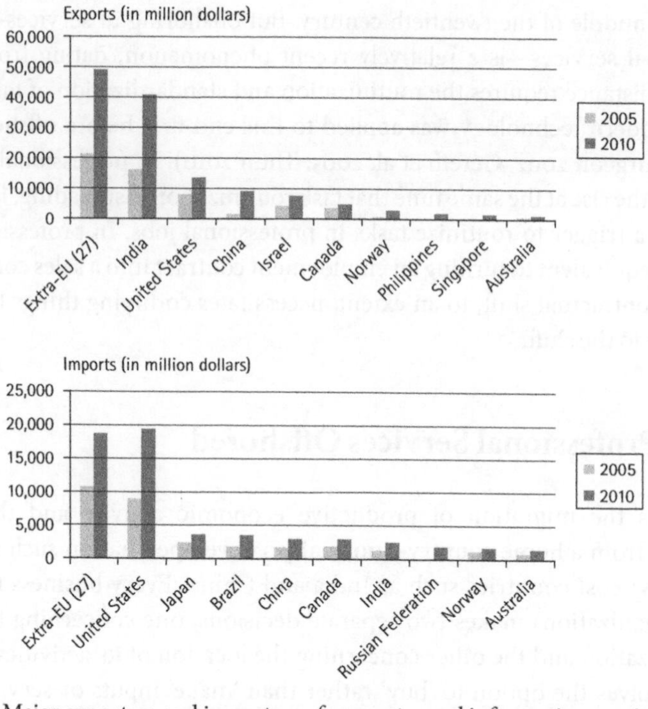

FIGURE 28.1 Major exporters and importers of computer and information services

Source: World Trade Organization.

for local firms to climb up the value chain in services, requiring higher levels of skills (Gereffi and Fernandez-Stark 2010). Starting with low value-added activities such as back office transactions and call centres, offshoring has expanded to include knowledge work in software programming, engineering design, R&D, radiology, accounting, human resources, financial modelling and analytics, market research, and legal support services (Piore 2004; Arora and Forman 2005; Sako 2006; Gospel and Sako 2010; Yu and Levy 2010).

Impact of Offshoring on Jobs

How many jobs are displaced by offshoring? McKinsey (2005) provided an estimate for service jobs in eight sectors (namely packaged software, IT services, banking, insurance, pharmaceutical, automotive, healthcare, and retailing).[4] The study calculated that 18.3 million jobs in these sectors could be done by people located anywhere in the world in 2003. They estimated that by 2008, 160 million jobs, or about 11% of total global service jobs, could be carried out remotely, but only 4.1 million of those would actually be offshored. This modest projected take-up was attributed

[4] A similar approach for IT jobs is taken by ACM (2006).

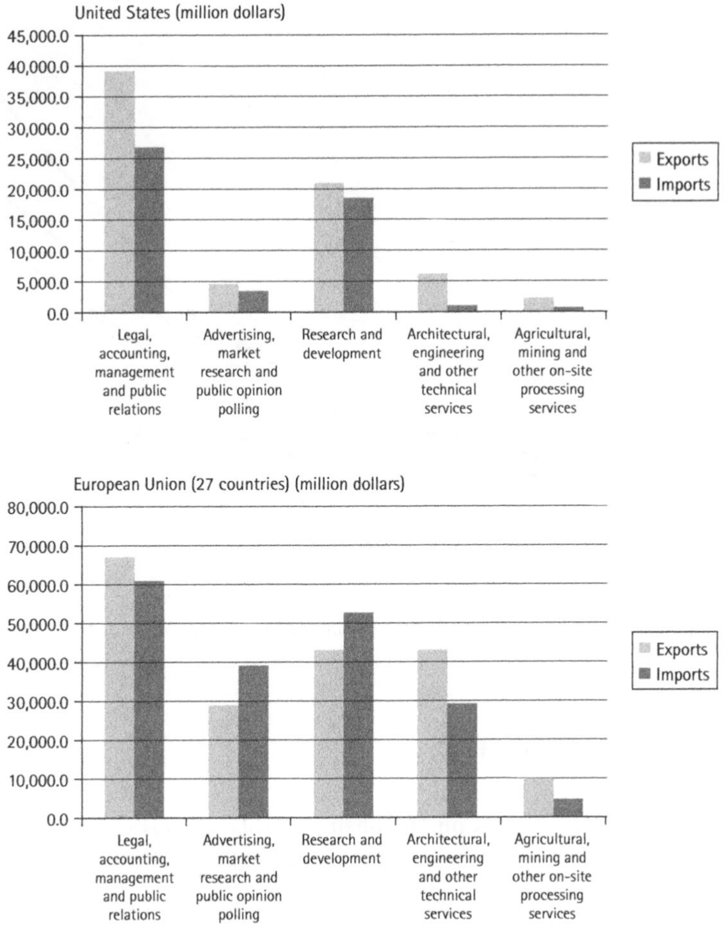

FIGURE 28.2 Trade in business, professional, and technical services 2010

Source: World Trade Organization.

to company-specific barriers rather than regulatory barriers. Such barriers were said to include operational issues, hostile management attitudes to offshoring, and insufficient scale.

The McKinsey study assumed that the nature of jobs that existed in the sectors they examined would remain unchanged as a result of offshoring. The same limitation is reflected in any analysis that is based on official employment statistics. However, the mix of tasks within jobs changes over time. There is evidence that such task changes within jobs have been quite large (Levy and Murnane 2004, 52). For example, in financial services, exceptions processing clerks in banks might have specialized in handling a single kind of exception, e.g. overdrafts. With digitization of checks, clerks' task scope expands to handle all types of exception—overdrafts, stop payments, address changes, etc. (Autor and Levy 2002). Thus, offshoring, just like digital technology, may bring about a change in the mix of tasks in jobs.

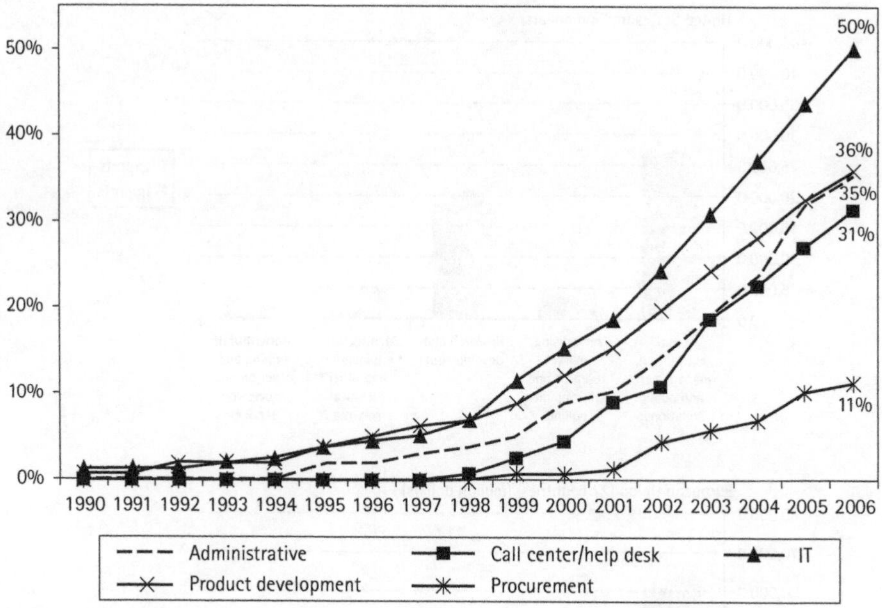

FIGURE 28.3 Cumulative percentage of firms initiating offshoring of functional category

Source: Lewin et al. (2009, figure 2).

Offshoring as Trade in Tasks

Building on this insight, studies on the offshoreability of jobs examine attributes of tasks and activities in jobs. Blinder (2006) began by making a distinction between 'personal services' requiring face-to-face contact and 'impersonal services' that do not and therefore can be delivered to, and from, remote locations.[5] He examined US occupational data (O*NET), and concluded that around 20% of all US employment in 2004 was potentially offshoreable. He also noted that both low-skilled jobs (e.g. hairdressing) and high-skilled jobs (e.g. court judges) require face-to-face interaction. Similarly, some low-skilled (e.g. typing) and high-skilled jobs (e.g. computer programming) may be in 'impersonal services'. Thus, jobs requiring higher skills are not necessarily more secure than those with lower skill content (Blinder 2009; Blinder and Krueger 2009). Other researchers use additional dimensions, such as an intense use of information and communication technology (ICT) and highly codifiable knowledge, to assess the offshoreability of jobs (Welsum and Vickery 2005; Jensen and Kletzer 2010).

These studies of offshoreability use a task-based model of jobs similar to the one originally developed to examine the impact of computer technology (Autor et al. 2003; Levy and Murnane 2004). They distinguish between routine (rule-based) and

[5] This distinction is, of course, not absolute and changes over time, as technology increasingly enables jobs previously requiring face-to-face interaction to take place via high bandwidth videoconferencing.

non-routine (pattern recognition) tasks. However, because routine tasks are in theory easier to computerize and offshore, the exact impact on offshoring is ambiguous. Either such tasks are offshored, or there is no need to offshore if machines onshore can substitute for the task more cheaply. More studies exist on the impact of technology on skills (and skill polarization) than on the impact of offshoring on skills and employment patterns. However, one relevant study by van Welsum and Reif (2006), using European data, finds that the import (equivalent to offshoring) of services has a negative impact on the employment share of potentially offshoreable occupations. Moreover, exports and ICT have a positive impact on the employment share of potentially offshoreable professional occupations.

Economists have also come to interpret offshoring as trade in tasks (Grossman and Rossi-Hansberg 2008). However, the notion of disaggregating jobs into tasks misses the point of what professional skills are about. Because people are not moving—international migration of professionals has not been very high with a few exceptions (e.g. nursing and engineering)—the discussion can be at the task-level. However, professionals, especially in sending countries, attempt to retain the whole occupational role without disaggregation into rule-based and pattern recognition tasks. For example, in the case of offshoring radiology services to India, Yu and Levy conclude that the world is not as flat for radiologists as it is for textile workers for two reasons (Yu and Levy 2010): firstly, tasks are on the whole not rule-based, but involve pattern recognition in CT, MRI, and PET scans that rely on extensive tacit knowledge and context. Secondly, there is asymmetry in the growth trajectory for sending and hosting countries. Sending countries such as the United States experience a loss of training grounds for future professionals who must start with simple tasks.

By contrast, for offshore-host countries such as India, simple tasks become the basis for building more complex skills and capabilities over time. For example, in legal services, graduates are hired by so-called legal process outsourcing (LPO) providers in offshore locations, initially to carry out simple tasks such as contract review and litigation support (Sako 2009). Whilst onshore law firms in the United States or Britain slow down or freeze the hiring of paralegals and entry-level associates, offshore LPO providers are hiring law and non-legal graduates to accumulate capabilities in higher-value-adding legal support work.

To conclude, it is difficult to single out offshoring as the primary driver for pressures to change professional skills and training, given other drivers such as digital technology. However, it is evident that the combination of offshoring and digital technology challenges the notion that whole professional roles would remain judgement-based. Consequently, some tasks in professional jobs are subjected to routinization and standardization, and are increasingly carried out by semi-professionals and non-professional graduates. Moreover, trade in tasks, due to a finer international division of labour, may lead to different trajectories of professional skill formation in emerging economies and advanced economies. Both offshore and onshore, potential opportunities exist for semi-professionals and non-professionals to take on tasks previously carried out exclusively by professionals.

Changing Models of Professionalization

Some professions (notably medicine and law) were born before the rise of corporate capitalism, whilst others (for example, engineering and marketing) came about in conjunction with the rise of the modern corporation. In the professionalization process, professions claimed legitimacy for their monopoly by connecting their power and status to the credentials attached to the mode of acquiring their knowledge, expertise, and skills. This last section takes stock of the link between the normative and cognitive dimensions of professions, and asks in what ways the mix of different types of professionals may change as the institutional model legitimizing professions changes over time.

In order to shed light on the extent to which professional skills and training may change in a more open economy, we need to examine the changing basis for legitimizing professional status and power over time. Historically, a dominant model of professions had been as callings for talented amateurs seeking to employ expertise to improve their station in life. Late nineteenth century Victorian England saw a shift to a more formal 'social trusteeship' model based on the creation of an orderly career grounded in higher education. Looking into the future, arguably, we are in the midst of experiencing another transition in the institutional model for legitimizing professions due to at least three factors: greater knowledge specialization, consumerism, and commercialism (Freidson 2001; Paterson 2012; Scott 2008). These factors are only obliquely related to globalization per se.

Firstly, as the knowledge base mastered by each type of professional has expanded, there is an inevitable drive towards differentiation and compartmentalization of expertise (Muzio and Ackroyd 2005). With 25 board-certified specialisms (encompassing over 125 sub-specialisms) for US physicians (Scott 2008), and 54 specialisms for lawyers in England and Wales, the greater division of labour within professions has also resulted in the proliferation of sub-professionals (e.g. ostepopaths and chiropractors in healthcare, paralegals and contract specialists in corporate law). There is also pressure to routinize and standardize professional tasks. Just like for craft skills a century ago, the ghost of Fredrick Taylor is in the air to blow the 'mysteries' out of professional work.

Secondly, societal norms espousing a service orientation are undergoing changes, from a public trusteeship model to a narrower conception of service based on expertise. The deregulation of legal services market in the United Kingdom, with the enactment of the Legal Services Act, is based on a logic that relies more on consumer power and market-based tests to verify the quality of professional services. In this world of 'consumerism', professionals listen to clients about what they want in a more literal sense, rather than act as custodians of clients' interest.

Last but not least, even independent professionals who value autonomy and collegial controls have come to rely more on hierarchical and managerial controls within large professional service firms as they grow in size. For example, we are seeing a major shift in the United States, accelerated by the Healthcare Reform Act, for doctors to go from self-employed professionals with their own practices to employees of large hospitals or healthcare systems. Similarly, in other areas, top-ranking law firms, accounting firms, and management consultancies employ several thousand. But most of these firms are still managed as limited liability partnerships, pushing to the limit the traditional authority structure of professional organizations, in which experts constitute the line (main authority) and managers the staff (Etzioni 1959).

Each of these three forces affects the four types of professionals identified earlier in a different way. By all accounts, organizational professionals already endorse knowledge specialization, consumerism, and commercialism. By contrast, independent professionals need to respond by readjusting their organizational logic. One insightful way of seeing professionalism is offered by Paterson who regards it as akin to 'a tacit concordat with the state by which in return for high status, reasonable rewards, limited competition (including monopolies) and self-regulation they would deliver expertise, a service ethic ... and public protection' (Paterson 2012, 3). However, this concordat requires renegotiation for independent professionals, as the state has become less willing to grant professional privileges and is keener to introduce market principles to improve the quality of professional services.

To conclude, different ideas at different times have shaped the incorporation of professionals by the state and business organizations. Will these ideas converge with international migration, international trade, and trade agreements in professional services? The three pressures appear to suggest a slow convergence of professionals across nations.[6] But professionals, with their role as institutional agents (Scott 2008), are unlikely to give up their privileges easily. The sheer fact that the tacit concordat remains with the national state implies that unless states get together to agree on mutual recognition or harmonization, convergence would not result from market mechanisms alone. For now, state-sponsored professionals would find it more difficult than other types to cross national borders. Occupational licensing, which involves the state as well as self-regulating professional associations, is also at the national (or sub-national state) level, and contributes to the immobility of professional labour across national borders. By contrast, independent professionals in liberal economies might potentially bypass the state to claim occupational closure at supra-national levels.

Conclusions

Research on professional skills and training has a track record in the sociology of professions and labour economics, but has been largely ignored thus far in the comparative

[6] Simultaneously, there is potential for divergence within professions, as the three forces reinforce star culture and inequality, with a small number of top lawyers commanding huge earnings whilst the average earnings fall sharply, or top professors becoming superstars whilst the average academic sees a move away from tenured employment.

analysis of political economies. The latter has focused on intermediate skills particularly in export-oriented manufacturing sectors, crucial to determining the international competitiveness of nations. This chapter demonstrated that a similar logic has begun to apply to hitherto non-tradeable service jobs in knowledge-intensive professional sectors. The diffusion of global value chains from agriculture and manufacturing to services requires a reconceptualization in the framework for analysing professional skill formation in a comparative manner.

Whilst some researchers discuss and analyse the impact of offshoring in terms of the migration of jobs from one place to another, what is moving across national borders is not the whole job but tasks within professional jobs. This has implications for the future of professions, which are facing the dual challenges of greater division of labour and offshoring. This simultaneity of disruptive forces for professional jobs stands in contrast to manufacturing jobs, which were divided and standardized first before offshoring became prevalent.

Moreover, different types of professionals—independent, state-sponsored, organizational, and knowledge-based—who dominate in different political economies have distinctive challenges, as the models for legitimizing professions change over time. The pressures for greater specialization, consumerism, and commercialism exist to a varying degree in some political economies, with LMEs taking a lead to undermine the traditional sources legitimizing professionals.

Given such trajectories, professional skills formation will continue to be profoundly shaped by a mix of institutions including the state, markets, and intermediate associations (including professional associations) in national political economies. A number of fruitful avenues for further research exist.

(a) Will the division of labour in professional work follow the industrial route, leading to more fragmented and routinized tasks that undermine control by professions? What is the impact of digital technology in making professional tasks more 'rule-based', and to what extent does technology continue to complement professionals' judgement-based 'pattern recognition' work?

(b) How are professional skills packaged and repackaged into professional roles as they appear in different contexts including large business corporations, professional services firms, entrepreneurial start-ups, the eco-system or cluster of firms, and in public sector organizations? Which context is most conducive to professionalizing new sets of skills?

(c) What is the impact of the routinization and repackaging of professional tasks on the status and income of professionals? If we require far fewer and only senior professionals, how will the next generation of professionals develop their core capabilities if the simpler tasks they had trained on are now automated or offshored?

(d) What is the relation between offshoring and international migration of professionals? Which types of professionals are most mobile, and which types of professionals are subjected most to offshoring? In what ways might digital technology lower national barriers to the globalization of professional labour market, given that professional certification and licensing remain at the national level?

(e) What is the impact of offshoring on the professional skill formation in host countries many of which are emerging markets? How will the huge growth in supply of graduates in emerging economies, like China, India, and Singapore, affect the global distribution of professional work? Would there be a different role of the state and associations in balancing the benefits of occupational licensing and of certification to ensure international relevance and mobility?

(f) What are the historical origins of national variations in professional skill formation and their social status? What factors have made lower level occupations move up, and others move down, the social ladder, and in what ways do these factors differ from country to country?

References

Abbott, A. (1988) *The System of Professions: An Essay on the Division of Expert Labor*, Chicago: The University of Chicago Press.

ACM (2006) *Globalization and Offshoring of Software: A Report of the ACM Job Migration Task Force*, New York: Association of Computing Machinery.

Adler, P. S., Kwon, S.-W., and Heckscher, C. (2008) 'Professional Work: The Emergence of Collaborative Community', *Organization Science*, 19(2): 359–376.

Arora, A., and Forman, C. (2005) 'Proximity and Software Programming: IT Outsourcing and the Local Market', Sloan Industry Studies Working Paper WP-2005-6.

Autor, D. H., and Levy, F. (2002) 'Upstairs, Downstairs: Computers and Skills on Two Floors of a Large Bank', *Industrial and Labour Relations Review*, LV: 432–447.

Autor, D. H., Levy, F., and Murnane, R. J. (2003) 'The Skill Content of Recent Technological Change: An Empirical Exploration', *Quarterly Journal of Economics*, November: 1279–1333.

Blinder, A. S. (2009) 'How Many US Jobs Might Be Offshoreable? *World* Economics, 10(2): 41–78.

Blinder, A. S., and Krueger, A. B. (2009) 'Alternative Measures of Offshorability: A Survey Approach', NBER Working Paper 15287, Cambridge, MA: National Bureau of Economic Research.

Brown, P., Lauder, H., and Ashton, D. (2011) *The Global Auction: The Broken Promises of Education, Jobs, and Incomes*, Oxford: Oxford University Press.

Busemeyer, M. R., and Trampusch, C. (2012) *The Political Economy of Collective Skill Formation*, Oxford: Oxford University Press.

Carr-Saunders, A. M., and Wilson, P. A. (1933) (1964) *The Professions*, 2nd ed., London: Frank Cass & Co.

Crouch, C., Finegold, D., and Sako, M. (1999) *Are Skills the Answer? The Political Economy of Skill Creation in Advanced Industrial Countrie*, Oxford: Oxford University Press.

Dore, R. P., and Sako, M. (1989) *How the Japanese Learn to Work*, London: Routledge.

Etzioni, A. (1959) 'Authority Structure and Organizational Effectiveness', *Administrative Science Quarterly*, 4(1): 43–67.

Finegold, D., and Soskice, D. (1988) 'The Failure of Training in Britain: Analysis and Prescription', *Oxford Review of Economic Policy*, 4(3): 21–53.

Forth, J., Bryson, A., Humphris, A., Koumenta, M., and Kleiner, M. (2011) *A Review of Occupational Regulation and its Impact*, London: UK Commission for Employment and Skills.

Freidson, E. (2001) *Professionalism: The Third Logic*, Cambridge: Polity Press.

Friedman, M., and Kuznets, S. (1954) *Income from Independent Professional Practice*, Cambridge, MA: National Bureau of Economic Research.

Galanter, M., and Henderson, W. (2008) 'The Elastic Tournament: A Second Transformation of the Big Law Firm', *Stanford Law Review*, 60(6): 1867–1929.

Galanter, M., and Palay, T. M. (1990) 'Why the Big Get Bigger: The Promotion-to-partner Tournament and the Growth of Large Law Firms', *Virginia Law Review*, 76(4): 747–811.

Gereffi, G., and Fernandez-Stark, K. (2010) 'The Offshore Services Value Chain: Developing Countries and the Crisis', Policy Resarch Working Paper 5262, The World Bank, Washington, DC.

Gereffi, G., Humphrey, J., and Sturgeon, T. (2005) 'The Governance of Global Value Chains', *Review of International Political Economy*, 12(1): 78–104.

Gilson, R. J., and Mnookin, R. H. (1985) 'Sharing Among the Human Capitalists: An Economic Inquiry into the Corporate Law Firm and How Partners Split Profits', *Stanford Law Review*, 37(2): 313–392.

Gospel, H., and Sako, M. (2010) 'Unbundling of Corporate Functions: The Evolution of Shared Services and Outsourcing in Human Resource Management', *Industrial and Corporate Change*, March: 1–30.

Gouldner, A. W. (1957) 'Cosmopolitans and Locals: Ttoward an Analysis of Latent Social Roles—I', Administrative *Science Quarterly*, 2(3): 281–306.

Greenwood, R., Li, S. X., Prakash, R., and Deephouse, D. L. (2005) 'Reputation, Diversification, and Organizational Explanations of Performance in Professional Service Firms', *Organization Science*, 16(6): 661–673.

Grossman, G., and Rossi-Hansberg, E. (2008) 'Trading Tasks: A Simple Theory of Offshoring', *American Economic Review*, 98(5): 1978–1997.

Hall, P., and Soskice, D. (eds) (2001) *Varieties of Capitalism*, Oxford: Oxford University Press.

Iverson, T. (2005) *Capitalism, Democracy, and Welfare*, Cambridge: Cambridge University Press.

Jensen, J. B., and Kletzer, L. G. (2010) 'Measuring Tradable Services and the Task Content of Offshorable Services Jobs', in K. G. Abraham, J. R. Spletzer, and M. Harper (eds), *Labour in the New Economy*, Chicago: Chicago University Press: 309–335.

Khurana, R. (2007) *From Higher Aims to Hired Hands*, Princeton, NJ: Princeton University Press.

Kleiner, M. M. (2000) 'Occupational licensing', *Journal of Economic Perspectives*, 14(4): 189–202.

Kleiner, M. M. (2006) *Licensing Occupations: Ensuring Quality or Restricting Competition?*, Kalamazoo: W. E. Upjohn Institute.

Krause, E. A. (1996) *Death of the Guilds: Professions, States, and the Advance of Capitalism, 1930 to the* Present, New Haven: Yale University Press.

Larson, M. S. (1977) *The Rise of Professionalism: A Sociological Analysis*, Berkeley: University of California Press.

Levy, F., and Murnane, R. J. (2004) *The New Division of Labour: How Computers are Creating the Next* Job *Market*, Princeton, NJ: Princeton University Press.

Lewin, A. Y., Massini, S., and Peeters, C. (2009) 'Why are Companies Offshoring Innovation? The Emerging Global Race for Talent', *Journal of International Business Studies*, 40: 901–925.
Mason, G., and Nohara, H. (2010) 'How Well-rewarded is Inter-Firm Mobility in the Labour Market for Scientists and Engineers? New Evidence from the UK and France', *Economics of Innovation and New Technology*, 19(5): 459–480.
Mills, C. W. 1951 (2002) *White Collar: The American Middle Classes*, New York: Oxford University Press.
Muzio, D., and Ackroyd, S. (2005) 'On the Consequences of Defensive Professionalism: Recent Changes in the Legal Labour Process', *Journal of Law and Society*, 32(4): 615–642.
Osterman, P. (ed) (1984) *Internal Labor Market*, Cambridge, MA: MIT Press.
Parsons, T. (1939) 'The Professions and Social Structure', *Social Forces*, 17: 457–467.
Paterson, A. (2012) *Lawyers and the Public Good: Democracy in Action?* Cambridge: Cambridge University Press.
Piore, M. (2004) 'The Limits of the Division of Labour in Design and the Prospects for Off-Shore Software Development in Mexico', MIT Working Paper, Cambridge, MA.
Rebitzer, J. B., and Taylor, L. J. (2007) 'When Knowledge is an Asset: Explaining the Organizational Structure of Large Law Firms', *Journal of Labour Economics*, 25(2): 201–229.
Reed, M. I. (1996) 'Expert Power and Control in Late Modernity: An Empirical Review and Theoretical Synthesis', *Organization Studies*, 17(4): 573–597.
Riain, S. O. (2011) 'Human Capital Formation Regimes: States, Markets, and Human Capital in an Era of Globalization', in A. Burton-Jones, and J. C. Spender (eds), *The Oxford Handbook of Human Capital*, New York: Oxford University Press: 588–617.
Sako, M. (2006) 'Outsourcing and Offshoring: Implications for Productivity of Business Services', *Oxford Review of Economic Policy*, 22(4): 499–512.
Sako, M. (2009) 'Globalization of Knowledge-intensive Professional Services', *Communications of the ACM*, 52(7): 31–33.
Sako, M. (2013) 'Professionals between Market and Hierarchy: A Comparative Political Economy Perspective', *Socio-Economic Review*, 11: 1–28.
Scott, W. R. (2008) 'Lords of the Dance: Professionals as Institutional Agents', *Organization Studies*, 29(2): 219–238.
Simon, H. A. (1951) 'A Formal Theory of the Employment Relationship', *Econometrica*, 19(3): 293–305.
Streeck, W. (2012) Skills and Politics: General and Specific', in M. R. Busemeyer and C. Trampusch (eds), *The Political Economy of Collective Skill Formation*, Oxford: Oxford University Press: 317–352.
Streeck, W. and Yamamura, K. (eds) (2001) *The Origins of Nonliberal Capitalism: Germany and Japan*, Ithaca, NY: Cornell University Press.
Sturgeon, T. J. (2002) 'Modular Production Networks: A New American Model of Industrial Organization', *Industrial and Corporate Change*, 11(3): 451–496.
Svensson, L. G. and Evetts, J. (eds) (2010) *Sociology of Professions: Continental and Anglo-Saxon Traditions*, Gotenborg: Bokforlaget Daidalos AB.
Thelen, K. (2004) *How Institutions Evolve: The Political Economy of Skills in Comparative Historical Perspective*, New York: Cambridge University Press.
Thelen, K. (2012) 'Foreward', in M. R. Busemeyer and C. Trampusch (eds.), *The Political Economy of Collective Skill Formation*, Oxford: Oxford University Press.
Thun, E. (2010) 'The Globalization of Production', in S. Ravenhill (ed), *Global Political Economy*, New York: Oxford University Press.

UNCTAD (2011) *World Investment Report: Non-equity Modes of Production and Development*, New York: United Nations Conference on Trade and Development.

Welsum, D. V. and Vickery, G. (2005) 'Potential Offshoring of ICT-Intensive Using Occupations', Digital Economy Papers no. 91, Paris: Organisation for Economic Co-operation and Development.

Wilensky, H. L. (1964) 'Professionalization of Everyone?', *American Journal of Sociology*, 70(2): 137–158.

Yu, K.-H., and Levy, F. (2010) 'Offshoring Professional Services: Institutions and Professional Control', *British Journal of Industrial Relations*, 48(4): 758–783.

CHAPTER 29

SKILLS AND TRAINING FOR THE OLDER POPULATION

Training the New Work Generation

WENDY LORETTO, CHRIS PHILLIPSON, AND SARAH VICKERSTAFF

Introduction

Against a backdrop of population ageing and its attendant problems of workforce shortages and economic burdens, more people are working into later life across many industrialized countries. Despite this increase, there is concern that workplace training and skills development do not mirror the increase in employment figures (Phillipson and Smith 2005). This chapter provides a focus on older-worker training, reviewing the experience of the over-50s in work, those unemployed but actively seeking work, and those on the way towards or in retirement. The empirical focus is on the UK experience, but this is placed in an international context by drawing on literature and studies from other nations so as to consider broader trends, problems, and possibilities.

The chapter commences with a brief overview of older-worker employment and training for those in employment, which shows clear and sustained gaps in training. The discussion then explores why these gaps matter and why they exist. It then tests some of these ideas using the latest Workplace Employee Relations Survey data from the United Kingdom. The focus subsequently moves to those older workers who are unemployed but would like to work, drawing upon a recent UK survey of over-50s job-seekers. Attention is then given to the role of education and training for over-50s who may want to improve their job prospects, take a 'bridge job' (part-time employment / self-employment) to full retirement, volunteer, or simply keep active through learning in retirement. The chapter concludes by assessing policy implications for the future of training for this new work-generation.

Overview of Older-Worker Employment and Training

Figures provided by the OECD from 34 industrial countries show a marked rise in employment rates of people aged 50–64 (the most common definition of 'older' workers), from 55.6% in 2001 to 61.2% in 2011 (OECD 2013). Beneath this average there is a large variation: only 54.7% of over 50s in France are in employment, compared to 65.1% in the United States and 77.3% in Sweden. The United Kingdom reported a figure above the OECD average, rising from 62.0% in 2001 to 65% in 2011 (although it should be noted that all but 0.5% of this increase happened before 2005). Additionally, in many countries state pension ages are rising, and it is expected that more people will continue to work or seek work *after* the age of 65 (OECD 2011). Employment rates past age 65 vary considerably across countries, with high rates of self-employment playing a major part in some countries such as Turkey and Portugal. Discounting self-employment, it is the Anglo Saxon and Scandinavian countries that have the highest rates of employment past 65 (Lain and Vickerstaff 2014).

It has been well established that older workers are less likely than their younger counterparts to receive training at work and training duration is shorter (Schuller and Watson 2009; Carmichael and Ercolani 2012), although there is some indication that the gap is closing (Urwin 2004; Felstead 2009; Canduela et al. 2012). The OECD's figures show that in both absolute and relative terms older-worker participation in training across their 34 member counties has increased. Regarding workers aged 55–64, data show that the percentage of those employed who participated in training rose from 6.6% in 2001 to 9.4% a decade later. Compared to the training participation of workers aged 25–54, this represents a rise of 0.44: 1 to 0.57: 1. The same figures show a closing gap for UK older workers (ratio increased from 0.6: 1 to 0.66: 1) but show a decline in absolute figures: only 11.6% of older employed people participated in training in 2011 compared to 15% in 2001 (and 23.7% in 2005). This would suggest that the provision of training has decreased for the whole UK workforce, regardless of age and that the over 55s may have been marginally less affected by this than their younger colleagues. Nevertheless, it remains clear that older workers are far less likely to receive training.

The limited involvement of older workers in training needs to be placed in the context of rapidly ageing populations across the OECD countries. Mature industrial economies will face increased pressures to support larger proportions of older and especially very elderly people. Delaying retirement is now viewed—across all OECD countries—as a means of mitigating the effects of worsening demographic ratios whilst increasing financial resources for later life. In its 2006 report, *Live Longer, Work Longer*, arising from a review of older-worker employment across 21 countries, the OECD concluded that weak employability was one of the major barriers to increasing employment rates of the over-50s. This weaker employability was reflected in a lower rate of tertiary education and lower participation in training. It thus argued that improving access to, and provision of, training for this age group would aid in helping unemployed older workers get back into employment and those in employment to be productive for longer. Longitudinal analysis from the US (Leppel et al. 2012) indicates that availability and quality of job-related training directly affects job satisfaction of older workers (although as they did not conduct an age comparison, it may be that job training affects satisfaction, regardless of age). Other arguments in favour of promoting training in later working life include encouraging the intergenerational transfer of skills, whereby older employees can pass on their skills and experience to younger colleagues (Felstead 2010). Furthermore, Phillipson (2013) has argued that supporting education and training of older workers will have a significant impact on their health and wellbeing, which may well bring benefits beyond employment, extending into a healthier retirement. Such wider benefits have been reflected in the emphasis on active ageing and are reinforced in the UK by government policy (see e.g. HM Government 2010).

Why Do Gaps Exist?

Reasons put forward to explain the lower incidence of training for older workers are varied. Some emphasize the personal circumstances and attitudes of the older employees themselves, whilst others focus more on the employers' position. The first group of reasons includes lack of confidence, lower 'basic' skills, health-related barriers, and restrictions arising from caring requirements outside of work (for a review, see Canduela et al. 2012). Research conducted amongst professional workers in Canada (Fenwick 2012a) suggested that as employees age they become more strategic in what learning they engage in and are more discerning about which training opportunities to participate in. On the other hand, a further body of work (e.g. Humphrey et al. 2003 and Felstead 2010) has shown that employers are less likely to encourage training amongst older workers, especially men (Canduela et al. 2012). This tendency to overlook older workers may arise from discriminatory attitudes (Loretto and White 2006) or because of the nature of the jobs they do (CIPD 2008). Occupation sector also appears to be influential: Schuller and Watson (2009) highlight the fact that working in the public sector gives a significant boost to accessing some form of training. Taking the proportion of people in employment aged 25 to retirement who received some form of training in the three months prior to interview, over 40% of public sector workers participated compared with 21% of those in the private sector. This is a highly significant contrast, given the projected decline in public sector employment, which has potentially serious consequences for access to training for older workers and other workers. Limited training may also be a feature of the so-called bridge jobs into which an increasingly large proportion move prior to eventual retirement. Cahill et al.'s (2006, 523) research using data from the US Health and Retirement Study found that the majority of older Americans leaving full-time career employment (about 60% of those leaving a full-time career job after 50 and about 53% of those leaving after the age of 55) moved first to a bridge job rather than directly out of the labour force. Analysis of the British Household Panel Survey, examining job movements amongst men in their 50s, indicated around one in five had spells of part-time, bridging forms of employment (Phillipson 2002). Yet these jobs tend to be concentrated in poorly paid work with limited opportunities for training or re-training to any significant degree (Vickerstaff et al. 2007; see further later in this chapter).

In their employer case studies, McNair et al. (2007) found that the decline of training with age may arise from 'collusion' between employer and employee, both parties tacitly agreeing to a winding down. The reluctance to invest in training for older employees appears to exist even when approaches to older workers are otherwise positive, and may reflect employers' concerns over rates of return of investment in training (Mayhew et al. 2008). Van Dalen et al. (2009) noted that although UK employers reported more positive attitudes to older workers than did those from the other countries, it was striking that the majority felt they were not responsible for lifelong learning. This may be a very short-sighted approach: more than one third of respondents in a survey of Belgian workers aged 40 and over claimed that extra training would influence them to postpone retirement (Buyens et al. 2009, 110). Furthermore, Fourage and Schils's (2009) analysis of 13 European countries indicated a positive association between provision of training and extending working lives.

It is also useful to deconstruct what we mean by training and development and the range of activities typically encompassed by the terms. Kooji and colleagues (2012) make the point that work motivations may change with age and thus the impact of different human resource (HR) management policies may similarly have differential impacts by age. They distinguish between two bundles of HR policies: those that seek to develop and improve performance such as training, and HR practices that are concerned to maintain performance such as appraisal and career management. In their empirical study they found that the associations between development practices and wellbeing weakened with age, whereas the relationship of maintenance practices with wellbeing increased with age. This suggests that we should avoid looking narrowly at the impact of access to training for older workers, but rather look more broadly at how their later-life careers are managed, whether they have access to meaningful appraisal and career advice. The picture here mirrors the position with regard to training: CIPD research reveals that older workers are also less likely to have informal conversations with their manager about their job or formal performance appraisals than prime-age workers (CIPD 2011). This suggests that there may also be an important role for mid- or later-life career guidance independent of the work context for those contemplating a change of direction. McNair (2010, 37) has suggested that governments should:

> create opportunities for career review for people in their late 40s, to enable them to plan for the last 15–20 years of working life, to raise skills levels or to change direction while it is still possible. This would encourage people to see work in their 50s as a continuing opportunity for progression and change, rather than a matter of 'serving out one's time.'

Theoretical Perspectives on Education and Training

The above findings would suggest that training and managing older workers has been a marginal area for employers over the past decade—despite policy moves highlighting the desirability of extending working life. Understanding the reasons for this has been complicated by the limited application of theoretical frameworks available to inform analysis in what has become a key area of public policy. Recommendations, however, about the need to encourage training amongst older workers will be restricted without theoretical insights about their role in the labour market. In this context there is a particular need for approaches that locate individual decision-making both within life-course transitions as well as the broader political and economic institutions underpinning later life (Phillipson 2013). The range of theoretical models that might be drawn upon include: human capital theory (Becke 1964), productive ageing theory (Bass and Caro 2001), life-course theory (e.g. Pillemer et al. 2000), organizational perspectives (e.g. Sennett 2006) and theories associated with the analysis of risk and 'individualization' (Vickerstaff and Cox 2005; Baars et al. 2013).

Human capital theory, as put forward by Becker (1964), has been a prominent approach from neo-classical economics. It argues that the returns to human capital investments are lower for older workers because productivity and wage gains are limited by impending retirement; or it may be the case that the job is not changing and hence established workers already have the appropriate skills. In either case, older workers are viewed as less likely to have an incentive to train and for employers to invest in their training. Lower training rates amongst older workers are thus consistent with arguments about the declining utility of investing in people coming towards the end of their work career.

The productive ageing approach has been the most explicit in theorizing about obstacles to continuing employment, with a particular focus on examining evidence for discrimination or 'institutionalized ageism'. This idea draws upon 'cultural lag' theory (Riley and Riley 1994) to explain the limited involvement of older people in the workplace. This theory suggests that whilst retirement was originally premised on a surplus of labour, employing institutions may be slow to adapt workplace practices to the reality of an ageing workforce. This model would also suggest that older workers may be viewed (as in human capital theory) as too costly to train, but also may encounter discrimination in respect of access to training and career management, which may create disincentives and limited opportunities.

Pillemer et al. (2000) put forward a life-course model that views the move from work to retirement as a process rather than a single or one-off event. They extend this model with the notion of 'linked lives' stretching across time and generations. Accordingly, 'retirement, family roles, community participation, and occupational careers are typically examined exclusive of other social roles and each other. What we do not know is how work and family experiences shape life after retirement' (2000, 76). Or to put this another way: how do attitudes towards retirement and the various events surrounding the transition from work to retirement influence approaches to later-life working and training in particular. Viewing training within a life-course perspective may be especially helpful for understanding variations in attitudes amongst employers and employees alike.

The possibility of later-life working will itself be influenced by a variety of organizational factors, not least the level of support provided within the work environment. Here, Ekerdt (2010, 74) poses the question: 'has the labour market become more welcoming to older workers, accommodating them in ways that could sustain an expansion in employment in later life'. The evidence would suggest in fact only limited movement in practical steps assists the extension of working life. Sennett (2006) argues that the collapse of the work-based bureaucracies associated with what he defines as 'social capitalism' has fostered a rise in 'precarious' and 'insecure employment', carrying negative implications for supporting older people in the workplace. In terms of the work–retirement transition, a number of research findings suggest the emergence of a more fragmented life-course, with the expansion of bridge jobs being an illustration of this development.

More generally, 'bridging' and related forms of employment might be seen as part of the shift from the highly bureaucratized transition from work to retirement characteristic of the 1950s and 1960s, as contrasted with the more 'individualized', negotiated form that developed over the course of the 1990s and 2000s (Vickerstaff and Cox 2005; Baars et al. 2013). On the one hand, this development suggested a new type of ageing—reflected in the idea of the 'third age with those moving from work to retirement 'richer, better educated and more culturally active ... than previous cohorts of retirees' (Gilleard and Higgs 2005, 14). On the other hand, there is evidence for increased inequality, with the scope for individual agency bounded or limited by extensive inequality within birth cohorts (Phillipson 2013). Vickerstaff and Cox (2005, 92) concluded that the consequences of individualization for many older workers was 'less to increase ... the range of alternatives and choices over when and how to retire and more to enlarge the risks they had to cope with'.

Older workers, based on some of these theoretical approaches, would appear to have been affected by a variety of structural, technological, and organizational forces placing constraints on training and career opportunities within the workplace. To investigate this further, the next section of this chapter examines evidence from the UK Workplace Employee Relations Study.

Training in the Workplace: Evidence from the United Kingdom

The Workplace Employment Relations Study (WERS) series is the most definitive and influential study of employment relations in Great Britain and one of the richest longitudinal datasets for analysing workplace trends in the world. The latest study was conducted in 2011 and collected data from nearly 3,000 organizations, covering both large and small workplaces across the private and public sectors. It comprises a series of linked studies, collecting information from managers, employee representatives, and a selection of employees. It is highly influential, as findings from previous waves of the study have been used to inform government policy on various aspects of workplace policy and practice. The data are publicly available via the UK data archive and the analysis represented here draws mainly on the employee survey, with appropriate weighting and links to the management survey. (Further statistical and technical details of all the analyses are available from the authors.) The employee survey included questions about amount of training over the previous year, satisfaction with training and skills development: the following findings are based on the 21,824 respondents who supplied their age details: of these, 30% (7,042) were aged 50 or over.

Quantity of Training

The headline figures on quantity of training in Table 29.1 support findings from previous work: a higher proportion of older workers received no training over the past year and a smaller proportion received five or more days of training. A regression model was constructed to control for the main factors that have previously been shown to affect participation in training and which may vary with age: educational attainment; nature of employment (full-time versus part-time and temporary versus permanent, length of service); trade union membership; caring responsibilities; nature of employer (workplace size and sector); and occupation (see Canduela et al. 2012 for a review). Whilst each of these had their own relationship with training, the age effect still persisted: incidence of training declined with length of service, and certain occupational groups—namely managers, professionals, and those in caring, leisure, and other services—were markedly more likely to have received training in the previous year. That is, the lower incidence of training amongst over 50s cannot be entirely accounted for either by the roles they occupy or the length of time they have occupied them.

Table 29.1 Number of days' training received in previous year

Number of days' training	Under 50	50 and over
None	29.2	38.1
<1 day	12.8	12.7
1 - <2	17.2	16.8
2 - <5	23.2	20.5
5 - <10	10.5	8.0
10+	7.0	3.9
	100%	100%

Satisfaction with Training

Despite these clear age differences, the older workers were more satisfied than their younger counterparts with whatever training they had received—56% reported they were satisfied or very satisfied, compared to 53% of under 50s. This overall figure is broken down by amount of training received in Figure 29.1, which shows the biggest difference amongst those employees who had received less than one day's training in the previous year: nearly 10% more of the over-50s in that group said they were satisfied or very satisfied with the training they received.

As regards the opportunities to develop skills on the job, exactly equal proportions (53%) of each age group reported they were satisfied or very satisfied. When this was broken down by number of training days received, a similar pattern to the above was seen, with an even bigger difference amongst those who had received less than one day's training (see Figure 29.2).

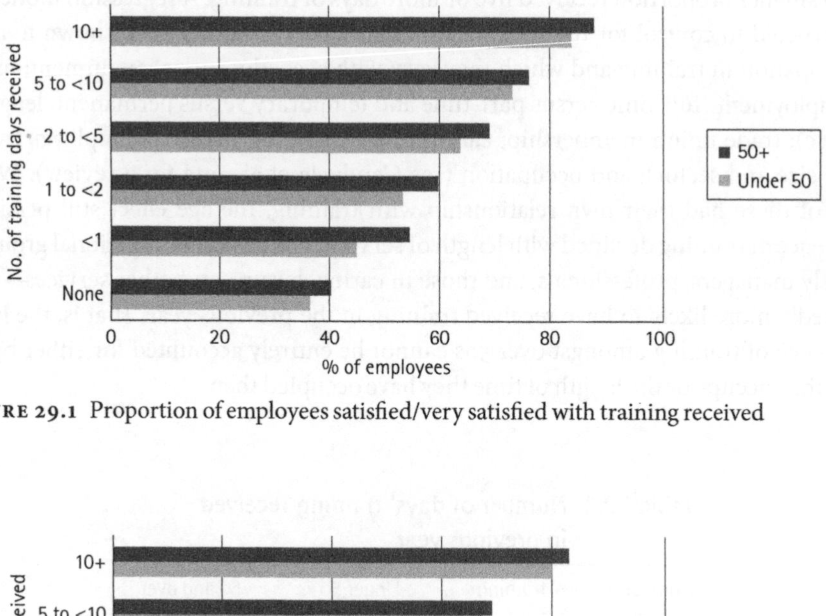

FIGURE 29.1 Proportion of employees satisfied/very satisfied with training received

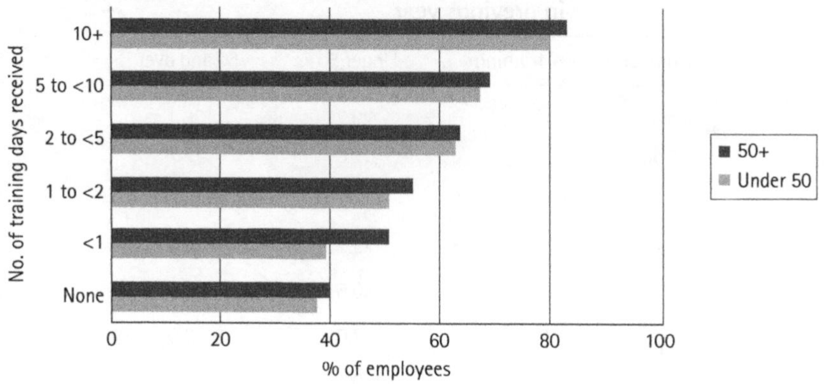

FIGURE 29.2 Proportion of employees satisfied/very satisfied with development opportunities

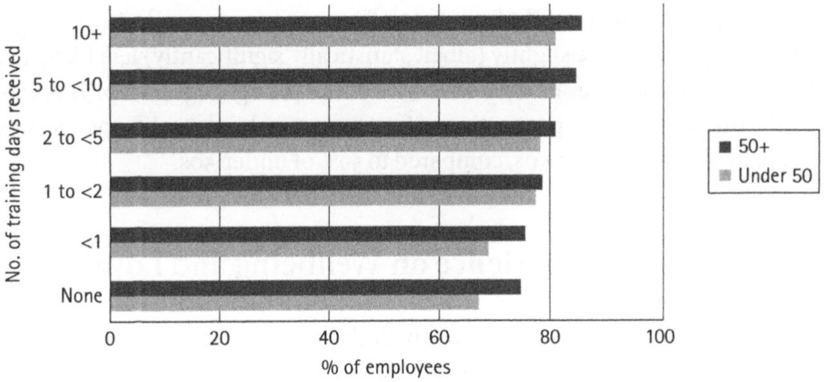

FIGURE 29.3 Proportion of employees satisfied/very satisfied with the work itself

The question arising is the extent to which these patterns merely reflect an overall higher job satisfaction rate amongst older employers. Previous research (Clark et al. 1996) has indicated that job satisfaction is U-shaped, with higher levels at the either end of the working-life course. To test this, it is interesting to examine employees' attitudes towards the work itself. Here, once again, overall satisfaction rates were higher amongst the over-50s (78% as opposed to 74% of under-50s) with the most substantial differences occurring between the subgroups who had no or minimal training (Figure 29.3). Thus it would appear that the older workers were more generally satisfied than their younger colleagues, but the amount of training received has more of an impact on satisfaction with training, development, and overall job satisfaction for the under-50s. This differential is most marked where training is absent or minimal.

Sufficiency of Skills

In terms of matching skills to jobs, a significant minority (44%) of both older and younger workers felt that their work skills were a good match for their present job, and less than 1% of each group felt under-skilled. However, what was notable was that the over-50s were more likely to say that their skills were much higher than needed for their present job—21% said this, compared to 18% of the younger respondents. There was no discernible relationship for either age group between the extent of match between skills and job requirements and amount of training received in the previous year.

Employer Provision and Encouragement

Younger employees (11.5%) reported that access to training in their workplace had been restricted as a result of the most recent recession. This was higher than the proportion (just under 9%) of older employees. All employees were asked the extent to which they thought managers in their workplace generally encouraged people to develop their skills. Older employees were slightly (albeit statistically significantly) less likely to agree with this—57% of over-50s as compared to 59% of the younger age group. This was mirrored by the difference in the proportions of each group who thought managers treated employees fairly—56% of over-50s, compared to 59% of under-50s.

Effects of Training Experience on Wellbeing and Loyalty

Workplace Employment Relations Survey includes measures of job-related stress, asking how often in the past few weeks the job has made employees feel tense, depressed, worried, gloomy, uneasy, or miserable. Overall, the older employees reported lower levels on each of these variables, and for older and younger employees, those who had received more training reported lower levels of wellbeing. However, the differences associated with training were much less marked amongst the over-50s: i.e. the amount of training did not affect their reported job-related wellbeing to the same extent as it did for their younger colleagues.

In contrast, the amount of training received had a more pronounced effect on the older age group in relation to another set of questions: those measuring more positive attitudes and behaviours relating to using one's initiative at work, sharing organizational values, loyalty, and pride in the workplace/employer. The differences between those who had received high levels of training and those who had received no or minimal training were greater for the over-50s, indicating that participation in training is more strongly associated with attitudes and behaviours amongst older employees. However, care should be taken in interpreting these results as the standard errors of the average (mean) values were in some cases larger that the modest differences according to training levels. Moreover, we cannot determine causality from cross-sectional data: in fact, there could be reverse causality, as suggested by a study of HR professionals in Italy (Lazazzara et al. 2012), which showed that training for older workers may be more a reward for good performance than a means of enhancing productivity.

In summary, findings from WERS confirm that, across Great Britain, older employees are less likely than younger ones to have received training over the past year. This lower incidence cannot be accounted for by factors such as the jobs they occupy, or the sectors they work in, or even a reduction in training arising from the recession. However, the over-50s were slightly less likely to report employer encouragement to participate in training and more likely to feel that their skills level exceeded the requirements of their job. Older workers were more generally satisfied with the training they had received than their younger colleagues, and this effect appeared whatever the training levels. This effect may in part reflect overall higher job satisfaction reported by the over-50s. Finally, there were some interesting indications that whilst the amount of training may not have much of an effect on improving wellbeing at work for the over-50s (at least as reflected in the measures adopted by WERS), training levels may have some positive benefits in encouraging older workers to use their initiative and promoting organizational pride, loyalty, and commitment.

Training and Skills for Older Adults Not in Employment

Whilst the increased employment rate of older workers has occupied much of the policy and media attention, the fact that unemployment rates have also increased should not be overlooked.[1] Across the OECD countries, unemployment amongst those aged 55–64 rose from 4.6% in 2001 to 5.8% in 2011; in the United Kingdom this rise was from 3.3% to 4.8%, with just over 40% of that group being long-term unemployed, i.e. unemployed for one year or more. The OECD's 2006 review recommended tackling the training and skills needs of this group as a priority. However, as this next section illustrates, this group remains under-served and to a large extent their needs and problems are hidden.

The next section draws on a survey of nearly 800 unemployed job-seekers aged 50 and over, undertaken between September and December 2012 (TAEN 2013). The sample came primarily from an online survey advertised through The Age and Employment Network's website and affiliated organizations, augmented by paper copies distributed by JobCentres. As such it is not a nationally representative sample; rather it aimed to provide some depth of understanding about the experiences of over-50s who were unemployed and seeking work. The profile of the survey respondents was 67% men of whom 35% were aged 50–54, 41% aged 55–59 and 24% aged 60+, giving representation across all occupational categories, albeit with an over-representation of managers and senior officials.

Exactly half were long-term unemployed. Most wanted to work for primarily financial reasons (89%), but nearly three-quarters (71%) also valued the sense of worth that working would bring. Around 70% were looking for a permanent and full-time role. When asked if they thought they had the right skills for today's labour market, nearly three out of four respondents (74%) said they did, with only 6% saying they felt they did not have the right skills. That so many people felt they were adequately skilled for work reflects the fact that 43% and 57% of respondents had a degree and/or professional qualifications respectively. In fact, those most confident that they had the right skills were managers and officials (84%) and professionals (78%), whilst the least confident were those who had last worked in skilled trades (40%) or elementary occupations (36%).

There was a significant contrast between the number of respondents who thought they had the right skills for today's labour market (74%), compared with those who thought employers recognized the skills they had (40%). Whilst there was no gender difference regarding responses about having the right skills, women were much less confident that employers acknowledge these skills: 37% of women felt that employers

[1] The group that has decreased is those termed economically inactive, i.e. neither in work nor actively looking for work.

would not recognize their skills, compared to 26% of men. Interestingly, whilst managers and officials were still the most confident about employers recognizing their skills (47%), and elementary occupations the least confident (14%), the variation is not as marked as it was for their own perceptions of the appropriateness of their skills.

> It is particularly difficult as an out-of-work professional to maintain CPD hours and activities which in turn causes skills to age and become less marketable.
>
> (Male, aged 55–59, business auditor)

This 'confidence gap' between individuals' assessment of their own skills and how they felt these skills would be received by employers perhaps explains why nearly one third of respondents (32%) felt that having outdated skills that didn't match the requirements of current jobs was an 'important' or 'very important' barrier to them re-entering employment. However, this figure is dwarfed by the 83% who felt that being seen as too old by recruiters was a major barrier, and it became clear from the qualitative comments that perceived ageism often lay behind stated 'skills gaps'.

> Since I've been out of work, I've passed my Level 2 I.T.C computer course, plus Business Administration and Management. I'm keeping up with the changing workplace, but the younger managers see me as a threat and not an asset.
>
> (Female, aged 55–59, administrative supervisor)

Women were significantly more likely than men to disagree with the statement, 'I have every opportunity to upgrade my skills to fit the needs of today's employers': 46% of women disagreed, compared to 31% of men. In terms of occupations, those last working in sales and customer services jobs were most likely to agree (45%), whilst those who were in associate technical and professional occupations were least likely to agree (21%). The qualitative comments provided insight into the nature of some of these barriers which often focused on cost, either to the individual or in respect of the priorities and rules of official government interventions.

> I am currently on the Work Programme with a well-known employment agency. However, they tell me they cannot pay for me to update my qualifications as they have not got any money. How am I supposed to pay to upgrade when I get less than £90.00 per month?
>
> (Female, aged 55–59, job search tutor)

> My particular employment background is working as a maintenance electrician in the petro-chemical industry. I diversified into other types of work 16 years ago, but would like to return to my trade. My Work Programme provider is unwilling to help me upgrade my qualifications on the grounds of cost.
>
> (Male, aged 55–59, process operator)

> My literacy, numeracy and IT skills are excellent, but the only back-to-work help I am offered is with basic skills—my high level of qualifications disbars me from financial assistance with any courses other than basic skills.
>
> (Female, aged 55–59, local government officer)

This discussion indicates that whilst access to (re-)training is vitally important for unemployed older workers, the barriers they face are more complex than simply whether or not training is available.

Education and Training for the Older Population

Current cohorts of older workers have typically had fewer years of formal education and are less qualified on average than more recent generations, so access to further and higher education and apprenticeships may offer important routes for the older unemployed to get back into employment or for the older employed to improve their job prospects. Research in both the United States and the United Kingdom indicate that those with low or no educational qualifications are the least likely to be working beyond the age of 65. Haider and Loughran (2001); Smeaton and McKay (2003). Hedge and Albright (2013) discuss the importance of broadening the focus to consider training of older workers given the changing nature of retirement, i.e. older workers who enter bridge jobs or who volunteer. Their review of the situation in the United States found that the volunteer sector was more adapted for training older workers than either the private or public sectors, and more likely to offer training and adapt that training to the needs of an older workforce. It is clear that access to education and training for the older population has a range of implications for both those in the labour market and those in retirement. As we live longer, more people may want to access further education in retirement not purely for utilitarian reasons related to job prospects, but also for leisure and wider benefits associated with wellbeing.

There has been a push to increase the number of apprenticeships in Great Britain and some discussion of 'older apprentices' although this typically refers to those over 25 years of age. The number of genuinely older apprentices has been increasing but still remains a small percentage of the overall total as indicated in Table 29.2. The growth of older apprentices is significant with over 65,000 people 45 years and older starting apprenticeships in 2011/12—a rise from 23,000 in 2009/10.

The picture in higher education (HE) is similar in that those over 45 years of age represent a small percentage of the total: in 2011/12 just 9% of first year students in higher education in the United Kingdom were over the age of 45. They were much more likely to be studying part-time and the overwhelming majority (94%) in non-STEM (science, technology, electronics and maths) subjects. A high proportion of

Table 29.2 Proportion of apprenticeship starts by specific age groups

Age	August 2009–July 2010	August 2010–July 2011	August 2011–July 2012
16	11	7	6
17	15	10	8
18	17	12	11
19–24	41	31	31
25–34	9	16	19
35–44	5	12	13
45–59	4	11	12
60+	0	1	1
Total	100%	100%	100%

Source: House of Commons Library Apprenticeships Statistics (BIS Data Service).

those over the age of 60 study through the Open University and are pursuing what might be described as recreational courses, such as Art History. In the context of dramatic changes to the HE sector in England little attention is currently focusing on the older student, but arguably improving access to further and higher education (FHE) could play an important part in improving the job prospects of older workers and their satisfaction in retirement. Lifelong learning then has a real meaning and potential to contribute to the realities of an ageing society. Biggs et al. (2012, 40) have argued that we are currently squandering the social capital of mature adults by failing to acknowledge, use, and develop their 'accumulated knowledge, experience, and continued ability to learn'. This would also encompass the intergenerational transfer of skills. Felstead (2010) found that older workers were very willing to pass on learning to newer and younger colleagues. A note of caution is sounded by Fenwick (2012b) who brings a more critical perspective to the issues surrounding older-worker training. She questions the extent to which the emphasis on lifelong learning is a reflection of the new capitalism and as such serves the position of the individual (older worker) poorly. Lower participation in training may be constructed as a problem, with the attendant expectation of continuous learning raising tensions between older workers as leaders and mentors, and older workers as competitive individuals striving to cope with work intensification and organizational change. Her own findings amongst professional accountants in Canada show how these older workers become more discerning about training and learning: 'Mainly they focus on learning as strategy, as approaches to getting what they want and need out of the system, and protecting for themselves what is important' (Fenwick 2012b: 1017).

Developing Training and Education: New Policy Initiatives

Developing new training initiatives targeted at the older population will require recognition of the different kinds of support likely to be required. For example, amongst those in their late-40s to mid-50s, demand for job training and professional courses is likely to increase, since many in this age group will have a substantial number of working years to complete before eligibility for a pension. Many in this age group will have been part of the expansion of FHE from the 1970s onwards and may view lifelong learning as an essential part of continued employment. Amongst those in their late-50s and 60s, the need for new skills may be an essential requirement if meaningful employment is to be secured. Mayhew and Rijkers (2004, 2), in a review for the OECD, stress the importance of 'continuous learning during the whole of working life as a means of reducing the dangers of labour market disadvantage in later years'. Policies for change will need to focus on the following areas:

- developing entitlements for 'third-age learning'
- re-assessing methodologies and techniques for training older workers
- expanding provision for those in non-standard forms of employment
- raising the quality of the general work environment
- developing the involvement of FHE.

The first of the above was addressed by Schuller and Watson (2009) as part of the UK *Inquiry into the Future of Lifelong Learning*. In their recommendations for change they set out a four-stage model to encourage learning across the life-course, recognizing different periods of development in the years up to 25, 25–50, 50–74, and 75 plus. They suggest that what has been termed the 'third age' (50–74) should be viewed as a central period for encouraging enhanced training and education opportunities, based upon a more even distribution of work across the life course. This would be buttressed by: (a) a fairer allocation of educational resources (public, private, and employer-based) to meet the needs of third- and fourth-age (those aged 75 plus) groups; (b) a legal entitlement of free access to learning to acquire basic skills (e.g. in literacy and numeracy); (c) a 'good practice' entitlement to learning leave as an occupational benefit; (d) specific 'transition entitlements', e.g. for people on their 50th birthday, to 'signal the continuing potential for learning of those moving into the third age' (Schuller and Watson 2009, 133).

The second area raises issues about developing more effective training programmes targeted at older adults. The research evidence reviewed above suggests that employer (or line manager) 'discouragement' partly explains decreasing participation in training. Yet it is also clear that this not a complete explanation for the problem. In particular, workers themselves may consider—after a certain age or stage in their career—that further training is unnecessary. Or, as is also possible, they may feel that the type of training and learning they are likely to receive is inappropriate given their level of skill and experience. Czaja and Sharit (2009, 266), in research from the United States, make the point that although many existing training techniques are effective for older adults we lack an adequate research database to: 'determine whether some training techniques are consistently differentially beneficial to older workers'. On the other hand, literature from work-based psychological studies has demonstrated the benefits as well as limitations of particular approaches to training involving older workers. Tsang (2009, 289), for example, cites a number of studies which demonstrate how relatively small amounts of training can reverse cognitive decline and assist the retention of newly acquired skills. Conversely, the limitations of training benefits are also noted, including reduced magnitude of learning and slower learning rates. Given the emergence of a more diverse ageing workforce, attention to new ways of delivering work-based training would seem an urgent requirement. One suggestion here would be to encourage a single organization to lead research and policy initiatives linking trades unions, business organizations, and government on the theme of training for an ageing workforce.

The third area concerns the need to encourage training programmes specifically targeted at those in part-time and flexible forms of employment, and with those older workers who are self-employed. The issues here have been summarized by Czaja and Sharit (2009, 259) as follows:

> as the number of workers in non-standard work arrangements ... continues to increase, one important issue confronting workers will be access to traditional workplace benefits such as training. [Such] workers will be less likely to receive structured company-sponsored training, and the responsibility of continuous learning and job training will fall to a greater extent on the individual. It is not yet clear how to best develop and disseminate training programmes to promote lifelong learning for these 'non-traditional' workers. This issue is especially pertinent for older workers, given that they are less likely to be provided with access to training and development programmes in traditional work environments where company-sponsored training is available.

There are no immediate solutions to the problems facing part-time and related groups of workers. On the one side, research already cited (e.g. Humphrey et al. 2003) highlights inequalities between full- and part-time workers in respect of access to training. Such difficulties are unlikely to have abated—they have probably worsened—in the period since the research was published. On the other side, opportunities from providers such as community and further education colleges have been steadily reduced, with the major focus now placed on preparing younger people for entry into the labour market. Some options for consideration here might include: firstly, adoption of Schuller and Watson's (2009) plan for legal and transitional entitlements (mentioned earlier), a proposal highly relevant to those entering non-standard and flexible forms of employment; secondly, more imaginative use of computer-based training or 'e-learning' to assist those working from home or those juggling work and caregiving responsibilities (Czaja and Sharit 2009); thirdly, specific obligations placed upon employers to expand training and learning as a pre-condition for creating non-standard forms of employment.

The fourth area concerns initiatives to improve the total work environment in which the older worker is embedded. An illustration of this approach is provided by the *Finnish Programme on Ageing Workers*, a joint intervention from government, pension companies, local authorities, and the Finnish Institute of Occupational Health. The aim of the programme was to address the whole work environment rather than isolated features, developing good practice around retention (including measuring people's capacity to work), as well as adapting employment services to the needs of older workers. Maltby (2013, 194) suggests that the experience of the Finnish Programme would appear to indicate that the: 'measurement of work ability, linked to improvements in age management, can lead to reductions in premature labour market withdrawal, as well as greater job satisfaction, improved health, and raised productivity'.

The final area for discussion concerns encouraging closer involvement from FHE in responding to the needs of older workers, with the development of new programmes or the adaptation of existing courses. Older students have always had an important presence in university adult education classes, with those over 50 comprising the majority of participants. They also form a significant group studying for part-time degrees and programmes related to continuing professional development (Phillipson 2010). The number of older learners moving into higher education (HE) will almost certainly increase given broader demographic and social changes. Key factors are likely to include, firstly, the demand for vocational and non-vocational courses coming from 'first wave' baby boomers (those born in the late-1940s and early-1950s), a larger proportion of whom—in comparison with earlier cohorts—have degrees and related qualifications; secondly, the need for new qualifications amongst those changing careers in mid and later working life. Reflecting this development, three pathways might be followed by higher education institutions (HEIs) to support older workers:

- *educational and personal development programmes*: these would build upon existing work in adult and continuing education, but would identify new types of courses and markets amongst a diverse and segmented post-50s market. An example of such an initiative is the Osher Lifelong Learning Institutes, which are located at over 100 US universities.
- *employment-related programmes*: these might support the policy objective of extending working life, although the extent of employer demand may be fragile in the context of high levels of unemployment. The development of courses

supporting people moving from full-time paid employment to various forms of self-employment may, however, remain a source of growth amongst HEIs.

- *social inclusion programmes*: substantial numbers of older people—in current as well as succeeding cohorts—remain educationally and socially disadvantaged. HEIs, with partners such as local authorities, further education colleges and the major national charities, should focus on a 'widening participation' agenda that covers all age groups and not just younger adults.

Conclusion

This chapter has reviewed education, training, and development for the over-50 population. Whilst there is general agreement that more training is needed for older workers there is little evidence to suggest that much is being done about it. In 2011 a follow-up questionnaire was sent to all 21 countries that had participated in the OECD's review some years earlier. The questionnaire was adapted to refer to the OECD's specific policy recommendations (OCED 2006) in each corresponding country report. For the United Kingdom they commented that no (relevant) action had been taken in the areas of increasing training for older, out-of-work adults. In part, this was because the specific initiatives they commented on in 2004 no longer existed at the time of the review.[2]

The discussion here has recognized that whilst there may be business case arguments for increasing access to training (increasing the productivity of older workers and extending working lives) these may be in tension with equal opportunities arguments about fair access and potential rights to education and learning in the third age and beyond (see also Canduela et al. 2012). Whilst we have outlined a range of policy initiatives that would improve the situation of the older population both in employment and in retirement, the scope for moving ahead on any of these is undeniably weak in the context of global economic turbulence and weak employment demand.

References

Baars, J., Dohmen, J., Grenier, A., and Phillipson, C. (eds) (2013) *Ageing, Meaning and Social Structure: Connecting Critical and Humanistic Gerontology*, Bristol: Policy Press.

Bass, S. A. and Caro, F.G. (2001) 'Productive Ageing: A Conceptual Framework', in N. Morrow-Howell, J. Hinterland, and M. Sherraden, M. (eds), *Productive Aging*, Baltimore, NJ: The John Hopkins University Press: 37–80.

[2] http://www.oecd.org/els/emp/Older%20Workers%20UK-MOD.pdf.

Becker, G. (1964) *Human Capital: A Theoretical and Empirical Analysis, with Special Reference to Education*, New York: Columbia University Press.

Biggs, S., Carstensen, L., and Hogan, P. (2012) 'Social Capital, Lifelong Learning and Social Innovation', in Beard, J., Biggs, S., Bloom, D., Fried, L., Hogan, P., Kalache, A., and Olshansky J. (eds), 'Program on the Global Demography of Aging', Working Paper no. 89, World Economic Forum, London. http://134.174.190.199/pgda/WorkingPapers/2012/PGDA_WP_89.pdf#page=42. Accessed 7 May 7 2013.

Buyens, D., Van Dijk, H., Dewilde, T., and De Vos, A. (2009) 'The Aging Workforce: Perceptions of Career Ending', *Journal of Managerial Psychology*, 24(2): 102–117.

Canduela, J., Dutton, M., Johnson, S., Lindsay, C., and McQuaid, R. (2012) 'Ageing, Skills and Participation in Work-related Training in Britain: Assessing the Position of Older Workers', *Work, Employment and* Society, 26(1): 42–60.

Carmichael, F. and Ercolani, M. (2012) 'Age-training Gaps in the European Union', *Ageing and Society*. Available on CJO 2012 doi: 10.1017/S0144686X12000852. Accessed 1 May 2013.

CIPD Research Insight (2008) *Managing an Ageing Workforce: The Role of Total Reward*, London: CIPD.

CIPD (2011) 'Focus on Managing an Ageing Workforce', *Employee Outlook* series. http://www.cipd.co.uk/binaries/Employee%20Outlook%20Focus%20on%20age.pdf. Accessed 4 May 2013.

Clark, A., Oswald, A., and Warr, P. (1996) 'Is Job Satisfaction U-shaped in Age?', *Journal of Occupational and Organizational Psychology*, 69: 57–81.

Czaja, S. and Sharit, J. (2009) *Aging and Work: Issues and Implications in a Changing Landscape*, Baltimore, NJ: The John Hopkins University Press.

Ekerdt, D. (2010) 'Frontiers of Research on Work and Retirement', *Journal of Gerontology: Social Sciences*, 65B(1): 69–80.

Felstead, A. (2011) 'The Importance of "Teaching Old Dogs New Tricks": Training and Learning Opportunities for Older Workers', in E. Parry and S. Tyson (eds), *Managing an Age Diverse Workforce*, Basingstoke: Palgrave Macmillan: 189–205.

Fenwick, T. (2012a) 'Learning among Older Professional Workers: Knowledge Strategies and Knowledge Orientations', *Vocations and Learning*, 5: 203–223.

Fenwick, T. (2012b) 'Older Professional Workers and Continuous Learning in New Capitalism', *Human Relations*, 68(8): 1001–1020.

Fouarge, D. and Schils, T. (2009) 'The Effect of Early Retirement Incentives on the Training Participation of Older Workers', *Labour*, 23 (Special Issue): 85–109.

Gilleard, C. and Higgs, P. (2005) *Contexts of Ageing*, Cambridge: Polity Press.

Haider, S. and Loughran, D. (2001) 'Elderly Labor Supply: Work of Play?' Center for Retirement Research at Boston College, WP 2001-4 (Ed, College, C.f.R.R.a.B.) Boston.

HM Government (2010) *The Coalition: Our Programme for Government*, London: The Stationery Office.

Hedge, J. and Albright, V. (2013) 'Learning and Training in Retirement', in M. Wang (ed.), *The Oxford Handbook of Retirement*, Oxford: Oxford University Press: 477–492.

HEFCE Equality Data Overview: students studying at English HEIs, http://www.hefce.ac.uk/media/hefce/content/whatwedo/leadershipgovernanceandmanagement/equalityanddiversity/equalities_summary_student.pdf. Accessed 4 May 2013.

House of Commons Library Apprenticeships Statistics. www.parliament.uk/briefing-papers/SN06113.pdf. Accessed 4 May 2013.

Humphrey, A., Costigan, P., Pickering, K., Starteford, N., and Barnes, M. (2003) *Factors Affecting the Labour Market Participation of Older Workers*, Leeds: DWP.

Kooji, D. T., Guest, D. E., Clinton, M., Knight, T. Jansen, P. G., and Dikkers, J. S. (2013) 'How the Impact of HR Practices on Employee Well-being and Performance Changes with Age', *Human Resource Management Journal*, 23(1): 18–35.

Lain, D. and Vickerstaff, S. (2014) 'Working beyond Retirement Age: Lessons for Policy', in S. Harper and K. Hamblin (eds), *International Handbook of Ageing and Public Policy*, London: Edward Elgar: 242–255.

Lazazzara, A., Karpinska, K. and Henkens, K. (2012) 'What Factors Influence Training Opportunities for Older Workers? Three Factorial Surveys Exploring the Attitudes of HR Professionals', *The International Journal of Human Resource Management*, iFirst: 1–19.

Leppel, K., Brucker, E., and Cochran, J. (2012) 'The Importance of Training to Job Satisfaction of Older Workers', *Journal of Aging and Social Policy*, 24(1): 62–76.

Loretto, W. and White, P. (2006) 'Employers' Attitudes, Practices and Policies towards Older Workers', *Human Resource Management Journal*, 16(3): 313–330.

Maltby, T. (2013) '"Work Ability": A Practical Model for Improving the Quality of Work, Health and Well-being across the Life-course?', in S. Vickerstaff, C. Phillipson, and R. Wilkie (eds), *Work, Health and Wellbeing: The Challenges of Managing Health at Work*, Bristol: The Policy Press: 187–206.

Mayhew, K., Elliott, M., and Rijkers, B. (2008) 'Upskilling Older Workers', *Ageing Horizons*, 8: 13–21.

Mayhew, K. and Rijkers, B. (2004) 'How to Improve the Human Capital of Older Workers, or the Sad Tale of the Magic Bullet'. Paper prepared for the joint EC OECD seminar on Human Capital and Labour Market Performance, Brussels, 8 December.

McNair, S., Flynn, M., and Dutton, N. (2007) *Employer Responses to an Ageing Workforce: A Qualitative Study*, Department for Work and Pensions Research Report no. 455, Leeds: DWP.

McNair, S. (2010) *A Sense of Future: A Study of Training and Work in Later Life*, Leicester: NIACE.

OECD (2006) *Live Longer, Work Longer*, Paris: OECD.

OECD (2011) *Pensions at a Glance*, Paris: OECD.

OECD (2013) *Aging and Employment Policies*. http://www.oecd.org/employment/emp/ageingandemploymentpolicies.htm.

Phillipson, C. (2010) 'Active Ageing and Universities: Engaging Older Learners', *International Journal of Education and Ageing*, 1(1): 9–23.

Phillipson, C. (2013) 'Education and Training in the Workplace', in S. Vickerstaff, C. Phillipson, and R. Wilkie (eds), *Work, Health and Wellbeing: The Challenges of Managing Health at Work*, Bristol: The Policy Press: 255–272.

Phillipson, C. and Smith, A. (2005) *Extending Working Life: A Review of the Research Literature*, Department for Work and Pensions Research Report no. 299, Leeds: DWP.

Pillemer, K., Moen, P., Wethington, E., and Glasgow, N. (eds) *Social Integration in the Second Half of Life*, Baltimore, NJ. John Hopkins Press.

Schuller, T. and Watson, D. (2009) *Learning through Life: Inquiry into the Future for Lifelong Learning*, Leicester: National Institute of Adult and Continuing Education.

Sennett, R. (2006) *The Culture of the New Capitalism*, New Haven: Yale University Press.

Smeaton, D. and McKAy, S. (2003) 'Working after State Pension Age: Quantitative Analysis,' Research Report 182, Leeds: Department for Work and Pensions.

TAEN (The Age and Employment Network) (2013) *Survey of Jobseekers aged 50+*, London: TAEN.

Tsang, T. (2009) 'Age and Performance Measures of Knowledge-based Work: A Cognitive Perspective', in S. J. Czaja, and J. Sharit, J. (eds), *Aging and Work: Issues and Implications in a Changing Landscape*, Baltimore, NJ: The John Hopkins University Press: 279–306.

Urwin, P. (2004) *Age Matters: A Review of Existing Survey Evidence*, Employment Relations Research Series no. 24, London: Department of Trade and Industry.

Van Dalen, H., Henekens, K., and Schippers, J. (2009) 'Dealing with Older Workers in Europe: A Comparative Survey of Employers' Attitudes and Actions', *Journal of European Social Policy*, 19(1): 47–60.

Vickerstaff, S. and Cox, J. (2005) 'Retirement and Risk: The Individualisation of Retirement and Experiences?', *The Sociological Review*, 53: 77–95.

Vickerstaff, S., Loretto, W., and White, P. (2007) 'The Future for Older Workers: Opportunities and Constraints', in W. Loretto, S. Vickerstaff, and P. White (eds), *The Future of Older Workers: New Perspectives*, Bristol: Policy Press: 203–226.

CHAPTER 30

RETHINKING SKILLS DEVELOPMENT

Moving Beyond Competency-Based Training

LEESA WHEELAHAN

Introduction

National governments around the world and international government organizations such as the World Bank and the International Monetary Fund have been seduced by the siren call of competency-based training as a 'cure' for 'problems' with skills. Competency-based training (CBT) will, it is believed: solve problems in poor and rich nations alike even though their problems are fundamentally different; support basic economic development and cutting edge innovation; 'upskill' the low skilled and high skilled; provide the basis for educational and occupational mobility; and, support people from disadvantaged backgrounds to have their existing skills recognized and gain new skills. In his critique of CBT, Norris (1991, 331) explains that competence:

> is an El Dorado of a word with a wealth of meanings and the appropriate connotations for utilitarian times. The language of competency-based approaches to education and training is compelling in its common-sense and rhetorical force. Words like 'competence' and 'standards' are good words, modern words; everybody is for standards and everyone is against incompetence.

The premise is simple and seductive: align the outcomes of training with the requirements of work, teach (or train) to those outcomes, and evaluate training through competent performance at work. In Australia, vocational education and training (VET) qualifications are based on 'units of competency', and each unit describes a discrete workplace requirement. Proponents of CBT argue that this is transparent, evidence based, responsive to 'industry' needs, and measurable because it is based on observable performance. A complicating factor is that the word 'competence' does indeed mean many things in different contexts. For example, Anglophone countries such as Australia and England have a narrow and restricted approach to competence that is task-focused, compared to richer and more holistic occupationally based notions in Northern Europe (Bohlinger 2007–8). Unfortunately, it is the Anglophone notions that are used in aid programmes to poor countries that are imperialistically coming to dominate international policy and government discussions. Anglophone notions of competency are critiqued in this chapter.

This chapter[1] argues that CBT contributes to fragmenting skills and work, that it deskills workers, and that it does not provide the basis for educational or occupational progression. It argues that we need to rethink the conceptual basis of qualifications in VET, and it suggests that the 'capabilities approach' that has been developed by economist and Nobel Laureate Amartya Sen (1993, 1999, 2009) and the philosopher Martha Nussbaum (2000, 2011) offers a promising alternative, although with some caveats. The first section discusses the 'social settlement' in VET to explain why competency training was introduced and it argues that the 'skills problem' has been misdiagnosed. This is followed by a discussion of the problems with CBT, whilst the next section explains why 'generic skills' cannot overcome the problems with CBT. The final section outlines what the capabilities approach is and how it may provide a conceptual basis for VET qualifications.

THE SOCIAL SETTLEMENT IN VET

The structure of VET, the way skill is envisaged, and the relationship between VET and work are always the outcome of a settlement between civil society (employers, labour, and occupational groups), the state, and educational institutions. Keating (2008, 3) argues that power is not equally shared in this relationship and that the key relationship is between the state and civil society. This is particularly clear in VET where educational institutions have less autonomy than in the higher education (HE) or the schools sectors, both of which are supported by very powerful, often overlapping, interests. Elite schools and universities train the social elites, are embedded in them, and mobilize them when needed. VET doesn't have friends like this; its relative lack of autonomy means that the pressure brought to bear by the state and employers and unions is much more direct and unmediated. And, whilst schools and HE are under pressure to be more relevant to the needs of work, VET comes under particular scrutiny and criticism because it is meant to deliver the skills that industry needs.

[1] Some of the ideas and formulations in this chapter are drawn from an earlier 'think piece' by Wheelahan and Moodie (2011) *Rethinking Skills: From Competencies to Capabilities*, New South Wales Board of Vocational Education and Training, but the initial ideas in that paper have been redeveloped for the purposes of this chapter and extended to reflect newer work on the ideas and concepts it contains.

VET is always subject to critique because it must serve a range of different purposes and different interests, and the interests of all constituents are not the same (Keep 2007, 2012). Clarke and Winch (2007, 1) explain that governments focus on the productive capacity of society; individuals focus on preparation for their working life and progression in the labour market; and employers focus on the immediate needs of their firms. They explain that these are conflicting interests, and as a result, the VET system represents a compromise and at the same time reflects the power attached to each of these different interests (Clarke and Winch 2007, 1).

Consequently, there have always been complaints about VET and always will be. Hyland (1999, 99) says that employers in the United Kingdom have been complaining about education and training since at least the time of the Paris Exhibition in 1867 when they argued that they were falling behind their industrial competitors. Debates over the extent to which VET should be directly tied to the needs of work are also not new. Hyland goes on to say that in 1889 the United Kingdom passed the Technical Instruction Act to improve this situation, but in 1901 (1999, 99), Lord Haldane:

still felt the need to remind politicians that the country had to train the minds of our people so they may be able to hold their own against the competition which is coming forward at such an alarming rate.

Not much has changed and we are still having the same debates today. VET will always be criticised, for three reasons. Firstly, if its purpose is primarily to prepare people for work, then it will be found wanting as the demands of work change and as a consequence of changing notions about appropriate preparation for work. Industries change at different rates and in different ways, and employers within the same industry often have different needs. It is not possible to reconcile these differences within one system. Secondly, the nature of the social settlement is always subject to negotiation and contest as the various constituents press for greater consideration of their concerns in response to broader changes in society and the economy. Thirdly, problems in the economy and mismatches between skills and work are attributed to problems with VET even though the relationship between VET and work is mutually constitutive, and problems also arise from ineffective deployment of skill in workplaces (Skills Australia 2010).

In other words, the skills 'problem' has been misdiagnosed (Keep 2012). Keep and James (2012) explain that it is the structure of the demand side, or the structure of the labour market and the economy, that is crucial in determining skill levels. Bad jobs provide poor incentives for individuals to train or employers to invest in training. In our work, we have found that the structure of the labour market shapes educational pathways and that the relationship between education and specific jobs is very weak (Wheelahan et al. 2012). Where there are strong occupational pathways, strong educational pathways will follow. Apart from the regulated occupations where criteria for entry and progression are specified by professional or occupational bodies, the Australian labour market is segmented and has weak occupational pathways (Yu et al. 2012). The relative absence of these pathways has been exacerbated by an increase in higher- and lower-skilled jobs, and a decline in jobs at the intermediate level. VET cannot substitute for the absence of occupational pathways and educational pathways created in the absence of occupational pathways are mainly a transition from lower- to higher-level studies and less a pathway to work. The policy implication of this analysis is that greater attention needs to be paid to the structure of occupations, jobs, and work.

CBT is the outcome of a low trust social settlement. It was introduced as part of broader neo-liberal reforms in the late 1980s and 1990s that sought to subsume education (particularly VET) as an instrument of micro-economic reform to tie it more tightly and directly to the needs of the economy. Reforms were seen to be needed because educational institutions are putatively not sufficiently responsive to the needs of industry and do not provide industry with the knowledge and skills that are needed. It is argued that educational institutions focus on inputs and are supply driven, so they offer what they think is important and not what the users (employers and individuals) think are important. As Bjørnåvold and Coles (2007–8, 227) explain, 'High on the reform agenda is institutional reform prompted by inflexibility of the education and training system to produce relevant programmes of learning.' The imposition of CBT is meant to break the power of institutions, teachers, and their unions and ensure education becomes 'demand-driven'. This was the explicit purpose of CBT in which learning outcomes are described as workplace tasks and roles. The broader context of CBT was that it was 'about giving industry more say' over the outcomes of qualifications in an industry-led system (Guthrie 2009). This is based on the notion that VET exists to serve industry as it currently exists, and it is a misattribution to VET of the short-comings in the structure of the labour market and in the way skills are deployed at work.

Competency-based Training

As in other countries, the introduction of competency-based training in Australia caused, and is still causing, major controversy. Debates and controversies have led to amendments in the definition of competency to address concerns. The current Australian definition (Department of Industry Innovation Science Research and Tertiary Education 2011) is that:

> Competency is the consistent application of knowledge and skill to the standard of performance required in the workplace. It embodies the ability to transfer and apply skills and knowledge to new situations and environments. (Department of Industry Innovation Science Research and Tertiary Education 2011)

Efforts have been made to develop a broader and more holistic definition of competency. The latest version of the *Training Package Development Handbook* (DIISRTE 2011) says that:

> Competency is a broader concept than the ability to perform individual workplace tasks and comprises the application of all the specified technical and generic

> knowledge and skills relevant for an occupation. Particularly at higher qualification levels, competency may require a combination of higher order knowledge and skills and involve complex cognitive and meta-cognitive processes such as reflection, analysis, synthesis, generation of ideas, problem solving, decision-making, conflict resolution, innovation, design, negotiation, strategic planning and self-regulated learning.

However, whilst the changes to the definition of competency over the years have been helpful, arguably CBT is intrinsically flawed because it is based on an atomistic notion of work and knowledge and skills. There are six key problems with CBT.

1. Units of competency are still tied to the specific. The *Training Package Development Handbook* explains that:

   > Each unit of competency identifies a discrete workplace requirement and includes the knowledge and skills that underpin competency as well as language, literacy and numeracy; and occupational health and safety requirements …
   >
   > Units of competency (DIISRTE 2011):
   >
   > - are nationally agreed statements of the skills and knowledge required for effective performance in a particular job or job function
   > - describe work outcomes
   > - can logically stand alone when applied in a work situation.

This is based on an atomisation of jobs in which jobs consist of an ensemble of workplace roles and requirements, and VET qualifications are made up of a matching ensemble of units of competence. CBT assumes that it is possible to break the whole down into discrete components, that it is possible to describe all knowledge and skill in statements, that knowledge and skills can be inferred from observation, and that the whole consists of adding up the parts (or different units of competency). It is assumed that the same units of competency can be used and described independently of contexts. This fragmentation is reflected in the composition of units of competency which include: elements of competency, performance criteria, required knowledge and skills, a range statement, and evidence guides. Such detailed specification is required because units of competency describe the outcomes of learning independently of processes of learning. This process of specification encourages reductive processes of learning that tick off outcomes rather than holistic learning. Moreover, the unitization of knowledge and skills results in the lack of a coherent knowledge base for a flexible workforce that is able to support change (Brockmann et al. 2008, 236). It makes the development of a theoretical basis for workplace practice more difficult by disaggregating elements of work rather than emphasizing their interconnectedness.

2. The outcomes of learning are tied to descriptions of work as it currently exists. They focus on the present (because outcomes must be related to a specific workplace activity) and thus emphasize tradition and inhibit the development of

innovative knowledge and new forms of practice (Wheelahan 2010, 2012). This results in:

> [a] rigid backward mapping approach, in which the state of the art on the shop floor is the untouchable starting point for the definition of occupational competencies, leading to routinised job descriptions, in which the proactive and reflective worker is left out. (Biemans et al. cited in Brockmann et al. 2008, 237)

3. CBT still does not provide adequate access to underpinning knowledge and it will not whilst it is still tied to specific units of competency. Knowledge is still restricted to that which is actually applied at work so that knowledge is tied to specific tasks and roles in the workplace. The *Training Package Development Handbook* says that:

> While knowledge must be expressed, units of competency, their elements or performance criteria should not be entirely knowledge based unless a clear and assessable workplace outcome is described. Knowledge in units of competency:
> - should be in context
> - *should only be included if it refers to knowledge actually applied at work*
> - could be referred to in the performance criteria and the range statement (DIIRSTE 2011 emphasis added).

This removes specific applications of knowledge from the applied academic disciplines which underpin professional and vocational practice. Students have access only to contextually specific elements of theory that are relevant to the particular context, so that the emphasis is on elements of content rather than the system of meaning. For example, a mechanic will learn that a particular formula applies in a particular context, but this does not tell them if the same formula will apply in a different context, or what to do if they are confronted with the unfamiliar. They need access to mathematics if they are to exercise autonomy and judgement. In contrast, Clarke and Winch (2004, 516) argue that students need to learn the relevant theory and then learn to recognize instances of theoretical propositions in practical situations to which they can then apply appropriate means. Moreover, it cannot be assumed that knowledge can be tied to specific events because events are complex outcomes. Understanding how events are constructed, identifying those components that are contingent and those that are necessary, the differences between events and their relationship to other events are critical aspects of understanding, particularly in allowing students/workers to discriminate, select, and apply knowledge in an appropriate way to particular contexts (Wheelahan 2012).

4. CBT is based on the simplistic notion that processes of learning are identical with the skills that are to be learnt. This is derived from behaviourist learning theory in which the outcomes of learning can be described in advance as observable behaviours that are aligned to a particular task, so if someone is observed undertaking a particular task, it is assumed that they have the knowledge they need (Jessup 1991). The conditions for learning are external, and what is to be learnt is a given (Smith and Ragan 2005). However, this underplays the complexity of learning and the

resources that people bring with them when engaging in tasks. Whilst there can be no learning without doing, underlying capacity lays the basis for new learning. This is widely recognized in the case of language, literacy and numeracy, but less acknowledged when it comes to systematic access to theoretical knowledge. Young (2010, 16), in drawing from the work of the Russian learning theorist Lev Vygotsky, explains that:

> access to higher order concepts ... [is] a complex two-way pedagogic process. Initially, the learner's everyday concepts are extended and transformed by pedagogy through engaging with the theoretical concepts of the curriculum. The process is then reversed; learners draw on their newly acquired theoretical concepts to re-engage with and transform their everyday concepts.

This allows students to 'think with' their ideas and concepts and not just apply them to specific situations. Theoretical knowledge becomes part of the lens through which they view the world. It is the basis for innovative learning in the workplace, and for educational and occupational progression.

5. Even though CBT is meant to certify that particular outcomes have been achieved, as Young (2003, 208) explains, this doesn't change the fact that:

   > the credibility, quality and currency of a qualification is only partly based on what it says the person qualified can do or knows; far more important is the trust that society in general and specific users in particular (those whom select, recruit, or promote) have in the qualification ... If one or other of these communities does not underpin a qualification, it will have a problem of credibility, however well specified its outcomes.

6. CBT models of curriculum in VET are premised on a different notion of the human actor compared to curriculum in HE. HE envisages autonomous individuals who are co-producers of their own learning, whereas VET envisages workers who are under the direction of others (Buchanan et al. 2009, 15). HE provides students with access to principled knowledge that promotes autonomous reasoning, whereas VET focuses on contextualized knowledge and procedural knowledge. Education for the professions focuses on the development of the person in the context of their occupation and the knowledge, skills, and attributes they need broadly speaking, whereas CBT focuses on workplace requirements and ties education to those requirements.

Why Generic Skills Don't Help

The loose fit between VET qualifications and particular jobs has been recognized in policy and this has led to growing emphasis on the importance of generic skills. In

Australia this emphasis on generic skills is expressed as employability skills, which must be included in all VET qualifications (DEST 2007). However, the notion of generic skills is intrinsically flawed and Australia's interpretation of generic skills in VET as employability skills is particularly narrow.

The argument for generic skills is exemplified by the World Bank (2007, 118), which says that people need 'new competencies' for the knowledge economy. These include cognitive skills (such as skills in language, communication, logistical, and mathematical thought); cognitive problem-solving skills; self-learning and self-knowledge; social skills (such as team working, negotiation skills, self-confidence, and developing social networks) and motivation for work (including initiative, responsibility, commitment, and interest). The OECD (2010, 58) posits a similar group of skills, which include basic skills and digital age literacy; academic skills; technical skills; generic skills; soft skills (appropriate emotions and behaviours, multicultural awareness and understanding, receptiveness, etc.); and leadership skills.

This is a common attempted resolution of the tensions between training for one and a range of workplaces and training for immediate and future relevance. But this resolution is illusory. Communication depends heavily on the subject since all skilled occupations have highly specialized language—jargon—and is also highly sensitive to context. Communicating with colleagues in a science laboratory is different to communicating with a two-year-old in a childcare centre. Similarly, solving an electrician's problem, such as calculating how many power points may be run off a cable, is different from solving a nurse's problem, such as ensuring a patient takes their medication. As Young (2005, 15–16) explains, 'there is no curriculum and no scheme of assessment that could teach or assess a form of generic problem solving that would apply to both'. The OECD (2010, 58) in citing debates about generic skills, says that 'Problem solving, for example, takes place within a certain work environment and culture and is influenced by routine procedures....' The common terms in which generic skills are expressed mask the differences they are trying to surmount. Consequentially generic skills either become so rooted in their immediate context that they are not transferable to other contexts or become so general that they lose their direct relevance to the workplace.

Moreover, emphases on generic skills tend to under-emphasize the technical or domain-specific knowledge of particular occupational areas. For example, Willingham (2007, 13) explains that 'knowing that one should think critically is not the same as being able to do so. That requires domain knowledge and practice'. In citing arguments about generic skills, the OECD (2010, 58) explains that critics argue that 'to solve anything but the simplest problem, expertise and specialist bodies of knowledge are likely to be required'.

Problems with generic skills in VET are compounded through being interpreted as core employability skills. In a report on the importance of 'core employability skills' for the ILO, Brewer (2013, 7) explains that the appellation given to these groups of skills differs between countries and that while the emphasis may vary between different jurisdictions, that nonetheless these skills can be 'pooled under four broad skill categories: learning to learn; communication; teamwork; [and] problem-solving...' These four headings are later broken down into specific skills or abilities, and they encompass personal attributes, dispositions and capacities and seek to mould and shape subjectivities in line with prevailing dominant conceptions of the ideal worker. For example, in Australia, the employability skills that must be included in all VET qualifications are defined as:

- communication that contributes to productive and harmonious relations across employees and customers
- teamwork that contributes to productive working relationships and outcomes
- problem-solving that contributes to productive outcomes
- initiative and enterprise that contribute to innovative outcomes
- planning and organizing that contribute to long- and short-term strategic planning
- self-management that contributes to employee satisfaction and growth
- learning that contributes to ongoing improvement and expansion in employee and company operations and outcomes
- technology that contributes to the effective carrying out of tasks (DEST 2007, 23–36).

These employability skills are premised on a unitary notion with an ideal worker in an unproblematic workplace in which workers and management all share the same interests, untroubled by problems of power or worker exploitation. Conflicts of interest are seen as arising from personal conflicts, rather than structured and conflicting interests arising from the employment relationship in capitalist society.

Can the Capabilities Approach Provide an Alternative?

The capabilities approach potentially provides a promising alternative as the conceptual basis of VET qualifications. However, like the term competency, the term 'capabilities' is used in many ways in different disciplines, and this creates similar problems for creating shared understandings. The capabilities approach, as used here, is drawn from the work of economics (Sen 1993, 1999, 2009) and philosophy (Nussbaum 2000, 2011). It is increasingly being used in economic and social policy (for example, it underpins the United Nation's Human Development Index).[2] The capabilities approach, as we are using it in our work, focuses on the development of the person and the knowledge, skills, and attributes they need for a broad range of occupations within loosely defined vocational streams (Wheelahan and Moodie 2011; Wheelahan et al. 2012). It is designed to support students to engage in occupational progression through a career, link occupational and educational progression, and help them adapt to meet new and emerging

[2] See http://hdr.undp.org/en/humandev/origins/ (accessed 29 January 2011).

needs. The capacity to exercise skill at work is an emergent property of more fundamental, complex, and wide-ranging knowledge, skills, and abilities. Capacity arises from the interrelationship between personal, social and working lives, and that means learning *for* work needs to go *beyond* work. Consequently, the capabilities approach starts with the person and not specific skills. It asks about the capabilities that people need in order achieve a range of outcomes and about the social, economic, and cultural conditions that are required to realize capability.

Robeyns (2005, 94) explains that 'The core characteristic of the capability approach is its focus on what people are effectively able to do and to be; that is, on their capabilities'. The capabilities approach distinguishes between *capabilities* and *functionings*. 'Capabilities' refers to people's capacity to act, whilst 'achieved functionings' refers to the outcomes that ensue when they choose to use their capabilities to achieve a particular goal. A complex set of capabilities provides individuals with the basis for making choices in their lives, whereas functionings are the outcomes when they exercise choice. A particular set of capabilities can produce any number of outcomes. Walker and Unterhalter (2007, 4) explain that 'The difference between a capability and functioning is one between an opportunity to achieve and the actual achievement, between potential and outcome'. Two people with similar capability sets may make choices that result in different functionings or outcomes. Sen (1993, 31) distinguishes between functionings and capabilities in this way:

> *Functionings* represent parts of the state of a person—in particular the various things that he or she manages to do or be in leading a life. The *capability* of a person reflects the alternative combinations of functionings the person can achieve, and from which he or she can choose one collection.

Sen (2000) defines social exclusion as 'capability deprivation' and this arises when people do not have the capabilities they need to choose how they will live their lives. He says that social exclusion can be both a cause and result of capability deprivation (Sen 2000, 5). For example, those excluded from education are generally disadvantaged to begin with, and continue to be so, in part as a consequence of their continuing exclusion from education. Far from being a deficit approach, the capabilities approach is based on human freedom and choice. Robeyns (2005, 95) explains that capabilities refer to 'effective opportunities to undertake the actions and activities that [individuals] want to engage in, and be whom they want to be'. As an illustration, those who have disabilities that limit their mobility will have a narrower capability set if they do not have access to transport or other resources they need to undertake the activities they choose (Terzi 2007). Capabilities are not solely an individual attribute; they also refer to access to the resources individuals need to make choices, and the extent to which individual, social, and environmental arrangements make it possible for them to exercise choice (Robeyns 2005). Education is not just a means to an end or an instrumental freedom; it is also a 'substantive freedom, a constituent component of development' (Henry 2007). Success and participation in education is what makes choice (capability) possible (Saito 2003).

Moreover, Sen's approach also takes us beyond a simple focus on human capital. He explains (2007, 99):

> At the risk of oversimplification, it can be said that the literature on human capital tends to concentrate on the agency of human beings in augmenting production possibilities. The perspective of human capability focuses, on the other hand, on the ability—the substantive freedom—of people to lead the lives they have reason to value and to enhance the real choices they have. The two perspectives cannot but be related, since both are concerned with the role of human beings, and in particular with the actual abilities that they achieve and acquire. But the yardstick of assessment concentrates on different achievements.

An Important Caveat

There is an important caveat in the way we use the capabilities approach in our work. This arises because the capabilities approach is a normative framework that is being used in policy to evaluate, assess, and provide the conditions for individual wellbeing and the social arrangements that are needed to underpin it (Robeyns 2005). It does not, however, provide a social theory that explains the causes of capability deprivation, or social arrangements and social distributions that cause inequality. This requires social analysis and social science (Sayer 2011, 238).

Social analysis is needed to provide the social context for the development of capabilities as it is this that gives capabilities their context. The absence of such an analysis can result, as Sayer (2011, 237) explains, in 'the application of context-insensitive norms or policies that are doomed to produce undesirable consequences'. This, in turn, can lead to lack of attention to the social conditions and social arrangements that are needed to realize capabilities. For example, whilst VET may provide education that helps students develop capabilities, these capabilities may not be able to be realized in workplaces that resist change, or fail to provide for the development and realization of autonomous practice. Moreover, unless the conditions for the development of capabilities and for the exercise of capabilities is considered, a capabilities approach could result in little more than the formal provision of opportunities, without the substantive means to result in opportunities. For example, disadvantaged students who are disengaged from education require complex support if they are to experience success, which goes beyond passive provision of opportunities, or even worse, making participation a condition of income support.

Capability is contextualized by the broader social and economic environment in which people live and work, and consequently, we need to focus on the capabilities that people need for work. If the focus is on the development of the individual and on work, then this means ensuring students have access to the knowledge, skills, and capabilities they need to work in a vocation or broad occupational field. Education policy that considers capabilities in the abstract will result in abstract lists—such as generic skills, employability skills, and graduate attributes. This problem is exemplified in some of the literature that explores the potential for the capabilities approach in HE. Much of the HE literature (but not all) refers primarily to individual attributes and not to the broader notion of capabilities as realized through individual, social, and environmental resources and arrangements. Consequently, it can focus on 'generic' aspects of capability without contextualizing them in vocational fields of practice which give capabilities meaning.

A contextualized approach to capabilities is needed because the development of skills is underpinned by complex capabilities that require an understanding of the nature of work, the relationship between education and work, and the 'kind of qualified person ... we want to produce' (Muller 2009, 217). Producing 'agential' workers who have autonomy goes beyond 'training' in units of competency that describe discrete workplace requirements, or learning bundles of skills. Winch (2010, 560) explains that:

> It is not the practice of a bundle of skills but the way in which they are integrated into a form of agency, involving independent planning, activity and evaluation, which is of a potentially very wide scope that is important to this type of agency.

A capabilities framework to support agency in this way will require access to the applied theoretical knowledge that underpins practice in occupations and professions, but also to industry-specific knowledge and skills that transcend particular workplaces and the tacit knowledge of the workplace (Barnett 2006). Effective VET pedagogy would explicitly orient to each whilst supporting students to integrate these different components of practice. Learning outcomes, curriculum, and pedagogy also need to be based on the notion of development so that a key outcome of learning is that students are able to progress to the next level of knowledge and complexity of practice. Barnett (2006, 152) explains that 'inevitably, the base-level activities in many workplaces largely involve situated knowledge, but in progressing to higher levels, a more even mix of situated and disciplinary knowledge becomes necessary.' Workers (and thus students) must continue to engage with the contextual at higher levels, but they use theoretical knowledge that is more complex and at higher levels of abstraction to do so.

The nature of qualifications and the design of the curriculum will differ within and between different vocational fields of practice. Muller (2009, 217) explains that there is not one kind of professional practice and that important curricular differences arise as a result. The body of knowledge underpinning practice varies in complexity, depth, and level of abstractness in different fields (Muller 2009, 219). Some qualifications will provide access to more strongly demarcated bodies of knowledge because this is needed as a precondition of practice, whereas others will have more emphasis on breadth of knowledge and contextual knowledge. However, whilst this is so, Muller (2009, 219) argues that the conceptual demands of all occupations are increasing and access to conceptual knowledge is important 'for epistemological, economic and social justice reasons.'

In VET, achieving agency as described above by Winch means moving beyond producing the 'supervised worker' to instead draw from the model used in education for the professions which focuses on developing the person in the context of their occupation and as an autonomous individual who co-produces their own learning (Buchanan et al. 2009, 15). A capabilities approach may help provide more curricular coherence between VET and HE and thus support pathways and help overcome discontinuities in flows in education particularly if both seek the development of practitioners capable of autonomous reasoning (Buchanan et al. 2009).

Conclusion

The problem with skills is that 'the skills problem' has been misdiagnosed (Keep 2012). Policy focuses on putative short-comings with VET, and does not adequately incorporate understandings of the way in which the demand side—employers—structures work and deploys labour. There is some evidence that this is starting to change (Keep 2012). For example, the Australian Workforce and Productivity Agency's (2012) analysis of the 'skills problem' in Australia identifies the way skill is deployed at work and the way work is structured as problems (but less so the way the structure of employment and the casualization of labour contributes to the skills problem).

The nature of skills has also been misdiagnosed. CBT is based on simplistic behaviourist principles that performing a skill is the same process as learning a skill. This fails to recognize that the exercise of skill is an emergent property that rests on complex, interacting, and broad ranging knowledge and skills. Whilst there can be no learning without doing, skilful practice requires integration of theoretical, procedural, and tacit knowledge. The capabilities approach may offer an alternative conceptual basis for VET qualifications because it emphasizes agency and focuses on the development of capability that can be used to result in a range of functionings. This provides a much better basis for the development of skills and for educational and occupational mobility. The important caveat is, however, that capabilities need to be developed within the context of broad occupations or vocational streams otherwise the end result will be a list of abstract generic skills. Generic skills cannot provide the basis for skills development, because skillful practice requires domain-specific knowledge and skill. The capabilities approach also emphasizes the interrelationship between the individual, and the social, economic, cultural and environmental resources that are needed to develop capabilities. These resources must include the workplace and learning in the workplace, but they also include access to education and to the applied theoretical disciplines that underpin practice. This provides the basis for rethinking the relationship between education and work, and between educational institutions and the workplace.

References

Australian Workforce and Productivity Agency (2012) 'Future Focus Australia's Skills and Workforce Development Needs: Discussion Paper', Canberra. http://www.awpa.gov.au/. Accessed 20 July 2012.

Barnett, M. (2006) 'Vocational Knowledge and Vocational Pedagogy', in M. Young, and J. Gamble (eds), Knowledge, *Curriculum and Qualifications for South African Further Education*, Cape Town: Human Sciences Research Council: 143–157.

Bjørnåvold, J. and Coles, M. (2007–8) 'Governing Education and Training: The Case of Qualifications Frameworks', *European Journal of Vocational Training*, 42/43(2007/3–2008/1): 203–235.

Bohlinger, S. (2007–8) 'Competences as the Core Element of the European Qualifications Framework', *European Journal of Vocational Training*, 42/43(2007/3–2008/1): 96–112.

Brewer, Laura. (2013) *Enhancing Youth Employability: What? Why? and How? Guide to Core Work Skills*. Geneva: International Labour Office, Skills and Employability Department, ILO. http://www.ilo.org/wcmsp5/groups/public/---ed_emp/---ifp_skills/documents/publication/wcms_213452.pdf. Accessed 22 May 2016.

Brockmann, M., Clarke, L., Méhaut, P., and Winch, C. (2008) ' Competence-Based Vocational Education and Training (VET): The Cases of England and France in a European Perspective', *Vocations and Learning*, 1(3): 227–244.

Buchanan, J., Yu, S., Marginson, S., and Wheelahan, L. (2009) 'Education,Work and Economic Renewal', An issues paper prepared for the Australian Education Union, Sydney, Workplace Research Centre, University of Sydney. http://www.aeufederal.org.au/Publications/2009/JBuchananreport2009.pdf. Accessed 26 August 2009.

Clarke, L. and Winch, C. (2004) 'Apprenticeship and Applied Theoretical Knowledge,' *Educational Philosophy and Theory*, 36(5): 509–521.

Clarke, L. and Winch, C. (2007) 'Introduction', in L. Clarke and C. Winch (eds), *Vocational Education: International Approaches, Developments and Systems*, London: Routledge.

Department of Education Science and Training (2007) *Training Package Development Handbook*, Canberra, Department of Education Science and Training. http://www.dest.gov.au/sectors/training_skills/publications_resources/profiles/Training_Package_Development_Handbook.htm. Accessed 16 March 2007.

Department of Industry Innovation Science Research and Tertiary Education (2011) *Training Package Development Handbook*. http://www.innovation.gov.au/Skills/About/Policy/TrainingPackageDevelopmentHandbook/Pages/default.aspx. Accessed 31 October 2012.

Guthrie, H. (2009) *Competence and Competency Based Training: What the Literature Says*, Adelaide, National Centre for Vocational Education Research. http://www.ncver.edu.au/publications/2153.html. Accessed 7 July 2009.

Henry, K. (2007) 'Creating the Right Incentives for Indigenous Development', Cape York Institute Conference, Strong Foundations—Rebuilding Social Norms in Indigenous Communities, Cairns. http://www.treasury.gov.au/documents/1275/HTML/docshell.asp?URL=070624_CYI.htm. Accessed 29 January 2011.

Hyland, T. (1999) *Vocational Studies, Lifelong Learning and Social Values: Investigating Education, Training and NVQs Under the New Deal*, Aldershot: Ashgate.

Jessup, G. (1991) *Outcomes: NVQs and the Emerging Model of Education and Training*, London: The Falmer Press.

Keating, Jack (2008) *Qualifications Systems and National Qualifications Frameworks*, Monash University-ACER Centre for the Economics of Education and Training Annual Conference, Melbourne. http://www.education.monash.edu/centres/ceet/docs/conferencepapers/2008jackkeating.pdf. Accessed 8 June 2009.

Keep, E. (2007) 'The Multiple Paradoxes of State Power in the English Education and Training System', in L. Clarke. and C. Winch (eds), *Vocational Education: International Approaches, Developments and Systems*, London: Routledge.

Keep, E. (2012) 'Education and Industry: Taking Two Steps Back and Reflecting,' *Journal of Education and Work*, 25(4): 357–379.

Keep, E. and James, S. (2012) 'A Bermuda Triangle of Policy? "Bad Jobs", Skills Policy and Incentives to Learn at the Bottom End of the Labour Market,' *Journal of Education Policy*, 27(2): 211–230.

Muller, J. (2009) 'Forms of knowledge and Curriculum Coherence, '*Journal of Education and Work*, 22(3): 205–226.

Norris, N. (1991) 'The Trouble with Competence,' *Cambridge Journal of Education*, 21(3): 331–341.

Nussbaum, M. C. (2000) *Women and Human Development: The Capabilities Approach*, Cambridge: Cambridge University Press.

Nussbaum, M. C. (2011) 'Capabilities, Entitlements, Rights: Supplementation and Critique,' *Journal of Human Development and Capabilities*, 12(1): 23–37.

OECD (2010) *The OECD Innovation Strategy: Getting a Head Start on Tomorrow*, Paris, OECD. http://www.oecd.org/document/15/0,3746,en_2649_34273_45154895_1_1_1_1,00.html#HTO. Accessed 7 February 2011.

Robeyns, I. (2005) 'The Capability Approach: A Theoretical Survey,' *Journal of Human Development*, 6(1): 93–114.

Saito, M. (2003) 'Amartya Sen's Capability Approach to Education: A Critical Exploration,' *Journal of Philosophy of Education*, 37(1): 17–33.

Sayer, A. (2011) *Why Things Matter to People: Social Science, Values and Ethical Life*, Cambridge: Cambridge University Press.

Sen, A. (1993) 'Capability and Well-being,' in M. Nussbaum and A. Sen (eds), *The Quality of Life*, Oxford: Oxford Scholarship Online.

Sen, A. (1999) *Development as Freedom*, New York: Anchor Books.

Sen, A. (2000) *Social Exclusion: Concept, Application and Scrutiny*, Asian Development Bank. http://www.adb.org/documents/books/social_exclusion/Social_exclusion.pdf. Accessed 25 January 2011.

Sen, A. (2007) 'Education and Standards of Living,' in R. Curren (ed.), *Philosophy of Education: An Anthology*, Malden, MA: Blackwell Publishing: 95–101.

Sen, A. (2009) *The Idea of Justice*, Cambridge, MA: The Belknap Press.

Skills Australia (2010) *Australian Workforce Futures: A National Workforce Development Strategy*, Sydney. http://www.skillsaustralia.gov.au/PDFs_RTFs/WWF_strategy.pdf. Accessed 9 March 2010.

Smith, P. L. and Ragan, T. J. (2005) *Instructional Design*, 3rd ed., Hoboken, NJ: Wiley-Jossey Bass.

Terzi, L. (2007) 'Capability and Educational Equality: The Just Distribution of Resources to Students with Disabilities and Special Educational Needs,' *Journal of Philosophy of Education*, 41(4): 757–773.

Walker, M. and Unterhalter, E. (2007) 'The Capability Approach: Its Potential for Work in Education,' in A. Sen (ed.), *Capability Approach and Social Justice in Education*, New York, Palgrave Macmillan: 1–18.

Wheelahan, L. (2010) 'The Toothless Tiger: Are Competency-based Qualifications Relevant in a 21st entury Knowledge Society?', TAFE Directors Australia National Conference, 2010: TAFE in the Year of the Tiger, Melbourne. http://www.tda.edu.au/resources/Leesa%20Wheelahan%20-%20Are%20Competency%20Based%20Qualifications%20Revevant%20in%20a%2021st%20Century%20Knowledge%20Society.pdf. Accessed 6 November 2010.

Wheelahan, L. (2012) *Why Knowledge Matters in Curriculum: A Social Realist Argument*, London: Routledge.

Wheelahan, L. and Moodie, G. (2011) *Rethinking Skills in Vocational Education and Training: From Competencies to Capabilities*, Sydney, Board of Vocational Education and Training. http://www.bvet.nsw.gov.au/pdf/rethinking_skills.pdf. Accessed 17 November 2011.

Wheelahan, L., Moodie, G., and Buchanan, J. (2012) *Revitalising the Vocational in Flows of Learning and Labour*, Adelaide: National Centre for Vocational Education Research. http://www.ncver.edu.au/publications/2535. Accessed 30 October 2012.

Willingham, D. T. (2007) 'Critical Thinking: Why Is It So Hard to Teach?', *American Educator*, 31(2): 8–19.

Winch, C. (2010) "Vocational Education, Knowing How and Intelligence Concepts', *Journal of Philosophy of Education*, 44(4): 551–567.

World Bank (2007) ' Building Knowledge Economies: Advanced Strategies for Development', http://siteresources.worldbank.org/KFDLP/Resources/461197-1199907090464/BuildingKEbook.pdf. Accessed 19 January 2011.

Young, M. (2003) 'Comparing Approaches to the Role of Qualifications in the Promotion of Lifelong Learning', *European Journal of Education*, 38(2): 199–211.

Young, M. (2005) 'National Qualifications Frameworks: Their Feasibility for Effective Implementation in Developing Countries'. http://www.ilo.org/wcmsp5/groups/public/---ed_emp/---ifp_skills/documents/publication/wcms_103626.pdf. Accessed 7 July 2009.

Young, M. (2010) 'Why Educators Must Differentiate Knowledge from Experience', *Pacific-Asian Education*, 22(1): 9–20.

Yu, S., Bretherton, T., Schutz, J., and Buchanan, J, (2012) *Understanding the Nature of Vocations Today: Exploring Labour Market Pathways*, Adelaide: National Centre for Vocational Education Research. http://www.ncver.edu.au/publications/2538.html. Accessed 4 November 2012.

CHAPTER 31

WHO PAYS FOR SKILLS?

Differing Perspectives on Who Should pay and Why

LYNN GAMBIN AND TERENCE HOGARTH

INTRODUCTION

GOVERNMENTS over the centuries have increasingly funded education to ensure that their economies possess the skills needed to meet the demands of industry. An implicit element of the social contract in most western economies is that compulsory schooling—which typically lasts between the ages of 5–6 and 15–16 years in most western economies—is publicly funded through taxation. There may be sound economic reasons for the state to fund and provide schooling to people in this age range, but over time it has become a societal norm to provide free schooling for children. Where there is less of a consensus relates to who should pay for post-compulsory education and training. This is an important issue for a number of reasons:

1. Youth unemployment has been a persistent problem in many countries, which has been managed to some extent by persuading young people to stay on in education and training beyond the compulsory minimum age.
2. There is a belief that relative productivity growth between countries is dependent upon the skills of the workforce typically acquired through participation in post-compulsory education and training.
3. Individuals are spending extended periods of time in the labour market, which means their skills will need to be updated at various points over the lifecycle (in other words, lifelong learning).
4. The benefit of education to the wider public has been a long-standing justification for state intervention in the funding of education and similarly for skills and

training. That there are returns to education and training which accrue to not just private individuals, as set out by human capital theory, but also to the public more generally has implications for the role of the state as there is a stronger incentive for ensuring the publicly optimal level of education and training is undertaken.

The above points need be seen in the context of the transition from school-to-work becoming more complex in many countries. Young people have the option of entering a variety of post-compulsory learning activities—some staying in full-time education either in vocational or academic study, others entering employment with training such as apprenticeship. Other young people will enter employment without training or become unemployed. Depending upon the post-compulsory pathway they take, young people are likely to attract differing levels of public funding to cover the costs of their education and training. How people equip themselves with the skills which will maintain their attachment to the labour market has also increasingly fallen within the purview of publicly funded active labour market policy.

In relation to the productivity issue noted above there are concerns that national training systems deliver sub-optimal levels of skill development, which places a constraint on productivity growth. This, for instance, has been an ongoing concern in the United Kingdom where analyses have pointed to a number of market failures affecting the supply of, and demand for, skills (Finegold and Soskice 1988; Wilson and Hogarth 2003). Accordingly, where market failures are suspected, policymakers have sought to identify mechanisms, institutions, and subsidies which may stimulate both the demand and supply sides. The trouble with market failures is that by the time they become apparent, they are exceedingly difficult to remedy.

If much of the initial focus of economics of education and training was on ensuring that the transition from school and in to work was effective—in other words an interest in initial vocational education and training—there is now much more interest in who should fund continuing vocational education and training, particularly as individuals spend a longer period in the labour market. This has been observed with reference to both the need to increase national competitiveness by raising the skill levels of all workers and the lengthening of working lives. If someone receives their initial vocational education and training at, say, age 18 years, this is unlikely to prepare them fully for an expected 50 years in the labour market to an average age of retirement at around, say, 68 years. Hence, over the past few decades the increased emphasis policymakers have placed on the provision of lifelong learning (Vogler-Ludwig et al. 2012). Clearly the economics of equipping someone in their mid-50s with various skills is different from that of supplying them to someone in their mid-20s, if only because the former will have less time remaining in the labour market to generate a return from the skills acquired and may have significantly greater financial and family obligations to fulfil. Vocational education and training, like other forms of education, has characteristics of a public good insofar as the provision of training prepares individuals to fill necessary roles within the market. Like other public goods, there exists the problem of free-riding in relation to training as some employers may decide to recruit already trained or skilled workers rather than investing in their training themselves. There is a risk then that investment in skills may be lower than what is optimal for the economy as a whole thus the state may step in to fund greater volumes of training. As will be demonstrated below, the issue of skills supply, and who should bear the cost of it, is not solely a question of economics. And even if it were, as will be revealed, there is not necessarily a consensus in the economics literature on this issue.

Any commentary which seeks to answer the question 'who should pay for skills', needs to set some limits on its ambitions. It is useful to make a distinction between the initial and its continuing vocational education and training system (IVET and CVET). IVET is likely to take place either within the school or college system (e.g. in vocational schools), be a mix of school-based and workplace learning (e.g. the dual system), or be wholly workplace based. The elements of training which require payment, in either IVET or CVET, include those activities which require the trainee to be engaged in non-productive activity (such as foregone earnings during off-the-job training), training delivery (e.g. by teachers and trainers, or supervisors of on-the-job training), and use of training materials and infrastructure. It is recognized that skill acquisition can be obtained through various forms of informal training—such as experiential learning—but, for the sake of brevity, the focus here is upon more formal learning that requires elements of off- and on-the-job training which are typically associated with readily identifiable costs.

In general, there is acceptance in many countries that the costs of funding IVET are to be shared between the state, the employer, and the trainee, whereas the costs of CVET are principally the responsibility of the employer and the employee. The exception in relation to CVET is those active labour market policies which are designed to move unemployed people back into work. In the main, however, CVET investment decisions are largely seen as private ones by public policymakers. For this reason, the focus in this commentary is on IVET. IVET also includes a multitude of activities in upper secondary and tertiary levels of education. In order to focus the discussion even further the emphasis is very much upon workplace-based IVET at the upper secondary level which incorporates apprenticeships and the dual system of IVET as well as education and training that is delivered wholly by vocational schools. Compared with higher education (HE), at the upper secondary education level there is less consensus about who pays and who benefits from IVET. Argubaly, in HE it is more straightforward to determine who should pay in that individuals themselves are the primary beneficiaries of their investment in learning. For upper secondary IVET, however, the direct involvement of employers in the provision of certain aspects of education and training, along with the productive contribution which learners may make in their employment whilst training, raises more questions about how the costs should be shared.

The commentary starts by providing general insights into the economics of funding skills drawn from the extensive literature on the economics of training, followed by a greater focus more on the issues which arise in relation to IVET. It considers the more market-driven approaches to the funding of IVET, which tend to draw on the theoretical insights provided by the human capital model, along with those which adopt a more co-ordinated approach through various labour market institutions. It also provides a case study of the UK system—or more precisely the system in England—which has over the past 50 years adopted differing approaches to the funding of IVET as it has responded to a number of perceived market failures. In so doing, it demonstrates the way in which the funding of skills is a question of political economy rather than just economics.

Who Should, and Who Does Pay, for What Skills?

Who should pay for skills largely depends upon which type of training is being considered. Even if agreement can be reached on what constitutes the concept of skill—and this is far from a settled issue (Payne 2000; Green 2011)—from the perspective of who should pay for its delivery, the evidence suggests several dimensions that need to be considered. This includes, amongst other things, the content of skill (for example, general versus specific, technical versus generic, initial versus continuing), the means through which the learning related to skill acquisition is transmitted (for instance, formal, informal, and non-formal learning),[1] the modes of delivery related to formal learning (on- and off-the-job training), and the level of skills delivered (that is, according to the level of conceptual difficulty). All these have implications for who can be expected to pay for skills.

The potential 'who' in the question here refers to the individual, the employer, and the state and asks how the balance of costs is to be shared amongst them. There is also the period over which the costs—and the benefits—associated with the acquisition of skills need to be considered. Ideally this needs to take a lifecycle approach. Individuals may have all or some of the costs related to their IVET paid for by the state or their employers, but there will be a flow of benefits which the state and the employer may both share in as individuals deploy the skills they have acquired. From the point of view of the state, these benefits may include increased tax revenues resulting from the enhanced wages of the individual or a reduced need for welfare payments if the individual is more likely to be in employment as a consequence of being more highly skilled and employable. For employers, there are the benefits which derive from the productivity gains associated with having more highly skilled workers, assuming they can retain the services of the employees for whom they have financed training.

The question of who should pay quickly boils down to assessing how the costs of skills training should be shared between individuals, employers, and the state so as to

[1] See Cedefop (2008) for a definition of these types of learning.

optimize the volume and type of skills training undertaken. This is where human capital theory associated with the economists Becker (1962, 1964), Mincer (1962), and Schulz (1963) provides useful analytical insights and, as will be discussed, controversies, too. As will be seen below, human capital theory is concerned almost exclusively with formal training and with skills training classified as being either general or specific. There are other dimensions of training and skills acquisition which might not fit neatly into these classifications.

The evidence on who indeed does pay for training illustrates how the theory about who should share in these costs is useful, but equally it shows that the theoretical predictions are not always fully reflected in reality. There is some degree of sharing in the costs of training in practice but the balance and involvement of individuals, employers, and the state in funding training differs according to many factors including the type of training, type of employer, and the nature of the labour market in which the various parties are located. How much each of the three players is likely to pay depends on the benefits which each can expect to accrue from training taking place, though for the state there are additional societal concerns which can drive its investment decisions.

The total costs of training are made up of various elements which are encountered by employers and employees (Gambin et al. 2010). In a series of studies on the net costs of training to employers, the estimated net costs of apprenticeships met by employers were significant, though they ranged considerably across businesses in different sectors and by the level of training (Hogarth et al. 2012; also Lerman, Chapter 9 in this volume). The state's main contribution in apprenticeships in England is paid directly to organizations which provide training rather than employers (though the intention is to fund employers directly in the future). Research from other countries similarly finds that employers are willing to invest in training staff through apprenticeship at significant net cost (e.g. Soskice 1994; Mohrenweiser and Zwick 2009; Ryan et al. 2011).

Table 31.1 provides an indication of the extent to which costs are shared between employers and the state in the publicly funded apprenticeship system in England. The employers' costs, before taking into account the work apprentices perform, include all the wages of the apprentices, the costs of training to be met by the employer, and an estimate of the apprentice's productive contribution which can be offset against the employer's training costs. In Table 31.1 this is considered relative to the wages of the fully experienced worker. It also provides an estimate of the costs met by the state in funding a training provider to take the employer and the apprentice through the apprenticeship. Estimates are provided for apprenticeships delivered in four sectors. In engineering and construction the estimates relate to more advanced apprenticeships typically taking between three and four years to complete; in retailing and hospitality they relate to lower- level apprenticeships, which typically take between a year and 18 months to complete. The data reveal, firstly, substantial differences in the overall net cost of delivering an apprenticeship, and secondly, that employers across all sectors meet around half the total cost of the apprenticeship. In hospitality and retailing, the relatively low overall cost of an apprenticeship reflects, in part, that the training

Table 31.1 Net costs of training in the UK: Share of overall cost of apprenticeships met by the state and the employer (2011 prices)

	(a)	(b)	(c)	(d)	(e)
Industry sector	Employer costs	Costs of Apprenticeship met by state	Total cost of Apprenticeship (a + b)	% costs met directly by employer (%)	% of costs met directly by the state (%)
Engineering (Level 3)	£39,500	£23,000	£62,500	63	37
Construction (Level 3)	£26,000	£29,500	£55,500	47	53
Retailing (Level 2)	£3,000	£4,000	£7,000	43	57
Hospitality (Level 2)	£5,000	£6,500	£11,500	43	57

Source: Derived from Hogarth et al. (2012).

is designed to give entry to relatively low- skilled jobs. But it also reflects the lack of strong internal labour markets within companies in these sectors. Employers are concerned that that their apprentices will move on to other companies once the apprenticeship has been completed, so they are keen to ensure that the overall net costs of training—once the productive contribution of the apprentice has been subtracted from the gross costs borne by the employer—at the end of the apprenticeships are relatively low or, preferably, zero. Similar results by sector have also been found for Germany (Mohrenweiser and Zwick 2009).

Why does it matter who pays? There are a number of reasons why it is important to address the question. From an economic perspective there is a desire to optimize the provision of training in any economy. Economies are increasingly seen to compete with reference to their stock of human capital hence there is a desire to increase investments in the skills supply. Depending upon the nature of the system in place to secure investments in skills, this is likely to affect the equilibrium position of demand and supply. The more co-ordinated approach adopted by countries such as Germany is considered to have optimized the level of skills investment for intermediate skills like apprentices at a higher level than more market oriented systems such as the United Kingdom and the United States (Acemoglu and Pischke 1999). From a socio-political perspective, there are issues of equity and fairness to consider. People are likely to exit the formal, compulsory education system having acquired differing levels of skills and qualifications. The reasons for this are multifarious but include the relative effectiveness of schools in ensuring that young people receive a good education, however that may be defined. Young people exiting the school system will, to differing degrees, face barriers to accessing HE and IVET because of, for instance, a lack of capital or access to finance to fund any training. This will affect the more socially and economically disadvantaged to a much greater degree. Accordingly, governments to differing degrees provide a range of subsidies to offset any market failures and ensure that young people have access to skill development. This may mitigate, to some extent, any disadvantage they experience as a consequence of the compulsory school system.

The Economics of Training

Historically, the economics of education was regarded as one explained by consumption theory. In many countries, post-compulsory education was seen as a consumption good explained with respect to the tastes of consumers and the costs of schooling (Blaug 1976). The level of this consumption was considered to be a function of wealth, personal tastes, and the costs of participation. Indeed, education (at least some types or aspects) exhibits the properties of a consumption good in that individuals derive utility from undertaking or consuming education and from the status it gives them (i.e. others perceive individuals with particular levels of education as being of a particular social status or quality). The consumption view of education may be effective in explaining the decision to stay on in full-time education and continue on to university, but it has relatively little to say about the determinants of training undertaken by people exiting school and entering employment. Human capital theory, which suggests that individuals and society more generally, stand to derive economic benefits from making investments in people, broke with the past in two important respects. Firstly, the theory specifies that individuals will make investments in education and training which will give them the highest pecuniary return. Secondly, human capital theory explains the different types of training for which employers and employees/individuals are willing to pay.

In specifying participation in post-compulsory training as an investment decision, human capital theory had little to say about IVET outside of the United States and a few other countries such as Japan and the Philippines (Blaug 1976). In the early 1960s post-compulsory education in much of Europe, for instance, was more or less wholly funded by government, which tended to set out the maximum number of places available in schools and colleges. More recently, however, countries such as the United Kingdom have sought to develop a training market which owes at least something to human capital theory.

The human capital model specifies the 'who pays for training' along the lines set out below (derived from Borjas 2002).[2] Assuming that companies are profit maximizing, their total labour costs (TLC) will be equal to the marginal product of labour (MP),

[2] See also Borjas (2002, chapter 7) for an excellent introduction to the wider economics of training.

suitably discounted over time at a certain discount rate (r). Over two periods (1 and 2), the relationship between MP and TLC can be denoted as:

$$TLC_1 + \left(\frac{TLC_2}{1+r}\right) = MP_1 + \left(\frac{MP_2}{1+r}\right) \tag{1}$$

Where employers provide training to employees in the first period, employment costs over the two periods will be equal to the wage of the employee (W_1) plus training costs (S_1) such that the costs of employment will be:

$$W_1 + S_1 = MP_1 + \left(\frac{MP_2}{1+r}\right) \tag{2}$$

In the second period, the training employer cannot avoid paying a wage which is equal to the marginal product of the employee in the second period because all employers, irrespective of whether or not they provide training themselves, will be willing to pay wages, X_2, at such a level (where training is general or transferable to be of benefit in other workplaces). Therefore the employer which provides general training needs to recoup the costs of the training it provides over the training period rather than relying on doing so in the post-training period. The wage paid in the first period (the training period) must be equal to the marginal product of the employee minus the costs of training:

$$W_1 = MP_1 - S_1 \tag{3}$$

If the employer attempts to recoup the costs of training in the latter period, it will by paying a wage lower than the employee's marginal productivity in that period. Other things being equal, so the employee can be expected to move to another employer which pays wages equal to MP_2.

The predictions of the model are somewhat different in relation to specific training (i.e. training that only increases a worker's productivity in the specific firm and thus is not transferable or valued by other employers). The employer in this case can recoup the costs of training in the post-training period by paying a wage (W_2) that is less than the worker's productivity (MP_2) in this second period. This wage is higher than that paid by other employers (X_2) as they would not see a productivity increase amounting from the worker being trained thus they would be willing to pay only up to the worker's previous marginal product (MP_1). In the period after training then the wages paid by the employer are:

$$X_2 < W_2 < MP_2 \tag{4}$$

This in effect shares the costs of specific training between the employer and the employee—the employees receive wages lower than their marginal product after training and employers pay for training (S_1). This sharing of costs arises because the employer cannot guarantee that the employee will remain with the company in the second period, and the employer cannot guarantee that it will not lay off the employee in the future. Because, in the second period, the employee's marginal product is greater than the employee's wage, this provides the employer with a buffer, should market conditions deteriorate, which may reduce the need for redundancies. Additionally, both employer and employee benefit from the training undertaken (employers receive higher marginal product and a rent by paying less than this after the training period and employees receive an increase in wages).

In the outline provided above it is assumed that employers are indifferent to the level of training provided. If employers are to engage in higher levels of training (i.e. training leading to higher levels of skills), they must have an incentive to do so. Training at a higher level will only take place if training at that level increases the marginal product of the employee more than training at a lower level.

The above model is a simple one but it suffices to illustrate the way in which the costs of training may be shared between employers and employees in theory. In practice, there are a range of factors which complicate the outcome. There is also evidence that countries have adopted differing approaches to sharing the costs of training between employers, employees, and the state which do not readily accord with the outline above.

Alternatives to the Human Capital Model

In a perfectly competitive market, investments in skills will be optimized according to the human capital model. There are two issues to consider, however:

1. markets are seldom, if ever, perfectly competitive in practice; and
2. the empirical evidence is far from unequivocal in its support of the human capital model (for example, Acemoglu and Pischke 1999; Blaug 1999).

These issues have helped to focus attention on the risk of market failure which can result from various sources, including (but not limited to):

- capital market problems and credit constraints such that individuals are unable to borrow to fund their investments in skills;
- imperfect information, including asymmetric information such that individuals do not know which skills to invest in so as to obtain the required return on their investment, and employers do not always know which workers will be the productive ones capable of acquiring skills they need; and
- externalities where others gain (or stand to gain) from the investments undertaken by a particular employer/employee. Other employers may poach trained workers

from the training employer. Wider benefits of training are experienced by communities or societies such that the benefits for employers stemming from training their workers do not capture the full benefit of that investment.

These (and other) failures or imperfections can result in employers and individuals investing in sub-optimal levels of training (from different perspectives). Under-investment in training is often attributed to the threat of poaching by non-training employers (e.g. Finegold and Soskice 1988). In response to such failures, there is much weight attached to ensuring that funding mechanisms are in place to allow individuals who wish to invest in their own general skills to do so. There is also an increasing emphasis on providing labour market information to allow would-be trainees and employers to make more informed investment decisions. Information asymmetries have also been suggested to turn 'general' training into 'specific' training; in practice the training in question does not transfer readily to other employers as recruiting employers do not have full information about the training that has been undertaken by a worker within another employer (Barron et al. 1999). In this situation, employers may be seen to fund all or part of general training for their workers.

Wage compression is also thought to arise due to labour market imperfections (including transaction costs and wage bargaining). In labour markets with wage compression, future employers are able to profit from the increased productivity of a worker who has undertaken training as they are able to pay the worker less than their marginal productivity (Acemoglu and Pischke 1999). This wage compression gives added incentive to other employers to poach trained workers from their existing employers. Where this compression is present and there are externalities of training for other employers, the policy solutions of dealing with credit constraints and providing full information will not overcome this further problem and thus employer investment in training may still be sub-optimal. As will be outlined below, wage compression can increase the amount of training funded by employers.

A further complication relating to the human capital model is being able to make a clear distinction between general and specific training, which proves difficult in practice. Employers often require a particular combination of specific and general skills, a combination which may be unique to their workplaces, rather the two being mutually exclusive. Additionally, evidence suggests that employers obtain higher returns from general training rather than specific. Barrett and O'Connell (1997) show that employees value general skills training more highly and, accordingly, reward the employer's investment in this form of training with increased effort on the job. This type of approach is consistent with the gift-exchange theories outlined by Akerlof (1994). Stevens (1994, 1996) sets out a further distinct category of skills that falls between generic and general: transferrable skills which are valued in other firms (so are not specific skills), but as they are traded in an imperfect labour market, the wage paid to the worker is lower than their marginal product (thus different from general skills). There are, especially so in the European Union, models of skills funding in operation which are not consistent with the human capital model but which are considered to work well insofar as they are seen to be relatively effective in producing the skills a national economy requires. The way skills are funded often has relatively deep historical roots in the industrial and employment relations systems of countries. This is seen most keenly in the German dual system where the costs of IVET, much of which is largely transferable in nature, is funded by the employer, the state, and the apprentice (Soskice 1994; Vogler-Ludwig et al. 2012). The employer is seen to fund training by virtue of the fact that at the end of the training period, once the productive output of the apprentice has been subtracted from all the costs borne by the employer (wages and non-wage costs), the employer is observed to be in deficit (Mohrenweiser and Zwick 2009). Soskice (1994) suggests that, in Germany, the costs borne by smaller employers may be over-estimated. Given relatively low post-training retention rates in smaller companies, employers would need to recoup much of their training costs over the training period in order for it to be economically viable. Soskice notes that apprentices in small employers can undertake both unskilled and (increasingly) skilled work, such that is beneficial for the employer to hire an apprentice rather than an unskilled worker. Moreover, much of the training can be done during slack periods by existing employees who are qualified to train, such that any loss to output resulting from a need to train is minimized. In is way, it is economically viable for the small employer to train.

A similar pattern emerges in the UK apprenticeship system as shown in Table 31.1 above (Hogarth et al. 2012). In sectors such as manufacturing and construction where employers do much to retain their apprentices post-training—and where apprenticeships are integrated into firms' internal labour markets—there is a substantial net cost to the employer. In sectors such as retailing, where there is substantial labour turnover post-training, employers ensure that the net cost at the end is relatively low. There are other similarities too. In Germany the state pays for the cost of the vocational schools where the apprentice receives off-the-job training. Again a similar pattern emerges in the United Kingdom where the state pays for training course fees and the apprentice is observed to pay for training by being in receipt of wages below their marginal product (or the wage paid to people in unskilled occupations).

The fact that the employer is willing to pay for general training is seen to stem from a number of factors:

(a) the existence of high-wage, high skill product market strategies;
(b) the role of labour market institutions and their impact on wage compression;
(c) the existence of relatively strong internal labour markets and the concomitant costs associated with recruiting skills in the external labour market; and
(d) the attractiveness of the IVET system to relatively able young people such that the costs associated with training are relatively modest.

In the first instance there has to be a demand for relatively skilled labour. In the German system this has been largely explained with reference to the system of industrial relations, combined with high-quality, high-value-added global product market strategies, which creates a virtuous circle: wage increases need to be paid for by productivity increases which, in turn, create a demand for higher levels of investment in skills and technical change to realize the productivity gains which will pay for the agreed wage increases. Additionally, the role of labour market institutions such as collective bargaining but also minimum wage legislation can set a floor for how far wages for low-skilled people can fall. In other words, the wages of low-skilled workers are likely to be in excess of their marginal product creating an incentive for the employer to employ relatively high-skilled workers because their wages are more likely to equal their marginal product (or exceed it). The existence of strong internal labour markets increases the likelihood that employers can retain their apprentices in the post-training period. This can work in a number of different ways. Employers can offer a range of non-pecuniary benefits, which can increase the attachment of the employee to the firm. There is also the possibility that employers will keep their more able employees after training and release their less able ones. If the more able employees leave, they are likely to be paid the wage associated with the less able workers' marginal product, so the more able employees will be incentivized to stay with their existing employer so long as their wage is higher than that associated with less able employees. There is also evidence that collective bargaining can limit the capacity of employers to offer higher wages than others in the same sector, so there are limited incentives for trained employees to leave the employment of the company which funded their training.

The willingness of the employer to fund general training is also facilitated by the attractiveness of the vocational training system to young people. This in turn helps drive down the costs of training since those young people who enter IVET are relatively able, and therefore can be trained more quickly and at less cost. In this way, the costs which are borne by the employer are constrained.

A recurring issue is how skills development can be maintained within a flexible labour market. In some countries, such as the Germanic ones, a feature of the industrial training system, where the social contract ensures that employers provide relatively high levels of IVET, is the existence of strong internal labour markets. This is thought to impose relatively high costs on the employer—and potentially the employee insofar as wages are likely to be paid below their marginal productivity over the training period—but relatively low levels of labour turnover within the enterprise ensures that the employer can recoup the costs of training over the longer-term (Gospel 1997; Mohrenweiser and Zwick 2009). German firms are able to achieve high levels of functional flexibility (where workers can move across different occupations), achieved through strong internal labour markets with broadly skilled workers. There are substantial rewards for the employee within strong internal labour markets, such as the prospects for promotion in a system which is oriented away from filling vacancies from the external labour market. Economies that rely more on flexible external labour markets, or numerical flexibility, may find it harder to ensure skills supply meets demand. To some extent, the apprenticeship system in Switzerland appears to have achieved the best of both worlds. Here, relatively high levels of training activity continue to take place in the context of a relatively flexible labour market. Switzerland has achieved this by ensuring that apprentices are relatively more productive than their German counterparts during training such that the employer breaks even on the training investment (Muehlemann et al. 2007; Dionsius et al. 2009). In this way, the employer is insured against the risks of training in a flexible labour market, but even in Switzerland an important element of the social contract would appear to be the employer's commitment to providing training. In countries with more flexible labour markets there has arguably been more reliance upon the market to sort out the issues of who pays and ensuring that supply meets demand. The United Kingdom proves to be an interesting case study if only because it has experienced a number of major transformations in the structure of its skills funding system and who pays for it.

The Political Economy of Funding Skills Training—The Example of the United Kingdom

Since the emergence of the human capital model in the early 1960s there has been a large volume of theoretical and empirical investigations into how the funding of skills can be organized to optimize skills supply. The essential problem which has faced policymakers is that, left to its own devices, the market will bring about a solution, or achieve equilibrium, at a level which is lower than that which policymakers, or indeed inhabitants of a country, would rationally desire (Finegold and Soskice 1988). Indeed this is a problem which has bedevilled countries such as the United Kingdom.

The UK system provides an interesting case study of how public funding of IVET has responded in relation to meeting market demand for skills and ensuring that that demand is sufficiently large. Over time, the UK system has veered from one which relied upon industry to self-finance vocational training via a system of training levies—to ensure sufficient skills development in the period before the mid-1970s, to one which during the 1990s and 2000s was increasingly dependent upon state funding of IVET at the upper secondary level, then to the 2010s when the aim is very much for employers and learners to bear an increased share of the overall cost of IVET. As an aside, HE in the United Kingdom from the mid-1990s onwards has become increasingly a private investment matter for the individual, with students (outside of science and engineering subjects) expected to meet more or less the full costs of their tertiary education. The reason the funding of IVET has vacillated so much between market solutions and state intervention is because it has been driven by concerns of under-investment by employers and individuals. This led to greater state intervention. Concerns that the content of training was not meeting the demands of the market meant the emphasis was once more placed upon handing more responsibility to the employer for determining the content and structure of workplace training, along with more responsibility for its funding (UKCES 2013).

A little history will demonstrate the points made above. The Industrial Training Act (1964) was originally implemented in the United Kingdom because of concerns that the market failure caused by poaching was leading industry to provide too little training. This led to the introduction of the levy-grant system, where all employers in a sector were taxed a percentage of payroll to fund skill development, and then, if they provided training, could apply for grants to cover the costs. This was used to fund, amongst other things, apprenticeships up until the 1980s. The evidence suggests that during this time apprenticeships were largely self-financed by industry (Haxby 1989). But participation rates remained low in part because there was limited demand from industry for a form of training which was considered expensive and of long duration. Low levels of post-compulsory participation in education and training and the rise in youth unemployment—an issue returned to below—led government from the 1970s onwards to increasingly provide grants to firms in order for them to fund apprenticeships and other forms of training. At the same time, the school leaving age was rising in the United Kingdom and other industrialized economies, with a shift towards more IVET in public further education colleges where the costs were largely borne by state (which covered tuition) and the learner (insofar as they were not provided with any funding to cover, for instance, living costs). It was this policy development which was behind the further demise of the UK apprenticeship system (Gospel 1997).

These reforms were not sufficient to head-off rising youth unemployment. This led the government at the time to re-establish workplace-based training initially with the introduction of the much maligned Youth Training System (YTS) and, following much fierce criticism about the negligible training content of YTS, the introduction of state-funded Modern Apprenticeships (MA) both of which were designed to get individuals, principally young people, into combined work and training (Fuller and Unwin 2003). With the introduction of MAs in 1994, the workplace-based pathway through further education was reinvigorated. From the mid-1990s onwards, considerable effort and funding was expended upon building employer participation levels in MAs such that school leavers who wished to pursue the vocational education pathway through upper secondary education had a range of options available to them including a relatively wide range of apprenticeships by subject, and a correspondingly wide range of vocational courses delivered by colleges offering full- and part-time vocational courses.

With YTS and MAs, the state took over responsibility for meeting a large share of the cost of providing IVET. Under the successor to MAs, Apprenticeships, the state has met around half the total cost of an apprenticeship through, primarily, meeting the costs of training courses (Hogarth et al. 1996, 2012). The impact of this was to substantially increase the number of apprentices, but at the same time it led to concerns about the extent to which skills being produced were ones which employers and, in aggregate, the economy required. Whilst there was a substantial group of employers which invested substantially in the training of their apprentices because they recognized that the costs would be recouped in the long-term, there were other employers which were making a much more modest investment and were able to ensure that the productive capacity of the apprentice more than compensated for the training costs borne by the employer.

If the challenge during the 1990s was principally that of ensuring that a sufficiently large proportion of young people continued in IVET, the more recent challenge has been that of ensuring that the vocational pathway is responsive to the signals from the demand side about the skills the economy needs. The concern has been that the provision of skills has been too supply-side oriented. In other words, too many employers have been passive participants in a system which acted more as a recruitment device through which employers could attract relatively good quality recruits. The employee would be trained—principally on-the-job in some sectors—and obtain qualifications which employers, again depending upon their sector, regarded as more or less essential to the needs of their business. A large training infrastructure, principally funded by the state, delivered the training and verified the competence of apprentices such that they could be awarded their vocational qualifications. This somewhat overstates the case insofar as there is plenty evidence that the apprenticeship system also delivered high-quality training, was able to actively engage employers, and met their business needs, as well as providing the learner with skills which had a substantial return attached to them (McIntosh 2007; Hogarth et al. 2012). But it captures the essence of the case made in various reviews of IVET in England, such as the Leitch (2006), Wolf (2011) and Richard (2012) reviews, respectively, that the upper secondary vocational education and skills system responded too slowly and inflexibly to the needs of the labour market and may have dampened the demand for vocational training. In the Leitch Review, the need for the skills system to become more responsive to the demand side was clearly spelled out (Leitch 2006). Implementation of Leitch's recommendations led to, amongst other things, greater employer involvement in the design and structure of programmes such as apprenticeships, and providers' funding being increasingly tied to achieving certain outcomes. As recently as 2011, the Wolf Report continued to question the economic value of many vocational qualifications (Wolf 2011).

The UK government policy papers in 2010—*Skills for Sustainable Growth* and *Investing in Skills for Sustainable Growth*—set out the principles for more far reaching change which would increase employer ownership of skills. The employer ownership of the skills agenda marked a substantial break with recent practice insofar as it assumes that the employer will take a larger share of the responsibility for meeting the costs of training. This was highlighted in the Richard Review of Apprenticeships commissioned by the UK government (Richard 2012). Apprenticeships are considered particularly important because, other things being equal, they deliver relatively high returns to employers and individuals compared with other forms of vocational training (McIntosh 2007; National Audit Office 2012).

The concern was that employers were delivering what various training providers—directly funded by the state—wanted them to, rather than what was relevant to the employer. Accordingly, policy has become increasingly oriented towards providing the employer with much more influence over the content and structure of apprenticeships. For this to occur, employers needed to be more active participants in the apprenticeship system. Accordingly, writ large into the new system of apprenticeships under consideration in England in 2014 is the notion of co-investment. At the time of writing the reform of the apprenticeship system and the implementation of the recommendations contained in the Richard Review (2012) are still to be fully worked out, but the state has been clear that it would like to see greater levels of co-investment by employers and, in certain instances, by individuals as well. Employer ownership is predicated on the idea that if employers are expected to make a direct financial contribution to the costs of training delivered by training providers (i.e. the element of training currently paid for by the state), then they will be more likely to take responsibility for ensuring that any training meets their needs and delivers value for money. In addition, the state's contribution to meeting the costs of their training providers may well be routed through the employer to give the employer purchasing power in the market. The employer will be able to obtain several offers from training providers willing to provide the training, and the employer will make a decision based on the quality and price of any offer (see BIS (2013) for an indication of the reforms of funding being considered).

The state's continued funding is, at least in part, designed to ensure a minimum level of skills training and to obtain skills which are likely to serve the trainee well in the wider labour market both now and in the future. Of course, this deals with only one side of the problem: ensuring that supply is responsive to the needs of the employer. It does not deal with the demand side and, as has been well documented, stimulating demand for training where firms' product market strategies are relatively low, is a problem (Finegold and Soskice 1988; Wilson and Hogarth 2003; Mason 2011).

Conclusion

The example outlined above drawn from the United Kingdom illustrates the way in which policymakers tend to take a pragmatic approach to the funding of skills where there are concerns that there is a significant risk of a market failure. The example of the UK case illustrates the wider set of problems which policymakers across many countries seek to tackle through funding IVET. These include:

- a recognition that future national competitiveness is dependent upon the supply of suitably skilled people who are able to design and produce high-value-added goods and services;
- concerns that, left solely to the market, the IVET system will not provide the skills required to safeguard national competitiveness because too few employers adopt the high-value, high-wage product market strategies which create the demand for the type of skills which a high-quality IVET system can produce;
- weak demand for IVET has implications for youth unemployment. Governments have tackled this by increasing the school leaving age and providing incentives to remain in education and training (such as limiting access to out-of-work benefits to 16 and 17 year olds);
- the risk that by the state increasing its role in the provision and funding of IVET it is not necessarily increasing the supply of skills which the economy needs because it has not been able to sufficiently engage employers in IVET.

These are formidable problems which countries face in finding a mechanism for funding IVET which will deliver economically valuable skills but at the same time will do so in sufficient volume to offset the risk of high youth unemployment emerging. Arguably Germany has been able to solve this issue through the way the industrial relation system and the pursuit of high-value global product market strategies reinforce one another in bringing about relatively high levels of engagement in a high-quality IVET system—which is underpinned by various labour market institutions—by both employers and learners. But the German system seems hardly transferable to elsewhere.

The mention of youth unemployment demonstrates that state funding of training is sensitive to conditions in the external labour market. Accordingly the state in many countries has always been willing to fund skills training through a range of active labour market measures. There is recognition that during periods of weak labour market demand, the state must step in to fund skills training to avoid mass youth unrest and assist the unemployed to get back in to work, even if the empirical evidence is somewhat sceptical about the effectiveness of such measures (Meager 2009).

Human capital theory now sets out well-established predictions about who pays for training of workers on the basis of the gains that can be accrued by employers and employees. There are, however, other issues to consider which can impact how training costs are shared. The example of Germany, as mentioned above, with labour market institutions which are mutually supportive in ensuring that skills development is optimal, is frequently cited as a model which does not conform to the human capital model, but which has been effective in developing the country's skills base. Perhaps the main issue on which the human capital model has little to say is how to shift an economy from being a relatively low skills equilibrium to a relatively high skills one. This is an issue which the United Kingdom, and other economies, has grappled with over the past 40–50 years, It is this, perhaps more than anything else, which has been the most significant market failure relating to IVET. Hence the state, especially where faced with high and rising youth unemployment, will tend to intervene to offset the worst effects of market forces.

References

Acemoglu, D. and Pischke, J-S. (1999) 'Beyond Becker: Training in Imperfect Labour Markets', *Economic Journal*, 109 (February): F112–F142.

Akerlof, G. (1982) 'Labor Contracts as Partial Gift Exchange' *Quarterly Journal of Economics*, 974 (November): 543–569.

Barrett, A. and O'Connell, P. J. (2001) 'Does Training Generally Work? The Returns to In-Company Training', *Industrial and Labor Relations Review*, 54(3): 647–662.

Barron, J., Berger, M., and Black, D. (1999) 'Do Workers Pay for On-The-Job Training', *The Journal of Human Resources*, 34(2): 235–252.

Becker, G. (1962) 'Investment in Human Capital: A Theoretical Analysis', *Journal of Political Economy*, 70(5): Investment in Human Beings: 9–49.

Becker, G. (1964) *Human Capital*, New York: Columbia University Press.

BIS (2013) 'Consultation on Funding Reform for Apprenticeships in England. London: Department for Business Innovation and Skills/Department of Education.

Blaug, M. (1976) 'The Empirical Status of Human Capital Theory: A Slightly Jaundiced Survey', *Journal of Economic Literature*, 14(3): 827–853.

Borjas, G. J. (2002) *Labor Economics*, 2nd ed., London: McGraw Hill.

Cedefop (2008) *Terminology of European Education and Training Policy*, Commission of the European Communties: Luxembourg.

Dionsius, R., Muehlemann, S., Pfeifer, H., Walden, G., Wenzelmann, F., and Wolter, S. C. (2009) 'Cost and Benefits of Apprenticeship Training: A Comparison of Germany and Switzerland', *Applied Economics Quarterly*, 55(1): 7–37.

Finegold, D. and Soskice, D. (1988) 'The Failure of Training in Britain: Analysis and Prescription', *Oxford Review of Economic Policy*, 4(3): 21–53.

Fuller. A. and L. Unwin (2003) 'Creating a Modern Apprenticeship: A Critique of the UK's Multi-sector, Social Inclusion Approach', *Journal of Education and Work*, 16(1): 5–25.

Gambin, L., Hasluck, C., and Hogarth, T. (2010) 'Recouping the Costs of Apprenticeship Training: Employer Case Study Evidence from England', *Empirical Research in Vocational Education and Training*, 2(2): 127–146.

Gospel, H. (1995) 'The Decline of Apprenticeship Training in Britain', *Industrial Relations Journal*, 26: 32–44.

Green, F. (2011) *What is Skill? An Inter-Disciplinary Synthesis*, Centre for Learning and Life Chances in Knowledge Economies and Societies. http://www.llakes.org/wp-content/uploads/2011/02/Green-What-is-Skill-reduced.pdf.

Haxby, P. (1989) 'Apprenticeship in the United Kingdom: From ITBs to YTS', *European Journal of Education*, 24(2): 167–181.

Hogarth, T., Gambin, L., Winterbotham, M., Baldauf, B., Briscoe, G., Gunstone, B., Hasluck, C., Koerbitz, C., and Taylor, C. (2012) Employer Investment in Apprenticeships and Workplace Learning: The Fifth Net Benefits of Training to Employers Study, BIS Research Paper no. 67, London: Department for Business, Innovation and Skills.

Hogarth, T., Siora, G., Briscoe, G., and Hasluck, C. (1996) *The Net Costs of Training to Employers*, London: Department for Employment Research Series, HMSO.

Leitch, S. (2006) *Leitch Review of Skills: Prosperity for All—World Class Skills*, London: Stationery Office.

McIntosh, S. (2007) *A Cost-Benefit Analysis of Apprenticeships and Other Vocational Qualifications*, Sheffield: Department for Education and Skills Research Paper RR834.

Meager, N. (2009) 'The Role of Training and Skills Development in Active Labour Market Policies', *International Journal of Training and Development*, 13(1): 1–18.

Mincer, J. (1962) 'On-the-Job Training: Costs, Returns, and Some Implications', *Journal of Political Economy*, Supplement, Part 2, 70(5): 50–79.

Mohrenweiser, J. and Zwick, T. (2009) 'Why do Firms Train Apprentices? The Net Cost Puzzle Reconsidered', *Labour Economics*, 16(6): 631–637.

Muehlemann, S., Schweri, J. Winkelmann, R., and Wolter, S. C. (2007) 'An Empirical Analysis of the Decision to Train Apprentices', *LABOUR: Review of Labour Economics and Industrial Relations*, 21(3): 419–441.

National Audit Office (2012) *Adult Apprenticeships*, Report from the Comptroller and Auditor General.

Payne, J. (2000) 'The Unbearable Lightness of Skill: The Changing Meaning of Skill in UK Policy Discourses and Some Implications for Education and Training', *Journal of Education Policy*, 15(3): 353–369.

Richard, D. (2012) *Richard Review of Apprenticeships*, London: Department for Business Innovation and Skills.

Ryan, P., Wagner, K., Teuber, S., and Backes-Gellner, U. (2011) *Financial Aspects of Apprenticeship Training in Germany, Switzerland, and Great Britain*, Hans Böckler Stiftung Arbeitspapier 241.

Soskice, D. (1994) 'Reconciling Markets and Institutions: The German Apprenticeship System', in L. Lynch (ed.), *Training and the Private Sector: International Comparisons*, Chicago: University of Chicago Press.

Stevens, M. (1994) 'A Theoretical Model of On-the-Job Training with Imperfect Competition', *Oxford Economic Papers*, 46: 537–562.

Stevens, M. (1996) 'Transferable Training and Poaching Externalities', in A. L. Booth and D. J. Snower (eds), *Acquiring Skills*, Cambridge: Cambridge University Press.

Stevens, M. (2001) 'Should Firms be Required to Pay for Training?', *Economic Journal*, 111 (July): 485–505.

UK CES (2013) *Employer Ownership of Skills: Building the Momentum*, Wath-upon-Dearne: UK Commission for Employment and Skills.

Wolf, A. (2011) *Review of Vocational Education: The Wolf Report*, London: Department for Education.

CHAPTER 32

CURRENT CHALLENGES

Policy Lessons and Implications

EWART KEEP

Introduction

As many of the preceding chapters have made clear, the nature of the challenges facing education and training (E&T) policy depends, to some extent at least, on the perceptions and interpretation of trends and events by the policymakers involved and the ways in which they then choose to frame both policy problems and the potential solutions that might be available (Keep and Mayhew 1999). How problems are 'named and framed' matters considerably, and policymakers in different countries will often have widely varying analyses of what the issues are and how they might best be tackled. In part, these differences reflect starting points dictated by national historical legacies (of policy and institutions), but also the economic, ideological, and cultural environment within which the naming and framing process is taking place (see Martin, Chapter 2 in this volume). For instance, in countries where there is a strong attachment to shareholder value models of capitalism, and neo-liberal, laissez-faire economic policies, perceptions of both the causes of the policy challenges around skill and the potential routes to salvation will be very different from the starting point liable to be adopted by a Scandinavian policymaker steeped in social democratic traditions.

The composition of the policy-making community that decides what the challenges are and how they might be addressed varies considerably. In many countries, the national E&T system is managed via elaborate social partnership arrangements alongside substantial devolution of decision-making powers to local and regional levels. This system produces a dispersed power structure. In others, social partnership traditions are lacking and local government and governance is weak or absent, with the result that central government and its agencies may be the main, sometimes the only, real actors within the policy sphere (Martin, Chapter 2, this volume).

At a simpler level, the state of a nation's economy and public finances and how badly these were affected by the global financial crisis (GFC) will also have a profound impact on the nature of the E&T challenges it faces and the options it has for dealing with these. In some cases, state spending on E&T is falling dramatically with profound impacts on the range of policy options that are available, whilst in others, such as China and India, rapid growth in E&T spending has continued.

Another key issue is the scale at which challenges are conceived of and policy responses operationalized—at one extreme lies a view of the national labour market and skills agenda as a single undifferentiated unit, which can be governed via national targets, and where categories such as 'employer' need no further disaggregation or unpacking. Skills policy in England under the New Labour governments (1997 to 2010) exemplified this approach. At the other end of the spectrum lie policies designed to deliver a high degree of granularity with differentiated interventions at sectoral and local levels such as the projects generated from 2000 by the Workforce Investment Act in the United States, and a relatively subtle understanding of how varied and diverse the range of demands covered by phrases such 'employer need' may be. All this suggests that a chapter trying to cover the global policy challenges can, at best, achieve a partial and selective take on the vast array of issues raised by earlier contributions to this volume. The aim, then, is to focus on areas where contention is greatest and/or where international bodies such as the European Union (EU), Organisation for Economic Cooperation and Development (OECD) and International Labour Organization (ILO) are focusing their attention.

The chapter's central argument is that E&T policy is reaching or, in some instances, has already reached a crossroads. One route is to continue down the traditional, well-travelled avenue of a simple, skills supply-led strategy driven by unsophisticated readings of human capital theory. The alternative is to branch out and to adopt policies that see E&T as a component within a much broader set of policies concerned with economic development, business improvement, workplace innovation, productivity growth, and job quality. Some countries (such as the Nordic states) are already quite a long way down this second track. Others, such as Scotland, are starting to follow suit.

Major Challenges

As earlier chapters have identified, there are a range of major trends and challenges that are impacting E&T policy and practice. These include mass unemployment, especially youth unemployment; the globalization of trade and economic activity, including the establishment of global value chains within large multinational corporations (Brown et al. 2011); the internationalization of some segments of the labour market; and technological change and the ongoing evolution of digital technologies (Frey and Osborne 2013). Given space limitations, only three of these overarching challenges will be discussed here—the funding of E&T, changing perceptions of the future shape of the labour market and of work, and over-qualification.

Funding E&T

The GFC created a skills funding crisis, which has had differential impacts across the developed and developing world. For those nations that were severely affected, ongoing deficit reduction policies are placing traditional skills supply models under significant strain. Examples here would be the United States (at both federal and state levels), Spain, Portugal, Italy, Greece, the Irish Republic, the United Kingdom, and many Eastern European members of the EU. For instance, the European Commission reported that in 2012, 19 member states cut their funding for education, and in six states (Greece, Spain, Portugal, Cyprus, Hungary, and Romania) funding fell during the year by more than 5%. In some instances, countries that already had comparatively low levels of spending in this area reduced them still further (EUA 2012; Katsinas et al. 2012; EC 2013, 2014). At the same time, even in countries where the economic shock was more limited, right-of-centre administrations are trimming back state expenditure, with implications for what skills policies can assay. Australia and New Zealand would be examples here.

As Gambin and Hogarth (Chapter 31, this volume) demonstrate, pressure on public budgets can lead to tensions and to a zero-sum competition for finite resources between different stakeholders and streams of E&T activity, such as pre-school programmes, apprenticeships, lifelong learning, and higher education. For instance, in Australia, funding for vocational learning has been cut to bolster spending on primary and secondary schooling. As a result, one important requirement within a resource-constrained policy environment will be the need for clearer cost/benefit analyses of the social and economic returns generated by investment in different forms of learning activity.

Moreover, economic slowdowns place all actors' ability to invest in skills under strain, not least by increasing demand from the unemployed for re-skilling. Both the state and employers simultaneously face spending pressures, which makes it much harder for government to shift the cost burden of training onto the private sector and, in instances where workers are unemployed or experiencing static or declining real wages, their ability to make larger contributions to the cost of skill formation is also going to be squeezed. This situation will make systems based on individual contributions more fragile and problematic, whether in terms of parental support for private forms of education, employee contributions or co-contributions towards adult training and learning, or state-backed loans systems which pay tuition and maintenance costs for various forms of further and higher education. Nevertheless, in England and Australia, public spending on vocational provision has been reduced and in part replaced with income contingent student loans. As a result, in some countries, E&T is facing a 'perfect storm', at the eye of which is funding (Gambin and Hogarth, Chapter 31, this volume).

It would be unwise to assume that this phenomenon will be temporary. Even as economic circumstances have started to improve, problems sometimes remain. The legacy of high levels of public debt and a host of competing demands from delayed infrastructure projects, depleted welfare regimes, the costs of caring for an ageing population, and rising calls on health provision all mean that it would be optimistic to assume that a more relaxed public spending envelope for skills provision is likely to emerge for a long time to come. Indeed, there is a strong possibility that for many national E&T systems the era of publicly-funded expansion is over and that in the future growth and improvement will have to be funded by actors other than the state.

The Future Nature and Shape of Work and of the Employment Relationship

Debates about the future and quality of work and how it is managed have formed the backdrop to thinking about E&T policy for the last quarter of a century or more. As Buchanan et al. (2013, 397) note, 'in modern capitalist societies the material welfare of the bulk of the population is delivered through the labour market'. For work to be effective in fulfilling this role, there has to be enough employment to go around (under and unemployment need to be avoided), and the jobs have to be of sufficient quality (Knox and Warhurst 2015). The dimensions of this include levels of pay to provide that material wellbeing and also intrinsic satisfaction and interesting work, and the degree to which an individual's skills are used (over or under-qualification is avoided), and the amount and patterns of work fit their needs. What jobs look like in future therefore really matters, not least in terms of creating demand for skill, offering opportunities to develop skill and their capacity to utilize skills effectively once created.

A key battleground focuses on the terms in which future skills and knowledge requirements are conceived. There are those who remain insistent that the much-vaunted, oft-heralded knowledge driven economy (KDE) is finally upon us, and that demand for higher levels of skill and far greater creativity, driven by technological change and the forces of globalization, is on an ever-upward curve, shifting the occupational structure towards more high skilled employment, whilst also increasing the skill requirements of lower-end work (Byrne 2014; Gratton 2014; Lawson and Elbaek 2014; Accenture 2015). These beliefs have played out at an international level via the work of global consulting organizations such as McKinsey (e.g. Manyika et al. 2012) and Deloitte (Erickson et al. 2012). It is also deeply engrained in the 'assumptive world' of many policymakers, not least in the United Kingdom (see CBI 2013; Byrne 2014).

What is striking about these often relatively rosy projections of the future is that they co-exist with news in countries such as the United Kingdom and the United States that for many workers in the present, low-skilled work, falling real wages, and minimal levels of creativity and job discretion are the norm, and seem liable to remain so for the foreseeable future. It is also apparent that although upskilling may have some role to play in helping to ameliorate this situation, it is liable to be confined to a relatively limited range of occupations and conditional on other factors (such as the availability of occupational progression routes and career pathways) (Bosch et al. 2010; Plunkett and Hurrell 2013; Tooley Street Research 2014).

As a result of this disconnect between optimistic visions of the future and rather starker current realities, the general tenor of the debate has shifted. Some of the sunnier readings of the future shape of employment and the labour market are now facing sharp and sustained criticism from analysts who see a more dystopian pathway emerging. There are still proponents of a happy, high-skills ending, but there are many others who see technology's ability to destroy jobs and de-skill and routinize work as a major threat (Frey and Osborne 2013; Keen 2014; Naughton 2014; Carr 2015). Instead of a KDE, technology and globalization, or at least some aspects of them, appear to be delivering 'disruptive' competitive strategies, one of whose side effects is often to downgrade earnings and job quality and move more workers into employment that has had large elements of skill and discretion 'disintermediated' or stratified (Brown et al. 2011 and 2015). Traditional conceptions of the relationship between skills and job status, job quality, discretion, earnings, and career progression are under serious threat (Sung and Ashton 2015; Brown et al. 2015). In essence, if the nature of the future of work is open to fundamental contestation, as a result, so too is the future shape and direction of skills policy.

Indeed, almost without anyone noticing it, the policy discourse on work and skills has begun to be shift. The traditional rhetoric focused on the ability of the E&T system to supply the general upskilling that it was assumed a burgeoning KDE would require; which, in turn, would enable more and more people to experience good jobs, higher levels of pay and creativity, and support greater participation in a 'middle class' lifestyle. However, in many developed economies, this dream has failed to materialize. Indeed, there is a growing realization that powerful counter-trends may mean that pay and job quality are, along with discretion and creativity, declining for many workers (Graeber 2013; Taylor 2014), with an accompanying sharp growth of inequality in income and wealth (Piketty 2014). As Krugman has noted (2015, 19), 'as for wages and salaries, never mind college degrees—all the big gains are going to a tiny group of individuals holding strategic positions in corporate suites or astride the crossroads of finance. Rising inequality isn't about who has knowledge; it's about who has power'.

As a result one of the key components of the traditional meta-narrative concerning skills is coming under increasingly serious threat. For example, the World Bank's (2012) *World Development Report 2013 on Jobs* notes that traditional beliefs in skills-led job growth and productivity and wage gains may be misplaced, and that there is a danger that the expected benefits may not always materialize.

Another major and related issue is the ability of the E&T system to cope with what, in some labour markets at least, is an ever-wider spectrum of employment strategies, new forms of employment relationship, and labour market polarization that encompass not just pay and conditions, but also skill levels and the models of work organization and job design that determine these (Brown et al. 2015). There are two challenges. The first relates to who pays for and provides E&T (both initial and continuing) for those who are employed in these new, non-standard types of employment. Research in the UK (Rubery et al. 2010) indicates that temporary and agency staff are substantially less likely to receive training than workers with traditional contracts. More generally, there is some evidence that employers, particularly from the United Kingdom, are stepping back from responsibility for training (CBI 2009; Green et al. 2013) and expecting the state or the individual worker to fund upskilling. This withdrawal suggests that new mechanisms may be needed to help support the funding of training for freelancers and agency staff, and this requirement comes just at the moment when many E&T systems are facing significant cuts in public funding.

The second challenge concerns the ability of E&T systems to cater for increasingly diverse employer needs. Put simply, good and bad jobs may each be clustering in some localities and occupations, and the gap between the most and least knowledge-intensive sectors, and between leading-edge and trailing-edge employers (across a range of factors, product market strategies, pay, working conditions, amounts of training offered, and levels of skills utilization) is arguably wider than ever. Much of the policy rhetoric has for the last two-plus decades implicitly (sometimes explicitly) assumed the widespread adoption of sophisticated, high performance models of work organization and job design. In instances where this is proving not to be the case, or where progress is patchy, there is a now a problem, not least in terms of where to pitch the goals of the E&T system. As long ago as 1999, Crouch et al. pointed to the issues that dispersed patterns and levels of employer demand produce for the public generation of collective goods (in this case skilled labour). Schemes that work for 'leading-edge' employers may be irrelevant for the 'long tail' of trailing-edge firms and vice versa. At the very least, one result may be the need for public policy to engage with employers at a finer level of granularity and to reduce dependency on large-scale, one-size-fits-all training schemes (Sung and Ashton 2015).

A final threat to traditional skills policy is that in some national labour settings the supply of more skills to more people appears to be having a limited impact in addressing the problems of those trapped at the lower end of the labour market in low-skill, dead- end employment (Wright and Sissons 2012; D'Arcy and Hurrell 2014; Schmuecker 2014; Dalziel, Chapter 7, this volume). It is now being recognized that the causes of these problems are not fading away and are indeed now deeply rooted within the power and wage/earnings structures of many economies and labour markets. One marker of this realization is the recent Anglo-American report on 'inclusive prosperity' by the Center for American Progress (Summers and Balls 2015).

Demand, Over-qualification and the Under-utilization of Skills

The final challenge to be reviewed here is qualification mismatch and over-qualification, which have long been a focus for academic research (see Livingstone 1999 and Chapter 14 in this volume), but only relatively recently been afforded much prominence in policy debates. In part, its identification as a problem for policy reflects the growing weight of evidence as to its incidence and scale (Livingstone, Chapter 14, this volume). For example, the OECD's 2013 Adult Skills Survey indicated that out of 22 countries, 20 had one in five or more workers who were over-qualified (14 had 20+% over-qualified, and 6 had 25+% over-qualified) (OECD 2013).

It is worth quoting from the highly prescient and still very relevant words provided in the abstract to Livingstone's 1999 article on lifelong learning and under-employment (1999, 163):

> The knowledge society is alive and well with adults engaged in unprecedented high levels of formal schooling, continuing education courses and informal learning. The 'knowledge economy', however, is still illusory. There is serious under-employment of people's learning capacities in current workplaces ... I suggest that this gap can be adequately addressed not by still more emphasis on lifelong learning, but by substantial economic reforms.

As his Chapter 14 for this volume indicates, these issues largely remain to be addressed. The underlying problem is that increasing the supply of skills without a concomitant rise in demand risks wasting scarce resources on creating skills that may not be required and which cannot be fully deployed. Furthermore, such gluts reduce the wage bargaining power of over-qualified individuals, as, for example, more UK graduates are discovering (de Vries 2014). Faced with this picture, it is becoming harder to make the case for another round of general expansion in skills supply.

As a result of these shifting perceptions of the evolution of the labour market, the political and policy 'moment' during which skills could credibly be depicted as a near-universal 'soft', non-conflictual solution that led to happy endings—in terms of better pay and higher quality jobs—for more and more workers and citizens, appears to be drawing to a close. Besides the fading of the KDE 'vision', the recession's boost to structural unemployment has weakened the recent prevailing policy narratives. In a world where there are currently around 200 million unemployed workers (ILO 2013), and where in some developed countries youth unemployment had by 2014 reached very high levels (Greece 62.5%; Spain 56.4%; Portugal 42.5%; Italy 40.5%), there are real issues about what, if anything, skills can do to help prospective workers gain employment. Many are unemployed not because they lack skills but because there are simply no jobs to go to. Indeed, unemployment and underemployment may put governments under pressure to change course on education and skills policy.

In labour markets where demand for skilled labour is static or only growing slowly, then further major increases in skills may lead to problems with their absorbtion and deployment, and also to what Brown et al. (2011) term 'opportunity traps'. As a result, the ability of upskilling to insulate individuals from the downward pressures on wages and job conditions and to deliver upward mobility is now open to serious challenge (Keep and Mayhew 2010; Brown 2013). As Buchanan et al. (2013) observe, in the United Kingdom and Australia at aggregate level, an ever more highly qualified workforce has witnessed a decline in the linkages between productivity growth and wages over time, and it is now an open question whether in general the bond between education, jobs, and income is tightening or loosening (Brown et al. 2011). Running through these challenges is a common thread—the growing realization that the supply of good jobs at any given moment is possibly finite (particularly within given labour markets), the supply of people qualified to undertake them is often in excess of demand, and that positional competition is increasing, with many people liable to be losers rather than winners (Brown 2013; Livingstone, Chapter 14 in this volume).

The overall outcome is that skills as a vehicle for soft, 'intervention-free intervention' within the productive process, and 'loser-free redistribution' within the labour market (Keep and Mayhew 2010) look less and less credible within many countries. In some parts of the world, the realization that the supply of good jobs is limited and that positional competition for them is increasing, is stoking further rounds of individualized 'arms races' for skills, as students and their parents compete to acquire what they see as scarce human, social, and reputational capital via participation in elite forms of educational provision (Anthony 2014). At the same time, social and political tensions with regard to employment, jobs, pay, and social status are becoming more marked and obvious. As Anthony (2014, 35) argues: 'in an age of economic uncertainty the social fault lines that prosperity had once concealed are now being exposed'.

Policy at a Crossroads

The Traditional Policy Narrative

The notion of skill levels as an indicator or emblem of national success, and the skills system as a key driver of economic growth and competitiveness, and as a means of securing social objectives, has over the last two to three decades become part of a universalized and often somewhat uncritical policy narrative (Keep and Mayhew 2010). For instance, the following quote (Putin 2012) could have come from the leader of almost any developed or developing nation:

> Investments in education will become our key budget priority. Education is not just training the workforce for the needs of the economy but an important factor of social progress and the development of values that unite us. Our system of education and training should meet the challenges of modern times. Schools no longer give people a chance to move to a higher social group. Instead, they reproduce and perpetuate social differentiation. Children should not be held hostage to (sic) social or cultural status of their families.

The rising salience of skills within national and international policy pertaining to economic growth and social justice meant that for a long time E&T policy, general and vocational, were on a supply side roll—able to secure larger amounts of both public funding and political capital.

As suggested above, in some countries this period may now either be, or be coming to, an end. The key reason for this potential passing of an era resides with a crisis of resources—of two kinds. Firstly, as noted earlier, for those nations badly affected by the

GFC, public finances will no longer easily allow significant further expansion of activity. For countries, such as England, that have relied upon a state-funded supply-push linked to ambitions to be 'world class' on skills (as evidenced in various OECD league tables), successive rounds of funding cuts are rendering these long-standing policy objectives increasingly unattainable and unrealistic. Moreover, as noted above, in some instances employers are seeking to minimize their responsibilities to contribute, declining levels of real pay are reducing the capacity of individuals to fund their own upskilling, and as a result major issues loom around attempts to shift more of the burden of cost onto employers or individuals (Keep 2015).

Secondly, and in many ways rather less visibly, the intellectual arguments to justify and sustain another round of large scale supply side measures are open to serious doubt. Increasingly, as noted above, both practical experience and research are raising questions about the case for investment in skills that has underlain policy. The standard human capital-based policy narrative is under sustained pressure for two sets of reasons. The first has been explored above in terms of changing visions of how the labour market and employment relationship are evolving and what these are delivering in terms of earnings, job quality, and the need for skills. The second set of reasons is bound up with the fact that, as many of the chapters in this volume reveal, there is a huge disconnect between the rich, complex, multi-faceted reality of how skills are created, measured, certified, and deployed to support competitive advantage and social goals, and the often simplistic and reductionist policy models of human capital theory upon which traditional skills supply interventions have usually been based. These two factors, taken together, represent a meta-level challenge to policy as previously conceived, albeit one of which some policymakers and commentators remain blissfully unaware.

Simple Human Capital Models Hit the Rocks?

The central assumption behind skills policy as it has been developed by bodies such as the OECD and many national governments for the last 30 years has been the explicit belief that (Keep 2013):

Participation = achievement = qualification acquisition = skill acquisition = higher productivity = wage gain

In at least some instances, this belief, derived from a relatively crude reading of human capital theory, is incorrect (Grugulis et al., Chapter 18, and Dalziel, Chapter 7, in this volume). For some kinds and levels of vocational learning, for significant numbers of individuals and those that employ them, the = signs are, in certain labour markets, highly conditional. For example, in the United Kingdom some forms and levels of vocational qualification generate nugatory gains within the labour market (Wolf 2011); moreover the causal linkages between skills and productivity are far more complex and conditional than policy often assumes (Keep et al. 2006).

Despite these problems, the traditional 'build and they will come' model of human capital supply and accumulation continues to have many steadfast supporters (as is explored by Holmes, and also Grugulis et al., Chapter 18 in this volume). A significant number of policymakers and analysts across the globe still argue for the existence of a direct causal relationship between skills and economic performance, whereby an increase in human capital of 'x' will produce a rise in output or productivity of 'y'. For example, the Boston Consulting Group (2010) argued, in a report written for a UK charity concerned with social mobility, that there is a simple correlation between education, economic performance and GDP, and therefore by 'boosting the educational outcomes of children from less educated families so that their absolute test scores are in line with the UK average—but without reducing the scores of those from the most educated families', the result would be a £14bn a year increase in GDP by 2030 (Boston Consulting Group 2010, 5). Precisely the same kind of arguments were recently deployed in the United Kingdom in relation to the case for expanding the apprenticeship system (Todd 2014), and on the international stage Andreas Schleicker, the OECD's director for education and skills, has argued that deficiencies in the UK's school system are resulting in £4.5 trillion worth of lost economic output over a lifetime (Wilby 2013). Indeed, some go further and hold to a belief in what the UK government dubbed a 'supply-push' model of skill formation, whereby publicly-funded increases in supply lead to subsequent, self-sustaining increases in demand for skills within the economy—in other words a form of Say's Law (Keep and Mayhew 2014).

The problem is that the gap between these happy stories and the actual economic and social outcomes that skills policies have generated within specific labour market settings is now wide and becoming more visible. For example, there is now a major question about the ability of skills to act as a distinctive, unique, and hard-to-copy source of competitive advantage (Brown et al. 2011). Whilst it might be true at the level of the individual organization in relation to skills, knowledge, and capacities that relate to its processes, products and strategies; it is extremely hard to see how much longer it can be held to be so in relation to nation states. As Brazil, Russia, India, and China (the BRIC countries) are demonstrating, high skill levels (at least at localized or sectoral levels) can be brought into being relatively swiftly. Thus, graduate skill levels are unlikely to form a distinctive source of competitive advantage when they are becoming increasing ubiquitous and relatively easily replicable (Brown et al. 2011).

Moreover, even before the GFC, it was becoming clear that skills supply was at best a necessary but not sufficient condition for progress; many other factors need to be in place to catalyse the full value of investment in skills, and in some circumstances there is a danger that supply could outstrip labour market demand with damaging consequences for many individuals and the societies in which they lived (Keep et al. 2006; Brown et al. 2011; OECD 2012; Grugulis et al., Chapter 18, this volume).

The case of New Zealand is instructive in demonstrating the practical limits of traditional policies based on human capital theory. Successive New Zealand governments have sought to follow the policy model set out by the OECD for securing higher productivity and competitiveness. Relatively flexible and deregulated labour markets have been one key component, alongside sustained investment in tertiary education. According to the OECD's own estimates, these policy settings should have resulted in New Zealand's productivity being as much as 20% above the OECD average. In reality, relative to many other OECD countries, both productivity and per capita income levels are weak, and New Zealand's productivity currently trails the OECD average by about 27% (de Serres et al. 2014). Its economy does not lack for skills rather it struggles to deploy them productively. As the evidence on over-qualification cited above suggests, this is a major and growing problem.

As a result, two competing meta narratives are now battling for supremacy. Firstly, is it simply a matter of a skills/human capital supply 'crisis', often supposedly caused by some form of market failure, which can be addressed by increasing human capital production (in terms of both quantity and quality), or, secondly, does the problem very often revolve around the interplay between various weaknesses in the supply of, demand for, and utilization of skill within the economy and labour market? This choice is a multifaceted one. At an initial level it is between an unsophisticated and very literal reading of human capital theory versus much more nuanced and complex narratives about how economic growth, innovation, and wealth creation are engendered and supported (Holmes, Chapter 17, in this volume; Brown et al. 2015). At another, it is between models of policymaking that are limited to or attracted by the idea of uncomplicated monocausal problems that can be addressed via simple, one-size-fits-all, centrally designed 'schemes'; and those that recognize that E&T policy needs to accommodate and mediate between the competing needs and goals of different stakeholder groups and where governance and policy instrument design needs to be shared and to differentiate between and react to varied demands (for example, between different sectors in the economy).

New Horizons versus Path Dependency?

Perhaps the key turning point in the international development of policy on vocational skills and indeed on investment in wider forms of education came with the publication of the OECD's new skills strategy in 2012. This moved the benchmark for debate beyond the traditional focus on supply and admitted that a new agenda that encompassed the demand for, supply of, and utilization of skills represented the new 'holy grail'. However, the OECD's own formulation of this model betrays signs of internal conflict and confusion about how far beyond traditional skills supply policies nations might need to move (see, for example, Schleicker 2014).

In deciding how to respond, if at all, to the OECD's revised policy model, countries have, unsurprisingly, reacted in different ways. For some still fast-developing nations, a primary focus upon a traditional supply-led approach remains appropriate. For others, such as the Nordic countries and Singapore, the OECD's new model simply reflects policy aims and approaches which integrate skills policy with wider employment, employee relations, innovation, and economic development policies in ways with which they are already familiar, although attempting to do so often raises major challenges (see

Sung and Raddon, Chapter 24, this volume). However, there is a group of countries, such as England, the United States, Australia, and New Zealand, where some elements of the new model have been tentatively tried (and in some cases also abandoned—see Buchanan et al. in the Introduction to this volume) and where policymakers are still struggling to come to terms with the scale and nature of the changes that would be required. In particular, for administrations wedded to a generally laissez-faire approach to the economy, the shift in policy emphasis from supply-side pushes to demand-side interventions has tended to be difficult to take on board and implement, and skills policies are currently exhibiting signs of path dependency.

That this situation should be the case is not entirely surprising, as what it suggests is the need for a painful and fundamental re-alignment of policy's strategic conceptual underpinnings, design principles, and management structures and routines. It also means developing institutions that can design and deliver an effective industrial policy. If strategy is to encompass demand, supply, and utilization, then the traditional policy model becomes at worst obsolete, and at best simply one component within a wider suite of policy considerations. Thus skills policy blurs into issues such as economic development, business improvement, labour and product market regulation regimes, work organization, job design, and workplace innovation (Sung and Ashton 2015). In other words, the new policy construct would need to be much more integrated and capable of significant levels of boundary crossing.

For government departments and agencies that have been used to designing and managing relatively simple skill supply systems and funding regimes, these unfamiliar and potentially challenging requirements may be impeded by capacity constraints. In other words, part of the skills challenge is governments' ability to develop and nurture the range of skills and experience needed to design and deliver new forms of policy (Brown et al. 2015). For instance, in England a long tradition of relatively narrowly framed, skills-supply focused policy moves has led to attenuation in both the breadth and depth of policy development and delivery capacity. Policymakers currently know how to design and manage a complex funding formula for E&T delivery; they have little or no idea how they might link skills development to workplace innovation and job redesign (Keep 2013; Keep and Mayhew 2014). For policy systems that find themselves bounded by these conceptual and capability constraints, the new model is often liable to be perceived as more of a threat than an opportunity.

Another issue that emerges, albeit obliquely, from some of the chapters in this volume is that E&T is now a major industry in its own right. It employs large numbers of staff, has institutions that are highly visible within their local communities, and are major providers of employment and spending power, and these institutions, whether public or private, are usually represented by regional or national lobbying organizations. This 'industry' often has a vested interest in maintaining and promulgating supply-led solutions as a means of securing resources and maintaining momentum and often 'captures' initiatives that initially seek to move beyond supply (Payne 2011).

The upshot of all this, as Buchanan et al. (Chapter 21 in this volume) demonstrate very clearly, is that even when policy attempts to re-frame the skills problem and to pilot a fresh approach—in this instance that afforded by skill ecosystems—there are a strong countervailing pressures that may lead to policy sooner or later reverting to a simple, traditional supply model. Australia's ecosystem approach, although an important experiment, ultimately struggled to bring about a fundamental and lasting re-orientation in the way the skills system defined its role and delivered its responsibilities, in part due to changes in government at both state and federal levels but also because many policy makers, delivery agents, and institutions proved resistant to the underlying philosophy, found the new model challenging to deliver, and ultimately discovered the means to revert to more familiar ways of framing the issues (Buchanan et al., Chapter 21, this volume; Eddington and Toner 2012). Thus, Australian policy regressed to fairly traditional concerns about establishing and maintaining a training marketplace, and the E&T system's ability to meet and match the needs of employers. The ecosystems projects' main impact was probably to make issues about demand for skill (and what factors might underlie and shape demand) more visible, but it did not lead to a sustained and widespread policy focus on areas such as skills utilization (Buchanan et al., Chapter 21, this volume).

What Now Constitutes Success for Policy?

As noted above, thinking in some countries and international organizations about E&T policy and practice has undergone gradual but radical change. The emergent approach brings with it a set of contests about what now constitutes good practice across many facets of E&T systems design and management. One example concerns what constitutes 'success' or successful performance by a national skills system or the institutions therein, and how best to judge this success. The tradition model, to which many cling quite tenaciously, is based upon key metrics that see measurement of student flows through the system (participation), and outputs in the form of certified stocks and flows of human capital (completed qualifications) as what matters. International qualification stock benchmarking exercises, such as the UK government's Leitch Review (2006), have helped drive this model (Keep 2008). In the same way, the OECD's extensive international testing regimes (PISA and PIAAC) also feed a model where national standing in the 'league tables' dominates public policy agenda setting in some nations (Sellar and Lingard 2014). Sellar and Lingard argue that this OECD testing and benchmarking system represents a form of global governance for education, whereby, 'we are seeing the constitution of a global policy field in education created through numbers, statistics and data' (2014, 931).

In the new policy environment there are major problems and weaknesses with both the OECD's outputs and stocks of skills/qualifications approach (Keep et al. 2006; Torrance 2006; Lingard 2011; Sellar and Lingard 2014), and with counting student participation. On this latter point, as Wolf and Jenkins (2014) demonstrate with regard to England's adult literacy strategy, participation in learning activity does not automatically equate with learning itself, nor with significant and lasting gains in skill levels. Being there and passing through is sometimes not enough.

More recently, in part in response to some of the problems that researchers have raised about the meaning and importance that can be attached to a stocks and flows approach, a somewhat more sophisticated variant has emerged which tries to move beyond outputs to see what outcomes (economic and social) the outputs actually generate (for example, wage gains). The problem, as much of the foregoing has indicated, is that the linkages between E&T outputs and economic and social outcomes is far more complex and conditional than simple-minded takes on human capital theory might suggest. As a result, finding reliable outcome measures and being able to calculate what proportion of any outcome is attributable to learning rather than to any other factors is often extremely challenging.

Countries seeking to adopt a new, broader model of E&T policy that bundles together training with other forms of business support and improvement require both government and intermediary agencies to think and act differently on two fronts. Firstly, government must work with and support industry and social partners on skills and industrial policy. Secondly, government must develop performance management systems and key performance indicators, as well as project management delivery systems, the architecture and management of intermediary bodies, funding regimes, policy design, and management skills and routines (in relation to experience with the ecosystems approach in Queensland: see Eddington and Eddington 2010). This kind of wholesale re-imaganing of E&T policy and practice is a demanding 'ask', since it requires individuals and organizations to re-orient thinking and behaviours in ways that are sometimes counter-intuitive given traditional policy assumptions about what skills policy and success therein are meant to look like.

Classroom versus Workplace (and How Do We Make the Workplace Better)?

The final policy challenge relates to the need to review the balance between classroom and workplace as the primary site for delivering initial and continuing E&T, and to re-think how policy can support more and better workplace learning. Competition between modes of provision matters, for at least two reasons. Firstly, in nations where public spending is under pressure, a shift towards more apprenticeship-style learning, where employers are liable to bear a proportion of the cost, makes good sense as the funding of full-time classroom-based post-compulsory provision generally falls on the state and/or the student and their families.

Secondly, in some instances, countries that have focused attention on expanding mass college- or higher-education-based provision have started to question whether this strategy is the most relevant and effective means of creating vocational skill. One example would be India, where the government has announced a programme that aims to train 500 million people in vocational skills by 2022 (Evans 2013; Liu and Finegold, Chapter 25, this volume) as a response to a traditional over-emphasis upon academic learning. How easy this target will be to achieve is an open question. As one commentator noted:

> There's a robotic fixation among parents to have their children go into higher education and a genuine apathy towards participating in vocational education. When it comes to encouraging young people to undertake vocational training, the natural position of many Indian parents is that they don't want their children to be plumbers or electricians because those jobs are seen as being for lower class citizens … the government will have to do more if it is to tackle this. India faces an enormous society-wide problem if it doesn't, because it will have so many people out of work. (Evans 2013: 20–21)

Evidence suggests that similar problems may pertain in countries such as China, Taiwan, and South Korea (see Sung and Raddon, Chapter 24, this volume; Liu and Finegold, Chapter 25, this volume). Meanwhile, for nations that have strong apprenticeship traditions, such as Germany, the challenge is to develop a new balance between this tradition and rising demand for HE.

As Unwin's chapter (Chapter 11, this volume) makes clear, work-based learning, formal and informal, is a vital means of creating skill, albeit one that is generally more complex to design and manage than classroom-based activity. In particular, in most instances it delivers the vast bulk of adult and continuing vocational upskilling and reskilling. Because this activity takes place within the firm, it is sometimes less visible to policymakers. Recent advances in our understanding of workplace learning, its linkages to how work is designed and structured, and how it can be expanded and improved (see Evans et al. 2006; Eraut and Hirsh 2007; Felstead et al. 2009) mean that it is likely that many of the next major advances in policy and practice will be focused on what happens within the organization and the workplace, rather than the external E&T system.

The other reason why workplace learning matters is because it is linked with those forms of bottom-up, employee-driven innovation that drive productivity gains (Lundvall et al. 2008; OECD 2010a, 2010b; Campbell 2012; Froy 2013). Indeed, it can be argued that by restructuring work it is possible to simultaneously boost the volume and quality of workplace learning, improve how skills are utilized within the productive process, and increase the potential for employee-driven innovation (Lundvall et al. 2008; Keep 2013). A focus on organizational development and the structure and quality of jobs means that policy needs to engage with employment relations policies and practices, and with what goes on within the 'black box' of the firm. This agenda requires a willingness to open the 'black box' and responsive policies and systems that are able to deliver bespoke interventions and support services at sectoral and sub-sectoral levels (see Ramstad 2009a, 2009b; Froy 2013).

Final Thoughts

This chapter has outlined a range of challenges to E&T policy, particularly as it has traditionally been conceived and framed. The seriousness of these will vary from nation to nation but most countries face at least some of them, and international bodies that have an interest in skills issues, such as the OECD, will need think about how to address the full spectrum of issues. For an example of one country's response in terms of grappling with these issues—Singapore—see Brown et al. (2015).

As a result of these challenges, this chapter has argued that in some parts of the world a spectrum of new models of policy are slowly and haltingly emerging. As a result, in the longer term it seems likely that at least some countries will re-think and re-orient their skills systems, both to stress the involvement of stakeholders other than the state and also to integrate skills issues within wider considerations of economic development, business improvement, work organization, job design, employee relations, and workplace innovation (Keep and Mayhew 2014). The re-focusing required means a reduced emphasis upon human capital accumulation and greater stress on demand and usage. In this new policy model, traditional skills supply issues represent not the end point but simply stage one of a suite of policies that reach deep into the firm and seek to influence its strategies (Sung and Ashton 2015) as well as into the surrounding labour market environment. As a result, the rules, goals and nature of the policy narrative and how it is enacted may be undergoing a paradigm shift.

These new models bring with them many fresh challenges. At national and subnational levels the capacity and resources (financial, political, organizational, and cultural) that can be marshalled to address these problems will vary very considerably, and some countries and their E&T systems will probably struggle to design and enact successful changes. In some instances it can be argued that the nations that face the largest challenges are those that will often have the weakest capacity for mounting a credible response. These countries include the former Communist states of Eastern Europe, and countries with weak trade unions and employer associations where the lack of collective organization renders many policy options hard to pursue, though even where relatively strong social partnership bodies exist, they may not always embrace change or support progressive policy developments.

In terms of how actors are responding to the new opportunities, it can be argued that there are potentially at least five groupings:

1. *Early adopters*, including the Nordic countries and Singapore. Scotland aspires to join this club but at present is probably in the next category.
2. *Experimenters*, who are testing out how the new model might be enacted. The OECD is an example here. The OECD's own internal debates about their skills strategy suggest that there is a strong desire on the part of many within the organization to cling on to the old supply-led model and also confusion about how best to design and deliver policy interventions that address demand and usage. The OECD's work with Norway on their new skills strategy (OECD 2014) illustrates that it is far easier to come up with new ways to supply skills and try and harmonize/match these with demand than it is to increase demand or improve how skills are mobilized within work.

3. *Discouraged experimenters*, who have decided that the road is too hard and who have reverted to the traditional policy model. Australia's experiences with skill ecosystems are an example here.
4. *The undecided*. England would fall into this category. At the level of superficial policy rhetoric, elements of the new model appear on the fringes of policy pronouncements but are backed by little concerted action. The vast bulk of activity remains focused on skills supply, although the public resources to make this approach work are rapidly dwindling.
5. *The unready*. This large category would cover much of the developing world, such as China and India, as well as developed nations that have remained focused on expanding skills supply or whose policy capacity has been paralysed by spending cuts and wider economic recession.[1]

The final point to make is that in seeking to bring about this re-focusing, a key issue concerns the aims of policy. What is E&T for? Is it, as many educationalists continue to claim, essentially concerned with an individual's search for knowledge and meaning in life, or, at the other extreme, is it concerned with economic efficiency whereby workers (prospective and current) equip themselves with the requisite skills needed to match their capabilities with demand within the labour market? Is E&T about personal fulfilment or economic competitiveness, or socializing and equipping people to perform as citizens, or some mixture of these different objectives—and if it is a blend, what is the optimal balance between the different components or objectives? For an interesting and insightful discussion of these issues as they relate to one country—Scotland—see Paterson (2014).

In contemplating these questions, there is a huge disjuncture and tension between the rich, multi-faceted reality of how E&T and skills impact upon both the social and economic domains at the level of individual, family, community, firm, locality, occupation, region, sector, nation state, and international trading bloc; and the more or less uni-dimensional, reductionist 'box' of human capital accumulation and market failure which forms the assumptive world within which traditional supply-led skills policies have been formed. In essence, the operating model that much policy has been based upon cannot cope with the real world, and therefore chooses to ignore it. In circumstances where resources are constrained, hard choices now have to be made, and non-state stakeholders are liable to have to invest more, understanding what the purpose(s) of such investment might be, and aligning provision with those objectives, would seem to make sense. Richer and more complex models of what is going on and what effects activity produces in the social and economic spheres would help.

[1] For an overview of approaches and trajectories across the OECD, see Campbell (2012).

REFERENCES

Accenture (2015) Accenture Technological Vision 2015, Digital Business Era: Stretch Your Boundaries. http://www.techtrends.accenture.com/us-en/assets/Executive_Summary_Technological_Vision_2015.pdf.

Anthony, A. (2014) 'The Class War is Back Again—and Haunting the Politicians', *The Observer*, 30 November: 34–35.

Bosch, G., Mayhew, K., and Gautié, G. (2010) 'Industrial Relations, Legal Regulations and Wage Setting', in J. Gautié and J. Schmitt (eds), *Low Wage Work in the Wealthy World*, New York: Russell Sage Foundation: 99–146.

Boston Consulting Group (2010) *The Mobility Manifesto*, London: Sutton Trust.

Brown, P. (2013) 'Education, Opportunity and the Prospects for Social Mobility', *British Journal of Sociology of Education*, 35(5–6):678–700.

Brown, P., Lauder, H., and Ashton, D. (2011) *The Global Auction: The Broken Promises of Education, Jobs and Incomes*, Oxford: Oxford University Press.

Brown, P., Lauder, H., and Sung, J. (2015) 'Global Value Chains and the Future of High Skills: Evidence from Singapore and Its Implications for the UK', UKCES Briefing Paper, Wath-upon-Dearne: UK Commission for Employment and Skills.

Buchanan, J., Dymski, G., Froud, J., Johal, S., Leaver, A., and Williams, K. 2013. 'Unsustainable Employment Portfolios', *Work, Employment and Society*, 27(3): 396–413.

Byrne, L. (2014) *Robbins Rebooted: How We Earn Our Way in the Second Machine Age*, London: Social Market Foundation.

Campbell, M. (2012) 'Skills for Prosperity?' A review of OECD and partner country skills strategies', LLAKES Research Paper no. 39, London: Institute of Education: LLAKES.

Carr, N. (2015) *The Glass Cage: Where Automation is Taking Us*, London: Bodley Head.

Confederation of British Industry (CBI) (2009) *The Shape of Business: The Next 10 Years*, London: CBI.

Confederation of British Industry (CBI) (2013) *Tomorrow's Growth: New Routes to Higher Skills*, London: CBI.

Crouch, D., Finegold, D., and Sako, M. (1999) *Are Skills the Answer?* Oxford: Oxford University Press.

D'Arcy, C. and Hurrell, A. (2014) *Escape Plan: Understanding Who Progresses from Low Pay and Who Gets Stuck*, London: Resolution Foundation.

de Serres, A., Yashior, N., and Boulhol, H. (2014) 'An International Perspective on the New Zealand Productivity Paradox', New Zealand Productivity Commission Working Paper 2014/01, Wellington: NZ Productivity Commission.

de Vries, R. (2014) *Earning by Degrees: Differences in the Career Outcomes of UK Graduates*, London: The Sutton Trust.

Eddington, N. and Eddington, I. (2010) 'Methods and Instruments for the Evaluation and Monitoring of VET Systems', SKOPE Research Paper no. 98, SKOPE, Cardiff University.

Eddington, N. and Toner, P. (2012) 'Skills Formation Strategies in Queensland', OECD LEED Working Papers 2012/07, Paris: OECD.

Eraut, M. and Hirsh, W. (2007) 'The Significance of Workplace Learning for Individuals, Groups and Organizations', SKOPE Monograph no. 9, SKOPE, Cardiff University.

Erickson, R., Schwartz, J., and Ensell J. (2012) 'The Talent Paradox, Critical Skills, Recession and the Illusion of Plenitude', in *Deloitte ON Talent: The Talent Paradox: A 21st Century Talent and Leadership Agenda*, Los Angeles: Deloitte University Press, 7–15.

European Commission (EC) (2013) *Funding of Education in Europe 2000–2012: The Impact of the Economic Crisis*, Eurydice Report, Luxembourg: Publications Office of the European Union.
European Commission (EC) (2014) *Education and Training Monitor 2014*, Luxembourg: Publications Office of the European Union.
European Universities Association (2012) *EUA's Public Funding Observatory (June 2012)*, Brussels: EUA.
Evans, D. (2013) 'Vocational Education Can Give People a Life of Dignity', *Times Educational Supplement*, 31 May, 5046: 20–22.
Evans, K., Hodkinson, P., Rainbird, H., and Unwin, L (eds) (2006) *Improving Workplace Learning*, London: Routledge.
Felstead, A., Fuller, A., Jewson, N., and Unwin, L. (2009) *Improving Working as Learning*, London: Routledge.
Frey, C. B. and Osborne, M. A. (2013) 'The Future of Employment: How Susceptible are Jobs to Computerisation?', Oxford Martin School Paper, Martin School, Oxford University.
Froy, F. 2013. 'Global Policy Developments towards Industrial Policy and Skills: Skills for Competitiveness and Growth', *Oxford Review of Economic Policy*, 29(2): 344–360.
Graeber, D. (2013) 'On the Phenomenon of Bullshit Jobs', *Strike Magazine*, 17 August. www.strikemag.org/bullshit-jobs/.
Gratton, L. (2014) 'Shifting Labour Landscapes', *Royal Society of Arts Journal*, 3: 10–15.
Green, F., Felstead, A., Gallie, D., and Inanc, H. (2013) *Training in Britain: First Findings from the Skills and Employment Survey 2012*, LLAKES, Institute of Education, University of London.
International Labour Organisation (2013) *World of Work Report 2013*, Geneva: ILO.
Katsinas, S. G., D'Amico, M. M., and Friedel, J. N. (2012) 'Workforce Training in a Recovering Economy', *Workforce Training*, Tuscaloosa: University of Alabama, Education Policy Centre (September): 1–16.
Keen, A. (2015) *The Internet Is Not the Answer*, London: Atlantic Books.
Keep, E. (2013) 'Opening the "Black Box": The Increasing Importance of a Public Policy Focus on What Happens in the Workplace', *SDS Skills in Focus Paper*, Glasgow: Skills Development Scotland.
Keep, E. (2015) *Employer Ownership of the Skills Agenda: What, Who and How?* London: Chartered Institute of Personnel and Development.
Keep, E. and Mayhew, K. (1999) 'The Assessment: Knowledge, Skills and Competitiveness', *Oxford Review of Economic Performance*, 15(1): 1–15.
Keep, E. and Mayhew, K. (2010) 'Moving Beyond Skills as a Social and Economic Panacea?', *Work, Employment and Society*, 25(4): 357–379.
Keep, E. and Mayhew, K. (2014) 'Industrial Strategy and the Future of Skills Policy', *CIPD Research Insight*, London: Chartered Institute of Personnel and Development.
Keep, E., Mayhew, K., and Payne, J. (2006) 'From Skills Revolution to Productivity Miracle: Not as Easy as It Sounds?', *Oxford Review of Economic Policy*, 22(4): 539–559.
Knox, A. and Warhurst, C. (2015) *Job Quality in Australia: Perspectives, Problems and Proposals*, Annandale, NSW: Federation Press.
Krugman, P. (2015) 'Knowledge isn't Power', *New York Times*, 23 February: A19. http://nyti.ms/1FNM7LT. Accessed 13 April 2015.
Lawson, N. and Elbaek, U. (2014) *The Bridge*, London: Compass.
Leitch Review of Skills (2006) *Prosperity for All in the Global Economy: World Class Skills*, London: H. M. Treasury.

Lingard, B. (2011) 'Policy as Numbers: Accounting for Educational Research', *The Australian Educational Researcher*, 38(4): 355–382.
Livingstone, D. (1999) 'Lifelong Learning and Underemployment in the Knowledge Society: A North American Perspective', *Comparative Education*, 35(2): 163–186.
Lundvall, B-A., Rasmussen, P., and Lorenz, P. (2008) 'Education in the Learning Economy: A European Perspective', *Policy Futures in Education*, 6(6): 681–700.
Manyika, J., Lund, S., Auguste, B., and Ramaswamy, S. (2012) *Help Wanted: The Future of Work in the Advanced Economies*, Washington: McKinsey's Global Institute.
Naughton, J. (2014) 'Meet Tech's New Concierge Economy: Where Serfs Deliver Stuff to Rich Folk', *The Observer*, 28 December: 29.
OECD (2010a) *The OECD Innovation Strategy: Getting a Head Start on Tomorrow*, Paris: OECD.
OECD (2010b) *Innovative Workplaces: Making Better Use of Skills within Organisations*, Paris: OECD.
OECD (2012) *Better Skills, Better Jobs, Better Lives: A Strategic Approach to Skills Policies*, Paris: OECD.
OECD(2013) *OECD Skills Outlook 2013: First Results from the Survey of Adult Skills*, Paris: OECD.
OECD (2014) *OECD Skills Strategy Action Report Norway 2014*, Paris: OECD.
Paterson, L. (2014) 'Competitive Opportunity and Liberal Culture: The Significance of Scottish Education in the Twentieth Century', *British Educational Research Journal*, 40(2): 397–416.
Piketty, T. (2014) *Capital in the Twenty-First Century*, Harvard, MA: Belknap Press.
Putin, V. (2012) 'My Goal Is to Make Russia a More Just Society', *The Independent*, 14 February. http://www.independent.co.uk/opinion/commentators/vladimir-... Accessed 17 February 2012.
Ramstad, E. (2009a) 'Expanding Innovation Systems and Policy: An Organisational Perspective', *Policy Studies*, September: 1–21.
Ramstad, E. (2009b) 'Promoting Performance and Quality of Working Life Simultaneously', *International Journal of Productivity and Performance Management*, 58(5): 423–436.
Rubery, J., Grimshaw, D., and Marchington, M. (2010) 'Blurring Boundaries and Disordered Hierarchies: Challenges for Employment and Skills in Networked Organisations', UKCES Praxis Paper no. 6, Wath-upon-Dearne: UK Commission for Employment and Skills.
Schleicker, A. (2014) 'Schooled for life', *Royal Society of Arts Journal*, 3: 40–43.
Schmuecker, K. (2014) *Future of the UK Labour Market*, York: Joseph Rowntree Foundation.
Sellar, S. and Lindgard, B. (2014) 'The OECD and the Expansion of PISA: New Global Modes of Governance in Education', *British Educational Research Journal*, 40(6): 917–936.
Summers, L. H. and Balls, E. (eds) (2015) *Report of the Commission on Inclusive Prosperity*, Washington: Center for American progress.
Sung, J. and Ashton, D. N. (2015) *Skills in Business. The Role of Business Strategy, Sectoral Skills Development and Skills Policy*, London: Sage.
Taylor, M. (2014) 'The Power to Create', in C. Umunna (ed.), *Owning the Future*, London: Policy Network: 81–90.
Todd, J. (2014) *Up to the Job*, London: Demos.
Tooley Street Research (2014) *Pay Progression: Understanding the Barriers for the Lowest Paid*, London: Chartered Institute of Personnel and Development/John Lewis Partnership.
Torrance, H. (2006) 'Globalising Empiricism: What, If Anything, Can Be Learned from International Comparisons of Educational Achievement', in H. Lauder, P. Brown, J-A.

Dillabough, and A. H. Halsey (eds), *Education, Globalization and Social Change,* Oxford: Oxford University Press: 824–834.
Wilby, P. (2013) 'The OECD's Pisa Delivery Man', *The Guardian*, 26 November.
Wolf, A. (2011) *Review of Vocational Education: The Wolf Report*, London: Department for Education/Department for Business, Innovation and Skills.
Wolf, A. and Jenkins, A. (2014) 'Do "Learners" Always Learn? The Impact of Workplace Adult Literacy Courses on Participants' Literacy Skills', *British Educational Research Journal*, 40(4): 585–609.
World Bank (2012) *World Development Report 2013 on Jobs*, New York: World Bank.
Wright, J. and Sissons, P. (2012) 'The Skills Dilemma, Skill Under-Utilisation and Low-Wage Work', A Bottom Ten Million Research Paper, London: The Work Foundation.

Author Index

Index